Praise for *I May Not Get There With You*

"Dyson is a prolific cultural critic who mixes journalism and scholarship to create a largely convincing portrait of the 'lost' King, emphasizing the years from 1965 to 1968, when he focused on race, poverty and militarism. . . . Dyson's achievement is to have recovered the discomfortingly radical core of King's message. . . ."

—Robert Boynton, *The New York Times Book Review*

"Dyson . . . emerges as a major American thinker and cultural critic. . . . We would do well to exchange the one-dimensional King we drag out every year for Dyson's multidimensional, flawed, but exceptional one."

—Farrah Jasmine Griffin, *The Philadelphia Inquirer*

"In this challenging study, Dyson sets out to retrieve the man behind the icon and clarify his legacy. He [reminds us] that King was no bland saint but a radical whose insistence on social justice entailed the overhaul (or perhaps even the abandonment) of contemporary capitalism."

—*The New Yorker*

"Brilliantly examines the foundation of King's profound social vision: his ideology, his identity, and his image . . . and painstakingly dissects the truth from growing folklore."

—*Los Angeles Sentinel*

"A bracing attack on sanitized and tendentious misperceptions of Dr. Martin Luther King. . . . Dyson succeeds in recasting King's message from a comfortingly unexamined myth to an enduring challenge by a great American provocateur."

—*Kirkus Reviews*

"A bracing, at times willfully subjective, political and cultural analysis in which Dyson's signature style is just as surprising and revolutionary as what he presents as King's true message. As usual, this Baptist minister employs poetic, sometimes acrobatic gospel rhetoric, with multiple references to black youth and music. . . . Dyson successfully proves how vital King's true political views and personality are to struggling and frustrated black youth today."

—*Publishers Weekly*

"Through crisp, engaging writing, [Dyson] challenges readers to remove the Nobel Prize winner from the holy historical pedestal and see King for who he really was: a socialist-leaning, God-fearing humanitarian with carnal weaknesses; an often depressed leader; and, still, 'the greatest American who ever lived.'"

—Rochell Thomas, *Vibe* Magazine

"Michael Eric Dyson wrests the safe Negro, Martin Luther King, Jr., from conservatives and restores his humanity. This conversation—provocative, wide-ranging, and occasionally playful—explores dimensions of King obscured by the icon. Black nationalist King? Maybe. Hip-hop King? Possibly. Flawed but heroic King? Definitely."

—Nell Irvin Painter, author of *Sojourner Truth* and
Edwards Professor of American History, Princeton University

"In the thirty-one years since Reverend Martin Luther King, Jr. was assassinated, his legacy has been pillaged by ideological grave robbers. In *I May Not Get There With You*, Michael Eric Dyson performs a vital act of restoration, showing that in Dr. King's hands, Christian love and nonviolent civil disobedience were not the passive choices of a pallid man but part of a radical vision of social activism. When you read this book, you will learn why Martin Luther King was a man who not only had followers among the lowly, but enemies among the powerful."

—Samuel G. Freedman, author of *Upon This Rock:
Miracles of a Black Church*

"Dyson brings to his treatment of King a rare and vital blend of keen objectivity, analytical depth, exciting prose and critical insights."

—Lewis Baldwin, *Christian Century*

"A thoughtful and provocative book that tries to put both King's accomplishments and his flaws in perspective. . . . Dyson has made a thorough study of King's own words and the interpretive literature about him. . . . Dyson's most original contributions, however, come . . . when he examines the ways in which King's reputation and legacy have changed during the past decade."

—David Garrow, *The New York Review of Books*

"A surprisingly entertaining read on King. . . . In a highly sophisticated, yet sort of newjack perspective on King . . . Dyson manages to take a story we're all familiar with and breathe new life into it. . . . [T]he strength of *I May Not Get There With You* is Dyson's rhythmic style of writing and unique street sensibilities merged with high scholarship and critical analysis."

—Trevor Coleman, *Detroit Free Press*

"Dyson crushes the rose-colored lenses through which the civil-rights martyr has been viewed since his assassination three decades ago. . . . In the tradition of jazz saxophonists John Coltrane and Charlie Parker, Dyson riffs with speed, eloquence, bawdy humor, and startling truths that have the effect of hitting you like a Mack truck."

—Venise Wagner, *San Francisco Examiner*

"In *I May Not Get There With You*, Dyson steps on toes, sets the record straight, airs dirty laundry, tells tales out of school, and compares King to the late rapper Tupac Shakur. Call it what you want, this look at King is not your typical academic tome. . . . Dyson analyzes them [King's virtues and flaws] and puts them into perspective, giving King's life more warts and substance, making it less of a glorified time line."

—Al Hunter, Jr., *Philadelphia Daily News*

"The book is intentionally provocative. Dyson wields his largely clear-eyed reverence for King to connect King's intellectual and moral dots and to speak for him on pressing issues of the day."

—Debra Dickerson, *The Village Voice*

"[Dyson] slings around the concepts of post-modern literary and philosophical thought with dazzling dexterity, something like a French neo-Marxist Eddie Murphy. Few can talk . . . with as much panache. . . . [But] the King book . . . is directed to an audience beyond [the] academic. Dyson is clearly gripped by a mission to integrate hip-hop's rebelliousness into . . . the civil rights movement."

—J. Linn Allen, *Chicago Tribune*

"There is a word for this alternative biography's stirring message: Corrective. This book scrubs away the thick layers of symbolism as well as the ideological muck piled on King since his death in 1968, offering instead the raw materials of a man labeled as 'the real Martin

Luther King, Jr. . . . ' In this intelligent, readable burst of controversial focus, Dyson insists on King's relevance; and in that argument Dyson succeeds."

—Juan Williams, *Black Issues Book Review*

"It would be a shame if Dyson's *I May Not Get There With You* were brushed aside with the sometimes facile productions of other public intellectuals. . . . [I]t is a significant essay. *I May Not Get There With You* engages an issue of real importance: Martin Luther King, Jr.'s image in contemporary politics, culture, and society. In a meditative critical spirit, Dyson's work examines not only a cultural icon, but also the society that has produced it. . . . Dyson's King is a blacker, more radical King than the figure who is currently commemorated in American culture."

—Phillip Richards, *The Journal of Blacks in Higher Education*

Other Books by Michael Eric Dyson

Race Rules:
Navigating the Color Line

Between God and Gangsta Rap:
Bearing Witness to Black Culture

Making Malcolm:
The Myth and Meaning of Malcolm X

Reflecting Black:
African-American Cultural Criticism

I May Not Get There With You

The True Martin Luther King, Jr.

Michael Eric Dyson

A Touchstone Book
Published by Simon & Schuster
New York London Toronto Sydney Singapore

TOUCHSTONE
Rockefeller Center
1230 Avenue of the Americas
New York, NY 10020

First Touchstone Edition 2001

TOUCHSTONE and colophon are registered trademarks of Simon & Schuster, Inc.

Book design by Ellen R. Sasahara

Manufactured in the United States of America

3 5 7 9 10 8 6 4 2

The Library of Congress has cataloged the Free Press edition as follows:

Dyson, Michael Eric.
I may not get there with you : the true Martin Luther King, Jr. / Michael Eric Dyson.
p. cm.
Includes bibliographical references and index.
1. King, Martin Luther, Jr., 1929–1968—Influence.
2. King, Martin Luther, Jr., 1929–1968—Political and social views.
3. Afro-American civil rights workers Biography.
4. Baptists—United States—Clergy Biography.
5. Afro-Americans—Civil rights—History—20th century.
6. Civil rights movements—United States—History—20th century.
E185.97.K5D97   2000
323'.092—dc21
00–40478
CIP

ISBN 0-684-86776-1
0-684-83037-X (Pbk)

For the
REVEREND MARCIA L. DYSON
Wife, Friend, and Lover

CONTENTS

FOREWORD TO THE PAPERBACK EDITION   ix

PREFACE   "We as a People Will Get to the Promised Land": Martin and Us   xv

INTRODUCTION   "You Don't Need to Go Out Saying Martin Luther King, Jr. Is a Saint": The American Hero   1

Part I. IDEOLOGY

CHAPTER 1   "I Saw That Dream Turn Into a Nightmare": From Color-Blindness to Black Compensation   11

CHAPTER 2   "Most Americans Are Unconscious Racists": Beyond Liberalism   30

CHAPTER 3   "As I Ponder the Madness of Vietnam": The Outlines of a Militant Pacifism   51

CHAPTER 4   "America Must Move Toward a Democratic Socialism": A Progressive Social Blueprint   78

CHAPTER 5   "We Did Engage in a Black Power Move": An Integrationist Embraces Enlightened Black Nationalism   101

Part II. IDENTITY

CHAPTER 6   "I Had to Know God for Myself": The Shape of a Radical Faith   123

CHAPTER 7   "Somewhere I Read of the Freedom
             of Speech": Constructing a Unique Voice   137

CHAPTER 8   "There Is a Civil War Going on Within All
             of Us": Sexual Personae in the Revolution   155

CHAPTER 9   "I Have Walked Among the Desperate,
             Rejected, and Angry": Two Generations
             of the Young, Gifted, and Black   175

CHAPTER 10   "The Primary Obligation of the Woman
             Is That of Motherhood": The Pitfalls of
             Patriarchy   197

Part III. IMAGE

CHAPTER 11   "Be True to What You Said on Paper":
             A Critical Patriotism   225

CHAPTER 12   "I Won't Have Any Money to Leave
             Behind": The Ownership of a Great Man   249

CHAPTER 13   "If I Have to Go Through This to Give
             the People a Symbol": The Burden of
             Representation   282

EPILOGUE   "Lil' Nigger, Just Where You Been?":
             Metaphors and Movements   307

NOTES   313

BIBLIOGRAPHY   376

ACKNOWLEDGMENTS   395

INDEX   397

"What risky, unfashionable research are we willing to undertake?"
—Toni Morrison

"Thanks for doing the white man's job for him," the elderly black man chided me as I left a prominent Los Angeles church.

I had just participated in an annual black books forum sponsored in part by the local branch of the Southern Christian Leadership Conference, Martin Luther King, Jr.'s organization. Many local folk had come to the Saturday forum to have a stimulating discussion of my book on King's career. My fellow presenter, a distinguished minister who had worked alongside King in the civil rights movement, suggested that my book dishonored the fallen leader's memory. I traded barbs with him in that nice-nasty fashion that sometimes characterizes strong disagreement in black Baptist circles. Nothing is healthier than an informed difference of opinion about a historical figure. However, few things get folks more worked up in black communities than arguments over whether we should "air dirty laundry," especially the faults of our heroic figures. The gentleman who took a parting shot at me at the black books forum had obviously decided that my truth telling was a destructive and traitorous act.

Of course, the older gentleman at the Los Angeles church was not the only black person to let me know how much he hated what I had done. On a live television show in Oakland, a black woman called up and let on how much she despised me. And on a radio show in Chicago, a black woman conveyed her loathing by wrapping it in a choice bit of homophobia: "You're a *homosexual*," she cried with contempt. And after I appeared on his show on Black Entertainment Television, Tavis Smiley told me that he had never received such strongly worded mail and comments, even when white bigots were featured.

The belief that it is harmful to our communities for authors to explore the humanity of our leaders can have troubling effects. At the least, it promotes the belief that black heroes have to be perfect to be useful. At worst, it censors our full investigation of black life. We are left with truncated visions of black culture and achievement. If the canvas on which we paint black life is stock and cramped, its colors drab and predictable, the representations of our culture are likely to be untrue. They will not capture the breadth and complexity of black identity. Some black folks' preoccupation with sanitizing King's life—which simultaneously mutes his challenging ideas—made it difficult for many audiences and readers to focus on my analysis of Martin Luther King, Jr.'s career. Never mind that I said that King was the greatest American this country has ever seen. Or that I proclaimed him the most important influence in my life. All that mattered was that I had told tales out of school about a few of his weaknesses. I could not in such a setting debate the merits or faults of my book. I was largely engaged in a fight-for-your-life defense of the *very idea* of discussing the leader's life by tackling the good, the bad, and the ugly.

The overwhelming good King did was a remarkable accomplishment, considering the awful odds he confronted in helping to bring racial justice to America. Although King's weaknesses were minimal, they merit exploration. Millions who share the same weaknesses may find consolation in examining these afflictions in one so great. As for the ugly, it involved the wounding hypocrisy of a nation obsessed with telling the truth about everything but itself. I set out to put the record right: King was no namby-pamby, we-shall-overcome-at-all-costs integrationist who advocated blindness to color, despite the twisted ends to which conservatives have turned him. He *was* the most courageous freedom fighter in our nation's history, despite the mean and duplicitous treatment he was sometimes accorded by supposedly "blacker" leaders. He was capable of calling a spade a spade, and accordingly, he mocked the self-righteousness of many white liberals by calling them racists too. And despite his genius, King was not God, but man. He had failings. But even his flaws are instructive.

Still, I am deeply sympathetic to the horror of what some folk wrongly suppose I am up to in my book. I love Dr. King deeply. My respect for his achievements only grew after sorting through the mountain of material that surrounds his life. Insulting his career by slighting his work or overplaying his faults is the furthest thing from my mind. However, I knew that to get his story right, I would have to detail the wonders and warts of the man. I know how white bigots stand at the ready to use any information they can to tear down King. In fact, in my book I defend King against the prejudiced assessments that eroded his reputation when he was alive and that have only gotten worse since his death. That is different from admitting that King gave in to his fleshly desires regularly, which hardly makes him unique. It does make him human, a thought that seems to frighten his friends as much as it makes him vulnerable to the attacks of his enemies.

I addressed King's sexual shortcomings because there is ample evidence they occurred. I could not conscientiously write a book about him without acknowledging King's promiscuity. King's sexual habits had been formed in a culture full of machismo and patriarchal posturing. To that degree, King was a product of his times, a fact that cannot be overlooked in a convincing portrait of his life and thought. A discussion of King's sexual practices highlights his moral struggles. King fought mightily against his urge to stray even as he slaked his sexual thirst. He was a man trying to live right while sometimes doing wrong, a common moral dilemma for most of us.

It is now a matter of record that King plagiarized big chunks of his graduate school course papers and his doctoral dissertation. Only by thoroughly examining King's case can we justly conclude that his intellectual habits were shaped by complex racial and cultural forces. And that his academic failings do not mar his monumental social and intellectual achievements. But we cannot take the ostrich approach to analyzing King's record. Either we are committed to examining as truthfully as we can what happened or we arbitrarily choose what we will and will not study. It is vital to recognize that we do not protect King by denying the truth. We must instead spell out as comprehensively as we can the conditions under which he acted and lived.

It is also vital to King's story to explore how his family has helped or hindered his legacy. To claim an exemption from scrutiny because they are the Kings runs counter to the democratic instincts that should govern our behavior. To be sure, the Kings are not the only ones who should be subject to criticism on this score. The entire nation has been a poor steward of King's legacy. In attempting to square King's life and what we have made of it—or off of it—the King family may be first in line, but they are by no means alone. Few can match King's sacrificial spirit or boldly embodied idealism. Not black intellectuals who make money and gain recognition by writing books about him. Not civil rights leaders who get rich while trumpeting black misery. And not politicians who cherish security above selfless service. Much of what we have done in King's name has compromised his legacy.

Of course, many folk felt that I sullied King's memory and did myself a great disservice by suggesting similarities between King and Tupac Shakur. King shared with some hip-hop stars a yen to destroy white supremacy, a strong focus on death, a sexist view of women, and a profound appreciation for black orality. What struck me most about the vitriolic response to such a comparison is just how much revulsion there is to black youth in black communities. It would be ludicrous to suggest that Shakur or any other hip-hopper should enjoy the affection or admiration we have reserved for King. But it is equally harmful to dismiss an entire generation, or at least some of its representatives, because they have failed to adopt King's lifestyle or outlook. King would have been the first to resist such an injurious position. Indeed, he spent a great deal of time reaching out to the most weathered young people in hopes of turning their cynicism into creative rage. King would have abhorred the sanctimony that has clouded his name and image.

This last point, I had hoped, would spare me the onslaught of the race protectors. They are the battalion of blacks whose self-appointed duty it is to rid the race of all poisons and distractions. To be sure, they are an inevitable, even necessary, consequence of a white supremacist culture that feeds itself by gorging on the heart of black identity and eating away black self-confidence. But racial protectors too often see only skin color where they should see the moral substance of race. Many of the racial protectors who attacked me shared a lamentable trait: they had not read the book. I realize that even those who read every word might still greatly dislike it. However, how could they form an opinion about something they had not even read, or from which they had read only an excerpt in a magazine? How could they debate what they had only heard or seen for a few minutes on radio and television?

Perhaps the attacks on me were harder to take since I am used to being praised by black folk for being a race defender, something that I hope is more profound than being a race protector. Black folk stop me on the street and say, "Brother, you handled your business with Ward Connerly," or "I'm so glad you stuck it to Dinesh D'Souza." They read my books and send me letters of support, more than making up for the hate mail I regularly receive from whites. The big difference between protectors and defenders is that the latter understand the contradictory conditions under which black life exists. By factoring in the malevolence of everyday assaults on black culture, they defend the right of blacks to live free of the myriad perils of racism. Race defenders embrace black life with informed zeal, even as they spurn romantic views of our race, culture, and condition. For instance, race defenders relentlessly oppose the bigotry of scientific theories that assail our native intelligence and fight doggedly for inclusion of folk whose feminist politics or sexual orientation alienates them from the mainstream. At his best, King endorsed the view that healthy blacks are only strengthened by self-criticism.

The self-critical instinct should surely shape the politics of portraiture in black culture. As intellectuals, we must examine black life in a fashion that flies in the face of black protectionism. It is a great disservice to scholarship and our history to paint King's legacy with a romantic revi-sionist's brush. We must indeed undertake risky and unfashionable research, if for no other reason than to combat the impulse to display sacred cows on shiny pedestals. The role of the black intellectual in black life is difficult and uncomfortable, but ultimately rewarding. It is difficult because one must be acutely aware that the ideal of critical investigation is mitigated by the harsh realities of bias, racial and otherwise, that suf-fuse the national landscape, and hence, shape the uses of intellectual pur-suits. Particularly when it comes to race, ideas are never just ideas, but active ingredients in the social intercourse that decides public policy and sets national agendas. There is no denying that segments of white Amer-ica relish the opportunity to assault black humanity. That realization should definitely influence how we think and write about black America. Only fatal naïveté could make us believe that our words and the choices we make do not affect our communities

Black intellectuals should take this into account as they read the cul-ture out loud. Still, we must never suppress the critical juices that are the lifeblood of serious scholarship. The black intellectual's craft will unavoidably cause discomfort, and sometimes, it may cause great dis-tress. It will predictably rattle those racists who believe that black life is strangled by a deficit of rational creativity. The substance of black critical reflection may also create unease in a majority culture unused to feeling the sharp edges of insight poking into the crevices of cherished beliefs and deflating long-held misconceptions. If done right, though, black intellectual scrutiny will bring the pain closer to home, causing black folk to take a harder look at the myths and fictions by which they live. Indeed, black intellectual life thrives in the embrace of a flinty paradox: the less we worship black life in our critical work, the more we will be able to inspire critical appreciation for the glories and virtues of black life.

One of the rewards of black intellectual investigation is that we gain a sense of our true greatness, which is never pegged on unwarranted praise, undeserved support, or uncritical celebration. In the end, black folk must love our heroes strongly enough to learn from their strengths and weak-nesses. We must resist the temptation to over-romanticize our stories or to lie about our journeys. We can love black folk and tell the truth about our-selves at the same time. That is the gift of our hard-won humanity. I would have to say to the elderly black man who stopped me at the door of the black church that I have not done the "white man's job for him." That would mean discussing the things about King I liked, while leaving aside the things I found troubling. That would mean sugarcoating history to satisfy the hunger for moral perfection in the present. For white Americans, such an approach to history denies that slavery was evil, that presidents slept with slaves, and that racial injustice cannot die in a few decades. In short, it is precisely the sort of history that denies history. What we must argue for is a history that embraces the truth, however we understand it, at the expense of prejudice or unreason. Such a history can never harm us. It can only aid in the war against the lies, myths, and half-truths that have made us suspicious to begin with. That is why King's true story is so much better and more meaningful than the one we can try to invent.

Michael Eric Dyson

"We as a People Will Get to the Promised Land"
Martin and Us

The prospect of another book on Martin Luther King, Jr., will prompt many readers to wonder, What is left to say about Martin? We certainly know the broad outlines of his story. And as a result of the work of imaginative King biographers, we are familiar with the intimate details of King's life. Still, most Americans have lost sight of King. They have forgotten what the details mean. I want to provide a fresh interpretation of a peculiarly American life and reconstruct its relevance to America today.

As we stand at the end of this wonderful yet troubled century, we don't recognize that King is, as I will argue, the greatest American who ever lived. What makes him the greatest? I contend that now, more than ever, King stands before us as a sublime mix of the profound and the profane. And in fact, the very dimensions of his gift that have disappeared in the thirty years since his death are what make him so unique. He was a man who was deeply human, deeply flawed, and yet truly amazing. In the last thirty years we have trapped King in romantic images or frozen his legacy in worship. I seek to rescue King from his admirers and deliver him from his foes.

Since his death, we have made three mistakes in treating King's legacy.

First, we have sanitized his *ideas*, ignoring his mistrust of white America, his commitment to black solidarity and advancement, and the radical message of his later life. Today right-wing conservatives can quote King's speeches in order to criticize affirmative action, while schoolchildren grow up learning only about the great pacifist, not the hard-nosed critic of economic injustice.

Second, we have twisted his *identity* and lost the chance to connect the man's humanity, including his flaws, to the young people of today, especially our despised black youth.

Finally, we have ceded control of his *image* to a range of factions that include the right, the federal government and its holiday, and even the King family themselves, who have attempted to collect a fee for nearly every word the great man gave to the world.

In a way, I have spent my entire life writing this book—since that evening in 1968 when as a nine-year-old black boy in Detroit I saw the King assassination seize up my family, my city, and my country. Although I grew up on the street, it was the rich tradition of the black church that saved me and led me to the world of words and ideas. For the past ten years, as a teacher, writer, and man of the church, I have traveled around the country speaking to large audiences, many of them young people, and I have witnessed a great need. I believe that Dr. King fills that need. His life teaches us that we cannot get to the promised land unless we are able to embrace contradictions.

Can you be as radical in your view of social injustice as Malcolm X, and still win the support of the white establishment? Yes.

Can you dedicate your life to the common good, and still give in to your own sexual appetites? Yes.

Can you be a creative master of language and rhetoric, while sampling the words and ideas of others? Yes.

Can you love white people and mistrust them at the same time? Of course you can.

Can you despise the unjust distribution of wealth and use its fruits to feed your own people? Yes.

Martin Luther King, a man who had as much in common with Tupac Shakur as he does with the Reverend Ralph Abernathy, teaches us that we must leave our most strident beliefs behind in order to move forward.

In 1998 Peter Jennings invited me to speak with him on the air on the birthday of Martin Luther King, Jr. Our discussion of Dr. King's legacy left me deeply troubled. Was the man disappearing before our very eyes? Had it come to this: a nod on network television about the dream deferred, the hopes shattered, the plans abandoned? What could be done?

Since that television appearance, I have lectured and preached around the country about the radical, human Dr. King. The exuberant response I receive, from people of all colors and all ages, tells me that there is a real hunger for a King who can lead us today. In this book I hope to resurrect that King, in whom humanity and greatness lived side by side. As he said that fateful night in Memphis before he was killed, "And He's allowed me to go up to the mountain. And I've looked over. And I've seen the promised land. I may not get there with you. But I want you to know tonight that we, as a people, will get to the Promised Land."

If we keep Dr. King alive, the way he really was, then we will get to the promised land. And he will get there with us. That is the aim of my book.

"You Don't Need to Go Out Saying Martin Luther King, Jr. Is a Saint"

The American Hero

I was sitting on the living room floor watching television. I can't remember what was on the tube, but whatever it was got interrupted by a news bulletin.

"Martin Luther King, Jr., has just been shot in Memphis, Tennessee," the newsman announced. His speaking was usually a lesson in good cadence and inflection. Now his voice dragged in somber monotone.

Behind me, sitting in his favorite chair, my father could barely manage a hushed but hurtful "humh." It was the sort of wordless expression that gathered into its dismal tone the horror and disbelief that black folk who loved King would surely feel when they learned that he had been mercilessly ambushed. King's mellifluous baritone had been silenced by a piece of metal that traveled with ungodly speed and accuracy to explode its message of death inside his neck.

After the newsman reported that King was seriously wounded and had been shot on a motel balcony (immediately an unholy shrine to the senseless murder of so many dreams and hopes), the television gave us an audience with King at a speech he had delivered the night before.

"We've got some difficult days ahead," King says as his eyes peer intensely into the audience. "But it really doesn't matter with me now, because I've been to the mountaintop."

King's audience erupts in cheers and verbal support. To my nine-year-old Sunday school–trained mind, his reference to the promised land was familiar, but I didn't ever remember it evoking that kind of response in church. Still, I could tell that something magical was happening between King and his hearers. The camera caught King at a side angle, his eyes blinking intently, his head shifting from left to right, and his mouth opened wide as his words spill forth in eloquent abandon.

1

"And I don't mind," he starts before the applause has completely subsided. "Like anybody, I'd like to live a long life," King yearns. "But longge-ve-ty has its place."

King stretched out the word, holding onto and savoring its ideal even as he perhaps felt his life slipping away. I began to get goose bumps. Did he know he was going to get killed? If he did know, did he have a special relationship with God? Does that kind of relationship mean that you know when you're going to die? I got a bit frightened, but I was riveted by King's words all the same.

"But I'm not concerned about that now," King insists. "I just want to do God's will. And He's allowed me to go up to the mountain." The audience senses King's climax, and they continue to perforate his speech with shouts of "Yes, sir!" "Oh yes!" "Go 'head," "Yes, doctor!"

"And I've looked over," King continues as the preachers behind him beg him to "talk to me!" "And I've s-e-e-e-e-n the promised land." King's intensity is imploding, his jaws extending to full range, his eyes almost teary as he gently frowns to concentrate his energy. "I may not get there with you. But I want you to know tonight, that we as a people, will *get* to the promised land." The congregation is collapsing in ecstatic verbal release around his every word, measured and articulated with stirring economy.

"And I'm happy tonight," King reassures his audience, perhaps worried that the weight of his possible death, his inevitable death, will push him into the ground. He stops to give them a boost as he seeks to boost himself. "I'm not worried about *anything*. I'm not fearing *any man*," he promises his flock. "'Mine eyes have seen the glory of the coming of the Lord.'" He begins the hymn he had quoted so often, turning suddenly on his heels, as much out of emotional fullness as out of a sense of dramatic ending.

The audience on television, and in my heart, exploded in thunderous applause. It was a life-shaping introduction to an ebony seer whose words fairly brimmed with the pathos and poetry of black life. After showing what turned out to be King's last speech, the television station resumed its regular programming. But in my own mind, I would never be able to switch back to the same channel, to pick up with the same program. I knew instantly that I was forever and unalterably changed. King's rhetoric electrified me, stood the hair on my arms at attention as he trumpeted a clarion call for freedom. Then, in what seemed a matter of moments, the newsman again broke faith with the printed program to announce the final tragedy.

"Martin Luther King, Jr., has been assassinated in Memphis, Tennessee, at thirty-nine years old."

Before that April night that changed my life, I had never heard King's name, had never heard of Memphis. But in the split second it took for King to enter my consciousness, he quickly dominated my thoughts. As an inner-city black boy, I had already survived the riot that blazed Detroit's ghettoes and killed forty-three people during the previous summer. I saw brothers and sisters loot neighborhood stores, hauling away televisions, stereos, and whatever else they could carry off before dusk fell and before the city-wide curfew was enforced. But even that seismic event, as riveting and as local as it was, failed to capture my attention the way King's death did. The bullet that shattered King's jaw ended his life; its shrapnel lodged deep in my psyche and burned me awake to race in America. This book is the most recent symbol of my awakening and the product of my struggle to interpret King's life and meaning in a new way.

For millions of others, King's death was undeniably a sad benchmark of racial desolation. His assassination sparked a profound period of national soul searching. We reluctantly revive that sort of introspection when catastrophes strike or official commissions beckon us to get things right. More recently, King's image is conjured to settle disputes on either side of a racial or political divide. King's words are also referenced to prove one's authenticity as a champion of truth and justice. It seems to matter little that few people actually read what King wrote or spoke. What counts is that one can marshal enough of King's sentences in isolation from their original contexts to justify one's beliefs or perspectives. Thus King becomes a convenient icon shaped in our own distorted political images. He is fashioned to deflect our fears and fulfill our fantasies. King has been made into a metaphor of our hunger for heroes who cheer us up more than they challenge or change us.

Using King in this way harms our nation's racial memory. Indeed, it feeds the national amnesia on which we desperately depend to deny the troubles we face, troubles that grow from our unwillingness to tell the truth about where we have come from and where we are headed. If we can employ King's words to whitewash our blood-stained racial history—use him to make it seem that racial progress, though painful, was natural, even unavoidable—then we can defeat efforts to extend King's work. We can even make his authentic heirs appear alien to King's moral vision. This is the perverse genius of making King the patron saint of the movement to destroy affirmative action. In these circles, King is portrayed as a color-blind loyalist at all costs. Perhaps the most tragic price paid for viewing King in this manner is that racial justice is trumped under the baleful banner of "true equality." Of course, what King understood as a culture blind to color is a universe away from contemporary refusals to take race into account in creating a just society. Reducing King's brilliantly disturbing rhetoric to sound bites lets us off the hook. It even causes us to forget his challenging ideas.

I May Not Get There With You is a work of biocriticism—a critical investigation of King's career and cultural impact through the analytical prism of biographical details and life episodes. It attempts to rescue King's memory from the image of romantic dreamer that obscures his embrace of challenging ideas. I try to extract King's flesh-and-blood achievements, and failures, from sanitizing hero worship. Ironically, King's friends sometimes shortchange his challenging legacy by forgetting that he made America better by disagreeing with it when it was wrong. That meant that he was sometimes seen as a threat to American values and perceived in some quarters as dangerous. King's love for America should never be questioned. Contrary to right-wing reports, King was a patriot's patriot. He loved his country so much that he was willing to sacrifice his life for his countrymen. Thanks to his religious beliefs, King refused to idolize the state. He shared a disdain for blind nationalism with the biblical prophets he strongly admired. And despite the charge that he subverted the social order, King was a tireless advocate of democracy. In fact, he was so devoted to democracy that he spent his life making sure that its fruits could be shared by those who had worked the hardest to nurture its growth.

King was at his best when he was willing to reshape the wisdom of many of his racial and national parents. He ingeniously harnessed their ideas to his views to advocate sweeping social change. He believed that his earlier views on race failed to change America fundamentally. He once believed that appeals to conscience would destroy racism. He later concluded that most Americans were unconscious racists. King confessed that he had underestimated how deeply entrenched racism was in America. Now America had to be forced to confront its painful racial legacy. If blacks could no longer depend on white goodwill to create social change, they had to provoke social change through bigger efforts at nonviolent direct action. This meant that blacks and their allies had to seize political power. They also had to try to restructure American society, solving the riddles of poverty and economic inequality.

This is not the image of King that is celebrated during annual holiday observances. Many of King's admirers are uncomfortable with a focus on his mature beliefs. They seek to deflect unfair attacks on King's legacy by shrouding him in the cloth of superhuman heroism. In truth, it is little more than romantic tissue. King was undeniably a great American hero, but he did not become great by denying his mortality. In fact, he eventually embraced his humanity with remarkable abandon. King concluded that his life was not his own. He knew early in his career that he would probably be sacrificed for the sake of both black and white America. This awareness released him into a powerful and sometimes perilous psychological freedom—the sort of freedom that makes those who haven't faced death for their beliefs extremely nervous. At times, King was personally reckless, even dangerously so. We do not have to make him a saint to appreciate his greatness. Neither should we deny his imperfections as we struggle to remember and reactivate his legacy.

King's image has often suffered a sad fate. His strengths have been needlessly exaggerated, his weaknesses wildly overplayed. King's true legacy has been lost to cultural amnesia. As a nation, we have emphasized King's aspiration to save America through inspiring words and sacrificial deeds. Time and again we replay the powerful image of King standing on a national stage in the shadow of the Lincoln Memorial mouthing perhaps the most famous four words ever uttered by a black American: "I have a dream." For most Americans, those words capture King's unique genius. They express his immortal longing for freedom, a longing that is familiar to every person who dares to imagine a future beyond unjust laws and unfair customs. The edifying universality of these four words—who hasn't dreamed, and who cannot identify with people whose dreams of a better world are punished with violence?—helps to explain their durability.

But these words survive, too, because they comfort folk who would rather entertain the dreams of unfree people than confront their rage and despair. That is why the ironic cycle of King's fame must be exposed. At first, he was viewed in many quarters of white America as a troublemaking, glory-seeking, self-promoting preacher whose racial opportunism was a plague on black-white relations. The logic ran that blacks and whites had worked out their differences to each other's satisfaction. The last thing they needed was for some Yankee-educated black preacher with highfalutin' words to threaten the segregated social contract of the South. One version or another of this story made fair book on King in even the most enlightened quarters of white Southern society. With the sudden and sharp rise of black militancy, King's challenging beliefs were transmuted into terms that white America fully exploited. With the emergence of Stokely Carmichael and especially Malcolm X, King was seen as the humble, nonviolent messenger of integration. His conciliatory views were contrasted to the supposed racial demagoguery and violence of black separatists. When King was suddenly crowned the Negro of choice within the white press, some blacks became suspicious of his authentic connection to the needs and interests of ordinary black folk. Two of the three major news magazines—*Time* and *Newsweek*—featured increasingly positive stories on King. *Time* even named King "Man of the Year" in 1964. King was made the poster boy for Safe Negro Leadership. His methods of social protest were embraced by millions of whites as the best route to racial redemption. By embracing King, many whites believed the threat of black insurrection could be contained, perhaps even shrewdly diverted.

To the chagrin of white leadership and the white press, King stepped out of character—at least the one they had written him into. He began to identify more strongly with the masses of black (and eventually, white and Latino) poor who had been invisible even within elite black circles. Moreover, King became increasingly anti-imperialist and chided the American government for its involvement in the Vietnam War. King's reproval bitterly stung civil rights stalwart Lyndon Baines Johnson. In King's mind, race, poverty, and war were intimately related. When King contended that all human life was tied together in a "single garment of destiny," he was lauded by liberal whites and integration-minded blacks. When he insisted that racism, economic inequality, and militarism were the "triplets of social misery," he was attacked for oversimplifying complex social issues. King paid dearly for his inevitable betrayal of Southern white interests, capitalist ideology, and black bourgeois beliefs. Financial support for his civil rights organization dwindled. Moral support for his war on economic inequality waned. And his antiwar protests caused him to be denounced by other black leaders. In 1967, for the first time in a decade, King's name was left off the Gallup Poll list of the ten most admired Americans.

This is not the King we choose to remember. The King we prefer is easily absorbed into fast-food ads for his birthday celebration. Or he is touted, even by political leaders who opposed him when he lived, as the moral guardian of racial harmony. In truth, political conservatives have more ingeniously than their liberal counterparts appropriated King's image, identity, and ideology. While such moves cause King's liberal admirers to cringe, they rarely enter the war of interpretation over King's legacy with the same gusto as their conservative opponents. One reason is that the times have turned against the sort of liberal ideology that they espouse, an ideology that has been brilliantly tagged by right-wing interests as un-American. Another reason that liberals fail to revive King's full legacy is that it represents a serious critique of many liberal racial remedies and goals. When King changed his mind about race and class, he both enraged conservatives and alienated liberals. While conservatives have zealously consumed King's earlier vision of race, even if to twist it perversely in a greatly changed racial era, liberals have refrained from appropriating King's rhetoric as aggressively. It is one thing to loathe taking King's words out of context to justify narrow interests. It is another thing altogether to understand the need to apply King's words skillfully, especially his more challenging words, to our current situation. Conservatives have retailed King's words. Liberals and progressives must retell his story. But we must make sure, in the interest of truth, to include the parts of King's vision that disturb us.

Why should we remember King's challenging legacy? Because Martin Luther King, Jr., is, arguably, the greatest American ever produced on our native soil. Figures like Abraham Lincoln and Thomas Jefferson seized the national imagination while holding public office. By contrast, King helped to redefine our country's destiny as a private citizen in a remarkable career that lasted a mere thirteen years. As a religious activist and social prophet, King challenged our nation's moral memory. He bid America to make good on promises of justice and freedom for all persons, promises that had been extended almost two centuries before. Part of King's enormous genius was the ability to force America to confront its conscience. He also brilliantly urged America to reclaim a heritage of democracy buried beneath cold documents and callous deeds. This book attempts to get at King's unique appeal to conflicting constituencies and seeks to explain the character of King's achievements, especially his later, more challenging thought and activity. While this book focuses on King, it attempts as well to place him in a broad network of social forces and movements that contributed to the black freedom struggle. King drew from a tradition of racial resistance that featured ordinary folk fighting for their freedom. My exploration of King's heroic stature by no means negates the achievements of folk who organized communities throughout the South without the aid of cameras or cash.

Martin Luther King, Jr., is the defining American of our national history. His social vision at its best captured the deepest desire for freedom that any other American has ever expressed. King's quest for true democracy is as great a pilgrimage as any American has undertaken. His hunger for real equality is as stirring a hope for national stability as any American has ever harbored. His thirst for racial redemption is as pure a faith in human morality as any American has dared to embrace. King's surrender of his life to the principles he cherished is as profound an investment in the worth of American ideals as any American ever made. King's career, with all of its flaws and failures, is simply the most faithful measure of American identity and national citizenship as we are likely to witness. As legendary jazz trumpeter Wynton Marsalis eloquently put it, "When I think of King, I think of a man who was the single person in the 20th century who did the most to advance the meaning and feeling of the Constitution, the Declaration of Independence and the Bill of Rights. He is the single most important person in the fight that America has to be itself."

As we begin the twenty-first century, in prosperous times that have widened the gap between rich and poor, in the era *Newsweek* (June 7, 1999) declared to be the best times yet for black America—while 15 percent of African American men go to prison—we would do well to turn to the true Martin Luther King, Jr.

Part I
Ideology

"I Saw That Dream Turn Into a Nightmare"
From Color-Blindness to Black Compensation

I am a mother with six kids," says the beautiful ebony-skinned woman adorned in batik-print African dress and silver loop earrings. "And part of the time I don't even know where I'm going to get the next meal for my children."

All Martin Luther King, Jr., can do is shake his head and utter, "My, my."

King was on a 1968 swing through rural, poor parts of the black South, drumming up support for his Poor People's March on Washington later that year. He had stopped at a small white wood-frame church in Mississippi to press his case, and to listen to the woes of the poor. A painting of a white Jesus, nearly ubiquitous in black churches, observed their every move. Later King would absorb more tales of Mississippi's material misery.

"People just don't know, but it's really hard," a poor woman in church pleads. "Not only me, there's so many more that's in the same shape. I'm not the only one. It's just so many right around that don't have shoes, clothes, is naked and hungry. Part of the time, you have to fix your children pinto beans morning, dinner and supper. They don't know what it is to get a good meal." King is visibly moved.

"You all are really to be admired," he compassionately offers, "and I want you to know that you have my moral support. I'm going to be praying for you. I'm going to be coming back to see you and we are going to be demanding, when we go to Washington, that something be done and done immediately about these conditions."

King couldn't keep that promise; his life would be snuffed out a mere three weeks before his massive campaign reached its destination. But King hammered home the rationale behind his attempt to unite the desperately poor. He understood that the government owed something to the masses of black folk who had been left behind as America parceled out land and money to whites while exploiting black labor.

"At the very same time that America refused to give the Negro any land," King argues, "through an act of Congress our government was giving away millions of acres of land in the West and the Midwest, which meant it was willing to undergird its white peasants from Europe with an economic floor." Building a full head of steam, King rolls his rhetoric down the track of just compensation for blacks by contrasting even more sharply the unequal treatment of the races in education, agriculture, and subsidies.

"But not only did they give them land," King's indictment speeds on, "they built land grant colleges with government money to teach them how to farm. Not only that, they provided county agents to further their expertise in farming. Not only that, they provided low interest rates in order that they could mechanize their farms."

King links white privilege and governmental support directly to black suffering, and thus underscores the hypocrisy of whites who have been helped demanding that blacks thrive through self-help.

"Not only that," King says in delivering the death blow to fallacies about the black unwillingness to work, "today many of these people are receiving millions of dollars in federal subsidies not to farm, and they are the very people telling the black man that he ought to lift himself by his own bootstraps. And this is what we are faced with, and this is the reality."

With one final fell swoop, King reinforces his identification with the destitute, reiterates his belief that the government has failed in its fiduciary obligations to blacks, and subverts the stereotype of blacks shiftlessly waiting around for government cash by insisting that blacks deserve what is coming to them.

"Now, when we come to Washington in this campaign, we are coming to get our check."

This is not the King whom conservatives have used to undermine progressive politics and black interests. Indeed, conservatives must be applauded for their perverse ingenuity in coopting King's legacy and the rhetoric of the civil rights movement. Unlike the radical right, whose racist motivations are hardly obscured by painfully infrequent references to racial equality, contemporary conservatives often speak of race in moral terms gleaned from the black freedom struggle. Thus, while the radical right is open about its disdain for social upheaval in the sixties, many conservatives pretend to embrace a revolution they in fact bitterly opposed. This is especially troubling because of the moral assault by conservatives on civil rights activists who believe that affirmative action, for instance, is part of the ongoing attack on discrimination. These same conservatives rarely target the real enemies of racial equality: newfangled racists who drape their bigotry in scientific jargon or political demagoguery. Instead, they hurl stigma at civil rights veterans who risked great peril to destroy a racist virus found even in the diseased body of ultraconservatism. Perhaps most insidious, conservatives rarely admit that whatever racial enlightenment they possess likely came as blacks and their allies opposed the conservative ideology of race. The price blacks paid for such opposition was abrupt dismissal and name calling: they were often dismissed as un-American, they were sometimes ridiculed as agents provocateurs of violence, and they were occasionally demonized as social pariahs on the body politic.

Worse still, when the civil rights revolution reached its zenith and accomplished some of its goals—including recasting the terms in which the nation discussed race—many conservatives recovered from the shock to their system of belief by going on the offensive. The sixties may have belonged to the liberals, but the subsequent decades have been whipped into line by a conservative backlash. After eroding the spirit of liberal racial reform, conservatives have breathed new life into the racial rhetoric they successfully forced the liberals to abandon. Now terms like "equal playing field," "racial justice," "equal opportunity," and, most ominous, "color-blind" drip from the lips of formerly stalwart segregationist politicians, conservative policy wonks, and intellectual hired guns for deep-pocketed right-wing think tanks. Crucial concepts are deviously turned inside out, leaving the impression of a cyclone turned in on itself. Affirmative action is rendered as reverse racism, while goals and timetables are remade, in sinister fashion, into "quotas." This achievement allows the conservatives to claim that they are opposed to the wrongheaded *results* of the civil rights movement, even as they claim to uphold its *intent*—racial equality. Hence, conservatives seize the spotlight and appear to be calm and reasonable about issues of race. In their shadows, liberals and leftists are often portrayed as unreasonable and dishonest figures who uproot the grand ideals of the civil rights movement from its moral ground.

At the heart of the conservative appropriation of King's vision is the argument that King was an advocate of a color-blind society. Hence, any policy or position that promotes color consciousness runs counter to

King's philosophy. Moreover, affirmative action is viewed as a poisonous rejection of King's insistence that merit, not race, should determine how education and employment are distributed. The wellspring of such beliefs about King is a singular, golden phrase lifted from his "I Have a Dream" speech. "I have a dream," King eloquently yearned, "my four little children will one day live in a nation where they will not be judged by the color of their skin but by the content of their character." Of the hundreds of thousands of words that King spoke, few others have had more impact than these thirty-four, uttered when he was thirty-four years old, couched in his most famous oration. Tragically, King's American dream has been seized and distorted by a group of conservative citizens whose forebears and ideology have trampled King's legacy. If King's hope for radical social change is to survive, we must wrest his complex meaning from their harmful embrace. If we are to combat the conservative misappropriation of King's words, we must first understand just how important—and problematic—King's speech has been to American understandings of race for the past thirty years.

As a nine-year-old boy, I saved money from odd jobs and sent off for a 45-rpm record containing excerpts of Martin Luther King, Jr.'s greatest speeches. Since King had been dead for only a few weeks and since I'd first heard about him the evening he was murdered, his recorded speeches had a great impact on me. Hearing the passionate words that King delivered as much as a decade earlier didn't at all diminish their powerful hold on my youthful imagination. I listened to his speeches over and over until his words were scorched into my brain. All I'd have to do was hear the beginning of a King excerpt, and I could immediately conjure the speech and the tumultuous verbal support of his adoring audience. King was constantly interrupted by a sweetly bellowed stream of "all right," "tell the truth," "yes, sir," "un hunh," "go 'head," "preach," "hah hah," and "speak." Besides "I See the Promised Land"—King's searing last speech that interweaved premonition of his death and the promise of black deliverance—I was thrilled the most by "I Have a Dream." King's best-known refrain echoed the longest on my recording since the compiler must have believed that it was King's most important speech.

"I Have a Dream" continues to draw millions around the globe to its hopeful vision of racial harmony. It is easy to see that many Americans identify with King through that speech. Many can recall where they were when it was delivered. Still others recall how reading that speech helped to locate them on the map of racial conscience. In a recent survey of the fifty most anthologized essays in American culture over the last half-century, "I Have a Dream" made the top ten list. King's towering oration shines alongside the essays of Jonathan Swift, Thomas Jefferson, and E. B. White. And as it skillfully did for me thirty years ago, "I Have a Dream" brings black suffering to the surface and tells us how racial healing can be embraced.

Of course, hearing that speech as a boy thirty years ago and hearing it now as a man makes a world of difference. King's radical tones are clearer. His rebellious flourishes defiantly leap to the foreground. And his dismay at America for denying prosperity to millions of blacks is now more sharply focused. Today I read even his labored restraint as a gesture of profound protest. We have surrendered to romantic images of King at the Lincoln Memorial inspiring America to reach, as he reached with outstretched arms, for a better future. All the while we forget his poignant warning against gradual racial progress and his remarkable threat of revolution should our nation fail to keep its promises. Still, like all other great black orators, King understood the value of understating and implying difficult truths. He knew how to drape hard realities in soaring rhetoric that won the day because it struck the right balance of outrage and optimism. To be sure, we have been long on King's optimism while shortchanging his outrage.

In ways that King could never have imagined—indeed, in a fashion that might make him spin in his grave—"I Have a Dream" has been used to chip away at King's enduring social legacy. One phrase has been pinched from King's speech to justify assaults on civil rights in the name of color-blind policies. Moreover, we have frozen King in a timeless mood of optimism that later *that very year* he grew to question. That's because we have selectively listened to what King had to say to us that muggy afternoon. It is easier for us to embrace the day's warm memories than to confront the cold realities that led to the March on Washington in the first place. August 28, 1963, was a single moment in time that captured the suffering of centuries. It was an afternoon shaped as much by white brutality and black oppression as by uplifting rhetoric. We have chosen to forget how our nation achieved the racial progress we now enjoy.

In the light of the determined misuse of King's rhetoric, a modest proposal appears in order: a ten-year moratorium on listening to or reading "I Have a Dream." At first blush, such a proposal seems absurd and counterproductive. After all, King's words have convinced many Americans that racial justice should be aggressively pursued. The sad truth is, however, that our political climate has eroded the real point of King's beautiful words. We have been ambushed by bizarre and sophisticated distortions of King's true meaning. If we are to recover the authentic purposes of King's address, we must dig beneath his words into our own social and moral habits. Only then can the animating spirit behind his words be truly restored. If we have been as deeply marked by his words as we claim, we need not fear that by putting away his speech we are putting away his ideals. After all, his ideals will have penetrated the very fabric of our personal and public practice. If King's speech has failed to reshape our racial politics sufficiently, it might be a good idea to huddle and ask where we have gone wrong. In the long run, we will do more to preserve King's moral aims by focusing on what he had in mind and how he sought to achieve his goals. That doesn't mean that King's words are scripture or that we cannot differ with him about his beliefs or strategies. We might, however, lower the likelihood of King's words being crudely snatched out of context and used by forces that he strongly opposed.

The great consolation to giving up "I Have a Dream" is that we pay attention to King's other writings and orations. Out of sheer neglect, most of his other works have been cast aside as rhetorical stepchildren. After devoting a decade to King's other works, especially his trenchant later speeches, we will grasp the true scope of his social agenda. We will also understand how King constantly refined his view of the American dream. As things stand, "I Have a Dream" has been identified as King's definitive statement on race. To that degree it has become an enemy to his moral complexity. It alienates the social vision King expressed in his last four years. The overvaluing and misreading of "I Have a Dream" has skillfully silenced a huge dimension of King's prophetic ministry.

Before putting away King's address and before attending to his other speeches, it will be useful to acknowledge "I Have a Dream's" true greatness and read it through the lens of King's mature struggles. True enough, on August 28, 1963, King stood at the sunbathed peak of racial transformation and at the height of his magical oratorical powers. King summoned resources of hope that took wing on carefully chosen words. He turned the Lincoln Memorial into a Baptist sanctuary and preached an inspiring sermon. "I Have a Dream" is unquestionably one of the defining moments in American civic rhetoric. Its features remain remarkable: The eloquence and beauty of its metaphors. The awe-inspiring reach of its civic ideals. Its edifying call for spiritual and moral renewal. Its appeal to transracial social harmony. Its graceful embrace of militancy and moderation. Its soaring expectations of charity and justice. Its inviolable belief in the essential goodness of our countrymen. These themes and much more came out that day.

King's delivery was equally majestic. His lilting cadences stretched along a spiral of intermittent sonic crescendoes. His trumpet-like baritone measured the pulse of his audience's fervor. He evoked his congregation's spiritual longing in sounds as tangy as Southern barbecue. His rhythms were brilliantly varied, a mix of blues and gospel. King encompassed his people's dashed hopes in slow, simmering drawls. He energized their yearning for deliverance in sharp pops of verbal intensity. And his performance was body-wide. His hands stabbed the air to highlight his points. His eyes squinted, then widened—not at all like the reflexive tics demanded by black stereotype—to underscore his propulsive moods. King reached to the heavens on tiptoe as his speech climaxed. King's enthusiasm raced through his limbs and circled his trunk as he was literally lifted by the crowd's momentum. It was a remarkable reflection of the levitating effect of his rhetorical genius. All of this made that speech what it has surely become: the defining oration of our age, the characteristic statement of King's career, and the oratorical taboo against which no other speech by King seems to prosper.

As great as the speech is, we have too often dulled its challenge beneath our overhearing of King's immortal cadences. To be sure, it is almost impossible not to be moved by King's vocal charms and intellectual inspiration. His clarion call for freedom rings in our ears each time the speech is replayed. "I Have a Dream's" condensing brilliance remains intact. King packs centuries of pain and possibility into nineteen minutes and thus makes brevity a servant of justice. But the greatest achievements of the speech are overshadowed by our admiration of its other great parts. King intended that day not simply to detail a dream but to narrate a nightmare. While the phrases that expose racial horror are as beautiful as the phrases that clarify hope, they are obscure because they are not as frequently excerpted. The simpler remedy to banishing King's speech for a decade might appear to be the application of an equal-time proviso: whenever the "dream" sentences are broadcast, we must broadcast as well the lines that speak of hurt and disappointment. But that will never work, in part, because it has not yet worked. One explanation is that the American hunger for amnesia is too great. And where amnesia fails, nostalgia succeeds. Our nation is too often overwhelmed by the desire for a past where racial issues, though desperate, were at least clear. For many, that beats living, as we do today, in an age of racial progress where many boundaries have been blurred and issues are much muddier.

The inclination in the past has been to seize on the positive, edifying portions of King's speech. The parts of the speech that address the terrifying and disheartening aspects of racism are suppressed. Plus, the cultural forces that seek to control King's image want to fix his image as a healer. They conveniently forget that King was seen by most whites as a troublemaker throughout his career. In that light, reciting the drearier sentences will never turn the trick.

Still, the metaphors King used to describe the nightmare are forceful. Despite the "momentous decree" of the Emancipation Proclamation, Negroes were not free. They were "still sadly crippled by the manacles of segregation" even as they lived "on a lonely island of poverty in the midst of a vast ocean of material prosperity." After noting that blacks were "languishing in the corners of American society," King concluded that the Negro "finds himself an exile in his own land." King announced to his civic congregation that the purpose of the march was to "dramatize a shameful condition." And then he evoked an arresting, extended metaphor to capture the frustration that blacks confront. America, he suggested, had failed to live up to its fiduciary obligations to black citizens. With this metaphor, King surgically penetrated the national conscience and sutured black suffering to America's identity as the wealthiest nation on the globe. King claimed that the signers of the Constitution and the Declaration of Independence were indeed signing a promissory note for all Americans. In the case of blacks, America was in profound default. It had issued blacks a bad check that had "come back marked 'insufficient funds.'" But, King declared, black folk refused to believe that "there are insufficient funds in the great vaults of opportunity in this nation." The march, then, was a march to collect on the promises that had been made, to cash a check, King argued, "that will give us upon demand the riches of freedom and the security of justice."

He was not finished yet. King chided those people who held that blacks should be satisfied with a gradual approach to social change, and he hammered away at such an idea by declaring "the fierce urgency of now," reminding America that the "sweltering summer of the Negro's legitimate discontent" would not pass until the coming of the "autumn of freedom and equality." King issued a warning that is still striking when it is shed of our suffocating distortions of his dream: "There will be neither rest nor tranquility in America until the Negro is granted his citizenship rights. *The whirlwinds of revolt will continue to shake the foundations of our nation until the bright day of justice emerges.*"

The militancy of these words can easily be relieved if one points out that King rushed to caution black militants against mimicking the hatred of white bigots. Predictably, that passage is often cited to douse the fire of black dissidents. But King's humanitarian urges, glimpsed in his warning against distrusting all white people—a warning that most black folk didn't need to hear, and one that King issued, perhaps, as a gesture of reassurance to white allies—do not quench his revolutionary thirst for justice. Thus, in answer to the rhetorical question of when black civil rights devotees would be satisfied, King thundered a string of resolute "nevers": black folk would never be satisfied as long as police brutality, disenfranchisement, lodging discrimination, black ghettoization, and attacks on black self-esteem were routinely practiced. Indeed, black folk would never be satisfied, King shouted, quoting the biblical prophet Amos, "until justice rolls down like waters and righteousness like a mighty stream." These passages have been virtually erased from our collective memory of that speech.

If such passages from King's most famous oration have been underplayed, many of his other speeches and writings have been unjustly neglected. In King's first visit to Washington to speak before the Lincoln Memorial, in 1957, he argued for black enfranchisement in the form of the ballot. In that speech, "Give Us the Ballot—We Will Transform the South," King also delivered a stinging rebuke to the sort of moderate neoliberalism that is now in vogue among Democrats. Terming it a "quasi liberalism," King indicts a political philosophy "so bent on seeing all sides that it fails to become committed to either side." King deemed such liberalism of little use to freedom struggles because it "is so objectively analytical that it is not subjectively committed," and because it "is neither hot nor cold, but lukewarm." In 1961, King addressed the AFL-CIO convention in Florida in a speech entitled, "If the Negro Wins, Labor Wins." Even then, King briefly outlined his dream while carefully linking it to social and economic justice. King claimed that the American dream is "a dream of equality of opportunity, of privilege and property widely distributed" and "of a land where men will not take necessities from the many to give luxuries to the few."

In his commencement address to Lincoln University in 1961, entitled "The American Dream," King warned that the "price America must pay for the continued exploitation of the Negro and other minority groups is the price of its own destruction." King also chided the critics of poor black communities who failed to understand that black criminality is "environmental and not racial" since "poverty, disease, and ignorance breed crime whatever the racial group may be." King argued against white supremacy and black inferiority, asserting that if "we are to implement the American dream we must get rid of the notion once and for all that there are superior and inferior races." In 1965, after the bloody march from Selma to Montgomery, Alabama, King, in his speech "Our God Is Marching On!" encouraged his listeners to "march on poverty, until no American parent has to skip a meal so that their children may march on poverty, until no starved man walks the streets of our cities and towns in search of jobs that do not exist."

In 1967, King delivered a speech at New York's Riverside Church in opposition to the Vietnam War exactly a year before his assassination. In "A Time to Break Silence," he scorned American imperialism and claimed that the war was stealing precious resources from the domestic war on poverty and racism. King urged a "revolution of values," a favorite theme of his later years, which he believed would "soon cause us to question the fairness of many of our past and present policies." In his last presidential address for the Southern Christian Leadership Conference (SCLC), "Where Do We Go from Here?" King laid out a daring social vision, a bold departure from his earlier civil rights focus, that joined concern for economic inequality to race and culture. King begged his organization to be possessed of a "divine dissatisfaction" that would lead them to be upset until "the tragic walls that separate the outer city of wealth and comfort and the inner city of poverty and despair shall be crushed by the battering rams of the forces of justice."

Two months before his death, King preached a sermon, "The Drum Major Instinct," at Ebenezer Baptist Church, which he copastored with his father, Rev. Martin Luther King, Sr. In this remarkable homily, King, a full quarter-century before "whiteness studies" became popular in American academic circles, gave a brilliant analysis of the cultural meanings of white identities. King spoke of how he talked to his white jailers in Birmingham, and how their pride and psychic investment in their whiteness was a self-destructive measure, not least because they were "living on . . . the satisfaction of [their] skin being white," when in reality they were as bad off as many blacks. Speaking of them, King said he informed them that "[you think] you are somebody big because you are white," but in fact "you can't send your children to school." In King's last Sunday morning sermon, "Remaining Awake Through a Great Revolution," delivered at Washington, D.C.'s (Episcopal) National Cathedral four days before his death, King was highly critical of the conservative self-help "bootstraps" philosophy, which held that "if the Negro is to rise out of poverty, if the Negro is to rise out of slum conditions, if he is to rise out of discrimination and segregation, he must do it all by himself." King sadly but forcefully observed that "the roots of racism are very deep in our country, and there must be something positive and massive in order to get rid of all the effects of racism and the tragedies of racial injustice."

The night before he was murdered, King warned, in his famous "I See the Promised Land" speech in Memphis, that "if something isn't done, and in a hurry, to bring the colored peoples of the world out of their long years of poverty, their long years of hurt and neglect, the whole world is doomed." And in "A Christmas Sermon on Peace," broadcast on Christmas Eve 1967 on the Canadian Broadcasting Corporation as part of the Massey Lectures, King acknowledged "that not long after talking about" the dream in Washington, "I started seeing it turn into a nightmare." He spoke of the nightmarish conditions of Birmingham, where four girls were murdered in a church bombing a few weeks after his speech. He spoke of the punishing poverty that he observed in the nation's ghettoes as the antithesis of his dream, as were the race riots and the Vietnam War. King confessed that while "I am personally the victim of deferred dreams, of blasted hopes," that "I still have a dream." King had stretched his dream by now to include the desire "that one day the idle industries of Appalachia will be revitalized, and the empty stomachs of Mississippi will be filled, and brotherhood will be more than a few words at the end of prayer, but rather the first order of business on every legislative agenda." His act of dreaming in 1967 was a courageous act of social imagination and national hope, perhaps even more so than when he dreamed out loud in Washington in 1963.

These few speeches, among King's myriad orations, sermons, essays, articles, lectures, and books, amply prove that giving up "I Have a Dream" does not prevent us from exploring King's dream. These speeches place King's dream in the broader context of his spiritual and moral evolution over the last three years of his life. Set free from the ideological confines of his "I Have a Dream" speech, King's true ethical ambitions are free to breathe through the words he spoke and wrote as he made his way to the promised land. If we have to do without "I Have a Dream" for ten years, we will be forced to pore over his other words, finding in them resources for the love and social transformation that were dear to King. If we are forced to live without that speech for a decade, we may be forced to live it instead. In so doing, we can truly preserve King's hope for racial revolution by wrestling with his less popular but more concrete solutions for equality and justice.

Conservatives and liberals alike have feasted on King's hunger for a world beyond race, a world where color will be neither the final sign of human identity nor the basis for enjoying advantage or suffering liability. To be sure, King's life and work pointed to such a day when his dream might be fulfilled. But he was too sophisticated a racial realist, even as he dreamed in edifying technicolor in our nation's capital, to surrender a sobering skepticism about how soon that day might arrive. His religious faith worked against such naiveté since it held that evil can be conquered only by acknowledging its existence. King never trusted the world to harness the means to make itself into the utopia of which even his brilliant dream was a faint premonition. The problem with many of King's conservative interpreters is not simply that they have not been honest about how they have consciously or unintentionally hindered the realization of King's dream, but more brutally, that in the face of such hindrances, they have demanded that we act as if the dream has become real and has altered the racial landscape. As an ideal, the color-blind motif spurs us to develop a nation where race will make no difference. As a presumed achievement, color-blindness reinforces the very racial misery it is meant to replace. Unfortunately, conservatives have not often possessed King's discerning faith or his ability to distinguish ideals from the historical conditions that make their realization possible. Most important, many conservatives lack the sense of poetic license that filled King's rhetoric. Instead they flatten his spiritual vision beneath the dead weight of uninspired literalism.

For example, William Bradford Reynolds, who served as assistant attorney general for civil rights at the Department of Justice under Reagan for eight years, attacked affirmative action as a cruel departure from King's uplifting vision of color-blindness. Reynolds contended that "the initial affirmative action message of racial unification—so eloquently delivered by Dr. Martin Luther King, Jr., in his famous 'I Have a Dream' speech—was effectively drowned out by the all too persistent drumbeat of racial polarization that accompanied the affirmative action preferences of the 1970s into the 1980s." Reynolds continued, writing that what had "started as a journey to reach the idea of color blindness" had been sidetracked by infighting among competing racial or ethnic groups. While excesses and mistakes of the sort that Reynolds outlined surely occur, they do not express the fundamental aims of affirmative action: the correction of past and present discrimination and the granting of equal opportunity to historically excluded minorities. Minorities who possessed merit in the past were unjustly treated. Merit, then, wasn't the crucial criterion that determined their participation or exclusion; race or gender was decisive. To pretend otherwise, and to discount race or gender now in combating patterns of racial or gender exclusion, violates common sense and impedes the sort of justice for which King fought. King argued that it "is impossible to create a formula for the future which does not take into account that our society has been doing something special *against* the Negro for hundreds of years." King went on to question how the Negro "could be absorbed into the mainstream of American life if we do not do something special *for* him now, in order to balance the equation and equip him now to compete on a just and equal basis."

In this light, it makes sense to conceive of merit as a dependent good. It functions according to its immediate environment of comparison. What is meritorious in one context—say, an ability to play violin in a high school symphony or to recite Shakespeare in a theater company—is irrelevant in the next—for instance, a soccer match, where neither skill is particularly useful. Besides, even in the same sort of environment, say a university setting, the same skills may be unequally prized at different schools. For instance, one university may need to fill a first-chair violin slot, where another is overrun with them. At another school, soccer is the sport of choice, offering scholarships to skilled players, while other schools don't field soccer teams. The problem with having used race so long as the sole criterion for participation in schools or jobs is that race wiped out any consideration of merit. Not to take that historical feature into account is not only to deny history, but to corrupt the potential for achieving justice. In fact, race became a kind of merit itself; put another way, if race functioned as a demerit, corrective justice dictates that for a time it serve as a merit. It was King who wrote that "the nation must not only radically readjust its attitude toward the Negro in the compelling present, but must incorporate in its planning some compensatory consideration for the handicaps he has inherited from the past."

Another conservative writer, Richard Bernstein, eloquently suggests that King and the civil rights movement would be opposed to contemporary multiculturalism and affirmative action, its social complement. Bernstein contends that the "obsession with the themes of cultural domination and expression justifies one of the most important departures from the principal and essential goal of the civil rights movement: equality of opportunity." He argues that multiculturalism, by contrast, "insists on equality of results." He maintains that King's "dream of a day when my four little children will not be judged by the color of their skin but by the content of their character" crystallizes in "one sentence the essential ideal of liberalism." Multiculturalism, however, reaches a directly opposite conclusion: "'Judge me by the color of my skin for therein lies my identity and my place in the world.'" And repentant conservative Michael Lind writes that King "publicly opposed racial preferences." But King's words contradict Bernstein and Lind. King said that whenever the "issue of compensatory or preferential treatment for Negroes is raised," many of our friends "recoil in horror." As King stated, the "Negro should be granted equality, they agree; but he should ask nothing more." King goes on to write that the "relevant question" is not what blacks want, but how "can we make freedom real and substantial for our colored citizens? What just course will ensure the greatest speed and completeness? And how do we combat opposition and overcome obstacles arising from the defaults of the past?" King advocated a strong multicultural approach that Bernstein claims he would have rejected. Further, King seems to have sided squarely with at least some version of multicultural emphasis on substantive, not just procedural, justice. As he wrote, the "Negro today is not struggling for some abstract, vague rights, but for concrete and prompt improvement in his way of life." King rejected the simplistic and ill-advised distinction between equality of opportunity and equality of results. "The struggle for rights is, at bottom, a struggle for opportunities," King wrote. But he warned that "with equal opportunity must come the practical, realistic aid which will equip [the Negro] to seize it."

Even black conservatives have attempted to wedge between King and affirmative action in the name of color-blindness. Shelby Steele wins the symbolic sweepstakes hands down. His book, *Content of Our Character*, lifts King's phrase as both the title and the basis of his argument for color-blindness and for his vigorous attack on affirmative action. And Boston University economist Glenn Loury quotes King's content of character phrase too, pointing out that today King's dream is "cited mainly by conservatives." Loury writes that the "deep irony here is that, while in the liberal mind a vigorous defense of the color-blind ideal is regarded as an attack on blacks, it is becoming increasingly clear that weaning ourselves from dependence on affirmative action is the *only* way to secure lasting civic equality for the descendants of slaves."

Perhaps the most controversial, and bitterly contested, appropriation of King's vital legacy by a black conservative is that of California businessman, and University of California regent, Ward Connerly. Connerly has gained national attention for his successful efforts to end affirmative action in California with the infamous Proposition 209. More recently, besides his antiaffirmative action forays into Washington State and Florida, Connerly officially opened his National Campaign Against Affirmative Action on the King holiday in 1997. He defended this symbolic gesture of identification with King's legacy by declaring that his actions were consistent with the martyr's goals, though to King's traditional admirers it smelled more like treachery. Connerly insisted that his group did "no disrespect to [King] by acknowledging what he wanted this nation to become, and we're going to fight to get the nation back on the journey that Dr. King laid out." Connerly contends that preferential treatment of minorities in college admissions and in the workplace undermines King's dream of a color-blind society and repudiates everything he stood for. Proposition 209 is certainly Connerly's crowning achievement to date, a piece of legislation that Connerly views as the natural extension of the Civil Rights Act of 1964. In fact, as printed on the ballot, Proposition 209 pilfered language directly from the 1964 bill, holding that "the state shall not discriminate against, or grant preferential treatment to, any individual or group on the basis of race, sex, color, ethnicity, or national origin in the operation of public employment, public education or public contracting."

Never mind that when those words were written, racial presumptions and practices were radically different. One major presumption was that the 1964 bill was marshaled to combat the forces of white supremacy that pervaded Southern government and civil society in de jure segregation, and in Northern states where de facto segregation reigned. Hence, the practice of whites' excluding blacks was outlawed. Blacks received newly granted citizenship rights that were framed in the universal terms that allowed them to be applied to blacks in the first place. In short, blacks should have already been included, and would have been, except for the racial distortion of the Constitution's original intent of freedom for "all men." The irony is that in order to protect the legal and civil rights of black citizens—after all, no such protection was needed, or granted, for white citizens, save in the Constitution and Bill of Rights— such protection had to be cast in language that suggested universal application. But everyone associated with the struggle for black rights understood three facts about such universality. One, universality was not a given, since it had to be fought for. Two, it was not self-evident, since it had to be argued for. And three, universality was not inalienable, since it had to be reaffirmed time and again. In other words, there were at least a few competing versions of the universal floating around. The trick was to incorporate one version of universalism, black rights, into the legal arc of another version of universalism, white privilege, while preserving the necessary illusion of neutrality on which such rights theoretically depended. Hence a philosophical principle—what the philosopher Hegel might call a "concrete universal"—was transformed into a political strategy, allowing both whites and blacks to preserve their specific stake in a universal value: democracy. To miss this process—that is, to mistake politics for philosophical principles, or, in turn, to disregard their symbiotic relationship in shaping American democracy—is to distort fatally the improvisational, ramshackle, halt-and-leap fashion by which American politics achieves its conflicting goals.

The great mistake of Connerly and his conservative colleagues is to think that American ideals, and the politics that support them, possess a neutral, universal meaning when in fact they are made up of specific, interest-driven priorities and arguments. We are on firm footing as long as we remember that the function of ideals is to govern political and social life or, more realistically, to provide an intellectual leg to stand on to argue for our view of the world. But if we collapse ideals and practices, if we mistake our views as eternal and complete, and the next person's or group's as imperfect and partial, we are on dangerous ground. Conservatives of Connerly's ilk have rarely proved their ability to make such distinctions when it comes to race. They are often bewitched by a stultifying literalism that leads them to invest in the crude reversal of fortune scenario Connerly painted when he imagined that opponents to his tactics would "stand in the doorways like the segregationists did in the 60s."

Such a literal failure of imagination also led California's Republican party to a devious plan: to employ the image of King at—where else?—the 1963 March on Washington delivering his most noted line about content of character, in a 1996 political ad urging voters to adopt the ballot measure targeting affirmative action. When civil rights leaders protested and the King estate threatened a lawsuit, the party relented, but not before the damage had been done. King had been the victim of an open surreptitiousness; his words had been twisted against their maker to justify a political policy that was underwritten by a philosophy he certainly opposed. If they were literary postmodernists, the Republican party might have been written off as a humorous attempt to "kill the author" and make merrily macabre uses of his "text." Alas, they were thudding literalists, arguing that King really believed what they made him appear

to affirm. Not even Connerly could stomach his comrades' display of ideological immaturity; he claimed he would have never used King in the ad,
since the backlash was predictable. Still, he fired his own political consul-
tant, Republican Arnold Steinberg, when he vigorously criticized the
Republican strategy. "The use of King," Steinberg emphasized, "was
juvenile at best and counterproductive at worst."

Connerly, however, remains staunch in his beliefs. "Every citizen
should have an equal chance at the starting line of life's race," Connerly
contends. "But there should not be a guaranteed outcome in the race. If
you discriminate for someone, you discriminate against someone else."
King, however, didn't buy the analogy or the logic by which it was supported. He wrote that on "the surface, this appears reasonable, but it is
not realistic." He believed that "it is obvious that if a man is entered at the
starting line in a race three hundred years after another man, the first
would have to perform some impossible feat in order to catch up with his
fellow runner." To underscore his point, King told of a visit with Indian
prime minister Jawaharlal Nehru during which he and Nehru discussed
"the difficult problem of the untouchables, a problem not unrelated to
the American Negro dilemma." Although many Indians were still prejudiced against the untouchables, it had "become unpopular to exhibit this
prejudice in any form." The reason for the changed climate was Gandhi's
great influence as well as the prohibition against discriminating against
the untouchables in India's constitution. Further, not only did the Indian
government spend "millions of rupees annually developing housing and
job opportunities in villages heavily inhabited by untouchables," but
when "two applicants compete for entrance into a college or university,
one of the applicants being an untouchable and the other of high caste,
the school is required to accept the untouchable." King indicates that his
colleague, college professor and King biographer Lawrence Reddick,
asked Nehru if such a practice weren't discriminatory. "'Well it may be,'
the Prime Minister answered. 'But this is our way of atoning for the centuries of injustices we have inflicted upon these people.'" King advocated
that America "seek its own ways of atoning for the injustices she has
inflicted upon her Negro citizens," as a "practical way to bring the
Negro's standards up to a realistic level."

Martin Luther King, Jr., has wrongly been made the poster boy for
opposition to affirmative action. His glittering moral authority has been
liberally sprinkled on conservative assaults on civil rights communities
and progressive black interests, all because of thirty-four words lifted out
of the context of his commitment to complete equality and freedom for

all Americans. Rarely has so much depended on so little. But to take full and just measure of King's views, we must read him, studying his words and his life as he evolved to engage the myriad forces that hinder the liberation of black and poor people. Unfortunately, King has been used to chide black and other humanitarian leaders who have sought, however imperfectly, to extend the views that he really held. If conservatives were to read and listen to King carefully, they would not only find little basis in King's writings to justify their assaults in his name, but they would be brought up short by his vision of racial compensation and racial reparation, a vision far more radical than most current views of affirmative action. King wrote in *Why We Can't Wait* that few "people consider the fact that, in addition to being enslaved for two centuries," that black folk were also robbed of wages for toil. It is worth quoting King at length:

> No amount of gold could provide an adequate compensation for the exploitation and humiliation of the Negro in America down through the centuries. Not all the wealth of this affluent society could meet the bill. Yet a price can be placed on unpaid wages. The ancient common law has always provided a remedy for the appropriation of the labor of one human being by another. This law should be made to apply for American Negroes. The payment should be in the form of a massive program by the government of special, compensatory measures which could be regarded as a settlement in accordance with the accepted practice of common law. Such measures would certainly be less expensive than any computation based on two centuries of unpaid wages and accumulated interest. I am proposing, therefore, that, just as we granted a GI Bill of Rights to war veterans, America launch a broad-based and gigantic Bill of Rights for the Disadvantaged, our veterans of the long siege of denial.

King ingeniously anticipated objections to programs of racial compensation on the grounds they discriminated against poor whites who were equally disadvantaged. He knew that conservatives would manipulate racial solidarity through an insincere display of new-found concern for poor whites that pitted their interests against those of blacks. King claimed that "millions of [the] white poor" would benefit from the bill. Although he believed that the "moral justification for special measures for Negroes is rooted in the robberies inherent in the institution of slavery," many poor whites, he argued, were "the derivative victims" of slavery. He conceded that poor whites are "chained by the weight of discrimination" even if its "badge of degradation does not mark them." King understood how many poor whites failed to understand the class dimensions of their exploitation by elite whites who appealed to vicious identity politics to obscure their actions. King held that discrimination was in ways "more evil for [poor whites], because it has confused so many by prejudice that they have supported their own oppressors." Hence, it was only just that a Bill of Rights for the Disadvantaged, intent on "raising the Negro from backwardness," would also rescue "a large stratum of the forgotten white poor." For King, compensatory measures that were truly just—that is, took race into account while also considering class—had the best chance of bringing healing to our nation's minorities and to the white poor. It was never one or the other; both were a moral priority for King.

Martin Luther King, Jr., hoped for a color-blind society, but only as oppression and racism were destroyed. Then, when color suggested neither privilege nor punishment, human beings could enjoy the fruits of our common life. Until then, King realized that his hope was a distant but necessary dream. As he lamented, the "concept of supremacy is so imbedded in the white society that it will take many years for color to cease to be a judgmental factor." As we interpret King's hope for a color-blind world, we must keep this in mind.

One of the greatest pitfalls of idolizing the "I Have a Dream" speech and failing to grapple with King's views on compensation to blacks is that it obscures King's dramatic change of heart and mind about the roots of white racism. Liberals and leftists often extol King's virtues as a racial healer and use his views to chide more militant blacks. They have little to say, however, about King's later-life contention that most whites were unconscious racists. For many Americans King's admission betrays his fervent commitment to racial reconciliation. That would be an unfortunate conclusion since King never shrank from racial healing. He simply believed that such healing could occur only after we acknowledged just how pervasive racism is in our nation. King's remarkable statement cannot be dismissed as the ranting of a reverse racist. We must consider what led him to such a stunning reversal of opinion. Perhaps in the process we can shed light on our own contentious racial debates.

CHAPTER 2

"Most Americans Are Unconscious Racists"
Beyond Liberalism

When Martin Luther King, Jr., was in jail in Selma, Alabama, during a 1965 voting rights drive, Malcolm X flew in to address a mass meeting at the request of the Student Nonviolent Coordinating Committee (SNCC). SNCC, which would soon elect Stokely Carmichael as its chairman, was more militant than its parent organization, the SCLC, headed by King. King had avoided meeting Malcolm in the past, since Malcolm relentlessly attacked King as an Uncle Tom. In fact, their paths had crossed only a single time, when they ran into each other at the U.S. Capitol as the Senate debated the civil rights bill early in 1964. Almost a year later Malcolm was in Selma to shake the rafters and stir the troops to fight segregation. Malcolm was introduced to King's wife, Coretta, who reports that she was "impressed by his obvious intelligence" and his gentle spirit. Mrs. King says that Malcolm indicated that he would not be able to visit King in jail since he had to catch a plane to New York in order to leave for London for a speaking engagement. Before he left, though, Malcolm made a startling revelation to Mrs. King that is still largely ignored. "'I want Dr. King to know that I didn't come to Selma to make his job difficult,'" Mrs. King says Malcolm told her. "'I really did come thinking that I could make it easier. *If the white people realize what the alternative is, perhaps they will be more willing to hear Dr. King.*'"

For most of their public careers, Martin and Malcolm brilliantly played off each other's strengths and weaknesses. They sparred each other through the media and chided one another for following the wrong path to black freedom. King practiced nonviolence and preached to blacks that they should love whites as their brothers and sisters. Malcolm fearlessly encouraged blacks to be self-reliant, reject white allies in a struggle for freedom, and, if necessary, take up arms against violent whites. But as most Americans know, Malcolm had a dramatic change of heart. After journeying to Mecca and after his stormy 1964 break with the Nation of Islam, Malcolm declared that he no longer viewed whites as "devils" but as ordinary, if flawed, human beings. Malcolm's martyrdom in 1965 brought a tragic sense of loss of a towering figure who was just coming into his own, a man who had only begun to fulfill his potential as an internationally minded leader.

Martin Luther King, Jr., experienced an equally fateful change of thinking about racism in American society. But unlike Malcolm, King lacked a dramatic event to parallel the Mecca conversion. If Malcolm was the prodigal son who strayed far from home before his partial return, then King was the son who never left but grew to question his inheritance. In some ways, King's change was even more startling and consequential than Malcolm's. Malcolm's shift to a friendlier view of whites was widely seen as a belated nod to the wisdom of the civil rights movement. Chalk one up for King, the logic ran. But what is little appreciated is how, even if indirectly and in a less pronounced fashion, an element of Malcolm's thinking got its hooks into King.

For the most part, King had been broadly trusting of whites. He believed that even the most vicious bigots would be won over by black suffering. But during the last three years of his life, King questioned his understanding of whites. Although he still believed in the possibility of transforming white society, his tactics shifted as his beliefs about white racism changed. In the past, King believed in the essential goodness of whites. Later he doubted if whites could respond adequately to appeals to conscience. King started to insist on large-scale protests and a chastened view of the desire of whites to change their behavior fundamentally. King's mature thinking depended on the skepticism that Malcolm engendered: blacks could not get very far, or at least not as far as they needed to get, by playing to white morality. King not only conceded the point, but went a step further: Most whites, he sadly concluded, were racists. Even when whites didn't intend or want to be racists, they often gave in to racist beliefs and actions. King still loved whites, but more wisely and with greater insight about their limitations. For King, this recognition was not a source of bitterness but a prompt to revised strategy. A belief that whites basically desire to do the right thing means taking one approach. But a belief that whites have to be made to behave in the right way means adopting an entirely different strategy. For the last three years of his life, this was one of King's mighty struggles.

King's revised beliefs fly in the face of his sanguine image. His beliefs certainly don't comfort liberals who deny, as King refused to do, the persistent, adaptive evil of white supremacy. Liberals and leftists alike trap

King in a view of race that he eventually discarded. As long as King waxed eloquent about how Southern segregation could be overcome with nonviolence, he was the darling of (Northern) white liberals. When he preached that blacks must sacrifice their blood and bodies to redeem whites, many liberals lauded his nobility. When he insisted that blacks love whites, even hateful and violent racists, King was crowned an epic moral figure by many liberals. And when he risked his life time and again to make certain that "the brotherhood of man [would] become a reality in *this* day," some liberals hailed him as a saint among mere mortals. The more King suffered and the more he encouraged black people to suffer, the more liberals praised King as a man who should be emulated by all blacks. (The distinction is crucial since many of these same liberals weren't about to implore whites to be beaten or killed for civil rights.) But when King began to say that racism was deeply rooted in our society and that only a structural change would remove it, he alienated key segments of the liberal establishment.

The left-liberal backlash against King was expressed in a biting passage written by cultural critic Christopher Lasch in 1991:

> In the early days of the civil rights movement, King had resisted the temptation to define black people simply as victims of white oppression. Instead he tried to encourage initiative, self-reliance, and responsibility. He understood that people who thought of themselves as victims either remained helplessly passive or became vindictive and self-righteous. His later attempt to organize a national alliance of "disadvantaged" groups, however, forced him to rely on just this kind of morally flawed appeal. . . . By taking up the charge of "white racism," he antagonized working-class and lower-middle-class whites without appeasing the black militants. . . . Instead of appealing to the nation's sense of justice, he now had to appeal to the mixture of pity and fear that came to be known, inappropriately (since it was activated less by conscience than by nerves), as "white liberal guilt."

Despite the harsh criticism of disappointed white liberals, King refused to shut his eyes or his mouth. It was his duty, he believed, to tell the truth about white supremacy in all its guises, including its softer, subtler surface as well as its hardened underbelly. Undoubtedly it was shocking to hear King reject his optimism about the "great resources of goodwill in the Southern white man that we must somehow tap." In the end, he branched beyond the South to criticize America's moral and racial illness, even as he predicted that recovery would consist of much more than tapping a vein of goodwill. In King's mature prognosis, nothing could heal the nation except radical moral surgery. This is crucial to remember today, when blacks and whites use the same water fountains but the color of a black man's skin can still cause him to be dragged to his death by a carful of white teens or brutally sodomized by white officers of the law.

What were the roots of King's earliest faith in the moral capabilites of whites? He had begun his journey to black leadership in traditional fash-ion. After pursuing seminary and doctoral degrees up North, King returned South in 1954 to accept the pastorate of Dexter Avenue Baptist Church, a small but prestigious congregation in Montgomery, Alabama. More than anything else, King wanted to improve black life in his native region. A little more than a year after going to Dexter, King won interna-tional acclaim for successfully leading the fight to desegregate public transportation in Montgomery through a widely heralded year-long bus boycott. King's reputation was powered by his charisma and his oratori-cal brilliance. He was most famous, however, for advocating nonviolent passive resistance. In the face of white violence, King counseled blacks to return good for evil. He criss-crossed the nation in one campaign after another, urging blacks not to hate whites even as he helped to unravel the tightly woven fabric of Southern apartheid. King viewed nonviolence as both a way of life and a way of undoing unjust laws. It was also an effec-tive means to challenge immoral social codes that made blacks second-class citizens. King's grasp of how widely he could apply nonviolence was tested in the numerous racial conflicts he engaged. King's hunger to find the best weapons of resistance was fed by his theology, a simmering gumbo of neo-orthodoxy, the social gospel, evangelical piety, liberalism, and, above all, radical black Christianity. King's social actions couldn't help but be improvised since they grew from the clashing forces that shaped the movement. But the moral core of King's activity lay in his vision of the "beloved community," where freedom and equality are ide-ally balanced.

King's confidence in nonviolence was helped by his belief that whites really wanted to change. Beneath their masks of racial hatred and the unseemly scowls that whites flung at blacks, King insisted, was a deep desire to repent. In King's mind, the depth of white bigotry was a sign of the great need for white forgiveness. The white soul slumped to repressed guilt for repressing blacks. Ironically, many whites often drowned their guilt by wading deeper in the fiery lake of hate. The sadistic habit of attempting to escape shame by repeating the act that causes it is one that King, a fellow Southerner and Christian, completely understood. King's claim that Southern whites really hungered for redemption was proof enough to his black critics that loving the hell out of bigots was a deluded, even destructive, strategy for social change. But to many whites, it revealed King's uncanny insight into the white psyche. It cannot be denied that whites were grieved by King and grateful to him at the same time. Although they resented being seen through, Southern whites were nonetheless comforted by King's emphasis on their humanity. In time, this led to a greater backlash because it suggested King's and black people's moral superiority, an idea that was hard for whites to accept since blacks were supposed to be inferior. But King didn't flaunt his ethical advantage in a game of racial one-upmanship. The point of the black freedom struggle, he argued, was not to embarrass whites but to embrace them along the road to equality. (King believed that the Negro's mission was to redeem America, a belief that surely presumed a special moral talent.)

Above all, King proved to be a master of the white psychology of race. He understood white racial anxiety and rescued whites by forcing them to face their spiritual contradictions. He encouraged whites to see themselves as participants in a cosmic struggle for right and wrong, even if they were often on the wrong side. The struggle to free blacks and redeem whites even gave white hatred a useful role. In King's drama, violent racism was not simply a dreadful denial of the moral order but a way to bring it into existence. Since it was inevitable, racial terror was made into an unintended ally in the fight for racial progress. In King's logic, obstacle was bent into opportunity. King depended on the expression of racial violence to dramatize the Negro's plight and to paint a searing portrait of American self-destruction. For instance, in 1963 he ingeniously wrung a moral and legal benefit for blacks out of the racial chaos of Birmingham. Through his dramatic efforts to contrast black dignity and white brutality sharply, King forced the nation to confront questions that it could no longer dismiss. Should America really seek to wash its hands of the whole racial mess by washing its black citizens off the concrete with firefighters' water hoses? Should our nation attempt to bite into our racial maelstrom by training the incisors and bicuspids of police dogs into the flesh of black men and women? Is Birmingham police commissioner Bull Connor, the violent, implacable defender of Southern segregation, really the sort of figure that we want our children to see as the family retires from dinner to watch the evening news?

Even the denouement of bigotry was useful to King's story of racial resistance. The possibility that prejudice could be partially resolved showed that blacks were willing to forgive whites and live peacefully. King's program of nonviolence was surely risky since it trusted whites and blacks to play their parts and then to treat each other as brothers and sisters. But King had a genius for making people believe that they had a moral gift they had forgotten, or never knew they possessed, and for making them proud to contribute to the common good. King, however, worked hard to deny whites the perverse pleasure of realizing that their bigotry was a spur to racial progress. He did this by suggesting that the moral values of American culture lie beyond race. Color-blindness so conceived was a crushing blow to the pigmented morality of white chauvinists. At the same time, King preached to blacks that their struggle was not between white and black but between right and wrong. By pegging black struggle to a universal moral foundation, King strongly affirmed black humanity, a fact that is today ignored by ahistorical advocates of color-blindness.

King's love of Southern whites drew in part from their mutual love of a region whose ancient and competing loyalties have imbued it with a spiritual geography that transcends land. He saw their souls and knew their pains, even their fears, because he ripened in the same soil that fed their moral imagination. King nodded to Southern white identity while undercutting it, building into his nonviolent protest a fierce belief in white redeemability. This notion ultimately won over whites but wearied blacks since the biggest burden was placed on their shoulders. Blacks had to love their hateful white neighbors. They had to "pray for those who spitefully use you." Black blood had to spill to wash away the sin of segregation. Black life was vulnerable to white violence. And black pain led to white gain, too, since, as King was almost too fond of quoting, "unearned suffering is redemptive."

King's Southern roots showed in the dramatic drawls that dotted his public speech. King's accent reminded the world of the negative hybridity of blacks in the minds of Southern segregationists: "They are *from* us but not *of* us." King's accent permitted him to lay claim to an identity that had visibly and violently tried to purge itself of its black trace. Whenever King opened his mouth, he was renewing his and black people's kinship with a tortured territory. Even as King necessarily harped on the South's bad qualities to promote black liberation, he hitched himself and his cause to the South's destiny by living, working, and, in the end, dying there. King seemed to understand how the South embodied social critic

Ernest Becker's observation that while character may be a lie, it's a *vital* lie. The South carefully shaped its character through byzantine social graces even as it teemed with suppressed longing and fear that were faintly disguised as courtesy and respect. For a long stretch of his crusade for justice, King seemed every bit the Southern gentleman. Above all, he understood how white nobility and honor worked: as a moral refuge for whites who felt betrayed by black freedom struggles and as a way for whites to save face as blacks challenged racist social habits.

It is not overstating the case to say that King was therapeutic for many Southern whites. He identified the psychic plagues that distorted Southern white culture. Many whites hated King for knowing them so well and for loving them just the same. Yet millions of Southern whites came to depend on a love they really didn't deserve from a figure their culture taught them not to respect. Somehow, though, his strange talk of redemption through black suffering proved, finally, to be irresistible even when it was morally incomprehensible. King's fight proved that although Southern blacks and whites in many ways lived in wildly different worlds, they had too much in common to make their quarrel easy or clean. They were joined by the Bible and the ham hock, by culture and cuisine. In fact, a mirror version of the Southern way of life operated in black life, even if it reflected a struggle against the inferiority imposed on it by white society. Black self-hatred often stemmed from the fear that what whites believed about blacks might be true. Black guilt, on the other hand, had to do with the failure to demand dignity and respect. The self-loathing that resulted was a faithful barometer of the great need for black liberation. But many blacks, convinced they were inferior and undeserving of equality, shrank further into a cocoon of self-hatred, denying their fitness to participate in the fight for freedom since they would be unworthy of its good results. They reinforced their chronic loss of self-worth by avoiding the struggle to achieve it. King understood both Southern white and black psychologies of race and worked to address the peculiar bruises of each community.

When King turned his attention North, he faced a far more brutal and complex terrain. King discovered the difference in the two regions soon enough when he made up his mind to conquer Northern bigotry. But his view of American racism suffered the biggest defeat. After a string of stunning Southern victories—and some notable setbacks—King temporarily moved his family to a Chicago slum for a run at Yankee apartheid. There he ran into a more stubborn force of racial resistance than he had met in all his years in the South. In applying his technique of nonviolent civil protest to Chicago, King uncovered the intransigence and intricacy of Northern racism. He was also shocked to discover the deep roots of black demoralization in the ghetto. Northern racism and black demoralization brought out the worst in King's strategies, bitterly reversing the usual success of his campaigns in exposing to the world the worst in segregated communities. He was hit in the head with a rock as he led a march for open housing in Cicero, Chicago's most notoriously racist community. He was outwitted in the media, and in political strategy, by Chicago's shrewd, hardball-playing mayor, Richard J. Daley, whose ruthless political machine counted key black ministers and politicians among its loyalists. And Northern blacks cared far less about integrating white neighborhoods than about surviving the social brutalities of ghetto life. In his last three years, white racism and black poverty changed King's mind about racism.

With the Civil Rights Act of 1964 and the Voting Rights Act of 1965 on the books, King sought to expand the scope of the civil rights revolution into the hearts and minds of black and white Northerners. King discovered very quickly that he knew neither group nearly as well as he did their Southern counterparts. The North was a far different country. It was an America whose rhythms and rituals were alien to King's slow speech and his "corny" appeals to conscience. The huge morality plays that King brilliantly staged in the South were stocked with antagonists who were beset by buffoonery or belligerence. These traits helped to underscore the dignity of black victims, whose only crime was the desire to eat a hamburger or ride a bus seated next to whites, or to vote for a mayor like their white neighbors did. If evil found brash flesh in such figures down South, up North it preferred to remain diffuse and anonymous. King didn't have a loopy sheriff to outfox after he had beat up defenseless blacks. Neither could he heavily draw on symbols of culture that transcended color and were rooted in the desire to harmonize the races, even if, ironically enough, white segregationists sought to achieve such a goal through dividing blacks and whites. Thus, the races could get along if each knew its place: whites on top, blacks on bottom. This was rough equality in Southern whites's minds, a view supported by their huge investment in the Jim Crow logic of "separate but equal." As hard as it is to admit, hierarchy was at least a hopeful sign since it grew out of a yen by whites to preserve their fragile society and defend it against Yankee hypocrisy. After all, what right did the North have to tell the South about racism when it couldn't acknowledge its own racial problems? At least the South came clean about its dirt. It consciously, if imperfectly, sought a way to live with the mess. The North, on the other hand, claimed that it was already clean, and thus largely sidestepped the always difficult task of fixing what doesn't appear to be broken.

King's open housing marches in Chicago were greeted with what he said was the most "hostile and hateful" demonstration of white racism he had ever witnessed, more violent than even Selma or Birmingham. King acknowledged that "we had not evaluated the depth of resistance in the white community," and he accused Northern whites of practicing "psychological and spiritual genocide," a stunning about-face on his earlier beliefs in the inherent goodness of whites. Not only in Chicago but in other Northern cities, like Cleveland, King faced a bewildering racial hostility. It gave him a greater appreciation for the rage of Northern blacks who doubted civil rights strategies because they didn't free blacks from economic misery. But King continued to blast away, digging himself deeper into psychological debt to a profoundly skeptical, even pessimistic, view of American race. He openly admitted that "I'm tired of marching for something that should have been mine at birth" and thundered that "if these agreements aren't carried out, Chicago hasn't *seen* a demonstration." Throughout the nation, King preached his new gospel of coming racial apocalypse if white supremacy was not destroyed. King confessed that he was "tired of race" and, anticipating the Kerner Commission, claimed that white racism was the "destructive cutting edge" that would split America into "two hostile societies." Before 1965, the imagery of a buoyant American democracy filled King's speeches and sermons. Now he lamented the loss of America's will to right its wrongs. In a remarkable sermon, King claimed:

> Our nation was born in genocide when it embraced the doctrine that the original American, the Indian, was an inferior race. Even before there were large numbers of Negroes on our shores, the scar of racial hatred had already disfigured colonial society. From the sixteenth century forward, blood flowed in battles over racial supremacy. We are perhaps the only nation which tried as a matter of national policy to wipe out its indigenous population.

In 1968, King claimed that the Constitution and Declaration of Independence were written by men who owned slaves and that a "nation that got started like that . . . has a lot of repenting to do." In a sermon to his congregation the same year, King questioned whether blacks would be able to celebrate the Bicentennial. "You know why," King asks. "Because it [the Declaration of Independence] has never had any real meaning in terms of implementation in our lives." In 1968, King made another stunning statement about why Negroes couldn't trust America, comparing blacks to the Japanese who had been interred in concentration camps during World War II: "And you know what, a nation that put as many Japanese in a concentration camp as they did in the forties . . . will put black people in a concentration camp. And I'm not interested in being in any concentration camp. I been on the reservation too long now."

King came to the conclusion that black oppression has generated a "terrible ambivalence in the soul of white America." And two weeks before his death, he announced that "yes it is true . . . America is a racist country." This is a far cry from the King who assured whites of their basic humanity, who was convinced that we must separate white sinners from the sin of white supremacy. Earlier in his career, King had said:

> And so we go this way, we can truly be God's children, and we can help America save her soul. Maybe God has called us here to this hour. Not merely to free ourselves but to free all of our white brothers and save the soul of this nation. . . . We will not ever allow this struggle to become so polarized that it becomes a struggle between *black* and *white* men. We must see the tension in this nation between *injustice* and *justice*, between the forces of *light* and the forces of *darkness*.

In his mature thinking, King grew bleaker about the possibility that whites could really change without a radical overhaul of their beliefs and values. As he told journalist David Halberstam, "For years I labored with the idea of reforming the existing institutions of the society, a little change here, a little change there. Now I feel quite differently. I think you've got to have a reconstruction of the entire society, a revolution of values." King also told Halberstam that he used to believe that most Americans were committed to racial justice and that although some white Southerners and a smattering of racist Northerners were bigots, the civil rights movement was "touching the conscience of America." After Chicago, King concluded that a small fraction of whites, largely college students, was committed to racial justice, lamenting that "most Americans are unconscious racists." In a May 1967 speech, "America's Chief Moral Dilemma," King argued that the "fact is that there has never been any single, solid, determined commitment on the part of the vast majority of white Americans . . . to genuine equality for Negroes." And in a speech delivered in August 1967, "Which Way Its Soul Shall Go," King declared that "I am sorry to have to say that the vast majority of white Americans are racists, either consciously or unconsciously."

King's change of heart about white racism reflected a huge shift in his understanding of the psychology of race. Near the end of his career, he no longer expended much energy figuring out the mood of white America. Only when one believes that bigotry flows from an unconverted heart does one work to transform an opponent's soul. But when one believes, as King did, that racial sentiments are shaped by deeply entrenched ways of life, one's moral obligation is to challenge the practices that preserve racism. King was dissatisfied with the important but limited gains that his earlier work had won. He believed that the civil rights revolution had struggled to realize rights already guaranteed by constitutional amendments for its black citizens. Though it was often bloody, that war got America to open the doors of opportunity for its ebony sons and daughters. As King envisioned it, the new war was to make America truly just, to make democracy more than words and promises. That would require the sort of broad revision of behavior that revolutions often promise but rarely deliver. For King, there was a grand precedent in American history: the creation of the United States. The American nation was born from the cruel denial of fair representation and the revolutionary desire for complete equality and radical democracy—for white men, that is. America's schizophrenia vexed King his entire career. He viewed the tension between America the Emancipator and America the Enslaver as the fundamental issue of self-identification that must be resolved.

King's radical views on race angered white liberals who felt that his earlier views were more helpful to bridging the gulf between the races. Then too, there are white liberals who might think that King's change of view is proof that even the most liberal black leaders resent white identity and culture. Other liberals were perhaps angry at King because he seemed to fantasize that blacks can be released from oppression in much the same way as one seeks release from a bad marriage: sue the injuring party for divorce or blame the person for destroying one's emotional and psychological well-being. On the first score, King's response might well be that only when the thick wall that separates blacks from whites is removed can the possibility of mutual goodwill be restored. It is, after all, a two-way street, a point that many liberals forget in their zeal to make interracial connections. From the liberal's point of view, such connections are often rebuffed for no good reason. Of course, from many black people's point of view, there is often a serious deficit of self-inventory among white liberals, a trait that might lead liberals to be more critical of their efforts to create racial healing. The lesson may be that goodwill without good work simply won't do.

On the second score, King might concede that the waters of rage sometimes flood the psyches of blacks who are presumed to be morally deficient or intellectually inferior. These presumptions, even when they are not explicitly stated, still form a painful point of reference for dialogue between whites and blacks. This certainly doesn't mean that most whites are bigots. What it does mean is that whiteness is powerful enough to do its greatest damage off the books, when no one is looking and when restraint is completely lost. Therefore, a general racial skepticism has often kept black folk alive. It is a mode of life that, should it become excessive, hurts the feelings of white allies. (Disinterested whites invest little emotion in discovering whether black conspiracy theories turn out to be true.) But why are white allies so easily offended? After all, in some instances, the failure to be skeptical has resulted in great harm to those blacks who ignore what Langston Hughes termed "the ways of white folk." In the long run, routine, benign racial paranoia (as opposed to destructive obsession with white life) appears to be worth the risk to many blacks, especially in the light of such incidents as the infamous Texaco case, where a secret tape-recording captured whites disparaging blacks and other minorities. Such instances of veiled white racism prove to many blacks that a hidden animus operates against them in influential pockets of white America.

On the final score, King might simply say that the state of race is so bad in our nation that no one metaphor could possibly capture the subterfuge and force of racial domination. One need not believe that racism completely denies black folk the freedom to act to acknowledge that, trendy academic theory aside, real victims do exist. It is true that black addiction to victimization has sometimes turned issues better suited to small claims court into federal cases. The exaggeration of perceived racial injury among some blacks has helped to ruin the sense of proportion that should make the identification of real suffering a fairly simple calculation. In truth, however, as King reminded us later in his life, America has rarely willingly acknowledged, much less responded to, black grievances. King made this point earlier in his career when he evoked the spirit of Frederick Douglass to remind blacks that freedom is never voluntarily given up but rather is taken from oppressors. All images of black suffering and the search for salvation fail, in the end, to convey fully the real experiences they represent. But the point behind every failed image is the same: the country must undergo a thorough reworking of its practices before justice is realized for black Americans.

Given the cultural amnesia that smothers King's radical legacy, it is not at all surprising that a group of liberal or formerly liberal commentators have assailed contemporary figures who warn of persistent racism or underscore the pervasiveness of white supremacy. This loosely defined group of commentators—including figures like Michael Tomasky, Tamar Jacoby, Christopher Lasch, Todd Gitlin, Jim Sleeper, and Stephan and Abigail Thernstrom—practices what may be termed the politics of racial evasion. In the politics of racial evasion, racial history is sometimes richly explored, but its effects are harshly minimized; responsibility for what is wrong is shifted from whites to blacks, or if white responsibility is acknowledged, it is in equal proportion to black culpability; and the punishing group identity imposed on blacks to limit their opportunities is neglected even as demands are made for blacks to claim a radical individualism they had been kept from enjoying by every resource of law and custom.

One of the reasons for these commentators' anger may be that when liberals were able to scapegoat unenlightened white Southerners as the source of black suffering, they could forge an alliance of conscience with blacks in opposing white supremacy. But with the claim that white liberals benefited in obvious and hidden ways from white supremacy and white privilege, and that they were themselves racist, even if unconsciously—a claim that King consistently made in his last four years—the relations between white liberals and blacks were permanently crinkled. Many white liberals lost the privilege of the outside insider status among blacks and were at times unceremoniously shed of both their innocence and their membership in black groups where their presence was a token of genuine integration and the discomforting realization among some blacks of the need for white help. For many white liberals, the best offense became a sharp defensiveness. Many white liberals launched retaliatory, and in some cases anticipatory, assaults on the psychic and cultural articulations of black difference: all-black organizations or schools, black middle-class claims of limited career opportunities, black rage vented in musical forums, extended-family forms, and civil rights leaders' claims of black erasure in Hollywood and on Wall Street.

There are many other reasons for the anger directed at blacks who argue for the lingering effects of white supremacy. Many angry critics ironically cite King as a source of reproach. To begin with, forgetting or denying King's later views permits even liberal or leftist defenders of King's legacy to pit him against contemporary advocates of his radical views. For instance, social commentator Michael Tomasky argues that King's success depended on "showing people outside the oppressed group how their interest lay in seeing members of that group lifted from oppression." In contrast are those who practice "particularist, interest-group politics," which, Tomaksy claims, are "politics where we don't show potential allies how they can benefit from being on our side," which "is a sure loser." Tomasky's point is true of the earlier King who, as historian and King biographer David Garrow argues, used nonviolent passive resistance to persuade white Americans to change. But in the early sixties, Garrow contends, King began to use nonviolence as a means to coerce social change. In short, King realized his strategy must be to make America live up to its promises of life, liberty, and the pursuit of happiness. If, in the process, people became convinced that it was in their best interests to side with blacks and the poor, fine; if not, King was prepared to argue, march, orate, and literally force the point. While it is easy for Tomasky to imagine that King would oppose contemporary interest-group politics, we should remember that King had that very charge leveled at him as he fought for justice and equality. (One of the familiar placards of protest that greeted King and his followers was, "They don't want *civil* rights, they want *special* rights"). To be sure, King never embraced racial chauvinism. To the end of his life, he eschewed vicious tribal loyalties. And he continued to embrace heartily white allies in the struggle against racial apartheid and class inequality. But the mature King insisted that America would never earn its title as the world's greatest country until it came to grips with its ongoing and pervasive racism.

If special-interest claims reflect black refusals of a universal moral impulse, then claims of white supremacy are surely a reflection of an even more disturbing black habit: playing the victim. To racial evasionists, claims of black victimization reek of an intoxication with self-righteous moralizing that avoids personal responsibility for one's own condition, a point hammered home by Christopher Lasch. Unlike most other racial evasionists, Lasch is willing to attack King for shaping many of the worst features of contemporary black racial politics. Lasch concedes that to the end, "King upheld nonviolence both as a tactic and as a principle (though with growing emphasis on the former)." If King's tactical nonviolence retained social usefulness, his move to indict white supremacy was clearly disturbing. For Lasch, "the definition of black people primarily as victims could only encourage a politics of resentment, with or without violence." Lasch writes that whether

> blacks rioted in the streets or merely demanded compensatory treatment in the courts—and the two strategies proved quite compatible—they now claimed a privileged moral position as the victims of "four hundred years of oppression." Their history of victimization, they argued, entitled them to revenge, although they indicated a willingness to settle for reparations. For obvious reasons, liberals could agree to reparations in order to escape reprisals; but their sponsorship of busing and affirmative action carried no moral weight as gestures of "compassion."

This is an extraordinarily cynical view of legitimate black moral claims rooted in the same rationale, one that Lasch endorses, for King's ethic of love. When King discouraged blacks from violently retaliating against the virulent white resistance of their Southern white brothers and sisters, Lasch seems not to have minded siding with black claims of white supremacy. Lasch says that by "addressing their oppressors not only as fellow sinners but also as fellow Southerners, King and his followers exposed the moral claims of the white supremacist regime in the South to the most damaging scrutiny." By a consistent and logical extension of the same reasoning, King came to understand the subtle enticements of racial domination that aimed straight for the liberal heart and pen: The claim of moral exemption. The insistence of a Manichean pitting "us" versus "them" and isolating bigotry in the Bubba-laden Bible belt. And the perpetuation of racial hierarchy in the belief that granting black equality would cost whites deeply entrenched ways of life, which King understood whites would believe.

But the more damaging insistence, carved from a deep and perhaps unconscious sympathy for even racist whites, is that black progress would burden not liberal whites but the poor whites who would have to pay for it with their schools and communities. Thus Lasch argued that those "who supported busing and affirmative action—comfortable members of the professional and managerial classes, for the most part—did not have to live with the consequences of their actions. The burden of busing notoriously fell on ethnic neighborhoods in the cities, not on suburban liberals whose schools remained effectively segregated or on wealthy practitioners of 'compassion' whose children did not attend public schools at all." What is especially damaging about Lasch's remarks is not his recognition of who would "pay" for black progress, although framing racial progress in such terms is more than a little revealing, particularly for a liberal. It is the radical identification with whites who benefited from racial and geographical segregation against the blacks who had been unjustly excluded from schools and neighborhoods. The identity politics—and, more relevant, ethnic victimization—that Lasch and other racial evasionists despise bleed ominously into the fabric of his arguments about the whites who will be victimized by the black progress promoted by white liberals. It is to King's credit that he not only discerned such a flawed perception in white liberalism, but that he was willing to say it out loud and make it the premise of his late-career lunge at the heart of white supremacy.

Another cause for the racial evasionists' anger is that claims of deeply entrenched racism mark uncomfortable differences between whites and blacks and complicate the proposition that "we are all alike under our skin." Hence white racial evasionists ask about blacks: "Why can't they be like us?" In other words, why can't blacks ignore race, be color-blind, and act as individuals? Critic Jim Sleeper contends that "America will make no sense at all in the years ahead unless it fulfills its destiny to become a society beyond race." As an ideal, that rings true to the aspirations of many blacks who are tired of the burden and stigma placed on race in America. But Sleeper is dazzled by the prospect of an earlier, more optimistic King when he writes of "the searing moral force of a Martin Luther King, Jr." Sleeper acknowledges that even "if every broken heart could be mended and every theft of opportunity redressed," there would still be "a black community of memory, loss, and endurance."

Sleeper has no problem with that, but he argues that "ultimately there can be only transcendence—and America becoming, without parallel, without equal. Pending that, nothing is more un-becoming than a sentimental, guilt-hobbled white liberalism." As are many other racial evasionists, Sleeper is trapped in a striking dualism: either one seeks to get beyond race or one is buried in its uncritical embrace. There is, however, plenty of ground between these positions, ground that is seeded with an awareness of the historical features and contemporary characteristics of race, as well as the recognition of other forces that shape human identity. King's recognition of white supremacy did not destroy his quest for a world beyond race. In fact, honesty about the real racial situation was the only way to arrive at such a destination. But it made no sense to board the train to racial harmony if the price of admission was a transcendence of the tracks on which one had to travel to get there.

Tamar Jacoby shares Sleeper's broad belief in color neutrality and a deep investment in a vision of racial integration that received its most eloquent expression in Martin Luther King, Jr., who more "than anyone" was "responsible for the blossoming of the word 'integration'—by virtue of sheer usage, but also because of the way he transformed its meaning." As a result, Jacoby finds disturbing the present fixation on "color-coding"— the relentless insistence that race will color human relations. As an illustration, Jacoby recalls an experience as a staff writer at *Newsweek* in the late eighties. Jacoby stopped by the desk of her researcher to check a reference. Her researcher, a "young black woman: attractive, able, personable, making her way up through the ranks at the magazine," had left her computer on and her e-mail open. As Jacoby recalls:

> The words jumped out at me, and though I knew I shouldn't, I couldn't stop myself from reading on. There were about two dozen messages sent and received over the past few weeks. . . . The difference was that, unlike my own stored mail, virtually all of hers made some mention of color: that white editor won't give me an assignment, that white scheduler put me on the late shift, that white librarian was rude to me, the white system will never be fair—to me or to us.

Jacoby recalls that she had met her share of black activists as a student in the sixties and seventies, and that as *Newsweek*'s law reporter she had encountered alienated black inmates, "kids who seemed to feel no sense of connection with the society whose laws they had broken." Her researcher was neither, but a "privileged insider" who benefited at school and work from the "racial changes of the past few decades." Since her researcher was like "other middle-class professionals her age" with a "promising career in mainstream journalism," Jacoby questions why she had "come to see this common professional problem in racial terms" and as a result felt "so irreparably cut off from her white peers."

What is striking about Jacoby's example is that she fails to understand how her act of unintended snooping provides an equally unintended metaphor for the way professional blacks feel in white corporate America: that they are forever on display, that their innermost thoughts must be policed unless they become subject to criticism or censorship, and that their alienation is increased by white liberals who fail to imagine a world where middle-class status is incapable of insulating even talented blacks from the effects of racism. Such a realization is even more ironic since another *Newsweek* colleague only a few years later published an acclaimed study of black alienation in the white workplace whose title was revealing: *The Rage of a Privileged Class.*

More revealing is the implicit ethical comparison that sets Jacoby off: "unlike my own stored mail" provides a plea for blacks to be more like her, a resolute individual. Color-coding is "playing with fire." Jacoby has no problem with a healthy celebration of one's group. As she writes, no one "who understands what makes America great can quarrel with ethnic pride." But it has its appropriate time and place, a lesson blacks must learn.

> At home, on the weekend, in the family and the neighborhood, Jews will be Jews, Italians Italian—and there is no reason blacks should be any different. . . . But when it comes to public life, even the benevolent color coding of recent decades has proved a recipe for alienation and resentment. Under the law and as people make their way up the ladders of school and career, they must operate as individuals, not members of a group. Society need not be color-blind or color-less, but the law cannot work unless it is color-neutral, and the government should not be in the business of abetting or paying for the cultivation of group identity. Nothing in the history of the past three decades suggests that American should stop requiring people to find a way of reconciling their ethnicity and their citizenship.

Few other groups have fought as hard as blacks for recognition of individual accomplishment and merit. The color coding of black identity is a historical process that occurred without black input. Blacks had little choice in how they were perceived by whites and even less choice about what features of their culture would be lauded or lambasted. In a culture where race has shaped the criteria by which blacks have been judged; where blacks have been denied the possibility of enjoying the fruits of their talents in a national vineyard they helped to plant and nurture to greatness; and where the rules of fair play have been rigged against blacks until less than forty years ago, it is disingenuous for racial evasionists to ignore that history and blame blacks for social conditions they had no hand in creating. The stinging paradox of being judged as a group and yet being expected to act like an individual meant that even excellence in a given activity

> made blacks exceptions to, not examples of, their race. Ironically, to be thought of as an exception to the race still denied a pure consideration of individual merit. As long as race colored the yardstick, a real measurement of individual achievements was impossible. It is a bitter paradox that the evaluation of individual achievement that blacks yearned for was subordinated to a consideration of any achievement's impact on, and relation to, the race. Blacks were routinely denied the recognition of individual talent that is supposed to define the American creed. This history is barely mentioned now that blacks are made by many whites to look as if they duck individual assessment while embracing group privilege.

Most racial evasionists adopt the fundamental principle of rough equality between the black and white races in calculating responsibility for our racial predicament. That is a fatal mistake, one that King refused to make. His indictment of white supremacy was driven by the realization that there is no easy equivalency between the experiences of blacks and whites. It is by now a commonplace among critics to say that how blacks and whites perceive race depends on where they fall in the racial order. This observation assumes that black and white perspectives on race share an equal starting place of reasonable bias—that is, that one's self- or group interest will color, but not control, what one thinks about racial issues. The problem with this assumption is that it neglects the history of how black and white interests were unequally weighted in determining what was viewed as reasonable to begin with. In other words, white perspectives on race have long set the limits for what is accepted as common sense or received wisdom on the subject. The success of this move among whites has hinged in large part on the power to deny the legitimacy, logic, or persuasiveness of black beliefs about race. Black folk have often been made to feel foolish, ignorant, or stupid—and in some cases, even insane—for the racial views they hold.

This history must be taken into account as we assess the radical discrepancy between white and black views of racial issues. To assign equal value to the perspectives of whites and blacks as a group— the suspicions they harbor, the skepticism they nourish, the biases they express—is to pretend that racial differences in opinion were given equal consideration in determining the course our country should follow in resolving its racial agonies. The tough truth is that the resolution of racial problems for whites often resulted in the deepening of racial problems for blacks. To take just one example, the dismantling of de jure segregation in American schools helped accelerate patterns of white flight from American cities and thus the deepening de facto residential segregation afflicting black communities.

There was no equal sharing, no equal bargaining, no equal arguing for positions about racial matters. In order to fix what is fundamentally wrong with race in America, those who had a lion's share in making things bad must bear a greater responsibility in making them better. Whites who have benefited, whether explicitly or unconsciously, from racial inequality must now be courageous in rejecting a belief in the moral equivalency of black and white views about race. Instead, they should acknowledge their obligation to give black beliefs the weight and consideration they justly deserve. Thus, when blacks view the criminal justice system with suspicion, when they are wary of white juries, when they believe that innocent blacks can be framed by police—for instance, as many blacks did in responding to the verdicts in the O. J. Simpson murder and civil trials—they are responding to a verifiable history of racial inequality. In such an unjust world, white skepticism about black juries' ability to convict black criminals does not have the same moral gravity as the claims of blacks victimized by a legacy of racial injustice.

To ask whites to understand this is not only counterintuitive; it demands a rejection of the claim to ethical innocence that masks white privilege and supremacy while reinforcing black inequality. That inequality brought into existence broadly differing group perceptions about what is good, what is normal, what is desirable, and what is achievable in regard to race in America. Short of acknowledging this truth, we will not get very far in bridging the enormous racial gap that recent polls and our social and political life prove to us exists.

If King's later views on white racism have, even posthumously, alienated many white liberals and leftists—or made them scamper to revise King's beliefs and saddle them with a more palatable outcome—then his views on the Vietnam War had an equally chilling effect. Overnight King became the most famous American to urge our nation to withdraw from Vietnam. Not only did King's antiwar activism outrage President Lyndon Baines Johnson, the civil rights movement's greatest political ally, but it brought King an unprecedented level of criticism from other black leaders. As if rethinking his views on the American dream and on racism weren't controversial enough, King bravely leaped into the heart of the issue that displaced civil rights as the defining American crisis. In retrospect, King turns out to have been right, but he clarified his views when it was riskiest to do so, long before anyone was sure what the outcome of the war would be. King's principled pacifism provoked cries of betrayal from critics who were suspicious of his radical political beliefs. Why did King jeopardize the fragile fate of the civil rights movement by opposing the war in Vietnam? By answering this question, we will learn more about King's valiant attempt to escape the moral ghetto and claim the full stature of the title he loved best: Baptist preacher.

CHAPTER 3

"As I Ponder the Madness of Vietnam"
The Outlines of a Militant Pacifism

At Martin Luther King, Jr.'s funeral on April 9, 1968, a tape-recorded excerpt of one of his last sermons, "The Drum Major Instinct," was dramatically aired. In the sermon, which he delivered at Ebenezer exactly a month before his death, King tells the folk how he would like his eulogist to remember him. Because the funeral was nationally televised, King's haunting words have become among the most famous that he uttered. King implored his eulogist not to mention his Nobel Peace Prize, the several hundred awards he had won, or where he attended school. Instead, he wanted the spotlight on what he thought were his life's deeper ambitions, its higher achievements. One can hardly escape the irony that the marvel of technology permitted King to say at his own funeral what he didn't want said at his own funeral, making him, in effect, dishonor his own wish. King said that he'd like his eulogist to say that he tried to feed the hungry, clothe the naked, visit the imprisoned, and "love and serve humanity." Before that, King said he wanted it mentioned that he tried to "give his life serving others," that he "tried to love somebody."

A single sentence captures King's struggle with his beloved country over what he had earlier in his sermon termed a "bitter, colossal contest for supremacy." Speaking of Vietnam, King begs his eulogist to say that "I tried to be right on the war question." What wasn't played at King's funeral was his declaration near the end of his sermon that nations were embroiled in the drum major instinct, an instinct that says, "I must be first," "I must be supreme," "our nation must rule the world." "And I am sad to say," King lamented, "that the nation in which we live is the supreme culprit." As if anticipating yet another wave of opposition to his antiwar sentiments, King quickly adds, in a tone both defiant and weary, that "I'm going to continue to say it to America, because I love this country too much to see the drift that it has taken." King assures his hearers that God "didn't call America to do what she's doing in the world today," that "God didn't call America to engage in a senseless, unjust war, [such] as the war in Vietnam." King rushes to make the even stronger claim that "we are criminals in that war," asserting that we "have committed more war crimes almost than any nation in the world." In redoubling his effort to oppose the war and draw strength and courage from repeating a danger-ous truth, King thunders again, "And I'm going to continue to say it."

The sermon passages that weren't played at his funeral make it clear that King's antiwar activism sprang from his belief that the gospel calls individuals and nations to repent of their sins and to serve humanity as best they can. King's views of Vietnam proved that his moral universe was complex. He refused to mold his conscience solely in the shape of a civil rights rally. Neither did his social analysis hinge exclusively on the levers of a voting booth. King was attacked within the civil rights move-ment and beyond for his daring opposition to war. He broke with other leaders in a dramatic but heartfelt gesture of moral independence. This side of King's public identity is rarely lauded, though his uncanny ability to stand alone made him even greater.

Martin Luther King, Jr., opposed the Vietnam War because he was a profound pacifist and proponent of nonviolence, because he was a Chris-tian minister, and because he was, as noted Jewish theologian Abraham Joshua Heschel said ten days before his death, a "great spiritual leader." King's pilgrimage to militant pacifism was a thoughtful one shaped by hard political choices and competing moral duties. Several myths cloud King's principled opposition to the Vietnam War: that he was always an absolute pacifist and immediately opposed the war; that he was a lone voice crying in the wilderness; that his militant pacifism was sparked by his white advisers; and that he turned to the white antiwar movement because there was little support for his beliefs in black and Latino com-munities. In truth, King's pacificist views became progressively more mil-itant as he took two years to condemn the war in public consistently; his antiwar activity was motivated as much by moral and political pressure from key black colleagues as by conscience and a commitment to nonvio-lence; his was not the only black voice (simply the most prominent) demanding an end to the war; and the strong antiwar sentiment in poor black communities fueled King's powerful protest against Vietnam, eliciting strong rebuke from many middle-class blacks and the white establishment.

As in most other areas of his social philosophy, Martin Luther King, Jr.'s pacifist beliefs evolved as he matured morally and as he confronted political situations that demanded his ethical attention. In contrast to such civil rights figures as A. Philip Randolph, Bayard Rustin, James Lawson, and his wife, Coretta Scott King, King was not in his early career a "strict pacifist." In 1960, King charted the growth in his thinking about what is known in theological and philosophical circles as "just war theory," which appeals to ethical reasoning to ground the belief that some wars are morally justified. King's positive experiences with nonviolence in the mass movement that sparked the Montgomery bus boycott convinced him of the reasonable application of nonviolence to international affairs, a new turn of thought for King. King admits that in his student days, he believed in "the power of nonviolence in group conflicts within nations," but he was "not yet convinced of its efficacy in conflicts between nations." Earlier, he had believed in the limited use of war to resolve international conflict:

> I felt that while war could never be a positive or absolute good, it could serve as a negative good in the sense of preventing the spread and growth of an evil force. War, I felt, horrible as it is, might be preferable to surrender to a totalitarian system. But more and more I have come to the conclusion that the potential destructiveness of modern weapons of war totally rules out the possibility of war ever serving again as a negative good. If we assume that mankind has a right to survive then we must find an alternative to war and destruction. In a day when Sputniks dash through outer space and guided ballistic missiles are carving highways of death through the stratosphere, nobody can win a war. The choice today is no longer between violence and nonviolence. It is either nonviolence or nonexistence.

King confessed that he was "no doctrinaire pacifist" and instead considered his position a "realistic pacifism" that was not "sinless" but the "lesser of evil in the circumstances." King thus disavowed making a "claim to be free from the moral dilemmas that the Christian nonpacifist confronts" while arguing that the church "cannot remain silent while mankind faces the threat of being plunged into the abyss of nuclear annihilation." King concluded that if the church "is true to its mission it must call for an end to the arms race."

King's growing political radicalism caused him to deepen his commitment to aggressive nonviolence as a remedy for social ills. More immediately, the bombing of North Vietnam and the buildup of American forces in 1965—with the ominous code-name "Rolling Thunder"—prodded King to reexamine his pacifist views. By 1965 he had concluded that America's policy on Vietnam had been since 1945 "morally and politically wrong." Despite his views, King's public criticism of the war was hampered by two factors. First, his evolving radicalism called for an independence from mainstream politics that the bulk of his followers were unlikely to embrace immediately or enthusiastically. Second, his open criticism of American foreign policy would alienate officials of the federal government on whom blacks depended to protect and extend their civil rights. This vicious double-bind effectively silenced King's opposition to the war and made it nearly impossible for him to generate sympathy for antiwar activities in broad segments of the civil rights community, including his own SCLC. Nevertheless, King sought to balance the racial realpolitik in civil rights circles that discouraged antiwar sentiment and the demands of his conscience and his commitment to nonviolence. In the beginning, it made for an awkward compromise of principles for politics, a compromise that eventually wearied King and led to his sharp break with civil rights orthodoxy. If his route to resistance began in confidence, only to be derailed by media and movement criticism, his eventual embrace of radical pacifism landed him in strange territory and brought him even stranger enemies and allies.

Beginning in the spring of 1965, King offered several public criticisms of America's foreign policy in Vietnam. At Howard University, he claimed that Vietnam was "accomplishing nothing." In a tour of Boston's predominantly black Roxbury, King called for the United States to end the war. At a SCOPE orientation, King called for a negotiated settlement and the end of American hostilities. At an SCLC meeting in Petersburg, Virginia, King pleaded for the end of the war and claimed that we "must negotiate with the Vietcong." Without the prior approval of his board or its members, King gave a speech at SCLC's annual convention in August 1965 calling for direct negotiations between Washington and the Vietcong's National Liberation Front and the halting of American bombing. King argued that North Vietnam would drop its demand for the immediate withdrawal of foreign troops and agree to UN mediation. After huddling with his advisers, King pledged to write letters to Lyndon Johnson, North Vietnam's leader, Ho Chi Minh, and leaders in Moscow and Beijing to garner support for his peace proposal. King even suggested that Americans should go to Vietnam to rebuild "some of the villages which have been destroyed."

Before the convention began, King discussed with his advisers, Stanley Levison, Clarence Jones, Harry Wachtel, and Bayard Rustin, the value of an SCLC resolution supporting his criticism of foreign policy in Vietnam. He was rebuffed by SCLC's board. Many of SCLC's black ministers were extremely loyal to Johnson because of his profound commitment to civil rights, a commitment that in action and scope far exceeded the achievements of his predecessor, John F. Kennedy. It made little sense to many of these ministers to antagonize the man who had arguably done more for black folk than any other president since Abraham Lincoln. Board member Benjamin Hooks, who would later succeed Roy Wilkins as the NAACP's executive director, cautioned the civil rights organization from going "too far in the international arena." King contended that "we have an obligation as individuals to express our concern about the peace question" and that there was "a need to call for a negotiated settlement." After a great deal of discussion, SCLC's board "issued a statement disassociating the organization from its leader's comments." For the time being, King was undaunted, and with his organization's blessing, he pursued his agenda of antiwar criticism as a conscientious individual, not in his official capacity as SCLC's head.

Although he was not alone in expressing antiwar sentiments, King raised his voice against Vietnam before such criticism was fashionable among liberals and long before it was viewed as a reasonable position that a true patriot might adopt. When he first criticized the war, King was immediately chastised by other civil rights leaders, who feared that his views would alienate the Johnson White House. Moreover, politicians and the media assailed King's antiwar statements as well. The NAACP's Roy Wilkins argued that "civil rights groups [do not] have enough information on Vietnam, or on foreign policy, to make it their cause." The National Urban League's Whitney Young argued that "Johnson needs a consensus. If we are not with him on Vietnam, then he is not going to be with us on civil rights." His own aides, including Andrew Young and Bayard Rustin, warned King that a direct confrontation with Lyndon Johnson would be unwise and costly to the black freedom struggle. Their fears were certainly not unreasonable. Johnson's support of civil rights legislation before Congress was crucial to its success.

Predictably, Johnson was in private both wounded and outraged by King's comments. Johnson was noticeably frosty to King in August 1965 at the White House ceremony, where the president signed the Voting Rights Act. Nevertheless, Johnson encouraged King to meet America's

UN ambassador, Arthur Goldberg, for a briefing on diplomatic initiatives to end the hostilities in Vietnam. When Goldberg postponed their planned late August 1965 meeting in New York, King still responded to reporters' questions about his Vietnam letter-writing campaign. He admitted that he had not yet followed through, but that it was "very urgent to work passionately and unrelentingly for a negotiated settlement of this very dangerous and tragic conflict." King disavowed any intention to act as a negotiator or to make SCLC a key player in peace efforts while emphasizing the prophetic duties that animated his ministerial calling, including the declaration that "war is obsolete" and that dissent over Vietnam was not disloyalty to the nation. Goldberg finally met with King on September 10, as King urged America to halt the bombing of North Vietnam and to negotiate with the Vietcong. At Johnson's request, Goldberg told King that secret negotiations were taking place between Washington and Hanoi and that peace was quite near. Further King was warned that "public utterances . . . which called for a laying down of arms would give aid and comfort to the enemy and stiffen [Ho Chi Minh's] position." Both Goldberg and King reported that the meeting was friendly and productive. The day after their meeting, however, Connecticut senator Thomas Dodd, a close friend of Johnson, sharply denounced King's views. Dodd lambasted King as having "absolutely no competence" in foreign policy and charged King with violating the Logan act prohibiting private negotiations with foreign powers. Dodd also argued that King's public comments had "alienated much of the support he previously enjoyed in Congress."

King believed that Johnson was behind Dodd's acrimonious attack. He also feared that the media assault in the wake of his criticism of foreign policy would unfairly overlook the merits of his arguments. King had good reason to lament the media bashing he endured. In the light of the unequivocal stand against Vietnam he took later, King's early opposition was certainly tame. The same was true in the Montgomery bus boycott: the early, relatively moderate demands of blacks were sharply rebuffed, leading to an escalation of response by the offended blacks. Similarly, King's early response to Vietnam—calling for a halt of the bombing, for all parties to huddle at the conference table, and for the Chinese and North Vietnamese to retreat from their demand for unilateral withdrawal of U.S. military forces—was by all measures a modest proposal. King's moderate views did not keep him from being attacked, not only by black leaders and white politicians, but by the national press as well, especially the news magazines. King's press secretary said that King was "just bombarded with criticism, both in the Negro press and the white press, . . . and it upset him very much." *Time, Newsweek,* and *U.S. News and World Report,* according to media critic Richard Lentz, held that "King should have . . . kept silent" and believed that "black leaders had no business speaking about such matters." *Time* repeatedly failed to mention King's doctorate or his Nobel Peace Prize, which should have qualified him to speak out on issues of war and peace, and ridiculed elements of his antiwar criticism as the work of a "drawling bumpkin, so ignorant that he had not read a newspaper in years, who had wandered out of his native haunts and away from his natural calling." The title of *Time's* article summed its position: that King was "Confusing the Cause." Although King was a powerful symbol of the "coalition of conscience" favored by the more liberal *Newsweek,* the magazine nonetheless criticized him for his antiwar posture since it threatened to deepen the rifts in the already deteriorating civil rights alliance. Hence, King was viewed as "opportunistic and meddling." Although the conservative *U.S. News and World Report* initially treated King less harshly than *Time,* it very quickly ran a series of articles that "painted King as an opportunist trying desperately to maintain his leadership of the civil rights movement and as one of the reckless black leaders 'exploiting dissatisfaction' in black America."

The harsh attacks on King by black leaders, white politicians, and the national press forced him into a self-described temporary withdrawal. He decided to drop his letter-writing campaign and concentrate on civil rights. In a conference call with his advisers, King reveals the sobering effect of the stinging rebukes he received from negative press coverage:

> I am convinced that the press is being stacked against me on this position. The criticism that affects me more is the one that says that I am power drunk and that I feel that I can do anything because I got the Nobel Prize and it went to my head and . . . that I am stepping out of bounds. No, I really don't have the strength to fight all these things. . . . I may feel a sense of guilt about the civil rights movement because this would take too much of my time to fight this. . . . I have to find out how I can gracefully pull out so I can get on with the civil rights issue because I have come to the conclusion that I can't battle these forces who are out to defeat my influence.

King disagreed with the notion that he must completely disengage, but he confessed that he needed "to withdraw temporarily." Aide Harry

Wachtel told King that "you don't have to withdraw, Martin, just sit back and let the bombshell you dropped have its impact."

King, however, was clearly wounded and fatigued. He reluctantly agreed to curb his criticisms of the war in the light of Goldberg's appeal on behalf of the president and due to the devastating dressing down in the national press. "They told me I wasn't an expert on foreign affairs, and they were all experts," King said in referring to the Johnson administration. "I knew only civil rights and should stick to that." King's awkward truce was troubled from the beginning, and it would not be long before he was pulled forcefully back into the stream of antiwar dissent. When former SNCC activist Julian Bond was in January 1966 unjustly denied the state senate seat in the Georgia legislature to which he was elected in the fall of 1965 because of his endorsement of SNCC's antiwar press release, King "put his pen, his voice, and his prestige at the service of the campaign to get Bond reinstated." Moreover, 1966 saw two forces that lent moral force and political urgency to King's full-fledged return to antiwar activism: the diversion of federal funds for domestic spending into the ever deepening war chest and the surge of antiwar passions, in both mainstream circles and the Northern poor black communities on which King was concentrating. In 1966, Congress cut funds for community action programs by one-third when it slashed half a billion dollars from the budget of the Office of Economic Opportunity, the primary vehicle of the government's War on Poverty. Congress's action rebutted the Johnson administration's boast that it could at the same time provide "guns and butter." Thus, a "distracted, uncaring President Johnson and spiraling war costs had turned the Great Society's war against poverty into a war against the poor; a war Republicans would later wage even more fiercely." King summoned an even more distressing metaphor as he testified before a Senate subcommittee at the end of 1966, saying that "poverty . . . and social progress are ignored when the guns of war become a national obsession. . . . The bombs in Vietnam explode at home; they destroy hopes and possibilities for a decent America."

Throughout 1966, the antiwar movement picked up steam and reflected the growing willingness of some Americans to challenge the nation's hawkish temperament and the unthinking link between patriotism and prowar passion. Of course, King continued to worry over Vietnam. His sermons and speeches reflected his disgust with American foreign policy, the lack of courage displayed by leaders unwilling to voice their antiwar views publicly, and the unwillingness of the press to entertain the possibility of a rational and principled opposition to the war. In their speeches and sermons, many SCLC staff members, including James Bevel, Hosea Williams, and Ralph Abernathy, spoke out against Vietnam. King eventually got the SCLC board to take a public stand against the war in strongly worded resolutions at it semiannual meeting in April and at the annual convention in August. Figures like prominent pediatrician Benjamin Spock, Yale chaplain William Sloane Coffin, and socialist leader Norman Thomas were helping to galvanize pockets of national opinion against the war. Spock had approached King on an airline flight in late 1966 to urge King to make a world tour for peace and to fill the sorely needed role of symbolic leader of the growing peace movement, a role that King could not at the time accept. But his encounter with Spock convinced King even more of the wrongness of official forces that would squash dissent in the name of national loyalty. In fact, when King managed an extremely rare vacation from his duties during the holiday season of 1966–1967, he was interrupted by adviser Stanley Levison with a request from Coffin, Thomas, *Nation* editor Carey McWilliams, and liberal activist Allard Lowenstein to take a more prominent role in the peace movement. Coffin, Thomas, and Lowenstein sought King's consent to run as a presidential candidate on a 1968 third-party ticket, an idea that King considered for its symbolic value for peace and justice purposes but eventually ruled out as unfeasible. More immediately, McWilliams wanted King to speak on Vietnam at an upcoming *Nation* forum.

King gave his first speech devoted exclusively to Vietnam, entitled "Casualties of the War in Vietnam," at a conference sponsored by the *Nation* magazine on February 25, 1967, arguing that American foreign policy was "supporting a new form of colonialism." This time there would be no stopping King as he lambasted American foreign policy with renewed moral passion and a commitment to showing the lethal links between racism, militarism, and poverty. King also locked arms with Spock, who was later paired with King on a presidential wish list by radical student activists, as they marched in the largest peace demonstration in history on April 15, 1967, sponsored by the Spring Mobilization to End the War in Vietnam, chaired by renowned pacificist A. J. Muste. The theme of King's speech that day was simple and eloquent: "Stop the Bombing." The demonstration was also attended by Harry Belafonte, Floyd McKissick, Stokely Carmichael, and a multicultural gaggle of activists largely on the very splintered left: Sioux Indians, hippies, militant leftists, communists, black nationalists, World War II and Korean War veterans, Puerto Ricans, actors, poets, musicians, pacifists, liberals, anarchists, and socialists. In May 1967 King spoke extensively about Vietnam

at the SCLC convention in South Carolina. On Memorial Day he addressed
a National Labor Leadership Conference at the University of Chicago. In
his speech, "The Domestic Impact of the War in Vietnam," he reiterated
his belief that the Vietnam War made the American War on Poverty, and
the Great Society that supported it, a flagrant myth. King insisted that
the war gave ammunition to reactionary forces at home, including those
opposed to blacks, labor, and humanism, providing this antidemocratic
bloc a "weapon of spurious patriotism to galvanize its supporters into
reaching for power right up to the White House." King included an
uncharacteristically scathing assessment of a public figure, saying of
Ronald Reagan, "When a Hollywood performer, lacking distinction even
as an actor, can become a leading war hawk candidate for the presidency
only the irrationalities induced by a war psychosis can explain such a
melancholy turn of events." (If Reagan had learned of King's statement,
it may help explain his disgruntlement with signing the King holiday legislation nearly fifteen years later.)

King's most famous statement of conscientious objection to the war,
"A Time to Break Silence," was delivered at New York's famed Riverside
Church on April 4, 1967, exactly a year before his martyrdom. King
detailed his reasons for opposing the war after noting the difficulty of
"opposing [the] government's policy, especially in time of war," and the
equally powerful obstacle of "the apathy of conformist thought within
one's own bosom and in the surrounding world." King made no secret of
his deep resistance to the war because it was stealing precious resources
from domestic battles against economic suffering, proving that the "Vietnam war is an enemy of the poor." King also noted the racial subtext of
the draft: black soldiers were being sent off by their government to perish
in "extraordinarily high proportion to the rest of the population." King's
double-barreled criticism was certainly not lost on the Johnson administration. King not only argued that the Vietnam War was an imperialist
assault on Third World peasants, but as far as he could tell, America's
prosecution of the war was racist as well. It was only after his death that
King was fully vindicated. Studies in the early 1970s show that while only
13 percent of the military was black, 28 percent received combat assign-
ments. Moreover, in 1965, the military lowered its educational standards
to increase its pool of soldiers, inducting blacks who had been previously
rejected—a case, it seems, of *affirmative retroaction*. In 1964, 18.8 percent
of eligible whites were drafted, compared to 30.2 percent of eligible
blacks. And in 1967, only 31 percent of eligible whites were inducted into

the military compared to 67 percent of eligible blacks. These numbers substantiate King's claim that black soldiers were being asked to sacrifice their lives to "guarantee liberties in Southeast Asia which they hadn't found in America." In this light, King says, he "could not be silent in the face of such cruel manipulation of the poor."

King argued that he could not encourage black youth to avoid violence while condoning its use in Vietnam, a contradiction many youth readily cited when King came crusading in their burned-up ghettoes. Moreover, the SCLC's motto was to "Save the Soul of America." If ever that needed doing, it was as America lost its political way and moral vision in Vietnam. King believed that winning the Nobel Peace Prize in 1964 commissioned him to guard the sanctity of nonviolence the world over. He felt that the gospel compelled him to tell uncomfortable truths about our nation's blood lust and international folly. King proposed a five-step plan for American withdrawal and called for "a revolution of values," even as he urged Americans to "rededicate ourselves to the long and bitter—but beautiful—struggle for a new world."

King's assault on America as the "greatest purveyor of violence in the world today" elicited a predictably furious reaction from the White House. Hardly anyone, however, could anticipate the sort of personal venom that Johnson expressed when he boiled with rage against "Martin Luther King, that goddamned nigger preacher." Johnson's confession to King during one of their last conversations was particularly odd: that his criticism of the war had the same effect on Johnson as if he had discovered that King had raped his daughter. In that anguished statement, Johnson tapped the tortured white male Southern soul: its jealousy and fear of black men, its selective rebuff to interracial sex (after all, thousands of white men aggressively pursued it), and its unquestioning use of white women to show how forbidden sexual desire is tied to political betrayal.

The polls were against King as well. In 1967, a majority of Americans, white and black, supported the war. In a Harris poll, only 25 percent of blacks supported King's stand on the Vietnam War. The response from civil rights quarters was swift and unsparing. NAACP head Roy Wilkins and National Urban League president Whitney Young charged that King's antiwar activities were thwarting the cause of racial justice. An April 12, 1967, resolution adopted by the NAACP said that to "attempt to merge the civil rights movement with the peace movement . . . is, in our judgment, a serious tactical mistake," concluding that it "will serve the cause neither of civil rights nor peace." Massachusetts senator Ed

Brooke, former UN undersecretary and fellow Nobel Peace Prize laureate Ralph Bunche, and baseball legend Jackie Robinson, then a special
assistant to New York governor Nelson Rockefeller, all agreed.

The news media chimed in. *The Washington Post* said that King's
Riverside speech was a "grave injury" to the civil rights struggle and that
King had "diminished his usefulness to his cause, to his country, and to
his people." *The New York Times* editorialized that King's speech was a "fusing of two public problems that are distinct and separate" and that King
had done a "disservice to both." This sentiment was echoed in the title of
Life Magazine's response to King's speech: "Dr. King's Disservice to His
Cause." If the three major news magazines had been deeply disappointed
with King's earlier antiwar activism—an activism they had helped to end
temporarily with their unkind digs—they now attacked King with ferocious abandon. *Newsweek* columnist Kenneth Crawford attacked King for
his "demagoguery" and "reckless distortions of fact." He contended that
King "seemed to have abandoned his dream—of an America in which people of all races and kinds would stand equal—in favor of a nation in which
a race-conscious minority dictated foreign policy." *Time* contended that
King's status as a black leader gave him no right to oppose the war, and
that by joining the peace movement, he had failed in his commitment to
"the entire cause of nonviolent Negro advancement." *U.S. News and
World Report* virtually accused King of treason by bitterly complaining
that he was "almost lining up with Hanoi." As Lentz notes, all three news
magazines shared a common theme in their attack on King: that he "was
ignorant of the best course to follow in settling the war; he was a source
of discomfiture to his 'liberal' allies [not so great a transgression in the
eyes of the conservative *U.S. News*]; and he was an ingrate, unapprecia-
tive of the rights won for him by other Americans willing to nourish the
Tree of Liberty with their blood." And black journalist Carl Rowan, writing in the *Reader's Digest*, launched an attack on King that was laced with
innuendo ("a more sinister speculation that had been whispered around
Capitol Hill . . . talk of communists influencing . . . the young minister)
and pettiness ("his trips to jail looked like publicity stunts"). Rowan claimed
that King's Riverside speech "put a new strain and new burdens on the civil
rights movement." He bitterly concluded that King had "alienated many
of the Negro's friends and armed the Negro's foes, in both parties, by creating the impression that the Negro is disloyal."

The perception that the Negro was disloyal when he dissented on war
derives from two interrelated forces: the long history of black commit-

ment to the national welfare in wartime efforts and the refusal to confront the national hypocrisy of deploying blacks to defend a democracy on foreign soil that they could not enjoy at home. Since slavery, blacks have actively defended the United States when it waged war to defend its national interests. In fact, the abolition of slavery and the promising achievements of Reconstruction were viewed in part as a reward for the indispensable service of over 200,000 black soldiers. Since the emancipation of slaves was a key factor in the Union's victory over the Confederates, black leadership has often conceived loyalty to the federal government as a crucial element in securing black liberation. In turn, black loyalty became a litmus test for black patriotism, a sticky situation at best since such loyalty was predicated on the willing suspension of dissent in the face of national crisis to unify around the common objective of protecting American interests. Even radical leaders like W.E.B. Du Bois argued that blacks should "forget our special grievances and close ranks . . . with our white fellow citizens." Du Bois's appeal was heeded: over 367,000 soldiers answered the call to armed service in World War I. But black soldiers did not reap the domestic benefits of their foray into European territory. Black patriotism had little effect in convincing the federal government to dismantle Jim Crow and to stem the rising tide of white supremacy. Nevertheless, black leaders and the black masses mobilized behind America once again in World War II. But sparks of dissent fueled some governmental change—especially as socialist labor leader and pacifist A. Philip Randolph threatened a massive march on Washington that led to an executive order from President Franklin Delano Roosevelt banning racial discrimination in the defense industry.

The interests of blacks suffered a slashing paradox during war: blacks were at once submerged in the larger pool of patriotism and thus identified as American, while the very act of such an identification nullified their appeals to racial distinctiveness as the basis of being granted the rights—of democracy, freedom, and justice—for which they fought. Thus, they were allowed to be fully American only when they abandoned their racial interests, or American soil, to fight for American sovereignty and support American allies. The natural inclination for most Americans, many of whom shaped their identities in the crucible of ethnic inheritance, is to assert that such a subordination of group interests to the national interest is the way of all loyalty. Such a judgment, however, overlooks a crucial distinction between racial and ethnic groups: that black interests were almost always the racial shorthand of a request to join

fully an American democratic experiment from which they had been systematically and unjustly excluded, but which they were expected to
defend fully. That their loyalty has been constant is a remarkable feature
of black American life.

King's dissent marked a departure from mainstream black leadership
and built on a tradition of principled pacificism and socialist resistance
within black life. When Du Bois urged blacks to close ranks with their fellow citizens in World War I and accepted a captaincy in the army, Randolph
and his colleague Chandler Owen criticized Du Bois for capitulating to capitalist interests that held little promise for the working masses. Randolph
and Owen objected to the physical abuse suffered by blacks and stepped up
their radical antiwar sentiments, "offenses" for which they were briefly
jailed in 1918. Similarly, King's charges of colonialism and genocide in
American foreign policy in Vietnam were linked to his profound concern
for poor blacks drafted to defend a nation that subjected them to racial
oppression and economic exploitation. King's views on Vietnam were
shaped by his growing racial militancy and economic radicalism. His
antiwar sentiments were also much more decisively shaped by black colleagues and the black poor than has been acknowledged.

Coretta Scott King played a crucial role in influencing her husband's
views on the war. From her student days at Antioch College, Coretta
King was active in the peace movement, joining the Women's International League for Peace and Freedom. She was an earlier and more
devoted pacificist than her husband, continuing throughout the fifties
and sixties her peace activity in the Women's International League for
Peace and Freedom and the National Committee for a Sane Nuclear Policy (SANE). Moreover, her grasp of nonviolent theory and her profound
personal commitment to the practice of peace and nonviolence influenced the development of King's thought. Coretta King joined SANE in a
picket in front of the White House in 1965, and she often participated in
peace demonstrations in place of her husband, especially during the
period when he refrained from public activism against the war. She
addressed a major antiwar rally in California in 1965 and continued her
activities while King became deeply entrenched in his campaign for economic justice in Chicago in 1966. And in 1967, as her husband addressed
the Spring Mobilization antiwar rally on April 15 in New York, Coretta
Scott King exhorted over 50,000 activists in Kezar Stadium in San Francisco. Her principled pacifism nurtured her husband's beliefs and were a
source of moral inspiration as King ventured further into the peace
movement that his wife had independently supported for years.

Within King's own civil rights organization, SCLC staffer James Lawson had earlier than King become an antiwar activist and urged King to oppose the Vietnam War. As a gifted theoretician of nonviolence and a loyal pacifist, Lawson exerted a profound influence on King's conceptions of nonviolent philosophy and strategy. In 1965, Lawson journeyed to Vietnam as part of a peace-seeking mission under the sponsorship of the pacificist organization Fellowship of Reconciliation. In February 1966 Lawson and four SCLC colleagues formed the Southern Coordinating Committee to End the War in Vietnam. Besides Lawson, Hosea Williams, and Ralph Abernathy, Andrew Young and James Bevel were crucial in solidifying King's commitment to antiwar activities. Young was initially skeptical of the antiwar movement, branding the antiwar activists gathered to discuss strategies for 1967's Spring Mobilization "a bunch of crazies," who were "uptight, high-strung, bitter." Young questioned King's wisdom in opposing the war, characterizing the peace movement as a "band wagon that's playing a 'square' tune." Young contended that only a long-term strategy of political action would change the militaristic views of Congress. In time, however, Young became deeply committed to the antiwar movement and offered valuable counsel to King about strategies to balance the demand for economic equality, racial liberation, and peace.

James Bevel was perhaps the most aggressive antiwar activist on SCLC's staff. A brilliant rhetorician, ingenious strategist, and eccentric, mystical theologian, Bevel was one of the most commanding presences in the Southern civil rights movement. It was Bevel's leave of absence from his SCLC staff position to spearhead the Spring Mobilization—he was offered the position by A. J. Muste in the hope that he could lure King and other civil rights activists to speak—that made King realize the brain drain from the civil rights to the peace movement. Bevel became obsessed with making King realize the importance of speaking out against the Vietnam War and to become a leader of the peace movement. Bevel's wife, legendary activist Diane Nash, had visited North Vietnam in the winter of 1966–1967, reinforcing Bevel's commitment to end the war. Bevel preached that the "Lord can't hear our prayers here in America because of all the cries and moans of His children in the Mekong Delta."

During SCLC's 1966 Chicago campaign that Bevel had "masterminded," Bevel collared Andrew Young in a fit of mystical revelation.

"Andy, we have got to stop the war in Vietnam," Bevel cried. "We've got to go. The Lord came to me and told me we've got to stop it."

"Calm down, Bevel," Young urged Bevel. "Tell me what this is all about."

"Well, last night I was in the laundry room in the basement of my building," Bevel replied. "You know, babies mess up a lot of clothes. When I looked up from loading diapers into the washing machine, there was the Lord, sitting on the drier. I said, 'Lord, what have I done now.' And the Lord told me, 'James Bevel, my children are dying in Vietnam, my children are suffering. They are your brothers and sisters too. You must help them.' Then, he disappeared."

It was Young who encouraged Bevel to visit King in Jamaica, where he was attempting to complete his book *Where Do We Go from Here?* Bevel's spell of divine inspiration deposited him on King's Caribbean doorstep unannounced and helped reinforce King's determination to take a more public stand against the war.

If Bevel's theological commitments fueled his passion for peace, Stokely Carmichael's more secular inclinations made him no less zealous about ending the war. As chairperson of the Student Nonviolent Coordinating Committee (SNCC), Carmichael was an important force in the organization's 1966 decision to criticize the draft and the Vietnam War, a year before King and SCLC followed suit. As Carmichael recalls:

> I was serving as chairperson of SNCC and, recognizing that we were being isolated politically, I instinctively understood that once King takes a position against the war in Vietnam, we will no longer be isolated. Thus, my task inside of SNCC politically was to put pressure on King to make him take a stand on the war in Vietnam. We understood from the people that I selected to help in this process that here we were going to use nothing but nonviolence, love, with him. You know, the statement was, "We're going to beat them with nonviolence and love." It was clear that his philosophy made it impossible for him not to take a stand against the war in Vietnam.

Carmichael's relentless criticism of the war, and his rising visibility as a leader of the controversial push for Black Power, forced King to come to grips with the growing radicalism of poor black communities and the destructive, even genocidal, relation between war and poverty. In fact, when King finally publicly opposed the war, he was viewed as one of a trio of troublemakers dubbed by *Time* as "King, Carmichael & Co," the third member the Congress of Racial Equality's (CORE) Floyd McKissick. Indeed, on the cusp of his April 30 return to Ebenezer to expand on the address he had delivered at Riverside three weeks before, King phoned

Carmichael in recognition of the latter's productive contribution to his views on Vietnam.

"What are you doing?" King asked when Carmichael picked up the phone.

"Tomorrow's Sunday," Carmichael replied.

"Are you going to be a good Christian and go to church?" King playfully asked.

"Well," Carmichael said, " like a good heathen, I'm going to work for the people. I've got office paperwork. I'll be working since six o'clock in the morning."

"Well, I want you to come to church," King said.

"Come to church, where?" Carmichael responded.

"The Ebenezer," King said.

"What's happening there?" Carmichael demanded.

"I'm preaching," King offered.

"Well, you know, okay, I can always come hear you preach, you know," Carmichael said. "Because even though I don't believe in your stuff, you make me tap my feet, you know."

Carmichael and King enjoyed a moment of levity.

"Well," King said, "I really want you to come tomorrow."

"Okay, I'll come," Carmichael assured him.

"Because tomorrow I'm going to make my statement against the war in Vietnam," King informed Carmichael. There was about thirty-five seconds of silence between the two men. Finally Carmichael spoke up.

"I'm going to be on the front seat of your church."

Carmichael kept his word. After King's impassioned plea for peace in Southeast Asia and after his stinging, bitter indictment of American policy in the region, Carmichael joined the Ebenezer congregation in giving King a standing ovation for, in Carmichael's words, "one of the most profound speeches."

The key figure behind King's analytical genius that day, as well as in his Riverside speech on April 4, was Vincent Harding, a prominent historian and minister who was then a movement activist and Spelman College professor. In 1965 Harding addressed a long letter to King and the SCLC convention since he was unable to attend. Harding, who had diligently studied American policy in Vietnam, urged King and other civil rights leaders "to put themselves out in the open in solidarity with the suffering of the people in Vietnam." Harding prepared a memo on Vietnam for King, and as a result of his thoughtful beliefs on the war, King asked Harding to draft the speech that he would give at Riverside, and

later, at Ebenezer. Harding is convinced that what he articulated in his
draft represented King's thinking, since "much of what I believed, he
believed. And it was simply a question of what do you say and when and
where and how." Harding recalls that

> what I was doing was really simply providing the . . . historical
> basis, for what he had to say about Vietnam. My sense was that
> because of who he was and because of what the situation was,
> that it needed to be as strong as it possibly could. And that it
> needed to be tied in as fully as possible with his role as freedom
> movement leader and religious leader and peace leader. The
> important thing was that this should be a reflection of the unity of
> his role in the struggle, rather than simply being seen as a kind of
> anti-Vietnam statement, but that there should be an attempt to
> indicate the organic nature by which this flowed out his concern for
> both the black struggle in this country and for the health of the
> country at large and for the well-being of the Vietnamese people.

Adviser Stanley Levison told King that the speech "had been unbalanced and poorly thought out." King disagreed with Levison, explaining
that while he had not prepared a full text in advance, he "spent a full
afternoon thinking about" the speech and thought he "had to say something." In the end, King agreed to allow Levison and Wachtel to prepare
his April 15 speech at the Spring Mobilization. That may explain King's
poor performance at the mobilization. His performance certainly suggests that his heart was much more in tune with Harding's radical indictment of American colonialism and genocide than the decidedly moderate
speech Levison and Wachtel had prepared for him. Carmichael's speech at
the Spring Mobilization provided perhaps the most memorable line,
when he characterized Selective Service as "white people sending black
people to make war on yellow people in order to defend land they stole
from red people." By comparison, King's speech was dull and uninspired.
Journalist David Halberstam began his noted article on King's late career
of fighting economic exploitation and militarism with an eloquent put-
down of King's speech:

> He is perhaps the best speaker in America of this generation,
> but his speech before the huge crowd in the U.N. Plaza on that
> afternoon in mid-April was bad; his words were flat, the drama
> and that special cadence, rooted in his Georgia past and handed

down generation by generation in his family, were missing. It was as if he were reading someone else's speech. There was no extemporizing; and he is at his best extemporaneously, and at his worst when he reads. There were no verbal mistakes, no surprise passions. (An organizer of the peace march said afterwards, "He wrote it with a slide rule.") When he finished his speech, and was embraced by a black brother, it seemed an unwanted embrace, and he looked uncomfortable. He left the U.N. Plaza as soon as he could.

King's best Vietnam speeches were his more radical ones, when his true passion could blush above the page and bleed into his improvised oratory.

If Stanley Levison opposed King's radical sentiments, Bayard Rustin was even more opposed to King's militant antimilitarism. As a well-known pacificist, Rustin might have been expected to embrace King wholeheartedly. But as his biographer points out, one could have expected Rustin to support King's stance only if one were ignorant of Rustin's ideological evolution. Rustin had changed his mind about his earlier radical pacifism and had become much more moderate by the time he began to advise King in the fifties. It is true that Rustin had encouraged King to criticize the Vietnam War in the early sixties. But as he became more prominent in civil rights circles, he cut official ties with the peace movement. In a manner, King's and Rustin's trajectories of antiwar criticism were inverted: as Rustin assumed leadership of the A. Philip Randolph Institute, his priorities accordingly shifted to racial and economic concerns. As King became immersed in the fight to end economic inequality and racial oppression, he embraced the peace movement as a logical and moral extension of his expanding social concerns.

In fact, King's work among the black ghetto poor reaffirmed his commitment to the antiwar struggle. His work in Chicago "demonstrated to King the depth of the hostility to the war within the urban ghetto and, more important, convinced him that the conflict in Asia was not an aberration but rather an extension of deeply ingrained American values." King was surprised by the strong reactions against the war in Northern ghettoes. Although a large number of middle-class blacks supported the war, King found enormous antiwar sentiment among younger and poorer black Americans. The FBI file summarized King's belief that "he gets more cheers in Negro colleges when he opposes the war in Viet Nam than he does when he talks about rights. He says they go wild about the Viet Nam issue."

Such facts contradict the perception that antiwar sentiment was a predominantly white, middle-class student affair. Although blacks may not have participated in overwhelming numbers in antiwar protests, they were nonetheless strongly opposed to the war. Opinion polls taken in the sixties prove that blacks were more likely than whites to favor total withdrawal from Vietnam and less likely to favor the escalation of aggression. In 1965, for instance, 25 percent of blacks supported withdrawal, 50 percent supported a cease-fire, and only 25 percent supported escalation. By comparison, 15 percent of whites favored withdrawal, 36 percent favored a cease-fire, and 49 percent favored escalation of hostilities. In fact, until 1970, "blacks, low-income families and the over-sixties were the only sections of the population in which greater numbers favored withdrawal than escalation." As King contended, "There is more discontent in the Negro community than most people realize." Although he failed to make class distinctions among the blacks to whom he refers, Andrew Young nicely summarized the political situation of black Americans in relation to the war:

> Martin's decision to oppose the war was courageous, but it did not run counter to the prevailing sentiment in the black community. Negative attitudes toward the war were widely prevalent among blacks well before massive protests began. Few black leaders, however, were willing to come out and give public expression to such community sentiments for fear they would alienate the president and the federal government and be charged with a lack of patriotism.

Neither was King's stand against the war the only criticism made by a noteworthy black public figure. Muhammad Ali, the heavyweight boxing champion whom King praised in his April 30 sermon at Ebenezer, was equally courageous in his stand against the war. Although Ali is famous for having said that "I ain't got no quarrel with them Vietcong," the self-proclaimed "the greatest" paid a steep price for his principles. He was convicted of draft evasion in 1967 and given the severest sentence possible: five years in prison and a $10,000 fine. He was stripped of his title, ridiculed in the press, attacked by hyperpatriots, condemned by middle-class blacks, and denied at least $10 million for the three-and-a-half years he was banned from boxing. On June 29, 1971, the U.S. Supreme Court overturned his conviction, paving the way for his return to boxing. By losing the prime years of his fighting, a paradox looms over Ali's career:

we may have never seen "the greatest" at his greatest. Like King, Ali endured bitter denunciations and claims of treason only to gain in illness what King gained in death: a vaunted spot in the pantheon of American heroes whose niche is preserved through amnesia and a willful disregard of his gleaming threat to narrow visions of American identity.

In hindsight, the uproar over King's peace activism seems jaundiced and obviously wrong. Not long after his death, the tide of public and professional opinion swept back to join King's ocean of opposition. His prophetic passion was never more righteous than when he took a swing at the false premises of war-mongering that were being pitched to the American public. Still, we can sympathize with civil rights leaders who feared the mean-spirited political reprisals in the offing if they did not stick to LBJ's demanding quid pro quo: "If you support my war," he seemed to say, "I'll support yours." Black leaders also legitimately worried that white radicals might siphon off the energy of the civil rights struggle without returning the favor or, worse, they might substitute their quest for racial justice in our country with a quest for justice in a distant land. Ralph Ellison said in 1973 that King's decision led to "a diffusion of interests" that "allowed a lot of nonblack people who were part of his support to focus their energies elsewhere." Ellison argues that it "let them off the hook when the going got hot in the racial arena." He traces "some of the defection of energies to ecology and antiwar protest back to people who realized when blacks started moving into their neighborhoods and their schools that they were dealing with something more difficult than just taking a high moral position as they looked toward the South." Ellison's sharp analysis makes even more sense now, when whites attack the racial basis of affirmative action while barely mentioning the white women who are its prime beneficiaries.

The limitations of historical perspective, however, don't nearly explain how King's severest critics lacked nerve and imagination. Some argued that King should have refrained from speaking out on the war in Vietnam because he was only a preacher and a civil rights leader. His bailiwick was the spiritual welfare of his congregation and the social welfare of blacks, not complex affairs of state and foreign policy. Not only did King have no business butting in on international matters, they charged, but he lacked the expertise to tell the American government what it should do in Vietnam. In rejecting such reasoning, King pointed out that his Christian ministry drove his dissent. The gospel led him to protest the egregious loss of life on foreign killing fields. King viewed unjust social customs and laws through the lens of divine justice. Moreover, King refused to segment his moral concern along lines drawn by the very forces that had been hostile to black liberation. To those critics who were clearly committed to racial equality, King replied that the same outrage that caused him to oppose racial oppression caused him to cry out against war. As King was fond of saying, "Injustice anywhere is a threat to justice everywhere."

Few could stomach King's insistence that America was a global bully who tagged its opponents as communists, a ploy that had been used against King's organization. King pointed out that the National Liberation Front had been called communist when that label fit only 25 percent of its membership. King further incensed the Johnson administration— and its rejoicing (Carl Rowan) and reluctant (Whitney Young) black apologists—by claiming that America must surely look like "strange liberators" to the Vietnamese. When the Vietnamese gained independence from French and Japanese colonialism in 1945, they quoted the Declaration of Independence. Later, however, America failed to recognize their right to freedom. Instead, it supported the ruthless dictator, Premier Diem. King also pointed out that America permitted the Saigon press to be censured by the military junta.

Further, the United States breached the Geneva agreement regarding foreign troops. And most telling, America failed to respond to Vietnamese peace overtures. To American nationalists, King's dissent was seen as poorly disguised betrayal. King had been applauded by these same critics when he adamantly opposed black nationalism and its cries for Black Power. Now he was shunned because he was morally consistent, following a belief about domestic affairs to its international conclusion. King's actions prove that he had a more compelling and complex view of American patriotism. His willingness to criticize his country when it was wrong proved his concern for its moral destiny. By insisting that America "live out the true meaning of its creed" not only in the South but in Saigon as well, King showed his love for his native land and for the documents of freedom that Americans hold dear. Not wanting the words that "all men are created equal" to be stained by neglect or hypocrisy, he underscored their global appeal. King was against colonialism and imperialism because he was for democracy and humanitarianism. When he sought to apply these virtues at home, King was at least partially supported. When he sought to give them international exposure, he was widely denounced.

As for the argument that King's peace protests hurt the civil rights movement, he could only reply, "I have worked too long now and too hard to get rid of segregation in public accommodations to turn back to the point of segregating my moral concern." He concluded, finally, that "justice is indivisible." The principle of desegregation that fired the quest for racial equality must now spark moral action in the political arena. A segregated conscience embodied the very moral schizophrenia that King detested. Other critics argued that King was naive to think that nonviolence could be applied to military conflicts. Nonviolence worked in a domestic situation, the argument went, but it failed to meet the test as a workable political strategy, a view summarized in Ralph Ellison's observation that "in a pulpit it's one thing," but when "you're leading a nation it's something else again." King reversed the logic: the very nonviolence that had helped save America from itself might now help save others from America. And in saving others from America, we might help save America's very soul. King claimed that if "America's soul becomes totally poisoned, part of the autopsy must read Vietnam." But he tied America's salvation to the salvation of people everywhere, arguing that the nation "can never be saved so long as it destroys the deepest hopes of men the world over." As King came to understand, and as Malcolm X had already announced, the civil rights movement was at its base a human rights struggle. In a speech delivered on February 23, 1968, to celebrate the centennial of W.E.B. Du Bois's birth, King lauded the radical scholar and activist for forging powerful links between American blacks and Africa, thus "alarming imperialists in all countries and disconcerting Negro moderates in America who were afraid of his black genius." Insisting that we remember Du Bois's radicalism and anti-imperialism, King argued that Du Bois "would readily see the parallel between American support of the corrupt and despised Thieu-Ky regime and Northern support to the Southern slave-makers in 1876."

Contrary to allegations that his militant pacifism hindered the struggle for racial justice, King insisted that the Vietnam War was hurting the civil rights movement because Congress would not support both the war on poverty and the war against the North Vietnamese. In the end, King claimed, Congress would not sacrifice its defense budget for the sake of racial or economic justice at home. King's attempt to link the civil rights and peace movements grew in part from his concern for the moral health of America and from his argument that the black poor bore a disproportionate burden in the nation's economy. But moderate black leaders who disparaged the thought and activism of blacks like Ida B. Wells-Barnett, Benjamin Davis, Paul Robeson, Ella Baker, Oliver Cox, Fannie Lou Hammer, and especially Du Bois—who long ago had seen the connection joining varied forms of oppression—failed to see how race shapes and is formed by a huge array of forces outside its boundary, like war and class, gender and sexuality. King's mature understanding of how injustices are interconnected set him apart from most other civil rights leaders, making him the odd man out even in his own organization.

A recent sign of King's influence on black beliefs about the relation of race, war, and economic inequality was glimpsed in black protest against the Gulf War. As was the case with the Vietnam War, there was greater support of the Gulf War among whites than blacks. A poll found that 83 percent of whites but only 43 percent of blacks supported President George Bush's decision to attack Iraq in the Persian Gulf War. What was especially troublesome to millions of blacks was the fact that King's January 15 birthday was chosen by the United Nations as the deadline for Iraqi withdrawal from Kuwait. Many black activists cited King as the inspiration for their opposition to the war. "I'd like to see the end of the war," offered portrait photographer Coakley Pendergrass at the Atlanta celebration of the King holiday. "If Martin were to return this day, he'd be very disturbed with what is happening in the Persian Gulf, in Russia and in America."

Black leaders, including Jesse Jackson, SCLC's Joseph Lowery, Coretta Scott King, former Atlanta mayor Andrew Young, and Atlanta mayor Maynard Jackson all criticized the Gulf War. Jackson argued that tens of billions of dollars would be spent on the war while funding for vital domestic programs would be slashed, an argument similar to the one King advanced during the Vietnam War. Lowery called for "a moratorium on the crippling and killing in Iraq." Coretta Scott King called for a cease-fire in the Persian Gulf. Andrew Young echoed Coretta Scott King's plea for a cease-fire, arguing that it "doesn't even have to be a permanent cease-fire. It could be a 48-hour cease-fire." Mayor Jackson was angered by polls revealing that many whites believed that blacks who opposed the war were unpatriotic, another reflection of a white belief held during the Vietnam War. "Let's set the record straight," Jackson declared in a rousing sermon at Ebenezer Church on the King holiday in 1991. "The ethnic group that has produced the fewest number of traitors in times of war is Afro-Americans."

Despite black patriotism, returning soldiers faced persistent patterns of racism, an argument made during the Gulf War by many black critics. "Black men and women have been in every war this country has ever fought," claimed Vietnam veteran Ralph Cooper. "These young Americans come back and find that they're still a nigger in America." According to research performed at Northwestern University cited during the Gulf War, even "retired black generals have a hard time finding a well-paid civilian job." In fact, many critics, including Jesse Jackson, argued that a dearth of domestic jobs forced blacks to become "cannon-fodder" for the American military. In St. Louis, Missouri, Rev. C. Garnett Henning, pastor of St. Paul AME Church, argued that King would be "outraged" by the armed forces "built on the back of poverty." Arguing that 30 percent of American front-line soldiers in Saudi Arabi were black, Henning underscored "the double whammy on those who fled from poverty and ended up on the front line in the desert." Henning asserted that American soldiers were the victims of "racism, classism and sexism" and that they could be ordered to "fight a war for their oppressors."

Finally, a group of black civil rights, labor, and religious activists—including United Church of Christ minister Benjamin Chavis, African Methodist Episcopal church Bishop John Hearst Adams, SCLC head Joseph Lowery, and Abyssinian Baptist Church pastor Calvin Butts—convened the National Emergency African-American Leadership Summit on the Persian Gulf War at Butts's New York church. The leaders decried the war, calling for a cease-fire and an end to what Adams termed the "racial immorality" of U.S. foreign policy that sent disproportionate numbers of blacks into combat. A look at the racial makeup of the armed forces in the Gulf War substantiated their criticisms. The marines were composed of 7.9 percent Latinos, 16.9 percent blacks, with other minorities comprising 2.6 percent, for a total minority makeup of 27.4 percent, and a total white makeup of 72.6 percent. The air force had 3.1 percent Latinos, 13.5 percent blacks, and 2.4 percent other minorities, for a minority total of 19 percent, and an 81 percent white force. In the army, Latinos were 4.2 percent of the Gulf forces, blacks were 29.8 percent, and other minorities were 1.5 percent, for a total minority population of 35.5 percent, with whites accounting for 64.5 percent of army forces. And in the navy, Latinos were 6 percent of the forces, blacks were 21.3 percent, and other minorities composed 4.6 percent of the forces, for a minority total of 31.9 percent, with whites constituting 68.1 percent. In 1990, the U.S. Census Bureau indicated that Latinos were 8.3 percent of the population and 4.9 percent of the overall military population. Blacks were 12.1 percent of the population and 23.0 percent of the overall military population. Other minorities made up 6.0 percent of the population and 4.4 percent of the overall military population. In short, minorities were 26.4 percent of the U.S. population but 32.0 percent of the overall military population.

Whites were 81.9 percent of the U.S. population and 67.7 percent of the overall military population. (These totals exceed 100 percent because the U.S. Census Bureau cites Latinos as a subcategory of either black or white).

As *Boston Globe* columnist Derrick Jackson argued, blacks who served in the military during the Gulf War were "people who simply want to get the most return for their labor at a time when it is increasingly difficult to buy houses and pay for college and health care." Jackson summarized the plight of blacks who are vulnerable to the pull of opportunity that military enlistment represents, an indictment of the lack of comparable opportunities in civilian life.

> Thus, many African-Americans, regardless of income, are so wary of taking out huge college loans that they are easy prey for the military's $2 billion-plus recruiting machine. The promise of free college tuition and free health and life insurance make the so-called diversity efforts of universities and corporations seem impotent. A 1989 National Academy of Sciences report found that 50 percent of African-American male seniors and 29 percent of African-American female seniors said they had definite or probable plans to enter the military. This compared with 21.3 percent for white male seniors and 5 percent for white female seniors with similar plans.

The criticisms put forth of the Gulf War were remarkably and depressingly similar to the ones King made in Vietnam. That the domestic racial condition for blacks has improved since King's criticism of the war is undeniable. That the racial condition is sufficiently desperate to funnel thousands of black youth into the volunteer armed forces is a stinging indictment of the persistent lack of opportunity that haunts the lives of millions of black and brown youth. It is a mark of our times that General Colin Powell, that exemplary personification of advancement through the military, has emerged as the black figure most palatable to whites in general and to conservatives in particular.

King shattered civil rights orthodoxy by linking pacifism and protest against American apartheid. He looked to the earlier examples of Gandhi, theologian and mystic Howard Thurman, pacifists and activists A. Philip Randolph and Bayard Rustin, and the pacifist organization Fellowship of Reconciliation in forging such a connection. But King's exemplary bravery marked him as the most controversial and visible figure in America to oppose the Vietnam War. King's boldness also led to a change of mind about the causes and consequences of racial suffering. He became convinced that racial inequality was entwined in economic roots. If King's antiwar activism led to his being branded a renegade and a traitor, his move to wrestle the demons of economic inequality and social class was even more unsettling. King believed that our nation's problems grew from the triplets of social misery: racism, militarism, and poverty. This trio of troubles also drove King's rapidly evolving social ideology. The bottom line of any ideology for King was its effectiveness in analyzing and relieving human suffering. Near the end of his life, King embraced what he privately termed "democratic socialism." He realized that saying so in public would only breed confusion and provoke hostility to an already beleaguered movement for racial and social equality. But that didn't stop him from pressing ahead, using the spirit of the gospel and the language of radical democracy to lessen the pain of the oppressed. He sought to galvanize the poor of all races in a March on Washington—the Poor People's Campaign, it was called—that would be far more creatively disruptive than the 1963 campaign. If King's views on race and war were jolting, his most radical plans were certainly his most ambitious: to establish social justice by destroying poverty. But as King was to discover, the unification of suffering groups across lines of race and ethnicity and region would provoke the greatest resistance he had yet encountered. Some even venture that in the end it got him killed.

CHAPTER 4

"America Must Move Toward a Democratic Socialism"
A Progressive Social Blueprint

Some of the least known but most remarkable film footage of Martin Luther King, Jr., captures him in Memphis, Tennessee, less than a month before he died. King has answered a plea from local civil rights leaders to come to Memphis to publicize the plight of striking sanitation workers, most of them poor black men.

"It is criminal to have people working on a full-time basis and a full-time job getting part-time income," King trumpets, his jawbone furiously rising then fading back into his chocolate cheek.

The camera loves King—loves the way the skin between his eyes furrows, loves the way he half-consciously licks his lips, loves the way his eyes twinkle and pierce as he recruits nearly every facial muscle to punctuate his sublimely intense preaching. As a seasoned orator, King soaks in the sights and sounds of his audience. He lets his listeners ratchet up the emotional pitch of his rhetoric in the verbal exchange that makes the best black preaching an electrifying experience. So King stares for a while, silently, knowingly eyeing the vast throng while his words ripple across the auditorium. As the gathering claps and shouts its enthusiasm, King tugs at his shiny, blue-gray suit jacket, a paradoxical gesture that suggests both supreme confidence and boyish shyness.

"One day our society will come to respect the sanitation worker, if it is to survive," King continues, his beefy palm sprouting sturdy fingers that stab the air in passionate rhythm. "For the person who picks up our garbage, in the final analysis, is as significant as the physician, for if he doesn't do his job"—and King drags job out in sweet, Southern melisma until it becomes *jaw-w-w-b*—"diseases are rampant." The camera pans the audience, and ordinary black folk in ordinary dress are standing to salute wildly and joyfully this black prince who has descended on their ravaged kingdom. Gray-haired black men and hat-wearing black women decked out in their Sunday best brim with pride as their golden-throated spokesman shapes words into weapons to defend their dignity. One can almost see a rising self-esteem straighten their deferential postures as they leap to their feet to collect money for their cause in garbage cans turned into makeshift coffers.

"Through our airplanes we were able to dwarf distance and place time in chains," King melodically reports, repeating a phrase he often used to great success. "Through our submarines we were able to penetrate oceanic depths." His audience can barely contain itself as an audible "talk, talk," rises above the din to push King on. "It seems that I can hear the God of the universe saying 'Even though you've done all of that, I was hungry and you fed me not.'" King relies upon his audience's deep biblical literacy and its keen sense of implied meaning to get the connection and to flesh out his prophetic message.

What is especially striking about the occasion is that King is documented in full transition from fighting segregation to opposing class oppression. King had retreated from focusing solely on race when he saw that blacks would continue to suffer if they lacked economic equality. As King told James Lawson, the shrewd civil rights leader who helped to spearhead the strike, he was drawn to Memphis as an irresistible testing ground for his national assault on poverty.

"He said to me, 'Jim, you are doing in Memphis what I hope to do with the Poor People's Campaign,'" Lawson recalls. "'You've gotten into one of the tough issues, that is, workers who need good work, and decency and living wages, while they work.'" Lawson says that King "saw Memphis as pulling the movement into the right direction." King may have believed that, but few others in the civil rights movement did, including many in his own camp. King's Poor People's Campaign was a hard sell, perhaps because it forced those who were used to thinking about race to think also about class, while forcing those who puzzled over economic inequality to think about race. King sought to forge a coalition of the truly disadvantaged by bridging the many gaps between poor whites, blacks, and Latinos. If King was already viewed as dangerous, then his stepped-up criticism of capitalism and the economic "manipulation of the poor" got him branded by conservative critics as a lethal troublemaker.

King's leadership of the campaign against poverty counters the view that he was always regarded as an American hero. As John Fisher, a white auto dealer in Memphis, put it, the "general sense, in the community in which I've lived, was that Martin Luther King was a troublemaker, that he was disruptive." Ironically, King's most bitter enemies perceived his true challenge to America in ways that his friends have scarcely acknowledged. Although his enemies often distort just how and why King was dangerous, they nevertheless help us see that King exercised a profoundly prophetic ministry. As painful as it is to admit, bigoted critics like J. Edgar Hoover and Jesse Helms put their fingers on a dimension of the martyr's career that his comrades have diligently avoided. Hoover's FBI tagged King "the most dangerous Negro in America," and Helms assailed him as "an action-oriented Marxist."

Given their political motives, there is little doubt that Hoover's and Helms's charges were way off the mark. King was not the "commie" subversive that Hoover made him out to be. Neither was he, as Helms supposed, an ideological zealot of Soviet Marxism. Still, a strong case can be made that, in his last three years, King was indeed the most dangerous black leader in America as he redreamed his dream, changed his mind about race, and linked the civil rights and peace movements. But King was also deemed dangerous, if not loony, because he began to analyze politics and society in a demonstrably radical fashion. True enough, King never publicly admitted his democratic socialism for fear that it would alienate allies and give his enemies more ammunition to attack him. But his demands for a "revolution of values" and society-wide economic change were driven in part by his democratic socialist principles. In effect, King was committed to acting on certain beliefs about class inequality that were at least partially inspired by Karl Marx. While King's retooled dream, revised racial beliefs, and antiwar activism have been hard enough for his followers to admit, the suggestion of King's democratic socialism is to them sheer blasphemy. In the effort to protect King from invidious figures like Hoover and Helms, his defenders have denied his turn to radical politics. But their doubled-edged strategy, although understandable, is harmful to history and politics. As they fight the caricatures of King's critics, they also deny the truth of King's ideological evolution. This denial also gives cover to civil rights activists who seek to shield themselves from the bothersome light of King's growth and from the challenge to turn away from a path that he blazed but abandoned when circumstances called for a new direction.

King embraced radical politics in earnest in 1965 when he confronted the crises of the Northern ghettoes. As he sought to transform black urban centers, King discovered tactical flaws in his endeavor to end racism. His experience in Chicago proved to be a successful failure, because he and his staff were forced to generate fresh strategies to cope

with the harsh realities they unexpectedly met. King was violently
rebuffed by working-class and lower-middle-class whites. Where Southern culture carved up social space through legal segregation, Northern
society charted a geography of racial separatism through informal codes
and unwritten rules. There was no need to name white and black water
fountains, restaurants, or department stores in Chicago. The disparate
communities that make up that city's population operated along invisible
racial lines that marked safe and dangerous territory. The threat of white
racist violence, or at times, black retaliation, was deeply etched in the
psychic map shared by Chicago's citizens. Such fears policed social contact much more efficiently than could a racist sheriff or a city council reg-
ulation. The North's topography of racial domination revealed huge
barriers to King's campaigns. As the Chicago movement proved, open
housing marches into rigidly segregated communities collided with the
inertia of local ways of knowing and making the world. In the absence of
formal restrictions against racial mobility—and in the light of the hidden
practices of redlining and steering, which in tandem stanched the bleed-
ing of black bodies into white neighborhoods—civil rights protests to
oppose legal segregation were out of rhythm with the subterranean flow
of racial commerce. And beyond the differences in Northern and Southern racism were differences as well in how blacks from each region
sought their liberty, a bitter lesson that King and his lieutenants were
soon to learn.

If King's Northern efforts, primarily in Chicago and Cleveland,
weren't the catastrophes the media reported them to be, they nonetheless failed to produce the results King and SCLC had hoped for. King
admitted that Chicago produced "no earth-shaking victories," but he
insisted that "neither have there been failures." That statement was at
least half right. King and SCLC forced the city to develop a Leadership
Conference to address their demands for fair housing, and they carried
out an aggressive program of tenant-union organizing and rentstrikes.
Their efforts led to a $4 million rehabilitation project that, King said, "will
renovate deteriorating buildings and give the tenants the opportunity to
own their own homes."

As King acknowledged, the "most dramatic success in Chicago has
been Operation Breadbasket," headed by then twenty-five-year-old Jesse
Jackson. Operation Breadbasket was the SCLC's beachhead in the North
(there was also a chapter in Cleveland) in the war to end economic violence against blacks. Under Jackson's leadership, Operation Breadbasket
garnered twenty-two hundred jobs that gave Negroes more than $18

million of new income. It also spearheaded the development of, in King's words, "Negro-controlled financial institutions which are sensitive to the problems of economic deprivation in Negro communities." As a result, several chain stores in Chicago agreed to deposit considerable sums in two Negro banks so that they could make loans to Negro businessmen with limited assets. It negotiated as well agreements with chain stores to strike contracts with Negro scavengers (to collect garbage), janitorial services, insect and rodent exterminators, advertising agencies, painters, masons, electricians, and construction firms. These developments reflected Operation Breadbasket's efforts to organize consumers in the fight for economic parity. They realized that Negro capital was the predicate for racial equality: if Negro consumers were spending money with white businesses, they should reap a larger share of the economic benefit of their consumption. As King said, the logic behind such efforts is "'if you respect my dollar, you must respect my person,'" and that Negroes "'will no longer spend our money where we cannot get substantial jobs.'" In Cleveland, Operation Breadbasket boycotted the dairy product company Sealtest, which, despite heavy black consumption, had only 43 blacks in a pool of 442 employees. It also boycotted the A&P grocery store chain because it refused to remove Sealtest products from its shelves in solidarity with aggrieved black consumers. The result was an agreement that brought more jobs, advertisements in Negro newspapers, and deposits of significant funds in Negro financial institutions. These Northern strategies, King said, "hold great possibilities for dealing with the problems of the Negroes in other Northern cities."

Beyond these victories, King faced black and white liberal resistance to his moves to unionize ghetto citizens. But King also had to weather an unfamiliar storm: the strong resistance of his own organization to his increasingly class-based analysis of racial suffering. King's growing radicalism brought him into sharp conflict with SCLC staff. Many of them believed, on the basis of their limited successes in Chicago and Cleveland, that blacks should develop strategies to increase their consumer power and to get a bigger piece of the existing economic pie. King, however, began to question the logic and the fairness of such an approach. Behind the muted successes of Chicago, King sensed the raging of a more powerful force than he had confronted in all the years of his civil rights struggles: structural economic inequality. While King's religion led him to side with the poor against the interests of the rich, he had yet to think in a sustained manner about the economic gulf between the have-gots and the have-nots. King saw that in the struggle to free Northern blacks, race

mattered, but class mattered more. By 1964, King had already reached
the conclusion that blacks faced "basic social and economic problems
that require political reform." But the vicious nature of Northern ghetto
poverty convinced King that the best hope for America was the redistribution of wealth.

In his 1967 presidential address to SCLC, King urged his colleagues to
fight the problems of the ghetto by organizing their economic and political power. He declared that from "the old plantations in the South to
newer ghettoes in the North, the Negro has been confined to a life of
voicelessness and powerlessness." The antidote, he said, was to acquire
power, which would give Negroes the "strength required to bring about
social, political, and economic change." King implored his organization
to develop a program that would compel the nation to have a guaranteed
annual income and full employment, thus abolishing poverty. He argued
that "dislocations in the market operations of our economy and the
prevalence of discrimination thrust people into idleness and bind them in
constant or frequent unemployment against their will." King preached
that "the Movement must address itself to the question of restructuring
the whole of American society." When such a question was raised, one
was really "raising questions about the economic system, about a
broader distribution of wealth," and thus, one was "question[ing] the
capitalistic economy." These words mark a profound transformation in
King's thinking.

No longer a liberal reformer who believed that the basic structures of
American society were sound, though in need of adjustment, King was
now a radical revisionist who argued that the fundamental institutions of
American life must be made over in fairness to the poorest citizens. King's
stringent dissent on the question of economic equality alienated him from
most of the few allies who remained, who believed that his new thinking
would only further loosen their already tenuous hold on the American
imagination. Besides, the ideological family of which SCLC was a part
appeared gravely fractured. The disintegration of the civil rights community, ripped by internecine squabbles and sundered by external hostilities,
was in process. The fraying of a liberal consensus on the best measures to
uplift the Negro had begun. And the white backlash against black
progress had already started to whip. In this light, King's development
was read as defection, a bitter betrayal of racial justice in pursuit of a pipe
dream, a far cry from his embrace of the American dream. The opposition didn't deter King. Instead, it drove him deeper into a depression
about the faint prospects of America's rediscovering its revolutionary

roots. The more America strayed from its noble heritage, the more King insisted that it change its wicked ways and cease poisoning the nation with racism, militarism, and materialism. King demanded that America, like the biblical character Nicodemus, undergo a profound spiritual and structural rebirth. As he stated in 1966, we must ignite "a restructuring of the very architecture of American society." King reiterated the point in his 1967 presidential address to SCLC:

> A nation that will keep people in slavery for 244 years will "thingify" them, make them things. Therefore they will exploit them, and poor people generally, economically. And a nation that will exploit economically will have to have foreign investments and everything else, and will have to use its military might to protect them. All of these problems are tied together. What I am saying today is that we must go from this convention and say, "America, you must be born again!"

It is clear that when it comes to dating the evolution of King's political philosophy, "B.C.," must refer to "before Chicago," before his encounter with persistent poverty, and "A.D.," must mean "after defeat," not simply of his programs in Chicago, but of his faith in American liberal reform to respond adequately to the needs of blacks and the poor.

The civil unrest that swept the country in the mid-sixties spurred King to deepen his analysis of structural inequality. According to the National Advisory Commission on Civil Disorders, better known as the Kerner Commission, there was an epidemic of violence as riots raged throughout the nation in 1967. In Newark, New Jersey, there were 23 deaths and 725 injuries from a riot that lasted from July 12 through July 17. In Detroit, the bloodiest of the riots lasted from July 23 to July 30; 43 died and 324 were injured. There were riots in Jackson State, Mississippi, on May 10; the Roxbury section of Boston, on June 2; Tampa, Florida, on June 11; Cincinnati, Ohio, on June 12; Buffalo, New York, on June 27; Cairo, Illinois, on July 17; Durham, North Carolina, on July 19; Memphis, Tennessee, on July 20; Cambridge, Maryland, on July 24; and Milwaukee, Wisconsin, on July 30. Altogether, there were seventy-five major riots in 1967, with 83 people killed. In 1966, there had been 11 killings in urban uprisings, and in 1965, 36 people were killed. Although King condemned the violence and reaffirmed his belief in nonviolence as the best means of achieving social change, he was even more critical of the social conditions that led to violence. Further, King acknowledged that nonviolence could work only in a just society. After his visit to Watts, King referred to the uprisings as a "holocaust," saying that Los Angeles should have expected them since "its officials tied up federal aid in political manipulation," "the rate of Negro unemployment soared above the depression levels of the thirties," and "the population density of Watts became the worst in the nation." A study of the Watts uprising conducted in 1970 confirms King's last point about population density. The study claimed that about 22,000 Negroes, or 15 percent of the black population, participated in the riots. A sample group was surveyed about their grievances, and leading the list were neighborhood conditions (33 percent), followed by mistreatment by whites (14 percent), and then economic conditions (13 percent); 21 percent listed no specific complaints. King, who famously said after Watts that "a riot is [at bottom] the language of the unheard," also claimed that "the looting in Watts was a form of social protest very common through the ages as a dramatic and destructive gesture of the poor toward symbols of their needs." In 1964, he had already pointed out the hypocrisy of white leaders' lecturing Negroes about nonviolence when it was "*Negroes* [who] created the theory of nonviolence as it applies to American conditions." King rejected the distortion of nonviolence by duplicitous civic leaders who failed "to perceive that nonviolence can exist only in a context of justice." If unjust conditions for Negroes prevail, the call for them to be nonviolent is a demand for them to submit to injustice. "Nothing in the theory of nonviolence," King argued, "counsels this suicidal course."

Ghetto poverty and civil unrest pushed King even further to the left. Inspired by a conversation with activist Marian Wright, King decided to launch a Poor People's Campaign to mobilize thousands of poor people to march to Washington, D.C., to demand economic justice. King attempted to forge a multiracial coalition of Puerto Ricans, Mexican Americans, Indians, blacks, and whites in his most strenuous effort to bring about radical democracy for what aide Michael Harrington called "the invisible poor." King sent out a team of forty SCLC fieldworkers to organize the poor in urban and rural communities across America. King's plan was to train three thousand poor people in the philosophy and tactics of nonviolence. They would be the first wave of the poor to march to Washington in April 1968 and eventually take up residence in a shantytown, entitled Resurrection City, to be erected along the Potomac River. King planned concurrent nationwide demonstrations and boycotts to aid the big march. With the civil unrest of 1967 heavy on his mind, King argued that "if this campaign succeeds, nonviolence will be once again the dominant instrument for social change." Moreover, the poor would receive jobs and income. He warned that if the campaign failed, "nonviolence will be discredited, and the country may be plunged into a holocaust—a tragedy deepened by the awareness that it was avoidable."

The version of nonviolence that King promoted was more forceful than the outlook that spirited his previous social campaigns. His language reflected his shifting mood. In response, it seems, to the stepped-up attacks on both the social effectiveness of nonviolence and poor communities, King announced a bolder initiative, calling it, alternatively, "massive nonviolence," "aggressive nonviolence," and even "nonviolent sabotage." King signaled his attempt to escalate his campaign to match the national escalation of racial violence. He also meant to counter the political opposition to his new direction by insisting that nonviolence would now contain "disruptive dimensions." (Memphis auto dealer John Fisher seems to have hit the nail right on the head about King's disruption, even if for the wrong reasons.) Protesters would engage in massive civil disobedience, tying up traffic, staging sit-ins in Congress and in government buildings, and shutting down business in the capital. The purpose of this massive, aggressive, disruptive, dislocating, sabotaging nonviolence was a protest "powerful enough, dramatic enough, morally appealing enough, so that people of goodwill, the churches, labor, liberals, intellectuals, students, poor people themselves begin to put pressure on congressmen to the point that they can no longer elude our demands." In 1967, King described how massive nonviolence flowed from linking civil disobedience to the new urban contexts into which he attempted to extend its influence.

Nonviolence must be adapted to urban conditions and urban moods. Non-violent protest must now mature to a new level, to correspond to heightened black impatience and stiffened white resistance. This high level is *mass civil disobedience*. There must be more than a statement to the larger society, there must be a force that interrupts its functioning at some key point. . . . To dislocate the functioning of a city without destroying it can be more effective than a riot because it can be longer lasting, costly to the larger society, but not wantonly destructive. It is a device of social action that is more difficult for a government to quell by superior force. . . . It is militant and defiant, not destructive.

Clearly this was a new King, a King waging warfare against the elite in the nation's capital on behalf of the beleaguered and forgotten poor. King said that he wanted SCLC to "go for broke" in pitting their moral and financial resources against the massive resources of the government. King confessed that "we've gone for broke before, but not in the way we're going this time, because if necessary I'm going to stay in jail for six months—they aren't going to run me out of Washington." As King admitted to *New York Times* reporter José Yglesias, "In a sense, you could say we are engaged in the class struggle."

Indeed, what may be termed King's revolutionary nonviolence was being fueled by his adoption of radical political beliefs and social analysis. This led King to focus on the plight of the poor, foreshadowing social democratic analyses like those of William Julius Wilson more than a decade later. King spoke of the "black underclass" on his last birthday, January 15, 1968, in a speech entitled "Why We Must Go to Washington." King said that "we have an underclass, that is a reality—an underclass that is not a working class" composed of "thousands and thousands of Negroes working on full-time jobs with part-time income," and often they had "to work on two and three jobs to make ends meet." In 1966, King admitted that the Civil Rights Act of 1964 and the Voting Rights Act of 1965 had not improved the condition of poor blacks in the South or North. These "legislative and judicial victories did very little to improve" Northern ghettoes, nor did they do much to "penetrate the lower depths of Negro deprivation." In fact, he argued, "the changes that came about during this period [1955–1965] were at best surface changes, they were not really substantive changes." In 1966, King acknowledged that the progress that had been made had been "limited mainly to the Negro middle class." In February 1968, King said that "the plight of the Negro poor has worsened over the last few years," and he called for "a redistribution of economic power." King also contended, in 1967, that "the roots [of economic injustice] are in the system rather than in men or faulty operations." In a remarkable statement in a speech he gave to his staff in 1966, King laid out the ideological basis for his deepened assault on poverty, economic injustice, and class inequality:

> We are now making demands that will cost the nation something. You can't talk about solving the economic problem of the Negro without talking about billions of dollars. You can't talk about ending slums without first saying profit must be taken out of slums. You're really tampering and getting on dangerous ground because

you are messing with folk then. You are messing with the captains of industry. . . . Now this means that we are treading in difficult waters, because it really means that we are saying that something is wrong . . . with capitalism. . . . There must be a better distribution of wealth and maybe America must move toward a Democratic Socialism.

This statement is remarkable since King rarely allowed his positive response to democratic socialism to be recorded. His usual practice, according to one of his aides, was to demand that they "turn off the tape recorder" while he expounded on the virtues of "what he called democratic socialism, and he said, 'I can't say this publicly, and if you say I said it I'm not gonna admit to it.'" King "didn't believe that capitalism as it was constructed could meet the needs of poor people," the aide said, "and that we might need to look at what was a kind of socialism, but a democratic form of socialism." Even in the speech that contains the passage cited above, King said he wasn't "going to allow anybody to put [him] in the bind of making me say every time" that he wasn't a communist or a Marxist. Still, as democratic socialist Michael Harrington said, King was highly reluctant to name his radical position in public. King didn't want to arouse suspicion and thus compromise the achievement of economic and racial equality. "Dr. King had a genius for this," Harrington said. "How do you phrase this message so that you don't betray the message but you put it in terms which are understandable and accessible to people on the street?" Harrington claims that King "certainly wouldn't use radical phraseology in many cases for that reason." The great Marxist historian C.L.R. James recalls that King told him that while he believed in radical ideas, he couldn't "say such things from the pulpit." James says that King "wanted me to know that he understood and accepted, and in fact agreed with, the ideas that I was putting forward—ideas which were fundamentally Marxist-Leninist." James concluded that King was "a man whose ideas were as advanced as any of us on the Left."

Referring to James's comments, Christopher Lasch contends that the "statement that [King] could no longer speak his mind to his own constituents indicates, however—if James's slightly melodramatic and conspiratorial account can be trusted—that his capacity for leadership was now exhausted." Such a criticism proves just how out of touch much of the white left is with the powerful currents of black religious and civic culture. Whites on the left have little respect for the way black religious or civic institutions function, nor are they often sensitive to how the black church presents ideas, especially troubling ones. Finally, they ignore the complex and varied constraints on political discourse for progressive blacks in the fifties and sixties. Many members of the white left undeniably chose their principles out of real conviction. Still, many could claim the security of wealthy families whose status belied their sons' or daughters' anticapitalist sentiments. King had no such resources to fall back on. His radicalism was born out of brutal oppositions. He had to master the media and the public in a fashion that cushy white leftists, for reasons of either cash or color, never had to consider. Moreover (as I will explore in greater depth in chapter 11), King was brutally harassed by the FBI for suspected communist ties. He also had to navigate a culturally conservative black church that could be twisted toward liberal, and occasionally, radical politics. Finally, he had to fight his own staff's stiff resistance to his political views. For instance, James Bevel, who in many ways was King's conscience on Vietnam, and Jesse Jackson, head of Operation Breadbasket, strongly opposed King on the Poor People's Campaign. They were joined by Bayard Rustin, Michael Harrington, Hosea Williams, and even Andrew Young, all of whom forecast inclement political weather for a march on Washington. They believed that President Johnson's anger and Congress's resistance would make the march a massive failure. Only Ralph Abernathy, King's trusted confidant and closest friend, stood with him.

Although the knee-jerk paranoia about communists, socialists, Marxists, and other leftists had certainly abated, it had by no means disappeared. In such a climate King could scarcely afford to share his views in public, even before a gathering of allies. But King understood what the left has too often forgotten: the failure to call an idea progressive does not mean it won't be effective to people—the very people the left claims it wants to reach—who might be open to such an idea shed of its ideological label. The left could learn from sophisticated radical black church leaders who have succeeded in masking or translating unpopular views to a public at first unwilling to hear them and yet who eventually become convinced of their absolute rightness. Many Americans violently resisted King's advocacy of desegregation, racial justice, and equal opportunity for blacks. Now these ideas are so widely accepted that it has often worked to the detriment of blacks. Many whites now assume such ideas were always warmly received and are therefore loathe to find new remedies for what they think are exaggerated or, worse, nonexistent problems. Christopher Lasch's criticism of King's "exhausted" leadership reveals the arrogance and amnesia that the liberal left, especially the secular, white liberal left, has often displayed when dealing with even progressive black religious figures or movements.

Was King, as Helms claimed, really an "action-oriented Marxist"? Although King admitted in private that he was a democratic socialist, he continued to declare that he was not a communist. Moreover, contrary to Helms's assertion, King never claimed to be a Marxist. Even if he had, it would by no means certify his communist standing. Many Marxists and post-Marxists have long since eschewed communism. They value the profound insights on class and economic inequality that Marx offered without embracing the political party he favored. In the same way that King was not a Hindu even though he was an advocate of Gandhian nonviolence, King can be said to have been a radical figure who appreciated Marx's insights about class and economic inequality and, more important, *put them into practice*, without being a communist. In the strict sense that King acted on Marxist insights about class—though he disagreed with Marx's "metaphysical materialism" and "ethical relativism" and said he could "never be a Communist"—he could be reasonably termed an action-oriented Marxist. By Jesse Helms's gnarled standards, King failed the test. But in a truly liberating and democratic sense, King passed with flying colors.

In the thirty-two years since his death, two of King's most talented aides, Andrew Young and Jesse Jackson, have taken very different paths in the fight to bring racial and economic justice to black Americans. Young, who knew King better and longer, was, with some qualification, deeply supportive of King's war on poverty through the Poor People's Campaign, and yet he has veered far from King's push for a massive redistribution of wealth. Jackson, who knew King for a brief but blazing four years, was vehemently opposed to the Poor People's Campaign on both strategic and substantive grounds, yet he has stuck much closer to the radical economic philosophy King favored.

Andrew Young was, "next to Abernathy," King's "closest colleague." As the SCLC's executive director, Young succeeded the gifted and combative Wyatt Tee Walker, a powerful preacher, ingenious strategist, and talented organizer who was one of the most original personalities to emerge in the Southern civil rights movement. Although not nearly as gifted an administrator or orator as Walker, Young's soothing personality and conciliatory, consultative administrative style ingratiated him to the SCLC staff. Young was jokingly known among SCLC staff as "Uncle Tom," the figure his peers, especially King, looked to to present the conservative view to the more militant inclinations of staffers James Bevel,

Hosea Williams, and Jackson. Ironically, however, Young was more dedicated to King's latter-day vision of democratic socialism than any of the
more radical staffers. Young aggressively sought to convince the other
staffers and key movement figures of the moral appeal and social feasibil-
ity of King's dream. And he expertly countered the criticisms launched at
what many considered to be King's romantic, deluded lapse into socialist
syncope. Young and King aide Stanley Levison encouraged King to adopt
even more radical tactics of aggressive, massive nonviolence in the Poor
People's Campaign. King drew satisfaction and energy from a Harris poll
published in an August 1967 *Newsweek* stating that whites "are ready and
willing to pay the price for a massive, Federal onslaught on the root problems of the ghetto."

Young advocated such tactics as "lying on highways, blocking doors
at government offices, and mass school boycotts" to provoke confrontation and dramatize the War on Poverty. He argued that the poor throughout the nation would march to Washington as SCLC demonstrators, part
of the "underclass that is locked out of the economy, people for whom a
spring in jail in Washington is heaven compared to a spring of hunger and
unemployment in Mississippi or Chicago." Young argued that the old-
style kind of March on Washington

> isn't sufficiently crisis-packed . . . people don't respond until their
> own self-interest is threatened. People don't give up power and
> money voluntarily. We have accepted the challenge to so threaten
> nonviolently the self-interest of the powers that be that they will
> be able to change, that they will see that a change is necessary.
> Our threat will be so pointed and well-defined that they will know
> that a change is possible and will change in the right direction.

Young's strong commitment to the vague but morally charged democratic socialism that King didn't live long enough to flesh out seems to
have slipped considerably. After enjoying a distinguished career as a congressman, UN ambassador, and mayor of Atlanta, Young has become
extraordinarily comfortable with the system of wealth and power that he
so heartily castigated when he marched with King in the sixties. It would
be too simplistic to suggest that in the absence of King's radicalizing
influence Young has taken too readily to the very boardrooms and halls
of power they once targeted as bastions of moral corruption. Young has
wrought too much important social change and done too much racial
good to justify such a reactionary appraisal. Still, his view of change is far

different from the vision of social change he nurtured by King's side. "I quantify revolution in dollar terms," Young says now. "Martin Luther King, when he was running the movement, never had more than half a millions dollars a year to work with. Now I see black people driving around Atlanta in cars that are worth one hundred thirty thousand dollars. That's integration. I keep running into young people who are starting their own businesses. That's integration. I used to know everyone in black Atlanta who could afford to take an airplane. Now I see black folks I don't even know flying first class. These people are carrying on the struggle."

Of course, it is by no means problematic to conceive of revolution in terms of dollars if the point is to redistribute those dollars in ways that benefit the neediest and lift the lowest in our nation. Such goals were embraced by King and Young in the Poor People's Campaign and in King's democratic socialist vision where material and economic resources were justly distributed. Further, the easy equation of integration with late-model cars and first-class flights reproduces the concentration of capital in the hands of the privileged—even if they are black—that King so vehemently opposed. Such blacks may indeed be carrying on a laudable struggle for economic security, but they are not necessarily carrying on *the* struggle: for economic justice, for racial parity, for democratic access to capital for poor citizens. Perhaps the explanation for Young's change of heart and thrust has to do with the failed politics of romantic revolutionary talk, a species of deluded discourse for which he nurtured a special disdain when it appeared in antiwar activists in the sixties. Rooting it out of his own vocabulary may have been a way to keep faith with his evolved, mature estimation of economic change and the pace and place at which such a prospect might occur: not all now, but some over time; not in the streets, but in the boardroom and in the political convention. Young's shift has been described as a "down-to-earth" view that has "minimal expectations":

His new idea of how to get to the future offered no false promise: no quick fixes, no automatic understanding, no instant equality. It didn't hinge on shared idealism or altruism. And it didn't count on people, black or white, to act like heroes—just ordinary folks pursing their self-interest. . . . More than anything, it was a view of change driven by personal striving: getting onto the old immigrants' escalator of schooling, a job and a stake in the system. Though less exciting than the vision Young and others had held out in the past, it also seemed potentially more practical.

If it is true that the high idealism of the past has been transmuted, not into practical politics, which are just fine if they have the chance to effect real change for real people, but into a dismally low-sighted acceptance of self-interest as the substitute for racial progress and economic equality, then such politics are a poor substitute for what came before. Fortunately, Young insists that he continues to "support the development" of programs like the Movement to End Slums, "whereby tenants collectively purchased their own buildings." As Young writes, rather "than build public housing projects that encourage the dependence of tenants, we should enable poor people to buy their own homes. If people, however poor, have an investment in their own living space, they will seek to enhance its value." This is a hugely scaled-back vision of what King aimed for—in Chicago, in Memphis, in the Poor People's Campaign—and if it is the best we can hope for from the politics of practicality, it is perhaps time again to seize the reins of possibility and dream outsized dreams of massive social transformation.

If Young has settled for less—less idealism and romance, less talk of complicating demands for radical economic redistribution, less social engineering—to get more of what is actually attainable—more cars, homes, jobs, businesses—then Jesse Jackson wants much more than he sought at the beginning of his civil rights sojourn. Unlike Young, Jackson was at strong odds with King's democratic socialist vision unfurled in the banner of the Poor People's Campaign. Jackson told King that "there is a problem with the staff not really being clear on this project." One staff member called James Bevel and Jesse Jackson the "greatest doubters" about the campaign at SCLC, as they argued that there was insufficient planning going into the march. Jackson's open opposition to the campaign greatly distressed King, a distress that was exacerbated by Jackson's ranging independence as the head of SCLC's economic arm, Operation Breadbasket. Young claims that Jackson in 1968 was

hung up on what Martin called "the image of Breadbasket" and what others of us used to call his "little Empire." He didn't want to leave Breadbasket-building to devote major time to the PPC. Martin was becoming a bit agitated with Jesse because he felt Breadbasket by itself was not going to solve major economic problems. He wanted to continue the program, but he felt, as I did, that a major structural reform of the American economy was needed, and that Breadbasket was too limited an approach to achieve this.

By contrast, Young argues, Jackson "dealt with neighborhood businesses and national franchises." Young says that by 1967, King "was convinced that a substantial increase in jobs would have to come from the public sector; private businesses simply weren't going to provide enough jobs to ease the huge problem of unemployment. Changes in priorities and policies must be effected." At an Ebenezer SCLC meeting less than a week before his death, King rounded up his executive staff to hash out the difficulties and opposition to the Poor People's Campaign. King was extremely agitated at staff resistance not only to the campaign but to his foray into Memphis to help striking sanitation workers, a project that Jackson and other staffers thought diverted attention from the already poorly thought out march for poor folk. But King insisted that "Memphis is the Washington campaign in miniature." King then allowed his rage to rip.

"Everyone here wants to drag me into your particular projects," King argued. "Now that there is a movement that originated basically from Mississippi-born folk, not from SCLC leadership, you don't want to get involved. Now that I want you to come back to Memphis to help *me,* everyone is *'too busy.'"* Young charges that some staff members succumbed to "their own egomania," feeling that "they were more important to the movement than Martin." Young says that when "they were really feeling their oats, Hosea, Bevel, and Jesse acted as if Martin was just a symbol under which they operated." Jackson was "busy building his own empire up in Chicago," using Operation Breadbasket to focus on the economy "and forcing white business to open its doors to blacks." Jackson, Young argues, "felt his approach was better than Martin's." But King appealed to Jackson to throw his support behind him.

"Look," King spoke sharply to Jackson, "whenever you needed me or wanted me to come to Chicago, I've always been there supporting your efforts. Now when we're trying to get a national movement going, I don't really have your support."

If Jackson's ego or entrepreneurial efforts kept him from giving King his full support when he lived, he has certainly compensated for his failed loyalty by brilliantly repackaging some of King's progressive ideas. Jackson's furiously improvised economic experiments of the seventies—an intriguing blend of capitalist enthusiasm and targeted boycotts of white businesses to compel their compliance with his vision of social justice— gave way in the eighties to an economic populism that has evolved now to a program of economic redistribution with an eye to democratizing capital. Jackson's current themes—waging class warfare, eradicating poverty, and democratizing capital—are huge themes carved from King's economic corpus: the quest to unite working-class people of all races, the desire to bring the poor into cultural focus and to dispel the myth of poverty as having a colored, and hence, easily dismissed and scapegoated face, and the fierce determination to make big capital accountable.

Jackson acknowledges King's "move toward a massive coalition of working class people," a theme reflected in his work as head of the Rainbow/PUSH Coalition, a multiracial political organization designed to leverage a moral lobby on behalf of working-class and poor people throughout the nation. Jackson says that he is convinced that

> working class black people and brown people have more in common with each other than they do with those who, in fact, downsize corporations, and what they call right-size, or what some might call downsize and out-source jobs. Wealth going upward, benefits and jobs going downward, and jobs going outward, is threatening to all of us. And to that extent, I think our whole language has to reflect more class inclusion.

In countering the vicious stereotypes that plague the poor, Jackson makes a point that many perceptive critics have underscored: that "most poor people are not on welfare." Jackson's sense of what may be termed the aesthetic dimensions of the working poor is compelling: "Most poor people work every day. They raise other people's children. They catch the early bus. They drive cabs. They work in fast-food restaurants. They work processing chicken at these meat plants. They work in hotels and motels. . . . So the charge that they are lazy or they need stimulation to work harder, is not true." Central to Jackson's encounter with class inequality is the relentless exposure of the racialization of welfare. Jackson contends that "the welfare debate has been stimulated or fed by images of race." Jackson is capable of puncturing the myths that surround the national discourse on poverty. Jackson illuminates how the terms of the debate are driven by unconscious racial allegiances and codes of identification that trigger social sympathy and public policy. In a vivid contrast, he portrays how such allegiances and codes work:

> So I remember distinctly in 1960, John Kennedy held up a black baby in his arm in Harlem. And the press dismissed it cynically. They said, "Well, one of these liberal guys from Boston, up north. He kind of talks funny. He's trying to get Adam Powell's vote. . . . And this is a symbolic gesture." It was kind of dismissed out of

hand. Robert Kennedy held up a white baby in his arm in
the Appalachian region of West Virginia. And that baby's belly
was bloated. That baby's nose [was] running. That baby's eyes
[were] running water. The imagery of Robert Kennedy and
that white baby in West Virginia triggered the War on Poverty, not
the black baby in Harlem held up by John Kennedy. Even white
southerners like Hollingsworth then helped lead the way for
addressing white poverty, but could not exclude blacks in the
process.

Such an awareness leads Jackson to advocate the politics of strategic deracialization: peering behind the demonized black face of social
misery to glimpse the white face that will drive the development of
social policies that benefit millions of blacks, a strategy advocated by
social democrat William Julius Wilson for contentious affirmative action
debates.

   Jackson's strategic deracialization has caused him to focus on the
plight of the poor, including the Appalachian poor. With the reminder of
the Kennedy brothers, their gestures of social compassion and the different results of their actions seared into his mind, Jackson's focus on
Appalachia is a political calculation rooted in a moral aptitude: what
works for the poor white will certainly work for the poor of every racial
and ethnic group. Jackson argues that Appalachia, "like urban ghettoes
and barrios, is on the wrong end of the new global economy." In the new
global economy, he says, the rich are favored, "the roof is off." But for the
poor, "the floor is gone," and the "middle class is left feeling shaky." What
Jackson aims to accomplish with such impressionistic language is the
sense of economic vertigo that haunts the poor and working. Further,
the depressed wages, high unemployment, poor health care, elevated
dropout rates, and depleted capital of Appalachia paint a picture of economic hardship that is difficult to dismiss on the basis of racial bigotry.
Jackson thus combines cunning and conscience. By sketching the existen-
tial and economic devastation of Appalachia on the canvas of American
social morality, he accomplishes a crucial aim: spotlighting the undeniable hurt experienced by hard-working, law-abiding, God-fearing white
Americans who through no fault of their own have suffered economic
misery makes a further argument by analogy of the comparably blame-
less suffering endured by black and brown people.

   I am not arguing that Jackson's focus on Appalachia is merely a
shrewd attempt to conflate white, black, and brown peoples or the obsta-

cles they endure, or a sneaky effort to deny the unyielding particularity of
their specific hardships or to deny the peculiar forms their suffering takes.
I am arguing, however, that Jackson's conception of Appalachia suffering
derives from a universal moral concern about economic inequality. Further, Jackson's journey to Appalachia reflects a distinctly Kingian theme:
the inescapable interconnectedness that characterizes human community at its best. Jackson's economic philosophy of radical redistribution of
wealth downward into ghetto cement, barrio sidewalks, and Appalachian
soil is driven by a common religious vision of the beloved community
that Jackson shares with King. King's vision of the beloved community
had more formal theological expression than Jackson's; Jackson's vision
has a more finely honed economic agenda that joins ideology, theology,
and materiality. In a sense, his attention to Appalachia represents a
maturing of the vision of King in its second generation. King had years
before urged the movement to forge connections with all oppressed peoples as an expression not only of economic exigency but of moral consis-
tency. Jackson has inherited such a calling, crafting it to fit his own gifts
and temperament.

Jackson's most ambitious attempt to date to unite King's socialist
surge with his own entrepreneurial evangelicalism is his Wall Street Project. On the face of things, Jackson's venture into the financial heart of
America, indeed the Western world, is a strictly capitalist affair. But it is
Jackson's attempt to democratize capital, to redirect its flow and to create
pockets of concentrated wealth from the application of a morally driven
economic tourniquet that holds the promise of making a real difference
for ordinary folk beyond the esoteric cloisters of ugly wealth. The creation of hundreds of more minority millionaires who care little for the
poor and despised is but the doubling of the devil's force. It will not only
circumvent the spread of wealth into black, brown, and poor white communities for high moral purposes, but it will, more grievously, arm to the
teeth insensitive soldiers in the war on capital who stand opposed to the
interests of working-class, middle-class, and poor people.

Jackson says that the mission of the Wall Street Project, launched on
January 15, 1997, is

> to work with business, labor and government to build those struc-
> tures that provide access to capital by ending the trade deficit with
> ethnic minorities. By building bridges to corporate America and
> new trading partnerships that are mutually beneficial. Both Wall
> Street and the underserved communities with underutilized talent

and untapped capital are equally distant from each other. Both stand to benefit from building bridges. By creating vehicles to transport capital to underserved markets with underutilized talent and untapped capital. To create economic growth that is shared and sustainable so that there are all winners.

The real challenge is to prevent poor, underserved communities from becoming exploitable markets that pay no dividends to any but a few ambitious capitalists intent on trading on skin color to economically marginalize further the minority communities from which they come but often do not return, except when it serves their interests. Jackson links his attempt to bridge the gaps between corporate capital and overlooked minority communities by appealing to King's vision of stuctural parity as the divining rod of his economic experiments. At the second annual meeting of his Wall Street Project, Jackson recalls how King spent his last birthday, making that memory the moral gestalt to which his project would return to define its spiritual boundaries:

> Perhaps what he did that day would be instructive for us. He had given me the assignment as national director of Operation Breadbasket—the economic arm of the Southern Christian Leadership Conference. He believed that the private sector had a major role to play in healing the breach, but that government policy and enlightened lawmakers would be the key in a partnership to make America the land of opportunity for all of its people. . . . Dr. King began his last birthday with breakfast at home with family. Later that morning, he pulled together the coalition—black, white, Jewish, Hispanic, Native American, labor—to work on the Poor People's Campaign. The object was to demand a job or an income for all Americans. He was driven by the moral imperative to include all and to leave no one behind.

Jackson draws a line from King's first foray into civil rights and its culminating moment in his Wall Street Project, a heady comparison to be sure, but perhaps an instructive one as well. He says, "So here we are on Wall Street, from the back of the bus in Montgomery to Wall Street 44 years later is a magnificent journey." Jackson claims that "31 years later after his last birthday, Dr. King would have been proud to be here to see the lions and lambs lying down together—multiracial, multicultural, corporate

executives, labor, Democrats, Republicans, Appalachia, ghetto, barrio—
under one big tent overlooking Wall Street—the capital of capital."

Jackson performs a majestic piece of rhetorical and ideological justification: by tying his drive to King's dream, Jackson takes the huge risk of
identifying King with the center of the economic processes that he so
desperately wanted to bring into line with an ethic of radical care and
rambunctious compassion. It is not yet apparent that Jackson's herculean
efforts to tame capital will in the end pay off for the people King loved
and whom Jackson loves: the poor of every race, the working class, and
the mightily assaulted middle classes. There are huge barriers to be overcome in convincing corporate capital to discover and obey its conscience.
Furthermore, King chose to prophesy to the powers that be in a fashion
that gave him room to be a lot more critical of capitalism's brutal effects
than either Jackson or Young did. Of course, King lacked the apparatus to
force the sort of economic change he vividly imagined should take place
in our nation, an apparatus that Jackson has seized by its bullish horns to
make it bear fruit for the structurally excluded. This does not mean that
Jackson has inherited King's democratic socialist mantle, with a corollary
obligation to chide capital relentlessly and provoke the American government to intervene on unrestrained capital and impose ethical boundaries
on its ceaseless activities. Of course, the defeat of communism and the
collapse of socialism worldwide makes that prospect much more difficult
in an era of ostensibly triumphant capitalism. Perhaps Jackson's odd
fusion of socialist sensibilities and market inclinations will pay off hand-
somely for the truly despised and disadvantaged.

However we come to think of King's ideological identity, it is clear
that he loved God, hated oppression, and sought to restructure American
society along radically democratic lines. At the heart of his democratic
socialist beliefs was a desire to square social reality with his deep religious
commitments to freedom and equality. King refused to view any political
ideology or party as the embodiment of the Kingdom of God. He was
too much of a skeptic about the possibility of human perfection to confer
divinity on even his own political beliefs. But as King reminded us the rainy
night before he was murdered in Memphis, he "just want[ed] to do God's
will." The tension between following God—into the ghetto, into sanitation
strikes, into military mishap, into rural Mississippi poverty, into the barrio,
into riots, into racial miasma, and into class conflict—while refusing to
follow conventional political logic, led King to radicalism, and perhaps to
his death. Ironically enough, even as King has been assailed for being too

radical, he has been attacked in some quarters for being a "sell-out" to real black interests. Such a conclusion could rise only from ignorance of King's profound love of black people. In other instances, it is the sign of an obstinate black bigotry that is both self-righteous and self-deluded— the former because it brooks no disagreement about how blacks should act or think, the latter because it believes it is the unerring expression of authentic blackness. In the past, some of the harshest criticism of King has come from self-styled "pork-chop nationalists," as Huey Newton termed them—a variety of Black Nationalism long on harangue but short on vision. What a surprise, then, for these critics, and for many others, to discover King's intriguing, and surprisingly complex, relationship to Black Nationalism. If one thinks that it is scandalous to call King a radical democrat, a democratic socialist, or an "action-oriented Marxist," what is one to make of the strong evidence that King was a proponent of an enlightened version of separatism and Black Power?

CHAPTER 5

"We Did Engage in a Black Power Move"
An Integrationist Embraces Enlightened Black Nationalism

"Fuck Martin Luther King," my younger colleague raged. "The nigga was the worst thing to happen to black people in the twentieth century."

I couldn't believe what I was hearing. After all, this was 1996, not 1966, when such rhetoric was much more common than it is now. I was visiting the West Coast to promote the paperback of my book on Malcolm X, a figure who certainly assailed King with colorful if caustic monikers in his own day. After my lecture, a few friends sought refuge in a soul food eatery where we could exult in the familiar smells of down-home cooking. Our conversation that evening ranged over the landscape of contemporary black culture, from sports to politics. Since I'd just talked about Malcolm X for nearly an hour, the discussion turned naturally enough to his peer in racial provocation, Martin Luther King, Jr. Judging by the dropped jaws of my friends, none of us was prepared for the acidic assault on King's career. To hear such an accusation spill from the lips of a brilliant thirty-three-year-old scholar whose work I admired was more than a little off-putting. It was simply shocking. But knowing how bright he was, I knew he would have plenty of reasons to back up his verbal tirade.

"Man, how can you say that about Dr. King?" I protested. "You can certainly disagree with his philosophy, and you can even question his tactics, but you can't just dismiss a man who gave his life defending black folk."

"Look," my friend responded, less out of exasperation than a fierce determination to make his point to nonbelievers. "I've got three reasons for what I'm saying. First, the nigga is an aberration. He didn't come from amongst the people. He had a Ph.D. when a nigga couldn't even get a drink of water."

My colleague knew from the "nigga, please" looks on our faces that we were ready to pounce on him—not only in defense of King's humility but to point out the obvious fact that he held a Ph.D. himself. He knew that we would believe it was a case of the pot calling the kettle black. But he read our minds instantly, and before we could offer a response, he parried our nonverbal blows.

" I ain't mad at him for *that*," he slyly retorted. "But what I am saying is that his connection to the people and their concerns could have never been genuine because he was never really part of the same thing he was rapping about."

My friend sensed that although we weren't satisfied with his response—after all, none of us was prepared to surrender so easily on the question of racial inauthenticity, especially since all of us had at one time or another been a victim of such a charge—we were still intrigued by the fact that an icon like King was being so baldly dressed down by a black man young enough to have been his son. He exploited our ambivalence and jumped immediately to his next reason for disliking King.

"Two, his pitch was all about white folks, in the very same way that early Motown and Berry Gordy [Motown's founder] were interested in targeting white listenership and the crossover market," he continued. "In Gordy's case, it was at the expense of the music. And in the case of your boy King, it was at the expense of black people being edified themselves before they integrated into white society. We needed to deal with our own self-image, our self-hatred and our knowledge of self before we dealt with white folks."

My friend was on a roll and gave no one in our party any time to interrupt his narrative. He knew we were nearly bursting to get back at him, but he seized the floor in the knowledge that once he shut up, he'd never regain his momentum. Given what he was about to say, he was surely justified in his belief.

"See, ten, fifteen, twenty years down the line, we're now wondering why we've got such a split in the black community," he fumed. "To me, King is responsible for niggas like Clarence Thomas."

A chorus of "Aw, naw, brother, you crazy," and "What, are you mad?" stormed at my friend, but he was undaunted.

"There's no way you can lay the blame for Clarence Thomas in the lap of George Bush or a right-wing agenda," he chided us. "We have to lay that in the lap of Dr. King. You couldn't have this all-out push to integrate mainstream society without at some level producing the ultimate integrated nigga, and that would be Mr. Thomas."

By now, our disbelief had only doubled. We questioned whether my friend really believed what he was saying or if he was merely trying to provoke us. But he put aside our queries and thundered through to his last point.

"In the black community, in essence, King has become something akin to Jesus," he lamented. "Or certainly a sacred cow. It's impossible to engage any sort of lasting critique of King because, by doing so, you automatically put yourself clearly outside of what is acceptable in black discourse. I don't think that's good at all to have a figure we can't critically interrogate."

Although I took strong issue with my friend, he set me to thinking hard about King's relationship to black folk. His last point was easy enough to concede. King, like any other figure, should be praised for his virtues and criticized for his failures. In fact, King is the last person to have wanted personal canonization. He was all too aware of his human frailty and had enormous guilt about his worldwide fame. And my colleague's first point, that King's concern for poor blacks wasn't genuine because his education alienated him from common folk, is amply repudiated by King's having committed "class suicide." More than any other black leader, King took to heart his profound devotion to poor folk by surrendering most of his yearly earnings to the movement, living in modest housing, owning no more than a few suits near the end of his life, and mounting one protest after another on behalf of the downtrodden.

But my friend's second point, that King's integration-mad policies led inevitably to the reactionary politics of Clarence Thomas, contained beneath its harsh polemic an insight more difficult to refute. Of course, it would be easy to argue that one species of Negro conservatism is as old as slave plantations, where rebel slaves were kept in check by "house Negroes" who informed on their radical brethren. And, it might be easier to trace Thomas's ideology to Malcolm more than Martin, since the Supreme Court justice fancied the *The Autobiography of Malcolm X* in his greener, militant days. Thomas's beliefs, ironically enough, may be the delayed elaboration of conservative cultural currents that have always circulated in militant black nationalism. Still, there is at least a kernel of truth, and perhaps much more, in the notion that blacks have lost a lot more than they have gained by pursuing integration at all costs. For instance, recent debates about school integration have focused on whether black and brown children have fared far worse in officially desegregated urban schools. Since these youth often make up the overwhelming majority of the schools they attend, they have in effect been resegregated. In such schools, which usually lack the resources of richer white suburban schools, black and brown children are often placed in special education classes or tracked as problem children without good reason. Moreover, they are denied access to cutting-edge technical resources. Martin Luther King, too, had second thoughts about integration, especially as he fell under the spell of black nationalist sentiment. But his views have not been nearly as publicized as his fight against racial apartheid. My friend's vehement attack on King convinced me that the civil rights leader's later views should be highlighted in any critical discussion of his legacy.

My friend is not alone in his steep criticism of King's racial politics. Critics who fly within a black nationalist orbit have been especially harsh. Malcolm X once said that King was a "twentieth-century Uncle Tom" who was the "best weapon that the white man has" ever had. Neither was King immune to criticism from other black clerics and politicians. Adam Clayton Powell viewed King as a moderate who catered to "whitey." And some youth consider King a sellout who "tommed" and "jeffed" for whites while betraying the strongest affirmations of blackness. Malcolm X eventually changed his mind, acknowledging that King and the integrationists were more militant than he had believed. Perhaps Malcolm realized the hypocrisy of calling King a chump while he hid in the bosom of black Harlem as King confronted police dogs and water hoses in acidly racist Birmingham. After all, what was to prevent Malcolm from taking a few busloads of the Fruit of Islam, the military arm of the Nation of Islam, to Alabama and giving Bull Connor three hundred things to think about? (The standard answer is that he was forbade from such action by Nation of Islam head Elijah Muhammad. But Malcolm, as we know, would disobey Muhammad on other matters. Why not at least make it count for something spectacular?) But for all of his bravado, Malcolm may have realized that he and his men would have been manhandled and dispatched if they dared to draw weapons on Connor's brigade of racist goons.

King's image as an integrationist Uncle Tom is sorely out of sync with the way his thought evolved during his last three years. King embraced powerful dimensions of enlightened black nationalist thought even as he remained outside its official borders. Although King surely didn't call himself a nationalist, he grew to appreciate the psychological and economic appeal of nationalist philosophy, elements that he easily absorbed into his eclectic radicalism. The great irony is that in his mature thought and radical action King proved to be much more faithful to some of black nationalism's tenets than many of its most ardent advocates. But more

than that, he has been unfairly attacked by black nationalists for arguing
that nonviolence was the best way to convert white America to his cause
and to defend the racial interests of blacks.

If King was an important therapist for white Americans, he was even
more cunning a therapist for black folk. King's philosophy of nonviolence addressed what Robert Jay Lifton, in writing about survivors of
war, terms "psychic numbing": King identified and attempted to relieve
the psychic suffering of black Americans. True enough, when he went
North, he ran into a cast of black characters he barely knew. To his credit,
he was a quick study. Although he made serious mistakes—for instance,
he took too readily to the language of pathology to describe black ghetto
families—few leaders, even those who had more progressive explanations of ghetto hardship, worked harder to relieve black suffering. King
warmed to dimensions of black nationalism to fight the psychic forces
that foil black self-esteem, and he sought to beat back the economic
forces that stymie black self-determination. But the key to his evolution is
his philosophy of aggressive nonviolence and his valiant efforts to defeat
the demons of racial oppression.

King was forced to grapple with black nationalism in earnest when he
took up residence in Chicago. He faced a struggle up North that he had
barely glimpsed in his Southern activism: the siege of black self-doubt
and self-destruction. It is not that these forces were unfamiliar to Southern blacks who lived in the shadow of white supremacy. Southern blacks
were reminded daily of their horrible insufficiency in the eyes of their
often uncultured despisers. But Southern blacks generated a culture of
survival through the invention of the *psychic doppelganger*, the shadow self
created to encounter the white world. The black who showed up to work
or play for "Mister Charlie" certainly resembled the black who returned
home to her community, but with a profound difference. In reality, blacks
acted quite differently around whites in public than they did around each
other in their own domain. The psychic doppelganger gave blacks mental
and moral refuge from the stormy blast of racism by splitting their true
selves from their public personas. The psychic doppelganger also gave
blacks the solace of quiet rebellion against white supremacy. Blacks gave
their songs double meanings, their jokes double entendres, and their
social behavior double uses in striking silent but powerful blows against
their oppression. To the white world outside, such behavior often
appeared diverting and innocuous. And to the black world that did not
share in its practices, it appeared offensive, even destructive. But blacks
who learned to mask their feelings and meanings generated an ingenious

culture of "signifyin'"—saying one thing but meaning something entirely different. Their artful duplicity allowed them to entertain whites even as they sought to help emancipate themselves. (The spirituals are a perfect example. While whites were being made happy, blacks were filtering information to each other about escape plots through their lyrics.) And while rituals of real or only apparent deference were undeniably taxing and demeaning, and certainly led to a punishing schizophrenic existence for many, they gave black folk enough room to breathe as they fought to create a world where such rituals were no longer necessary.

What King faced up North was as harsh as it was unfamiliar. The New Breed Negro was no longer vested with the garb of formal debasement, but his soul dragged beneath the weight of displaced kinship and degrading social structures. Housing arrangements diminished privacy and led to a desperation for space that didn't exist. The cussing and carousing that were more easily absorbed in segregated Southern spaces often brought black life to a brutal end along a razor's edge or in the barrel of a policeman's pistol. The Great Migration had deposited millions of black souls in cities with the promise of money and freedom. They were often quarantined in tenements and slums with low-paying jobs and very little freedom, except the freedom to choose their form of bondage— drugs, crime, or sex. But like their Southern counterparts, Northern blacks created a culture of survival through the *myth of the authentic Negro*: the invention, and in some cases, reinvention of archetypes of cultural identity used to resist the definition of blackness by whites or bourgeois blacks.

As with the psychic doppelganger, the authentic Negro manipulated masks. But unlike their Southern soulmates, Northern blacks no longer wished to depend on artful duplicity. The North's strong suit was subversive exaggeration. The mack, the pimp, the hustler, and the player grew from urban mythologies of a "real" blackness that countered the shuffling, sniveling, deferential, conciliatory, and compliant blacks who lived for white approval. The authentic Negro generated a culture full of bluster and boast. He reveled in the sort of psychic posturing that was meant to stave off the corrosive self-doubt imposed by a society too mean to care about how it slashed black self-esteem. Thus, overdoing became a way of undoing. To be sure, since most of the Northerners were transplanted Southerners—Chicago, after all, was a bustling suburb of Mississippi—there was overlap and interweaving of survival cultures. But the emphases in each were clearly marked, reflecting the differing style of white response in the South and North. The psychic doppelganger relied on wit shaped by religious inspiration. The authentic Negro drew his steely defiance mostly from secular sources. Gospel music filled Southern houses of worship and wafted across fields of frolic and labor. The blues were belted in Northern sanctuaries: clubs, basement parties, and ghetto garages. And while the psychic doppelganger aimed for the white man's back, the authentic Negro lunged straight at his face. Thus, black habits of deference directed at taming the beast of white supremacy soared in Southern circles, but the aggressive Northern defenders of authentic blackness threw stereotype and hyperbole into the open, as if to dare white folk and bourgeois blacks to beat them at their own game of self-definition.

Of course, there was dissension within each region's approach to survival. King and his colleagues sought to rework the rituals of artful duplicity. They wanted to increase their effectiveness by stripping them of their harmful residue. By lying to the white world, the Negro was of necessity lying to himself. King had a genius for linking the helpful features of the psychic doppelganger—especially its cool calculations of what it took to survive Southern apartheid—to a strategy of resistance that depended on telling the truth. Before the civil rights movement, few Southern blacks could be honest in public about white supremacy or black suffering and expect to live. To millions of Southern blacks, King's nonviolent direct action was scandalous and scary. Telling white folks what they really wanted to do, and what was really on their mind was downright dangerous.

But King's movement didn't intend to be naively self-disclosing, even if it was at first painfully modest in its ambitions. Initially, King and his comrades did not angle for racial justice. "We are not asking for an end to segregation," King said in 1955. Instead, blacks sought the right to sit, not stand, in seats that were not occupied by whites, because, as King said, "we don't like the idea of Negroes having to stand up when there are vacant seats." Even that tiny gesture of open rebellion provoked fear in millions of Southern blacks. Of course, King didn't want blacks simply to say what was on their minds. King and his comrades never wanted to leave to chance what organization, strategy, and propaganda should accomplish. Instead they sought to shape a tradition of revolt through telling stories of black overcoming in the past. They also worked to link memories of black revolt to the nonviolent struggle for freedom. Thus, they were not simply refusing, as some revolutionaries rightly refuse, to pour new wine into old wineskins, but they were, even more ingeniously, using new wineskins to transport the old wine. "Gimme dat ol time 'ligion . . . it's good enough for me," might as well have been their theme. The black movement might look different on the outside, but inside was the same desire to be free that had rung in the breast of slaves in the fields and kept sharecroppers company on tenant farms. Part of King's enormous talent as a leader of the movement was to help shape a new self-understanding for black Southerners, bringing his education to the aid of blacks who were formally uneducated but by no means stupid. These same folk had, after all, tricked mean white men, trained white children, and treated the ills of white women with grace and skill that belied their lowly stations. And the work of indigenous black leaders like Fannie Lou Hamer and Ella Baker had already revealed the depth of Southern black ingenuity. The goal now was to turn that energy loose on themselves, for themselves, for the world to see.

King's movement challenged black Southerners to revise their use of the psychic doppelganger. Instead of hiding their pain through dual personas and artful duplicity, he said they must now bend their outer self in a different moral direction. Moreover, King helped redefine what was at stake when blacks distinguished between their inner and outer selves. Now the struggle was over how blacks should respond to white supremacy while preserving their dignity and, indeed, their lives. The outer self might want to return a blow from a white racist, but the inner self must act in discipline, in *self*-discipline at that, in refusing to do harm. Eventually the inner and outer selves will fuse in the determination of blacks to live a life that is morally and psychically unified. For King, the unity of black selves was not merely a means to achieve racial revolt. Instead, it was an end in itself, a way to embody the goal of liberation for which blacks hungered. The need to mask would be reduced, though not destroyed, since racism still existed. But the result of black self-unity would be the ability of blacks to tell whites what was on their minds, especially since it could now be expressed as a moral appeal to dignity and self-development, huge themes in the American experience. King understood that real black self-unity could come only as blacks threw off the shackles of oppression and redefined themselves through their moral aspirations. And blacks could love whites only if they respected and loved themselves. A large part of self-love is the strength, even if momentary or episodic, to shed the mask of the outer self and reveal in public the inner desire to be free. King's philosophy of nonviolence had ingeniously taken into account the virtues and limits of the psychic doppelganger. He knew that the only way black folk could survive long enough to rebel against apartheid was if they remained calm and absorbed the worst that whites could throw at them. King's philosophy of nonviolence was at least partially built on the belief that violent revolt was self-destructive, and hence, ultimately futile. In King's world, desire was linked to potential: what *could* be done determined what *should* be done. King knew how far to push, when to pursue change, at what pace, and when to fall back, all elements that gave such force to the psychic doppelganger. But King pushed beyond the psychic doppelganger's strategic ceiling. He insisted that the dangerous-to-know truth and the even more dangerous-to-tell truth be made public and, equally important, serve as the basis of negotiating a new society.

Within the North's edgy cultural rebellion of fighting stereotype with stereotype—for that was the logic, after all, of subversive exaggeration, using ever bigger versions of the feared black identity to make whites believe that it was worse than they could imagine, since out-imagining whites was a key part of the strategy—emerged a powerful voice of dissent belonging to black nationalists. Many of these figures claimed to be the spiritual children of Marcus Garvey and Elijah Muhammad, and for some, even Booker T. Washington. In truth, their heritage was more numerous and ancient, including figures like David Walker, the early Frederick Douglass, Martin Delaney, Alexander Crummell, Edward Wilmot Blyden, Henry McNeal Turner, Daniel Payne, and W.E.B. Du Bois. Black nationalism for the most part took a dim view of subversive exaggeration. It failed to see the connection between the authentic Negro and a noble black heritage. For many black nationalists, the authentic Negro was decidedly inauthentic, a projection of racial stereotypes that did the white man's job for him.

Black nationalism's psychology of race insisted on the upright posture of black manhood. Given the context of its times, this was meant to signify the entire race, but its references to the restored egos of black *men* is unmistakable. As was the case with the civil rights movement, the metaphors, images, and symbols of liberation were carved from a masculine worldview. Black nationalists often viewed the subversive exaggeration of authentic Negroes as less a useful strategy of survival than a fatal surrender to the very vices from which blacks sought escape. But black nationalists, who shared a rabbinical seriousness with most civil rights leaders, had little appreciation for the complex and dynamic expressions of popular culture. Black nationalists failed to see the emancipating effect of dramatic excess and playful hyperbole that were common to the toasts, boasts, and bravura of feigned or real hustlers. The hustling lifestyle was read flatly: hustlers were moral casualties in the struggle for the black mind, a black mind that must resist the lure of immediate gratification and an addiction to white approval. The former warning was directed to authentic Negroes, the latter to civil rights defectors from the "true" struggle for black liberation.

In fact, King and crew were just taking to the ground that nationalism had already covered in its attempts to redeem black people from the hell of hating and destroying themselves. If King's extended visit to Chicago awakened him to the harsh realities of the Northern ghetto, these realities had always been front and center for black nationalists, especially Elijah Muhammad's Nation of Islam with its fiery spokesman, Malcolm X. But King and Malcolm never traded notes about their perceptions of black struggle. One of the bitterest ironies of King's and Malcolm's talk about self-love and racial pride is that they never were able to find more than a few minutes to speak briefly. If King could sit across the table from rabid racists, some of whom sought to murder innocent blacks, and if Malcolm could meet with violent white hate groups to reinforce each other's separatist efforts, then surely they might have discussed their mutual commitment to black freedom. It is easy enough to see how King might have found the notion unappealing, since Malcolm's attacks on him as an Uncle Tom—or as "Rev. Dr. Chickenwing," an epithet perhaps matched in black circles only by Congressman Adam Clayton Powell's vicious dig, "Martin *Loser* King"—were aggressive and unsparing. Malcolm's attacks on King were part of the symbolic warfare that black nationalists, especially the Nation of Islam, were waging against nonviolent civil rights struggle. Malcolm was a crucial figure in expressing black nationalism's resentment of the ink and blood spilled around King's organization. For most of his career, Malcolm viewed King as the antithesis to black manhood because he put women and children on the movement's front line. In Malcolm's mind, real black men kept their families out of harm's way. Thus the patriarchy that plagued the black freedom struggle on all sides was evoked as the litmus test for authentic rebellion. For Malcolm, King's repression of rage in nonviolent strategies scarred the black psyche as much as the white supremacy against which they both fought. Malcolm believed that nonviolence would never make whites love blacks. Love, in any case, was beside the point. The aim was to make whites respect blacks, and if need be, fear them, since fear appeared to be the only force to which Northern whites responded. King wrote Malcolm off as a firebrand of black hatred, an emotion King sought to avoid since it multiplied the forces of evil instead of relieving the oppressed's suffering.

For King, Malcolm's advocacy of even defensive violence would lead only to illusory freedom. No one could be free, King believed, as long as he was in debt to distress, as long as he was bound to his oppressor by identical cords of hatred. King claimed that because the Nation of Islam was "nourished by the contemporary frustration over the continued existence of racial discrimination," it had "concluded that the white man is an incurable 'devil.'" But King claimed this was a self-defeating proposition, that there was "the more excellent way of love and nonviolent protest."

In truth, civil rights activists and black nationalists fought for the black soul with competing theologies, cosmologies, and moralities. They put forth beliefs about God and how the world works and, hence, ought to work. If King sought to destroy the need for artful duplicity, Malcolm sought to counter subversive exaggeration, since as a black puritan all such strategies were for him the devices of the devil. Then, too, Malcolm waged war against King because he believed the nonviolent apostle undermined black self-determination. To be sure, Malcolm's self-determination was not primarily a philosophical resolution of moral tensions generated by black strategies of survival. Rather, Malcolm's self-determination expressed a will to self-creation. The black self must be conceived in the womb of black consciousness even as black culture must be purified in the crucible of self-love. From these principles would flow economic control, cultural recreation, social cohesion, spiritual rebirth, psychic regeneration, and racial unity. This too was the message behind Stokely Carmichael's cries of Black Power. To black youth in particular, Black Power represented a promise of control after forever being controlled, of power after being powerless, of embracing the beauty of blackness after being told for so long that black is ugly. "We feel that integration is irrelevant; it is just a substitute for white supremacy," Carmichael argued. "We have to go after political power." But King claimed that integration's moral appeal was fundamental to arguments for black equality. King sought to convince Carmichael that the terms "Black Consciousness" or "Black Equality" were "less vulnerable [to misunderstanding] and would more accurately describe what we are about." King argued that the words "'black' and 'power' together give the impression that we are talking about black domination rather than black equality." Carmichael persisted, contending that neither of the alternate phrases that King suggested had, in King's words, "the ready appeal and persuasive force of Black Power." Then, too, as long as King stayed in the South, he failed to hear the desperate Northern cry for deliverance, not only from white supremacy but from a nonviolent philosophy that, to its critics, would gain freedom at the expense of self-regard.

It seemed that King understood the argument against his philosophy only when he experienced firsthand the deep wounds to the minds and hearts of Northern Negroes. Like many puritan black nationalists, King failed to see little more than pathology in the cultures of Northern blacks. Still, he gained an empathy for black suffering that was not possible before his move to Chicago. What King saw surely haunted him. "The shattering blows on the Negro family have made it fragile, deprived and often psychopathic," he wrote in summoning a remarkably depressing image. "Nothing is so much needed as a secure family life for a people to pull themselves out of poverty and backwardness." If this sounds like a passage from the infamous 1965 Moynihan report on the black family, it should come as no surprise that King read the document but, unlike other radicals, refused to condemn it. King said that the report offered "dangers and opportunities." The opportunity was to gain support and resources for the black family. The danger was that "problems will be attributed to innate Negro weakness and used to justify, neglect and rationalize oppression." Still, there is little difference between King's views and the views he feared would gain authority over Moynihan's signature. King's aide said the ghetto was filled with "jammed up, neurotic, psychotic Negroes" who were "forced into violent ways of life."

King sought to destroy the ghetto through open housing ordinances and heavy federal intervention regarding poverty. After spending only a month in Chicago, an aide said that "I have never seen such hopelessness." He said that the "Negroes of Chicago have a greater feeling of powerlessness than any I ever saw," drawing an implicit comparison between Southern blacks subject to segregation and Northern blacks supposedly free from such horrors. The aide said that they "don't participate in the governmental process because they're beaten down psychologically," and, speaking for his colleagues, concluded that "we're used to working with people who want to be freed."

King's disagreements with Stokely Carmichael and other black militants forced him to call for measures that would enhance black self-esteem and pride, virtues that had been systematically denied to blacks. Even *Newsweek* magazine detected the influence of Carmichael and others on King when it said of his Chicago campaign that "integration is out: The rallying cry for King's own campaign in Chicago is not 'integrate' but 'end slums'; the means, in effect, is Black Power without calling it that."

King's rhetoric was laced with responses to the new mood set by the black nationalists. In 1968, he declared, "Over the last ten years, the Negro decided to straighten his back up, realizing that a man cannot ride your back unless it is bent," familiar words given new meaning in the context of Black Power. King claimed that the Negro had "stood up and confronted his oppressor" and that the "courage with which he confronted enraged mobs dissolved the stereotype of the grinning, submissive Uncle Tom." King got new fuel from black nationalism for fighting the harmful features of the psychic doppelganger. He claimed that blacks "gained manhood in the nation that had always called us 'boy.'" He also claimed that "the ghetto is a domestic colony that's constantly drained without being replenished" and that America is "always telling us to lift ourselves up by our bootstraps and yet we are being robbed every day." King pleaded to America, then, to put "something back in the ghetto," a statement clearly reflecting the influence of economic radicalism and black nationalism.

King was equally sensitive to the psycho-racial dimensions of freedom that nationalism and his Northern experiences forced him to engage. King remarkably claimed that white Americans had practiced "psychological and spiritual genocide" against black people. In his last presidential address to SCLC, King took full measure of the destructive psychic forces that melt black personal resolve and erode self-esteem. He claimed that the "tendency to ignore the Negro's contribution to American life and to strip him of his personhood" was an ancient tradition in America. In response to these forces—what King strikingly, and bitterly, termed "cultural homicide"—he said that "the Negro must rise up with an affirmation of his own Olympian manhood," a sentiment that might have been taken from the works of Malcolm X, Stokely Carmichael, or, in our own day, many Afrocentric scholars. King asserted that any "movement for the Negro's freedom that overlooks" this need is "only waiting to be buried." And in a phrase that anticipated George Clinton's famous aphorism, "Free your mind, and your ass will follow," King claimed that as "long as the mind is enslaved, the body can never be free." "Psychological freedom," he continued, "a firm sense of self-esteem, is the most powerful weapon against the long night of physical slavery." King claimed that neither Lincoln's Emancipation Proclamation nor Johnson's civil rights bill could grant the Negro true freedom:

> The Negro will only be free when he reaches down to the inner depths of his own being and signs with the pen and ink of assertive manhood his own emancipation proclamation. And, with a spirit

straining toward true self-esteem, the Negro must boldly throw off the manacles of self-abnegation and say to himself and to the world, "I am somebody. I am a person. I am a man with dignity and honor. I have a rich and noble history. How painful and exploited that history has been. . . . Yes, we must stand up and say, "I'm black and I'm beautiful,"and this self-affirmation is the black man's need, made compelling by the white man's crimes against him.

King's statement brilliantly mimics nationalism's belief that racism has a devastating impact on young and old black minds.

Ten days before his death, King said that the positive elements of Black Power included the "psychological call to manhood," "pooling black political resources in order to achieve our legitimate goals," and "pooling of black economic resources in order to achieve legitimate power." "All too many have had a deep sense of inferiority," he said, "and something needed to take place to cause the black man not to be ashamed of himself, not to be ashamed of his color, not to be ashamed of his heritage." King also claimed that the election of Carl Stokes as mayor of Cleveland was an example of political power, admitting that "we did engage in a Black Power movement. There's no doubt about that." King said as well that blacks "can pool our resources, we can cooperate, in order to bring to bear on those who treat us unjustly." Then he made this astonishing statement in support of strategic black separatism:

> When we see integration in political terms, then we recognize that there are times when we must see segregation as a temporary way-station to a truly integrated society. There are many Negroes who feel this; they do not see segregation as the ultimate goal. They do not see separation as the ultimate goal. They see it as a temporary way-station to put them into a bargaining position to get to that ultimate goal, which is a truly integrated society where there is shared power. I must honestly say that there are points at which I share this view. There are points at which I see the necessity for temporary segregation in order to get to the integrated society. . . . We don't want to be integrated *out* of power; we want to be integrated *into* power.

King still lauded the goal of ultimate integration but conceded the need for temporary forms of separation as a means to preserve political power, consolidate economic resources, and shore up psychological strength.

Recently there have been vigorous renewals of the spirit of black nationalist sentiment among black communities. Some of the nationalist sentiment marks generational differences. Then there are huge ideological and political gulfs; many younger blacks favor self-segregationist strategies for racial uplift that fly in the face of the radical integrationism of earlier generations. And the popularity of minister Louis Farrakhan among younger blacks has caused no little consternation among older blacks who embrace a civil rights agenda. A central conflict has to do with the meaning and purpose of black freedom struggles in the fifties, sixties, and seventies. Many younger blacks believe that older blacks are caught in an ideological time warp, which can be caustically summed up as, "It don't mean a thing if it ain't about marching." Strategies for social change that were relevant and effective then simply don't have much power now. Crack epidemics don't yield to sit-ins; economic restructuring is impervious to boycotts. There is, too, a feeling among many younger blacks that older blacks were, and remain, too white obsessed, too worried about what the majority culture thinks about black life. Hence, blacks have given whites too much power in determining black progress, as with the NAACP (which has large numbers of white board members and financial support). Or they have ceded whites too much influence within black institutions, as with the National Baptist Convention (where Revelation Corporation, the investment arm of the largest black religious body, was poised to give white conservative evangelicals a ruling interest in an economic partnership).

Moreover, the dominant liberal paradigm that propelled the civil rights movement, especially an unshakable belief in the virtue of integration, has come in for severe criticism by many younger (and some older) blacks. By questioning the logic and legitimacy of integration, younger blacks appear naive or ungrateful, or both, in the eyes of many of their elders. Many blacks who endured great risks to fight Jim Crow laws in the fifties, struggle against segregation in the sixties, and establish affirmative action in the seventies are sometimes infuriated at young blacks who jettison integrationist strategies for survival while embracing nationalism or, at the least, self-segregationism. Perhaps nowhere has this generational gulf proved more painful than in recent debates surrounding an issue widely regarded as a bedrock of civil rights ideology: the desegregation of public schools. While disputes over school desegregation cannot be framed as exclusively generational, strong age cohorts often shape black responses to the viability of desegregation as a tool for racial mobility, enhancement, and liberation. But as with all of the other thorny issues facing black Americans, tense disagreements over integration and desegregation reveal the complex character of the choices that shape black generational perceptions of the best route to racial redemption. This was made especially clear when the NAACP, the leading civil rights organization—and to many younger blacks, a symbol of the implacable, stagnant forces of a bygone era—announced, prior to its 1997 convention, that it would rethink perhaps its most time-honored and sacrosanct goal: the racial integration of American public schools. Just the idea that the NAACP would even consider the idea dismayed some black communities (while delighting others).

In retrospect, the news was less shocking than it first appeared, particularly if we recall that the painful questions posed by integration really are at the center of the African-American experience. In 1944, Swedish economist Gunnar Myrdal wrote that the monstrous gulf between our nation's claim of practicing democracy while denying it to blacks—along with the hypocrisy and hostility such a denial breeds—is "the American dilemma."

But for blacks, the real dilemma has been whether to integrate into American society—which, as James Baldwin said, without adequate black economic resources and white goodwill, is like integrating into a burning house. The alternative strategy currently under debate, especially by millions of younger blacks, is to preserve separate black institutions that would sustain dignity and social identities. In the abstract, this dilemma has been framed throughout black history as an ideological conflict, pitching integration against nationalism, racial assimilation against separatism. In practice, however, the choices have never been as pure or as rigid as such labels suggest. The history of black struggles against white oppression and structural inequality is steeped in ideological promiscuity, a frenetic and often heroic amalgamation of ad hoc strategies for black liberation.

But these hybrid strategies have also exacerbated the terms of the dilemma. American blacks have forged their daily lives in a zone of frustrating paradox, from which there is little, if any, relief. Even at the height of the civil rights movement, many of its leaders advocated integration as they presided over what was arguably the most successful nationalist institution ever: the black church. Meanwhile, many of the most ardent black nationalists have maintained their jobs in the bowels of the white mainstream, from corporations to universities. Still, it can't be denied that the desegregation of public schools has symbolized, and in many ways defined, the aggressive integrationist mission of the NAACP. For many of the group's stalwarts, the fight to desegregate public schools, which culminated in the monumental 1954 *Brown v. Topeka Board of Education* decision, argued before the Supreme Court by NAACP lead counsel Thurgood Marshall, was a major stride in the bitter pilgrimage to a truly just and integrated society. After all, black children had been the victims of a two-tiered educational system sanctioned in the 1896 Supreme Court "separate but equal" ruling in *Plessy v. Ferguson*. After *Brown*, many believed that the nation would move, as the Supreme Court ordered, with "all deliberate speed" to create an equitable, racially balanced school system. But it was not until the hyperintegrationist policies of the early 1970s, especially court-ordered busing, that the ideal of an integrated school system was given more than emergency federal support. It has been rough traveling for the ideal of integration ever since.

Advocates of integration blame the ill fortunes of public school desegregation on the conservative turn in electoral politics. The country's meaner racial politics has produced reversals in the judiciary and raised the enormous cost, psychic and financial, of fighting de facto segregation in supposedly desegregated school districts. These factors, coupled with everyday white hostility at the idea of artificial integration, have fueled a striking resegregation of public education for black and Latino children. While racial segregation dropped dramatically in the South between 1964 and 1972, and gradually in the West and Midwest between 1964 and 1989, segregation in public schools has once again increased in the South and, especially, the Northeast. In the Northeast, 70 percent of urban black and Latino students populate schools that enroll between 90 percent and 100 percent blacks and Latinos. By 1991, two-thirds of all black students and nearly three-fourths of all Latinos attended schools that are predominantly black and Latino, while one-third attended schools that are more than 90 percent black and Latino. These levels reflect the same proportions that existed prior to court-ordered busing in the early seventies.

These numbers have prompted younger blacks, and even former advocates of public school desegregation, to question its effectiveness, while provoking its long-term critics to step up their demands for all-black schools. We might call this postintegration position "neoseparatism"—a stance that recognizes the reversals that integration has suffered without endorsing the sometimes-shrill utopian nationalism of Louis Farrakhan and the Nation of Islam. The neoseparatist critics of integration argue that public school desegregation is a flawed strategy because it rests on

what may be termed the proximity premise: just being in the same class-
room as white children guarantees that black children will get a quality
education. The neoseparatists claim that the proximity premise ignores
(among other factors) the current de facto resegregation of black and
Latino children in integrated schools.

The neoseparatists have a point. Black and Latino children are consistently scapegoated and otherwise stigmatized in integrated settings. They
are put on lower academic tracks than white children. They have higher
suspension rates from school than the majority population. And in situations of borderline academic performance, they are more readily shunted
to special education, remedial, and compensatory classes than are white
children. The neoseparatists also argue that black Americans have been
saddled with an unfair share of the burden of desegregation. Predictably, a
far greater proportion of black students get bused from the inner city to
suburban schools, thanks largely to the Supreme Court's 1973 *Milliken v.
Bradley* decision, which struck down metropolitan busing plans that moved
students from suburban into urban school districts. The closing of finan-
cially strapped black schools and the firing and demotion of black educa-
tors have also accelerated the growth of separate and unequal schooling.

Equally poignant, the psychic tax on black children was severely
underestimated in the strong push for desegregation. Segregated black
schools provided a culture of expectation in which black students were
taught that they could perform well despite radical social and economic
inequalities. Of course, we must not romanticize black schools, which
were often economically starved of support. And we should never forget
the vicious culture of apartheid that enforced discriminatory educational
practices. But neither should we treat neoseparatist claims about the high
value of black schooling as the misguided efforts of ethnosaurs or crack-
pots. Desegregation has produced serious and undeniable failures, but
neoseparatism comes with pitfalls of its own. Studies show that black students in integrated schools complete more years of schooling, are more
likely to secure white-collar and professional employment, and make
higher wages than their segregated peers.

So what should we do? First, we should make a distinction between
self-segregation, where groups choose to coalesce for mutual benefit, and
the coercive racial segregation that was supported by social prejudice and
sanctioned by law. If the ultimate goal is quality education for black children, we have a moral obligation to test a variety of means of achieving
that purpose. If self-segregation is a viable option in helping some black

children reach the pinnacle of their educational possibilities, such means must be responsibly supported. Of course, we must match resources with remedies. That means that black schools are not merely theaters of therapy, although an obvious desideratum for such schools is that they strengthen black students' self-esteem and will to perform. More important, however, is the imperative to reinforce the strength of these black institutions as schools: places that promote disciplined learning and pedagogy and equip black children for suitable employment and self-enjoyment.

We should be aware that arguments for self-segregation may be deployed by many white opponents of desegregation as an excuse to defund black education in integrated settings or to curtail severely the quest for justice in public schools. Thus, we must also push for integrated education to be supported when such efforts have been hampered by administrative and political resistance to the law. Here we must make a fine but necessary distinction between desegregation and integration. The former is the absence of apartheid-like conditions that prohibit educational equity. The latter is the active pursuit of a multiracial educational politics that acknowledges the hybrid character of American identity and democracy.

Such careful insights can help us avoid the tired and in some ways false clash of ostensible opposites: separatists versus integrationists. One can believe in the ultimate politics of integration while affirming that one must practice, at least for a while, the self-affirming politics of self-segregation. No less an integrationist than Martin Luther King, Jr., after all, touted the virtues of "temporary segregation." And as NAACP founder W.E.B. Du Bois said, blacks must never be "against association with ourselves because by that very token we give up the whole argument that we are worth associating with." On another occasion, Du Bois warned:

> What we must remember is that there is no magic, either in mixed schools or segregated schools. A mixed school with poor and unsympathetic teachers, with hostile public opinion, and no teaching of truth concerning black folk, is bad. A segregated school with ignorant placeholders, inadequate equipment, poor salaries ... is equally bad. Other things being equal, the mixed school is the broader, more natural basis for the education of all youth. ... But other things seldom are equal, and in that case, Sympathy, Knowledge, and the Truth, outweigh all that the mixed school can offer.

If black leaders, parents, and teachers proceed with sympathy, knowledge, and truth into a provisional neoseparatist politics, we should appreciate that they are only continuing to work through the twinned American and African-American dilemmas. As such, a new position on desegregation would help us to redefine the terms of these dilemmas in a way that could be a model for the much-touted national dialogue on race. And in the long run, that may help us reach a point where other things could finally become equal.

One of the remarkable features of King's last years is that he grew to embrace powerful aspects of enlightened black nationalism while chiding its ethnic absolutism and its hateful, disharmonious incarnations. It is equally remarkable that many critics counterpose King to those blacks who delight in just the sort of identity politics that King advocated in the passages cited above. King surely reveled in the new sense of personhood that certain varieties of nationalism seemed to offer, but he also had an ecumenical vision of blackness. Without donning dashikis or wearing a big afro, King taught America, including millions of black folk, about the value and beauty of blackness. Much more consistently than many aerial nationalists—those fly-by-night figures who make their judgments about "fake Negroes" from their perches of comfort and convenience in the white world as they dash in and out of black communities—Martin Luther King loved blackness; he loved, and even died, for black people.

When King died, he still lived modestly in Atlanta, with little money for his family, since he gave nearly every cent he earned to his black organization. When he lost his life, he was staying in a humble black hotel in Memphis supporting poor black working men, while copastoring a black church, the most successful black institution that black folk have ever produced. Indeed, the black church was the basis for King's radicalism. Its history is full of figures, admittedly on the margins, who embraced revolt as the righteous fulfillment of religious faith. In the black sanctuary King learned to love freedom so much that he could declare with his ancestors, "Before I'd be a slave / I'll be buried in my grave / And go home to my Lord and be free." King's rejection of racial idealism—his postliberalism, his militant pacifism, his radicalism, and his enlightened nationalism—drew from a vision of social change developed by the militant margin of the black church. If we are to understand the moral thrust behind King's ideological evolution, we have to understand the complex components of his identity. And nothing was more important in shaping his identity than the radical remnant of the black church.

Part II
Identity

CHAPTER 6

"I Had to Know God for Myself"
The Shape of a Radical Faith

The sight of Rev. Henry Lyons sobbing as he pleaded for the mercy of the court at his 1999 sentencing hearing was painful not only for him but for millions of other black Baptists throughout the nation. Two weeks before his appearance, Lyons stepped down from his post as beleaguered head of the National Baptist Convention, the country's largest black religious body. His controversial tenure ended with Lyons being convicted of racketeering and theft and with a cloud of alleged infidelity hanging over his married head. Now he was pleading for leniency from the judge who was unpersuaded by his mea culpas and sentenced Lyons to five and a half years in prison. As Lyons bowed his head in shame, I couldn't help but think of how the organization that he guided for four years had so harshly mistreated Martin Luther King, Jr. Under the brilliantly conservative leadership of Joseph H. Jackson, the National Baptist Convention robustly resisted King's civil rights agenda and blocked his allies from influential positions at the convention's top levels. As a result, King threw in with other disgruntled ministers in 1962 to form a rival group, the Progressive National Baptist Convention.

Lyons's downfall reminded me too of how King had chided black ministers who betray their vocation by embracing a toothless piety or giving in to materialism. Some of King's sharpest criticism of the black church was delivered to a February 1968 SCLC meeting of ministers in Miami, sponsored by the Ford Foundation.

"We didn't come to Miami to play," King reminds his fellow clergy. "We came to Miami to see how we could develop a relevant and a creative ministry for the valley." King hammered relentlessly at the theme of his sermonic address, "To Minister to the Valley." He had already warned his colleagues that they must return to valleys filled with "men and women who know the ache and anguish of poverty," with "welfare mothers who'll not be able to feed their little children," and with "black people who are in moments of despair because of their circumstances." King reassures his intimate audience that they have the moral force to transform America. "You know we have in this room the power, if we really mobilize it, to *compleat-lay* change the course of the United States of America," King emphatically proclaims. "*Brotheren*, you don't know how powerful you are. We don't need everybody." King understood that a militant minority in the black church had always led the way to moral and political change. "We will influence the politics of every city," King announces, "if we in this room will just stick together, and work together, and love each other."

King implores his listeners to confess their failures as well. "Let us admit that even the black church has often been a tail-light rather than a headlight," King argues. In the face of social injustice, these minsters remained silent "behind the safe security of stained glass windows," as King strung together synonyms for safety to underscore his point. King also scores black ministers for standing "in the midst of the poverty of our *ow-w-w-n-n-n* members" and mouthing "pious irrelevancies and sanctimonious trivialities." He then bears down on his brethren as he points to the ugly, self-serving practices of some black ministers. "Let us honestly admit," King rhythmically repeats, "that all too often we've been more concerned about the size of the wheelbase on our automobiles, and the amount of money we get in our anniversaries, than we've been concerned about the problems of the people who made it possible for us to get these things." King insists that his relatively few colleagues can "make the church recapture its authentic reign," that they "had the power to change America," and that they could "give a kind of new vitality to the religion of Jesus Christ." King laments, however, that in the competition with secular ideologies, "the great tragedy is that Christianity failed to see that it had the revolutionary edge."

King's belief in the revolutionary potential of Christianity contrasts sharply with the tenor of so much of contemporary black religion. The black church is too often mired in navel-gazing piousness and undisciplined materialism. But King's vision of social change was inspired by the radical remnant of the black church. Although he has been rightly associated with the genius of black religion, he has not often gotten credit for challenging the conservative drift of the black church. He skillfully molded the moral energy of mainstream black religion into a prophetic stance against oppression. King represented black religion at its best even as he resisted the pressure to soften his radical positions. But King did not erupt from a vacuum. Although he was paradoxically in the bosom and on the borders of black religion, his revolutionary vision of Christianity took shape in a religious womb that was centuries old. To take full measure of King, we must understand the radical remnant of the black church.

From the beginning of black folks' conversion to Christianity during slavery, critics have questioned how adopting the oppressor's religion could free blacks from the yoke of white supremacy. It is true that many white slave owners believed that conversion to Christianity would make their slaves docile. In fact, Frederick Douglass wrote that he met "many good, religious colored people who were under the delusion that God required them to submit to slavery and to wear their chains with meekness and humility." Many slaves, however, believed that their religion encouraged them to rebel against slavery's brutal restrictions. Indeed, one of the reasons so many slaves converted to evangelical Protestant Christianity is the vision of radical equality that the religion promoted. Snobbish Anglicans viewed early Southern white evangelicals as rude, disorderly sorts, a real threat to religious and civic order. Their ranks were swollen with unlettered folk, even servants, who were welcome to speak at their meetings. During the 1780s and 1790s, the worship services of Baptists and Methodists reversed the racial and social status quo. Some members even advocated the abolition of slavery. Predictably, as Baptists and Methodists became upwardly mobile and more respectable in the 1800s, they rejected their antislavery commitment. But black slaves clung to the egalitarian vision that they believed was revealed to them by God. In any case, by the 1800s slaves had started their own churches, where they aggressively advocated a gospel of freedom.

Black churches nurtured the defiance of white supremacy. Insurgent slave ministers like Gabriel Prosser, Denmark Vesey, and Nat Turner hatched revolts against ruthless slave masters. They may have lost their lives, but they gained "a better reward" in preferring death to slavery. And Harriet Tubman drew from black religious belief the inspiration to lead hundreds of black souls out of slavery. She dramatically embodied the prophetic spirit of rebellion. The black church was greatly hated and feared by many powerful whites. After Turner's revolt in 1831, the *Richmond Enquirer* wrote that the "case of Nat Turner warns us" that no "black man ought to be permitted to turn a preacher through the country" or else the "tragedy of Southampton appeals to us in vain." A New Orleans newspaper even ventured in 1839 that the black church was "the greatest of all public nuisances and den for hatching plots against [the] masters." Besides the heroic efforts of Prosser, Vesey, Turner, and Tubman, blacks found other ways to resist, some mundane, others more dramatic: work slowdowns, singing spirituals with dual meanings, embracing atheism, urinating in food, aborting babies, and committing suicide. Although black Christians obviously did not support all these measures, the black church supported their ultimate aim: to liberate slaves from bondage.

The history of black religion since slavery has largely been the history of black people struggling to free themselves from oppression. In this light, a small but significant segment of the black church has agitated for radical social change. Of course, there is little doubt that former Morehouse College president Benjamin Mays was right when he observed that the antebellum Negro's idea of God "kept them submissive, humble and obedient." Equally true is sociologist E. Franklin Frazier's observation that religion made black slaves turn their minds from the suffering and privation of this world "to a world after death where the weary would find rest and the victims of injustice would be compensated." Unfortunately, the same may be said of some quarters of the black church today. In fact, Mays's prized student, Martin Luther King, Jr., complained in 1967 that too many black churches were "so absorbed in a future good 'over yonder' that they condition their members to adjust to the present evils 'over here.'" As rare as they might appear to be, King's radical religious ideas were not without precedent. Figures like Bishop Henry McNeal Turner, Bishop Alexander Walters, and the socialist preacher Reverend Reverdy C. Ransom had sought to radicalize the black church more than a quarter-century before King was born. Moreover, courageous black women have profoundly shaped the black church from its beginnings. As historians Sylvia Frey and Betty Cotton argue, black women formed the black church's revival culture, structured its rituals of worship, gave it secure institutional grounds, spread its religious values between generations, and forged the link between the spiritual and social realms.

Even in this century, the politics of black radicalism has fed the hunger for justice and equality. For instance, the black church has often been an unsung partner in the struggles of black radicals in the labor movement. In Memphis, decades before King led his last march in solidarity with striking sanitation workers, the black church helped to form and mobilize a working-class left. The black church provided a place for white unions to meet and organize when no one else would have them. It helped to establish buying clubs and cooperatives. It agitated to increase wages for workers. It helped to improve federal agricultural policies. Black church leaders argued for sensitivity to the plight of woodworkers, mineworkers, and agricultural workers. And the black church pushed for better schools and black voting rights. In fact, union culture was shot through with black religious sentiment. Black laborers appealed to God to help them and their white counterparts, who were often racist, to organize unions. They inserted union lyrics into religious songs, blending the quest for working-class solidarity with the quest for black freedom. As historian Michael Honey relates, black Southern Tenant Farmers' Union (STFU) organizer John Handcox turned the black gospel song, "Roll the Chariot On," into "Roll the Union On." It became, Honey says, "an anthem for southern unionism." And black preacher-laborer Rev. Ernest Fields was instrumental in the International Woodworkers of America. He led the union organizing committee, preached a healthy social gospel, and appealed to "God's will" to justify the improvement of living standards for workers. When black and white laborers worked together to organize unions, they showed the great potential of uniting the labor and civil rights movements. Their connection also prodded some white workers to change their racist beliefs.

Explorations of the link between religion and radicalism often note that black freedom struggles in the sixties were led by gallant ministers like King. But this is only partially true. The civil rights movement was shaped by ordinary black folk whose often unheralded bravery and sacrifices make them all the more remarkable. Only recently have we had detailed histories of grass-roots leaders—often church-based women—who worked in local communities to make the black freedom struggle effective, even radical. Though not as famous as their male counterparts, Fannie Lou Hamer, Ella Baker, Jo Ann Robinson, and Septima Clark were invaluable in helping black communities muster their moral might to resist white supremacy.

King played a unique role in the black freedom struggle. He was above all its most popular—then its most misunderstood, and finally, its most prophetic—symbol, a man whose willingness to burn bridges in order to bring justice is nearly unparalleled in American history. His faith gave King the will not to settle for less than full equality for blacks and the poor. It also gave him the strength not to sell out his beliefs for popularity or material benefit. Throughout his career, King stayed rooted in his religious base, although he shed the fundamentalist garbs of the religion in which he was reared to take on a more liberal theological outlook to combat black suffering and, eventually, class oppression. King was profoundly influenced by the militant minority of the black Baptist church. He readily took to its theology of love—not the sappy, sentimental emotion but the demanding, disciplined practice of social charity—and to its theology of racial justice and social liberation. Since the church was at the heart of the black community's resistance to racism, King's efforts to transform American society were founded on his prophetic faith. The radical remnant—or, as I use them here interchangeably, the prophetic brigade or militant minority—of the black church taught King how to translate his faith into the language of social justice and civic virtue.

These acts of translation were driven by the belief that the universe belongs to God, that truth is not trapped in church sanctuaries, and that God transmutes hostile powers to achieve the divine will. This truth is captured in a favorite scripture of black Christians, recorded in the book of Genesis in the Hebrew Bible, which in the Revised Standard Version states: "You meant evil against me; but God meant it for good." Besides reflecting a strong doctrine of providence, this scripture reflects a grass-roots strategy used by millions of black Christians to interpret suffering and evil. It is clear from such a strategy that black religious beliefs sustain black survival. A crucial function of the black preacher is to retell powerful stories of the oppressed who overcame opposition through belief in God. King was no exception. His powerful social speech was laced with biblical allusions. His civil rights orations were rife with the themes of faith. His brilliant public use of rhetoric inspired by religion allowed him to forge a style of communication that was doubly useful, satisfying the demands of civic rhetoric while meeting the spiritual needs of his black brothers and sisters.

The radical remnant of the black church usefully adapts the language of civil society. They believe that God's will is glimpsed in preaching and theology and unleashed in politics, culture, and social struggle. Since God's spirit pervades the world and shapes the powers that exist, the world's evil forces may even be turned to good use. God can choose any event or force to confer blessing or deliver judgment. That's why, when the Supreme Court decided in 1956 that segregated transportation in Montgomery, Alabama, was unconstitutional, some black soul shouted, "God Almighty has spoken from Washington, D.C." As King understood, black religion is constantly in tension with all political systems, even those favored by the church's prophetic brigade. But the radical remnant tirelessly works to make politics reflect the justice that prevails in God's kingdom. Long before King, the militant minority in the black church labored to make democracy both noun and adjective, an achievement and a process. That explains why King and the radical remnant could never believe, as some conservative Christians do, that the state is, by definition, the black church's enemy. King was even more convinced that the state should be the black church's ally when he bitterly observed the white church's repeated failure to side with their black brothers and sisters. Many of these whites, and a fair number of blacks, believed that faith should be quarantined from politics. They criticized black religious leaders for their social and political activism.

A great deal of King's genius lay in his unique ability to extend the public witness of radical black Christianity throughout the nation. King used the language of civic piety to express the goals of black religion and radical democracy. He sought to transform society by appealing to a broadly shared set of beliefs that hold together political identity and national citizenship. In the process, King avoided the treacherous path of seeking to enshrine his faith as law, a route that some conservative Christians have not resisted. King ably used two rhetorical strategies gleaned from black religion to stimulate social change: he underscored the power of speech to help change human behavior, and he fused sacred speech with civic rhetoric.

The gist of the first strategy is to use rhetoric to convince participants of a moral crusade, that inspired speech can lead to purposeful action. The power of speech can also make people change their destructive ways. In short, the rhetoric of King and his allies could lead citizens outside their moral arc to change their speech and behavior. Of course, King's rhetoric would have been ultimately useless without the supporting action of the movement, but he ingeniously interpreted that action through his soul-shaking rhetoric. King shaped how the nation understood its racial crisis through the ceaseless stream of words that poured from his tongue. Since the nonviolent movement forbade retaliation to racial violence, rhetorical resistance became that much more important in bringing about social change. King also understood that rhetoric had moral uses inside the civil rights camp, as movement devotees encouraged each other through countless speeches and made use of songs to revive their flagging spirits.

The belief in rhetoric's power to change human behavior and social relations grew from black Christian encounters with a hostile white world. Religious speech helped black Christians to express many goals. It allowed them to tout personal transformation through trial and error. It encouraged adherents to reinvent themselves through moral self-examination. It facilitated spiritual conversion through interaction with God. And it permitted them to spread the message that redemption comes through unearned suffering. King and his comrades believed that their rhetoric had moral authority because they enjoyed what King termed "cosmic companionship."

The second rhetorical strategy that King employed was equally remarkable. He insisted that civic and political life desperately needed the moral resources of black religion. He even made what to some was an outrageous argument: that the black freedom struggle could refashion American democracy. King argued that black resistance allowed America to test its ethical resolve to be a great nation and to recover the original meanings of the American republic. King shrewdly appealed to the Constitution and the Declaration of Independence, highlighting their celebration of democracy and equality. He made religious uses of the secular documents that support civil society and embody national beliefs about citizenship. King also used these documents to ground his civil religious interpretations of justice, freedom, and equality. His religious beliefs drove his public efforts to link love and justice. Through the rhetoric of civil rights, King argued that racial revolution was crucial to the common good.

Had King been more receptive, he might have gained great insight from Karl Marx's radical critique of religion. But King was opposed to Marx on this score because of Marx's supposed antipathy to religious faith. The proof for King was Marx's belief in "metaphysical materialism." Moreover, King, like many other critics, believed that Marxist ethics was an oxymoron. Hostility to religion and ethics, however, derived from a reactionary hard line in orthodox Marxism. In truth, King had a rather flat and unreflexive reading of Marx's views of religion and ethics, a trait he shared with many on the right. At the same time, King's reading of Marx made him miss just how faithfully he embodied progressive Marxist principles in his own fight for the poor against capitalism. King claimed that his principles came from Jesus, not Marx.

King said that "you don't have to go to Karl Marx to be a revolutionary," claiming that "I didn't get my inspiration from Karl Marx. I got it from a man named Jesus." Jesus was "anointed to heal the broken hearted" and "to deal with the problems of the poor, and those in captivity." King concluded that "that's revolutionary. And that is where we get our inspiration." But to return to the example of Gandhi, King often said that when it came to nonviolence, Jesus supplied the inspiration and Gandhi supplied the method. Although an exact analogy between Gandhi and Marx would not work—after all, Marx certainly didn't supply any methods to which King might subscribe, except methods of social analysis—it is fair to say that King actualized, through his strategic social actions, some of the best insights about class warfare and economic inequality about which Marx wrote.

But if the right has garbled Marx's interpretation of religion, so has the left. The left's well- known antipathy to religion hinges on a sophisticated tradition of misreading Marx's famous statement that religion is the "opium of the people." Contrary to the notion that Marx detested religious passion or mistook it for yet another form of "false consciousness"—another misreading, to be sure, since Marx never used the term— he understood that religion was a crucial human response to oppression and a protest against suffering. The proof is in what Marx wrote in the few sentences that precede and follow his fateful declaration: *"Religious* suffering is at the same time the expression of real suffering and also the *protest* against real suffering. Religion is the sigh of the oppressed creature, the heart of a heartless world, as it is the spirit of spiritless conditions. It is the *opium* of the people." Marx also wrote that to "abolish religion as the *illusory* happiness of the people is to demand their *real* happiness," and that to "give up illusions" about the state of existing affairs is to *"give up a state of affairs which needs illusions."*

Clearly religion for Marx was a symptom of an unacceptable state of affairs that demanded radical change. But the meaning of the religious suffering that Marx noted was a powerful, if insufficient, response to horrible conditions that he thought communism might fix. Plus, the religion that needed to be criticized was the sort of religion that created disillusion in the people because it hurt them when it should have helped, especially when it promised a heaven it couldn't deliver. Marx didn't live long enough to see his words boomerang on him in the name of communist dictatorships that promised bread but instead brought (prison) stones. It's clear that Marx and Engels—and a whole lot of oppressed folk before and since them—were outraged by religion's refusal to engage the social and economic forces that harm human community. At best, religion had become passive or otherworldly in the face of suffering. At worst, it had become an agent of human oppression. King was profoundly influenced by a radical black religious tradition that had much in common with Marx's analysis. In fact, many of King's own criticisms of white and black religion square perfectly with Marx's judgments.

Given its grand legacy, especially during slavery and the civil rights movement, the black church seems to have strayed from its radical roots. The National Baptist Convention is mired in a leadership crisis. Black Christians seem to be growing more politically and socially conservative, glimpsed in anecdotal reports of their beliefs about abortion, premarital sex, school prayer, and gay rights. This is certainly a bad sign for extending the radical agenda that King envisioned for the black church. But there are glimmers of hope. For instance, Jesse Jackson continues to be a beacon for progressive black Christian interests and a vital link to the greatly diminished radicalism of American politics. As we move to reclaim the energy King devoted to the church's militant margin, we must revive his bold witness. The radical remnant must learn again to become, like King, prophetic pests in the public sphere. Like King, we should translate our beliefs about love into concrete action. Justice is what love sounds like when it speaks in public.

King might say to the radical remnant of the black church if he were alive today that we shouldn't give up on the black church, especially not the part that supports a radical black agenda. Thus, the black church should oppose white supremacy and address the failures of welfare reform. It should forge class solidarity among the working class and help to shore up national unions. It should promote school reform. It should defend reparations and affirmative action. It should advocate environmental justice. It should support full employment, argue for national health care, and assert the need for reform of the death penalty. It should work vigorously to end police brutality. Then it should join with committed activists around the nation to push for progressive political change.

The black church continues to be a sleeping giant when it comes to tapping its potential to lobby and mobilize its voter base. The religious left could learn a lesson in political mobilization from the religious right. According to a 1984 National Black Election Survey, only 22 percent of blacks attended a church meeting in support of a candidate. Only 19 percent of churches took up collections for candidates during an election year. Only 10 percent worked for a candidate through the church. And in a 1983 survey of eighteen hundred black ministers, only half supported the use of the church as an instrument of social and political change. Of course, radical democratic efforts should not be exhausted in electoral politics. Grass-roots efforts by black churches, especially the delivery of social services to local communities, are important expressions of black radicalism. But until the black church flexes all of its political muscle, it will continue to squander its great influence.

The prophetic brigade must block the religious right from making even more detrimental inroads in the black church. The right appeals to the black church's homophobic inclinations, its sexist sentiments, and its nostalgic hunger for a golden era of "family values" that never existed. To be sure, the black church has enough regressive morality without the assistance of the religious right. But it is troubling how the religious right snares black Christians in the trap of transcendence: the illusion that they can do away with the racial history that colors the interpretation of the gospel. The right also wields its biblical literalism as a bludgeon, convincing many black Christians that progressive views on sex, gender, race, or class betray the faith (this even as white conservative evangelicals aggressively pursue their own political agenda). That is a far cry from the gospel of freedom embraced by early black Christians. It also is a tragic confirmation of Marx's and King's indictment of the obsessive otherworldliness of some religious communities.

King might also argue that the radical remnant must oppose what social ethicist Robert Franklin terms "positive-thought materialism." Positive-thought materialists believe that their own health, wealth, and success are the keys to salvation. They neglect the social transformation, political activism, and moral vision advanced by the church's prophetic brigade. Positive-thought materialism has taken hold of many black Americans just as they enter the middle class. It may provide a way for many religious blacks to justify their upward mobility without feeling responsible for their less fortunate kin. In such a pernicious social vision, the poor are viewed as being unhealthy, unsuccessful, and unwealthy because they are morally flawed. To put it crudely, the poor are seen as spiritual failures because they do not think right, pray right, or live right. Positive-thought materialists are thus relieved of the burden of brotherhood imposed by the gospel. They fail to shoulder any responsibility for the less well off while shirking the pursuit of social justice on behalf of the poor. Why should they? If the individual is at fault, the remedy surely will not come through social or political measures.

In the light of his mature thought, King would undoubtedly urge the radical remnant in their thinking and activity to be race specific without being race exclusive. It is true that in forging coalitions with other progressive groups, racial minorities are often encouraged to surrender the particular claims they might press as a group in deference to a misleading definition of "universalism." This, I believe, is precisely the argument we are now getting from left-leaning figures like Todd Gitlin, Michael Tomasky, and, to a lesser degree, Richard Rorty. Such critics argue that the scourge of identity politics has torn apart a plausible left movement. They hold that the focus on special interests, especially the interests of racial, sexual, and gender minorities, has undermined a viable radical politics. But this can make sense only if one ignores the tremendous struggle for human and labor rights that progressive blacks have always backed. The radical remnant must surely call on black folk to underscore their varied identities—just as the white mainstream does, but without the same stigma as blacks because white identities have been made the basis for what is universal in our culture. The radical remnant must continue to join struggles against homophobia, gender oppression, class inequality, and the like. Such linkages should be made because they are the right thing to do. But it is also a way of enlarging our awareness of the various ways black folk cut our identities. All of those ways should be affirmed within black culture, especially in religious bodies.

Perhaps the biggest challenge facing the radical remnant is to reform the National Baptist Convention. The recent troubles of Henry Lyons have once again thrust the group into an unwanted spotlight. To be sure, the National Baptist Convention has garnered its share of bad press in the past. Perhaps the ugliest headline came in 1961, when a minister was pushed from an auditorium stage to his death as delegates to the annual convention literally struggled over who would lead the group. The convention's problems certainly reveal the religious and moral turmoil at its center, but they also underscore the huge stylistic and symbolic battles in black circles over how black leadership should behave. The National Baptist Convention must reclaim its relevance to blacks who are skeptical about religious institutions.

In large part, Lyons's problems bring to light the unjust exercise of charismatic authority. Lyons first came under severe scrutiny in 1997 when he was charged with misusing church funds to purchase a $700,000 Florida home with an associate, Bernice Edwards, with whom he was suspected of having an affair. Despite vigorous protest at the 1997 annual meeting from a vocal minority within the National Baptist Convention— led by New York's Rev. Calvin Butts, North Carolina's Rev. Matthew Johnson, and Atlanta's Rev. Jasper Williams—Lyons managed to preserve his position by shrewd politicking and mobilizing members who were sympathetic to his presidency.

Lyons held on, too, because he is a gifted preacher. The talent to "tell the story," as black preachers phrase it, is the most useful, and misused, ability of black religious leaders. The gift of sacred speech has been used to lift the sagging souls of parishioners damned by disbelief in themselves and to rally bewildered troops in the war for racial and social justice. But black religious oratory has too often been employed to line the pockets of materialistic ministers or cause vulnerable women to swoon and sexually submit under the hypnotic sway of eloquence. And the genius of black rhetoric has also been used to obscure personal and professional misconduct. Of course, such abuses of religious leadership are not peculiar to black churches. Sinclair Lewis's novel *Elmer Gantry*, Robert Duvall's film *The Apostle*, and the real-life foibles of televangelists Jim Baker and Jimmy Swaggart amply illustrate the sins of white preachers. But the failures of the black ministry reverberate widely because the church remains the dominant institution in black culture and the black preacher a staple in sacred and secular affairs.

The National Baptist Convention's problems will not be solved with Lyons's departure. True enough, most black preachers won't be convicted, as Lyons has been, for defrauding corporations, stealing funds from B'nai B'rith intended to help burned black churches, taking a million dollars from a Canadian funeral home in exchange for help in a court case, or inflating membership numbers to hike fees from companies for endorsing their products and services. (But to be fair, more harmless lies have been told by pastors about the number of members they have than about anything else in the black church!) Lyons's alleged abuses underscore a need for the National Baptist Convention to overhaul and update its structures of accountability. The group's relatively loose organizational design, its open-ended process for dispersing finances at the top, its culture of glamorizing personality-driven loyalties, and its strict adherence to models of priest-as-chieftain and church-as-fiefdom have all eroded the group's greater impact on black America.

Most sharply, the culture of sexual privilege encouraged within most religious quarters—where ministers, priests, and rabbis expect carnal rewards for spiritual service—must be openly addressed. The doctrine of sin in most black Baptist circles counsels forgiveness in the face of failure because human vulnerability is universal. But that's different from the moral hypocrisy that often haunts black religious circles. While black ministers rail against the sexual deviance of rappers, teen mothers, and gays and lesbians, they often fail to confront the rituals of seduction they practice from the pulpit. Bedding women is nearly a sport in some churches.

In the end, the situation in black churches won't be rectified until justice for women is the rule in black churches, where black women make up over 70 percent of the membership. Because black women are largely excluded from leadership in the very institution they numerically dominate, many choose to compete sexually for access to a leadership they could otherwise earn through spiritual service and sacrifice. When black women are routinely ordained as ministers and assume strong leadership in churches, the potential for sexual misconduct by male pastors will certainly be minimized.

While King did not have a shred of Lyons's unseemly malfeasance, he shared with many a minister a weakness for the flesh. An extraordinary culture of justification throbs in religious circles around the sexual practices of preachers, or, for that matter, of rabbis, priests, and gurus. King's moral status shrank even more in the eyes of his critics with the revelation that his cheating did not end with women but extended to the written word. What are we to make of King's behavior, and how does it square with his public commitment to social justice? In the next two chapters, I explore King's plagiarism and promiscuity, twin evils that fatally wound King's reputation in the minds of his detractors. Of course, if the measure of any great person is taken over the entire sweep of her life, then surely revelations of King's failures cannot cancel our appreciation of his extraordinary career. But neither will it do any good for his admirers to avoid his flaws. By refusing to engage his weaknesses, we fail to learn the true nature of King's achievements since we deny ourselves complete knowledge of what he was up against. All along, King insisted that he was unworthy of the public praise that he received. By acknowledging his warts, we might better understand his greatness. In the end, we might honestly conclude, with both eyes open, that King was far too harsh in judging his own worth.

CHAPTER 7

"Somewhere I Read of the Freedom of Speech"
Constructing a Unique Voice

At a recent conference on black males, I shared keynote responsibilities with two other speakers. One of them was a forty-something civil rights leader and Baptist preacher. It was February, known in my circles as "National Rent-a-Negro Month" in homage to the flurry of Black History Month activities that colleges and corporations cram into those twenty-eight days (as if no other time was appropriate to recognize black achievement). I hustled into the conference late, arriving just in time to hear the closing comments of the civil rights leader, who by now was "putting on the rousements"—firing the crowd up with his astute analysis of the crises confronting black men. He was sailing fast now, punctuating his speech with powerful phrases he knew would elicit the audience's approval, an old trick that we Baptist preachers use to send our congregations out to do the Lord's work.

Just as the speaker reached the climax of his oration, I was whisked to the back entry of the stage to await my turn to speak, since all three keynoters were presenting in rapid succession. As I watched my colleague finish, I got an even better sense of the glorious rapport he had established with his audience, a sublime connection that gives both parties a rush that few other events can match. As he offered his husky-voiced parting thoughts, the crowd leaped to its feet, and so did I, gleefully grabbing him as he came off stage in a brotherly bear hug, wrapping him in the audience's affection as their unofficial emissary.

"Hey, Doc, how ya doin?" my colleague brightly greeted me.

"Man, you tore it up," I enthused. "I got a hard act to follow, boy."

"Aw, man," he graciously responded, "you know you gonna turn it out."

"I don't know, brother," I shot back. "You look like you killed every-*thang* in there. And what ain't dead, you done put in intensive care."

We both cracked up, bathing each other in the occasionally obnoxious mutual admiration to which Baptist preachers are eagerly given. As I was being introduced, my colleague offered his regrets about having to leave for another engagement. I readily understood, since I would have to leave right after my speech for the next town in my Black History Month tour.

As the crowd warmly greeted me, I let on that my colleague was difficult to follow but that I'd try to do my best (a Baptist preacher way of begging for sympathy and winning the crowd). My grasp at pity seemed to be working, as the crowd urged me on with "amens" and "go 'heads." I slid easily enough into my speech, but at a crucial period—or, more exactly, at a crucial three-minute passage that I had used in many of my speeches over the past year—I felt the enthusiasm of the audience flag. Usually my passage drew uproarious guffaws and penetrating "humhs," but now I was greeted with sprinkled laughter and moderate "huhs," the kind that feel more obligatory than genuine. I pressed on, not giving it much thought, chalking the lukewarm response up to my poor delivery or to having misjudged my audience. But the rest of my speech went well. I too got a standing ovation and was grateful for the audience's loving endorsement. But after my speech, I wondered again why my passage hadn't gone over as hugely as it usually did. Not until later did I discover what had gone wrong.

Three weeks after my keynote speech, I had a speaking engagement in a nearby town. The woman who picked me up from the airport for the hour-long drive to the university remarked that she had attended the conference on black males and had enjoyed all of our speeches.

"I know you must have wondered why, when you got to a certain point in your speech, people didn't respond as enthusiastically as you perhaps thought they would," my host offered, impressing me with her savvy while piquing my interest.

"Yeah, I did wonder what had happened," I confessed.

"Well, the speaker before you had gone through the same routine in his speech," she revealed. "And since the audience had just heard it, their response was certainly muted."

"O-h-h-h-h," I said. "Now I get it."

Although I was friendly with the civil rights leader, I took it as a matter of pride to point out to my host that *he* had ripped *me* off, and not vice versa. As soon as my host's comments hit my ears, I recalled that the civil rights leader's wife had heard me preach a few months before at a black Baptist church, and since her husband couldn't attend, she promised that she would give him a tape of my sermon. I had used my dramatic passage in that sermon, and of course, he had obviously listened to the tape and lifted my passage for his speeches. In spite of my brief fit of ego, I couldn't stay sore at my colleague. After all, Baptist preachers are always ripping each other off and using the stories, illustrations, phrases, verbal tics, mannerisms, phrases—and in some cases, whole sermons—we glean from other preachers. That's how we learn to preach—by preaching like somebody else until we learn how to preach like ourselves, when our own voice emerges from the colloquy of voices we convene in our homiletical imagination. And in the end, the only justification for such edifying thievery among preachers is that the Word is being preached and the ultimate author of what we say is being glorified.

In fact, the line I had used about the civil rights leader having "killed every*thang* in there" was torn straight from the transcript of a thousand other conversations between black Baptist preachers congratulating one another for their rhetorical might. Then, too, I knew the humorous three-step rhetorical rule of citation by which many black Baptist preachers operate. The first time they repeat something they hear, they say, "like *Martin Luther King* said . . ." The second time they repeat it, they say, "like *somebody* said . . ." The third time they repeat it, they say, "like *I* always say . . ." None of this means that there aren't rules of fair play—that one shouldn't work exceedingly hard in preaching with a Bible in one hand, the newspaper in the other (an idea ripped off from theologian Karl Barth), that one shouldn't hunt for inspiration in all sorts of unusual places, and that one shouldn't feed one's flock with the fruits of rigorous intellectual and spiritual engagement. At their best, the practices of black Baptist preachers remind us that knowledge is indeed communal, that rhetoric is shaped in the interplay of a rich variety of language users, and that what is old becomes new again by being recast in forceful and imaginative ways.

All of this is crucial if we are to make sense of the recent revelation that Martin Luther King, Jr., borrowed other people's words in his published and preached sermons. Of course, nothing I have said can account for the even more disturbing charge that King was a plagiarist in his academic work. It is now clear that he plagiarized huge chunks of his dissertation and graduate school papers and that he carelessly cited sources in his seminary and undergraduate papers. This news is especially jarring to those who view King as an American original, a figure whose social vision came wrapped in brilliant metaphors and memorable phrases. The notion that a figure who commanded the English language with such authority was in truth a borrower of other people's words is too hard for King's admirers to swallow. For many Americans, King's example is law, his words scripture. In fact, King's memory has become a racial Esperanto. His life has been made into a moral language that allows whites to translate their hopes and fears about black life into meanings that black folk intuitively understand. Much of King's power hinged on his use of language, indeed, his use *as* language. His moral authority was largely rooted in his unique ability to express eloquently the claims of black freedom.

In that light, understanding what King did with language—that is, getting at his complex rhetorical habits and the presuppositions he brought to his spoken and written work—will give us a better sense of how to judge his achievements and failures. By explaining how King absorbed and recycled rhetorical sources and how he creatively fused a variety of voices in finding his own voice, one may be charged with excusing his verbal theft by "converting King's blemish into a grand achievement." Worse yet, one may be charged with appealing to some mythic racial practice to justify his borrowing, but certainly not borrowed, genius. But that is to confuse explanation with justification. Such a conclusion clings desperately to the naive belief that we must ignore context and circumstance in making moral judgments.

King's borrowing, and at times, outright theft, of others' words must be viewed in two arenas: his sermons in the pulpit and in print and his scholarly writing in the academy before that. The most sophisticated arguments to date about King's use of language in the pulpit and in print have been made by scholars Keith D. Miller and Richard Lischer. Miller, in his insightful *Voice of Deliverance*, persuasively argues that King heavily borrowed from white liberal preachers in his published sermons to further the cause of civil rights. He ingeniously seized on the ethical and political dimensions of white liberal sermons—including their emphasis on the Christian social gospel, their antimilitarism, their critiques of capitalism and communism, and even their inchoate antiracism—to cast his own arguments for black emancipation in terms that white liberal listeners would find irresistible. By fusing his voice with white liberal voices, King practiced, in Miller's term, the black oral art of "voice-merging," an ancient practice in black religious circles. Miller argues that in such circles, speech is seen not as private but as communal property. In black oral culture black folk learn to refine rhetoric and shape identity by joining their voices to the voices of their ancestors and their contemporary inspirations. Thus, King didn't view such an art as verbal theft but as a time-honored, community-blessed tradition with deep roots in black culture.

Richard Lischer agrees in substance with this aspect of Miller's argument. His brilliantly argued *The Preacher King* explores the rich rhetorical resources that King inherited as a prince of the black church. While Miller analyzes King's written sermons and speeches, Lischer pays close attention to King's spoken word, poring over the unedited audiotapes and transcripts of King's sermons and speeches. Lischer argues that King's real voice was edited out of his published sermons as he and his publisher sought to appeal to as wide an audience as possible. Where Miller finds virtue in such a strategy, Lischer smells trouble. Not only is King's spoken voice missing—a voice full of cultural allusion, racial wisdom, and black rhythms that were muted under the dogma of pen and page—but his theological and ideological evolution—a full-blown radicalism that was especially apparent in his highly personal, magnificently improvised, and deeply colloquial black sermonizing—is completely whitewashed. Lischer disagrees with the notion that "in his plagiarism King was simply adhering to the standards of African-American . . . preaching." He claims that it "is one thing to assert" that language is a shared commodity in black culture, which he concedes, but "it is quite another to translate that generalization into a rationale for academic falsification." Finally, Lischer thinks that Miller overstates the extent to which King borrowed. After all, he argues, white liberal ministers borrowed freely from each other (Miller also makes this point).

Despite their disagreements, Miller and Lischer offer persuasive arguments about how King used his intellectual and rhetorical gifts to bring about social change. Both authors help us understand exactly how King went about the formidable task of drawing on black cultural and religious traditions while shaping a message of liberation that could sway the conscience of white America. By digging deep into the history of black oral traditions, they help us understand a much celebrated but little understood practice: black preaching. Their brilliant explorations of the mechanics, methods, and modes of black sacred rhetoric help us see that black preachers often give their listeners reason to hope and fuel to survive by spinning words into the Word. Black preachers coin phrases, stack sentences, accumulate wise sayings, and borrow speech to convince black folk, as the gospel song says, to "run on to see what the end is gonna be." King had a genius for knowing what intellectual and spiritual resources to bring together, and to know when such a fusion would make the most sense and the greatest impact on his hearers.

As Miller and Lischer make clear, King's borrowing had a noble purpose. For Miller, it was nothing less than the reflection back to liberal white America of the ideals it cherished in comforting and familiar language. For Lischer, King's borrowing helped to subvert the status quo as

King's speech progressively filled with rage in denouncing racial optimism. Miller is right to emphasize King's brilliant reworking of white liberal religious themes and to suggest that King's success, at least the success of his early years, was surely linked to the perception by liberal whites that he and, by extension, most other blacks, was very much like them. King possessed the unique ability to convince liberal whites through phrases and sermon plots they were familiar with that black freedom was a legitimate goal because it was linked to social ideals they embraced each Sunday morning. By embracing liberal orthodoxy through the rhetoric of its main exponents, King was able to send the message that he and the blacks he represented were committed to the same goal of social reform as white Protestants. Miller also convincingly argues that through the rhetoric at hand, King constructed a public persona—a social self—that expressed blackness in a fashion that appealed to the white mainstream.

Lischer complains that Miller's notion of self-making makes King appear duplicitous. But Miller discerns in King's public persona the tough but inevitable choice that all minorities in a dominant culture face: how to put one's best face forward. Given that King was concerned or, early on, even obsessed with what would work in white America, he was perhaps compelled to mold a public persona that pleased liberal whites while reinforcing black self-respect, a virtually impossible task. But Lischer usefully reminds us that King faced Du Bois's famed dilemma of twoness—to be "an American, a Negro." Even in this light, mask wearing or self-making need not be read as mere duplicity. Instead, it may be viewed as a renewal of the ancient black effort to survive through creating durable, flexible personalities. Making selves and wearing masks is not merely a defensive device to deter white intrusion. It is also the positive means by which blacks shape their worlds and make their identities. Lischer is right to argue that Miller's reading skews King's later, more radical preaching by not attending to the sermons and speeches that rarely made it to print. And he renders invaluable service by excavating a neglected version of King's public persona that remains buried beneath the rubble of feel-good rhetoric that distorts his memory. Like Miller, Lischer shows us how King used rhetorical formulas to argue for racial justice, but with a different bent. He explores how King ingeniously employed the rhythms, cadences, and colloquialisms of the black vernacular to inspire his black audiences to disobey unjust laws. Thus, King made speech a handmaiden of social revolution.

Both authors' arguments illumine King's borrowing habits by placing his speech making and sermon giving in broad cultural and racial context. Black preachers—for that matter, all preachers—liberally borrow themes, ideas, phrases, and approaches from one another, although most would not pass off in print a sermon heavily borrowed from another preacher as their own. But many of the same preachers would not hesitate to preach a heavily borrowed sermon in their pulpits. Many critics are skeptical about the claim that speech is so freely shared in black communities, and even more skeptical of the notion that cribbing others' work is such a common practice. But in an oral culture where, as Miller argues, authority is prized above originality, the crucial issue is not saying something new by saying something first, but in embracing the paradoxical practice of developing one's voice by trying on someone else's voice, and thus learning by comparison to identify one's own gift. If imitation and emulation are the first fruits of such an oral culture, its mature benefits include the projection of a unique style—a new style—that borrows from cultural precedents but finds its own place within their amplifications.

King spoke much the way a jazz musician plays, improvising from minimally or maximally sketched chords or fingering changes that derive from hours of practice and performance. The same song is never the same song, and for King, the same speech was certainly never the same speech. He constantly added and subtracted, attaching a phrase here and paring a paragraph there to suit the situation. He could bend ideas and slide memorized passages through his trumpet of a voice with remarkable sensitivity to his audience's makeup. King endlessly reworked themes, reshaped stories, and repackaged ideas to uplift his audience or drive them even further into a state of being—whether it was compassion or anger, rage or reconciliation—to reach for justice and liberation. King had a batch of rhetorical ballads, long, blue, slow-building meditations on the state of race, and an arsenal of simmering mid-tempo reflections on the high cost of failing to fix what fundamentally ails us—violence, hatred, and narrow worship of tribe and custom. King knew how to play as part of a rhetorical ensemble that reached back in time to include Lincoln and Jefferson and stretched across waters to embrace Gandhi and Du Bois in Ghana. But he played piercing solos as well, imaginatively riffing off themes eloquently voiced by black preachers Prathia Hall and Archibald Carey. In the end, King brilliantly managed a repertoire of rhetorical resources that permitted him to play an unforgettable, haunting melody of radical social change.

Even if one holds that King's creative uses of borrowed words amounted to verbal theft (a view I heartily reject), one might still conclude that, in King's case, there was a moral utility to an immoral act. A greater good was served by King's having used the words of others than might otherwise have been accomplished had he not done so. This utilitarian calculus takes into account Miller's insistence that King was weighed down with so much to do that it would have been impossible for him to achieve the worthy goal of racial revolution without appealing to such resources. And even if one concludes that King's unattributed use of sentences and paragraphs from others' sermons in his printed sermons was plagiarism (a view I do hold), one can still acknowledge the pressures under which King performed—not simply pressures of time and commitment, but the pressure to resist white supremacy in a manner that maintained black dignity while appealing to white conscience. As if that were not formidable enough, King also had to balance the militant demand for social change early on while making certain that the manner in which black folk demanded their due would not lead to mass black destruction. Given such pressures and in the light of King's moral aims, it is certainly not unforgivable to produce a book of sermons, *Strength to Love*, that includes unacknowledged sources. In fact, there is some poetic justice in King's use of orthodox liberal ideas to undermine orthodox racial beliefs and even more justice in his having breathed new life into these words while expanding their moral application, fulfilling them in ways their owners might never have conceived but to which they would certainly have no objections. As Lischer argues, *Strength to Love* was published to consolidate King's white liberal audience, a goal he certainly achieved. But as Lischer also notes, unedited audiotapes of King's sermons and speeches are not only more representative of King's rhetorical output, but are a more reliable index of his sophisticated oral practices. In the main, King was more Miles Davis than Milli Vanilli.

King's academic work is another matter altogether. From the scant evidence that exists, even in his undergraduate days at Morehouse College, King was sloppy in formally citing the sources of ideas he propounded in his papers. King began college at age fifteen, swept in on an early admissions policy for bright students to compensate for the drain of black men during World War II. King graduated from college at nineteen, the same age at which he preached his trial sermon. The sermon that King would preach that night became one of his favorite homilies and was greatly dependent on a sermon by a well-known white minister. King sailed into seminary with supreme confidence, the son of a solidly middle-class minister whose future promise had begun to blossom as he embraced graduate school at an age when most male students were gearing up for girls and guzzling beer. King's work at Crozer Theological Seminary in Chester, Pennsylvania, was often distinguished enough to earn him high marks from his professors (except, ironically enough, in a couple of public speaking courses) and the confidence of fellow students, who voted him class president. But King's formal citation habits continued to be sloppy. In most cases, his errors might have easily been corrected had he taken more time to place quotation marks around material amply cited in his notes and had he refined his skills of paraphrasing others' work. King's work at Crozer, especially his use of books and articles from which he drew many of his ideas, proves that he used these sources to bolster his burgeoning theological beliefs about God, human nature, evil, and sin.

The same holds true for his work at Boston University, where King matriculated after graduating from Crozer. Initially enrolled in the philosophy department to work with renowned philosophical theologian Edgar Brightman, King transferred to the school of theology when Brightman died. There King worked under the tutelage of L. Harold DeWolf and, to a lesser degree, S. Paul Schilling, both of whom were influenced by Brightman's conception of personalism, which holds that God is a living being with the characteristics of human personality. King put his own stamp on personalist theology even as he wrestled with other great theological and philosophical figures, some of whom he first read in seminary—Kant, Hegel, Marx, Nietzsche, Barth, Niebuhr, Tillich, and Wieman. Throughout his Boston University career, it is now evident that King plagiarized large portions of his course papers and his dissertation, "A Comparison of the Conceptions of God in the Thinking of Paul Tillich and Henry Nelson Wieman," completed in 1955. King plagiarized the two principal subjects of his dissertation, but the bulk of his theft concentrated on large portions of Jack Boozer's dissertation, "The Place of Reason in Paul Tillich's Conception of God," written just three years before King's thesis and supervised by L. Harold DeWolf, King's major adviser. Interestingly, King used plagiarized thoughts to reinforce his theological convictions. He stole words for at least three reasons: first, to explore the character of a God who was personal and loving, and not simply, as Tillich argued, the "ground of being"; second, to investigate the complex nature of human identity and sinfulness, as King struggled between neo-orthodox theology, with its emphasis on original sin, and liberal religious views, which hold that myths and symbols dot the biblical landscape; and, finally, to probe the origin and persistence of evil—was it allowed by God, who in yielding to human will, decided to limit herself, or was God not really all-powerful? As historian Eugene Genovese notes, King's plagiarism contained a "curious feature" since it was not characterized by "laziness and indifference" but showed that King "constantly wrestled with difficult subject matter." And most of his teachers agreed with his seminary professor's assessment that King possessed "exceptional intellectual ability." Moreover, there is no evidence that King cheated on his examinations, which he constantly passed with high marks. Then why did he plagiarize?

No one knows, although many scholars and critics across the ideological spectrum have ventured reasons. Theodore Pappas's edited volume, *Martin Luther King Plagiarism Story*, is a relentless assault on King's reputation, a bitterly moralizing anthology that assays to unveil King's moral deficits through his stolen words. Instead, Pappas's tome, with the exception of contributions by Genovese, Gary Wills, and Jacob Neusner, is a throb of journalistic overkill with little relief or balance. Its ominous blue tones seek to warn us that King's sordid act of intellectual treachery reveals his inherently flawed character—information intended, no doubt, to flatten King's naive boosters. Pappas's attack reveals just how persistent are the pockets of intellectualized attacks on Martin Luther King's reputation in our nation, although he does document the reluctance of media and academic critics to publicize King's plagiarism. King's first scholarly biographer, David Levering Lewis, was "appalled" at the news of his virgin subject's literary misdealings, decrying King's "repeated act of self-betrayal and subversion of the rules of scholarship," which, in the light of Lewis's estimate of King's ability, was wholly unnecessary. Lewis detects in King's psychic makeup the "angst of strivers in the melting pot," whether they came by immigration or slavery. He plausibly posits that an "alert striver" like King might have sensed a racial double standard in his professors' treatment of him, and thus, "finding himself highly rewarded rather than penalized" for his apparent mistakes, "he may well have decide[d] to repay their condescension or contempt in like coin." That may be true, although it may not help us understand why King cheated in the first place. Then, too, such a reading depends on denying that King's scholarly habits were influenced by the verbal promiscuity of black culture, an argument Lewis finds "wholly incredulous." Another exhaustive King biographer, David Garrow, is more willing than Lewis to concede the relevance of black cultural factors in understanding King's practices, at least on the sermonic front. Garrow holds that the discovery of King's plagiarism will not only "alter our understanding of the young Martin Luther King," but that the consequences of such a finding will "complement and further strengthen two interpretive themes" that have found support among civil rights scholars. The first is that King "was far more deeply and extensively shaped" by the black church tradition that nurtured him than by the thinkers and teachers he engaged in graduate school. And second, "the black freedom movement was in no way the simple product of individual leaders and national organizations." Like King scholars James Cone, Lewis Baldwin, and Taylor Branch, Garrow underscores the powerful influence of the black church on King's theological framework and his habit of verbal borrowing. Although none of these scholars is an apologist for King's scholarly plagiarism, they bring a vital balance to criticism that fails to acknowledge the cultural and racial forces that shaped King's rhetorical choices.

Still, it is one thing to argue that King's habits of verbal borrowing drew from cultural practices (which I think is true) and another to argue that King simply carried these habits into the academic arena. Such an argument dishonors King's sophistication and shrewdness and ignores the intellectual gifts and scholarly talents that got King admitted to graduate school in the first place. But even those who argue that King's academic habit of taking others' words without attribution was pure and simple plagiarism (which I believe it was) have unconvincing arguments about what drove him to do it. The suggestion that King's teachers gave him a break because he was black—that they engaged in "reverse racism" or, even worse, as Lewis and Genovese argue, that his professors engaged in racial paternalism—seems implausible. After all, Boston University produced, during or immediately after King's tenure, distinguished scholars like Major Jones, Samuel Proctor, Evans Crawford, Cornish Rogers, and C. Eric Lincoln. That does not rule out the possibility that King's case was an exception, but for that logic to work, King would had to have been a marginal student whose limited skills prevented his success. There is too much evidence that King mastered the mechanics of academic survival and was bright, diligent, and highly disciplined. David Garrow's surmise that King was in his Boston years "first and foremost a young dandy whose efforts to play the role of a worldly, sophisticated young philosopher were in good part a way of coping with an intellectual setting that was radically different from his own heritage and in which he might well have felt an outsider," may go further in capturing King's conflicting emotions about graduate school and his doubts about whether he belonged. The most highly gifted black student could harbor insecurities about his talents in a white world that insisted on his inferiority, even in a relatively benign environment like Boston University, which had a reputation for nurturing bright black students. Garrow suggests that the King of Boston University may have been "a rather immature and insecure man," who did not fully become "himself" until he left graduate school, a reasonable speculation not only in the light of King's subsequent career but in the light of how most of us who have trod a similar path have developed. (Did anyone really expect Michael Jordan to become the greatest basketball player ever after viewing him in college, where he never averaged twenty points a game?) We often forget that King was only twenty-six when he became what Hegel termed a world-historical figure. Boston University certainly was a proving ground for him, a place where he fought personal and institutional demons and succumbed to the temptation to represent others' work as his own. I think there are at least two complex and interrelated reasons behind King's scholarly plagiarism.

First, part of the explanation may reside in what Cornish Rogers, a contemporary of King at Boston University, says was King's primary goal: to become a first-rate preacher and pastor of a distinguished black Southern church. Rogers says that "King told me the main reason he was getting a doctorate was so he could get that church—Dexter Avenue, which wanted a minister with a doctorate." Rogers says that despite the fact that King's application for Boston University indicated his desire to become a scholar of theology, it was not surprising that King "changed his perspective as he got older and sensed where his real heart and best gifts lay." This confirms Miller's and Lischer's arguments that King was first and foremost a preacher of extraordinary skill and resources, and by comparison, at best a competent theologian. Rogers also argues that theological education was "alien in the sense that it really did not provide [King] with the tools for ministry in the black community," even though King would use "some of the titillating ideas that he got in his studies if he thought they would preach well." For King, as for many "evangelical divines," preaching was the supreme skill one must possess and develop to render the greatest service as a Christian minister. Among black preachers, there is the often repeated mantra dressed up as a question: "But can he tell the story?" referring to homiletical skills honed in the black pulpit. And, as Lischer argued about King, every item of experience is made grist for the preacher's mill, as preachers often remark about a compelling story or idea "that will preach."

Undoubtedly, there is a profound conflict in such circles about formal theological education. Although it is viewed as necessary to critical thinking about religious matters, theological education is often viewed as a hindrance to the true worship of God, since liberal scholarship in particular challenges evangelical faith. This skepticism often translates into a paralyzing anti-intellectualism, a phenomenon not unknown in black and white preaching circles. But even as such preachers despise the process of theological education—both its demanding intellectual regimen and its relentless criticism of received theological views—they cherish its value to their upward mobility and hunger after its symbolic rewards. This is why, perhaps, there are so many self-anointed, self-appointed, self-administered "doctors" in the Christian ministry, including the black pulpit (especially, perhaps, the black pulpit). The doctor deficiency among black clergy—the result of racist strictures against formal and higher education for most of our history—has led to its diseased exaggeration in such quarters. King certainly got major cachet from his degree. How many times would black folk derive pride from announcing that their leader was "*Doctor* Martin Luther King, Jr.," almost as if his title were part of his given name? And liberal white folk were pleased with themselves in pronouncing a title that King had collected from one of their schools. Calling him "*Doctor* King" was a way for them to participate vicariously in his achievement while perhaps unconsciously lauding themselves for having had the good sense to recognize his gifts. The anti-intellectualism of the clergy, the alienation of a white academic setting, the appeal of becoming a "doctor," the desire to serve the black church, and a change in vocational aspiration in midstream might certainly have ganged up on a young black scholar who sought to relieve the intense pressure of being simultaneously vain, gifted, ambitious, and insecure. Neither can we gainsay King's pride in being able to pull it all off—not simply the deception that the work he stole was his, which wasn't difficult (after all, as his dissertation's second reader, S. Paul Schilling commented, there were other student-scholars whose plagiarism was far worse than King's) but the more difficult task of managing the competing demands of two worlds that, in the words of Bernice Johnson Reagon, King sought to "straddle." In this sense, King's plagiarism, though still tragic, was among the least of his worries. That is a profound commentary on the racist world King sought to penetrate, the conflicted black world from which he emerged, and the uncertain world into which he would be thrust as an educated agent of social change. Not to get the degree would be a greater failure than cheating to get it. The fault lies not simply with King, although he bears a lion's share of the blame, but with a world that demanded that he and others perform under such conditions. The wonder is not that King cheated under these conditions, but that C. Eric Lincoln, Samuel Proctor, Evans Crawford, Cornish Rogers, Major Jones, and thousands of other blacks did not.

Second, King's plagiarism may have had to do with his aversion, one shared by many black students of his generation, to write a dissertation on race. Of course, that aversion is not the driving force in King's cheating but its symptom. The racial climate that made race a scholarly taboo and encouraged the embrace of already validated European subject matter might have been the predicate for his plagiarism. The aversion to write about race was not accidental, but reflected the dilemma that all black students faced: if they wrote about race, they risked being pigeonholed or stereotyped; if they avoided it, they risked failing to develop critical resources to combat arguments about black inferiority. Even today, such a stigma persists, particularly in the light of the bitter culture wars still being fought. For instance, Eugene Genovese, in an otherwise tough and eminently fair review of King's work, let slip that "King passed over the chance to take courses on social Christianity, Gandhi, race relations, and other trendy subjects, preferring courses on Plato, Hegel, formal logic, and modern philosophy." If such courses were deemed trendy then, it is no wonder that rigorously exploring the ideas that pushed or prevented racial justice would be strongly discouraged in white academic settings. At Boston University, the stigma of "race scholar" was one that few students appeared willing to risk. As James Cone notes, King did "not even mention racism in most of his graduate papers that dealt with justice, love, sin, and evil." Cone also argues that in "six years at Crozer and Boston, King never identified racism as a theological or philosophical problem or mentioned whether he recognized it in the student body and faculty."

Such issues were broached in the Dialectical Society, an organization of black graduate students founded by King and Cornish Rogers to offer their peers an intellectual forum to debate ideas relevant to black communities. The need for such a group underscores the schizophrenia that many black scholars faced, and often still do, in seeking to address the painful circumstances of black life while satisfying the demands of a white academy. Cone's conclusion that King, like most other integrationists of his time, "appeared to be glad merely to have the opportunity to prove that Negroes could make it in the white man's world," is borne out by Rogers's observation that "the only reason many students stuck around (and did everything that was required of them) was to get the degree which in the black community makes you equal to the man, to white folks, if you've got your degree from a white institution, the same degree that whites get." In such an environment, King concluded that he would never set the world on fire with his scholarly gifts. And as he perhaps battled his own self-doubt in confronting the rigorous demands of scholarly work—work he couldn't do as well as the work his genius had suited him for in the pulpit and the public stage, work of which he was not yet fully aware or capable—it is likely that cheating became a way to save face back home, satisfy "the man" at school, and sail off into the sunset of pastoral duties with no one having been the wiser about his grave sin. After all, as David Levering Lewis points out, no one, not even King himself, knew then that he would become *Martin Luther King, Jr.* Neither did King or, for that matter, his admirers and detractors, realize that his failures, like his successes, would gain such wide attention.

Recent scholarship in the psychology of race may provide a small glimpse onto King's tortured psychic landscape. This is by no means an attempt to excuse King's misdeed. Neither is it an attempt to suggest that most of those blacks victimized by the problem I will discuss would ever resort to stealing others' words as their own. Still, I think it opens a window onto King's mental processes that might help us understand a bit better why he cheated. Studies by Stanford University psychologist Claude Steele and his colleagues suggest the existence of a problem that King most likely engaged. Steele and his colleagues have attempted to answer a difficult question: Why do able black college students fail to perform as well as their white colleagues? Throughout the 1990s, Steele says, "the national college-dropout rate for African-Americans has been 20 to 25 percent higher than that for whites. Among those who finish college, the grade-point average of black students is two thirds of a grade below that of whites." Steele says that "the under-performance of black undergraduates is an unsettling problem" that may "alter or hamper career development, especially among blacks not attending the most selective schools."

Steele says the answers have resulted in an often "uncomfortably finger-pointing . . . debate. Does the problem stem from something about black students themselves, such as poor motivation, a distracting peer culture, lack of family values, or—the unsettling suggestion of the *The Bell Curve*—genes?" Steele adds to that list a host of other factors relating to the "conditions of blacks' lives: social economic deprivation, a society that views blacks through the lens of diminishing stereotypes and low expectation, too much coddling, or too much neglect?" What stumped researchers even more is that middle-class black students, who have had the social and economic resources to lift them above the social plight of their poorer peers, underperform as do disadvantaged blacks, garnering lower standardized-test scores, lower college grades, and lower graduation rates than their white peers. What forces could possibly account for such underperformance, even among middle-class black students? At the risk of oversimplifying and reducing Steele's argument, it all boils down to what he and his colleagues termed "stereotype threat": the "threat of being viewed through the lens of negative stereotype, or the fear of doing something that would inadvertently confirm that stereotype."

Steele develops his theory to apply to differential performance among black undergraduate students and their white peers. I apply it to King's own possible mind-set and suggest that he cheated in part to escape or relieve "stereotype threat"—the enormous pressure of feeling under relentless white scrutiny and living with the fear of confirming stereotypes of black identity. In a telling passage, nineteen-year-old graduate student King (at an age when most young men are college sophomores) is described as being

> terribly tense, unable to escape the fact that he was a Negro in a mostly white world. He was painfully aware of how whites stereotyped the Negro as lazy and messy, always laughing, always loud and late. He hated that image and tried desperately to avoid it. "If I were a minute late to class, " he said, "I was almost morbidly conscious of it and sure that everyone noticed it. Rather than be thought of as always laughing, I'm afraid I was grimly serious for a time. I had a tendency to overdress, to keep my room spotless, my shoes perfectly shined and my clothes immaculately pressed."

King was certainly not alone as a black student who confronted an egregiously unfair academic situation. Neither can we be sure that he wasn't simply the sort of person who would have cheated no matter his race or age. But since we only know him as we did—a black man confronting his self-doubt in a majority white culture—we can only reasonably speculate with the facts at hand. From King's own description of the psychic and emotional torture he confronted, I think it is reasonable to suggest that a possible reason for his cheating had to do with the attempt to please the white professors who judged him and to measure up to the standards of the white society in which he competed academically. I am not suggesting that most black students respond similarly; they obviously do not. I am, however, arguing that it is plausible that King responded to stereotype threat, perhaps even "stereotype fatigue," and surrendered the fight on the academic end to preserve his mental health on the emotional end. The fight was just that costly that plagiarizing course papers and a dissertation—as awful and lethal a flaw as it is—was deemed less harmful than facing the consequences of failing to meet the challenges of the white world.

King's plagiarism at school is perhaps a sad symptom of his response to the racial times in which he matured. His plagiarism is made even sadder by the realization that King's heroic efforts as a civil rights leader relieved for others some of the pressures that he faced as a graduate student, pressures that no one should have to face but that thousands of blacks have managed with amazing grace. It is not unbelievable that such figures were gifted, but that they could perform under the punishing conditions of rigid racial apartheid. Their success deflects attention from the horror of the conditions they learned to master. It is bitterly ironic that of all people, Martin Luther King, Jr., should be found out as a plagiarist since his huge rhetorical gifts helped to create a world of opportunity for millions. But then his genius for mastering the white world through mastering its languages, and for portraying so compellingly the pained psychic boundaries of black life, may derive from the tortured memory of his sore temptation on an isolated battlefield of conscience where he wrestled with, and failed, himself. As a *New York Times* editorial eloquently reminded our nation, King may have plagiarized words, but he could never plagiarize the courage he displayed on countless occasions:

> But however just it may be to denounce his scholarship, that should not be confused with his leadership. Whether or not, as a student, he wrote what he wrote, Dr. King did what he did. . . . Some say he solicited the assistance of others . . . but even if so, that's no more to be faulted than John Kennedy turning to Theodore Sorensen, or George Bush to Peggy Noonan. . . . What the world honors when it honors Dr. King is his tenacity on behalf of racial justice—tenacity equally against gradualism and against violence. He and many with him pushed Americans down the long road to racial justice. That achievement glows unchallenged through the present shadow. Martin Luther King's courage was not copied; and there was no plagiarism in his power.

King's punishing gift for guilt may have had its roots in his Boston mendacity, an infraction that may have haunted him into ego deflation, a sin that may have made him worry that he was supremely unworthy of the accolades he would later win. It was perhaps not only the sins of the intellect that made King feel at times like an impostor, but also his prodigious sins of the flesh. But even King's sexual indiscretions are not as simple as many of his critics make them out to be. It is one of the cruel consequences of white supremacy that whites sought not simply to control where blacks ate and drank, but where and with whom they slept as well. Beyond being an obvious source of his moral failures, King's sexual sins were an often crude, occasionally pathetic, and at times sadly ironic attempt to seize back a privacy that had been forcibly mortgaged to Southern segregation. While white men in King's lifetime could freely and with little moral stigma violate black women as a matter of course, King's consensual trysts have been read as a sign of his fundamental perversion. Such a view is not only vulnerable to a charge of hypocrisy, but underscores as well that in the sixties in the South, where sheets were used to make love and cover hate, sex was never merely sex.

CHAPTER 8

"There Is a Civil War Going on Within All of Us"
Sexual Personae in the Revolution

It is a scene that is too painful to conjure for many of Martin Luther King Jr.'s supporters. After spending his last night delivering one of the most brilliant speeches in his career—a moment comparable to Michael Jordan's fending off a swarming opponent to sink the winning shot in the Chicago Bulls' sixth championship series and thus immortalizing the image of his last play before his final departure from basketball and his team's certain disintegration—King allegedly rendezvoused with two women at different points of the night and in the early morning fought with a third female "friend" before being gunned down later that evening at the Lorraine Motel. The source of this shattered image of King's Memphis martyrdom is not J. Edgar Hoover, Jesse Helms or Ronald Reagan. It is none other than Ralph David Abernathy.

If Martin Luther King was the civil rights movement's Michael Jordan, then Abernathy was surely King's Scottie Pippen (Jordan's superstar teammate). At midcentury, King and Abernathy formed a formidable one-two lineup in the agitation for freedom. When King was jailed, Abernathy was jailed. When King spoke, Abernathy often introduced him. When King couldn't speak, Abernathy often spoke for him. When King headed the SCLC, Abernathy was chosen by King to succeed him. When King stayed up late at night, Abernathy often kept him company. When King traveled to Norway to collect his Nobel Peace Prize, Abernathy was there. They ate in each other's homes, kept each other's kids, preached in each other's pulpits, and built each other up over nearly fifteen years of friendship and professional fraternity. And when King breathed his last breath in Memphis, it was in the arms of Abernathy, who also officially identified King's body at the morgue and presided over his friend's funeral a few days later. The two shared ideas back and forth until it was nearly impossible to discern where one man's thinking began and the other's ended. On this score, Abernathy is hardly accorded the credit he deserves for his contributions to King and to the cause they both championed. If King was the movement's most valuable player, then Abernathy was, by King's own account, a sturdy source of comfort and "the best friend that I have in the world."

When Abernathy, in his 1989 best-selling autobiography, *And the Walls Came Tumbling Down*, divulged secrets about Martin Luther King, Jr.'s, sex life that had until that moment rested with him in his grave, he was widely viewed by movement veterans as a traitor to King's memory. All along, there had been rumors among civil rights cognoscenti that Abernathy loved King even as he was jealous of his more famous friend. In their eyes he waited until King could no longer defend himself before offering damaging details of King's Promethean trysts. To be fair to Abernathy, he faced a difficult choice in telling the story of the movement and his friendship with King. In an introduction to the paperback edition of his autobiography, Abernathy answers his critics. He argues that in writing his book, he wanted to "let Americans—particularly black Americans—in on a secret: Martin Luther King, Jr. was not just a great public hero but an extremely attractive human being as well—a man whom they would have loved to have as a friend." Besides the portrait of a great defender of justice, Abernathy "wanted to show the private man as well," the "mimic who was so funny he could render his friends helpless with laughter," the "young soldier who loved life and was afraid to die, but went into battle anyway," and the man "who on the last day of his life worried about hurting the feelings of a tired waitress who had brought the wrong order." Abernathy thinks that controversy greeted his book because he "wanted to portray Martin as a believable human being." Therefore, he "had to deal with certain personal weaknesses (which others had already written about)." Abernathy believes that it is important to tell the whole story so that future generations can truly appreciate King's genuine greatness as an epic hero on the order of "Washington, Lincoln, and a handful of other leaders." Since his friend has become a legend, Abernathy wants to set the record straight so that King's legend will be useful to Americans in the centuries to come. Abernathy argues that "legends are important to give people a sense of who they are and what, in their best moments, they can become." But Abernathy wants "to let everyone know that this legendary figure was also a human being, and that his humanity did not detract from the legend but only made it more believable for other human beings."

If we take Abernathy at his word, King's memory will not be besmirched by his best friend's revelations. Moreover, even King's severest critics cannot prevent his ascent to the pantheon of American heroes, figures whose clay feet and singular flaws have not prevented a nation from strongly embracing their legacies. But even if we doubt Abernathy's motives—he only obliquely referred to his own philandering, an alleged instance of which produced the famous photo of King having his youthful arm twisted by the police as he seeks to support his best friend in court against a charge of cuckolding—we can still endorse his belief that the more honestly we confront King's moral lapses, the more we are able to extract from his failings a sense of his authentic humanity and a fuller grasp of his towering achievements. To avoid exploring King's weaknesses is to deny him the careful consideration that should be devoted to any historic figure. And to pretend King didn't sin is to subvert the healthy critical distance we should maintain on all personages, the lack of which leads to charges of uncritical black hero worship. As Abernathy suggests, King "will grow in the hearts of future Americans regardless of what I or other biographers have to say about him."

If Abernathy is right, the charge of plagiarism cannot blot King's achievements from the pages of history. Neither can King's adultery reduce his reputation to the shape of a bed. Only advocates of moral perfection will seek to deny King his high place in history because of his sexual sins. This does not mean that we cannot or should not criticize King for his rampant womanizing and his relentless infidelity (although one is tempted to cry with Alfred Lord Tennyson in his defense of fellow poet Lord Byron: "What business has the public to know of Byron's wildnesses? He has given them fine work and they ought to be satisfied"). But as with the good things in King's life, we must place the bad things in context as well. King was certainly reared in a preacherly culture where good sex is pursued with nearly the same fervor as believers seek to be filled with the Holy Ghost. And the war against white supremacy in which King participated was thoroughly sexist and often raucous; men who had a symbolic, and sometimes literal, bounty on their heads mistreated female soldiers and sought refuge in the fleeting pleasures of the flesh. But in the comparative moral context in which we inevitably view history, their sins were far less grievous than the racial apartheid that led figures like King to spend most of the year away from home, making them more vulnerable to their weaknesses. White supremacy didn't cause their sins, but it surely gave King and others ample opportunity to succumb to temptations that they may have otherwise been spared.

King's true greatness can be understood only when we get rid of the false expectations of human perfection in our heroes and leaders. King was a spiritual and moral genius, but his genius had nothing to do with unrealistic notions of purity. King's was, paradoxically, an imperfect perfection. To paraphrase singer Grace Jones—who sang that "I may not be perfect, but I'm perfect for you"—King may not have been perfect, but he was perfect for Americans who desired racial justice. His moral aim of transforming America was perfectly suited for the times and places in which he acted with decisive courage. And if King was pure, it was in the biblical sense of being "pure in heart"—that is, obsessively single-minded about the greatest good: loving God and one's neighbor. King was so committed to that good that he died for it, a death that revealed the astonishing oneness of his speech and his life. To be sure, the sense of hurt, even betrayal, evoked by King's shortcomings partially underscores just how morally useful he has been in our culture. King is for many whites the ideal expression of black identity—whether that means speaking "standard" English, refusing to hate bigoted whites, refraining from listening to violent rap music, or shunning Louis Farrakhan. The early King also symbolizes for many whites how black folk should behave in the aftermath of the racial revolution that King helped to ignite. Never mind, of course, that many of these same whites opposed King and the civil rights river as it began to flow. They have now been baptized in its redeeming currents and have had the sins of their resistance washed away. King reigns, then, as the Black Moral Messiah, the prophetic figure whose loving insurgence led many whites to a new faith in blacks.

As great as King's achievements are, they fail to silence his severest critics. King's good works are lost on those who were never satisfied with his moral goals or who rabidly opposed the civil rights movement. These critics are easily dismissed as bigots, folk who, in Howard Thurman's revealing definition of the term, "make an idol of their commitments." Then there are critics who believe that King's failures symbolize his essential perversion. In their eyes, King's theft of other men's words and their wives revealed his deep moral corruption. Although there are bigots in this group, it contains many others who simply believe that one can never be a good person if one is an adulterer or plagiarist. These folk are less easily dismissed. For one reason, King often spoke against the sins he committed, at least against adultery, and he insisted that ethical means and ends must hang together in a meaningful moral universe. Still other critics claim that one or another of King's sins is the defining feature of his character. And then there are those who oppose King out of civic duty. They claim that King was a hypocrite who is undeserving of national honor because he failed to, as the gospel song phrases it, live the life he sang about in his song. Some of these claims are surely repulsive, self-righteous, and overly simplistic, but they should nevertheless be met head-on with a sober grasp of King's successes and failures. In making a mature and balanced moral judgment of King, we have to acknowledge the enormous odds that were stacked against King and his colleagues throughout their lives. As King's life heroically suggests, morality is sized up and situated within messy personal and historical borders. The contours of a good life never trace the anatomy of perfection. The outlines of a life well spent are more likely composed of jagged edges and interrupted lines silhouetted against a backdrop of moral aspiration. Indefensible as it is, even King's philandering may suggest more than rakishness or depravity because of the unique conditions under which he conducted his career.

We have known for a while that King was at once a guilt-stricken, grief-engulfed, and, paradoxically, vigilant adulterer. Jesse Helms and J. Edgar Hoover (the latter's double life as gay, cross-dressing "Mary" was a bigger and longer-held secret than King's philandering, and was no doubt the spur of Hoover's self-hating puritanism) tried to soil King's legacy by publicizing his peccadilloes. David Garrow has brilliantly documented the FBI's evil assault on King's life and reputation, including the use of illegally acquired electronic evidence of King's "compulsive sexual athleticism" to dissuade King from his civil rights leadership. The FBI's immoral and relentless pursuit of King—at first on the grounds of his alleged communist activity, next for nonexistent financial malfeasance, and finally for nothing short of a voyeuristic campaign to discredit King and destroy the civil rights movement—reflected the highly conflicted emotions of segments of white society around the issue of black sexuality. Andrew Young, King's trusted lieutenant and former Atlanta mayor, Georgia congressman, and U.N. ambassador, argues that "the campaign against Martin and the movement was less about sex than about fear of sexuality." Young powerfully summarizes this fear when he writes:

> Deeply buried but intense sexual fear of black males, illustrated by the sexual nature of the attacks on black men by whites who seek to control or destroy black aggressiveness, has been a persistent pattern in the South since the advent of slavery. From the systematic destruction of the black family during slavery to contemporary barriers for black males attempting to protect and provide for their families via the imposition of strong societal and economic proscriptions, there is a recurrent theme: controlling

black men. The theme was ever-present at lynchings of black men for allegations of rape or for flirtation with white women, and is always evident somewhere in the heavy punishment awaiting black men who assert or advocate the interests of their people. The FBI campaign was very much consistent with this neurotic white Southern racist tradition.

At the same time, there is little doubt that, like his habits of verbal borrowing, King's sexual practices were nourished within a powerful pocket of the church. His sexual habits grew in part out of a subculture of promiscuity that is rampant among clergy and religious figures in every faith. As David Levering Lewis remarks, sexual license is a "chronic avocation among evangelical divines, black and white." As surely as King learned from the black church the use of brilliant rhetorical strategies that would help change America, and as surely as he was shaped in its crucible of biblical interpretations of social sin and suffering, he learned in the same setting about the delights of the flesh that were formally forbidden but were in truth the sweet reward of spiritual servants. As the writer Marcia L. Dyson observes, there is a tradition in Christian churches of ministers who "exploit this power [over women] and even take it for granted, as if it were an entitlement—sometimes preying on vulnerable and lonely women, at other times seeking out accomplices in sexual misconduct who are quite willing or, at best, self-deceived." King was no exception. But it must be said that as an internationally famous figure, King was a sexual magnet for women of every race, from every walk of life, who longed to bask in his limelight and in his affectionate, lustful embrace.

Undeniably one of the great ironies of King's sexual failings is how they embodied the conflicted uses of black privacy. King fought against the ruthless restrictions imposed on black public life, which led black folk to use their private spaces as both incubators of political activism and protection from the tyranny of apartheid. King opposed the lethal limits that denied blacks full citizenship and equality before the law. Thus, black private and public spaces acquired heightened importance and took on multiple uses under segregation. These spaces were at once outlet and refuge, providing sanctuary and solace from the bruising public humiliations brought on by white supremacy. These spaces were a site for refining the moral narratives of social rebellion that black folk expressed in the white public. They also provided blacks a place to rebel against black immobility in the white world.

In King's case, the varied functions of black privacy were even more highly charged. During much of his career, King's private time was spent on the road in black homes or in the few black public accommodations, where he and his colleagues sharpened strategies for social change. King's time at home was severely curtailed by the inhuman demands of the movement. He spent nearly twenty-seven days of most months in pursuit of the prize of black liberation. Inevitably, this separation weakened King's sexual bonds with his wife and eroded the quality of time and affection he could devote to her and to their children. To be fair, King's habits of sexual adventure had been well established by the time he was married. His personal and public circumstances only amplified his sexual indiscretions.

It is clear that King was both tortured by his adultery and awkwardly comforted by its serial anonymities and episodic thrills. As a Christian minister, King was constantly reminded, if not by history or scripture then by circumstance, of the perilous traps of the flesh. In a remarkable 1966 interview with King conducted by Hugh Downs on NBC's *The Today Show*, King addressed what Downs termed the "loose sex relations and problems of the quite young" with calm and balance. King suggested that in "the past, too often the church has taken a kind of prohibitive attitude on the whole question of sex, a hush-hush attitude, rather than trying to honestly discuss sex and deal with the problems surrounding it." King said that the "only answer is for the church through its channels of religious education and other methods to bring this issue out into the open, and reaffirm once more that what God creates is good and that it must be used properly and not abused." Although ostensibly addressing the evils that young folk face, King was surely thinking during the interview of his own compromised situation. King perhaps provides a poignant glimpse into his own psychic and moral struggles when he argued:

> I think it is also necessary to bring out this point that sex is basically sacred when it is properly used and that marriage is man's greatest prerogative in the sense that it is through and in marriage that God gives man the opportunity to aid him in his creative activity. Therefore, sex must never be abused in the loose sense it is often abused in the modern world. I think the other thing that is necessary to say here is that it is necessary to move to the causal basis of sexual promiscuity, the deep anxieties and frustration and confusion of modern life which lead to the abuses, and the church must not only work on the level of condemnation, but it must

seek to get at the causal basis and work to remove these causes and deal with the psychological problems that bring the looseness into being, rather than making a general condemnation and not be concerned about the causal basis.

But the more recriminations he had over his sexual surrender—he said in a sermon that his congregation need not "go out this morning saying that Martin Luther King is a saint" but that he was "a sinner like all of God's children"—the more he was oddly driven to seek the satisfaction and relief that could come only from falling in sin and rising up to fight again. In his carnal escapades, King ritually reenacted the storyline of racial redemption: we attempt to do good, we fall, we rise again, we succeed for a while, we feel guilty for failing again, we get pleasure from our guilt, we feel remorseful for our pleasurable guilt, and we punish ourselves by reengaging the source of our suffering. King's private space provided him little relief from the unforgiving demands of representing the race. In his privacy, he was constantly consumed with how he might make a better world for blacks, even as he sought in vain to escape through sexual release the magnitude of his duty, the burden of his role, and the unrelenting pace of his quest for freedom.

King realized the moral schizophrenia produced by his prolific infidelities. He acknowledged them in a veiled way before his congregation at Ebenezer when he declared that "each of us is two selves" and that the "great burden of life is to always try to keep that higher self in command." King admonished his hearers not to "let the lower self take over," but that occasionally one will "be unfaithful to those you should be faithful to." Of course, King realized that adultery was more than a failure to be faithful to one's partner. Because marriage is a profoundly sacramental relationship, it was also a repudiation of God's law. But to his glory, and grief, King could not resist representing God even in his most private domain at his most profane moment. King is said to have uttered during one of his sexual romps that "I'm fucking for God," suggesting that, in the lowest moment of moral alienation from his personal values, and when he was furthest from his vows of fidelity, King could not shake the consciousness of his representative duties: to his race, to the civil rights movement, and above all to God. Instead of bringing his duties and desires into conflict, King momentarily fused them. His attempt at such a union symbolized his temporary rejection of the idea that his duties and desires were incompatible. King's desperate hedonism was also a profound gesture of sanity making as he sought release into the forbidden realm of erotic excess as an escape from the unbearable heat of white hatred. It was perhaps a convoluted way of keeping in touch with his own flesh—flesh that was being ransomed to redeem racial justice as a condition of his commitment to black freedom. Indirectly, and unconsciously, King's exuberant extramarital affairs may have expressed anger at a God who would thrust such an onerous duty on him. At the height of his infidelity, King calls God's name in vain to bless his fleshly frolic as a way to call attention to his paradoxical predicament: by invoking the divine presence, he is both seeking sanction and inviting scorn on his divided soul. Even though he is breaking God's law in committing adultery, his reckless invocation of God is at once profane and the ultimate predicate of his existence. No matter what, King's theology reminds him that God "promised never to leave me, never to leave me alone."

King spiritualized his fleshly faults not so much to justify them as to bring them into even a tenuous relation to his higher urges. After all, David, a likely model for King, said in Psalm 139, "if I make my bed in hell, behold thou art there." King flipped the logic of representing God and took it to its literal climax: King explodes in orgasm to keep his spirit from exploding, since, as he claimed, "fucking's a form of anxiety reduction." But if he couldn't escape the heavenly hound, at least he might be able, through his sexual profligacy, to shift momentarily the burden of representing the race. King often attempted to drown in a sea of sensuality all the demands of being the good, upstanding Negro, the shining embodiment of black perfection, the exemplary exhorter of moral excellence—as he ejaculated during one encounter, "I'm not a Negro tonight."

Carl Rowan has also made disturbing claims about King's sex life. In his 1991 memoir *Breaking Barriers*, Rowan says that in the sixties, Congressman John Rooney informed him that "a lot of congressmen had been inflamed by an alleged FBI tape recording" of what J. Edgar Hoover had termed an "orgy" in King's suite at the Willard Hotel in Washington. This was one of the scenes of the scandalous FBI tape that had been sent to King as he departed for Europe to receive his Nobel Peace Prize. And there is a possibility that the tape that Rowan reports was exercising the congressmen was the very tape, or a version of it, sent to King. Rowan asked Rooney what was on the tape that had everyone up in arms.

"He looked at me as if doubting whether he should answer," Rowan writes. "He looked at his notes, which someone already had typed out for him. Then he replied: 'Hoover played us a tape with sounds indicating that someone was having intercourse in one room of the King suite. But it clearly wasn't King, because we hear him saying to a man Hoover identified as Abernathy, 'Come on over here, you big black motherfucker, and let me suck your dick.'"

Rowan writes that he thought to himself that an "FBI director who is suspected of being a homosexual has gone to Congress to try to destroy our greatest civil rights leader by portraying him as a homosexual!" Rowan says that he defended King to Rooney, arguing that he couldn't speak against a tape he hadn't heard. Rowan also argued that "whenever black men gather in a party, the language, the back and forth, may have no relationship to reality." Rowan suggested to Rooney that after a few drinks, black men and many others lie about their sexual prowess. "They throw the word 'motherfucker' around like 'buddy' or 'pal,'" Rowan writes. "They talk about sucking dicks or cocks, which meant a vagina in Tennessee, the way they talk about eating a watermelon. And it may not have a damned thing to do with any behavior they intend to carry out."

It is obvious that in Rowan's explanation of the behavior that he was told was captured on tape, he is quite uncomfortable with the possibility that King's alleged sexual activity involved another man. This is the vicious bind that Hoover's dirty tricks trap us in. If we decry his ruthless manipulation of the facts—after all, that is the point of spliced tapes— and if we protest his unprincipled use of private affairs, then it is reasonable to insist that painting King as a homosexual pervert is no worse than painting him as a heterosexual pervert. Of course, in the sixties, it was certainly the case that painting King as a homosexual was equal to labeling him a pervert. But what is also at work here is the deliberate attempt to smear a black leader's character by whatever means were available. In the sixties, it was King's sexuality—and in this case the implication that he engaged, or intended to engage, in gay sex—that had the desired effect of further damaging King's reputation. To defend King by suggesting that he was not gay, in this context, is not a knee-jerk homophobic response, but a desire to clarify his sexual practices on the basis of what we otherwise know about his sexual behavior. That information is important precisely because its source was not a disinterested observer of human behavior but a federal bureau out to do in a leader of global importance. Of course, the rush to disprove King's homosexuality may indeed indicate a homophobic streak. On the other hand, given the context of the repressive sixties, when sexuality was a highly charged issue that intersected in complex ways with race, the use of sexuality of whatever sort to stigmatize a black leader is simply wrong. Furthermore, the undeniable existence of homophobia does not mean that clarifying King's preferences for the sake of historical accuracy is a homophobic act. To extract the debate about King's sexuality from its racial and cultural context is to do a grave disservice to the causes of racial and sexual liberation.

In our attempt to get the facts of the case, we should not suppress any feature of the truth. It may be that FBI tapes, when they are unsealed and if they are proved to be reliable, will reveal that King did engage in a homosexual act. That will not make King a pervert, as the FBI forces wished to portray him, but it may also be revealed that King did not engage in a homosexual act, in which case his heterosexuality will be insufficient grounds to suggest his virtue. In a world where sexualities are equally valued, sexual preference will never automatically indicate one's perversity or purity. But in a world where sexuality, like race, continues to mark human identity in strange and powerful ways, we must pay attention to how those identities are manipulated by destructive forces. This is true today; it was even truer in the sixties. Even if Rowan's motivation for offering a plausible explanation of King's behavior is homophobic, it does not mean that his explanation is not legitimate. In other words, black men who have been drinking often lie about their sexual powers and engage in same-sex references for comic effect. Even if the reason for saying that is driven by homophobia, the truth is that the facts of the case remain unchanged. What is changed is the context of our interpretation of those facts. Such a context was provided by Hoover: King is an unrepentant pervert. A counterargument can appeal to King's true sexual preferences and practices without necessarily falling into the trap of homophobia.

Neither should Rowan's possible homophobia obscure an essential element of his defense of King: that the government was illegally listening in on King for no other purpose than to destroy him by destroying his reputation and, ultimately, his family life. "All this stuff about King's sexual appetite is of trifling consequence," Rowan says, "compared with the still-chilling reality that under Hoover the nation's highest law enforcement agency tried unlawfully to destroy his reputation in hopes of thwarting the movement toward racial equality in America." Besides, as Rowan said, it is impossible to speak against something one has not heard. And Rowan's explanation about black male humor, whatever the motivations that underlie his makeshift apologia, should remind us that as with anything else, context and circumstance are crucial in understanding and explaining behavior. To rely on J. Edgar Hoover as even an informal ethnographer of black sexuality is surely misleading.

In the end, King's adulterous liaisons are both a sign of his deeply flawed sexual ethics and a product of his unique role as the most renowned twentieth-century crusader for racial justice. If we read King's sexual practices merely as a response to his enhanced opportunity for licentious behavior, we ignore the keen moral sensitivity that made him conscious of his shortcomings. But if we deny that King's courageous pursuit of freedom and equality led him to live most of his life on the road, away from hearth and home and, hence, a loving environment where he might nurture marital fidelity, then we deny history and truth. King's fight against white supremacy not only cost him his life but a great deal more: his privacy, as he was recklessly pursued by an out-of-control government agency; quiet time to collect his soul and share his life with his family and friends; the enjoyment of the normal course of human events, since his mission to mold America into a greater nation intruded on nearly every waking moment of his life; and the constant threat and fear of death, for simply, plainly, and honestly striving to make democracy a reality for all of this country's citizens. In such a context, King's failures are not the greater evils, but the racial fascism and economic violence that made his career a necessary risk and, in the end, an unavoidable sacrifice for this nation's best interests.

For critics who insist that King's plagiarism and promiscuity signal a tragic lapse in judgment, they may be right. But critics who insist that his sins signal a *fatal* flaw in character—so that the good that King did is nullified by his failures—are absolutely wrong. The debate about character must be wrested away from *virtuecrats* who espouse a narrow view of character and the qualities that feed it. Character cannot be understood through isolated incidents or a fixation on the flaws of a human being during a selected period in life. Assessment of character must take into account the long view, the wide angle. Character is truly glimpsed as we learn of human beings negotiating large and small problems that test moral vision, ethical creativity, and sound judgment. Character cannot be grasped in disjointed details or sporadic facts. Character can only be glimpsed in a sustained story that provides plausible accounts and credible explanations of human behavior. Of course we can and often do draw inferences about a person's character based on a phrase here and an action there. These reactions may certainly be useful in casual relationships, but they are shaky grounds for choosing a life partner or, for that matter, a president. Character is undeniably an important ingredient in judging the worth of public figures like King. But character is hardly reducible to personal life. Personal matters surely count in assessing character, but so do courage, integrity, sacrifice, and love as they are expressed on the battlefield of public conscience. King possessed these traits in abundance, and arguably, they are the character traits most relevant to judging his effectiveness in the public realm. I am not suggesting that we jettison considerations of private virtue or personal character. I am arguing, however, that we should have a more encompassing vision of character, one that embraces personal and social features, as we judge the worth of a human being's life.

Inevitably, King's flaws will be compared to those of Bill Clinton. Of course, King was a private citizen and Clinton held the nation's highest office. Further, King matured during an era when standards for judging the faults of public figures were considerably more discrete, at least for a white man. And color is not an inconsiderable feature of their difference. Whereas Clinton's Bubba legend is an index of the persistent bigotry toward the South, King's blackness and Southern heritage carry even more complicated resonance. What is intriguingly similar about Clinton and King, however, is both have received enormous black support despite their failures. And I think it is in probing this black support that the crucial differences in King's and Clinton's character shine.

Martin Luther King, Jr., struggled mightily against his sins even as he indulged the sexual excesses available to him. He constantly worried if his decisions were right, if they had moral substance, and if their impact on his flock would be productive and uplifting. Guilt plagued King at every step—not simply at the door of his sins, but even more cruelly on the thrones of his myriad successes. King was never able to bask completely in the sweet aura of his triumphs because he was forever pushing forward with a moral ambition to change the course of racial history. King was thoroughly preoccupied with opening his soul to the guidance of his God, no matter what his crude departures from the path of faith were. And when King was forgiven, when he enjoyed a brief respite from his own ruthless self-criticism, he used his psychic freedom to imagine how much more he could pour into the movement.

His life was spent in the relief of suffering for millions who looked to him as the symbol of changes they neither completely understood or entirely embraced, at least not immediately. King was therefore a moral pioneer for blacks and whites, leading the way with a torch held up against the surrounding darkness of bigotry and hatred. But he forged ahead, standing with others whose courage lent energy to a movement that was from the beginning on a historical timer. The movement's in-built obsolescence was guaranteed by a culture that threw every weight it could muster in his way: the FBI, police dogs, halfhearted allies, scarily bigoted politicians, reckless rednecks, brutally anarchic mobs, scholarly digs, and ad hominem media. Yet he pressed forward toward the high mark of his calling. And for that, black folk loved him. After his death, these same folk forgave themselves their ignorance because they realized King would have wanted it. Surely such a recognition was a sign of the triumph of his way of thinking long after he melted into the Georgia dust from which he sprang.

Every celebration of King is a gesture of defiance against the powers and principalities that dared rise up to strike him down. In such a context, King's sins can be more than forgiven. They can be remembered as a mark of his profound humanity and a measure of the forces against which he struggled, both external and internal, that make his achievements even more resonant. This is not to be confused with celebrating King's weaknesses. Rather it is a celebration of the unique oneness of his outward and inward life. It is remarkable that he was able to overcome sexual and textual sins, as well as the cruel opposition he faced, to speak lucidly and compellingly for millions he had never met, except in the heated chambers of a longed-for freedom that united blacks across the nation, indeed across the globe.

Bill Clinton too enjoyed wide black support during his sex scandal and impeachment trial after he first lied and then admitted that he indeed had a sexual relationship with White House intern Monica Lewinsky. Despite his sins—although cynical anecdotal reports throughout the nation in country clubs, bars, and talk shows suggested that it was *because* of his sins that black folk were attracted to him, given the lower character of black people—Clinton basked in the love consistently shown him by his most loyal base of black supporters. Perhaps black folk identified with Clinton because he was viciously attacked, as his wife, Hillary, suggested, by a "right-wing conspiracy." Or blacks may have been grateful that here finally was a president who was comfortable around black folk, familiar with their songs and in tune with their spiritual yearnings since he shared in the common culture that binds white and black Southerners in poignant and peculiar ways. Or perhaps Clinton benefited from the forgiveness that blacks have been taught to extend to sinners who fall. Some famous black supporters like novelist Toni Morrison suggested that, skin color notwithstanding, Clinton was our nation's first black president. (This is a perfect example of how the swirling current of black speech is communally conveyed, and at points, corporately owned, since comedian Chris Rock had argued, in *Vanity Fair* before Morrison and in much funnier fashion, that Clinton was our first black president, and who knows where he got it from?)

What seems to be at the core of black sentiment toward Clinton, however, as Harvard Law School professor Randall Kennedy has argued, is an "undue gratitude." Kennedy says the fact that many blacks "feel truly beholden to Clinton for his racial policies is a sign of how little they expect from the political Establishment: accustomed to being dealt with as outsiders—particularly after 12 years of Reagan-Bush administrations—they are overwhelmed with gratitude for a president who treats them as significant members of the American polity." Kennedy suggests that black folk ought to stop feeling overly grateful to Clinton because, after all, when he rewards blacks for their support, he is doing nothing more than any other politician who acts accordingly and pays "back those groups that supported him."

Kennedy raises an even more serious challenge to black support for Clinton and in the process provides a peek into Bill Clinton's character: that Clinton's "special" concern "with racial justice for blacks" and his "special" ability to "heal racial wounds" is an assessment "larded with large dollops of sentimentality." Kennedy argues that Clinton's support of civil rights has coincided with his "advancing his own political career." His support for affirmative action was motivated by the recognition that he would lose a lot more by ending affirmative action (strong black support) than by keeping it in place. Furthermore, Kennedy argues, if Clinton were really committed to advancing black interests, he would take on North Carolina Senator Jesse Helms over the senator's effective blocking of the appointment of "progressive jurists to the Fourth Circuit Court of Appeals—a pathetic state of affairs which has meant that no black has ever sat on the federal appeals bench that oversees the federal trial courts in Maryland, Virginia, West Virginia, North Carolina, and South Carolina."

In judging Clinton's character, blacks have committed a grave error: they have often confused the perception of a warm feeling from Clinton toward black folk with a set of political practices that reveal a much more disturbing view of Clinton's character. Blacks were right to support Clinton through his impeachment trial. A great deal of black support was principled, rooted in the belief that in taking stock of political figures, personal flaws of a sort that are not relevant to the offense in question should not discount a consideration of public virtue. Blacks showed political maturity when they were willing to judge Clinton not on his illicit and private activities in the Oval Office but on his record of stimulating the economy, appointing blacks to high political positions, and being sensitive on racial issues. In short, blacks understood that character, especially the character of a public man, can never simply or even primarily be judged on the basis of personal features but on public facts and political factors. For instance, assessing character in a president does not hinge primarily on determining the occurrence of sexual trysts, but in determining if a president orders mines to be placed in the harbors of South American countries or if a president exploits racially divisive agendas for political gain.

But it is precisely here that blacks faltered in our moral duties, reneging on the wise reversal of the conventional—or at least partisan—thinking about political character. Blacks have mistaken Clinton's ease with them as a sign of his good, trustworthy character, when in fact Clinton's racial politics are among the most destructive among recent presidents, precisely because they depend on an exploitative duplicity. When it benefits him, Clinton reaches out to blacks; when it hurts him, he withdraws the hand of racial charity. All the while, he employs a racial cunning that belies his public persona as honorary homeboy. With Bill Clinton, blacks have lowered their guards, and they have been repeatedly disappointed. This is why he is much more problematic than a president like Ronald Reagan, from whom blacks expected little and got less. With Clinton, it is just the opposite, and here is where his bad character shows through. He is willing to turn every speck of black familiarity into a political advantage and hold black folk hostage to a corrupt racial politics that says, in effect: "I'm all you've got, so take me or lose progress." Only someone familiar enough with black culture—only a person intimately acquainted with black folkways and mores—could be so abusive.

Clinton is not the great racial healer blacks have taken him to be. In fact, he has considerably poisoned the well of race relations by, conveniently and with little cost to his political fortunes, evoking race as a way to shape a legacy, win a campaign, or forge a connection with whites disaffected from a political mainstream polluted by "special interests." There is no gainsaying Clinton's knowledge of black styles and feelings, black patterns of thought, and cultural response. When he wrote a now-famous letter to Colonel Eugene House about his draft status and the Vietnam War, Clinton said, genuinely, that he opposed the war "with a depth of feeling I had reserved solely for racism in America." When Martin Luther King was assassinated and Clinton had volunteered to work for the Red Cross in the riot-torn sections of Washington, a next-door neighbor heard him reciting snatches of King's "I Have a Dream" speech when he returned home that night. He knew it by heart. And when Clinton and his future wife, Hillary, were law students at Yale, she helped to monitor the New Haven trial of several Black Panthers, including Bobby Seale, activities flagged by the FBI.

But when Bill's political career took off, he took off the racial compassion he had worn like a merit badge and replaced it with a racial
realpolitik that would eventually make George Bush at his Willie Horton
prime look like a bush-leaguer. Bill Clinton was determined to become a
New Democrat, and a large part of that entailed a paradox: finding a way
to get distance on the most loyal constituency—liberal black voters—to
secure the loyalty of disaffected, moderate Democrats who had fled what
renowned funk musician George Clinton termed "chocolate cities" to
seek refuge in what he called the "vanilla suburbs." When Clinton ran for
president in 1992, his much ballyhooed bus tours were lily-white, as was
the segregated Little Rock country club where he "mistakenly" played
nine rounds of golf a day after the Illinois and Michigan primaries. Clinton also sought to send a message when he refused to stay the execution
of brain-damaged black murderer Rickey Ray Rector, providing Clinton
yet another "photo-op execution" in the effort to convince America that,
unlike 1988 presidential candidate Michael Dukakis, he wasn't soft on
crime. When he and Al Gore published their campaign book, *Putting People First*, they barely mentioned race; it got less mention in a chapter on
civil rights than sexual preference or physical disability.

Clinton's now-infamous mangling of Jesse Jackson—going to the Rain-
bow Coalition at Jackson's invitation, only to attack Sister Souljah based on
a phrase he quoted from a speech she'd made the night before, when she
said, "I mean if black people kill black people every day, why not have a
week and kill white people?"—revealed a racial legerdemain that was not
only cynical but ruthless. As Mary Matalin, Bush's campaign director for
the 1992 election, said, it was a stroke of evil political genius:

> Trust me, you *never* get that lucky in politics. Everyone in politics
> understood their continuing need to assuage Jackson, still a phe-
> nomenal force in their party, while simultaneously backing away
> from him. . . . We thought it [the Souljah assault] was a stroke of
> genius. Clinton was running as a so-called New Democrat while
> the Democratic party had previously been captive to minority
> extremists, mostly identified with the leadership of Jackson. . . .
> We wondered from the beginning how they were going to deal
> with the Jesse Jackson factor, and they did it all in one fell swoop.
> Not only did they not kowtow to him, they publicly humiliated
> him. I don't know how that traveled in the electorate, but in polit-
> ical circles the Clintonistas got a lot of points for courage and for
> staying in the mainstream. It was a particularly creative coup.

Clinton's refusal to stand behind Justice Department nominee Lani
Guinier and his summary dismissal of Surgeon General Jocelyn Elders
for her plain-spoken lectures about safe-sex alternatives, including auto-
eroticism (to which a strong listening might have spared Clinton his subsequent impeachment ordeal) reveal a remarkable willingness to manipulate
race much more harshly than many of his Republican predecessors did.
But because Clinton knows all three verses to "Lift Every Voice," the so-
called national Negro anthem, he is exempt from the sort of close scrutiny
another figure with his track record might receive.

Then too, Clinton's insistence on personal responsibility usually finds
its way into a speech or action directed, at least symbolically, at black
America. Clinton's crime bill and welfare reform were widely perceived
as an attempt to get black folk to clean up their ugly social pathologies
since they threatened to overrun the national moral landscape. Here
Clinton has been especially damaging in sending a signal of black cooperation with and perpetuation of social evils that plague the nation's life.
To come full circle, Clinton went before a conservative body of black religious believers in 1993, at the very church auditorium in Memphis—
Mason Temple Church of God in Christ—where King delivered his last
speech, to lecture black folk about their morals. It was his biggest speech
ever on the subject, and no one could hardly mistake the subtext he was
sending: I will be brave in representing white America as I tell black folk
the truth about their families, values, and their moral condition. Of
course, a convention of Church of God in Christ members are among
the last audiences on earth for whom that message will be new or
prophetic. What was especially troubling was Clinton's assumption of
King's mantle to deliver "a report card on the last 25 years."

After briefly praising the job of electing formerly unelectable black
officials and securing open housing and getting black folk into the military, the middle class, and at the top levels of government, Clinton/King
rips into black America with a message of moral responsibility. "I did not
live and die to see the American family destroyed," Clinton/King remon-
strates. "I did not live and die to see 13-year-old boys get automatic
weapons and gun down 9-year-olds just for the kick of it. I did not live
and die to see people destroy their own lives with drugs and build drug
fortunes destroying the lives of others. That is not what I came here to
do. I fought for freedom." Few would argue with Clinton/King about the
need for just the sort of moral policing at which most of his listeners
were extremely skilled. What was troubling was the venue and the message Clinton was sending to his silent white constituency fed up with the

plagues of inner city poverty, and fed up with trying to correct mistakes in Washington that should be fixed in the home or school. But when Clinton was confronted with a rash of shootings around the country by largely middle-class white males, Clinton was unwilling to go to a white high school—or a white church convention—to lecture them about the erosion of family values, the erotic appeal of gun ownership, or the lure of violence that was being reproduced in the white family structure.

In the end, the question of character takes into account private and public features; personal and political considerations must be weighed in assessing the quality of a figure's character. While on the surface King and Clinton appear bound by their weaknesses, the relationship is only on the surface. As Clinton ruminated on what King might say to black America if he were alive, one can also speculate that King would surely take Clinton to task for his racial bad faith. If King was willing to confront Lyndon Baines Johnson on a matter of principle—his prosecution of the Vietnam War—he most certainly would have criticized Clinton for his seductive and damaging manipulation of racial passion and for his exploitative relation to black culture and identity. Where it concerns Clinton, black communities have forsaken the sort of insightful moral critique that King practiced. King rarely failed to distinguish the personal from the political in judging political character. No contemporary black leader or black intellectual has had King's courage to confront Clinton in public and address his pernicious racial politics. Indeed, engaging in a discussion of character that gets mired in sexual habits and avoids political practices only lets him off the hook. If it is true that Clinton is the first black president, he acts more like Clarence Thomas than Martin Luther King, Jr.

Martin Luther King, Jr., was a great but flawed man. George Santayana put his pen on the pulse of true greatness when he wrote: "A great man need not be virtuous, nor his opinions right, but he must have a firm mind, a distinctive, luminous character; if he is to dominate things, something must be dominant in him. We feel him to be great in that he clarifies and brings to expression something which was potential in the rest of us, but which with our burden of flesh and circumstance we were too torpid to utter."

King's failures were significant, but they pale in comparison to the majestic good he did. As King knew, character should never be judged in Manichaean terms. Human striving to do right must balance human wrongdoing, since at its best, life is a tattered quilt of the good and the bad. King lived a life obsessed with helping others. He loved when he was hated. He forgave when he was despised. He worked when he was tired. He prayed when he was cursed. He sang of peace when others shouted violence. And he refused to retaliate when he was stabbed, slapped, hit in the head with a rock, and repeatedly threatened with death. If he could forgive his enemies and friends their faults, we can certainly forgive him his. We need not idolize King to appreciate his worth; neither do we do honor to him by refusing to confront his weaknesses and his limitations. In assessing King's life, it would be immoral to value the abstract good of human perfection over concrete goods like justice, freedom, and equal- ity—goods that King valued and helped make more accessible in our national life.

Having a more balanced view of King may help us appreciate the value of black youth who are often dismissed for their moral flaws, espe- cially by older, middle-class blacks who defend King. Of course, we do not have to deny the huge differences between King and many contem- porary black youth, but both have good and bad things in common: how they view women, how they borrow and piece together intellectual sources, how they view sex, and how they confront the evils of racism and ghetto oppression. If King's weaknesses can be balanced against the good he did, perhaps we can take a second look at youth who sometimes have been profoundly criticized without being fully understood. While black youth easily embraced Malcolm X a few years ago as a griot, it may turn out to be Martin Luther King, Jr., who in his successes and failures, is the true spiritual father of the hip-hop generation.

CHAPTER 9

"I Have Walked Among the Desperate, Rejected, and Angry"

Two Generations of the Young, Gifted, and Black

"Professor Dyson, what's the answer?" Tim Russert, host of *Meet the Press*, asked me. "Ban video games, ban violent music lyrics?"

Russert was referring to the tragic school shootings in spring 1999 in Littleton, Colorado, which left thirteen students and a teacher dead. In the eyes of many critics, the shootings were largely instigated by the violent influence of video games, movies, the Internet, and popular music. I had encountered this argument before when I testified in the U.S. Senate about the impact of rap music on American youth. This Sunday morning, I appeared on *Meet the Press* with a panel of commentators that included Surgeon General David Satcher, Kansas Republican senator Sam Brownback, America Online CEO Steve Case, and author David Grossman, to try to unpack the meaning of the mayhem in Colorado.

"That might lead to a resolution of the crisis in Kosovo," I retorted, trying to suggest the often overlooked relationship between war—in this case, NATO's bombing of Serbia—and problems of violence closer to home. "We don't know."

I realized that my off-the-cuff retort might be perceived as a smart-ass stab at the sensational or the too-easy explanation, but it was a lesson that I had learned from Martin Luther King, Jr. One of King's central reasons for opposing the Vietnam War was the moral hypocrisy of trying to convince ghetto youth that "Molotov cocktails and rifles would not solve their problems" without having "first spoken clearly to the greatest purveyor of violence in the world today—my own government." I felt certain that were King around and had he been pressed about the violence that saturates American society, he might have similarly pointed out the relationship between international and domestic violence, especially since the first half-hour of *Meet the Press* had been devoted to the NATO bombings.

But I also suspect that King might have objected to how the violence that pervades poor communities is ignored—or when it is addressed, it is blamed on black or brown youth themselves—while violence that sweeps through suburban white communities is made the source of a national crisis and the cause for intense hand wringing, finger pointing, and soul searching.

"I think that the reality is that all of us as human beings are trying to make suffering make sense," I offered. "Violence has enormously and precipitously risen in the last, say, thirty to forty years. I think what we have to do is look for other factors that are much more relevant to how we understand what's going on in this world."

After pointing out that video games were certainly not responsible for the brutal police killing of African immigrant Amadou Diallo in New York City, I argued that the "social pathology of racism in this country" should be taken into consideration, as well as the "gender oppression of women—most of the victims [of violence] happen to be women and children in our society."

I argued that the steep rise in violent deaths of minority youth was stunning. "And in black communities—I think we have to pay attention to this—young black men are eight times more likely to die at the hands of firearms than are white kids." While acknowledging the responsibility of "video-game makers, the music-makers, the filmmakers, and us as parents," I said that "we have to pay attention" to the "hierarchy of privileges assigned to some kids and not to others."

As I spied Russert gently raising his hand to interrupt me, I held the floor for one last flurry of words aimed at getting the hard truth on the table. Russert graciously relented.

"Littleton, Colorado, is not an exception in American society," I stated. "But when crime affects the larger community, then it becomes a subject for roundtable debates. Think about Yummy Sandifer, the young black kid in Chicago who was killed by fellow gang members. He was eight years old and already had 23 arrests. By the time he was 11, he was shot for—his fellow gang members believed—for telling the police about what he was doing. We didn't have a roundtable on Yummy Sandifer. You know what we said? We said it was black cultural pathology. We said the family structure of African-Americans was deteriorating."

I knew I was pushing the envelope, but I resolved to break, even if temporarily, the sordid silence in this debate about the suffering of black and brown youth.

"If we were to be fair, we would apply this same analysis to white culture," I provocatively proffered. "Can we find a white family pathology going on? I think not. What we have to say then is that the incentives for violence are extraordinary in this country. And what we have to do is stop scapegoating and stigmatizing, and figure out a way to make us corporately responsible for the enormous rates of violence. The troubled youth who committed murder in Littleton were obsessed with black kids. They were worshiping Nazi symbols and so on. Those are the real culprits, and the access to firearms. That is very important."

I argued so passionately that morning because I have too often been involved in panels, conferences, and scholarly conversations where black youth were demonized for their social distress. To be sure, white youth are taken to task for their moral and social shortcomings. Still, they are not reprimanded with nearly as much anger, or the occasional hatred, that is directed at minority youth. How many times had I heard even black adults repeat in discussions about the hip-hop generation that if King were alive, he would be greatly troubled by them? They contend that King would be opposed to rap music and the violent imaginations of the youth who make and consume this dubious art. That may indeed be true, but it would not be all that King might have to say. He would at least attempt to understand the rage that burns in areas of hip-hop culture before he condemned its cultural expression. Surprisingly, King and prominent members of the hip-hop generation have a lot in common that is worth examining.

Although it may seem blasphemous to say so, there is a great deal of similarity between Martin Luther King, Jr., and a figure like Tupac Shakur. They both smoked and drank, worked hard, and with their insomnia waged a "war on sleep." King and Shakur cursed, told lewd jokes, affectionately referred to at least some of their friends as "nigger," had fierce rivals, grew up in public at the height of their fame, shared women with their friends, were sexually reckless, wanted to be number one in their fields, occasionally hung out with women of ill repute, as youth liked nice clothes and cars, were obsessed with their own deaths, made a living with words, lived under intense scrutiny, allegedly got physical with at least one woman, had their last work published posthumously, and died before reaching their full potential. As with many other hip-hop artists, King shaped and revealed his persona through a name he was not born with. (His name was legally changed from Michael to Martin when he was five years old.) Like many hip-hop stars, King preferred the company of light-skinned black women and was accused of fathering a child out of wedlock. As a youth, King, like some hip-hop figures, twice attempted to commit suicide. And like some hip-hop artists, King during his last four years was often morose and even deeply depressed. Finally, King was, like hip-hop's greatest DJs and producers, a gifted sampler who recombined rhetorical fragments in an ingenious fashion.

That said, there are also huge differences between King and many hip-hop artists. The most obvious is King's rejection of violence as a philosophy of life or as a means to freedom. Neither do I mean to suggest that hip-hop artists are engaged in a profound mission to change the world nor to argue that they should receive the sort of tribute paid to King. (I can't help but think here of comedian Chris Rock's acidly humorous observation that while he "loved Tupac and Biggie," we shouldn't exaggerate their importance. Rock says that fans lament that "Biggie Smalls was *assassinated*. Tupac Shakur was *assassinated*. They weren't assassinated. *Martin Luther King* was assassinated. . . . Those brothers just got shot! . . . School is still going to be open on their birthdays.") Nor am I arguing that if one multiplies King's weaknesses and then adds loud music, one can get a clear picture of hip-hop culture at its best. What I am arguing is that the politically correct and puritan urges of especially the black bourgeoisie lead them to attack black youth for some of the same shortcomings that they deny King had. Or, in the interest of King's reputation, they simply overlook his faults. King's less savory habits, or even his revealing erotic preferences, may indeed yoke him to despised black youth who share these same traits. It is often ignored how many rappers entertain King's ambition to stamp out the evils of racism and class oppression. Often King is set off in bold relief from such youth. But his personal and political struggles suggest that he was closer to black youth than we might admit.

If we acknowledge that King was an extraordinary man despite his faults, perhaps we might acknowledge that some of our youth have the same potential for goodness that King possessed. (We must remember that if King had died at age twenty-five like Shakur, or at twenty-four like Notorious B.I.G.—or after his first fame as a boycott leader at twenty-six—he might now be remembered as a promising leader who was shown to have borrowed other people's words and wives, infractions that in the absence of his later and greater fame we might be less willing to forgive.) In the process, some of these youth, by identifying with King, might rise above their limitations. They might also see that they can remake their lives and place their skills in the service of social transformation. Or we may realize that they do not have to be Martin Luther King, Jr., to be accepted or affirmed. At the very least, we must be willing to criticize and embrace them in the same spirit of understanding and forgiveness that we extend to King. King did as much when he confronted and mentored black youth who were gang members or ghetto residents.

King's brilliant uses of black orality link him to hip-hop culture. He drank from the roots of black sacred rhetoric within his own genealogical tree—he was the son, grandson, and great-grandson of Baptist preachers—and from legendary figures who branched into his youthful world, including William Holmes Borders, Sandy Ray, and Gardner Taylor, who is widely viewed as King's preaching idol and the "poet laureate of the American pulpit." Before King was baptized in the waters of liberal white theological education, he drew deep from the well of wisdom contained in the words of his church elders. King also learned the art of masking hard truth in humor. He learned how to dress cultural observation in the colorful cadences of tuneful speech. King gleaned these lessons from the foremost artisans of the black folk pulpit, including renowned revivalist and civil rights activist C. L. Franklin. From these figures, King learned to weave penetrating and eloquent liberation stories by threading into his sermons extensive allusion to the Bible and keen political and social analysis.

Hip-hop's obsession with word-play, verbal skills, and rhetorical devices marks its best artists' performances. Hip-hop is deeply indebted to the secular elements of black music and oral culture. Its departure from religious rhetoric is glimpsed in its embrace of blues themes (the unfaithful lover, sexual prowess, the moral outlaw) and older oral forms such as toasts and "the dozens," playful verbal put-downs. Hip-hop culture's celebration of irreverent folk and popular identities—the thug, the pimp, the mack, the hustler, the player, and the like—too freely play on racial stereotypes for the liking of black church members. Hip-hop also fuses the rhythmic and percussive elements of the spoken word with the syncopations of African-American music and thus reveals the inherently musical qualities of black speech. As with black preaching, hip-hop's repertoire of styles is distinguished by idiosyncrasies, derivations, and transformations within the boundaries of a given genre. These similar features allow a preacher or hip-hop artist to establish a unique sound while blending with, and stretching out, the art form. For example, C. L. Franklin's sermons are characterized by sonic hiccups, verbal gyrations, soul-shaking shrieks, and lightning-quick rhythmic shifts. By contrast, Caesar Clark's preaching thrives on guttural ellipses, densely layered melodies, multioctave moans, and a labored buildup of pace. Both are past masters of the chanted sermon, known colloquially as the "whoop." Similarly, Snoop Dogg's rap styles feature a feather-thin legato, deeply melodic flow, tender tenor tone, and Southern-drenched cadences. His approach rubs sharply against Ice Cube's stentorian baritone, staccato rhythms, sharply energetic delivery, and ominous tone. But each has been viewed as a gifted performer within the gangsta rap genre.

Hip-hop has come under severe criticism for its practice of "sampling"—borrowing older sounds or contemporary beats without attribution and without generating original music. Sampling, however, is more technologically sophisticated and intellectually creative than the mere sonic piracy suggested by its critics. For instance, when rap producer and mogul Puff Daddy lifts the Ashford and Simpson–penned Diana Ross anthem, "I'm Coming Out," he does not merely reproduce it note for note. Instead, he slows the beat and loosens the tightly coiled rhythmic release into the bridge, then builds an infectious hook by looping a break beat from the original song, giving rapper Notorious B.I.G. a complex aural landscape on which to shape his lyrical message. Because early hip-hop producers and DJs often were forced for lack of technology to sample less creatively than in the present—that is, they literally lifted or duplicated lines of rhythm and looped them as the song's primary beat—rap's musical foundations were accused of being parasitic on existing music or merely imitative. Moreover, older artists like James Brown, whose sampled beats provided early rap its rhythmic backbone, sought financial compensation for the unlicensed use of their music. While the charges of theft and imitation were being leveled at early hip-hop, few considered its winning features: Its brilliant reworking of musical identity. Its creative recoding of sounds. Its powerful fragmentation of vocal images. Its relentless drive to give rhythms and harmonies new aural contexts. Its flawless merging of voices from the past and present. Its edifying disruption of settled musical ideas. Its revival of long-forgotten melodies and discarded breaks to renewed popularity. Its miniaturization or exaggeration of sonic signatures. And its endless experimentation with and remaking of musical personae.

Of course, King has been assailed for rhetorical borrowing, for verbal sampling. Although the comparison is much too overworked to avoid derision, he may be understood as a postmodern rhetorician. In this sense, King completely understood and accepted the conditions for generating oratorical originality. First, one must excavate sermons that have settled into the homiletical substrata. One must then dynamite and sift through the sermons' inessential features and clarify the potential to connect their themes to the goal of racial redemption. Then one must recast the sentiments such sermons express in the styles that make up the black sermon. To shift and mix metaphors, King cut and spliced others' voices, ideas, and images into his own reel of rhetoric to project a compelling picture of racial resistance. King expanded the ethical arc of white liberalism by sampling its root metaphors and its guiding visions. King reshaped liberalism's words and images within a fresh and exciting rhetorical context that fused white preaching and black religious traditions. He elevated and extended the rhetoric he borrowed; using it for even higher purposes and greater aims than suggested by its original intent.

Renowned preacher Harry Emerson Fosdick certainly did not intend to subvert the racial hierarchy with his homily, "On Being Fit." But once parts of his sermon found use in King's rhetorical universe, it gained a moral gravity it would have otherwise failed to achieve. King deconstructed white supremacy by reconfiguring the words of white authorities—ministers mostly, but theologians and philosophers too—within the bounds of his social and racial message. King's originality had nothing to do with saying words first and everything to do with how he said what he said. King's originality also had to do with how he backed up words with incomparable courage and actions and seamlessly stitched together disparate sources. Such a practice allowed him to say, more brilliantly and breathtakingly than he might otherwise have done, what needed to be said during the few years the world listened to him in person. King breathed into the formulations he borrowed the moral inspiration for black freedom and set the world on fire with his vocal magic. At the same time, he constantly remade his public persona. He found the appropriate rhetoric to forge his identity as the times and his purposes demanded, as his ideology shifted and evolved.

The bridge between King and contemporary rappers is built not only on the forms of hip-hop culture but on some of its themes as well. As was true of King, hip-hoppers are enraged by racist oppression and angered by the economic inequality that often makes black life miserable. King was concerned, as are many rappers, with the plight of black males. Such a concern is easy to understand given the masculine emphasis, even obsession, of both the black freedom struggle and hip-hop culture. King argued, for instance, that the "ultimate way to diminish our problems" would be a "government program to help the frustrated Negro male find his true masculinity by placing him on his own two economic feet." But perhaps one of the most intriguing and undervalued areas of overlap between King and contemporary rappers is in their struggle with the problem of evil. In formal theological circles, the branch of thought that addresses this question is called theodicy. Theodicy attempts to understand and explain why bad things happen to good, or at least, innocent, people. It also tries to understand human suffering in the light of asserting that God is good. How can a good God allow evil to exist and to harm her children?

King's professor, L. Harold DeWolf, who greatly influenced King on this score, examined at least four solutions to the problem of evil and found them all wanting. The first solution holds that evil is a mere illusion in human beings' minds, an error in perception. Hence such evils are not real to God. In DeWolf's view, empirical evidence disproves that claim. Second, human suffering serves to warn us of the existence of even greater suffering and evil from which we are mercifully spared. DeWolf maintains that this argument is theologically wrong because it fails to address where the greater evil came from in the first place. Third, the sufferer deserves her suffering since a just God would mete out punishment only to the evil. DeWolf argues that this solution is contradicted by the fact that so many good people have suffered for no reason. The final solution holds that human suffering results from our failure to take proper advantage of the scientific resources that might prevent or alleviate our pain. DeWolf rejects this solution for two reasons: it depends on the benefits of scientific techniques that are not permanent, since we eventually die despite their application, and it fails to account for why the world was designed in a manner to keep millions ignorant of such techniques. DeWolf attempts to solve the problem by suggesting the careful synthesis of two more plausible solutions. First, the so-called finitistic view holds that God chooses to limit herself in power in order to give real power to her creatures, thus respecting their free will. The next argument, the so-called absolutist view, holds that God's transcendent power assigns purpose to human suffering that falls beyond human reason. In the end, DeWolf affirms the belief that unearned suffering can become redemptive because it can help bring about God's ultimate purpose.

King reflected his teacher's thinking on this score. In a brief 1960 essay in *Christian Century*, he underscored his faith in just such a resolu-

tion of the problem of evil and the place of unearned suffering in the
struggle for freedom:

> My personal trials have also taught me the value of unmerited suf-
> fering. As my sufferings mounted I soon realized that there were
> two ways that I could respond to my situation: either to react with
> bitterness or seek to transform the suffering into a creative force. I
> decided to follow the latter course. Recognizing the necessity for
> suffering I have tried to make of it a virtue. If only to save myself
> from bitterness, I have attempted to see my personal ordeals as an
> opportunity to transform myself and heal the people involved in
> the tragic situation which now obtains. I have lived these last few
> years with the conviction that unearned suffering is redemptive.

It is also clear from this passage that King strongly believed in making
a virtue of necessity. Since suffering and evil are unavoidable, one must
transform them into tools for good. His philosophical approach to suffering and evil was part of a crucial survival technique. Those who believe
that suffering and evil have an ultimately good purpose can counteract the
fear, anxiety, or resentment that eats away their moral resolve. Unearned
suffering is ultimately redemptive because it is aligned with God's power
to bring about good in the universe. King often reminded his followers
that they had "cosmic companionship" in their struggle for freedom and
justice. King believed that nonviolence, which often entailed suffering and
brutality, was the best way for oppressed blacks to achieve their liberation.
Resort to violence would inevitably lead to massive destruction of black
life. King warned blacks that "if you use violence, he [your opponent]
does have an answer. He has the state militia; he has police brutality."
Thus nonviolence was philosophically sound and eminently practical to
combat the vicious force of white hatred. It matched such violence with
black moral power. King realized that evil is "stark, grim and colossally
real," and that it "is recalcitrant and determined, and never voluntarily
relinquishes its hold short of a persistent, almost fanatical resistance." In
his later years, King sought to change white America by forcing it to
come to grips with his massive, disruptive campaigns of nonviolent sabotage. Although far more aggressive than before, he still held out the wan-
ing possibility but absolute necessity for nonviolent social change.

Hard-core rappers, including Notorious B.I.G., Tupac Shakur, Snoop
Doggy Dogg, and Bone, Thugs N Harmony, have all, in varying ways,
grappled with the problem of evil. Interestingly, this salient dimension of

hard-core rap has been overlooked, perhaps because it is hidden in plain sight. In addressing evil and hard-core rap, it is helpful to remember that theodicy also has a social expression. One of sociology's towering thinkers, Max Weber, conceived theodicy as the effort of gifted individuals to give meaning to the suffering of the masses. Indeed, the appeal of King and Malcolm X rested largely on their abilities to make sense of the suffering that their followers endured. Of course, King's and Malcolm X's theodicies had vastly opposed orientations. King argued that the unearned suffering of blacks would redeem American society. Malcolm believed in mutual bloodshed: if blacks suffered, then whites ought to suffer as well. More recently, black leaders as diverse as Colin Powell and Louis Farrakhan have urged blacks to take more responsibility in dealing with the suffering in their communities. Hard-core rappers, by contrast, dismiss such remedies. They celebrate the outlaw as much as they denounce the institutions they view as the real culprits: the schools, churches, and justice system that exploit poor blacks. Paradoxically, the fact that rappers are struggling with suffering and evil proves that in fact they are connected to a moral tradition, one championed by King, that they have seemingly rejected. Moreover, the aggressive manner in which rappers deal with evil—putting forth images that suggest that they both resist and embrace evil—is disturbing because it encourages us to confront how we resist and embrace evil in our own lives.

The suffering masses that concern hard-core rappers are almost exclusively the black ghetto poor. According to many gangsta griots, the sources of this suffering are economic inequality, police brutality, and white racism. These forces lead to a host of self-destructive ills: black-on-black homicide, drug addiction, and the thug life that so many rappers celebrate and, in a few cases, embrace. For instance, on his "The Ghetto Won't Change," hard-core rapper Master P expresses the widely held belief among blacks that the carnage-inducing drug trade flourishes in the ghetto because of government complicity and white indifference. On "Point Tha Finga," Tupac Shakur gives voice to the rage many blacks feel when they realize that their hard-earned wages are subsidizing their own suffering at the hands of abusive police. For Shakur, the ethical line drawn between cops and criminals is even more blurred by the police's immoral behavior.

But blurring the lines that divide right from wrong is what seems to set these urban theodicists apart from their colleagues in traditional religious circles. Even Martin Luther, who shook the foundations of the

Catholic church, dropped his moral anchor as he launched his own theodicy in the form of a question: "Where might I find a gracious God?" As Luther understood, the purpose of a theodicy is, in Milton's words, to "justify the ways of God to men." This is especially true when a God whom believers claim to be good and all-powerful allows evil to occur. The problem with most thuggish theodicies is that their authors are as likely to flaunt as flail the vices they depict in music. Unlike traditional theodicists such as King, hard-core rappers maintain little moral distance from the evil they confront. Instead, they embody those evils with startling realism: guns, gangs, drugs, sexual transgression, and even murder are relentlessly valorized in the rhetoric of gangsta rappers. Although gangsta rappers are not the only popular cultural figures to do that, their words provoke a special outrage among cultural critics. For instance, although the 1996 film *Last Man Standing*, starring Bruce Willis, was filled with gratuitous violence, it was not denounced nearly as much as Snoop Doggy Dogg's equally violent 1993 album, *Doggystyle*. Neither did the Arnold Schwarzenegger vehicle *True Lies*, which was swollen by crude ethnic stereotypes, come in for the bitter attack aimed at Tupac Shakur's "2Pacalypse Now." When it comes to guns, we still feel safer when they are in the hands of white men, even if they are thugs.

Moral ambiguity is at the heart of hard-core rap's struggle with evil. When it comes to dealing with that idea, hard-core rappers are treated far differently by critics than are the creators of gangster films. In *The Godfather*, for example, Francis Ford Coppola's characters pay lip-service to a code of respect, loyalty, and honor. Still, they are ruthless murderers. Coppola is considered a brilliant artist and his characters memorable creations. The hard-core rapper and his work are rarely credited with such moral complexity. Either his creations are taken literally and their artistic status denied, or he is viewed as being incapable of examining the moral landscape. It is frightening for many to concede hard-core rap's moral complexity. An equally frightening prospect may be that its moral ambiguity—in truth, it is more like moral schizophrenia—points up two disturbing truths. One, our theodicies might lead us to conclude that life, or our faith in God, is meaningless. Two, the big difference between saints and sinners is not achievement but effort. Theodicy is a cry from the heart of hurt. Some religious thinkers have argued that what hurts us most is our belief in God. Therefore, we should surrender our belief and stake our future on how humans treat each other. As Master P suggests on "The Ghetto Won't Change," life in the ghetto is occasionally absurd.

In the absence of life's meaning, many embrace one extreme of the thug's theodicy: hustling and heartless behavior are life's only rewards.

A remarkable feature of the thug's theodicy is the energy she expends to hold on to belief in God in the midst of suffering and evil. This is so even if one is torn between accepting or rejecting evil behavior. On his rap "Things Done Changed," The Notorious B.I.G. claimed that his rap career was a direct outgrowth of a moral choice: pursue hip-hop or be a hoodlum. Tupac Shakur, perhaps the theodicist laureate of gangsta rap, was obsessed with God in his albums. Although he often expressed the belief that there was "a heaven for a G," he could not free himself from the evil, pain, and suffering he saw around him, a conflict elegiacally expressed in "Only God Can Judge Me." On this song, Tupac's plea for divine guidance is cast in thugs' terms. Still, it touches a universal nerve. Even if they had vastly different answers, such a perspective binds Shakur and other hip-hoppers to King. Both participated, in different ways, in a powerful tradition of reflecting on suffering and evil.

The ultimate symbol of suffering and evil is death. By engaging the forces of social chaos in our nation's urban centers—from drug addiction to AIDS, from mugging to murder—many black youth have been inducted into a culture of death. Many hip-hop artists are obsessed with death, especially the violent death of black males at the hands of their own number. Hip-hoppers evoke a continuum of emotions to confront death—from anger to rage, from regret to surrender. They also don a variety of rhetorical masks in facing the loss of life: as perpetrator or victim, as mourning relative or friend, or often as consoling survivor. Hip-hoppers are romantic, realistic, reactionary, or retributive when they speak of death. Often they combine some or all of these moods. Hip-hop's rhetorical modes of response are an attempt to understand and resist the psychic and moral devastation of death. Ironically, such an attempt often leads hip-hoppers to an apparently deeper embrace of the ethic of destruction that breeds violence and death. The contempt that hip-hoppers feel for the forces that make their friends suffer is revealed in the lyrics of rap's Jeremiahs. The hip-hop jeremiad both rejects and embraces suffering. The urban prophet lodges a stirring complaint against the destruction of his friends even as he calls down destruction on the heads of his foes. The hip-hop jeremiad is, to a degree, a secular expression of the Hebrew Bible's *lex talionis*—the principle of an eye for an eye that characterized ancient justice. And hard-core hip-hop's resistance to *and* advocacy of violence compose a modern gangsta's midrash. Hip-hoppers seek to combat suffering and evil by interpreting their existence in the light of the moral priorities of urban black life. In the inventive if torturous logic of hard-core rap, urban prophets seek to end carnage by pointing to how carnage ends life. At the same time, they seek to show cleverly the futile ends of carnage, its sick purposes. The moral message is often muddled, and the resistance and ratification of death are often confused. But too often the complicated narratives of hip-hop that address the culture of death are dismissed as merely glorifying or glamorizing violence. Glorification and glamorization of death in hip-hop certainly thrive as often flawed but important rhetorical strategies designed to bring visibility to the suffering of poor black and brown youth. Scholar Crispin Sartwell argues that such "lyrics do not glorify violence, unless you take the position that to *notice* violence linguistically, to admit that it exists, is to glorify it." Sartwell says that these lyrics "tell about violence, mourn it, object to it, and rage against the conditions that make violence a day-to-day reality."

To be sure, a great deal of death dealing, dying, and mourning occurs in hip-hop. Some of rap's most poignant narratives are elegies for fallen friends. Ice Cube's "Dead Homiez" is a path-breaking example of the genre, as Cube seeks an answer to why a funeral is "the only time black folk get to ride in a limo." Tupac Shakur's "Life Goes On" is a haunting, mellow paean to departed homeboys. And few can match the Notorious B.I.G. when it comes to knowing how death can at once create and destroy black identity. For B.I.G., death can bring a person fame even as it wipes out the personality on which the fame descends. His perspective is brutally summarized in the title of one of his last songs, "You're Nobody Til Somebody Kills You." The song was contained, in tragic sync with Notorious B.I.G.'s untimely death, on his posthumously released compact disk, *Life After Death*. In Scarface's "Never Seen a Man Cry," the rapper powerfully evokes the experience of simultaneously dying and watching death. And Snoop Doggy Dogg's "Murder Was the Case" is a powerful example of imagining one's own death. In the rap, Snoop is critically wounded by gunshot. His story tells the dread he feels in the face of his impending death. Unexpectedly his death is interrupted as God steps in to save him. For both Scarface and Snoop, the experience of death is narrated in its totalizing horror: it brings an end to life and the possibility of sharing joy or pain with loved ones. Or, for that matter, it saves one from knowing the wrath of one's enemies. Oddly enough, both death narratives reflect the pressure of sacred presence. God intervenes directly to stop Snoop's demise, and in Scarface's song, God is manifest as the peaceful spirit. In both cases, as in Tupac's narrative, hard-core theodicy is linked to an unshakable sense of God's active intervention in human suffering. In Snoop's case, God is a spiritual mediator. In Tupac's lyrics, God is a moral adjudicator (especially in "Only God Can Judge Me"). And in Scarface's scenario, God is a divine healer in the world to come.

King was shadowed by the threat of death from the beginning of his public career. He was hounded, really, by a nearly palpable certainty of his own demise. But from his Montgomery days, King was convinced that even death might be used to assist providence. His viewpoint was characterized by a statement he made in 1960:

> We will always be willing to talk and seek fair compromise, but we are ready to suffer when necessary and even risk our lives to become witnesses to the truth as we see it. I realize that this approach will mean suffering and sacrifice. It may mean going to jail. If such is the case the resister must be willing to fill the jail houses of the South. It may even mean physical death. But if physical death is the price that a man must pay to free his children and his white brethren from a permanent death of the spirit, then nothing could be more redemptive. This is the type of soul force that I am convinced will triumph over the physical force of the oppressor.

From this passage it is clear that King linked his view of death to his vision of theodicy, since death might lead to the fulfillment of God's purpose. Five years later, King even more strongly reiterated his view of redemptive death while providing personal insight into death's meaning:

> If I were constantly worried about death, I couldn't function. After a while, if your life is more or less constantly in peril, you come to a point where you accept the possibility philosophically. I must face the fact, as all others in positions of leadership must do, that America today is an extremely sick nation, and that something could well happen to me at any time. I feel, though, that my cause is so right, so moral, that if I should lose my life, in some way it would aid the cause.

During his Chicago campaign, King emphasized that he had "no martyr complex." He confessed that he was "tired of living every day under the threat of death," echoing a statement he had made years before to his

Montgomery congregation. While in public King remained philosophical about his death, he was left exhausted and often depressed by the inhuman crush of his schedule, the erosion of nonviolence as a viable strategy of social change, and the escalation of death threats. It is a measure of his remarkable will and a tribute to his ability to recover from self-doubt that King was able to function at all during his final four years. For instance, after a plane King had boarded received a bomb threat in 1964, he remarked to his wife and to aide Dorothy Cotton that "I've told you all that I don't expect to survive this revolution; this society's too sick." When Cotton tried to console him, King replied, "Well, I'm just being realistic." Increasingly, King felt more isolated, even alienated, from his close circle of associates. He began to eat and drink more as his depression grew heavier. Neither activity seemed to assuage his melancholy. King longed for "somebody you can sit with and discuss your inner weaknesses and confess your agonies and your inner shortcomings, and they don't exploit it, they listen to you and help you bear your burdens in the midst of the storms of life." This perhaps helps to explain King's extramarital affairs as well: he sought consolation in fleeting moments of affection in the embrace of a kind, warm soul. But little really worked; King became more depressed. Amazingly, he pushed on. The source of King's survival was his religious faith, which motivated him never to surrender hope. As King stated in a BBC interview, "I have my moments of frustration, my moments of doubt, and maybe temporary moments of despair, but I have never faced absolute despair because I think if you face absolute despair, you lose all hope, you have no power to move and act, because you really feel there is no possibility of winning."

Still, journalist and historian Roger Wilkins says that beginning in 1966, King had become a "profoundly weary and wounded spirit" and had been engulfed by "a profound sadness." His closest friend, Ralph Abernathy, confessed that in 1968 King "was just a different person"—"sad and depressed." A former staff member of Summer Community Organization and Political Education (SCOPE) said that King "was depressed," that he "was dark, gaunt and tired," that he "felt that his time was up. . . . He said that he knew that they were going to get him." King friend Deenie Drew claimed that in his "last year or so, I had a feeling that Martin had a death wish. . . . I had a feeling that he didn't know which way to turn." John Gibson says that in his last years King could relax only in a room that had no windows, since he feared being vulnerable to an assassin's advances. He relentlessly searched people's eyes, ceaselessly wondering who would

kill him and how and when he would meet his death. In such an atmosphere pervaded by paranoia and fear, King's tragic death was surely at
some level also a great relief. Unlike hard-core hip-hop, King saw suffering as a route to divine destiny, not its insuperable obstacle. Unlike many
hard-core hip-hoppers, King believed that death might bring a more positive outcome. (At the end of his song "Only God Can Judge Me," Tupac
and a guest lament that their only fear of death was the possibility they
had to "return to this bitch.") He embraced its inevitability, at least initially, as a means to the greater good of black liberation. Hard-core hip-
hop's use of death, alternatively, is rooted in a theodicy that often spurns
black suffering and views death as a painful hindrance to personal and
social freedom. A huge difference occurs, too, in the identities of their
respective opponents. King's mortal enemies were white supremacists.
Hip-hop's sworn enemies, both within its camp and beyond its bounds,
are as likely to be black competitors and critics as white opponents.
Nearly a decade ago, the Stop the Violence Movement released an antivi-
olent song where rapper Kool Moe Dee lamented running from a black
criminal when he had never had to run from the KKK.

If their obsession with death at least partially unites King and hip-
hoppers, they are also bound by their sexual mores and practices. The
sexual transgressions of rappers, on record and in life, are well publicized
and widely denounced. Hip-hop has been rebuked for its vulgar lyrics,
explicit speech, crude and profane gestures, and publicizing of private
sexual matters. At times its actions have brought cries of censorship.
Many black critics in particular have called for rappers to return to an earlier epoch of moral discipline, when filthy sentiments were banned from
public view and quarantined in juke joints, pool halls, blues clubs, or bed-
room walls. Many black critics are especially ashamed of the raunchiness
that is being passed off as authentic black culture. They claim that true
representations of blackness have nothing to do with hip-hop culture's
commercially driven images. According to critics, these images often do
little more than repackage high-gloss stereotypes of black identity. Further, the misogyny and sexism that rip through hip-hop culture are
viewed by many blacks as a radical departure from the norm in black
communities. They think that black youth culture has embraced a
deviant morality that devalues black female identity. Moreover, the repulsive images of black males as studs and black females as "bitches" and
"hos" contrast sharply with how blacks of previous generations viewed
themselves. Such images also play to the racist beliefs about black identity and behavior that members of the civil rights generation bitterly

opposed. The irony of fighting for black youth to have a voice in civic and national life, only to have them use such freedoms to denigrate black women and to belittle and reject the cultural mores that sustained blacks from the plantation to the ghetto, is more than most black critics can abide.

Indeed, critics often point to the black freedom struggle as the basis of their criticism of hip-hop culture. These critics argue that if Martin Luther King, Jr., were alive, he would oppose the violence, misogyny, and vulgarity that for many youth marks "real" black identity. There is little doubt that they are right. In one of his "Advice for Living" columns that he penned for *Ebony Magazine* in the late fifties, King argued that rock music "often plunges men's minds into depravity and immoral depths." Unquestionably King was publicly opposed to moral decadence and cultural violence. He would have been much more sympathetic than current critics to the causes of what he might have thought of as youthful pathology. He would have certainly opposed hip-hop's crude misogyny and its public displays of shameless sexual lust. In fact, the use of the public sphere signifies a huge difference between black generations.

For older blacks, the public realm marked a sacred social boundary in which sexual interactions or passionate processes were kept private. Neither dysfunction nor delight—and sometimes the borders between the two were admittedly blurred—was to seep beyond the sanctified seal of domestic space. In the public square, private discourse was hushed. Private passion was muted. Harmful and exploitative stereotypes of black sexuality already soured black public interactions with white society. Therefore the less raw material that black folk provided to substantiate white claims, the better off the race would be. Even if one engaged in the very acts that to the white world proved black savagery—acts that many blacks knew defined *all* racial communities, including white ones, but which some blacks internalized as the mark of their own moral inferiority—they were to be hidden. On the surface this seems like hypocrisy, but it was a necessary hypocrisy, geared to survival in a highly charged racial atmosphere. It is a hypocrisy forced into existence by the greater hypocrisy of a white world that practiced criminal sexual acts against blacks without punishment or remorse. The best safeguards blacks could manage as they engaged the white world were the self-disciplining practices of sexual purity and repressed desire—qualities irrelevant to lustful whites. Blacks were always on sexual display, whether they liked it or not. They always operated under the harmful moral surveillance of white culture. Thus, blacks often lived their public lives at a remove from their private passions.

They knew that those passions, whether they involved sex or civil rights, had better be kept under lock and key. As King himself demonstrated, the private lives of blacks often found many uses. One of them was certainly to blow off steam and let down hair that had been pinned up for public purposes. Keeping his private life private was in many ways a moral and racial priority for King. Of course, the two priorities often inevitably merged.

Ironically, black youth feel nothing near the level of sanction or outrage faced by their forebears because of King's and civil rights struggles to remove racial double standards. Still, the reactions to rap's sexual ethics are remarkably strong. Indeed, it is undeniable that black youth face severe social sanctions of their own. They live under constant surveillance, whether in South Central Los Angeles or in malls in suburban Maryland. Poor black youth are subject to forms of public surveillance that are hugely different from middle-class blacks under apartheid thirty years ago. These youth are both worried over and resented by older blacks. The cruder forms of hip-hop culture evoke the resentment of the black bourgeoisie, a powerful sentiment fueled by several forces: the deterioration of relations between the generations, the expression of revulsion to black ghetto styles, and the expression of class conflict in black communities. Thus, there is a huge lag between civil rights and hip-hop styles and sensibilities in black culture (although there have always been class tensions in black communities, as witnessed, for example, in the deep resistance, even by black elites, to King's movement in Northern ghettoes). In their own minds, hip-hoppers are "keepin' it real." This means they are telling the truth as best as they can about what they like and what they hate, even if it is relentlessly crude and all too often obnoxious. In seizing the microphone to speak their minds, black youth often forget, if they ever knew, how recent is the freedom to narrate publicly the pains and predicaments of poor black communities. But their black critics often fail to acknowledge that while hip-hop's rhetorical freedom may be put to troubling uses, its existence is a significant sign of the emancipation for which black elders fought.

Moreover, black youth should not be written off as simply pathological or morally corrupt unless we are willing to apply the same litmus test to King's life. True enough, King's attempt at discretion meant that he made a moral distinction between private and public behavior. But that distinction was as much a sign of the racial times in which he lived as it was an ethical prescription drawn from his religious beliefs. For that matter, his religious beliefs forbade the sort of behavior in which he, and many, many more black leaders privately engaged. The bitter truth is that at a certain level, Snoop Doggy Dogg wants what Martin Luther King, Jr., enjoyed: sexual freedom. Because of King, Snoop can now choose to say so. King never had, nor would he probably have ever wanted, the chance to do the same. But their differing philosophies about public and private morality do not prevent us from exploring just how similar were King's and hip-hop's sentiments about sexuality and about women. If we can agree that King is not a deviant because of his behavior (a view I heartily endorse), then we must entertain the same possibility about black youth.

From his teens, King enjoyed sharp suits and light-skinned women. Nicknamed "Tweedie" because of his sartorial splendor, King learned about the love of women, or more likely, the tantalizing sexual treats of female surplus, in the black church—where women outnumber men three to one. King's erotic preferences and treatment of women were solidified at Morehouse. As his college friend Larry Williams recalled, "M.L. could get involved with girls, and most of the girls he got seriously involved with were light." Williams and King formed a bond around their boyhood flirtations. They named themselves "Robinson and Stevens, the wreckers" after an Atlanta wrecking crew. When asked the logic behind their names, King replied it was because "we wreck girls," bragging that we "wreck all the women." King continued his ways with women in seminary and graduate school. Outfitted with a wardrobe of fine suits and a new car, a rarity for graduate students, King played the field as he pursued his degrees. Even after he met his future bride, Coretta Scott, he satisfied his ample sexual appetite. King confessed to Coretta that he had cheated on her with an Atlanta girl over the 1952 Christmas break. They quarreled and then reconciled, and then announced their June 1953 wedding. But even after their marriage, King continued to stray. A family friend admitted that King "loved beautiful women," and that the "girls he 'dated' were just like models," that they "were tall stallions, all usually were very fair, never dark." The friend says that King was "really a Casanova" but with "a quiet dignity," since he "would give the girls respect." A woman who claimed to have known King "as a man" was described as "extremely fair . . . [with] freckles."

King preferred very light women. That preference had everything to do with light-skinned blacks' being extended more privileges than dark-skinned blacks because they were closer in hue to whites as the obvious product of miscegenation. Hence they were assigned a higher position on the racial totem pole. According to one friend, King "said that he was willing to fight and die for black people, but he was damned if he could see anything pretty in a black [dark-skinned] woman." Such a self-hating sentiment is all the more stunning since its alleged source was a leader of the fight for black psychic freedom and dignity. King obviously had a great deal of distortion and miseducation to conquer in himself as he sought to bring psychic healing to blacks en masse. Tragically, too many hip-hop artists have enlarged King's narrative of disdain for black women. In their videos, they prefer light-skinned black women—or Asian or white women—to their darker-hued sisters. Having been for so long exoticized and demonized at the same time, dark-skinned black women still find themselves at the bitter heart of intense racial conflicts over self-worth, self-esteem, and true self-love—and that from black hip-hoppers who claim to "keep it real."

King's sexual pace did not slow even when he realized that J. Edgar Hoover was waging an ugly, evil campaign to destroy his reputation. One figure claims that King "had a chick in every town." Despite his prominence, King at times appeared defiant in his affairs, donning sunglasses in the deluded belief that they would mask his famous face. At other times, he cavalierly introduced his flings as relatives. On the trip to Scandinavia to pick up King's Nobel Peace Prize, King and his party encountered an embarrassing situation. Several local women who had slept with some men in King's entourage afterward made off with several of their possessions and wallets. To quiet the potential fallout, King aide Bayard Rustin refused to press charges when the authorities arrived. But as one aide later explained, "All the guys were putting it to them [women in European countries] that, if the girls gave them pussy first, they'd see that she got to Martin." As Notorious B.I.G. rapped about his woman-sharing habits in a hotel with his friend Lil' Caesar:

> Cease know
> All his hoes go to my door
> Then they go to his floor
> To fuck some more.

And like hip-hoppers, King's sexual liaisons were even finding their way into his spoken work. King once made improper sex an analogy for segregation, saying that "segregation is the adultery of an illicit intercourse between justice and immorality," which "cannot be cured by the Vaseline of gradualism."

Not only were King's sexual relations remarkably like hip-hop culture's, but his views toward women were not much more enlightened. In fact, he was solidly chauvinistic. In another of his "Advice for Living" columns for *Ebony*, for instance, King responded to a woman's query about how to handle her husband's extramarital affair. He placed the responsibility for her husband's straying squarely on the wife's shoulders. King asked the wife to consider what faults she might possess to cause her husband to stray—"Do you nag?" he asked—and to reflect on the qualities that the other woman might possess that she was lacking. In an earlier column, King had expressed the belief that "the primary obligation of the woman is that of motherhood." As King's only high-ranking female staff member, Dorothy Cotton, put it, when it came to women's rights, King "would have had a lot to learn and a lot of growing to do." King was in constant conflict with his wife about her role. She wanted to become much more involved in the movement; he wanted her to stay home and raise their children. Further, King was "somewhat uncomfortable around assertive women." His own strained relationship with Ella Baker is exemplary. As Baker noted about SCLC:

> There would never be any role for me in a leadership capacity with SCLC. Why? First, I'm a woman. Also, I'm not a minister. And second . . . I knew that my penchant for speaking honestly . . . would not be well tolerated. The combination of the basic attitude of men, and especially ministers, as to what the role of women in their church setups is—that of taking orders, not providing leadership—and the . . . ego problems involved in having to feel that there is someone who . . . had more information about a lot of things than they possessed at that time. . . . This would never have lent itself to my being a leader in the movement there.

Andrew Young confirms King's difficulties with strong, independent women, claiming that they "had a hard time with domineering women in SCLC, because Martin's mother, quiet as she was, was really a strong, domineering force in the family." Young provides perhaps an unintended insight about the politics of female blame that often drive the patriarchal logic of black liberation movements when he adds, "She was never publicly saying anything but she ran Daddy King, and she ran the church and she ran Martin, and Martin's problem in the early days of the movement was directly related to his need to be free of that strong matriarchal influence. This is a generality, but a system of oppression needs strong women and weak men." King's outlook on women was only barely better than many black youth have today.

King is indeed much closer to hip-hop cultural sentiments than we have up to this point admitted. As Dorothy Cotton suggests, King would have had to make huge adjustments in his outlook to address effectively contemporary social ills such as gender oppression. Still, there will be many critics who claim that in spite of his sexism, he otherwise treated women with dignity and respect. To a degree, that is the case. But King's private sexual dealings with women, and his public discomfort with female authority, suggest otherwise. Moreover, the allegation that King may have engaged in a shoving match or a fight with a woman the night before he was murdered underscores how arbitrary are our distinctions between King and hip-hoppers.

King's views of women certainly affected his wife, though she claims that she and King never discussed his indiscretions. Yet King's womanizing and his largely coerced neglect of domestic duty left its mark on his family. Of course, King's relationship with his wife was shaped by his chauvinistic beliefs about the role of women. King's painfully narrow view of gender roles also strained his relationship with powerful women in the civil rights movement. King routinely overlooked the achievements of the black women who pioneered the path of racial and sexual liberation. He neglected the brilliant insights and courageous actions of his female contemporaries who were amazingly effective in shaping strategies for social change. While King has transcended his own era as the surpassing symbol of social struggle in the twentieth century, he proved to be in his relationship to women very much a man of his times.

CHAPTER 10

"The Primary Obligation of the Woman Is That of Motherhood"
The Pitfalls of Patriarchy

It was a tender and sad scene that choked with foreboding, as did so much of Martin Luther King's last year. Because of his relentless pace, King had again become exhausted and even more vulnerable to an intermittent but deepening depression. He finally yielded to a physician's request to take a few days to mend, and in mid-March, less than a month before his murder, he prepared to take a brief respite. Working at his office before his scheduled rest, King telephoned his wife, Coretta.

"Did you get the flowers?" she recalls King asking her.

Mrs. King told her husband that no flowers had come. King explained that while he was downtown shopping for clothes, he had stopped by the florist next door to purchase her flowers. The owner assured King that they would be immediately delivered.

"I was touched by his gesture of love," Mrs. King remembers. "By the time he had come home to pick up his bag to leave for the airport, the flowers had arrived."

Mrs. King says that King sent her "beautiful red carnations," but when she touched them, she realized they were artificial.

"In all the years we had been together," Mrs. King says, "Martin had never sent me artificial flowers. It seemed so unlike him."

When Coretta kissed Martin and thanked him for her flowers, she remarked on their beauty and their artificiality.

"I wanted to give you something that you could always keep," Mrs. King says her husband told her.

"They were the last flowers I ever got from Martin," she says. "Somehow, in some strange way, he seemed to have known how long they would have to last."

In the light of Coretta Scott King's herculean efforts at guarding and extending her husband's legacy, King's flowers have had to last more than twice the length of their marriage and nearly as long as the thirty-nine years he lived. But the flowers' artificiality, the very basis of their durability, meant that from the start they would carry no fragrance to sweeten the foul and uncharted passages that King's widow and their children would have to navigate. Coretta has garnered admiration in many quarters, but she has also been seen as living off King's legacy, invoking his words to smooth her path to leadership by proxy. More damaging, she has been accused of making a killing off her dead husband's image, and with her family has been charged with making a commodity of King's legacy, packaging and selling his face and tongue to the highest corporate bidder. I explore these last charges in Chapter 13.

Now, however, I focus on King's relationship with Coretta and through it view his understanding and treatment of women, issues that are indivisible from the times in which King lived. King's views on women were shaped by ideas and practices that were common in the thirties, forties, and fifties. Ironically enough, the movement he led would eventually spark the rise of modern feminism in the late sixties and early seventies. But the religious and academic subcultures that nurtured King rarely challenged traditional gender values that enhanced men's lives while curtailing the social possibilities of women. Moreover, the civil rights movement at midcentury was hardly a model of female inclusion, especially in leadership roles. All of these factors must be taken into account in judging King's views on gender and, consequently, how he treated his wife.

Coretta King is perhaps the most prominent member of a trio of Famous Black Widows—"our three Queens" activist C. Delores Tucker calls them—that includes Medgar Evers's widow, Myrlie Evers, and Malcolm X's widow, Dr. Betty Shabazz. To some critics, these women command attention primarily because they are projections of the personalities of their martyred mates. While such an idea may thinly masquerade as feminist—after all, its implied premise is that women should earn respect independent of the men to whom they are connected—it ignores three factors. First, each of these talented women has more than held her own since her husband's death. Evers, for instance, has served as chairwoman of the NAACP, helping it to regain stature after the erosion of its prestige and influence. She also worked tirelessly for thirty years to bring her first husband's murderer to justice. The only one of the widows to remarry, Evers has written powerfully about her attempts to redefine her spirituality and sexuality as a mature black woman. And after Malcolm X's death,

Shabazz reared their children under difficult circumstances and returned to school to earn a doctorate in higher education. Until her tragic death in 1997, Shabazz worked as a college administrator and effective community activist in extending Malcolm's memory and addressing the needs of unfortunate black youth. Second, to criticize the Famous Black Widows is to punish them for accidental events. None of these women married their husbands when they were famous, so they had no intention to use them as springboards to fame or fortune. Finally, to attack King, Evers, or Shabazz for capitalizing on her husband's legacy to promote the social good of black communities reveals a paradox: if they failed to use their visibility to help other blacks, they would be accused of squandering their good fortune and the legacy of their husbands. If, on the other hand, they employ their privileged posts as spokeswomen—a position acquired through great sacrifice, including the sacrifice of their husbands' lives— then they are often charged with recklessly throwing around their name and the privilege it entails. We make a serious mistake when we assume that the sorts of privileges these women inherit automatically causes them to abuse their positions or to exploit a fortune wrung from pain.

Coretta Scott King's relation to Martin Luther King, Jr., before and after his death, tells a powerful story of gender and race. It illumines the sexist character of black culture and the movement in general, revealing the consequences of pursuing racial justice while leaving aside considerations of gender equity. King's sexist beliefs not only had a profound effect on his organization but also caused trouble in his marriage. His relationship with Coretta symbolizes the difficulty faced by black leaders who attempted to forge a healthy life with their loved ones while the government aimed its huge resources at destroying their families, a sure metaphor for how the state has often abandoned or abused the black family with cruel social policies.

King's beliefs about women faithfully reflected the insensitivity and indifference of many black men to the plight of black women. Many black men before the seventies simply lumped together the concerns of black communities, without carefully distinguishing the effects of class and gender on one's racial status. The struggles of black women for both racial freedom and gender equity have been amply illustrated in black history, even if their contributions often went unrecognized by black men. In the nineteenth and early twentieth centuries, for instance, the National Association of Colored Women (NACW) provided black women of means and social standing an outlet to fight stereotypes of black female immorality. This organization also allowed them to pool their resources to resist racial tyranny, uplift the black race, and demand racial and gender justice. And in our own century, the organization of black welfare recipients in the National Welfare Rights Organization (NWRO) gave poor and working-class black women a means to reform welfare laws and bring the issue of urban poverty to the forefront of the national agenda. From the beginning of black America, black women have fought valiantly for themselves and their race. Although their efforts have had a great impact on the liberation struggles of black people, black women often have been denied due recognition for their achievements. They have also been systematically excluded from the top tiers of formal leadership in civil rights organizations and in the central institution of black culture that black women overwhelmingly populate: the black church.

King resisted giving women leadership roles in his own group even though he was deeply aware of the importance of black women like Mary Church Terrell, the first president of the NACW, who enjoyed a distinguished career as a clubwoman, educator, writer, lecturer, and social activist for over sixty years. Terrell's social activism was jump-started in 1892 by the tragic death of her friend Thomas Moss at the hands of a white lynch mob enraged by his success as a grocer in her native Memphis. By the time of Moss's lynching, Terrell had relocated to Washington, D.C., with her husband, jurist Robert Heberton Terrell. Mary Church Terrell and Frederick Douglass met with President Benjamin Harrison in the aftermath of Moss's lynching to complain of the rise of racial violence. The same year, she also became the leader of the Colored Women's League and, subsequently, in 1896, the NACW. For Terrell and her fellow NACW members, the fight against racism and the uplift of black women went hand in hand. After she was elected to three consecutive terms as president of the group, Terrell was named an honorary life president in 1901. Afterward, as a writer and lecturer, Terrell promoted racial equality and interracial cooperation. She had already delivered a speech, "The Progress of Colored Women," before the 1898 convention of the National American Woman Suffrage Association. In 1904, Terrell was the only black representative at the International Congress of Women in Berlin, Germany, where she addressed the gathering in German, and was invited to address the second Congress of the Women's International League for Peace and Freedom in Zurich in 1919. She also served as the first black woman member of the Washington, D.C., Board of Education, from 1895 to 1901 and again from 1906 to 1911. As a social activist, Terrell and her fellow National Woman's party members picketed the White House for female suffrage.

In 1940, Terrell, who was born in 1863, published her autobiography, *A Colored Woman in a White World*. During the late 1940s and early 1950s, Terrell encouraged the blacklisted, imprisoned, and harassed liberal victims of McCarthyism to "keep on insisting—keep on fighting injustice." Her advanced age did not slow her civil rights activism. In 1942, she became chair of the Coordinating Committee for the Enforcement of District of Columbia Anti-Discrimination Laws passed in 1872 and 1873. The laws "required all eating-place proprietors to serve any respectable well-behaved person regardless of color, or face a $1,000 fine and forfeiture of their license." Although the laws had not been repealed, they were uniformly ignored, and from the 1890s until the 1950s, the district public facilities were segregated. Blacks who tried to integrate public facilities were fined or jailed. When she was eighty-six years old, Terrell led two other blacks and a white to request service at a segregated Washington, D.C., restaurant. They filed suit when the owner refused to offer them service. Eventually the case went to the Supreme Court. In the meantime, Terrell helped to boycott, picket, and sit in at several other Washington, D.C., eateries. The Supreme Court ruled in 1953 that segregated eating facilities in Washington, D.C., were unconstitutional. A year later, on July 24, Terrell died, just two weeks after the Supreme Court outlawed segregated public schools in *Brown v. Board of Education* and one year before Rosa Parks sparked the Montgomery bus boycott.

Of course, Terrell was well known to King and other black activists. Her courage and commitment to black freedom and women's rights provided a strong example of leadership. The same is true of Mary McCloud Bethune, another black woman warrior who blazed the way for King and other freedom fighters. Bethune was a famous educator and activist who also served, from 1924 to 1928, as president of the NACW. In 1904, Bethune found the Daytona Educational and Industrial Institute for Training Negro Girls, molded on the mind-hands-hearts paradigm: educational instruction that included teacher training, vocational education that included sewing and food production and preparation, and intense religious instruction and outreach. Bethune's racial politics shone through in her insistence that all institute functions be desegregated. It also surfaced in her organization of Daytona blacks to vote in 1920 in the face of threats by the Ku Klux Klan. In 1923, Bethune merged her school, know by then as the Daytona Normal and Industrial Institute, with the Cookman Institute, which began as a facility for black boys under the auspices of the Methodist Episcopal church. In 1929, the school was renamed Bethune-Cookman College, and in 1943 it offered its first bachelor degrees. But

Bethune had already given up the presidency of the college and in 1936 was appointed director of the Division of Minority Affairs at the National Youth Administration (NYA) under President Franklin Roosevelt, serving until 1943. When she was president of the NACW, Bethune helped the group in 1928 to become the first black organization with permanent headquarters in Washington, D.C. Still, she clashed with the NACW over its decentralized activities, and in December 1935, a frustrated Bethune founded the National Council of Negro Women (NCNW) in New York City.

Bethune stayed at the helm for fourteen years, bringing twenty-two national professional and occupational groups under NCNW's umbrella during her tenure. Beginning with Calvin Coolidge, Bethune served five presidents as an adviser on black issues, particularly education. Already serving as one of thirty-five members of the advisory committee of the NYA, Bethune was appointed in 1936 as administrator of the Office of Minority Affairs in the NYA, making her the first black woman to hold a federal post. Eventually Bethune became Roosevelt's unofficial chief adviser on racial issues, and in August 1936, she organized the Federal Council on Negro Affairs, dubbed the "Black Cabinet." The group included more than one hundred advisers drawn from the NAACP, the Urban League, the black press and other civic and social groups. The Black Cabinet convened two groundbreaking conferences in Washington, D.C., in 1937 and again in 1939. As an independent activist, Bethune also endorsed A. Philip Randolph's 1941 March on Washington, which resulted in an executive order banning racial discrimination in employment in government and defense industries. Even after the NYA was dismantled, Bethune advised Presidents Truman and Eisenhower on race relations. She died in 1955, the year of King's rise to national prominence.

These strong, powerful women are just two of the battalion of black women who would have inspired King as a budding black prophet. Moreover, their bourgeois base and appeal among influential white Americans should have endeared them to King because of his middle-class values and because of his thirst at the beginning of his career for a method of black revolt that still allowed blacks to love whites. These women's heroic example helped win the acceptance of black intelligence and skill in the councils of power, even as they expressed the deep desire of ordinary blacks to be free from legal and social restrictions. Their examples also fueled the social imagination of Rosa Parks, the spunky Montgomery, Alabama, seamstress whose refusal to give up her seat in the white section of the city bus as mandated by law was a flashpoint in the modern civil rights movement.

Parks had been a veteran of black women's organizations, was a strong member of the St. Paul AME church, and was a longtime member of the NAACP, serving as secretary to E. D. Nixon, the Montgomery branch president. She was solidly anchored in black revolt and had sought several times since the 1940s to resist the segregation of public transportation. Parks was also a member of Montgomery's Women's Political Council (WPC), which had been organized in 1946 by Mary Fair Burks, an instructor at Alabama State College, to enhance the educational opportunities of black youth. It was reorganized in 1949 to register black women to vote and became a political force to be reckoned with under the presidency of Jo Ann Robinson, an English teacher at Alabama State College. At the Montgomery city commission, the WPC agitated for the repeal of segregated laws and practices in the public sphere. They demanded that black policemen be hired and organized protests against woefully inadequate recreational facilities for black youth. Most important, the WPC had long before Parks's arrest concluded that a bus boycott would be an effective means of ending segregation. As Robinson says, a bus boycott would be a way "not to just teach a lesson but to break the system. We knew if the women supported it, the men would go along." After Parks's arrest, Robinson led the WPC in announcing to students and colleagues that it would begin a bus boycott to end segregation. Robinson wrote a leaflet to explain Parks's arrest and galvanize the black community for strategic social action. Without WPC's ingenious tactical maneuvers, quick response, and organizational efficiency, the Montgomery bus boycott may have never occurred. But beyond a token nod to their efforts and those of Rosa Parks, King barely recognized WPC's achievements in his account of the year-long boycott, *Stride Toward Freedom*.

Moreover, without the spur of grass-roots leaders like E. D. Nixon, the ministers who seized the helm of leadership—or were forced to take up the reins of the boycott—might never have acted bravely to exploit Parks's act of social rebellion for the black community. As Nixon recalls, at a key point when decisive action was called for from several black leaders, including ministers like King, Ralph Abernathy, and H. H. Hubbard, they wanted to distribute leaflets endorsing the boycott but without letting white authorities know of their support. Nixon gave them a tongue lashing, accusing them of acting like "little boys."

"What the hell you tallkin' about?" Nixon quizzed them. "How you gonna have a mass meeting, gonna boycott a city bus line without the white folks knowing about it?" And that wasn't all. Nixon connected the black ministers' livelihood to the poor black women who supported them but whom the ministers in turn now waffled in supporting.

"You guys have went around here and lived off these poor washer-women all your lives and ain't never done nothing for 'em," Nixon chided them. "And now you got a chance to do something for 'em, you talkin' about you don't want the white folks to know it." Nixon threatened to tell the black community that the boycott would be canceled because the ministers were "too scared" to stand up for them. As social historian Paula Giddings memorably sums it up, faced "with a choice of confronting either the wrath of white racists or those black women, they chose the safer course." The Montgomery Improvement Association (MIA) was orga-nized, and King was named its president.

In the aftermath of the bus boycott, King was fortunate to have work-ing with him one of the foremost organizers in radical politics and civil rights, Ella Baker. Even before the boycott was completed, Baker lent her expertise to the efforts in Montgomery, joining her comrades and King aides Bayard Rustin and Stanley Levison to generate strategies and dis-cuss ways to transform the moment of racial rebellion to a genuine mass movement for social change. When Baker came to Montgomery, she often stayed with Rosa Parks, whom she met in 1946 when Parks attended a leadership training session Baker had conducted in Jack-sonville, Florida. In fact, when Parks ignited the boycott, she had recently returned from a civil rights workshop led by Ella Baker at the Highlander Center. Baker was reared in North Carolina and migrated to New York in 1927, where she helped to develop the Young Negro Cooperative League. She was national field secretary for the NAACP from 1941 to 1942, jour-neying throughout the South to conduct membership campaigns and develop branches of the NAACP. When she became the NAACP's direc-tor of branches, Baker attended more than 150 meetings and logged over ten thousand miles within a year's time. By the time she began to work with King, she was a seasoned organizer with important contacts throughout the South.

Furthermore, she was ideologically committed to the empowerment of ordinary figures to make social change, a viewpoint that later landed her in trouble as she worked with an organization of male ministers beset by charismatic, top-down and personality-driven leadership. When Baker, Rustin, and Levison, in Levison's kitchen, cooked up an institutional framework through which the movement might be extended, they came up with the idea for what eventually became the SCLC. Initially Baker, Rustin, and Levison helped to organize the Southwide Institute of Transportation, which later became known as the Southern Negro Leaders Conference on Transportation and Nonviolent Integration, whose first meeting was held in 1957 in Atlanta. For that meeting, which inaugurated the SCLC, Rustin wrote a set of conference working papers that were edited by Levison and Baker. At the meeting, Baker recalls that more than one hundred ministers "were willing to do something I had never seen Negro ministers do before: they were willing to analyze each of the papers we presented." But in Baker's estimation, King failed to study and learn. She argued with Rustin and Levison over her suggestion to confront King and force him to "face up to the potential that was in the movement." Baker felt that the black ministers' problem lay with the organizational structure of black churches, where one didn't need to learn how to organize "so all you need to do is carry on as before." In lamenting King's negative effect on the group, Baker observes, "I think they would have been willing to learn had their 'leader' had the understanding."

With the Atlanta conference completed and a follow-up meeting in New Orleans done, King pressed Rustin to take the leadership of a voter registration drive, the Crusade for Citizenship. But King quickly realized that Rustin had three strikes against him: he was gay, he had former communist ties, and he had been a conscientious objector to World War II. Although Ella Baker was reluctant to take the post, she agreed to head the Crusade for Citizenship at Rustin's and Levison's urging. It was a decision that she would soon regret. Baker was largely successful in her efforts to organize voter registration drives in as many cities as possible by the deadline of February 12, 1958. According to an SCLC memorandum from King that was likely drafted by Baker, the crusade's goal was "to set up at the local level the type of action and organization that can struggle, come what may, to obtain the right to vote where it does not exist." From her base in Atlanta, where she relocated in January, Baker encouraged SCLC board members to carry the campaign into their communities. She also traveled to cities identified by the crusade for intense voter registration efforts, wrote countless letters to inspire local workers, supplied necessary literature, and expertly informed the press of their efforts. Contrary to news reports of the crusade's weak effect, Baker indicated that "reports from the cities I have reached show that some good sound work has been and is being done, and that the results are far from negative." She reported to King that "I talked with New Orleans, Baton Rouge, Shreveport, Mobile,

Tallahassee, Jacksonville, Nashville, Chattanooga, Knoxville and Durham. All of these places had something to report." After successfully completing her work with the crusade, Baker was encouraged by SCLC board members and allies, including Rustin, Levison, Abernathy, Fred Shuttlesworth, and C. O. Simkins, to remain in Atlanta and run SCLC. Baker agreed to remain until SCLC found an executive director.

From the start, there was tremendous tension between Baker and the black male ministers. She was relegated to performing mundane chores as the ministers ignored her vast organizational skills and her talent for institution building. Also her profound belief in the equality of women put her at odds with the sexist attitudes of the male ministers. Besides, her constitutional inability to show unprincipled deference and to become a "yes" woman made her tenure at SCLC rocky. Mainly Baker clashed with SCLC's cult of personality. The group was driven by an unshakable belief in the sort of religiously inspired leadership that emanates from gifted individuals at the top and trickles down to the waiting masses below. In a succinct comment that characterized Baker's clash with SCLC, leader C. T. Vivian said, "She wasn't church."

In sharp contrast to SCLC, Baker believed in group-centered leadership that enables individuals to identify their leadership talents and encourages ordinary people to perform extraordinary feats. Her belief in democratic leadership rubbed crudely against the hierarchical habits of black male ministers. She was extremely critical of King's leadership style, offending the taboo in most black religious circles against criticizing the leader—unless, of course, you were a male with some authority. Nevertheless, Baker was able to muster the SCLC's resources to encourage the youthful leadership of the civil rights movement that she glimpsed in student sit-ins across the South. Baker helped to organize the historic conference where the SNCC was launched. SNCC finally provided an organizational outlet for her ingenious gift of helping others help each other while nurturing their own leadership gifts. But Baker remained an acerbic critic of King's leadership, a trait that would be moderated and adopted in later years by their colleague, Bayard Rustin.

Baker and other black and white women faced in SNCC the same sexism that riddled older civil rights organizations. Although SNCC leaders were influenced by Baker's insistence on stimulating group leadership, they often resisted the leadership of women. True enough, Baker and legendary grass-roots activist Fannie Lou Hamer became identified with SNCC's political radicalism and its deft occupation of the movement's left wing. Hamer was a sharecropper and time keeper on a Mississippi plantation. She was severely physically abused for her heroic fight for freedom, especially when she lost her job after attempting to vote. Hamer served as field secretary of SNCC from 1963 to 1967. In 1964, when the Mississippi Democratic party rebuffed black participation, Hamer helped to form the Mississippi Freedom Democratic party, serving as its vice chair. She led a delegation of fellow Mississippians to the 1964 Democratic National Convention in Atlantic City, challenging the seats of the all-white Mississippi Democratic party delegation. As a result, she helped to extract an unprecedented pledge from the national Democratic party: that starting with its 1968 convention (in Chicago), it would not seat delegations to the national convention that excluded black members.

Despite the courage and vision shown by black female staffers, SNCC's gender politics were anything but democratic and just. At a staff retreat in Waveland, Mississippi, several position papers were presented. None was more explosive than a paper written by female staffers assailing the group for its pervasive sexual discrimination. The paper, presented anonymously at the time but later revealed to be the work of white female staffers Mary King and Casey Hayden, compared female oppression to black suffering. "Assumptions of male superiority are as widespread and deep rooted and every much as crippling to the woman as the assumptions of white supremacy are to the Negro," the paper maintained. It claimed that male members were "too threatened" to face their own sexism, while female members were "as unaware and insensitive as men, just as there are many Negroes who don't understand they are not free or who want to be part of white America." The authors argued that SNCC should "force the rest of the movement to stop the discrimination and start the slow process of changing values and ideas so that all of us gradually come to understand that this is no more a man's world than it is a white world." In response, the question was asked about the proper position of women in SNCC, to which Stokely Carmichael infamously and half-jokingly replied, "Prone." His answer outraged the female staffers and was immediately and widely repeated in feminist communities, causing Carmichael no little embarrassment. As Clayborne Carson notes, although "the paper on women effected no noticeable changes in SNCC's policies, it was an opening salvo of the feminist movement of the 1960's." (One effect noted by John Lewis, the Georgia congressman and once a courageous student activist and the former chair of SNCC, is that some of the women "staged what they called a 'pussy strike,' refusing to have sex with any of their boyfriends [or men] in the group until they were treated with more respect.") As Carson argues, Hayden and King, and "other women brought many of the values and tactics of the civil rights struggle into the nascent women's liberation movement."

Like his male colleagues, King's sexist beliefs were nurtured in a black religious culture that depended largely on the labor of poor and working-class and middle-class Southern black women. These women infused black culture with spiritual fire and moral imagination. They also placed their enormous skills and talents at the disposal of the movement. Then too, because providing civil rights workers with housing and food was viewed as threatening to the economic order, the skills of black female domestic workers were spotlighted and valued. Since many of the black women who attended church and supported the movement were employed by white people, their social rebellion in boycotts riled white landlords and housewives, making their actions that much more remarkable. And black Southern working women poured out stories of their trials and tribulations, as well as their small triumphs and quiet courage, inspiring their fellow participants in social change movements. Despite their extraordinary achievements and service to the church and the movement, these same women were denied leadership roles in either camp.

Equally disappointing, King's sexist beliefs prevented him from forging stronger connections with radical black women who were his great ideological allies in the struggle against economic oppression. For instance, King met in 1967 with several welfare activists from the NWRO, including Johnnie Tillmon, Beulah Sanders, and Etta Horn, to discuss the Poor People's Campaign. As Paula Giddings states, the NWRO "had actually come up with the idea of a poor people's campaign before King did," and they "were peeved when King started to beat that drum without even acknowledging their efforts—or their knowledge of the issue." Tillmon and her sister activists were outraged that the Poor People's Campaign had ignored welfare issues in their drive to dramatize the plight of the poor, and they called a meeting with King and his aides to question their actions. King responded, in part, because he needed the NWRO's connections to poor blacks: their organization in 1968 exceeded ten thousand members, with national chapters throughout the nation.

At their Chicago meeting, Andrew Young recalls that the women made King extremely uncomfortable and "jumped on Martin like no one ever had before." After introductions, King proceeded to give his take on the Poor People's Campaign and solicited their support. When Etta Horn, NWRO's first vice chairman, asked King his views on Public Law 90–248, he was dumbfounded. Johnnie Tillmon informed King that she "means the Anti-Welfare Bill, H.R. 12080," which had been passed by

Congress in December and signed into law by Lyndon Johnson in January. Tillmon then pointedly asked King, "Where were you . . . when we were down in Washington trying to get support for Senator Kennedy's amendments?" It quickly became apparent that King had no idea what they were talking about, and he, along with his staff, became quite defensive. "You know, Dr. King," Tillmon chimed in, "if you don't know about these questions, you should say you don't know, and then we could go on with the meeting." King finally confessed, "You're right, Mrs. Tillmon, we don't know anything about welfare. We are here to learn."

If King's relations with women in the movement were deeply flawed, his relationship with his wife underscored his patriarchal beliefs about marriage and women's roles. To be fair, there were areas of friction between King and Coretta that had nothing to do with his tradition-bound gender beliefs. For instance, King's philosophy of material sacrifice clashed with Coretta's understandable hunger for financial security. King's radical democratic philosophy of economics, his adoption of a nonviolent lifestyle, buttressed by his visit to India in 1959, and his theological beliefs about sharing and redistributing material resources led him to adopt a progressively simple lifestyle. King had already rejected his father's pro-capitalism, and according to Coretta, his progressive view of economic justice was apparent "when I first met him"; she insists that it "wasn't something that he learned later and developed." As she states:

> And he talked about working within the framework of democracy to move us toward a kind of socialism. I say this very advisedly because I think that people misunderstand the word "socialism," but in the sense that Martin used it—he said a kind of socialism has to be adopted by our system because the way it is, it's simply unjust. He looked at the poor and the fact that so many people were in ill health with no way for them to pay for their medical expenses. He asked, how do you catch up on all these things? There's got to be some kind of concern within the nation. . . . Now this was within the first month or so of our meeting.

When King's crew of graduate student friends met Coretta, many thought she was more formal than King's other girlfriends, and some of them even thought she was "bourgie," black shorthand for being refined and stiff in the face of "regular" black folk. The irony, of course, is that Coretta, the daughter of poor Alabama farmers, was denied the comfortable existence that King, by his own admission, enjoyed for the first twenty-six years of his life. King perhaps had the luxury of renouncing the material security that Coretta had never experienced. He took his radical democratic beliefs so much to heart that he increasingly shed himself of personal belongings and even felt uncomfortable owning a house. That explains why the King family lived in a rented home until 1965. King's aversion to private property was reinforced after his 1959 trip to India. Even after Coretta finally convinced him to buy a home, King was ashamed of what he felt were his prosperous appointments. But no one who saw King's home then or since could believe it was anything but a modest structure in a part of Atlanta that most folk with money avoided. As Andrew Young says, there was "nothing fashionable about his neighborhood, it was all but a slum." Moreover, Coretta could barely keep the children in adequate shoes and clothing. She was also anxious because she was left alone with the children most of the time as King traveled. She had not grown up in that neighborhood, and her experience of their house bombing had a lingering effect.

Aside from his theological convictions and economic philosophy, King's disdain for personal comfort drew from his enormous guilt in being featured as the premier leader of black America. King believed that others deserved praise for the movement's success—although it did not lead him to give black women their due. Undoubtedly King's strict fiscal self-discipline was another way to punish himself for what he felt was undeserved credit for sparking and sustaining the racial revolution. King was extraordinarily scrupulous about his personal finances. Incredibly, he gave the movement most of his income, including the more than $200,000 he earned in annual speaking fees. In fact, King kept only $4,000 of this money, gained no less at a time when, as Andrew Young says, "the huge speaking fees of today were unknown." That meant King gave over three hundred speeches a year to raise money for SCLC. He kept the few thousand dollars of his fees to supplement his copastor's salary of $6,000, an unprincely sum even in the sixties. King took no salary from SCLC, and his father, a board member, pleaded with the organization to provide life insurance for his son. King's habits rubbed Coretta the wrong way. They constantly quarreled about his financial choices.

Perhaps the most poignant instance of their disagreements about money involved the $54,000 King won in 1964 when he was awarded the Nobel Peace Prize. King believed that the prize recognized the movement's importance, not simply his individual leadership genius, and he decided to donate the entire purse to the civil rights movement: $12,000 to SCLC, $17,000 to the Council for United Civil Rights Leadership, and

$25,000 to a special fund associated with SCLC. King's decision greatly disappointed Coretta, who argued that they should set aside $20,000 for the education of their four children. Coretta's suggestion was a compromise of sorts, a way to bargain for the equally crushed Abernathys, who contended they deserved half the money since Ralph was equal partners with King. Such internecine squabbles marred King's trip to Oslo to receive his prize. On the trip, the Abernathys insisted that they be treated on par with the Kings. This petty bickering left King even more depressed than he had been when he set out for Scandinavia.

Money was not the only source of tension between King and Coretta. King had a rather narrow and typically sexist view of the wife's role in the family. As his aide Bernard Lee recalls, "Martin . . . was absolutely a male chauvinist. He believed that the wife should stay home and take care of the babies while he'd be out there in the streets." King's stubborn and hurtful gender beliefs are often obscured by the sunny descriptions of his decision on their first date that Coretta was the woman he wanted to marry. King's recall of their courtship and the rehashing of his seductive moves in countless biographies have enlarged his story into myth and solidly lodged his narrative in the annals of black romantic folklore. After getting Coretta's telephone number from a mutual friend, King called her to invite her on a date. Coretta was pursuing her graduate degree at the New England Conservatory of Music with an eye to concert performance. After a bit of chit-chat—Coretta remembers that King talked "very easily and smoothly" and that she had "never heard such talk in all my life"—King tried one of his lines on her.

"You know every Napoleon has his Waterloo," he offered. "I'm like Napoleon. I'm at my Waterloo, and I'm on my knees."

"That's absurd," Coretta said, resisting his charm. "You don't even know me."

King persisted, and got Coretta to agree to a luncheon date the next day. As they talked, exchanging information about their backgrounds and laying out their career plans, Coretta overcame her initial concerns about King's short stature and his average looks, confessing that as he spoke, his eloquence and charm made him "grow in stature" and made him become "increasingly better-looking." Obviously King was equally impressed, for when he drove her back to the conservatory, he surprised her with his serious comments.

"Do you know something?" King offered after he suddenly became very quiet.

"What is that?" Coretta asked.

"You have everything I have ever wanted in a wife," he said with quiet intensity. "There are only four things, and you have them all."

Coretta was "flurried." "I don't see how you can say that," she responded. "You don't even know me."

"Yes, I can tell," King replied. "The four things that I look for in a wife are character, intelligence, personality, and beauty. And you have them all. I want to see you again. When can I?"

Coretta said she'd have to check her schedule and asked him to call her later.

King made a powerful impression on Coretta. When he called the next day to invite her to a weekend party, she readily consented. A glimpse of his views on women flashed when King exulted in the women who swooned over him when they arrived at the party.

"He was always popular with the girls," Coretta recalls, "and was completely relaxed and free and unself-conscious." But Coretta's comment about King's explanation to her of the reason for his popularity is telling.

"You know women are hero-worshippers," King explained. It may indeed explain King's easy exploitation, even then, of the shortage of educated black males and his manipulation of his charm as a leader, and eventual hero, to his erotic advantage.

As King pursued Coretta and as she fell for King, there was a major obstacle: her planned career as a concert singer. After King made it clear that Coretta was his choice of mates—King was consciously seeking marriage and was weighing Coretta's candidacy against that of other women, making their courtship, as Taylor Branch terms it, "an odd mixture of romance and pragmatism"—he was concerned about her ambition. King glowingly recalled that "the first discussion we had was about the question of racial and economic injustice and the question of peace. She had been actively engaged in movements dealing with these problems." Moreover, King claimed that he "didn't want a wife I couldn't communicate with" and sought a mate "as dedicated as I was." Yet he wanted to restrict her expertise to the domestic domain, propping him up when he needed help and giving him advice when he sought it. Coretta's resourceful knowledge and her commitments to peace and justice would be used to mostly sharpen the thought and buttress the activity of her husband.

"Martin had, all through his life, an ambivalent attitude toward the role of women," Coretta says. "On the one hand, he believed that women are just as intelligent and capable as men and that they should hold positions of authority and influence." King, of course, was more than willing to make an exception in his own case.

"But when it came to his own situation," she recalls, "he thought in terms of his wife being a homemaker and a mother for his children. He was very definite that he would expect whoever he married to be home waiting for him."

Coretta prayed to God, consulted her sister Edythe, thoroughly analyzed her situation, met King's family, and decided to change her plans. After all, her sister reminded her "how difficult it is to find a stable, intelligent, dedicated man." So Coretta switched her major at the conservatory from performing arts to musical education with a voice major, believing that she could teach wherever they chose to live. But even after she made such a huge concession, King would later thwart Coretta's modest teaching ambition with an all-or-nothing insistence of her dedication to the home. Having made her decision, Coretta says that she would adjust to King's career, and that in their marriage, "there was never a moment that I wanted to be anything but the wife of Martin Luther King."

Although no one can challenge Coretta's claim that no matter what, she always wanted to be King's wife, it seems that she did want a lot more than simply being his wife. Coretta says that the "amazing and wonderful and terrible things that came later in our lives created no problems between us," but that seems to be untrue. How could it have been otherwise? The pressures of a movement that neither King nor Coretta could have anticipated would change their lives so dramatically bore in on them with merciless force and speed. And the aim of a racist society to put down the rebellion of blacks that King brilliantly symbolized meant that they were constantly shadowed by the fear that King's life would likely be snuffed out before he reached old age. While her husband dreamed of a brighter future for their children, Coretta had a recurring nightmare in which her husband was killed. And neither could she really console him when he bluntly confronted the probability of his own premature demise. When John Kennedy was shot in Dallas, King viewed the news on television with Coretta. She reports that when it was announced that Kennedy was dead, King grew quiet. Finally he spoke.

"This is what is going to happen to me also," King somberly stated. "I keep telling you, this is a sick society." One can feel the heartbreak and horror that grasped Coretta when she admits to herself that her husband had spoken the truth.

"I was not able to say anything," she confessed. "I had no word to comfort my husband. I could not say, 'It won't happen to you.' I felt he was right. It was a painfully agonizing silence. I moved closer to him and gripped his hand in mine."

These pressures exacerbated the damaging effect of King's rigid rules of homemaking for Coretta. Movement pressures also undoubtedly robbed King of any inclination to figure out a way to make his marriage as meaningful and satisfying as possible for them both. An early sign of Coretta's chafing under the marital harness came when she demanded that Martin Luther King, Sr., known affectionately as Daddy King, strike the obedience clause from their vows before he officiated at their wedding ceremony. Although Coretta maintains that King "allowed me to be myself and that meant that I always expressed my views" and that he "always sought my views because he valued them and so I felt an equal to Martin," it seems clear that King sought to contain his wife in a velvet cage of domesticity, even as he escaped the demands of home life in service to his race and nation. In 1960, *Life* magazine profiled King and also spoke with Coretta. Already she noted that her husband's work "takes a toll on the family. We like to read and listen to music, but we don't have time for it. We can't sit down to supper without somebody coming to the door." Of course, Coretta knew that her husband on another occasion had lamented the "frustrating aspects" of leadership that deprived him of time with his family. "It's just impossible to carry out the responsibilities of a father and husband when you have these kinds of demands," King stated. "But fortunately I have a most understanding wife who has tried to explain to the children why I have to be absent so much." If she was able to explain King's extended absences to the children, Coretta was increasingly incapable of explaining them to herself. As Andrew Young recalls of King and Coretta, it was "with great difficulty that he kept her in the house. He insisted both of them couldn't be gone all the time."

King was largely successful in suppressing Coretta's public activity, but it came at a great price. Coretta became increasingly angry at King for his absentee parenting and his haphazard husbanding. It is not that she did not understand the impossible task her husband faced in giving his life to a movement that was jealous of any moment of respite from its agitated center. Neither did she seek the pampering of a prima-donna, beyond the normal affectations of "first ladies" in the church or in the civil rights movement. She simply wanted to share her gifts with the movement—not only her singing, which she did on occasion, but her determination to speak and rebel to enhance her people's quest for free-dom. Ideally, Coretta would do this while standing at "the side of a man who would change the course of the nation's history and have an impact upon the thought of Western civilization to the extent that the most renowned scholars still have not determined what that impact really is or will finally be." But King stubbornly insisted that she remain at home while he fought the forces of evil.

King's heavy outside involvement derailed his devotion to home mat-ters. When Coretta tried to involve King in the decision of what school his eldest daughter, Yoki, should attend to begin first grade, he was unin-terested. "I spoke to my husband about it," Coretta later remembered, "and he said he would leave it up to me because those were the things that I had to deal with and he was very busy and so on." Years later Yolanda recalled "a household where my mother basically called the shots because Daddy was away *so* often," and how her mother "was run-ning the house" and making "all the decisions" because her father "was not there to actively participate in those." Coretta's great unhappiness occasionally bled into print; she once told a reporter, "I've never been on the scene when we've marched. I'm usually at home, because my hus-band says, 'You have to take care of the children.'" On another occasion, King had promised to call home to check on his children's hospital visit to have their tonsils removed. King forgot, reminding Coretta of the painful gulf that continued to widen between her husband and his family. King even confessed in a 1965 sermon that his secretary had to remind him of Coretta's birthday and their wedding anniversary.

Perhaps one of the greatest blowups King and Coretta experienced was captured by the conscienceless snooping of the FBI. Their taps caught King and Coretta in full throttle as they thrashed one another in an ugly dispute. In part, their fight was fueled by the savage schedule he maintained and the threats of death under which he operated. It was also fed by the unforgiving demands of her restricted role. Usually Coretta kept a careful lid on her emotions, even when it came to King's neglect of his family. But in a Sunday telephone conversation in the middle of 1964, King and Coretta had it out. She was profoundly upset by King's extended absence from home. For his part, King had just been told of Klan death threats in his St. Augustine campaign in Florida. He had little tolerance for her uncharacteristically vehement criticism. Their anger boiled and splashed hurtfully on one another. They blamed each other for making the stress of the movement that much more unbearable.

Their argument left King even more exhausted and tense and undoubtedly sent Coretta further into despair about their failed emotional intimacy. Coretta later remarked in the *Baltimore Sun*, "Every now and then he gets peeved and I get peeved. He can shout. Every now and then he'll blow up." But this was not King's normal pattern of response. As Coretta confessed to the *Arkansas Gazette*, "When we get in an argument, usually he just stops talking."

King may have stopped talking to Coretta, but he talked with many other women, sharing with them as well his libido, and sometimes his affection. King's chronic womanizing was a complex affair that allowed him at once to reinforce his ministerial machismo, satisfy his lust, assuage his loneliness, temper his fear of death, provisionally escape his burden of racial representation, and reduce his anxieties. All the while, Coretta insists that she never had a conversation with King about his alleged philandering:

> During our whole marriage we never had one single serious discussion about either of us being involved with another person. . . . If I ever had any suspicions . . . I never would have even mentioned them to Martin. I just wouldn't have burdened him with anything so trivial . . . all that other business just didn't have a place in the very high-level relationship we enjoyed.

This may be hard to believe, but it is made more credible by Coretta's having spared King as much as she could the burden of rearing their children. It is also supported by her worried telephone calls with her husband's associates about his growing depression and mental weariness. Perhaps her pleas for King to return home were a way of acknowledging the probability, maybe even the inevitability, of his frantic infidelities while sparing herself the torture that actual knowledge would bring. Until Coretta Scott King speaks in greater detail about how she coped, we may be held in tantalizing mystery or tempted to overinterpret her assertion that she and her husband never had "one single discussion about *either of us* being involved with another person."

A pivotal moment in King's and Coretta's relationship occurred when the FBI sent King a cut-and-spliced tape-recording that allegedly captured King on several occasions in sexual trysts with numerous women. The thin box package had been anonymously mailed from Miami to SCLC headquarters before King and his entourage headed to Oslo to collect his Nobel Peace Prize in December 1964. Now, in early January, the package had been shipped with other mail to the King household, where Coretta retrieved it. Thinking it contained a recording of one of her husband's speeches, Coretta discovered her mistake when she opened the package, listened to a brief portion of the reel of tape, and immediately called King. The recording was accompanied by a vicious letter encouraging King to kill himself since his sexual exploits and moral decadence were about to be exposed. In the presence of Young, Abernathy, Joseph Lowery, and Coretta, King played the tape. This episode would lead to a meeting between King and Hoover, and their aides, at FBI headquarters. On the home front, Coretta humorously brushed the tape aside, saying, "I couldn't make much out of it, it was just a lot of mumbo jumbo." Ralph Abernathy claimed that "such accusations never seemed to touch her. She rose above all the petty attempts to damage their marriage by refusing to even entertain such thoughts." But she probably heard more than enough to identify her husband's voice and detect his familiar moans of sexual ecstasy. How painful it must have been to imagine King enthralled in erotic entanglements as he increasingly withdrew his body and, it appears, parts of his soul from her. Besides his many casual carnal connections, King had established relationships of significant affection with three women. One of the women, in fact, had become King's de facto wife, a spousal equivalent upon whom he became emotionally dependent as she replaced Coretta as the primary focus of her husband's intimacy and affection. The government's unseemly role in sinking King's relationship with his wife fused with King's patriarchal beliefs to twist his marriage into a caricature of domesticity.

But it was more difficult for Coretta to laugh off a visit by new SCLC executive director Bill Rutherford and King confidant Chauncey Eskridge to her home, since King had often invited Rutherford to his house. When Rutherford greeted Coretta and asked her where Martin was, she replied that he was in a meeting at Bill Rutherford's house. Rutherford says he "gulped," and said, "'Oh yeah, sure, sure, that's right, but it wasn't a meeting I had to be in.' She looked with a very penetrating glance—looking right through me—and we changed the subject, and walked out. I could have died." Rutherford also claims of King, "That poor man was so harassed at home" and that one "cannot write about Dr. King without dealing with the reality." Rutherford says of King's wife in relation to staff members who bucked King's leadership: "She was as much a part of his depression as his staff. . . . Coretta was a part of the problem, but . . . also in many ways she probably was a much put-upon person." Of course, Rutherford and other aides recognized that Coretta's unhappiness with her husband's patriarchal posturing made his home life hell. One staff member ventured that had King lived, "the marriage wouldn't have survived, and everybody feels that way." Rutherford acknowledged that Coretta envisioned for herself a public role that King refused to accept. Another staffer summarized her fate: "Coretta King was most certainly a widow long before Dr. King died."

Since his death, Coretta has endured a stunning round of revelations and allegations about her husband's sexual escapades and intimate interactions. A former Kentucky state senator, Georgia Davis, wrote a memoir in 1995, *I Shared the Dream*, built around what she claims was an extended relationship with King. Davis defends her decision to tell her story by appealing to King's heroic stature: "If Dr. King had been an ordinary man, the telling of my story wouldn't make much difference." Davis says that King's extraordinary life will be studied "by scholars long after I'm gone," so she wants to set the record straight, since she has been written about by others, like Carl Rowan and Ralph Abernathy, who got the story wrong. "When Dr. King's life is researched," Davis writes, "I want the part relating to me to be available in my own words." Davis seems to lack a sense of irony or self-deprecating humor about her decision to unveil so private a part of her life and King's life as well. Before she wrote her book, Davis's story had not created a media stir, mandating that she get her side of the story in print. Neither had the exposure of her alleged secret love affair with King been so hotly debated that she had to step in to settle disputes about her actions. Abernathy, in his own memoir, never mentions her by name, saying only that on the last night of King's life, "a black woman" had come to visit him in Memphis, that they "had known each other before," and that their "relationship was a close one." On face value, Rowan's comments about Davis in his memoir are vague, and at their strongest, they may imply a tryst between King and Davis, but even that conclusion is open to interpretation. Rowan says that an account by Mrs. Davis given to the FBI, a report that Davis claims is fabricated, says that after King spent time with his brother A. D., and Mrs. Davis and Mrs. Ward, that he later "visited with Mrs. Davis for approximately one hour." Whether sex or other intimacies were involved is not clear. So a report that Davis claims is entirely made up is the only public witness to her presence at King's motel the night he was murdered. And Abernathy's discretion—an odd one indeed, since he was not nearly so discreet about his best friend, King—left us in the dark about the mystery woman.

Davis's claim that she wanted to set the record straight has the effect of creating a record out of obliqueness and discretion that bears no direct

testimony to her affair with King. She has created the very scenario she
claims to want to dispel. Perhaps another motive besides clarification is at
work. Perhaps it is to come clean about her former folly and confess her
sins. Perhaps it is a venal desire to reap financial reward from telling a sensational story about yet another King tryst. Perhaps it is to tie her life to
King's legacy and cement her place in history, despite her admirable
career as a public servant and politician, as one of King's many women,
or more precious still, one of his "special" women. Or perhaps she wants
to suggest that King was, after all, a man who needed love like any other
mortal. Maybe she just wants to tell the truth about her loving relationship with a great man. Or perhaps it is a complex combination of all of
these reasons. Whatever merits her book may have—shedding light on
King's mood near the end of his life, showing how gleeful he was to be
considered an author, displaying his love for his young brother, A.D., who
suffered in his older brother's shadow, revealing how predatory lust can
be moderated by human vulnerability, cataloguing the difficulties that
bright women have in being accepted in the black freedom struggle—are
overshadowed by the limiting premise of her book's appeal. After reading
the parts about King's interactions with her, readers may not want to stick
around to hear her own interesting and instructive story. While Davis may
not intend to one-up Coretta—or to fight with her, even posthumously, for
King's affection, a widow-competition, even widow-substitution, that
inscribes her name above his wife's in the eyes of those who may be per-
suaded by her testimony that King cheated as much out of hunger for affection as out of wanton lustfulness—the effect is the same.

In the light of what she has had to contend with, Coretta Scott King's
behavior since King's death, and perhaps the behavior of her children in
recent years, is more broadly illumined. Coretta surely protected her own
self-esteem, and that of her children, by publicly denying and avoiding
the truth of her husband's sexual and familial failures. In that way, she
also offered posthumous protection to her husband, despite the overwhelming evidence that he routinely cheated on her. But Coretta's
motives for such action are nearly as complex as her husband's reasons
for straying. Her love for her husband is abundantly apparent. Her care
for his unique place in history, as we shall later see, is iron-clad. Her faith
in his mission is unshakable. But she bears the burden of knowing, along
with the cruelly conflicting emotions of relief and guilt that such knowledge imposes, a harsh reality: his death gave her life. King on countless
occasions had bravely remarked that if he had to die, then nothing could
be more redemptive to the movement. But he certainly had not imagined

that his death would redeem his wife from the limits he placed on her while he lived. Coretta's forgiveness of King's sins—her utter denial that they even existed—is not only a gesture of her genuine unconditional love; it is also the predicate of her contemporary career as King's soulmate and surrogate. Despite King's emotional distancing and displacing of his wife, she has won public respect for her role as a leader in her own right, a role that her husband vigilantly prevented her from achieving. It is also ironic, and perhaps poetically just, that Coretta, *as King's widow*, should get from the public what King near the end of his life often denied her: genuine affection, and in some quarters, true devotion. Although Coretta is mocked as "My husband" behind her back, a nod to how she sows influence and opens doors with the magic wand of King's golden name, it is rather simplistic to berate her appeal to authority, even if it is a borrowed one, by neglecting how she came into her Martin Luther Kingdom to begin with. To twist the blues anthem against its gender bias, she paid the cost to be the boss.

Coretta has ingeniously transformed the boundaries of her former existence as solely a wife and mother into a celebration of her domestic duties now that she has, since her husband's death, been free to pursue public service and leadership. In this way, Coretta deflects the arrows of verbal assassination aimed at her husband by hypocritical enemies. Thus, she trumps the self-righteous ploys of critics who feign an understanding of her plight by using an alleged empathy to take vicious swipes at her husband's reputation. It may be argued that she is still in death tethered to King in an unhealthy manner—that she is posthumously codependent on an image that still binds and exploits her. Such an insight may carry metaphysical weight, but it evaporates in the face of the concrete war of position that Coretta Scott King has had to wage—whether lobbying the government to celebrate her husband's birthday as a national holiday or extending King's vision of racial justice in South Africa. If she is codependent, it is a genuine two-way street; Coretta has given as good as she has taken from King. She has provided for her children by providing for their father, and in turn, allowing him, posthumously, to finally, and forcefully, provide for them.

But she has also translated her yearning for the spotlight into substantive social action. On April 8, 1968, only four days after her husband's assassination and at the prodding of Harry Belafonte, Coretta and her children led the march her husband was to have guided in Memphis. She gave a keynote speech at the Cardozo High School Stadium in Washington, D.C., on May 12, 1968, to kick off the Poor People's Campaign. Most dramatically, in 1969, Coretta founded the Center for Nonviolent Social Change in Atlanta to honor the work and life of her husband, and as a vehicle to teach the principles of nonviolence that governed his life. Coretta emerged as a force to be reckoned with on her own terms, becoming a leader by performance more than by proxy, although, admittedly, her almost exclusive appeal to her husband's legacy has furthered her leadership ambitions. Still, she has carved out a niche of public service that must be judged on its own merits. In a poll of the attendees of the 1995 Million Man March, Coretta polled a 34 percent acceptance rate as a black leader. In the seventies, and early eighties, Coretta gave speeches, wrote nationally syndicated news columns, and lobbied for her husband's birthday to become a national holiday. She also became a prominent anti-apartheid activist in the eighties, protesting South Africa's policies in demonstrations in Washington, D.C., and later traveled to the African nation to analyze apartheid up close. She used her influence to pressure Ronald Reagan to grant sanctions against Botha's despotic South African regime. Coretta did not restrict her interest to Capetown; in 1990 she traveled to Namibia, Zambia, and Zimbabwe and then met with recently freed political prisoner Nelson Mandela. Recently Coretta served as cochair of the Full Employment Action Council and regularly participated in the Black Leadership Forum. In 1995, with Coretta's full support, her youngest son, Dexter, succeeded her as the head of the Center for Nonviolent Social Change.

After being made marginal in the movement by her husband—its greatest, most enduring symbol—Coretta King has come into her own. To be sure, she has pegged her leadership on his ideals and pursued his principles of nonviolence and racial and economic justice with true devotion. Of course, inheriting the mantle of leadership from her husband, and now passing parts of that legacy along to her children has certainly led to serious mistakes by Coretta King and her family, issues I take up in Chapter 12. But having suffered the indignity of King's myriad infidelities and neglected domestic duties, she may feel that she can certainly gain from him in death what he failed to provide in life: a place in the spotlight and a useful role as a social servant. Martin Luther King's relation to his wife grew out of profound gender and sexual conflicts in American life that are reflected deep in black life. While he bravely sacrificed his life for his nation and his race, it came at great cost to his wife and family. King neglected to learn from the heroic examples of brave black women leaders, and at points it certainly hampered his leadership in the civil rights movement. King also failed to free himself or his wife from the binds of patriarchal beliefs about female roles. His wife paid dearly, but so did King in the diminished intimacy that might have been replenished had he torn loose from his punishing presumptions about women. In the end, King and Coretta, like all other married couples, had legitimate reasons to resent one another, even as they had powerful reasons to support one another and stay together despite the storms they weathered. We will never know if their marriage would have survived had King lived. But we do know that Coretta Scott King has entered a domain of opportunity for public service that has given her the chance to reclaim the beautiful and edifying dimensions of her union with Martin Luther King.

If King's identity is much more complex than we have up to this time allowed for, his image is even more a cultural and racial battlefield where competing visions of King's career are vigorously contested. King's religious beliefs were certainly at odds with elements of his sex life and his writing practices. But they also bolstered King in the midst of his moral failings as he kept his eyes on the ultimate prize of justice despite his dramatic surrenders to temptations of the flesh and pen. We have been less successful in maintaining our cultural focus on King's real significance. We have too often failed to keep the powerful forces of historical amnesia from purging King's challenging meanings from his public image. The battle over King's image is really a struggle over memory and metamorphosis—over how we will remember King's discomforting past and what continually changing uses we will make of his memory in the future. Whether involving his image as a patriot (or traitor), a meritocrat, a saint, or an icon, King has been fashioned to calm rather than trouble the waters of social conscience in the post–civil rights era. But he was no Safe Negro. His image has too often been used to repudiate the very ideas for which he gave his life. If we are to comprehend fully King's orbit into the outer spaces of cultural influence, we must first test the gravity of cultural images that keep him bound to puny, parochial, and perverse visions of his true meaning.

Part III
Image

CHAPTER 11

"Be True to What You Said on Paper"
A Critical Patriotism

It was a brief but telling moment, one of those almost happenstance occurrences that reveals a far greater subterranean fury than what shows above the surface. In November 1983, President Ronald Reagan was set to sign the legislation making Martin Luther King, Jr.'s birthday an official holiday. Reagan had vehemently opposed civil rights. In 1964, as a private citizen, he supported Proposition 14, a statewide ballot initiative in California to repeal the 1963 fair housing law. In 1982, as president, Reagan restored federal tax exemptions for segregated private schools that had been ended by Richard Nixon in 1970. And between 1981 and 1985, he reduced the number of lawyers in the Justice Department's Civil Rights Division from 210 to 57. But now he was forced to co-sign a movement that he despised by supporting a law to fête its most heralded champion. It was a delicious sight for ardent King supporters who had almost helplessly witnessed Reagan's heartless dismantling of the gains that King had given his life to preserve. Reagan gave the requisite presidential remarks in support of King's ideas.

"Traces of bigotry still mar America," he proclaimed. "So each year on Martin Luther King Day, let us not only recall Dr. King but rededicate ourselves to the commandments he believed in and sought to live every day: 'Thou shalt love thy God with all thy heart and thou shall love thy neighbor as thyself.'"

That is about as bland an endorsement as possible of the revolutionary ideas that had made Reagan recoil, seeking refuge in a blistering conservatism that had little sympathy for blacks. Now, against his will, he affixed his signature to a bill that would honor a man who was his bitter ideological enemy.

Although he praised King greatly in his formal statement at the White House's Rose garden, Reagan had already gotten in a final dig that briefly opened onto the disdain he held for the fallen American hero. At an October press conference, when asked a question about King's alleged communist politics, Reagan responded with the wise-cracking, "We'll know in about 35 years, won't we?" He was referring to the FBI surveillance of King that was sealed until 2027 according to a 1977 federal court ruling. But Reagan had been hoodwinked by Jesse Helms. The sealed surveillance of King is about sexual matters. All the relevant FBI files on King's political beliefs are available. They don't substantiate Helms's charges or Reagan's suspicions. Although Reagan called King's widow, Coretta Scott King, to apologize for his remarks, his insincerity was quickly exposed. Former New Hampshire governor Meldrim Thomson revealed that Reagan had written him about King's character and political affiliations, confiding that he had "the same reservations you have."

It seems strange and not a little ironic that Martin Luther King, Jr.'s loyalty to America should ever be questioned. After all, King belongs to the heroic pantheon of martyrs who fell during America's Second Revolution, the bitter and often bloody war to end American apartheid and to invite black people into the sanctified arena of full citizenship. King displayed his patriotism in countless gestures of dramatic courage. His was a patriotism of flesh and blood, born of the holy obligation to provide a bridge over which the words of democracy might march from parchment to pavement. His most enduring trophies were the calluses he gathered from marching for justice in merciless heat and the sore knees he gained from bending to pray for enemies he defiantly loved. As King marched and prayed, he willed into existence—even, finally, in the hearts of many of his fiercest opponents—a view of our nation that was counterintuitive: America's revolutionary birthright could be extended by those black sons and daughters it had treated as orphans. King relished the irony of such an achievement. It was one of the singular benefits of the black investment in what the Bible terms "hope against hope." King's version of love of country was certainly challenging. It drew a contrast between belief in the strange providence of God, which is often disguised in unpredictable events, and the idolatry of nation that is a damaging counterfeit of true patriotism. King understood that authentic patriotism depends on telling the truth about the nation in an effort to help it achieve its highest destiny.

Yet the radical right has attempted to portray King as an enemy of liberty and democracy almost from the time he was propelled into our nation's racial vortex in the mid-fifties. Although fringe extremists certainly don't dominate the war of interpretation over King's legacy, they have helped to taint the perception of King's commitment to his country. The radical right—composed over time of Southern segregationists, extreme political conservatives, unrestrained governmental agents, and even antistatist rebel "patriots" who bomb federal buildings—has consistently ridiculed King's efforts to make democracy work for all of the nation's citizens. Much of the anecdote and folklore that fuel King's image as an unpatriotic American draws from the FBI's atrocious assault on King's reputation at the height of the civil rights movement in the sixties. Under the ruthless rule of J. Edgar Hoover, the FBI haunted, and in some cases persecuted, those it considered dangerous black leaders. The list ranged from W.E.B. Du Bois and Paul Robeson to Martin Luther King, Jr., and Malcolm X. Besides the intrinsic fear that black rebellion to white authority evoked in millions of white Americans in the fifties and sixties, the red scare seized the political horizon and exacerbated tensions between progressives and conservatives. The Soviet Union's challenge to America's emergence as the dominant world power produced the cold war. Joseph McCarthy became the cold war's most searing symbol in conducting a phobic and crazed witch-hunt for suspected or certified communists. If the civil rights universe was caught in McCarthy's anti-communist orbit, Hoover was the destructive meteor that rocked their world. McCarthy's House Un-American Activities Committee (HUAC) certainly undermined civil liberties and induced fear and paranoia, even in the civil rights community. But Hoover had a more damaging effect: his FBI used repressive tactics, including personal intimidation, libelous press leaks, and illegal microphone plants, to conspire against alleged conspirers. King became Hoover's most hated and harassed victim.

In the beginning, King did not attract much notice from the FBI. A petition he signed urging clemency for Carl Braden, imprisoned for contempt of court due to his refusal to testify before the HUAC, drew little response. Neither was the FBI riled by King's nominal support for the Committee to Secure Justice for Morton Sobell, who was convicted of espionage along with the Rosenbergs in 1953. The FBI wrote off King's patronage as a naive response to a call for help from an organization that was in truth a communist front, never really fearing that King had communist ties. And no one in the FBI attributed any conspiracy to well-known black communist Benjamin Davis's donation of blood to King when he was stabbed in Harlem in 1958 by Izola Ware Curry, a demented black woman. The FBI became more suspicious of King when he criticized the bureau in an article he penned for the left-liberal magazine *The Nation* in 1961. But with the FBI's discovery in 1962 that New York lawyer

Stanley Levison had been a close aide to King for nearly six years, their pursuit of the civil rights leader roared to full blast. The FBI believed that Levison was a communist in the early fifties who "severed" ties with the Communist party USA (CPUSA), only to join King's movement in 1956, at the prodding, the bureau contended, of the CPUSA. The FBI maintained that Levison's influence was the ideological hinge on which the CPUSA swung King's SCLC to the poisonous precincts of Soviet sympathy.

After Hoover leaked his alleged findings to the Kennedy brothers— first to the attorney general, Robert, and then to the president, John— they both warned King of the danger of his intimate association with Levison and another King aide, Hunter Pitts "Jack" O'Dell, a staff member in the SCLC's New York office. The Kennedys feared that King's contact with communists would threaten the civil rights legislation that President Kennedy had sent to Congress in 1963. King was aware of O'Dell's Communist party activity in the fifties, but stated that "no matter what a man was, if he could stand up now and say he is not connected [to the Communist party], then as far as I'm concerned, he is eligible to work for me." King eventually made O'Dell his executive assistant. The Kennedys' warnings were followed by an FBI leak trumpeting O'Dell's communist past. For strategic advantage and public relations, King was forced to accept O'Dell's resignation from the SCLC, declaring his organization's opposition to communism's "crippling totalitarianism." Levison, on the other hand, continued to deny any involvement in the Communist party, even after King's assassination. Indeed, despite Levison's association with several members of the Communist party, there was never any proof that he actually joined the organization. Later, however, he too was forced to disassociate himself publicly from King and the SCLC. But as the FBI discovered, he continued to provide King advice and guidance through their mutual friend Clarence Jones, the head of the Gandhi Society for Human Rights, a fund-raising arm of the SCLC. The FBI suspected Jones of being a communist because of his leadership in the Labor Youth League in the mid-fifties, where he had, according to the FBI, "denounced the State Dept. ban on travel behind [the] iron curtain in May '52." Eventually the FBI sought and gained the reluctant approval of Robert Kennedy to wiretap King's office and home telephones. Levison's office and home telephones had already been tapped. The FBI never acquired any damaging evidence of King's alleged communist affiliations. Instead, through illegal surveillance of King's hotel rooms, the FBI gained unexpected booty: knowledge of King's extramarital affairs, a knowledge that Hoover recklessly wielded in seeking to undermine King's leadership.

After King's death in 1968, the radical right revived the belief that King's organization was little more than a communist front. The John Birch Society, founded in 1959 to defend extreme conservatism, argued through its major ideologues, including Robert Welch, Dan Smoot, and Alan Stang, that King's aim in protests and civil disobedience was, contrary to his nonviolent rhetoric, the violent overthrow of the American government. King's ultimate purpose, they contended, was not black advancement but communist revolution. They pointed to King's association with alleged communists Carl and Ann Braden, Jack O'Dell, and Bayard Rustin, architect of the 1963 March on Washington, as solid proof that King took his marching orders—all the way from Montgomery to Memphis—from Moscow. In *It's Very Simple: The True Story of Civil Rights*, the Birch Society's bible on civil rights, Alan Stang wrote that King sought communist collaboration and communist advice. Dan Smoot praised Alabama governor George Wallace for his actions to maintain peace amid King's calculated violence through his nonviolent protests in Birmingham. In the aftermath of the racist bombing of a Birmingham church that killed four black girls, Smoot proclaimed that "King's 'non-violent' agitation triggered violence which brought death to five children and one adult in Alabama during 1963." And Scott Stanley, Jr., wrote in 1965 that King's march to Selma "was obviously about revolution. It was in fact about Communist Revolution." Perhaps the most intriguing claim of all is that King's death was ordered by the communists to create greater sympathy for their cause. Writing in 1968, Alan Stang warned the radical right that this is why "we must continue telling the truth about Martin Luther King; not for revenge, or just to destroy a phoney reputation, but because of the use to which his murder . . . is being put." Stang contends that while communists might refrain "from assassinating their enemies for fear of martyring them," they might "arrange assassinations that would create sympathy for something communists want." By murdering King, Stang writes, they could rehabilitate the reputation of a figure who had grown ineffective, make a strike against "white racism," and helped pass "Communist legislation."

The FBI and John Birch Society ruminations may sound far-fetched, but in many radical right circles, including those that spawn figures like Timothy McVeigh, they still carry significant weight. Beyond that, their pernicious musings color the arguments of even right-wing politicians.

Predictably, in 1963, Mississippi governor Ross Barnett said that the civil rights movement was "part of the world Communist conspiracy to divide and conquer our country from within." And South Carolina senator Strom Thurmond the same year declared that "there is some Communist conspiracy behind the movement going on in this country." To his credit, twenty years later Thurmond endorsed the King holiday bill "out of respect for the important contributions of our minority citizens." But there would be no similar change of heart for rabid segregationist and Dixie loyalist Jesse Helms, North Carolina's symbolic beachhead of bigotry.

Helms objected to King's birthday's becoming a national holiday in 1983 because of King's sordid private life, because he was influenced by Soviet loyalists, and because his political beliefs were un-American. Helms contended that King "kept around him as his principal advisers and associates certain individuals who were taking their orders and direction from a foreign power." He also asserted that "King may have had an explicit but clandestine relationship with the Communist Party or its Agents to promote, through his own stature, not the civil rights of blacks or social justice and progress, but the totalitarian goals and ideology of Communism." Helms's beliefs partially parallel Alan Stang's contention fifteen years earlier that "King has no real interest in the real welfare of black—or white—Americans," except to trick "them both into civil war" and to lift "their money." And while most of the relevant FBI files on King were by then available, Helms argued in 1983 that all FBI surveillance on King should be released before the Senate voted on the King holiday. Helms contended that the items contained in that surveillance were crucial to proving his point about King's communist connections. But two different Ford administration Justice Department task forces reviewed the materials and concluded not only that they contained no evidence of King's communism but that they were "scurrilous" invasions of King's privacy. The allegations of King's communism reached, finally, to the highest office in our nation, when Reagan offered his ill-tempered remarks.

The truth is that the early public King was as much a knee-jerk reactionary to the alleged communist threat as many other Americans were during the fifties and sixties. His comments after the Jack O'Dell "resignation" bear this out. Apart from Paul Robeson, Benjamin Davis, and the latter-day W.E.B. Du Bois, it was rare in the fifties and early sixties to find black American leaders who endorsed communist ideology or even socialist politics. King was sorely compromised in his progressive thinking by the realpolitik of the civil rights movement. In order to fight the White Beast of racism, he had to agree to the hard line on the red scare.

In a 1965 interview in *Playboy Magazine*, King stated that there "are as many Communists in this freedom movement as there are Eskimos in Florida." But King moved toward a less reactionary view of communism. At the same time, he contended that capitalism was as much wrongly celebrated as communism was rightly opposed. King argued in a 1961 speech that "I think with all of the weakness and tragedies of communism, we find its greatest tragedy . . . under the philosophy that the end justifies the means that are used in the process." King went on to say that the student and nonviolent movement "would break with communism and any other system that would argue that the end justifies the means." It became increasingly clear to him, however, that capitalism too used its ends to justify its means. In his book, *"Where Do We Go from Here?"* King wrote that we must admit "that capitalism has often left a gulf between superfluous wealth and abject poverty" and that it "encourages a cutthroat competition and selfish ambition," while communism "reduces men to a cog in the wheel of the state." Even as King grew more politically radical, he never embraced communism. Still, he acknowledged that truth "is found neither in traditional capitalism nor in classical communism," that capitalism "fails to see the truth in collectivism," and that communism "fails to see the truth in individualism." For King, the "good and just society is neither the thesis of capitalism nor the antithesis of communism" but "a socially conscious democracy which reconciles the truths of individualism and collectivism."

A crucial component of King's patriotic vision was the appeal to religious faith and Christian beliefs to shape his critique of American society. For King, patriotism did not involve an uncritical celebration of American social and moral habits. He believed that true patriotism motivated citizens to work for social change through analyzing the shortcomings of our society and working to strengthen the nation's moral and political life. In King's thinking, authentic patriotism was expressed in the willingness to engage in unpopular forms of social action, especially edifying forms of nonviolent civil disobedience—including protests, rallies, marches, freedom rides, being jailed—in order to underscore the gulf between American ideals and their failure to be implemented in the social order. More crucial, a profound love of nation meant that citizens were willing to suffer for their beliefs in the social and political arena in order to compel the nation to behave according to the principles of freedom, justice, and equality embodied in the Declaration of Independence and the Constitution. For King, religious belief was a profound source of moral support for citizens who engaged in civil disobedience. By appealing to religious views of personal dignity, social justice, and corporate moral responsibility, King and his religious colleagues shaped their social protest with a view to bringing society into line with what they conceived to be the ideal expression of humanity: community.

Moreover, King believed that unjust laws must be broken in order to realize the ultimate goals of justice and equality for all citizens. Thus, civil disobedience was a challenge to those American legal and political practices that contradicted the ideals of life and liberty that undergird national self-identity. Civil disobedience was not a wanton disregard for law and order. But civil rights activists refused to elevate law and order above the social welfare of citizens—in this case, oppressed black citizens—whose citizenship rights were undermined by unjust laws (Jim Crow laws mandating segregation), and immoral social practices (unleashing fire hoses and police dogs on protesting citizens). Laws were meant to extend and preserve American ideals; they should not be seen as immutable features of the social order. In short, laws should serve social ideals and should not be idealized. Laws are means to social and political ends, not ends in themselves. This crucial distinction allowed King and his colleagues to appeal to their religious beliefs as the inspiration to change unjust laws and social practices. But they never sought to enshrine their faith in law. They simply sought religious support as they reshaped the social order by grounding their protest in the ideals expressed in those documents that are central to American life.

King conceived civil disobedience to be an important means by which patriotic American citizens—citizens who loved their country so much they were willing to shore up its strengths and remove its weaknesses—helped to correct the errors of our nation's social and political behavior. Civil disobedience was a way to suggest to the country that it had taken the wrong path in its effort to expand citizenship opportunities for all Americans. As such, civil disobedience was a hopeful social practice; underpinning its expression in the social order was the belief that America was a nation worth fighting for, that it was a nation whose social ideals should be preserved and promoted even if its unjust practices should be discarded. For King, even the aggressive civil disobedience he advocated near the end of his career had the goal of restoring to American social life a regard for civic equality and radical democracy that animated the founding fathers to establish the nation.

Given King's conception of nonviolence civil disobedience, true Americans were those who were willing to work to change unjust law in order to defend the democracy that law should serve. The distinction

between just and unjust laws was a way to distinguish between a healthy
regard for legal processes that embody precious American ideals and an
unhealthy preoccupation with legal processes that undercut those ideals.
For King, religion was a way to make such a distinction. God stands
behind the quest for just law as the expression of the divine will in political community. King argued that a

> just law is a law that squares with a moral law. It is a law that
> squares with that which is right, so that any law that uplifts
> human personality is a just law. Whereas that law which is out of
> harmony with the moral law is a law which does not square with
> the moral law of the universe. It does not square with the law of
> God, so for that reason it is unjust and any law that degrades the
> human personality is an unjust law.

King realized that the appeal to moral law as the grounds for civil disobedience would not necessarily convince those for whom such an ideal
was hopelessly abstract. He also understood that religious belief, while
sufficient for people of faith, might be conceived as an untenable source
of social reform. Thus he emphasized the need to translate religious
belief into political terms—majority versus minority, democratic versus
totalitarian, just versus unjust—that were rational even to those who
stood outside the circle of such beliefs. A common religious belief was
unnecessary to sustain a common political practice. King anticipated
such charges when he rhetorically imagined that

> somebody says that that does not mean anything to me; first, I
> don't believe in these abstract things called moral laws and I'm not
> too religious, so I don't believe in the law of God; you have to get
> a little more concrete, and more practical. What do you mean
> when you say that a law is unjust, and a law is just? Well . . . an
> unjust law is a code that the majority inflicts on the minority that
> is not binding on itself. So that this becomes difference made
> legal. . . . An unjust law is a code which the majority inflicts upon
> the minority, which that minority had no part in enacting or cre-
> ating, because that minority had no right to vote in many stances,
> so that the legislative bodies that made these were not democrati-
> cally elected. . . . An unjust law is a law that individuals did not
> have a part in creating or enacting because they were denied the
> right to vote.

King not only argued that those who subscribed to a belief in a moral law that trumped unjust man-made laws must be willing to translate their beliefs into political language. He also suggested that such citizens were authentic patriots whose civil disobedience was not intended to be anarchic, as some charged, but to preserve the social order by making it more just. Those who had unjust law on their side, or who appealed to immoral social codes to justify their political practices, were the real antipatriots and anarchists. Such figures were the greatest threat to American democracy. King contended that

> individuals who stand up on the basis of civil disobedience realize that they are following something that says that there are just laws and there are unjust laws. Now, they are not anarchists. They believe that there are laws which must be followed; they do not seek to defy the law, they do not seek to evade the law. For many individuals who would call themselves segregationists and who would hold on to segregation at any cost seek to defy the law, they seek to evade the law, and the process can lead on into anarchy. They seek in the final analysis to follow a way of uncivil disobedience, not civil disobedience. And I submit that the individual who disobeys the law, whose conscience tells him it is unjust and who is willing to accept the penalty by staying in jail until that law is altered, is expressing at the moment the very highest respect for law.

In the final analysis, King argued that those who practiced civil disobedience were superior citizens because they were willing to suffer for their beliefs by submitting to legal punishment for breaking bad laws. Civil rights activists helped to bring about just laws by drawing attention to the harmful consequences of unjust laws.

What is especially intriguing, and more than a little disturbing, is how King's patriotic example of religiously based political activism and civil disobedience has recently been co-opted and sometimes twisted in the grasp of the religious and militant right. In the mid-1990s, Ralph Reed, executive director of the Christian Coalition, a predominantly white group of conservative evangelicals founded by religious broadcaster Pat Robertson in 1989, appealed to King's fearless fusion of religion and politics to justify his organization's patriotic vision of political activism. Reed criticized liberals who issued dire warnings about the "improper" use of religion in national politics now that the most politically active people of faith are largely conservative. Reed contended that liberal critics ignored the religious inspiration behind such political forces as abolitionism in the 1830s and the antiwar and civil rights movements under the leadership of Martin Luther King, Jr., in the 1960s. But with the swing toward conservatism, Reed argued, liberal critics demonized conservative figures who sought to bridge faith into the domain of politics with a view to reshaping American social practice.

Reed and the Christian Coalition raised even more eyebrows—and suspicion—when it attempted to enhance its image and broaden its appeal by courting blacks and Latinos. Both groups had been previously neglected in the legislative action and political purview of the conservative organization. Sandwiched between black and Latino clergy at a January 1997 press conference announcing the initiative, Reed quoted Martin Luther King, Jr., in pledging to make racial reconciliation the "centerpiece" of the Christian Coalition's legislative agenda. The Christian Coalition's program of outreach to racial and ethnic minorities, named the "Samaritan Project," included urging Congress to pass bills offering scholarships, tax credits, urban empowerment zones, and other action geared to developing poor black and Latino communities.

The Christian Coalition also aimed to improve poor black and Latino communities through measures designed to enhance education, lower inner-city crime, and reduce minority unemployment. "For too long our movement has been primarily—and frankly almost exclusively—a white, evangelical, Republican movement, whose political center of gravity focused on the safety of the suburbs," Reed admitted. "The Samaritan Project is a bold plan to break the color line and bridge the gap that separates white evangelicals and Roman Catholics from their Latino and African American brothers and sisters." Reed also indicated that his organization intended to ease racial tension by raising at least $10 million over a three-year period to be used by one thousand black and Latino inner-city churches in outreach ministries. Reed admitted that white evangelical Christians had too often focused on conservative social and moral values to the exclusion of issues that occupied blacks and Latinos. "If we went out and talked about abortion and divorce and the traditional family and didn't do anything about those left behind," Reed offered, "I think we would be open to a legitimate criticism by the left that we had blinders on." Those blinders began to fall off, he said, when a rash of church burnings consumed black houses of worship. As a result, the Christian Coalition raised funds to assist in the effort to rebuild burned churches.

The use of King to justify the Christian Coalition's appeal to blacks and Latinos, and the organization's aggressive outreach to minority communities after the widespread perception of its hostility to black interests, elicited skepticism from progressive black leaders. Laura W. Murphy, executive director of the American Civil Liberties Union's Washington office, argued that the Christian Coalition's agenda was "window dressing." Murphy also suggested that it was "conceivable that black leadership could be siphoned off by Ralph Reed because this is a very slick and sophisticated snow job. . . . But it's a Trojan horse." And Jesse Jackson accused Reed of attempting to extend his right-wing agenda.

Conservative black figures, however, embraced Reed's efforts. Black pastor Earl Jackson, who headed the coalition's burned-church assistance efforts, suggested that a summit of coalition leaders and black pastors in Atlanta underscored the common objectives of black and white Christians. "The moment was so pregnant with poignancy and emotion and connections between people," Jackson related, "that all that other stuff—conservative and liberal, Republican and Democrat—just dissipated. All that was left was human beings expressing deep concern for one another." Jackson said that it "was a kind of epiphany. There's no question in my mind that was a transforming moment." An equally enthusiastic if more hyperbolic black supporter suggested that Reed was the leader blacks were searching for, thus making him a possible successor to King. "We in the black community were looking for a leader to come from the black community," effused Lawrence F. Haygood, founder of a church-based community college in Tuskegee, Alabama. "But that leader didn't appear. *He appeared in a white form in the image of Ralph Reed.*"

Despite using King to reach out to blacks and Latinos, Reed sent a signal to his core constituency that the coalition was not surrendering its primary political objectives: opposing abortion, gambling, and a big-government response to social problems. But he reaffirmed the coalition's commitment to oppressed minorities. "This crisis of the soul presents us with the question that Martin Luther King called 'the most persistent and urgent question': What are you doing for others?" Reed asserted.

If Reed's appropriation of King to legitimate the Christian Coalition's conservative social agenda seems odd, it is a theme that Reed thoughtfully developed in his 1996 book, *Active Faith*. Reed confessed that

I draw much of much own inspiration from the example of Martin Luther King, Jr. He faced this difficult dilemma of balancing a movement's passionate faith with the requirements of political sophistication. His response varied, but one of the things he did say in no uncertain terms was that his must be a movement defined by love. . . . King and his army were able to move out in love, transforming the country and bringing to fruition the dreams of tens of millions of Americans—a transformation whose spirit has outlived both King and the movement he led. I am not comparing our movement to King's. . . . But we can seek to make this creed our own, and hope to wield a fraction of the influence that they had on the hearts of their fellow citizens.

If Reed has drawn inspiration from King's commitment to social transformation informed by love, the Christian Coalition's political agenda, and that of the religious right in general, has not often wrestled creatively or perhaps justly with the themes of racial and economic injustice that vexed King his entire career. Of course, Reed has conceded the point, but concession alone is an insufficient basis for shaping social policies that overcome both the history of the religious right's neglect of racial and economic justice and the barriers to full equality that remain for blacks and the poor. Neither will outreach to black and Latino churches sufficiently address the structural obstacles to equal opportunity that prevent the flourishing of millions of black and brown religious believers. While the coalition's goal of securing government-supported scholarships that would enable low-income students from the country's one hundred worst districts to attend private schools, a program with a $500 million annual price tag, is certainly enticing and potentially quite useful, it fails to address the bulk of poor black and brown children left behind by such measures. The devastating consequences of poor schooling on the employment opportunities and social well-being of minority children means that voucher programs may function as a tool of social selection: the gifted student will thrive; the marginal and the slow-to-develop student will be swept away by the undertow of frustrated scholarly ambition, social inequality, and limited economic mobility. In the end, the recent racial outreach proffered by the coalition may unintentionally be of greater benefit to those who serve the poor than the poor themselves. The coalition advocated a $500 tax credit for those who donate ten hours of volunteer time working for the poor and promoted state and federal tax breaks in empowerment zones in one hundred poor communities to stimulate the growth of new businesses.

Reed's appropriation of King is complicated by his use of the civil rights leader to support contradictory claims about King: that he acted outside the political arena and that his engaged faith led him to operate within political borders. The distinction is not just an academic one, but drives Reed's claim of the uniqueness of his own organization in the history of Christian involvement in politics. Reed argues that the Christian Coalition was

> founded upon the same religious principles that fueled those massive involvements of churches and synagogues, and of pastors, priests, and rabbis, in some of the greatest social reform movements in American history. For the most part, those movements existed outside the political mainstream and created pressure from without. Even Martin Luther King, Jr., spent most of his active years marching and demonstrating, not organizing precincts or electing politicians. The Christian Coalition . . . represents a new thing in American politics: the marriage of a sense of social justice with the practical world of modern politics. It has mainstreamed the voice of faith through its political effectiveness, challenging the political system to confront issues of moral and transcendent significance that might otherwise be ignored or swept aside by purely economic concerns.

By overlooking the rich history of black figures like Henry Highland Garnett, Adam Clayton Powell, William Gray, and Jesse Jackson who combined social justice, religious faith, and electoral politics, Reed makes claims for the uniqueness of the Christian Coalition that simply don't hold up. More relevant, Reed correctly asserts that King's activity was outside the realm of electoral politics. For Reed, that limits the political effectiveness of King's tradition of social activism because it had not "mainstreamed the voice of faith," and neither had it challenged "the political system to confront issues of moral and transcendent significance." But figures like Walter Fauntroy, Andrew Young, and John Lewis, all ministers and colleagues of King in the civil rights movement, have done just that as members of Congress. At the same time, Reed acknowledges that in the debate between a tradition of "self-help and education as the surest road out of poverty for blacks, versus the more radical and overtly political wing," that King "chose the more political route of protests, petitions, and marches." Reed quickly adds, however, that King "always acknowledged that hearts and souls could not be changed by ballots alone." Thus, when Reed is arguing for the distinctiveness of his organization's role in fusing faith and politics, King is viewed as less politically engaged than the coalition. But when Reed is making an argument for the uniting of cultural and political action—particularly in "the pro-family movement"—King is a crucial figure. For Reed to have it both ways, he must overlook King's moral complexity: his relentless judgment of politics through a religious lens and his constant willingness to view religious institutions critically through the prism of politics.

To be sure, Reed appreciates King's "indispensable" genius in providing "the vision and leadership that renewed and made crystal clear the vital connection between religion and politics." Reed also acknowledges that "King considered his duties as proselytizer and political player insep-arable." Further, Reed admits that the Christian Coalition "has adopted many elements of King's style and tactics." He argues that

> just as he spoke as a black man to a largely white society, we have tried as Christians to speak in a language that could be heard by a secular society. King used the church and the pulpit to give moral force to what was essentially a political movement. . . . Most impor-tant, King allied himself with the Democratic party in passing civil rights laws, while maintaining strong relationships with liberal Republicans like Nelson Rockefeller to give his movement a non-partisan cast. We have done the same by building alliances with . . . pro-life Democrats in the House of Representatives. . . . King's movement was a religious movement from the start. It influenced an entire generation of future leaders to view their religious beliefs as informing and shaping their political involvement.

What Reed seems to miss in his often perceptive analysis of King's uniting of faith and politics is King's insistence on the dialectical method in thought and social practice. King believed in the dynamic process of synthesizing conflicting, even contradictory, elements. In this case, it meant merging useful features of religious and secular thought in ana-lyzing social problems and in seeking to implement social change. Fur-ther, King was much more willing than Reed to use secular arguments to criticize religious parochialism and to appeal to non-Christian moral resources to judge the weaknesses and limitations of religious behavior. For instance, although he disagreed with Marxist materialism, he found certain elements of Marxism's economic critiques of capitalism quite insightful. And while Gandhi was not a Christian, King made skillful use of his views on nonviolence and mass civil disobedience. King was much more willing than Reed to indict the racial caste of modern Christen-dom, an insight that Reed and his compatriots have only recently begun to address. King's disappointment with white Christianity was rooted in its appeal to religious dogma to sanctify segregation and to legitimate bigotry. It will take much more than Reed and the radical right's appealing to King's moral example and political activism to eradicate the legacy of conservative white religious cooperation with racist oppression. And what must not be discounted is the severe price paid by civil rights activists for supporting the social truths they advocated. In our nation's profoundly conservative climate, the Christian Coalition's social agenda is much more widely embraced than was true of the civil rights revolution. The risks of faith incurred by black Christians who sought racial liberation in a political climate that frowned on their moral aspirations were immeasurably greater than those taken by the religious right. (Reed, to his credit says so.)

Further, the moral myopia of making one's positions on abortion the litmus test of authentic Christian identity—while slighting the crucial moral and social issues that afflict the vulnerable poor and oppressed—severely limits the possibility of forging connections among a broad range of believers, much less between all citizens of conscience. While Reed is right to point to King's appreciation for matters of the heart and spirit, King believed such matters only made sense in a world where the right to flourish was protected by the government and supported by a just social order. King was much more interested in a society where no form of bigotry would prevail—even a form of religious parochialism that might have supported his own beliefs. Unlike most religious conservatives, for instance, King opposed school prayer. When asked about the Supreme Court decision outlawing school prayer, King replied,

> I endorse it. I think it was correct. Contrary to what many have said, it sought to outlaw neither prayer nor belief in God. In a pluralistic society such as ours, who is to determine what prayer shall be spoken, and by whom? Legally, constitutionally or otherwise, the state certainly has no such right. I am strongly opposed to the efforts that have been made to nullify the decision. They have been motivated, I think, by little more than a wish to harass the Supreme Court. When I saw brother Wallace [Governor George Wallace] going up to Washington to testify against the decision at the congressional hearings, it only strengthened my conviction that the decision was right.

In the end, the religious right's appropriation of King will be incomplete until it is willing to advocate attacking systematic racial injustice through the compensatory measures favored by King; establishing economic justice through creating social programs that guard the social welfare of the poorest; and creating long-term prospects for social welfare through the restoration and strengthening of social programs aimed at protecting the family, including Head Start, youth-employment incentives, a raise in the minimum wage, universal health coverage, and widespread child care assistance.

If the Christian Coalition's efforts to use King to illumine their fusion of faith and politics is problematic, it is even more disturbing to witness figures in the radical antiabortion movement justify their militant resistance by appealing to King's example of civil disobedience. Leaders in Operation Rescue, a militant antiabortion group that blocks entry to abortion clinics, often cite Martin Luther King and the civil rights movement as an inspiration for their acts of civil disobedience. The group, which has the backing of televison evangelists Jerry Falwell and Pat Robertson, was founded in the late eighties by Randall Terry to dramatize the plight of the unborn and to focus critical social attention on abortions nationwide. Operation Rescue first gained prominence in 1988 for staging a series of blockades at abortion clinics in Atlanta, New York, and other cities around the country, where thousands were arrested. The organization also sponsored "a National Day of Rescue," consisting of sit-down protests in abortion clinics in thirty cities. All the while, activists draped themselves in "the rhetoric and tactics of the civil rights struggle."

When Operation Rescue founder Randall Terry went on trial in 1989 in Los Angeles for charges of trespassing and conspiracy during a blockade of a women's clinic, Terry compared himself to civil rights and feminist leaders who courageously confronted forces of oppression. He represented himself at his trial, as did two of his four other codefendants, and during the closing argument, he said that there were periods of history when blacks had to sit at the back of the bus and women could not vote. "But during these dark hours, there were people who stood up to the tyranny," Terry argued. "And what did these people have in common? Susan B. Anthony arrested, Rosa Parks arrested, Dr. King arrested. But being arrested is not a crime." At a 1989 California antiabortion rally held at a Baptist church just hours after four Operation Rescue members had been convicted and sentenced to jail for trespassing at a doctor's office in San Marcos, a spokeswoman for the organization argued that the people who jailed antiabortion activists would one day look as shameful as the people who jailed Martin Luther King, Jr.

Randall Terry says that his organization's "acts of civil disobedience, which we call rescues, are designed to save lives by preventing abortionists from entering their death chambers, and to dramatize for the American people the horrors of the abortion holocaust." Terry argues that antiabortion activists who are jailed and refuse to give their names to the courts "focus attention on the nameless victims of abortion." By blocking the entry to abortion clinics, Terry argues that Operation Rescue activists "seek to persuade the other victims of abortion, the mothers about to lose their children, to rethink their decision and choose life." Terry says that his organization is "committed to nonviolence of word and deed," and Operation Rescue activists "resist passively" and "treat policemen with respect." He writes that the rescue movement has been inspired by examples of civil disobedience "such as the Underground Railroad before the Civil War." He suggests that this "period of history is one of Christendom's great examples of sacrificial love and the need to obey God rather than men."

Perhaps the most controversial claim to inspiration made by the rescue movement involves the black freedom struggle of the late 1950s and early 1960s. Terry says that

> by enlisting the black church leadership and then mobilizing thousands of churchgoers, Dr. Martin Luther King, Jr. and other civil-rights leaders were able to overcome decades, if not centuries, of racial prejudice, and break the back of segregation and its unjust laws. . . . The peaceful, nonviolent, nonretaliatory suffering of the black civil-rights activists, many of them Christians, helped win the hearts of millions, and was the catalyst for the passage of the Civil Rights Act of 1964 and the Voting Rights Act of 1965. Blacks, willing to suffer and risk arrest in order to stand for what was right, created a tension in the nation that forced politicians to take action.

Terry is right to emphasize the nonviolent philosophy that the civil rights and rescue movements have in common, although extremists in the rescue movement have resorted to bombing abortion clinics and murdering doctors who perform abortions as a violent measure of deterrence. While it would be unfair to hold Operation Rescue directly responsible for actions its members did not participate in, it is fair to argue that the organization has helped to create a climate of fascist intolerance for opposing points of view in the abortion debate. While devotees of the civil rights movement were convinced of their moral rightness in the cause of black liberation, very few resorted to demonizing their opponents or to murder. Moreover, the near-fanatical devotion shown by adherents of the rescue movement makes the rational debate and compelling moral justification that almost always accompanied the civil disobedience of civil rights activists all too rare. "This is not a game," a southern California representative of Operation Rescue argued. "This is a life and death struggle. There is no place you can hide as a Christian and be left alone; they will come find you and seek to exterminate your Christianity." Not only did King relentlessly and patiently explain the purposes of the nonviolent civil disobedience he encouraged, but the reasoned passion of his rhetoric embodied the moral aims he sought to bring into existence.

There is a huge difference between the civil rights movement and the antiabortion rescue movement. Where the civil rights movement struggled to gain constitutional rights that were being unjustly denied to millions of black citizens, the antiabortion rescue movement aims to deny the constitutional rights of women to exercise reproductive choice. In such a light, the brand of civil disobedience practiced by the antiabortion rescue movement is morally flawed; it lacks a compelling ground of justification that respects the human dignity of its opponents. The civil rights movement sought during the fifties and sixties to achieve its goals while respecting the humanity of even its fiercest opponents. Many participants in the movement sought to spread love and refused to return evil for good. Many participants in the antiabortion rescue movement seek to impose moral sanctions on opponents—in this case, prolife advocates—while often demonizing them as the agents of moral evil and social harm.

The antiabortion rescue movement is also legally destructive. By attempting to prevent the equal application of law and constitutional right to one's opponent, the rescue movement subverts the profound respect for law that characterized civil rights activists. As King argued, the willingness to break an unjust law—and to suffer the consequences for such behavior—is the highest respect for law. Although the antiabortion rescue movement has shown a willingness to fill the jails to protest what it views as an unjust law, it has erred in resisting legitimate authority, refusing to go to prison willingly for infringing on the rights of others, a pillar of nonviolent civil disobedience. Finally, a crucial component of civil disobedience is the requirement of its adherents to break the law they deem unjust. That option appears unavailable to the antiabortion rescue movement. Hence, it is not only morally incoherent to equate the civil disobedience of the civil rights and antiabortion movements; it is technically and philosophically incorrect to apply civil disobedience to the actions of the rescue movement.

The appeal to Martin Luther King, Jr., by the religious and militant right often obscures the moral complexity and political ingenuity of the civil rights movement. King and his comrades sought to transform American society by inviting it to live up to its best destiny. King urged America to forsake the unjust social and legal practices that contradicted its own stated goals of granting equality, freedom, and justice to all of its citizens. Unlike the religious right, he fought for equality and justice in the face of massive resistance from the majority culture. And unlike the militant right, he sought to realize, not restrict, the constitutional rights of fellow citizens. His vision of civil disobedience is a glorious tribute to the American tradition of democracy.

If King's vison of civil disobedience had a peculiar American twist, he refused to subordinate his moral concern to narrow national interests. As he matured politically, he became resolutely international in thinking about social change. He increasingly linked domestic problems in American society, including racial oppression and economic exploitation, to their manifestation on foreign soil. King's encounters with African independence movements in the late fifties, for instance, deepened his understanding of the connection between European colonialism and American racial oppression. Further, he began to discern in African revolts against European domination a model for black American struggles against apartheid. King said in 1960 that one of the factors

that has accounted for the new sense of dignity on the part of the Negro has been the awareness that his struggle for freedom is a part of the worldwide struggle. He has watched developments in Asia and Africa with rapt attention. . . . For years they were exploited economically, dominated politically, segregated and humiliated by foreign powers. Thirty years ago there were only three independent countries in the whole of Africa—Liberia, Ethiopia, and South Africa. By 1962, there may be as many as thirty independent nations in Africa. These rapid changes have naturally influenced the thinking of the American Negro. He knows that his struggle for human dignity is not an isolated event.

At an SCLC African Freedom Dinner held in Atlanta in 1959 for Kenyan leader Tom Mboya, King reinforced his views about the link between African resistance to colonial domination and black resistance to segregation. "I am absolutely convinced," King told Mboya, "that there is no basic difference between colonialism and segregation. They are both based on a contempt for life, and a tragic doctrine of white supremacy. So our struggles are not only similar; they are in a real sense one." In fact, through his international lens King was able to view the striking differences between black American and African struggles for liberation, and he evoked Africa as a yardstick to measure American racial enlightenment. "The nations of Asia and Africa are moving with jetlike speed toward the goal of political independence, and we still creep at a horse and buggy pace toward the gaining of a cup of coffee at a lunch counter." King also became increasingly knowledgeable about the plight of blacks in South Africa, and especially after he received his Nobel Peace Prize in 1964, King became extremely critical of American foreign policy in Southern Africa. As Thomas Noer notes, King's social concern became more global in the early sixties, embracing not only Africa but other non-European countries as well:

> Aside from Africa, other issues most important in King's early dissent from American diplomacy were world poverty, nuclear weapons, and neutralism. King's visit in 1957 first shaped his view that poverty was the direct result of colonialism, and his trip to India in 1959 reaffirmed this judgment. King was overwhelmed by the misery he observed in India and outraged that wealthy nations allowed it to persist. He claimed that the former colonial powers and the United States had a moral obligation to share their wealth with the poor.

All of King's international concerns—colonialism, white supremacy, poverty, nuclear weapons, the failures of American diplomacy, and cold war ideology—blossomed in his criticism of the Vietnam War. His antiwar activism and critiques of American foreign policy in Vietnam were not only morally motivated, but they were rooted in King's understanding of the strong tie between American racism and Western colonialism. He saw Vietnam as a tragic metaphor of America's undisciplined imperialist impulses. For him to remain silent on Vietnam meant that he would have to remain silent about racial oppression closer to home. To his way of thinking, neither prospect was desirable or defensible.

In truth, King's international social vision was another way to render service to his country. His radical moral criticisms were motivated by one

overriding desire: to view human behavior in the light of religious principles that were politically expressed. Even as a radical democrat in his later
years, it is clear that Martin Luther King, Jr., loved America deeply and
courageously. More than J. Edgar Hoover or the John Birchers, King
served his nation with a view to loving it to its greatest stature, which
meant criticizing it when it was wrong so that it might grow in the right
direction. In fact, what King said about the John Birchers is true of much
of the rabid right: that they "thrive on sneer and smear, on the dissemination of half-truths and outright lies." King concluded that they "are a
very dangerous group—and they could become more dangerous if the
public doesn't reject the un-American travesty of patriotism that they
espouse." King's warning is still apt today.

King's most famous speech, delivered in 1963 on the steps of the Lincoln Memorial, forever etched into our collective consciousness his reverence for the vital meanings of the American dream. His voluptuous
phrases that day matched his keen appreciation for the beauty of America's physical landscape, an appreciation that served as a powerful
metaphor for the hallowed legacy of American democracy and freedom
that his speech sought to conjure majestically. This is why he could call
for freedom to ring "from the prodigious hilltops of New Hampshire,"
from the "mighty mountains of New York," and "from the curvaceous
slopes of California." Even before his legendary oration in 1963, King, in
a commencement address in 1961, evoked the American dream as the
sacred canvas on which the character of national destiny was colorfully
illustrated. Referring to the words of the Declaration of Independence,
he stated that very "seldom if ever in the history of the world has a
sociopolitical document expressed in such profoundly eloquent and
unequivocal language the dignity and the worth of human personality."
King went on to say that the "American dream reminds us that every man
is the heir to the legacy of worthiness." And in his famous "Letter from
Birmingham Jail," King spoke of how protesting blacks who "sat down at
lunch counters" were "in reality standing up for the best in the American
dream" and were "carrying our nation back to those great wells of
democracy which were dug deep by the founding Fathers in the formula-
tion of the Constitution and the Declaration of Independence."

In the best sense of the word, King was an American patriot. His was
a complex and vigorous patriotism—one of the head and heart. King's
loyalty to America persisted in the face of its bitter unfaithfulness to his
flesh and blood. King profoundly loved a country that despite his unerr-

ing fidelity, denied him and millions of other loyal blacks the right to exist on the same terms as white Americans. Still, his disappointment with America took the form of a lover's quarrel. Time and again, King proclaimed his love for his country by seeking to make it truly just, forcing it to take seriously the creeds by which it claimed to live, demanding that it "be true to what [it] said on paper." It was a patriotism of loyal opposition, a love of nation so enduring that King, when posing to himself the possibility of psychically or even physically removing himself from the source of his people's suffering, declared, "I'm not going anywhere." King's critical patriotism helps to explain why he could acknowledge that "America is essentially a dream" and in the same sentence conclude that it is "a dream as yet unfulfilled." In fact, King believed that those who heroically suffered America into its noblest expression of its ideals are the real patriots, "the true saviors of democracy." In this light, King's criticism of American racism or, for that matter, his reluctant but valiant criticism of America's participation in the war in Vietnam, grew from an undying hope that America could correct itself, or at least yield to the correction pointed to by its faithful critics.

Beyond his prophetic speech, King proved his tenacious fidelity to American ideals. Indeed, he choreographed his commitment to America in the ultimate act of sacrifice in the nation's war against its worst half and in defense of what Abraham Lincoln called "the better angels of our nature." When King's blood was spilled in Memphis in 1968, it stained the American conscience and rallied the American spirit like few other events in our nation's history. In fact, King's was a peculiarly American martyrdom. In a way no other public death has done—except, perhaps, Lincoln's—King's slaying simultaneously relieved and reinforced racial difference, illuminating a painful paradox of American race: that blacks must often be *rejected into* the American creed, that they are often included only after their alienation from America reveals America's alienation from its social ideals. Hence, race is often the vehicle of a clarifying crisis, a means of testing the mettle and malleability of national self-identity. Black America's racial revolution in the sixties gave flesh to a questioning, critical patriotism. King's assassination embodied his ultimate sacrifice for God, country, and race as he unified in death, if only for a moment of triumphant epiphany, what he had sought to bring together in life.

But if conservatives and the right wing have misused King's image, forces closer to home have also, even with good intention, hampered the quest for a fully accessible King. Coretta Scott King has admirably carried on King's legacy, shielding her husband from historical amnesia and making sure that the country honors his uniqueness and brilliance. But the King family's role in King's memory is a mixed one. Its role in promoting King's image is full of the same complex amalgam of high purpose, hidden heartbreak, and inevitable self-interest that often surround the contested legacies of the great.

CHAPTER 12

"I Won't Have Any Money to Leave Behind"
The Ownership of a Great Man

In the summer of 1991, I made my way to Memphis to attend the opening of the National Civil Rights Museum. The museum was literally carved out of the Lorraine Motel, on whose balcony King had been assassinated twenty-three years before. The motel had been one of the few places that accommodated black lodgers in 1968. Now, in 1991, only the facade remained as the motel was gutted and rebuilt to house the museum dedicated to documenting the civil rights struggle. Located on Mulberry Street, the motel had languished for years in the midst of dilapidated warehouses in a neighborhood jammed with prostitutes and drug dealers. White businesses and foundations had chipped in $1.3 million of the museum's $9.7 million price tag, with the rest of the funds coming from city, state, Shelby County, and various private donations. The museum wasn't quite ready to open on its scheduled date of July 4, 1991, but it still held celebrations starting on June 30.

As I wandered around the museum's 10,000 square feet, I caught a glimpse of the city bus imported from Montgomery that was similar to the one that Rosa Parks boarded in 1955, when she refused to surrender her seat to a white passenger and sparked the 381-day bus boycott. There was also space for a lunch counter like the one that students occupied as they led the sit-ins in the early sixties. Video screens would play footage of actual demonstrations behind the installments. But I was most intrigued by the restoration and preservation of the two rooms King rented as a base to lead the march for striking sanitation workers. One of the rooms had the original furniture arranged as it was on the evening of April 4, 1968, when King stepped onto the hotel balcony. I was saddened by seeing the reset bloodstained concrete slab where King had fallen when he was shot by James Earl Ray from a building across the street.

A citywide worship service to launch the week's activities was organized at Mason Temple, where King gave his last, immortal speech, "I See the Promised Land." Jesse Jackson, who along with Abernathy received King into his arms after he orated his last will and testament that night in Memphis, preached at the service. He spoke about the importance of the museum, comparing it to the liturgical seasons of suffering and celebration in the Christian calender.

"To not have this museum in Memphis would be like the Christians celebrating Christmas and never celebrating Easter," Jackson insisted to a thousand congregants.

"Memphis, his last sermon. Memphis, the vision of the mountaintop. Memphis, the last march. Memphis, the last interruption. Memphis, the last breath," Jackson rhythmically pounded out his point.

But the euphoria of the day's events was not universally shared. A former hotel employee and sixteen-year resident, Jacqueline Smith, who had been evicted in 1988, had camped out across the street from the hotel for three years to protest turning the Lorraine into a museum.

"These people are playing with history in order to make a buck," she said. "It should have been converted into housing for the poor, the homeless or the elderly. That's what we need in this neighborhood."

And Mohandas Gandhi's grandson, a journalist who was opening the Gandhi Institute for the Study of Nonviolence at Christian Brothers University in Memphis, was also critical of the museum.

"I think my grandfather and Martin Luther King had the same dream," Gandhi offered. "And they didn't want people to erect statues and museums in their memory. It's a waste of money."

Smith's and Gandhi's comments underscore how difficult it is to convert memory into fitting memorials for fallen heroes. Each gesture of remembrance inevitably invites accusations of abusing the hero's image or misusing her identity in the effort to celebrate her greatness. Furthermore, one runs the risk in memorialization of turning a hero into a mere commodity, a commercial interest stripped of redeeming social and moral value.

Such a charge, and many more, have been leveled at the King family in their efforts to preserve the legacy and polish the image of Martin Luther King. In the years since King's death, the King family has risen to royal status in black America. But they have recently tumbled from their privileged perch with charges of commercializing the fallen leader's image. They have also been accused of attempting to control how his life story will be shaped by scholars and how his legacy will be shared with future generations. The King family, for its part, believes that it has been exploited through the commercial exploitation of Martin Luther King's legacy. In their efforts to reclaim legal control of King's voice and image, they have have declared an all-out war on illegal profiteering at Martin Luther King, Jr.'s expense. But many critics charge that the King family has neglected King's social and moral legacy in favor of exploiting for themselves his commercial appeal. The King family has waged a war on several fronts: the legal battle to get the papers King produced up until 1964 returned to Atlanta from Boston; an even more aggressive legal campaign to enforce strictly copyrights on King's intellectual property and to collect fees for the commercial use of King's image; an ugly public battle with the National Park Service over its plans for a visitor center; and striking a deal with Time Warner to consolidate the King legacy in multimedia—from books and audiotapes to cyberspace.

Perhaps the King family's resolve to seize control of Martin Luther King, Jr.'s legacy was fueled by a bitter court battle in the early nineties. Coretta King sued Boston University in December 1987 for the return to Atlanta of her husband's personal papers dating from his graduate school days at the university until the height of his international fame in 1964. The Martin Luther King, Jr., Center for Nonviolent Social Change, which Coretta founded in 1968 to carry on her husband's legacy, already had more than 100,000 King papers. The center, composed of exhibit rooms, libraries, archives, and a bookstore, is a vital part of the King Historic District a few blocks from downtown Atlanta. The district, also known as Sweet Auburn, encompasses Ebenezer Baptist Church, which King copastored, the memorial crypt where he is buried, and the modest home where he was born.

After six years of legal maneuvers and a countersuit by Boston University to have King's Atlanta papers turned over to it in accordance with King's wishes—and after negotiations to settle out of court broke down—the case went to trial at Suffolk Superior Court in Massachusetts. Although there were several witnesses, the case hinged on a gigantic struggle between two strong-willed personalities: Coretta Scott King and controversial Boston University president John Silber. At the two-week trial, Coretta King testified that her husband had reluctantly sent his papers, including 83,000 letters, documents, notes, and manuscripts, to his graduate alma mater for safekeeping during the turbulent days of the civil rights movement in the South. With their home being bombed and their safety constantly threatened, King says that her husband finally acceded to the wishes of his beloved former Boston University professor, Harold DeWolf, and shipped his papers in a big truck to his alma mater for safe, but temporary, haven. Coretta argued that her husband had no

intention of permanently leaving his papers in a Northern white institution, preferring instead a Southern black institution to house his intellectual output, which largely grew out of his struggle for liberation in the
South.

John Silber proved to be every bit as wily and ruthless in his own way
as any sheriff she or her husband had faced in the South. Criticized by
some for his brusque demeanor, intemperate rhetoric, and demagogic
style, Silber and Boston University had the upper hand from the start. Silber testified that his concern about the shabby state of the King papers in
Atlanta prompted him to write to Coretta King in 1981, suggesting that
the papers be sent to Boston University as her husband had obviously
intended. (Silber's letter was important, since it was written prior to
Coretta King's assertion that one of the reasons for seeking the return of
her husband's papers to Atlanta was their poor upkeep at Boston University.) Silber says that he proposed to Coretta that photocopies of the
papers, as well as Dr. King's trophies and memorabilia, should be kept at
the King Center. "I pitched her a hardball," Silber testified. "I put the
issue as clearly as I could. I had no idea what her response would be."
Coretta wrote several letters to Silber between 1981 and 1984, inviting
him to visit her at the King Center in Atlanta to discuss how the university and the center "could work together." She did not want to strain her
"cordial relationship" with Silber and sought a face-to-face meeting
because, as she testified, "whenever there is a serious matter to discuss,
it's better to meet one to one." Silber testified that King in her letters
showed "no trace of anger or disappointment or opposition in any way."

Still, Silber skillfully rebuffed Coretta King's overtures—he testified
that they could never reconcile their schedules in four years—and in 1985
she decided to travel to Boston to meet him on his own turf, a tactical
advantage that Silber must surely have relished. Their meeting, according
to Coretta, went poorly; she testified that Silber was "very, very hostile."
It was certainly not the sort of treatment to which the dignified Coretta
King had become accustomed as the matriarch of black America's first
family of civil rights. According to King, Silber summarily dismissed
Coretta King's claim that her husband had changed his mind about his
papers before he died and wanted them returned to his native region. Silber testified that he found it difficult to take "that claim seriously in the
absence of any action or any word by Martin Luther King Jr. himself."
Silber said that for "some strange reason, despite the claim of some people
he had changed his mind, we don't have the slightest shred of evidence

from him that he had changed his mind." Coretta King said that Martin Luther King felt awkward in asking for the papers back in the light of his friendship with DeWolf and had established a committee at SCLC to obtain the papers, even though the committee never officially notified the university. But a lawyer for Boston University argued that SCLC representatives, including Coretta King and New York lawyer and former King aide Harry Wachtel, failed to meet with Boston University as planned. Further, they never mailed a letter that was allegedly drafted in September 1967 stating that King desired the return of his papers.

Coretta's encounter with Silber also provided bitter proof that he held at least a legal advantage. "Before I could finish," she testified, "he interrupted me and said 'I have this letter here'—and he held it up—'that Dr. King wrote in 1964 and his papers belong to Boston University and I would like for you to send those papers up right away.'" The letter to which Silber referred was a 1964 letter King had written to the university stating that the papers he had deposited would become the university's "absolute property" in the event of his death. Silber claims that he showed Coretta the letter in their 1985 meeting, and that she was "very distressed," "utterly surprised," "sort of dumbfounded," and "almost thunderstruck." Silber testified that it was "as if she didn't know I had it or as if she didn't know she had seen it." When she claimed at trial that she had no knowledge of the letter until she saw it during depositions for her lawsuit, a lawyer for Boston University produced a letter written by Coretta King to a friend in 1967 that proved that she did indeed know about her husband's letter. "I still don't recall having seen that letter at that time," she testified.

In the absence of any evidence that King had changed his mind—and after a Boston University lawyer all but implied that Coretta King was lying—the entire matter turned on King's 1964 letter. Unsurprisingly, the jury, which included two blacks and a Latino, voted ten to two in favor of Boston University. After her bitter defeat, Coretta King took little solace in the fact that the copyright to her husband's papers remained with the family, an issue that was never in dispute. She appealed to the state supreme judicial court, which in 1995 upheld the lower court decision. After the higher court ruled against her, Coretta King declared that the "decision is tragic." But her true feelings, and perhaps the motivation for her pursuit of King's papers, are glimpsed in her response to the lower court ruling, when Coretta King stated that she was disappointed that "moral justice" had not prevailed. King knew from the beginning that the legal merits of her case were weak; she commented when the case went to jury that while she hoped the overriding issue would be moral, "in the real world it's a legal one." But she believed that the sort of moral suasion her husband had so brilliantly used to change unjust laws might once again prevail. As Martin Luther King III lamented, it "seems tragic that one would have to legally argue for things that belong to them." His statement provides perhaps a window into the feeling of unjust exclusion from a vital part of Martin Luther King's legacy that would drive their later efforts to recoup King's image, and the payment for its commercial uses, in the public sphere.

To be sure, Coretta King's sense of moral justice was shaped by the interests of her center, interests that converged with the desires of her family. But other civil rights veterans and scholars sided with her struggle to regain physical custody of her husband's papers. Their arguments moved beyond the narrow self-interest of the King family, or at the least, hinged on the belief that, in this case, what was good for the King family was good for the movement and the memory of the man over whom a legal and symbolic battle was being waged. "It's really about owner-ship—not so much in the proprietary sense, but in the political and intel-lectual sense," Julian Bond, the brilliant activist and intellectual argued. "Who's going to tell the future generations what it was that he did? Just as the Kennedy Library exercises control over the Kennedy legacy, the King center wants to do the same." Activist and comedian Dick Gregory argued as well that the papers should be returned to the South, the site of King's mammoth struggles against white supremacy. "It's like saying the Pyramids should be in London," Gregory colorfully commented.

To Gregory and many other critics, Boston University, a Northern white institution, lacked the symbolic and racial cachet that the black South conjures. "When you think about the civil rights struggle," Gre-gory argued, "BU doesn't jump out in your mind. Martin Luther King is synonymous with Atlanta." Gregory also stated that people are "looking at this big institution not just picking a fight with Coretta, but the whole movement." Lewis Baldwin, author of several highly regarded scholarly studies of King's life, said that the King Center is the best place for King's writings since it "is dedicated to keeping alive the work, teachings, dreams, and legacy of Dr. King." And Baldwin agrees with theologian James Cone, author of an acclaimed comparative study of King and Mal-colm X, that the "center is a gold mine on the civil rights movement." It holds the papers of the Congress of Racial Equality, the Southern Christ-

ian Leadership Conference, and the Student Nonviolent Coordinating
Committee. The King Center also keeps files collected by the FBI surveil-
lance of King, as well as the personal papers of civil rights veterans Andrew
Young, Fred Shuttlesworth, Fred Gray, Septima Clark, and Hamilton
Holmes. Even the *Atlanta Journal-Constitution*, whose editorial page editor
would later charge the King family with exploiting the commercial value of
King's legacy, supported Coretta Scott King under the heading: "King
Papers Belong in the South." The paper contended that "it was never
[King's] intent to bequeath them permanently to a predominantly white
institution . . . and he never intended to leave them in a region other than
that which spawned the civil rights movement." They concluded that
"the original works of Dr. Martin Luther King belong in the South—the
birthplace of the man and the movement and the keeper of the flame."

In truth, an even more complex and painful reason explains why
King's papers ended up at Boston University in the first place. When
Harold DeWolf visited Martin and Coretta in 1964, he urged King to
deposit his growing volume of papers at Boston University. King was flattered by the offer, but indicated that he had always believed that he would
give his papers to his undergraduate alma mater, Morehouse College.
Nevertheless, King had doubts about whether the college's tenuous
financial condition made it a likely or logical home for his papers. Even
more prickly was the slightly strained relationship between King and
Morehouse president Benjamin E. Mays. For years, Mays had refused to
place King on Morehouse's board of trustees. Mays justified his decision
by arguing that King was viewed by some black and white members of
the board as a bad example because he had often been jailed and because
his controversial status would jeopardize the college's fund-raising efforts
among influential patrons. So Mays claimed that he avoided submitting
King's name for consideration—despite the importunings of Daddy
King, a thirty-year veteran of the board—because he didn't want to
embarrass King with anything less than overwhelming support for his
candidacy. King was disappointed and insulted by Mays's justifications,
although he continued to support the college and admire Mays. But as is
true of so many conservative black institutions that favor innocuous persons, safe practices, and unthreatening policies, Morehouse was denied
the benefit of progressive black thought and redemptive social action.
The bitter irony is that the King family may have been spared expensive
legal and emotional wrangling with a white institution that eagerly
embraced its former student had his black undergraduate school proudly

claimed him. After all, without King, Morehouse's national reputation and global fame would be considerably diminished.

But if the King family viewed itself as the keeper of the flame, they were also viewed in some quarters as hogging the light for themselves. Or they were charged with seeking to control tightly how King's light would be shared with the rest of the world. The battle over King's papers, then, was also a battle over who had the authority to shape King's legacy. Julian Bond, who would later criticize the King family's stewardship of the late leader's legacy, defended the family with a generosity that some felt was unwarranted. "It's not a question of whether these papers will be available to the public," Bond said. "I take that for granted. They aren't attempting to hide any of his warts, and they shouldn't get into the business of censoring. But they do have an interest in being the intellectual custodian of his memory." But for many critics, public accessibility of King's papers was centrally at stake. In fact, the King Center's dwindling resources made the papers in their possession, a full two-thirds of King's correspondence, notes, manuscripts, sermons, and speeches, virtually inaccessible. Only scholars with longstanding requests were allowed access to King's words.

Ironically, in their war to get back King's papers, the King family sought to portray the upkeep of Boston University's collection as woefully inadequate. In 1985, Pulitzer Prize–winning King biographer David Garrow, who would also later quarrel with the Kings, in response to a request from former King Center archivist Louise Cook, wrote a letter stating that during several visits in 1979 he observed that some of the Boston University King papers had "substantial damage" resulting from "complete lack of care" and "heavy usage." Garrow, whose letter was entered into evidence during the trial by Coretta King's lawyers, indicted Boston University's handling of King's handwritten papers as "a professional scandal of the highest order." But Taylor Branch, himself a Pulitzer Prize winner for his work on King and the civil rights movement, declined Louise Cook's request to write a letter denouncing the condition of the Boston collection as "substandard." "I didn't think, in good conscience, it was true," Branch said. Instead, the author appeared at the trial as the first witness for the defense of Boston University. Branch testified that he found the papers at Boston University, where he visited in 1983 and 1984, "perfectly usable." The condition, handling, and security measures for the Boston University collection mirrored the King's Center's, he said. After his testimony, Branch explained that he agreed to testify for the defense because he feared the scholarly repercussions of the

King Center's gaining control of all of King's papers. "This is about control," Branch said. "The King Center is mostly about promoting the legacy of Dr. King through them, and that means their interpretation of it. . . . But people should be concerned about the monopoly control of historical materials if it's used to control how it's presented to the world."

Less than a week after his appearance in court, Branch received a letter from lawyers for the King estate reminding him that King's words were copyrighted and that "no commercial or proprietary usage may be made without prior written licensing from the heirs of Dr. King." The threat could hardly be missed. And author Richard Lischer states that his study of King's preaching vocation was held up for a year as the King estate scoured his scholarly monograph for potential copyright violations. In addition, the King estate extracted unwarranted compensation for his use of King's unedited audiotapes. "I thought their demands for payment for quotations in a serious study of King were excessive." The convergence of commerce and control is ominous in the King estate's attempt to determine King's legacy in scholarly and popular circles.

The King papers are valuable assets in both monetary terms and the prestige they bring to its holders. Although the King family credibly claimed that in seeking to regain King's papers they were concerned with the best space and region for his intellectual contributions to shine, they were also undoubtedly conscious of the added financial value of consolidating King's papers at their center. As sociologist David Reisman said at the time of the trial, Boston University, and we may assume, the King Center as well, had a lot at stake. "It's a question of ethics in a way," Reisman said, referring to the conflicting legal and moral issues of the case. "But the fact is BU would be giving up a lot. It would be a wounding generosity for BU to surrender the papers. It's not trivial." Moreover, the university could brag that it retained the papers of the most significant public figure in twentieth-century American life, a certain draw for academic conferences, funding sources, black students, and scholars of American politics and race. The King papers are acknowledged as the crown jewel of Boston University's collection, worth a mere eighteen thousand dollars when they were deposited and now deemed priceless.

Not everyone connected to the King family believes that the family has been a good steward of its resources. Even Louise Cook, the former King Center archivist, argues that in the 1970s and 1980s Coretta King failed to live up to pledges—including moving documents from her home to the center—that she made to federal grant-makers who have supported the King papers with gifts totaling almost a million dollars.

"Mrs. King always said to me that she felt the only inheritance left by Martin to his children were his papers," Cook said. That belief may well explain how the King family confuses private interest and public trust, issues that are intimately linked to who is granted access to King's papers and what commercial or scholarly uses are made of that access.

It is even more curious, then, perhaps even cruelly ironic, that the King estate has recently decided to sell off much of its collection to one of two vying universities: Stanford University, the professional home of King Papers Project director Clayborne Carson, or Emory University, in Atlanta. In fact, in its public relations efforts to acquire the King papers, Emory University appealed to the very argument the King family made when it earlier sued Boston University for the return of Dr. King's papers: that they belong in the South. But in a stunning about-face, the King estate now insists that King's legacy is national and not confined to one region. On its face, such an argument makes a great deal of sense—especially since, as Julian Bond says, the ideal place for the King papers is "someplace where proper care, stewardship and availability are prominent, and none of those things is true at the King Center." But in contrast to the King Center's earlier claims and the claims of its supporters that the Boston papers should return to Atlanta on the morally compelling grounds that the South was King's home and the site of his greatest struggles, the argument smacks of opportunism and rationalization. Philip Jones, hired to manage the King estate, argues that Emory University, in making the same argument the King family and its supporters made a few years before, was engaging in an orchestrated effort to pressure the Kings into accepting its bid. "Dexter King and I, and the Center and the [King] family, have taken a number of black eyes in the past for things we believed in," Jones says. "Certainly they are not going to frighten us into doing a deal with them because they feel the papers shouldn't leave the South." Jones fails to understand how his own argument contradicts the King family's logic in its earlier public relations campaign to garner sympathy for its efforts to regain King's Boston University papers.

More damaging is how Jones now ingeniously, though unpersuasively, twists Boston University's *legal* arguments for keeping King's papers—an argument the King family had assailed as perhaps legally correct though morally deficient—into the *moral* basis for justifying the King family actions. It is not simply that the King family appropriates Boston University's legal argument for its own moral purposes that makes its actions questionable; it is that the family appropriates the moral core of

Boston University's argument, a position the King family and its allies demonized, to buttress their own legal arguments. "It's not a Southern situation for us," Jones says, "because, obviously, Dr. King himself gave Boston University the right to archive his papers and we have been working with Stanford for many years. We see Dr. King's legacy as a national legacy and not just a Southern legacy." But isn't that precisely what Boston University had argued in its fight with the King estate four years earlier, even if indirectly and with less moral urgency? In Boston University's eyes, its claim to King was legitimate because he trained there and because he gave the university his papers as a gesture of confidence in its ability to husband his work for the future. In that light, Coretta King's earlier arguments—especially with no explanation of her family's changed position that acknowledges the moral appeal of arguments made earlier by Boston University, arguments they now apparently embrace—fly in the face of the King estate's unprincipled turnaround, even if that turnaround will have wide-ranging and largely salutary effects on King scholarship. (For instance, it would be good for the papers to be removed from the King Center, where low budgets put the papers at risk: a leaky roof threatens the safety of the papers, which often have to be covered with a tarpaulin when it rains, limiting scholarly access to the papers.) It also casts doubt on the noble and high purposes that the King family claimed to be at the root of its resistance to the papers remaining at Boston University. In fact, when challenged by Emory's assertion that the papers belong in the South, Phillip Jones unfavorably compared university officials to hip-hop artists who engage in turf wars between the East and West coasts. Emory's fight is comparable to "these black kids killing each other [and saying], 'You are East and we are West,'" Jones says. "The same immature behavior is saying, 'This is Southern, this has to stay in the South.'" At one point, Jones said that the papers might remain at the King Center, and that talks with Emory and Stanford, which had stalled when the controversy broke, might not resume.

Whoever gets the papers would have only administrative control, housing them and making them available for scholarly research. The King family would retain licensing rights to the use of King's words. Stanford University professor Clayborne Carson, the editor of the King Papers Project, believes that Emory University's motives were less than noble. "My own personal opinion is that [acquiring the papers] only became an urgency at Emory when they learned that Stanford was in the picture." Carson points to the fact that Emory seemed uninterested in assuming the management of the papers, at his suggestion, when he served as a visiting professor at the school in the fall of 1996. "So this fear about the papers leaving the South, all they had to do was stay in contact with me, and make use of me." Even more ironic, Jones suggested the possibility of combining the King Center papers with those at Boston University, which expressed interest in the papers "in principle," although they admitted they were "a little unclear as to what is going on."

In the aftermath of the King papers dispute with Boston University, the King family members seem to have made up their minds to pursue a legal route to gain control over Martin Luther King's legacy. The moral claim lost out in court, and in any case, they seem to have concluded that morality doesn't pay the bills. (When Martin Luther King, Jr., faced the dilemma of cash or conscience, he opted for the bills' remaining unpaid. When financial support for SCLC dramatically declined because of his stand on the Vietnam War and his promotion of the Poor People's Campaign, he said he would continue to say what he had to say even if no one agreed, and if the checks stopped coming in. "I do not determine what is right and wrong by looking at the budget of the Southern Christian Leadership Conference," King said.) In some cases, of course, it is eminently fair and entirely reasonable for the King family to sue to keep commercial interests from corrupting King's legacy. For instance, the King family successfully litigated the violation of their copyright of King's image in 1982, when a decision by the Georgia Supreme Court ruled that the selling of plastic King busts by Ohio-based American Heritage Products, Inc., was illegal. The company never received permission from the King estate to sell its $29.95 statuettes. That decision legally established the King family's inheritance of the right to control the commercial exploitation of King's image. The King estate also filed suit in Los Angeles Superior Court to prevent the 1992 auctioning of a rare outline—on pages ripped from a reporter's stenographer pad—for a speech, "The Roots of Racism Are Very Deep in America," that King gave at a 1966 SCLC staff retreat. They have waged legal war on companies that have placed King's image on switchblades and refrigerator magnets or, in equally poor taste, that have attempted to market an ice cream product called the Dream Cone.

Although the King Center claims to allow educational and nonprofit institutions to reproduce King's words and image without charge, three recent cases have raised questions about the sincerity of their motivations, or at least their definition of what constitutes public education.

The King estate sued CBS in November 1996 for copyright infringement. CBS was marketing a videotape that contained extensive excerpts of King's "I Have a Dream" speech that the network filmed in 1963 when King originally delivered the speech. CBS did not pay the King estate a licensing fee. The CBS case is not a straightforward one involving a clear commercial interest. Excerpts of the speech were included in a five-part documentary, The 20th Century with Mike Wallace, which sells for $99.95. As a news organization, CBS was attempting to market film footage of a copyrighted speech that it recorded without paying licensing fees. The King estate suit argued that the videotapes are not exempt from requirements for licensing fees that are mandated under the fair use doctrine of copyright law. As CBS president Andrew Heyward argued, the age of news should be irrelevant when courts make decisions about whether the tapes violate copyright law. "Just as it is important to cover significant public events at the time they occur," Heyward said, "so too is it important to preserve the historical record and memory of those events by communicating their significance to later generations." The CBS case is complicated by the fact that while copyright law makes an exception for the gathering of news, in this case, strictly speaking, it is not the news at issue but a commercial use of news. In the end, the federal court decided in 1998 that CBS had not violated copyright law since the speech belongs to the public, clearing the way for the network to continue disseminating its videotapes with the King excerpts intact. The King family in 1999 appealed the decision to the Eleventh U.S. Circuit Court of Appeals.

The King family also sued USA Today for reprinting King's most famous speech in 1993, on the thirtieth anniversary of the March on Washington, without paying the King estate a licensing fee. The estate claims it informed the newspaper that a $1,700 licensing fee was required to reprint the speech for commercial use. USA Today bargained for a $450 reduction and reprinted the entire speech—but without payment to the King estate. The newspaper settled the case in 1993 and paid the King estate a $1,700 licensing fee as well as legal costs. The Atlanta Journal-Constitution claims that the King estate sent a letter threatening the paper when it published excerpts of "I Have a Dream." The newspaper also reported that King family members have attempted to wrest huge fees from foreign journalists for interviews. A German television charged that the youngest King, Bernice, "wanted to have $4,000 or $5,000 for one interview, ten minutes," a charge that Dexter King bitterly denies, charging the Atlanta Journal-Constitution with "viciously attack[ing]" his family.

As with CBS, it might be argued that in the cases of the *USA Today* and *Atlanta Journal-Constitution*, the intervention of a commercial interest legitimated the King estate claim for compensation. But it can also be argued that the newspapers performed a valuable educational service by distributing to a new generation, perhaps unfamiliar with King's work, a historic speech that many consider to be part of the public legacy of the civil rights movement. The King family balks at this idea, claiming through Jones that King himself copyrighted his speech, and that shortly after its delivery on August 1963, King successfully sued a company that had produced and sold a recording of it without his permission. "Dr. King had a literary agent, he had a record deal, he had a publishing deal, and he profited off of his work during his lifetime," Jones said. What Jones neglects to mention is that King donated all of those profits to the civil rights movement. The FBI surveillance of King, with no interest in portraying his good qualities, testifies to his motives for filing a suit to stop the distribution of "I Have a Dream":

> On October 3, 1963, a confidential source, who has furnished reliable information in the past, furnished information which indicated that on that date Clarence Jones was preparing a complaint to be filed on behalf of Martin Luther King. Reverend King is setting a temporary restraining order against Twentieth Century Fox and Mr. Maestro, Incorporated to prohibit them from selling recordings of King's speech "I Have a Dream," which he recently made in Washington, D.C. *King wants any proceeds received from this recording to go to the United States Civil Rights Leadership to be used for the Civil Rights movement.* (italics added).

Furthermore, after indicating that he accepted only a dollar from SCLC annually in order to qualify for its group insurance plan and after revealing that he gave most of his annual income of over two hundred thousand dollars to his organization, King told interviewer Alex Haley that "I get a fairly sizable but fluctuating income in the form of royalties from my writings. *But all of this, too, I give to my church, or to my alma mater, Morehouse College, here in Atlanta*" (italics added). To claim that King filed suit to reclaim lost income for his personal benefit is plainly wrong and sullies the memory of King's singular altruism, which led to several clashes with his wife and closest friends about how best to distribute his income.

Perhaps no other action of the King estate is as painful or problematic as the one it took against Blackside, Inc., the black-owned independent production company run in Boston by the late Henry Hampton. Blackside produced the widely heralded documentary series, *Eyes on the Prize*, which led to a bitter conflict with the King family. The case did not receive wide publicity, or it might have helped to expose the hunger for profit from a prophet that at times makes the King family confuse justice and avarice. First broadcast in 1987, with a sequel in 1990, *Eyes on the Prize* traces the development of the civil rights movement through footage of the struggle combined with contemporary interviews of participants and analysts. The series is widely used in American classrooms and has received global distribution. In 1992, King family attorneys dispatched a letter to Blackside claiming that films of the slain leader had been illegally used. (The King family seemed not to have noticed or cared about this offense when Coretta appeared in the first series to comment on the Montgomery bus boycott and other key events.) As a result, the Public Broadcasting System (PBS) became wary of the dispute and refrained from showing the series during 1993's Black History Month, a sure travesty for the interests of the civil rights community and African-American history, not to mention King's legacy. In response to the King estate action, Hampton offered the family $100,000 in hopes of avoiding a nasty public dispute. The King family rebuffed his offer and instead mounted "an aggressive attempt to get an enormous amount of money," Hampton said. "They seemed to have the notion that millions of dollars were available." Hampton also said that the family sought to exercise control over the material, a prospect that Hampton found distasteful and unacceptable, as have many other scholars and researchers. When negotiations stalled, Hampton filed a lawsuit against the King estate in U.S. district court in Boston, alleging that the family's threats "had a chilling effect on Blackside's right of free speech."

Dexter King at the time contended that Hampton's suit was an attack on his family, an increasingly tired and self-righteous claim made by the Kings to deflect attention from their misdeeds in Martin Luther King's cherished name. Dexter also revealed one of the real reasons that the King estate sought to control Blackside's use of King footage: it conflicted, and perhaps in their minds, superseded, a documentary, *Montgomery to Memphis*, that is shown at the King Center. Dexter claimed that "our documentary was usurped by 'Eyes on the Prize.'" Dexter also refuted the claim that the Blackside production was a nonprofit venture when he discovered that cassettes of the program "were being sold at Blockbuster Video. It was no longer educational." But that is a ludicrous argument and fails to see that the wide distribution of *Eyes on the Prize* series could only broaden public education about the civil rights movement and was by no means a vast money-making product that warranted legal action by the King estate. Hampton countered Dexter's claims that *Eyes on the Prize* usurped *Montgomery to Memphis* and suggested that Dexter was perhaps motivated to target Blackside aggressively because *Eyes on the Prize* bit into profits the King estate reaped through royalties on *Montgomery to Memphis*. (That tape too is available at Blockbuster.) The King estate and Hampton eventually struck an out-of-court settlement for what both figures said was less than Hampton's original offer of $100,000. Hampton was crushed by his exasperating experience with the King family. He genuinely believed that *Eyes on the Prize* had, in his words, "regenerated Dr. King's role."

If the shameful actions of the King estate toward Blackside escaped wide notice, its bitter fight with the National Park Service was observed by millions. It was this battle perhaps that shattered the King stronghold on the American public's sympathy and eroded its standing as the first family of civil rights. In January 1995, the King family banned the National Park Service from conducting tours of King's birthplace, a two-story Queen Anne house, and his crypt, the result of a heated dispute between the King family and the federal agency over how best to exercise custody of King's legacy. Specifically, the dispute centered on a new congressionally appropriated $11.8 million visitor center that was being constructed on Auburn Avenue in the King Historic District, or the Sweet Auburn neighborhood, across the street from the King Center. The city gave the land to the Park Service in exchange for the rights to revenues reaped by a parking lot the agency was building. Ebenezer, King's home church, worked out a deal for its current historical site to be taken over by the Park Service in exchange for land on which it has since built a larger sanctuary.

For fourteen years, the King family and the Park Service enjoyed friendly relations. In fact, the King family had invited the Park Service in 1980 to help it administer every aspect of the King Historic District except the King Center itself. The federal agency's faithful stewardship of the site helped to make it, after the Statue of Liberty and Independence Hall in Philadelphia, the third most popular historic attraction in the country. Coretta King originally supported the visitor center, which was conceived as a way to alleviate the severe shortage of parking and toilet facilities before the arrival in Atlanta of the 1996 Olympic Games. In November 1994, the Park Service began construction of the visitor center, from whose plans the King family claims it was excluded. With construction underway, the King family claimed—in an argument similar to the one Dexter King made against Henry Hampton and Blackside—that the visitor center would cut into King family plans for an allegedly income-producing interactive museum. Dexter King consulted with Oppenheimer Capital in an effort to capitalize his dream through structuring a tax-exempt bond offering that would make the King Historic District self-supporting, since it was being partially supported by Park Service funds, another bone of contention in the dispute. In 1994, the King family demanded that the Park Service triple its annual $535,000 payment to the King Center to $1.5 million, despite the fact that the rangers already provided upkeep and tours of King's birthplace and tours of his tomb as well. When the government turned the King family down, their showdown with the Park Service quickly followed.

The King family argued that the Park Service had spread false stories about the proposed interactive museum's being a profit-making venture, even as King estate executive Philip Jones accused city officials of "trying to sell off the Historic District." The King family called a press conference in January 1995 and lambasted the federal agency. "The same evil forces that destroyed Martin Luther King," Coretta dramatically claimed, "are now trying to destroy my family. We are more determined than ever that they who slew the dreamer will not slay the dream." It is easy enough to imagine that Coretta believed such harmful hyperbole, but her misplaced appeal to racial loyalty—especially since it was really loyalty to her family being sought in the guise of loyalty to her husband—largely failed to spark outrage in black or white communities. Indeed, it had the opposite effect: the King family was subject to an unprecedented level of scrutiny and criticism over their custodianship of the King legacy. As Georgia state Senator Bob Holmes, who also runs Clark Atlanta University's Southern Center for Studies in Public Policy, commented, "I don't think there is this continued level of support [in Atlanta] for the King family . . . because people now feel it's long past the time when they should be deferred to in terms of what should be done regarding Dr. King's legacy."

Sadly, it seems that for the King family, Martin Luther King, Jr.'s legacy has been reduced to recent efforts to fill their coffers and support their dwindling programs. Coretta King argued that the National Park Service's visitor center would slash the crucial revenues she gains from the King Center gift shops, whose operations would be neutralized by competition with the federal agency. When Dexter King proposed his alternative interactive museum on the visitor center site, the National Park Service, the neighborhood association, and even Interior Secretary

Bruce Babbitt declared that it was too late to change plans. And John Lewis, the Georgia congressman and former SNCC president who had marched with Martin Luther King, Jr., and a key figure in the congressional appropriation in support of the visitor center, sided with the Park Service. Lewis even organized a meeting between the King family and the Park Service in an effort to help them resolve their dispute. "None of us who marched with Dr. King will be here forever," Lewis claimed. "If we want something to be here for future generations, then we have to make way for it." Lewis also offered in response to the King proposal that Martin Luther King's legacy should not be "up for sale like soap."

But Dexter King was less charitable in his assessment of the Park Service plans, ascribing to the federal agency the intent of undermining the memory of King's radical social legacy.

> If the Park Service gets its way, a majority of the tourists who come here will leave with a superficial understanding of my father's teachings, history and legacy. They will learn about the Martin Luther King Jr. of "I have a dream" but they won't learn much about his leadership of labor struggles [or] protests against the Vietnam War. They won't learn much about what he said about racism, economic oppression and the power of nonviolence.

And instead of seeing the Park Service's renovation of dilapidated housing as a boon for neighborhood revitalization, Dexter viewed their actions as an effort "to annex this area to control the dissemination of history. Our history has always been diluted. We can tell our history. We know best."

Dexter is certainly right that the federal government has not been a reliable ally in fostering progressive social action—and indeed, in his father's case, the government has not only failed to stimulate the remembrance of King's challenging actions; it had earlier spied on him and tried to ruin his life and, by extension, the lives of his family. It is more than reasonable for the King family to be suspicious of the role of government in preserving and promoting Martin Luther King, Jr.'s memory (although when it suits their interests, the Kings don't hesitate to use the government to achieve their goals). But in the case of the National Park Service, the government has appeared to be a friend. The Kings, by their own admission, were instrumental in getting the federal agency to assist them in crafting suitable ways to honor King's memory. For them to attack the federal agency they worked with for nearly fifteen years as "evil," without compelling evidence of its wrongdoing, and primarily out of self-interest, is unconscionable.

Further, the King family also fails the litmus test of historical preservation that it accuses the Park Service of failing to pass. Many critics, even those close to the Kings in the past, have accused the family of failing to carry out the mission of the King Center. "If they are the repository of King's legacy, I don't see much being done to spread the message of his life and work," Julian Bond lamented. He was not alone in his criticism. "The center is not addressing the issues of the day," notes Joseph Roberts, the pastor of Ebenezer. Roberts says that the King Center is painfully absent in terms of debates over welfare and church burnings. He argues that "it is incumbent upon somebody representing the King center to instruct us, albeit conjecturally, on what Dr. King's position might have been on those issues according to his principles." In a show of bold independence, Roberts, though pastor of the church where many of the Kings still worship, had earlier termed the King family's actions in the Park Service debacle "high-handed, dictatorial and undemocratic." While Roberts had no quarrel with Dexter King's proposed interactive museum, he suggested that the efforts of the King family might be better placed in educating the public about how to tackle critical social ills. "History is all right but there are some challenges we face now with the problems of labor, low-paying jobs for people even though the economy is allegedly good." Cynthia Tucker, the first black to become the editorial page editor of the *Atlanta Journal-Constitution*, criticized the Kings for "years of short-sighted leadership" while accusing them of "profit mongering" with their allegedly money-making interactive museum proposal, which Tucker tagged as "a sort of I Have a Dreamland." One scholar surmised that the Kings "are trying to polish and protect [King's] image, but actually they are making it very fragile and short-lived."

As for Dexter King's claim that the Park Service was attempting to co-opt his family's control of the King legacy, neighborhood activists and other critics often applauded the Park Service efforts to rejuvenate the Sweet Auburn community while assailing the King family's poor record of social responsibility. Based on its record of real interest and investment in the Sweet Auburn neighborhood—it renovated many neighborhood homes and became active in the low-income area even as the Kings were increasingly perceived as uninterested outsiders—the Park Service garnered wide sympathy among local citizens and leaders. For instance, Mtamanika Youngblood, the director of the Historic District Development Corp., an Atlanta historic preservation program in the neighborhood, claims the King family was on weak grounds in its opposition to the federal agency. "We hardly see any of these people," Youngblood says, referring to the King family. "For them to unilaterally decide that the National Park Service cannot stay in this community is not acceptable to us." Even Atlanta city councilwoman Debi Starnes doubted the sincerity of the King family's plans for an interactive museum, claiming that "we have seen no plans, no timetable, no financing package." As Howard Spiller, the president of the Sweet Auburn Area Improvement Association, lamented, it was tragic "that this [Park Service dispute] came up because all we wanted was to lift up the life of Dr. King."

Young also expressed a sentiment that many others have long held but rarely publicly stated. "The trouble with Mrs. King," Young states, "is that she thinks she's a head of state. We used to ignore them, but we always kind of resented their attitude toward the community." Perhaps Coretta felt that way because she has by and large been accorded that kind of respect throughout the nation and around the world. In fact, when her fight with the Park Service heated up, Nelson Mandela, with whom she danced at his victory party in Johannesburg, asked if he could help, as did President Clinton. But even more telling, the exploitation of her royal status outside Atlanta, and until recently inside as well, seems to have made Coretta and her family suspect carriers of King's legacy. "I believe the dream is still alive in everyone else," Starnes said. "People are just wondering what happened to the dream in the King family."

Mrs. King bristles at the suggestion that her family is attempting to cash in on her husband's legacy. "This line about my family profiteering is nonsense," she says. "We're the only ones who haven't profited. I've never had a salary in all these years. How they've brainwashed so many people, I don't know." Coretta King accused the Park Service of exploiting an invitation from the King family to help the neighborhood and afterward pushing out the very folk who invited them in to begin with. She also accused her neighbors of forgetting all the good work that she has done on their behalf through the years. As a *U.S. News & World Report* story summarized it:

She accuses the park service of trying to destroy her family for reasons she can't understand. She accuses her neighbors of forgetting that she lobbied three mayors and numerous federal officials to get money for the community center and virtually everything else that has come to Auburn Avenue. She says the community has forgotten the voter education drives, the work with the elderly and the early childhood center she started, preferring instead to suggest that her motive is greed rather than commitment. "I had a commitment even before I met Martin," she says. "If I didn't believe in this, I wouldn't be working 18-hour days. I don't have another life. This is my life. I'd like to see the legacy prevail because if it does, we would have a better world."

Coretta Scott King is certainly right that for most of the years since King's death, her family has not reaped a financial windfall from King's legacy. Coretta King never moved her family from the humble brick home she shared with her husband before he died. When King was murdered, Coretta was left with few resources to support her children. When checks poured into the SCLC from all over the world in Coretta's name, the organization's leadership claimed that the money should be used to further King's legacy within SCLC. Ralph Abernathy and SCLC board members were largely insensitive to her need for help. But Coretta had come to see herself as a worthy leader in her own right, and she wanted to carry her husband's legacy in a direction that she determined was faithful to his social vision. As Andrew Young says:

There were a lot of contestants for Martin's legacy and Coretta wanted to take up the mantle, too. She had always seen herself as a civil rights leader, not just as a wife in the background. . . . Martin could keep her "in her place" so to speak, but there was no way Ralph, Joe Lowery, Hosea Williams, or any of us were going to tell Coretta what to do. . . . Ralph and the board wanted to use Coretta to raise money for SCLC, but they didn't want her to play any kind of policy role in the organization. The men in SCLC were incapable of dealing with a strong woman like Coretta, who was insisting on being treated as an equal . . . she perceived her role differently from the role of SCLC. . . . Almost unavoidably, Coretta became a prominent spokesperson for Martin's legacy and many people resented her because of it.

Young also laments that it was "painful to see people that Martin nurtured openly criticizing his widow. But Coretta tenaciously set about establishing the Martin Luther King Center for Nonviolent Social Change to preserve and share Martin's legacy into the twenty-first century."

Coretta established the King Center in 1968. She raised funds from the private sector as well as from the government to finance the building of the complex in 1981 on Auburn Avenue. The King Center eventually grew to seventy employees with an annual budget of $5 million. It received grants for its programs, especially its archive of King's papers, with nearly a million dollars in aid. Coretta used her center as a base to lobby for her husband's birthday to become a national holiday, an effort that came to fruition in 1986 and ranks among her most notable accomplishments. The King Center sponsored King Week, an annual celebration of King's life and legacy. But grants have dried up over the years, and the King Center ran a deep deficit; in 1993, it was $400,000, and in 1994, it rose to $600,000. As a result, Coretta King spent most of her time and energy raising funds for the center. After a disastrous first attempt to run the King Center for four months in 1989, Dexter King was named to succeed his mother in 1995. "I was ready before, but the timing wasn't right," the younger King said. "At that time, I was probably moving faster than the board was ready to; I don't know if I'm really slower now, but I have a better understanding of how to get things done in a complex environment."

Dexter King certainly moved with speed and skill to shore up the King Center's sagging finances and to redefine the center's operations and intellectual focus. He immediately consolidated his family's strength by appointing them to a majority of the board's seats. He engineered the early closing of the Martin Luther King, Jr., Federal Holiday Commission, which had been authorized by Congress and headed by his mother. Dexter felt that the commission cut into the fund-raising efforts of the King Center. Dexter moved to streamline the King Center operations, reducing the staff from seventy in 1993 to fourteen in 1997. Dexter also closed a child care center (the one his mother implied her neighbors should be grateful to her for opening). In effect, he shifted the focus of the center away from conventional movement-centered activities to an emphasis on preserving his father's legacy through the Internet and exercising strict control over his intellectual property rights. Although the King Center's mission statement contends that it is dedicated to "research, education and training in nonviolent philosophy and strategy," it no longer presents workshops on nonviolence. Dexter created a separate unit, the National Institute for Community Empowerment, to take up the center's programs, which previously taught nonviolence and helped with community development efforts.

The center now primarily plans annual commemorations of the King birthday, maintains King's crypt, manages the archive and other buildings, operates a gift shop, and oversees public appearances and other activities by family members. "We were not being very effective in carrying out our mission and purpose, primarily because we were too broad-based," Dexter said. "The King center became kind of all like an all things to all people organization, and that's always a handicap." The center deteriorated to the point where the elevator did not work, and the center was on a "cash-only business with vendors" and had trouble paying employees. "I used to get knots in my stomach every time I had to make payroll," confessed William "Sonny" Walker, who served the center as executive director from 1993 to 1995. Dexter King's efforts reduced the deficit considerably, from $600,000 in 1994 to $50,000 in 1996, but in 1996 the center still got half of its $4.2 million budget from federal grants. Dexter sought a way to make the center self-supporting and to abstain from the guerrilla fundraising tactics deployed out of necessity by his mother, begging a benefactor here, bagging some cash there. Further, he aimed to free his family from people in business, politics, and civil rights who were out to exploit their connections to his mother for self-promotion, political advantage, or upward mobility. "Everybody for the most part that came here to do something did it at her expense," Dexter claims, "because they were coming to take more away from the table than they brought."

Philip Jones says that Dexter King has "determined that the King Center should be part of the national park and should be a tourist attraction," and that the family wants to cede much of its programming to other institutions. Jones claims that the King family "would prefer the center become institutionalized so that they don't have to always raise the money, always greet the dignitary, always be at the center of every possible thing that goes on there." That represents a keen difference between Dexter and his mother, who sought to keep King's legacy alive and hence keep her own flame bright. As Clayborne Carson says, the King Center "programming is very localized, labor-intensive and the impact is quite limited. What Dexter senses is that the intellectual property has almost infinite potential for impact." And profit. As Jones contends, he and Dexter are part of "the new paradigm" in business that pays attention to marketing on the basis of "added value." Jones's estimation of his colleague seems to be borne out by Dexter's insistence that "I have never seen myself they way the media has portrayed me, as a leader. I'm not trying to have a constituency. I'm not trying to be preachy or be on a pedestal. I'm not trying to effect change on that level, not because it's not something that should be done, but that's just not my best destiny."

It is perhaps Dexter's paradigm shift, at the strong bidding of Jones, that has resulted in the King family's aggressive attempts to seize control of its financial possibilities. Dexter was the guiding force behind the King family's tussle with the Park Service, which was a public relations fiasco. The Park Service built its visitor center, but some of its exhibit space is empty because the King family has refused to lend it notable King artifacts like his clothing, his Nobel Peace Prize medal, and the funeral wagon that carried his casket. Dexter became executor of the King estate in 1991 and shortly after began a business relationship with Jones, his former Morehouse College classmate and president and CEO of Intellectual Properties Management (IPM), which Dexter retained to oversee a King family corporation created in 1993, the Estate of Martin Luther King, Jr. Jones's partnership with the Kings has had far-ranging consequences on how they perceive themselves and are in turn perceived by the public. Not only has he spurred them on to be aggressive about selling off the King papers, but he has prodded them to become much more conscious and protective of the commercial value of the King image, name, and copyright. In essence, the King estate was out to protect Martin Luther King, Incorporated.

As a result, in 1996, the King family announced a reversal of opinion about commercializing Martin Luther King, Jr.'s persona, a move they had resisted in the past. The family agreed to license merchandise containing King's image and words, from compact discs of King's speeches to a Hollywood movie possibly directed by Oliver Stone. A line of personal checks were among the first products, as well as a limited-edition Llandro statuette of the fallen leader. And to take advantage of the 1996 Olympic Games, the estate offered Olympic pins and medallions containing King's image. IPM arranged to handle the licenses and agreed to pay the King estate 6 percent to 10 percent royalty on each deal, as well as donate a substantial percentage of its profits to the King Center. The King family defended its move as an attempt to offer "high-quality and tasteful" products in the face of overwhelming demand for such merchandise; more than a thousand requests are fielded each month, according to Jones. Such a demand was not new, but Jones's presence prompted the Kings to capitalize on the interest in King merchandising while also countering a black market of bootleg merchandise being illegally produced and sold. "I want it clear that all of this was born out of reaction," Dexter said. "We didn't set out to duplicate Elvis Presley Enterprises." (The younger King did, however, visit Graceland to get an idea of how to market an icon.) Dexter claims that his family didn't look at Presley and conclude, "'We're going to start Martin Luther King Enterprises and figure out how we're going to make money.' We are on the reverse side. There is a demand for these products." Moreover, Dexter intended for the money to reduce the King Center's deficit and relieve its dependence on foundation grants. The family insisted that nonprofit organizations and noncommercial entities could continue to use King's image and words without charge. Still, the Kings' move provoked predictable suspicion and skepticism among critics. "You run the risk of turning King into a commodity," said Charles Jones, chair of the African-American Studies Department at Georgia State University. "You run the risk of the message being lost to the product. King was not the only leader in the civil rights movement, but he symbolized that movement. The mass selling of King would cheapen what he stood for."

Charles Jones's criticism was perhaps made even more powerful in the light of the King family's latest venture: a 1997 blockbuster deal with Time Warner that by 2000 should net the King estate about $10 million a year, making it worth an estimated $30 to $50 million in less than five years. The Time Warner deal includes new books of King's writings (including the already published *The Autobiography of Martin Luther King, Jr.*, culled from King's writings and speeches and sermons and edited by King Papers Project director, Clayborne Carson, as well as *A Knock at Midnight*, a collection of King's sermons also edited by Carson), a memoir by Coretta and a book by Dexter, recordings and CD-ROMs of King's speeches, and a King-related Web site. Time Warner also intends to publish the first complete collection of King's sermons, including previously unreleased homilies, and to reissue a backlist of King's HarperCollins books that will be now be packaged as a boxed set from Book-of-the-Month Club. When the deal was struck, Time Warner Trade Publishing chairman Larry Kirschbaum claimed that King's works are "a national treasure . . . a gift we will take into the 21st century. We will use it as wisely as possible." Kirshbaum ventured that there is "an enormous audience, both here and abroad, for the legacy of Dr. King."

Time Warner chairman and CEO Gerald Levin claimed the deal was "a distinctive relationship—I won't even call it a transaction" and referred to their agreement as "personally meaningful." In describing the deal as unprecedented, Levin said, "I don't think you've had the circumstances that would permit it. That is, where there is a relatively unexplored treasure that has been aggregated by a family that really understands the historical importance of it and is also inspired by a new generation and new technologies." Coretta King was equally ecstatic. "Today is a great day for the legacy of Martin Luther King, Jr.," she said. "I believe that this historic agreement will make an extraordinary contribution to promoting my husband's teachings in print and electronic media and lead to a better understanding of his life, work and the continuing effort to fulfill his dream." She also claimed that now "Martin's legacy will be disseminated widely throughout the world."

Other King observers were not so elated. David Garrow demurred, saying, "I think the family has some right in a royalty sense, of course, to receive income from his writings, from his literary rights. But it's a question not just of degree or scale but of at what point does commercial aggressiveness rub against the essence of King's impressively selfless legacy?" Joseph Roberts was troubled by the message being sent by the King's aggressive enforcement of their commercial interests: "What you see now is more and more of an emphasis on developing the fiscal basis of the estate." He noted the split between King family members who want to perpetuate King's legacy and King friends and supporters who would like to see the center work diligently for the issues King championed: racial justice, economic opportunity, and radical democracy. "He was far more universal in scope than the center appears to be," Roberts said, adding that it "would be good for them to sort of share their vision." According to some of his allies, Dexter King's vision is rooted in bringing financial solvency to the King Center and then reviving the programs that have historically defined the King mission. In such a scenario, Dexter and the King Center could be freed from corporate blackmail should he refuse to defer to a company's demands. The fact that Ford, British Petroleum, and Coca-Cola withdrew their generous support underscored for Dexter the need to attain financial independence. Furthermore, Dexter viewed the national landscape and saw the economic exploitation of his father's image and decided to rein in the financial forces that dwindled his center's gross benefits. "If people are going to exploit it, do we turn a blind eye and say, 'Well, we don't mind if you make money, but if you think about us down the road and you want to help us underwrite our overhead, send us a check?'" Dexter stated. "We have a legal right to protect what is ours, but whether it's morally right, some people would question. I think it's both."

Dexter found support in his beliefs from Andrew Young and C. T. Vivian, civil rights veterans who fought side by side with Martin Luther King, Jr. "People look with a jaundiced eye at the Time Warner deal, but Time Warner will get Martin Luther King's words distributed better than all the nonprofits and churches have done in the last 30 years," Young said. "There's nothing wrong with a free-market approach to an essentially humanitarian vision." And Vivian, who was struck on the face by Sheriff Jim Clark in Selma as he protested for the right to vote, supports the King family's move to make money: "Martin had to spend most of his life away from his family. Being able to secure their future with his own labor and creativity and intellect would be his way of trying to make up for anything he did not give them as a result of giving all of us his life." Vivian concluded that if there "is money to be made, some of it should go to his family. Martin could have quit and made millions in corporate America or he could have traveled, giving speeches. But he gave his life to the movement. There are millions of people—black and white—reaping the rewards of Martin's work. There is no reason why his family shouldn't live comfortably."

Few would begrudge the King family's making some money from King's estate. Nor could anyone justly criticize the King family for living comfortably, since for most of their lives they resided in a modest home as Coretta worked extremely hard to provide her children with a decent life. For the thirty years since Martin Luther King, Jr.'s death, none of the Kings has gotten rich off of his legacy, and not until the Time Warner deal has that possibility been genuinely within their grasp. It certainly would not be immoral for the Kings to get rich off King's legacy, but it would be immoral for them to pretend that such a state of affairs would please Martin Luther King, Jr. King was notoriously uncomfortable with money—not making it, but keeping it.

To be fair, we must remember that King was not always opposed to comfort. Indeed, until the early sixties, he was accustomed to and avidly indulged the material and social accoutrements that flooded the province of ministerial royalty, for which he certainly qualified. King was the beneficiary of fortunate birth. His father, Martin Luther King, Sr., struggled against mighty odds as a sharecropper's son in rural Georgia to gain formal education and, later, a degree from Morehouse College, on his way to marrying the daughter of an Atlanta minister and inheriting from him a church that Daddy King made into one of that city's most prestigious pulpits. Alfred Daniel Williams took on the pastorate of the fledgling eight-year-old Ebenezer Baptist Church in 1894 and pastored for nearly forty years until his death in 1931. His daughter, Alberta, later married Daddy King and bore him three children, Christine, Martin (originally Michael), and Alfred Daniel, after his maternal grandfather. King was reared in quaint comfort in postdepression Atlanta, and enjoyed the perks of being a "p.k." (preacher's kid) and a member of the black petite bourgeoisie. As a youth, King took quickly to the relative ease of his middle-class station and eagerly exploited its attendant luxuries. He was known as a teenager for his sartorial spunk, so much so that he was nicknamed

"Tweedie" for the stylish tweed suits he sported. And when he was enrolled at Crozier Seminary, he wrote his mother that he "met a fine chick in Phila who has gone wild over the old boy," and notes that since family friend and local pastor "Barbour told the members of his church that my family was rich, the girls are running me down," though he denies to his mother that anything came of the female attention. As a doctoral student in Boston, King's distinctly bourgeois life—nice apartment, fancy car, splendid threads—contrasted sharply to the modest means of most of his peers.

But as a mature minister and civil rights leader, King forsook his middle-class upbringing and lived simply and modestly. King's beliefs have been immortalized in his famous sermon, "Drum Major Instinct," delivered at Ebenezer, exactly two months before his death. King reminds his congregation about his wishes for his funeral during the climax of his sermon. He also registers a few disclaimers that illustrate his hallmark generosity.

"Yes, if you want to say that I was a drum major," King declaims, "say that I was a drum major for justice; say that I was a drum major for peace; I was a drum major for righteousness. And all of the other shallow things will not matter. I won't have any money to leave behind. I won't have the fine and luxurious things in life to leave behind. But I just want to leave a committed life behind." It is clear from King's sermon that he had amassed no great fortune, indeed, not even a meager one, to give his family. Instead, he sought to leave them a legacy of selfless service to humanity.

If the King family benefits from King's unselfish legacy and builds an empire of private wealth from his speeches and sacrifice—and ultimately, his death—they will not only turn his charisma into vain commodities, they will bury his challenge to capitalism and his embrace of democratic socialism in a golden tomb of social neglect. It is not the making of money that holds peril for the King family; it is the keeping of money to build the King estate, which benefits them personally, and not the King Center or other groups, that benefit the public and the causes for which King gave his life. King expressed his views in a *Playboy* interview with Alex Haley: "I believe as sincerely as I believe anything that the struggle for freedom in which SCLC is engaged is not one that should reward any participant with individual wealth and gain. I think I'd rise up in my grave if I died leaving two or three hundred thousand dollars. . . . If I have any weaknesses, they are not in the area of coveting wealth. My wife knows this well; in fact, she feels that I overdo it."

Coretta and Dexter and the rest of the King family are not Martin Luther King, Jr. They are not bound by law to embrace his views. But when they make public claims about their right to control King's legacy, they invite the sort of comparison that is double-edged: while comparison to the most extraordinary figure American life has produced may be unfair to most persons, including his own family members, such a comparison also unfairly benefits the King family since they are associated with Martin Luther King, Jr.'s profound legacy. Moreover, the King family often exploits the conflation of two competing personas: the public figure King who served the common good through his civil rights career, and the private citizen Martin Luther King, Jr., whose public image is privately owned for the commercial advantage of his kin. Moreover, they have failed to distinguish King's intellectual and moral legacy from a body of public works—books, speeches, sermons—that are the property of his estate. The King family has often confused the two. Often in their efforts to enforce their rights as owners of King's commercial image and voice, they have been pricked by the sharp edges of social conscience coming from other quarters that claim to have inherited King's spiritual and moral legacy. If the Kings think that by owning King's words they own what his words mean to millions who have no material stake in his legacy, they are profoundly mistaken. Further, if by exploiting the commercial value of King's intellectual property they claim to have done anything more than make a commodity of King's legacy—as opposed to upholding his wish to undermine capital by giving it away to groups that sorely need it to mount a fight against the forces that destroy blacks and the poor—then they are tragically deceived. In order to clarify how the Kings have legitimate legal ownership of King's intellectual property, but not necessarily ownership of his true intellectual and moral legacy, we must consider how the two are often confused.

A great deal of the grumbling about the King family grows from two necessarily contradictory claims: that they have departed from Martin Luther King, Jr.'s path of selfless service and that they have tried to hog his legacy for themselves while cashing in on a martyr's memory. For the first claim to make sense, it means that King's family has a special obligation to fulfill the sort of call to public service that Martin Luther King, Jr., answered. According to such logic, his wife and offspring have a unique charge to carry on the work that their loved one began. Some mystical, magical property of inheritance (but not succession, as the resentment of the King family shows, although the two are often confused in the minds of both his family and the public) appear to be at work through the biological ties of kinship. If such a claim is true, then the second claim makes no sense. Of course, his loved ones would then have the right to shape King's memory and profit from his legacy since their ties to King should benefit them in precisely such a manner.

But an even more complicated issue arises: Does his family make claims on the King name—and therefore benefit from commercial association with Martin Luther King, Jr., by literally trading on his image—on the basis of his public career, or on the grounds that he was their husband and father, or both? Do King's public and private roles unavoidably intersect? Or do they merge at points that can be conveniently manipulated by either the family or the public? The family claims ownership of King's voice and image while also distinguishing between the King Estate, the private concerns of the King family, and the King Center, the public face of the King legacy, in seeking compensation for profitable uses of his image or words. The public demands that his family be accountable to King's legacy but sometimes objects to the use by the family of the means to control his legacy and consolidate his image, including suing for-profit corporations that exploit his image, and producing authorized commercial images of King. If King's family has a genetic claim to ownership, then the grumbling about their handling of his image, while perhaps persuasive on aesthetic or moral grounds, is mute. To put it crassly, they are the beneficiaries of gilt by association. But if they have a moral obligation to pursue with dignity the preservation of King's memory, then the basis of such an obligation cannot involve either their claims to direct inheritance or the claims made on them by a public that points to their blood ties to King. It must be on the basis of their participation in the moral drama of social redemption in which King brilliantly performed.

After all, if they don't have suitable talents to extend King's legacy, they should no more be expected to answer the call to public leadership than Michael Jordan's children are expected to lead the NBA in scoring because their daddy was a great player. In the case of both civil rights and basketball, the relevant qualities for leadership have nothing to do with blood and everything to do with talents and gifts that are mysteriously allotted to the most unlikely men and women. Civil rights heroes and basketball legends can neither will their successors (think of how disastrously things worked for Ralph Abernathy in King's stead) or appoint their kin as keepers of the flame (think of how basketball star Rick Barry's sons have not inherited his glorious gifts). Of course, our national history is cluttered with offspring and wives, and in some cases, husbands, who have been called on to finish the term of a deceased politician, fill the shoes of a departed spouse, or inherit the public affection of a fallen parent. Sometimes it works. Sometimes it collapses on the weight of its own inherent contradiction. No one should be expected to speak well, think sharply, or act bravely because her husband or wife or mother did.

By right, too, no one should be able to exploit the public affection built up by a relative for personal gain. But Jimmy Carter's brother did, and so did Bill Clinton's brother. Even more tricky, though, is when the offspring of famous families have shown—by virtue of association with the movers and shakers of society, or by being reared in an environment where certain skills are cherished and refined—great, or even greater, gifts for just the sort of practices in which their parents or siblings engaged. Think of the children of George Bush, or John and Robert Kennedy, or Jesse Jackson, or Ken Griffey. While it is rightly assumed that they benefited, perhaps even unfairly, by being born fortunately into their families, it is often wrongly assumed that fortunate birth alone is capable of producing the qualities of leadership demanded by politics, sports, or public service. Michael Jordan is the least likely of champions, not simply because he developed relatively late in the physical stature on which basketball thrives, but because no one in his family is very tall or displayed the sort of skills by which he mastered his sport. In the end, even though we often place unreasonable demands on the kin of the great, we simply don't have a reliable calculus of who will or will not be able to perform under such expectations. But if we are to generate fair rules of assessing the responsibilities of the inheritors and guardians of the great, we must gain clarity on just what is at stake and how we determine good from bad behavior.

This is especially true of King's family, whose claims to public ownership of King's legacy have often depended on their appeal to blood lines—"my husband," "my father"—more than shared philosophy or similar sacrifice. The King family seems to have confused defending their commercial rights with defending King's legacy of hard work for the poor and beleaguered. If they have sought legitimate power to curtail illegal profit at the expense of King, they have also upped the stakes of how a family balances the demands of representing an icon's legacy while profiting themselves in the name of that legacy. If there has been a shift from legacy keeping to license provision—or, worse yet, an identification of legacy with licensing— then the moral claim to representing King's ideals has been at least partially forfeited. It now belongs, as it always really has been, in the hands and hearts of those whose are spiritually and morally committed to King's ideals. Although they did not invent such a distinction, the King family has benefited from the split between King's public persona as a property of moral identification with his social ideals and King's image as an intellectual property subject to legal claims. Once they chose to enforce aggressively and primarily embrace the latter, they no longer had exclusive, or even privileged, claim to the former. They may have legal supremacy, but they no longer have (if they ever did) moral or intellectual supremacy in claiming his legacy. Once we accept that, we should no longer demand that the King family be the bearers of King's legacy in the way Coretta claimed at first to represent it. But if that is the case, then we can no longer defer to the King family in fostering, enlarging, and claiming King's spiritual and moral legacy. The problem is that the King family has attempted to have it both ways: to exercise legal claims while exercising moral authority. It is not that it is impossible to do both; it is that once a legal and commercial claim becomes primary, the moral primacy withers by comparison. The King family can no longer claim, by definition of biological kinship, to be the arbiters of King's social or moral legacy; they are, at the least, his legal and commercial legatees. This does not mean that they are not also King's moral legatees, but only in the sense that anyone who subscribes to his beliefs can be. Their bloodline cannot guarantee their moral pedigree. As Gary Pomerantz said, "Because they are King's blood does not make them the proper custodians of his legacy. But then the question is what determines who the proper custodians shall be and who determines it? This legacy is larger than any one family."

The King legacy is indeed larger than the King family. By aggressively pursuing their commercial interests in King's memory, they have at times sought to control the King legacy by determining, even if indirectly, the scholarship that addresses King's life and thought. Further, their attempt to enforce strictly the licensing of King's voice and image has at times severely hampered efforts to educate the public about, and with, King's wonderful words. Neither have the Kings in their attempt to cash in on King's legacy figured out how to legally divide the spoils legally among the many people and sources from which the great leader borrowed his ideas, and often, his words. Did they split the fee they collected from USA Today, for reprinting King's most noted oration, with the brilliant preacher and professor Prathia Hall, from whom King pinched his famous "I Have a Dream" phrase when she was a student activist saying a prayer in Albany, Georgia? Did they contact the estate of Chicago preacher and jurist

Archibald Carey to pay fees for the "let freedom ring" portion of King's speech that he lifted from Carey? The list goes on and on.

In the end, King's legacy is larger than his words, even the words he brilliantly sampled from others as he shaped them into weapons to free the victims of racial and economic oppression. His death at Memphis bore greater testimony to his transcendent appeal than even his speech before the Lincoln Memorial. But those words are important vehicles through which to recall King's legacy. They should not be controlled by anyone, even his family, more interested in their commercial value than their moral appeal. Although the King family certainly has a legal, and in some instances, even a moral right to make a living off King's voice and image, they have no monopoly on the social and ethical dimensions of King's legacy. His legacy belongs to the ages. It is in the hands of those who pursue justice and who work for peace to triumph over violence and hate. It is a legacy that can neither be bought nor sold. King's grand legacy is the inheritance of every man and woman who is willing to sac-rifice personal advantage for the common good, who is willing to place the needs of community above property, and who is able to share unselfishly the fruits of his labor with the lowliest creature. It is no won-der that few can claim to be in genuine league with King, even those who bear his name.

If the King family has too often sought to control the King legacy, cul-tural forces have too often undermined his radical legacy by portraying him as an honored sage who aimed to charm the world with his wise words. King's fire has often been quelled by the very corporate forces he opposed when he lived. His social legacy has been undercut by political amnesia. Predictably, the King holiday, while bringing just recognition to King and the civil rights movement, has often been used to sweeten his bit-ter presence as a searing prophet of edifying rage. If King cannot be taken hostage by his family, he surely cannot be imprisoned by the bland images and toothless mythologies that temporarily trap his true meaning.

CHAPTER 13

"If I Have to Go Through This to Give the People a Symbol"
The Burden of Representation

My wife and I dashed the long block from our apartment on Riverside Drive to the magnificently imposing Gothic structure of Riverside Church, pastored by the distinguished preacher, and our friend, James Forbes. I had read in the paper that Charles Adams, another friend and brilliant preacher, would be speaking at Riverside this July morning in 1998. Since it offered us the opportunity to enjoy fellowship with these great masters of sacred speech, I made my way to the church with my wife to hear "the Harvard whooper," as Adams is known, deliver the word.

I was intrigued by Adams's published topic, "Faith Critiques Faith," and I had listened to his preaching growing up in Detroit. Along with my pastor, Frederick Sampson, and Aretha Franklin's daddy, C. L. Franklin, Adams formed a trio of homileticians who thrilled me with their astonishing artistry. Adams is a formidably erudite but lucid preacher who is also a master of riveting, rapid-fire rhetoric that he delivers in a high, clear tone that often rushes into song when he reaches the climax in his sermons. He is as well a consummate liturgical dramatist whose instincts for edifying theater in the pulpit never betray a desire to play to his congregation. As usual, Adams brought insight and fire, or as black preachers say, the "learnin' and the burnin.'" The Riverside congregation was mesmerized by his verbal dexterity and his ability to join theological sophistication to spiritual yearning and, equally important, social analysis. Adams unfailingly reveals how the Bible speaks to politics and culture, and he didn't disappoint us on this brisk Sunday morning.

Near the middle of his sermon, I got an unexpected treat. Adams turned his attention to the King holiday and brilliantly dissected the forces that seek to twist King's memory and thwart his progressive agenda.

"I was somewhat taken aback when my friend, Harvey Cox, said to me that he could not celebrate the mandating of Martin Luther King's birthday as a national holiday," Adams stated, referring to the well-known religious scholar. "He took all the air out of my celebrative zeal when he reminded me that the holiday bill was passed by essentially the same Congress, and signed by the same President, that had refused to pass a new civil rights bill in the 1980s." Then Adams launched into one of his dizzying, nonstop verbal tirades that brilliantly illumine a subject through his panoramic view and exhaustive exegesis.

"They mandated that Martin Luther King, Jr.'s birthday be a federal holiday," he continued. "But they refused to demand the immediate release of Nelson Mandela; refused to protect affirmative action; devastated the Civil Rights Commission; amputated the legs and arms of the Equal Employment Opportunity Commission; cut off necessary support systems for the poor; snatched fifteen billion dollars away from poor babies, in order to reduce the tax liabilities of the wealthy; took away seven hundred and fifty billion dollars from the cities; cut off anti-poverty programs; polluted the air; destroyed jobs; carried on an illegal war in Nicaragua; despoiled the environment; de-neutered public education. And these are the same *people*, that made Martin Luther King Jr.'s birthday a paid federal holiday!" Riverside was delirious with joy as Adams barely gave us room to breathe, poignantly peppering us with a question that was more righteous than rhetorical.

"Now why did Ronald Regan sign that bill?" he demanded to know amid our laughter. We knew he'd quickly tell us.

"Could it be that Mr. Reagan understood that the *ease-ee-est* way to get rid of Martin Luther King, Jr. is to worship him? To honor him with a holiday that he never would have wanted. To celebrate his birth and his death, without committing ourselves to his vision and his love. It is easier to praise a dead hero than to recognize and follow a living prophet. The best way to dismiss any challenge is to exalt and adore the empirical source through which the challenge has come."

Adams's prophetic words are a useful reminder that King's legacy is bitterly contested in our nation. The struggle to make King a national icon has often ended in the effort to curb his challenging legacy, to make him a Safe Negro. In order to wrest King's memory from the cultural energies that would deny how he upended the status quo, we must understand why and how his birthday became a national holiday. We must also clarify how we can use the holiday to celebrate the concerns for which King died. In the process, we will have to confront the seductive amnesia that draws our nation away from the memory of King's challenging legacy.

The struggle to make Martin Luther King, Jr.,'s birthday a national holiday was fueled by longstanding efforts to find a public vehicle to celebrate black heroism. In the past, black heroism was conferred on figures who bravely and imaginatively confronted problems that bewitched black life—chattel slavery, black codes, Jim Crow law, lynching, castration, and the like. Denmark Vesey, Gabriel Prosser, Nat Turner, Sojourner Truth, and Harriet Tubman became heroes for resisting racial domination through slave insurrections, plantation rebellions, work slowdowns, running away, or hatching escape plans for hundreds of slaves. When slavery was abolished, blacks still faced huge obstacles to equality and freedom. Black heroes effectively battled the forces of persistent white oppression. Frederick Douglass and Booker T. Washington sealed their heroism through autobiographical narratives that detailed their rise from slavery to racial leadership. Henry Highland Garnett acquired mythic status by helping to rehabilitate black culture through politics. And Henry McNeal Turner achieved heroic stripes by appealing to religious faith and spiritual devotion to elevate the moral vision of black America during Reconstruction.

In each era, black heroes help to preserve the collective memory of black culture against racial oppression and amnesia. Collective memory was a crucial means by which blacks resisted racism and expressed their newfound freedom after slavery. As historian Eric Foner notes, long after "the end of the Civil War, the experience of bondage remained deeply etched in blacks' collective memory. . . . In countless ways, the newly freed slaves sought to 'throw off the badge of servitude,' to overturn the real and symbolic authority whites had exercised over every aspect of their lives." The collective memory of blacks attacked the racial amnesia of the dominant society. Collective memory also allowed blacks to shape a compelling story of racial struggle to counter the selective memory of white America. Historian Michael Kammen has explored how blacks used collective memory to celebrate themes that are crucial to their survival. Kammen argues that the dominant society's selective memory "kept African-Americans outside the mainstream of retrospective consciousness," motivating blacks to create and pass on their own heroic "traditions and memories." Kamen says that from "the mid-1880s onward, therefore, African-Americans largely celebrated their heroes and pursued their own historic occasions alone." African-Americans' "collective memory of slavery remained vivid," and "what they chose to emphasize by means of traditional activities each year was the memory of gaining freedom." Indeed, Frederick Douglass carved out his heroic niche in black culture by promoting a tradition of collective memory that fought the amnesia of the dominant society:

> It is not well to forget the past. Memory was given to man for some 'wise purpose. The past is . . . the mirror in which we may discern the dim outlines of the future. . . . Well the nation may forget, it may shut its eyes to the past, and frown upon any who may do otherwise, but the colored people of this country are bound to keep the past in lively memory till justice shall be done them.

In the light of these definitions and functions of black heroism, Martin Luther King, Jr., was undoubtedly a great black hero. What is also intriguing about King, and the source of no little consternation and suspicion in some black circles even today, is his appeal as well to mainstream society. Part of the trouble is quite understandable. If the black hero achieves his stature by pressing the full weight of black complaint against the lethal limits of white oppression, how can the white mainstream from which such oppression originates genuinely love this dark son of thunder? Either something is awry in the white mainstream's embrace of such a figure—their motives are impure, their intent of use is flawed, or their acceptance of him as the right sort of black is a rejection of the wrong kind—or he is surely to be regarded with the most heartfelt skepticism one can manage. From the beginning of his career, King has evoked violently conflicting responses, and continues to, as he is canonized in our national culture as the Great Black Man. Equally intriguing is how the same blacks who regard King with skepticism, or at least they do his avid reception by whites, are put off when those same whites question King's fitness, not as a Black Hero, which after all is just fine with them, but as an American Hero. That is as close a substitute for a Great White Man that any black could hope or, more likely, dread to get. Whether these blacks liked it or not, even if they found such a prospect distasteful and altogether undesirable, they knew in their hearts that for King to be accorded such respect in the white world—even if it is begrudging, and all the better if that is true—means that something large and meaningful, and perhaps unpleasantly so, will have been achieved. And that achievement is the due recognition that a black man meant as much to the future and salvation of white America as he did to blacks, and that his achievements drew from the same hunger for moral decency and political democracy that drove the founding fathers into nationhood. Even if some blacks didn't wholly accept King as the best of what blackness can be, they did accept him as the best that a black person can be when seeking to live with and love whites.

These and many more conflicting views swirled around the fierce debate that tapped an even more ferocious groundswell of emotion: Should we make Martin Luther King, Jr.'s birthday a national holiday? The gauntlet was thrown fast and decisively. On April 8, 1968, four days after King was assassinated, Michigan congressman John Conyers introduced legislation seeking a King federal holiday. According to scholar William Wiggins, Conyers's gesture boosted a fourteen-year three-act play that dramatized the quest for public recognition of black achievement. Wiggins maintains that King's holiday celebration marked "a historical reenactment of the drama originally played out in Abraham Lincoln's issuance of the Emancipation Proclamation." He argues that for the "second time in a little more than a century, Washington, D.C., was the center stage upon which this Afro-American morality play of freedom and justice was performed." The initial drama, he says, was Lincoln's signing of the Emancipation Proclamation, with Lincoln as the hero. The second drama began with Conyers's foray into legislative waters. It ended with Ronald Reagan's signing a bill declaring King's birthday the tenth federal holiday. Altogether, Wiggins says, there were three acts.

The first act of the second drama broke out in the streets and in the midst of Washington, D.C.'s monuments during a four-year period lasting from 1978 to 1982. During this time, blacks from across the country journeyed to Washington to commemorate King's birthday. They also expressed "their demands to have this date declared a national holiday by marching to the Lincoln Memorial and cheering rousing speeches from Afro-American spokespersons as Mr. Stevie Wonder, the singer/composer, and Mrs. Coretta Scott King, Dr. King's widow." The second act took place in congressional debates between 1975 to 1983 as a variety of witnesses passionately attacked or defended the idea of a national holiday for King. Wiggins notes the wide-ranging group of "blacks and whites, men and women, Jews and Christians, conservatives and liberals, young and old, northerners and southerners, laborers and executives, Nobel laureates and governmental bureaucrats, racists and integrationists, patriots and Communists" who voiced their support or disdain for the proposed federal holiday. The final act of the King holiday drama took place in the Rose Garden at the White House, where the mass media created a spectacle of American collective memory. The news corps heavily covered the event. Photographers flashed pictures of Reagan signing the bill into law, and television cameras captured for posterity the image of Mrs. King and other supporters looking over the president's shoulder as he gave flesh to distant dreams with a stroke of his pen. Wiggins cites the irony of a drama where the hero never appears on stage. Still, "his presence is felt in pictures of him that the demonstrators carried and in his ringing words of freedom which were quoted by those who testified before the various House and Senate subcommittees."

If this three-act play seems too neatly to summarize the tumultuous events that crowded onto the historical stage, there were certainly other fits and starts, other stage directions uttered behind the curtains in *sotto voce*, while some actions occurred very much in the public eye. In 1971, SCLC delivered to Congress petitions filled with 3 million signatures supporting the King holiday, though Congress neglected to take action. In 1973, Harold Washington, later mayor of Chicago and then a state assemblyman, sponsored a state King holiday bill that was signed into law in Illinois. In 1974, Massachusetts and Connecticut followed suit and enacted statewide holidays. In 1975, the New Jersey State Supreme Court ruled that the state must provide a paid holiday in honor of King to accord with New Jersey's labor contract with the New Jersey State Employees Association. In 1978, the National Council of Churches encouraged Congress to pass the legislation for the King holiday. In 1979, Coretta King testified for the King holiday before the Senate Judiciary Committee and before joint hearings of Congress. She also employed the King Center to mobilize a nationwide citizens' lobby for the King holiday. The King Center gathered over 300,000 signatures in a national petition campaign to establish a federal holiday in recognition of King's achievements. The same year, President Carter appealed to Congress to pass legislation for a King holiday, as the bill began to move through congressional committees. Later that year, the King holiday bill was defeated in a floor vote in the House. In 1980, Stevie Wonder released his hugely popular "Happy Birthday," a song dedicated to King's memory and to mobilizing public support for the King holiday. Later that year, the bill once again failed to pass, but this time the margin of defeat was only five votes, a hopeful sign for King supporters. In 1981, the King Center organized a holiday coalition whose office and staff in Washington, D.C., were funded by Stevie Wonder. In 1982, Coretta King went again to Congress to testify for the holiday bill before the House Committee on Post Office and Civil Service's Subcommittee on Census and Population. In the same year, Coretta King and Stevie Wonder gathered and delivered King Center petitions bearing more than 6 million signatures supporting the holiday legislation to Speaker of the House Tip O'Neill. In August 1983, the House of Representatives passed the holiday bill by a vote of 338 to 90, a dramatic turnaround from its first vote four years earlier. Later that same month, at the demonstration commemorating the twentieth anniversary of the 1963 March on Washington, over 750,000 marchers urged the Senate and the president to pass the federal holiday legislation honoring King's birthday. More than a year later, in October 1983, the Senate heeded the demonstrators' call and passed the bill by a vote of 78 to 22. And on November 3, 1983, Reagan signed the bill establishing the third Monday of each January as the Martin Luther King, Jr., national holiday.

Many of the arguments in the broader culture against having an official King holiday—that King was undeserving because his actions led to violence, that the birthday was too expensive, that there should be a commemorative holiday instead, that it was too soon after his death to honor him, that a black other than King should be feted, that his appeal was limited to blacks—surfaced in congressional chambers. Each argument was met with reasoned rebuttal by members of Congress, their aides, and other activists and leaders. For instance, the twisted reasoning that portrayed King as unworthy of honor because his nonviolent campaigns led to violence—an argument made by right-wing zealots who hated King—was aired by opponents to the bill. E. Stanley Rittenhouse, a legislative aide for the conservative Liberty Lobby, not only told committee chairman Strom Thurmond that the bill was "a thoroughly bad piece of legislation," but he asserted that it would "sanctify and justify a man who deliberately brought violence to American streets, a subversive who was called 'the most notorious liar in America' by J. Edgar Hoover—who was in a position to know—It is a very one-sided, racist legislation." Rittenhouse's bitter declaration was quickly supported by Democratic Georgia congressman Larry P. McDonald, who argued that King was "not the caliber of person suitable to be made into a national hero . . . his teaching of contempt for the law and legal process makes it most unsuitable for his anniversary to be made a national holiday." But an aide to Democratic senator Birch Bayh challenged McDonald by suggesting that laws that corrupt the principles of life, liberty, and the pursuit of happiness are bad laws that need to be changed.

Later Rittenhouse argued that the King bill "would be very costly to the citizens and taxpayers of America." Senator Bayh compared the cost of a King holiday to the cost of a black or Latino child's being denied a full sense of citizenship and cultural belonging:

> The cost? What are the costs of a national holiday? Perhaps more rightly, what are the costs of not having a holiday? What are the costs of second-class citizenship? What are the costs of a little black boy or a little black girl or a little brown boy or a little brown girl not having the opportunity to share in a national holiday of some great leader that happens to look like them, to come from the same heritage that they came from?

Coretta King seconded Bayh's comments, pointing out that slave labor financed the expansion of American industry. Although denying that she sought black reparations, she said in the light of the "hundreds of years of economic sacrifice and involuntary servitude of American blacks, is it too much to ask that one paid holiday per year be set aside to honor the contributions of a black man who gave his life in an historic struggle for social decency?" And after arguments were put forth that perhaps Booker T. Washington or the late General Chappy James were more deserving of honor than King, Coretta King admitted that although "there have been many black historical figures other than Martin who deserve to be honored with a holiday," they "necessarily addressed issues that tended to concern blacks exclusively, while Martin Luther King, Jr., spoke to us all."

Holiday opponents denied King's universal appeal and instead attempted to portray him an unpatriotic communist sympathizer. Julia Brown, a black woman and a former member of the Communist party, testified that King was "closely connected with the Communist Party" and that if the bill passed, "we may as well take down the Stars and Stripes that fly over this building and replace it with a Red flag." John Bircher Alan Stang was presented as a "professional journalist and writer" who charged that King "collaborated intimately with the Communists from the very beginning of his career to its end." But senatorial aides' and subcommittee staff's close questioning of those who accused King of being a communist revealed that no one had ever seen King at a Communist party gathering. In the end, the legislation passed, and Reagan, himself a disbeliever in King's worth as a national hero deserving a federal holiday, signed the bill into law.

If the bitter battle to squeeze King into the cycle of public holidays that cement citizenship seemed to be a significant victory, as I believe it was, an even bigger challenge looms in keeping King's birthday from being turned into a festival of forgetting his challenging legacy. Neither is the motivation to forget King's radical dimensions a simple, singular one. All sorts of amnesia compete to rob the King holiday of its potential to remind us of what practices angered and grieved King and what issues made him care the most. King's obsession with wiping out racial oppression, poverty, militarism, and violence and his love for young people and the poor of every race who were trapped in ghettoes or shotgun shacks are often clouded by a haze of recalling King's wish to overcome bigotry and his early dream of racial harmony. Those ideas certainly deserve mention and often warrant praise. But their imbalance in the rituals and celebrations that fix King's legacy in the public mind threatens to diminish his true legacy, one that I have explored throughout this book.

Ironically, a good deal of the amnesia that displaces our collective memory of King's challenging legacy is meant to spare our nation the prospect of reliving the agony that made the King holiday necessary. *Reverential amnesia* is the sort of forgetting that seeks to avoid harm, in the present, to aggrieved victims of injustice by repressing the memory of past pain. In this case, the individuals or culture associated with the offense—economic inequality, sexism, white supremacy—place themselves in the shoes of the person or group that is hurt and imagines what it must feel like to have to live every day with the consciousness of past suffering. The advantage is that the offending party does not have to assume responsibility for the hurt inflicted or in any way seek to address the ongoing expression of the original offense. Still, the motive is noble, if misled.

Repentant amnesia, on the other hand, seeks to forget the pain of the past as a gesture of reconciliation for the harm inflicted by an individual or group. In repentant amnesia, the emphasis is on the individual or group that inflicted harm; they forget the past in order to avoid the embarrassment or discomfort of remembering a prior injury or injustice. If the mode of reverential amnesia is, "I want to forget because it will cause the offended party embarrassment," the mode of repentant amnesia is, "I want to forget because it will cause me embarrassment." In the case of repentant amnesia, forgetting is an attempt to reconcile with the offended party through a relationship of goodwill based on repressed memory. It is forgiving by forgetting. Again, such a gesture relieves the offending party of responsibility. And while the attempt to establish healthy relations with the offended are welcome, the pain that is repressed often roils beneath the surface. Such repressed pain often infects the relations between the two parties in strange and sometimes unpredictable fashion. The burden is shifted to the offended. She is viewed as hostile or, more important in repentant amnesia, as unforgiving, should she bring up the past or assert how it is connected to present problems.

Revisionist amnesia achieves its effect, ironically enough, through manipulated memory, through selective retrieval of the past that changes the tint and tone of what actually happened. Of course, all memory is filtered through the prism of the present, affected by its priorities and its chosen points of view. But in revisionist amnesia, the present is much more important in determining the past. In revisionist amnesia, past pain is never denied. The catch, however, is that the past is never viewed as causing the degree or depth of injury claimed by the offended party. The mode of revisionist amnesia is, "I do not forget what happened and I am accordingly embarrassed, but you should be comforted by realizing that it is not nearly as bad as you remember." In revisionist amnesia, the contested terrain of memory is the political battlefield where the war to interpret the past and the present is fought. If the past wasn't as bad as the injured claimed it to be, then surely the present cannot be as bad as they say it is. The burden is shifted again to the injured. Now they must compete with both the faulty memories of the offending party as well as the idealized—read, forgotten and distorted—practices of their predecessors. A different twist on revisionist amnesia permits the injured party to focus on one part of the past while negating others. This is especially true of racial issues that bring discomfort or embarrassment, like the specific suffering of darker blacks or antipathy to "lower" classes. It is also true of social issues that challenge a particular political or religious value—for instance, the existence in black culture of black conservatives or black gays and lesbians. This selective retrieval of the legacy of pain protects the injured from having to search his own conscience or challenge his own privilege as a member of the injured party: the privilege to sanctify one's pain, say as a middle-class male, while denying the pain of others, say a poor single mother.

Recalcitrant amnesia is the most virulent, obvious, and, as a result, perhaps the most easily combated form of forgetting. It is the effort by individuals or groups to forget the past pain of parties they have offended by flatly denying that they were connected to such pain. Their mode is, "I do not remember causing any pain and therefore I will not be embarrassed." It is apparent that such persons or groups have no intention of assuming responsibility for injuries or injustices that they deny they inflicted. This sort of amnesia is akin to the credo of the cheating husband: "Deny everything," even those things, perhaps especially those things, that are obviously offensive and that violate one's partner.

Resistant amnesia, finally, is the forgetting of past and present pain by the offended party. The intent of such amnesia is to relieve the stress and fatigue brought on by the memory of oppression. Resistant amnesia is primarily aimed at survival of the injured party. The mode of resistant amnesia is, "I have to forget what has happened in order to live." Often, too, there is an element of shame, a shame that sometimes translates into bitter denials of the force of oppression caused by one's identity. At other times, there is a grave discomfort with one's very identity, since the act of calling attention to one's identity is perceived by the injured party as the source of one's suffering. There is in resistant amnesia a confusion between the sort of attention to one's identity that is diseased and destructive and the sort of self-identification that is healthy and a source of pride. This grave identity discomfort and confusion, or outright denial of the historical effects of blackness, can be termed *Aframnesia*. The deliberate repression of painful memory is intended to give the injured person or group the time to mend and to fashion an existence that depends less on the past and more on the present. The danger of such an approach, of course, is that the injured party fails to grasp the important lessons of one's suffering for one's group but also for the nation. Thus the helpful dimensions of past struggle are lost, as well as hints about how to handle current difficulties. Of course, such difficulties are downplayed, if not dismissed, in resistant amnesia, creating tension between the members of the injured group who hold that the only way to get past the pain is through recalling and thereby defeating its force and those who believe that recall and reinjury are indistinguishable. Tragically, resistant amnesia frees the injured party from responsibility for fighting in the present over the interpretation of the past and, hence, for how it will be used to aid or hinder the liberation efforts of the injured group.

The struggle to interpret and celebrate King's holiday celebration shows how different features of amnesia fuse, then flare, to distract our attention from King's challenging legacy. For instance, in a study of King ceremonies in three distinct venues—school assemblies and after-school programs, community observances, and federal governmental agencies— political scientist Richard Merelman discovered a big difference when whites and blacks were in charge of the celebrations. When whites led the King celebrations and were its major performers, white discrimination against blacks was mentioned only one-third of the time. Merelman writes that whites "obviously prefer less threatening . . . depictions, such as poems by black writers, or songs by black composers." Merelman states that whites "thus help to project black culture but avoid the most painful aspects of domination *or* resistance." By contrast, blacks who were in charge of King celebrations and acted as its major performers emphasized the theme of white discrimination against blacks, even as their presentations contained "little black resistance." Merelman pointed to the ironic absence of resistance as a theme in King celebrations since King was a "leader of black resistance to white oppression, a man who achieved great success in voting rights, school desegregation, and access to public accommodations." In the case of whites' leading King celebrations, it seems possible that a combination of reverential, revisionist, and repentant amnesia may have prevented them from emphasizing the effect of white domination on black life. By not mentioning such white discrimination, they may have intended not to reinjure black psyches by replaying dreadful scenes of past bigotry. Then too, they may have avoided an emphasis on white discrimination because they deemed it a much less harmful barrier to black achievement than do blacks. Or they may have deemphasized white domination as the terms of an implicit social contract with blacks of forgiving the past, and themselves, by refusing to mention its heinous dimensions.

In the case of the black celebrations, perhaps a version of revisionist amnesia is at work, leading blacks to lament white domination while failing to emphasize the political agency in the hands of even oppressed people to shape their destinies and work against the forces that hurt them—hence, the struggles of Fannie Lou Hamer, Septima Clark, Bob Moses, Julian Bond, John Lewis, and for that matter, Martin Luther King, Jr., not simply to complain of white domination but to do something about it, to take strong and strategic actions against it, is forgotten or dismissed. By stressing white discrimination while leaving aside the powerful ways that blacks acted to free themselves, blacks not only miss an opportunity to stress their strength but they slide precipitously close to victimizing self-pity. As Merelman suggests:

> To be sure, blacks as victims, not resisters, may heighten white guilt. After all, there is pathos in the exploitation of the weak. And white guilt conveys a strategic advantage to blacks in the struggle between the two racial groups. But guilt has its limits; moreover,

this self-portrait as victim suggests weakness—even fear—on the part of blacks. Thus, the theme of victimization diminishes whatever strength the ceremonies might create in blacks.

Although too many white critics complain that blacks exploit victimization discourse—a rhetorical ruse that makes fresh victims out of injured blacks because they are again blamed for being victimized to start with—Merelman's criticism is on target and a healthy reminder of the need to emphasize King's, and other black folks', heroic resistance to white oppression. All that is remembered of King in the ceremonies Merelman studied was his nonviolent civil disobedience and his great oratorical talent. Again, revisionist amnesia seems to have undermined an appreciation for how King deployed a broad measure of tactics and strategies to resist racial oppression, including voter registration drives, marches, boycotts, and strikes. Besides, a wide range of resistance techniques were employed by a host of black participants in the civil rights movement that have been largely forgotten or overlooked: mass picketing, public protests, strategic voting, the creation of independent political parties, political lobbying, legal maneuvers, petitioning, sit-ins, and the orchestration of civil disorder. Amnesia has kept America from coming to grips with the sorts of complex practices that black folk engaged in to resist white supremacy, economic inequality, class exploitation, and social suffering.

Amnesia also makes it easier for Americans to believe that racial progress was an inevitable feature of American history. In revisionist amnesia, brutal racial atrocities—rape, lynching, castration, savage gun assaults, burnings, fire-hosing of children and women, police dog assaults on men and women, police brutality—withered away as a bad piece of fruit on the vine of democracy. Furthermore, repentant amnesia in particular keeps many whites from admitting that it was their fathers, grandfathers, uncles, granduncles, aunts, grandaunts, mothers, and grandmothers who not only committed many of these unspeakable acts but abided their ugly persistence in custom, law, and culture. The point, of course, is not to shame whites by scoring them for bad behavior; the point is to acknowledge the depth and complexity of racism and to acknowledge that it has flesh and blood. Indeed, a large part of the affirmative action debate draws from such repentant amnesia, with a good deal of recalcitrant amnesia thrown in as well. Amnesia makes people forget that the specific problems between blacks and whites are not faceless, nameless, voiceless, and raceless. It can also make us forget that racial problems are not self-resolving. Amnesia makes us forget that particular groups collectively bear responsibility for such actions because they collectively bene-fited from legally sanctioned racial inequality. Further, racial amnesia makes us believe that the attempt to assign responsibility to dominant society for actions taken in its name is an act of self-righteous blame or finger-pointing ridicule, which too many blacks have themselves suffered. Instead, it is an attempt to craft social policies and political measures that bring sane solutions and just balance to insanely unfair social situations. But many citizens believe that the advocates of such measures and poli-cies are the source of the problem and not its solution. This is surely the strong wind of revisionist and recalcitrant amnesia having its way with history and truth. The truth is that heroic black and white Americans engaged in brave and formidably imaginative acts of resistance, organiza-tion, mobilization, and rebellion against social injustice that was main-tained to help some and hurt others.

Of course, if the opposite of black victimization is the celebration of black resistance, we must admit that such resistance has never been strongly encouraged in our nation. That is why the King holiday is an even more important jog to the nation's collective memory. King holiday cele-brations must therefore give quite a different picture of King's heroism—one that emphasizes his strong resistance to oppression. But the holiday celebrations must move beyond the charismatic center of King's person-ality to emphasize the resistance movements of ordinary black folk in the sixties and still today. Surely in the cultural consensus that was needed to make King's birthday a national holiday there evolved a great deal of amne-sia—reverential, resistant, revisionist, and repentant. For instance, the need to clarify King's heroism, and therefore to articulate why he deserved national honor, focused on his individual achievements at the expense of the traditions that produced him and the other elements of the move-ment that inspired him, often pushed him, and at times even bettered him in their substantive contribution to the black freedom struggle. Too many King celebrations portray him as a Lone Ranger out to rescue his people from the ravages of racism. Before his arrival they were helpless, and after his departure they were hopeless. But only a virulent strand of revisionist amnesia can make us believe that. King came from a culture of social valiance and quiet heroism that mounted resistance to racial oppression during each era. Undeniably, King occupied a key role—I would argue, the most important symbolic one—in the history of that resistance. But the very fact that such a distinction is made—between symbolic and sub-stantive contributions to the movement for black freedom—underscores how King was used, by blacks and whites, as a representative figurehead in the civil rights movement. Understanding King's role doesn't diminish his importance; it simply suggests that his role was unique and that it was made possible because he answered the needs of blacks and whites at *the* crucial time of remaking the moral and social practices of race in America.

King was the defining figure of his age. He was, by any measure, a great American hero who was able to alter substantially and influence the course of events because of his mix of skills, talents, and visions. That definition derives from Sidney Hook's famous distinction between two types of potential heroes: the "eventful" and "event-making." Hook defined the hero in history as "the individual to whom we can justifiably attribute preponderant influence in determining an issue or event whose consequences would have been profoundly different if he had not acted as he did." Hook said the *"eventful* man in history is any man whose actions influence subsequent developments along a quite different course than would have been followed if these actions had not been taken." On the other hand, the *"event-making* man is an eventful man whose actions are the consequences of outstanding capacities of intelligence, will, and character rather than of accidents of position." For Hook, the distinction between the two was more than academic. In his mind, the distinction underscores the notion that "a hero is great not merely in virtue of what he does but in virtue of what he is." In the light of Hook's definitions, King certainly qualifies as a person whose combination of intelligence, moral imagination, and action changed the course of history. This does not mean that King was the only figure in the civil rights movement who possessed the gifts he brilliantly displayed or, for that matter, that he had the best skills to organize and stimulate social movement. But the force of his personality, intelligence, and gifts helped in a decisive way to catalyze social change and symbolize the broad black struggle for human rights.

Further, as historian Lerone Bennett argues, King's ability to create the conditions that led to social change was clearly demonstrated in Birmingham, Alabama, where the movement King symbolized gained one of its greatest victories in the fight against legal segregation. Bennett acknowledges that no leader can "create an event the time is not prepared for," but he contends that great leaders apprehend "what the times require," and thus act in the face of great opposition to change the times: "In Birmingham, King approached that kind of greatness, creating the occasion of the 'Negro Revolution' by an act almost everyone said was ill-timed and ill-chosen. Birmingham . . . was *chosen*, not stumbled upon. It was created by a man who knew exactly what he wanted and how much he would probably have to pay to get it."

Unfortunately, the declaration of King's undeniable heroism has depended on revisionist amnesia to forget the crucial contributions of ordinary folk who struggled mightily against oppression. In a way, the Lone Ranger theory of historical change is the flip-side of the victimization argument; either way, black folk are denied agency in their own interests. Either they failed to resist in the face of overwhelming odds, or they waited for a messianic figure to set them free. I think there is a way to acknowledge King's individual genius—even his strong sense of religious call that involves elements of messianism—while also accentuating the courage of ordinary black folk whose actions were just as important in helping black folk to realize the racial revolution for which King is almost always given exclusive credit. Of course, in a one-man show, by getting rid of him—that is, by first assassinating him and then honoring him—we can do away with the demands he brought. But King is a vital symbol of the ongoing demands for freedom. He is as well a symbol of the extraordinary genius of a host of black folk who invested their lives in the struggle to be free.

King was surely no solo prophet. His brilliant beliefs about black resistance were nurtured in him by the prophetic brigade of the black church as well as the traditions of critical social reflection given him by theological study. Equally important, King was part of a broader social movement for justice during the sixties that he did not always justly acknowledge or help the public to comprehend. In a sense, his amnesia about others who struggled for social change has been passed along and ritualized by journalists and historians, with the exception of writers who are unearthing the histories of Southern communities that struggled for their freedom largely beyond the television glare that trailed King—and which often blinded others to their presence—and beyond the ideological orbit in which he circulated. For instance, SNCC organizers had been working in Albany, Georgia, to get out the vote and confront segregation in a systematic fashion long before King came to Albany to stir things up and meet what is widely regarded as one of his greatest defeats. What angered many of the SNCC organizers is that when King held a press conference after being released from jail, he excluded SNCC from the proceedings, a move that further alienated them from his leadership and created even more resentment of King's camera-hogging strategy of social change. As one SNCC organizer, Cordell Reagon, put it, "I don't think that anybody appreciates going to jail, getting their balls busted day in and day out, and then you don't even get to speak on it."

Of course, we can draw a line between King before 1965 and afterward, when his understanding of leadership broadened and deepened.

But from the time of the Montgomery bus boycotts until Selma, he was imbued with a rigid, hierarchical, top-down conception of leadership. A large part of King's beliefs were gender coded, since he failed to recognize women as leaders. King's sexism meant that he would overlook not only the brilliant organizing of Ella Baker, but the leadership of women throughout the South who organized local communities for social change. Baker was one of King's most vocal and insightful critics. Most of her criticism had to do with King's failure to nurture leadership in others, the key to her philosophy of organizing and empowering others to become leaders and to effect social change. King's insistence on a top-down leadership style rubbed Baker raw in all the wrong places. As Baker said, "I have always thought what is needed is the development of people who are interested not in being leaders as much as in developing leadership in others." Baker was critical as well of the unhealthy dependence that most traditional leadership instilled in people because she insisted that "strong people don't need strong leaders." Baker urged skepticism about charismatic leadership, the sort that King represented and that to her was fundamentally antidemocratic:

> I have always felt it was a handicap for oppressed people to depend so largely on a leader, because unfortunately in our culture, the charismatic leader usually becomes a leader because he has found a spot in the public limelight. It usually means that the media made him, and the media may undo him. There is also the danger in our culture that, because a person is called upon to give public statements and is acclaimed by the establishment, such a person gets to the point of believing that he *is* the movement. Such people get so involved with playing the game of being important that they exhaust themselves and their time and they don't do the work of actually organizing the people.

Baker tried to get King to resist what she thought was a "cult of personality" as early as Montgomery, but to little avail. She recalled an anniversary celebration in Montgomery that failed to mention the role of ordinary people and instead concentrated on King, "our great leader." Baker recalls that everything was "a reflection of the greatness of the individual." After speaking to King, which she said "was not very bright," she claimed that he rejoined, "Well, I can't help what people do." On another occasion, Baker suggested that King share speaking duties at a mass meeting in Clarksdale in the hopes that the meeting would not only inspire folk but help them get organized. "I know that you would hesitate to be the only speaker," she wrote him, "and would like to suggest the possibility that one or two other speakers be requested to deal with specific points, such as explaining the provisions of the 1957 Civil Rights Act and procedure for making use of the act or similar informational emphasis." Baker's fundamental clash with King, and the issue that led to her resignation as executive director of SCLC, was that she "did not envision the SCLC as a leading civil rights organization with national recognition, but rather as a vehicle for the creation of a mass movement with indigenous leadership."

Baker's work with SNCC allowed her to encourage leadership by teaching young people to lead themselves, to show no deference to charismatic authority, and to organize communities into forces for social change. She deeply influenced a number of leaders, from Julian Bond to Diane Nash, from John Lewis to Bob Moses, to take into their hands the reins of group leadership as they sought to resist racial domination. Such group leadership had its own perils. Former SNCC chairman John Lewis praised the "very noble concept, the idea of a leaderless movement, of a truly indigenous, nonviolent revolution." But he also squarely faced the eventual collapse:

> Anarchy and chaos. Freedom and openness. It's amazing how one set of values can slide almost imperceptibly into another, how principles that are treasured at one moment as positive and healthy can, with time and a shift in circumstances, become forces of destruction and divisiveness. That was what happened to SNCC by the fall of 1964. The precepts that had been so fundamental to us when we began—decentralization, minimal structure, a distrust of leadership—were now beginning to tear us apart.

SNCC's brilliant experiment with "democratic charisma" eventually led to its expansion and subsequently to its demise in 1969. But it remains one of the most profound and progressive attempts to share the decision-making process in a way unheard of in antidemocratic, top-down organizations like SCLC. And further, beyond the genius of King's personality and his symbolic authority, factors that shaped and drove SCLC, SNCC was able to do more organizationally to bring about racial justice for ordinary black folk than its parent body. National leadership of the sort King symbolized did far less than local, largely anonymous, female leaders of the nitty-gritty work of organizing poor people to take their destinies in their own hands. As Bob Moses argued, there was a key difference between a mobilizing tradition of social change—where the emphasis was on stimulating social rebellion through demonstrations and other dramatic efforts to challenge racial domination—and an organizing tradition that sought to help people develop indigenous leadership in order to tap local community resources in the fight to transform their way of life. While mobilizing and organizing were certainly complementary functions, the national leadership got most of the ink, while the organizers who labored in the trenches got most of the dirt. Their efforts went largely unrecognized. Yet the mobilizing work of the national leadership would have been impossible without local organization. King would certainly learn this lesson as he sought to organize communities in Northern ghettoes and as he sought to organize and mobilize the poor to march on Washington, taking a page from the playbooks of groups like SNCC and CORE.

King's symbolic dominance of the civil rights movement, and hence his preeminence as the leader of black revolt, has led to spirited debate as to whether his style of charismatic leadership helped or harmed the civil rights movement. Sociologist Charles Payne, in his brilliant analytic history of the Mississippi movement, points to how an exclusive engagement with national leaders gives a misleading portrait of social change. In speaking of King's first crusade for justice in Montgomery, Payne eloquently defends ordinary local folk against an emphasis on the elite national figures:

> Finding Dr. King to take the leadership of the movement was fortuitous, but the local activists had put themselves in a position to be lucky through lifetimes of purposeful planning and striving. . . . Taking the high drama of the mid-fifties and early sixties out of the longer historical context implicitly overvalues those dramatic moments and undervalues the more mundane activities that helped make them possible—the network-building, the grooming of another generation of leadership, the sheer persistence. . . . The popular conception of Montgomery—a tired woman refused to give up her seat and a prophet rose up to lead the grateful masses—is a good story but useless history.

At a 1986 conference on King held in the Caucus Room of the Russell Senate Office Building in Washington, D.C., Bob Moses and historian

Clayborne Carson were rightly critical of the dependence on the single, messianic deliverer encouraged in top-down views of leadership. Both criticized the view that King was the only significant leader to emerge. As Carson warns, even "the most perceptive King-centered studies will have limited value unless they acknowledge that the black struggle was a locally-based mass movement rather than simply a reform movement led by national civil rights leaders." He also warned that King-centered scholarship ran the risk, if it wasn't careful, of reinforcing "the tendency of many Americans to see him not only as the exemplar of the modern black leader, at least in the pre–Jesse Jackson era, but as a charismatic figure who single-handedly directed the course of the civil rights movement." Bob Moses was blunter: "I never thought of the movement in terms of King. It never occurred to me to think about the movement in terms of King. I lived and breathed the *movement*." Moses said that historians should offer histories of the movement, and not a man, so that "through that history of the movement we can then understand the relationship of Dr. King to the movement." Moses argued that without such a history, "trying to understand King is as meaningless as trying to understand the wave without the ocean." Moses reveals a crucial predicate of such a new history of King: that it can relieve the "frustration with young people who don't know how to relate to Dr. King because they see him as a god, so they have no concept that they, too, can be like him."

The late Nathan Huggins, while agreeing with Moses and other critics that one must emphasize organizations and movements, warned against viewing the people who participated in the movement as "interchangeable parts. You cannot remove Martin Luther King from that picture and have the story happen more or less the same way." Since that is the case, Huggins argued that it is precisely King's personality and character that are significant in explaining his role in history. Although he acknowledged the need for balance between impersonal forces and personal characteristics, Huggins stressed King's unique charisma, his emphasis on love, and his sense of call to leadership as key to explaining his career. Huggins took issue with Moses's metaphor of the ocean's being the movement and the individuals in it the waves. Huggins argued that "just as the charismatic individual gets himself killed or his life ends, so in reality movements ebb and flow." Huggins found a degree of mystery in both movements and charisma in both oceans and personality. "If it's misguided to wait for the next charismatic leader to come along," Huggins argued, "it's also misguided to expect the lunar cycle to work so that the ocean will crest, to wait for the ocean to crest." Huggins warned that "it's possible to create gods out of movements, too, just as it is out of people."

It is crucial, then, to balance an appreciation for the social forces that made King's emergence possible—the end of World War II and the eclipse of European colonial powers, the rise of independence in African and Asian nations, the growing black dissatisfaction with American apartheid, and the politicization of black Southern populations—and the organizing activities of local leaders in grasping the true nature of social transformation in the sixties. But we must also pay attention to King's peculiar genius, to the extraordinary charisma and gift of leadership that, beyond the undeniable lift he received for a while from the white media, made him an extraordinary symbol of social change, and in the end, a symbol of radical challenge to the racial and economic status quo. Of course, we must underscore King's own sense of destiny. Time and again he reminded his hearers, and the nation, in a paraphrase of theologian Reinhold Niebuhr, that "the battering rams of historical necessity" had thrust him into his leadership position. And like many charismatic religious figures before and after him, King appealed to a notion of providence, a sense of call, to justify his ascent to leadership. Too often such an appeal is used to cloak calculated misdeeds and sanctify the acquisition of social power and religious authority. These claims are often used to accumulate wealth or expand the minister's cultural influence.

King had a complete conviction that God had called him to his task of sacrificial leadership, which helps to explain partially his rigid, initially authoritarian leadership style. When you're being led by God, it's hard to listen to mere mortals. From the very beginning of his public ministry, King's sense of call was reaffirmed in his own personal religious experiences and through other friends and supporters across the nation. Five days after King's home was bombed in Montgomery, a Crozer classmate sent him a telegram, urging him: "Fight on Amos, God is with you." In 1956, King received a letter from a Baptist minister in Baltimore who affirmed him: "You are becoming a prophet of this day and age. . . . Lion King is on the march." Another Baptist minister wrote to him in 1956 that "I have longed for a Baptist Messiah like you since 1932!!" When King made his way to a mass meeting the evening he was convicted of conspiracy for leading the bus boycott, a preacher heralded him: "He who was nailed to the cross for us this afternoon approaches." And in May, King received a letter from Shreveport, Louisiana, whose writer proclaimed: "You're a leader, yes leading 16,000,000 Negroes to the Promised Land. Hold your *head* up if you do die *hard!*" Throughout his career King conceived of himself as a Moses figure; he said in 1957 that "if I had to die tomorrow morning I would die happy because I've been to the mountaintop and I've seen the promised land and it's going to be here in Montgomery." In his last speech in 1968, he said, "I just want to do God's will. And He's allowed me to go up to the mountain. And I've looked over. And I've seen the Promised Land." He was constantly told by a stream of well-wishers and followers that he was Moses or, sometimes, a Christ-like Messiah sent from God to do God's will. If King was convinced, like Jesus, that his death could be redemptive, it was not out of arrogance, but a hard-headed, clear-eyed belief that his martyrdom could drive home the very cause for which he was willing to die.

Still, too many King supporters believe that to proclaim his genius is to assert his perfection, or worse yet, that he was a figure who remained the same throughout his career. But only the worst sort of amnesia can make us forget that King was supremely human and full of the same fears and frustrations that all human beings endure, except his were magnified a thousand fold by the weight that he carried as he made his way to Memphis and martyrdom. King was a complex figure who changed his mind—about race, about class, about leadership, and about poverty—as he matured into the powerful, disturbing figure he was to become. It is convenient to forget that in 1967, King failed to make the Gallup Poll's list of the ten most popular Americans. His growing radicalism was spoiling the canonization that had begun in earnest in 1964, when he won the Nobel Peace Prize. In fact, when he was murdered, King was unpopular with white America and had lost his sure hold on huge segments of the black population as well.

These are crucial facts to remember as we celebrate the King holiday. We should neither be ashamed to celebrate his greatness nor afraid to point to his limitations, taking them both into consideration as we figure out how to use the King holiday better to serve the cause of justice for which King died. Sadly, King did not give full due to those nameless, faceless women and young people who deserved the credit for social change in communities throughout the South. And though for most of his life he had a limited, rigid view of leadership, King was a brilliant, bold, sacrificial, charismatic leader whose career symbolized the ingenuity of the people he dearly loved and whose cause he proclaimed for most of his tragically shortened adult life. From the time he was twenty-six, he lived nearly every day in the shadow of death, alternately embracing its inevitability with uncommon courage while fearing its approach in mortal terror. King came from strong black religious leadership, but he increased the world's faith in its social possibilities. He emerged from a brilliant womb of civil rights agitation, but he gave it new birth. King's career was enabled by the often unsung efforts of local leaders and community activists, but he brought global attention to their common struggle for freedom. King came from comfort but rejected it in favor of identifying with the poor. He was produced by the movement, but he gave it the sort of legitimacy that it would have never enjoyed without his life. Ella Baker has famously said that "the movement made Martin rather than Martin making the movement." In many ways, she is absolutely right. Truly, without the raging urge to be free that tore through Southern black breasts in the fifties and sixties and without the apparatus of social transformation that gave King a vision and vehicle to realize his desire to serve, then he would have gotten nowhere. But as Richard Lischer reminds us, King's unique genius helped to make the movement:

> But the Civil Rights Movement did not "make" King any more than the Civil War "made" Lincoln. Admittedly, like Lincoln, King was summoned by events he did not initiate and exposed to conditions he did not create, but his response was so powerful an *interpretation* of events that it reshaped the conditions in which they originated. His answer was so true that it reframed the question. Martin Luther King, Jr. was not the first Negro to champion the cause of civil rights in the twentieth century. He was merely the first to name the struggle and to declare its meaning.

When we celebrate the King holiday, we do not simply celebrate the life of Martin Luther King. We celebrate individuals like Ella Baker and Fannie Lou Hamer, Bob Moses and Charles Sherrod, Septima Clark and Harry Moore, Emmett Till and Medgar Evers, Victoria Gray and Malcolm X, Roy Wilkins and Whitney Young, Angela Davis and Huey Newton, Mickey Schwerner and James Chaney, Andy Goodman and Bayard Rustin, Viola Liuzzo and James Reeb, Addie Mae Collins and Carole Robertson, Denise McNair and Cynthia Wesley, Julian Bond and John Lewis, Andrew Young and Ralph Abernathy, Hosea Williams and Jesse Jackson, Diane Nash and James Bevel, Dorothy Cotton and Johnnie Tillmon, and legions of other souls who sought to bring justice and freedom to Southern black doors and Northern project apartments. We celebrate King's willingness to surrender security and throw safety to the wind as he and many more crossed this nation in pursuit of peace and love. We celebrate King's insistence that "injustice anywhere is a threat to justice everywhere," as we extend his radical legacy to embrace citizens who are oppressed because of their sexual orientation or their gender. We celebrate King's ability to lay everything on the line, including his reputation, to do what he deemed was right in the eyes of God.

We must rebel against the varieties of amnesia that compete to reduce King to an icon for the status quo or a puppet of civil and social order. We must combat corporations like the ones he fought for the last four years of his life that seek to turn King into a commodity. We must insist that instead of making commercials to celebrate his life, these corporations pay their workers a humane wage in honor of King's vibrant memory. No amount of mythology will make King any larger than he was, for he long ago surpassed the need to be immortalized by the feeble romance of distorted memory. King as he truly was is enough for us now, perhaps even too much—a fact that drives us to sanitize his image with soapy tales of how he wanted us to like each other very much. King was much more dangerous than that. He is a much more demanding hero, a fiery icon whose hot breath continues to melt plastic portrayals of his social intentions. King meant nothing less than to change the world. He was out to make America behave against its will in a way that is cherished by people who love each other enough that they argue and fight for what is right before they will tell lies and live in false peace. Through our amnesia, we have attempted to portray King as a meek and mild savior sent to spin beautiful stories about birds and flowers. But King has entered the temple of our conscience and turned over the tables where moral commerce has been cheapened and the tales of justice have been sold for a price. He is a hero who loved America so much that he became full of rage and anger for our failing to treat the least to the best our nation can offer, whether that meant money or enough space to live without cramped ambitions or stunted hopes. We have attempted to make King in our own image, but he is, as historian Vincent Harding reminds us, "an inconvenient hero." Even from his grave, King challenges our desire to manipulate his image since that desire feasts on ethical laxity, a failure of nerve to do what is right in favor of doing what is easy and familiar.

Martin Luther King, Jr., is the greatest American in our history because in his life the contradictory meanings of American democracy found a perfect and healing embodiment. King is the great thesaurus of American identity; his many ideological shifts and moral evolutions are alternative ways of reading and understanding our national history. King did more to help America discover its own voice and rhythm in thirty-nine years of life than any other citizen in our nation's brilliant but bothered heritage. King's genius was the willingness to risk everything he was—a preacher, a leader, a husband, a father, a son, a brother, a black man—to make America all that it could become. Within a nation that had sutured his destiny to his pigment, King severed identity from its base in color. He freed the American soul to love its black self and, hence, to love itself wholly and universally. He embraced the best of America and made it better.

It is to his everlasting credit that King assaulted the dominion of excluding pronouns, insisting that "we" no longer meant one's group but the whole republic. He united Whitman and Baldwin in a metaphysical union of American idealism and racial tragedy: He brought them to each and into each other, refusing to differentiate their defining trajectory since neither made sense without the other. Thus the vision of American identity that seized King was both poetic and prophetic: it built out from the Given—where one lived, what one's color was, what language one spoke—and built up to the Giver: if God is the author of our human drama, we must read our divine destiny in each other's hurts and triumphs.

King was great because, as he liked to preach, he was willing to serve. His life continues to speak to all of us because he is the truest bellwether of our moral possibilities. Without his spirit, we cannot comprehend our national destiny. Without his voice, the tainted glories of citizenship rust into burdensome routine. And without his love, we might perish from lack of noble striving. He is the language we speak to understand our deepest wishes, not only about race but about human conscience in the crucible of choice. King ushered us into the sublime realm of moral agency—making us see that we do make a difference when we decide to stand, to work, to fight, to love, to resist, to sing, to march, and in the end, to die for the truth. His example is timeless because his energy is boundless, forever present through the renewing kinship of memory. We can claim his brand of heroism by fully and honestly embracing the cantankerous differences that unite us in our constant pilgrimage to America: With King as a guide, we can discover America again, and set off to conquer nothing less than the ignorance and fear that keep us from and not with one another.

"Lil' Nigger, Just Where You Been?"
Metaphors and Movements

In 1939, Martin Luther King, Jr., took his first bow on the national stage in a setting that was symptomatic of the cruel Southern racial politics he would help to change fifteen years later. As a ten-year-old child, King had snagged what was, sadly, considered to be something of a plum part in a celebration of a national phenomenon that had local roots. The film version of Atlanta author Margaret Mitchell's epic Southern historical novel, *Gone With the Wind*, was being feted in an Atlanta premiere.

Predictably, the film's black actors were barred from participating in the week-long festivities marking the film's opening, so organizers of the week's events hit on an ingenious idea: they could throw a bone to local blacks by recruiting them to supply the absent color created by the ban on the film's black actors. The Junior League Charity Ball was the perfect occasion to showcase the local blacks, but not as party participants. Instead, before a replica of Tara, the famous mansion of the film's protagonists, local blacks appeared in a slave choir. Martin Luther King sat poised between two huge white columns of the mansion, surrounded by his fellow "slaves" and a sprinkling of white actors, singing, if not the songs of Zion, then at least darky ditties. But as with the spiritual and gospel numbers that blacks often sang, King and his cohort were indeed singing their songs, as the Bible says and black folk like to repeat, in a very strange land.

If the thought of King appearing as a "happy darky" is jarring—an unintended but perfectly drawn symbol of how white culture often savaged the splendor of black life through crude stereotype—the thought that black youth might now do the same thing to black culture's heroes and icons is almost unbearable. Such a feeling led Rosa Parks—the widely heralded "Mother of the Civil Rights Movement" who recently had bestowed on her gray-haired halo the Congressional Gold Medal—to sue the hip-hop group Outkast for $25,000 for using her name in its song "Rosa Parks," without her permission. The Atlanta-based group, composed of rappers Big Boi and Dre, claimed that it only wanted to pay homage to a great role model when it named its song after Parks. But Parks's lawyer, Gregory Reed, claimed that his client was offended by Outkast's homage.

"You have her name associated with lyrics that contain vulgarity and profanity that she does not appreciate," Reed said.

Outkast claimed they never intended to defame Parks, since she has "inspired our music and our lives since we were children."

Reed admitted that the song was not about Parks and that the lyrics don't contain her name. Still, he claims that Parks was upset that her name was used to boost record sells.

This brief but bruising incident offers a peek into the huge gaps that divide blacks as they seek to honor the heroes and legacies of social change. While Parks certainly has a right to ask Outkast not to use her name, and while it is quite understandable that she wouldn't want her name associated with vulgarity and profanity, her suit against Outkast is a tragic one. Outkast is among the most progressive and culturally sensitive hip-hop groups now recording, one of the few rap groups that perhaps knows or even cares who Rosa Parks is or what she accomplished. Their song "Rosa Parks" invokes her presence as a metaphor for insight and wisdom, as a cautionary tale against an uninformed obsession with the past. They also appeal to her symbolic presence to warn all pretenders to their hip-hop throne that they would have to move to the back of the bus—in other words, that they would have to take a back seat to Outkast's preeminence. In the world of hip-hop verbal battles, that is indeed a gentle boast. Even more heartbreaking is the realization that Outkast's homage to Parks had the great potential to awaken a new generation to her achievements, or to the movement that she inspired with her act of singular courage.

By interpreting Outkast literally, failing to understand that she had become a transcendent metaphor for social change, Parks was not alone. Late Yankee legend Joe DiMaggio was quite peeved when he heard singer Paul Simon ask in a song where he had gone. DiMaggio took offense at the lyrics because he heard them literally, and not as they were intended by Simon: as a metaphor of an era when heroism of the sort that DiMaggio inspired had receded from cultural view. It is a shame that Parks misunderstood Outkast and, in a way, ironic as well, for Parks's fame derives from a symbolic gesture of freedom that seized the imagination of a people and then a nation as black folk refused any longer to sit still for injustice. Parks may have sat in her seat, but she inspired millions to rise in defiance of apartheid. As she has admitted, "I understand that I am a symbol." It is unfortunate that Parks, or her lawyer, cannot understand her symbolic importance to some of today's black youth.

Martin Luther King, Jr., also understood Parks's symbolic value. It caused him to comment that Parks was "a victim of both the forces of history and the forces of destiny," that she was "ideal for the role assigned to her by history," and that she was "tracked down by the Zeitgeist—the spirit of the times." Of course, such a comment can easily be interpreted to deny wrongfully that Parks "spent much of her adult life actively seeking levers of change, not waiting until the times were right." But I think what King was underscoring was a sense of divine destiny that works even as humans work their hardest to bring about change. After all, when Parks was arrested, it was not the first time she had sought to challenge the system of segregation through the buses. In fact, she was so well known that when they spotted her, many drivers simply passed her by. But all of her hard work and that of local activists, as well as the hand of history, met on a fateful day in 1955, and Parks's symbolic gesture of refusal brilliantly captured the spirit and destiny of a people.

Outkast's song "Rosa Parks" registers the changed terms of struggle for contemporary black youth. Many are robbed, deprived, or simply bereft of a sense of history, even that history that made their achievements possible. Many poor youth are also alienated from the civil rights generation. Although they certainly respect Martin Luther King, Jr., they may not understand his complexity or his undying relevance to their condition as a figure who took up residence in the ghetto to see up close the trouble they see. If it was only for a while, it was still much longer than many other leaders are willing to spend there. Moreover, King committed his life to eradicating poverty and organizing poor people to speak and act for themselves. While their language is different and their demeanor is surely changed, Outkast and Martin Luther King, Jr., have more than Atlanta as a birthplace in common. They share, as do Rosa Parks and a host of civil rights soldiers, a desire to see justice prevail for the forgotten black poor.

Parks has worked hard in her life to defend black youth. After she was assaulted in a cowardly attack by a black youth a few years ago outside her Detroit home, she courageously asked that the public be careful not to stigmatize all black youth. It was a profoundly loving gesture, one that signaled Parks's understanding of just how much young blacks are ravaged by stereotype and unfair criticism. One fears that Mrs. Parks has been victimized by well-meaning but misled counselors who fail to understand that Outkast and Parks are on the same side.

If Martin Luther King, Jr.'s legacy and the legacy of heroes like Rosa Parks is to thrive, it will have to be adapted, translated, and reinterpreted by a new generation whose words are often angry, whose ways are often crude. (Interestingly, the song "Rosa Parks" is remarkably free of curse words; in any case, if curse words are the standard of associating with Parks's legacy, then surely King's private discourse would have ruled him out as well. But the rules for public discourse among blacks have changed from the fifties to the nineties. Neither is cursing an automatic sign of unintelligence or unrighteousness. Those stereotypes must be broken in order to open communication between the civil rights and hip-hop generations.) As King did, and as Parks has often done, we must meet youth where they are to challenge—and be challenged by—them.

When Rosa Parks joined the 1965 march from Selma to Montgomery, she already felt alienated from a new generation of activists who were more vocal and angry and full of rage and curse words. She recalls that she had been out of Alabama for only a short while, "but so many young people had grown up in that time." As Parks recalled, this new generation had already forgotten its heroes:

> They didn't know who I was and couldn't care less about me because they didn't know me. Marchers on the final lap were supposed to be wearing special-colored jackets or other clothing, and I wasn't wearing the right color. They just kept putting me out the march, telling me I wasn't supposed to be in it. . . . I remember I marched for a while with Dick Gregory's wife, Lillian. . . . But somehow or another I couldn't hold on to them, or couldn't keep up with them, and then some of these youngsters just sort of pushed me out of the way. But I kept getting back in anyway and I struggled through that crowd until I walked those eight miles to the capitol.

Like so much else about Parks's life, this scene is powerfully symbolic. Old soldiers in the fight for justice are often shunted aside by younger soldiers who often have no idea that they wouldn't exist, couldn't exist, without those seasoned souls. These veterans are often told to get out of "the way," a way they helped to pave with blood, imagination, and sacrifice. But heroes must hang in there. They must insist on their right to participate in the long march to freedom, a march that is still winding through communities where people with the wrong colors are put out or, more tragically, even killed. Perhaps in the throes of such insistence, the heroic example of veteran freedom fighters will inspire the younger ones to learn something about their roots in order to travel different routes. Rosa Parks has been in the struggle for the long haul. Outkast has been inspired by her example and has expressed its gratitude by making her a useful hero, a working icon, a meaningful metaphor. The only way her legacy, or King's legacy, or the legacy of a brave generation of freedom fighters will stay alive is if the rest of us, young and old alike, follow suit.

Preface: "We as a People Will Get to the Promised Land"

ix *"We as a People"*: King, "I See the Promised Land," in King, *A Testament,* p. 286.

x *"And He's allowed me"*: Ibid.

Introduction: "You Don't Need to Go Out Saying Martin Luther King, Jr. Is a Saint"

1 *"You Don't Need"*: King, "Unfulfilled Dreams," in Carson and Holloran, eds., *A Knock at Midnight,* p. 198.

1 *"We've got some difficult days"*: King, "I See the Promised Land," in King, *A Testament,* p. 286.

6 *Two of the three major news magazines*: Lentz, *Symbols, the News Magazines, and Martin Luther King.*

6 *"single garment of destiny"*: King, "The American Dream," in King, *A Testament,* p. 210.

6 *In 1968, for the first time*: (January 1967 Gallup Poll) Lewis, *King,* p. 358.

8 *As Wynton Marsalis eloquently: Jet,* Jan. 25, 1999, p. 9.

Chapter 1: "I Saw the Dream Turn into a Nightmare"

11 *"I Saw That Dream"*: King, "A Christmas Sermon on Peace," in King, *A Testament,* p. 257.

11 *"I am a mother"*: ABC News Special, "The Century: Memphis Dreams: Searching for the Promised Land," hosted by Peter Jennings, 1999. Also see Jennings and Brewster, *The Century.*

11 *"People just don't know"*: PBS Special, "Frontline: The Two Nations of Black America," hosted by Henry Louis Gates, Jr., Feb. 10, 1998. All quotations from King in this section are from the same source.

12 *Unlike the radical right:* I address the right-wing attack on King, especially from far right groups like the John Birch Society and the J. Edgar Hoover–era FBI in Chapter 11.

13 *Newfangled racists:* A long list of figures in Western intellectual history have appealed to scientific discourse to justify and legitimate their bigoted beliefs, the surly precursors to today's apologists. For a small sample of historical figures, including Carl von Linne, Georges-Louis Leclerc, David Hume, Immanuel Kant, Johann Gottfried Herder, Johann Friedrich Blumenbach, Thomas Jefferson, Georges Leopold Cuvier and Georg Wilhelm Friedrich Hegel, see Eze, ed., *Race and the Enlightenment.* For more contemporary figures, see (for Shockley) *U.S. News and World Report,* Aug. 28, 1989, and *Business Week,* Nov. 7, 1994; Jensen, "How Much Can We Boost I.Q.?" Jensen, "The Differences Are [unreadable]," in Jacoby and Glauberman, eds., *The Bell Curve Debate;* Jensen, *Genetics and Education;* Jensen, *Bias in Mental Testing;* Jensen, *Straight Talk About Mental Tests;* and Herrnstein and Murray, *The Bell Curve.* As for political demagogues, the most obvious figure is David Duke. But recent revelations about the close ties between Senate Majority Leader, Mississippi Senator Trent Lott, and the Council of Conservative Citizens, "a White Supremacist group that espouses anti-black views on its Internet Web site," reveal disturbing patterns of persistent bigotry in Dixiecrat politicians. (The

portion in quotes is from Fulwood and Lin, "Two in GOP Join Fight Against Racist Group.") Also see Ian Brodie in Overseas News, *The Times* (London), Jan. 15, 1999.

13 *Now terms like:* In the early sixties Senator Strom Thurmond had claimed that the civil rights movement masked a communist conspiracy. But in 1983 he supported the King holiday bill "out of respect for the important contributions of our minority citizens" (Garrow, "The Helms Attack on King," *Southern Exposure*, Mar.–Apr. 1984, p. 12). And former FBI agent and then last-term congressman Ed Bethune supported the King holiday because it would "give us an annual opportunity to recommit ourselves to the proposition that all men are created equal" (Branch, "Uneasy Holiday," *New Republic*, Feb. 3, 1986, p. 27). Even more recently, conservative policy wonk Clint Bolick, in the April 30, 1993, *Wall Street Journal*, spearheaded the attack on Justice Department nominee Lani Guinier as a "quota queen," effectively torpedoing her chances for serving as the Justice Department's civil rights leader in 1993. See Guinier, *Tyranny of the Majority*, pp. ix, x. And conservative figures like Linda Chavez and Ward Connerly have ingeniously wrested terms from the civil rights community to name their organizations, hence confusing unsuspecting advocates of racial opportunity while twisting the themes of the civil rights movement out of their original context. Chavez heads the Center for Equal Opportunity, and Connerly heads the American Civil Rights Institute. (In an equally cruel gesture, Clint Bolick is director of litigation for the Institute of Justice.)

14 *these thirty-four:* In most transcriptions of King's speech—whose most famous part was extemporized—there are thirty-five words in the sentence I have quoted, reflecting the addition of a conjunction, making it a grammatically tighter rendition of his phrase. It usually reads, "I have a dream *that* my four little children . . . " But in audio- and videotaped recordings of King's speech, the conjunction *that* is never stated.

15 *In a recent survey:* Heller, "Essays That Live On," p. A-20.

15 *"I Have a Dream":* King, *A Testament of Hope*, pp. 217–220. The following quotations from King's speech in this section are from the same source.

15 *later that very year:* King says that he first saw his dream turn into a nightmare "just a few weeks after I had talked about it" in Washington, D.C., when "four beautiful, unoffending, innocent Negro girls were murdered in a church in Birmingham, Alabama." "A Christmas Sermon on Peace," in King, *A Testament*, p. 257. Also see King's brief but pungent Sept. 29 essay for the *New York Times Magazine*, "In a Word: Now," which sums up the edifying impatience of black protesters with, among other issues, the denial of the right to vote, the lack of federal protection against police brutality, and the unpassed civil rights bill, in King, *A Testament*, pp. 167–168.

16 *an inspiring sermon:* I am certainly not claiming that this was one of King's most powerful sermons, a church address with the purpose of informing, inspiring, and instigating the congregation to action. Nor am I suggesting that this was one of King's most fully realized public orations, where the sweep of his eloquent vision dominates the speech from beginning to end, as he did in his last speech, "I See the Promised Land." What I am arguing is that King's "I Have a Dream" speech was neatly tailored for the occasion on which it was delivered. Its eloquence and inspiration draw from two points: its summary of the Negro demand for racial justice with an appeal to sacred documents in the civil and political order in its first parts and its shrewd identification of Negro social and political aspiration as the dominant shape of American democracy in the last half of the twentieth century in its closing sections. Nicolaus Mills argues that until King's "I have a dream" passages, "there was little in King's speech that moved his audience. He had tried too hard to write an updated *Gettysburg Address*." Mills argues that what "emerged from his prepared text was not moral passion but historical self-consciousness. It was a speech so dominated by carefully worked out metaphors that it left little room for spontaneity" (Mills, "Heard and Unheard Speeches," p. 285). Although King's earlier passages don't have the ingenious rhetorical formula of his "I have a dream" peroration, they were nonetheless

crucial in articulating the Negro demand for freedom and justice. They also revealed the revolutionary hunger for true equality that possessed millions of black citizens. The careful and extended metaphors of the first sections are just as crucial to King's message for the balance of his career. The low appeal of the earlier passages of King's speech can be ascribed to their relative stiffness or uninspiring language—a charge that may be true in spots—and is also perhaps linked to their more radical and uncompromising commitment to seeking black liberation in the political, civic, and social realms. For further discussion of King's speech and how Mahalia Jackson may indeed be responsible for urging King to lift off from the printed page and preach by capping his oration with the soaring peroration "I have a dream" ("Tell 'em about the dream, Martin"), see Branch, *Parting the Waters*, pp. 881–883. Also, John Lewis argues that King's speech, "despite its lack of substance, was magical and majestic in spirit." (This view is shared by David L. Lewis, who wrote about key passages of King's speech that this "was rhetoric almost without content, but this was, after all, a day of heroic fantasy," in *King*, pp. 228–229.) The lack of substance to which John Lewis refers is King's failure to criticize the government for *its* failure to grant and protect the equal rights of black Southerners. Lewis maintains that although "I Have a Dream" was a "good speech," it was "not nearly as powerful as many" that King had made before. The awareness that he "hadn't locked into that *power* he so often found," Lewis surmises, drove King to adapt his dream discourse, a rhetorical strategy that he had used many times before. While Lewis admits that he didn't hear her say it, he says that Mahalia Jackson apparently did suggest to King to "tell them about the *dream* Martin." See Lewis, *Walking with the Wind*, pp. 225–227. Writer John Williams heard a different response to King's peroration. "'I have a dream,' M.L. said again, and behind us, his voice lost to all but those close to him, a man screamed, 'Fuck that dream, Martin! Now, goddamit, NOW'" (Williams, *This Is My Country, Too*, cited in Williams, *The King God Didn't Save*, p. 63).

17 *nineteen minutes:* According to varied sources, King, as were the other speakers, was to have had either eight minutes (C. King, *My Life*, p. 236, and Oates, *Let the Trumpet Sound*, p. 256), seven minutes (Branch, *Parting the Waters*, p. 873), or only three minutes (Young, *An Easy Burden*, p. 271). King was positioned at the end of the lengthy list of speakers for at least two reasons. First, since they knew the cameras would be focused on the early speakers, Whitney Young and Roy Wilkins successfully lobbied for the early slots (Young, *An Easy Burden*, p. 271). But perhaps equally compelling was the fact that no speaker wanted to follow King, who was by then the preeminent black leader and America's finest orator. As Bayard Rustin recalled, "Almost all the speakers had asked me to make sure they didn't follow King," since they realized his status and knew "that the minute King finished speaking the program would be over, that everybody would be heading home" (Anderson, *Bayard Rustin*, p. 261). But King's disadvantage ultimately worked in his behalf. By the time he spoke, ABC and NBC had preempted their normal soap operas to join CBS's continuous live coverage of the march (Branch, *Parting the Waters*, p. 881). Now, all three networks would beam King's thrilling oration around the nation. In the hours after King delivered his historic address, his wife and colleagues kidded him in his hotel suite about exceeding his time limit, humorously warning him to "watch out for Roy [Wilkins] now" (Oates, *Let the Trumpet Sound*, p. 263).

17 *where amnesia fails:* I have in mind here the hunger for the sort of amnesia that buries the awareness of past pain as the predicate of present race relations. I address this matter in far greater detail in Chapter 13. For a discussion of the nostalgia for the sort of racial clarity that prevailed during our nation's brutal, bloody past, see Dyson, *Reflecting Black*, pp. 146–154. And for a discussion of how such nostalgia functions in black communities to romanticize history and confer heroic moral values on people from the past, see Dyson, *Race Rules*, pp. 109–149.

18 *as a troublemaker:* Not only J. Edgar Hoover, whose FBI famously tagged King the most dangerous black man in America, but many rank-and-file whites, such as auto

dealer John Fisher whom I cite in Chapter 4, viewed King with great suspicion and as a source of racial trouble.

19 *"Give us the Ballot"*: King, *A Testament*, pp. 197–200.

19 *"quasi liberalism"*: Ibid., p. 199.

19 *"is so objectively analytical"*: Ibid.

19 *"If the Negro Wins, Labor Wins"*: Ibid., pp. 201–207.

19 *"a dream of equality of opportunity"*: Ibid., p. 206.

19 *"The American Dream"*: Ibid., pp. 208–216.

19 *"price America must pay"*: Ibid., p. 209.

20 *"environmental and not racial"*: Ibid., p. 211.

20 *"we are to implement the American dream"*: Ibid.

20 *"Our God is Marching On!"*: Ibid., pp. 227–230.

20 *"march on poverty"*: Ibid., p. 229.

20 *"A Time to Break Silence"*: Ibid., p. 231–244.

20 *"revolution of values"*: Ibid., p. 240.

20 *"soon cause us to question"*: Ibid., p. 241.

20 *"Where Do We Go from Here?"*: Ibid., pp. 245–252.

20 *"divine dissatisfaction"*: Ibid., p. 251.

20 *"the tragic walls that separate"*: Ibid.

20 *"The Drum Major Instinct"*: Ibid., pp. 259–267.

20 *"living on . . . the satisfaction"*: Ibid., 264.

20 *"Remaining Awake"*: Ibid., pp. 268–278.

21 *"bootstraps" philosophy*: Ibid., p. 271.

21 *"the roots of racism are very deep"*: Ibid.

21 *"I See The Promised Land"*: Ibid., pp. 279–286.

21 *"if something isn't done"*: Ibid., p. 280.

21 *"A Christmas Sermon on Peace"*: Ibid., pp. 253–258.

22 *evil can be conquered only*: For a discussion of King's views on evil and the influence on his thinking of his Boston University professor and thesis adviser, L. Harold DeWolf, see Chapter 9.

22 *color-blindness reinforces*: See my discussion of how an investment in the presumed achievement of color-blindness affects political and legal decisions in Dyson, *Race Rules*, pp. 213–224.

22 *Reynolds contends that "the initial"*: "An Experiment Gone Awry," in Curry, ed., *The Affirmative Action Debate*, pp. 132–133.

22 *"started as a journey"*: Ibid., p. 133.

23 *the fundamental aims of affirmative action*: Lawrence and Matsuda, *We Won't Go Back*; and Ezorsky, *Race and Justice*.

23 *"is impossible to create"*: King, *Why We Can't Wait*, p. 134

23 *"could be absorbed into"*: Ibid.

23 *even in the same sort*: For a brilliant and exhaustive discussion of affirmative action in higher education and its positive impact on our culture, see Bowen and Bok, *The Shape of the River*.

23 *"the nation must not only"*: King, *Why We Can't Wait*, p. 134.

23 *"obsession with the themes"*: Bernstein, *Dictatorship of Virtue*, p. 58.

24 *"insists on equality of results"*: Ibid.

24 *"dream of a day"*: Ibid.

24 *"Judge me by the color"*: Ibid.

24 *"publicly opposed"*: Lind, *The Next American Nation*, p. 109.

24 *"issue of compensatory"*: King, *Why We Can't Wait*, p. 134.

24 *"Negro should be granted"*: Ibid.

24 *"relevant question"*: Ibid., p. 135.

24 *"Negro today"*: Ibid.

24 *"The struggle for rights"*: Ibid., p. 136.

24 *"with equal opportunity must come"*: Ibid.

24 Content of Our Character: Steele, *Content of Our Character.*

24 *"cited mainly"*: Loury, in Curry, ed., *The Affirmative Action Debate*, p. 60.

24 *"deep irony here is that"*: Ibid.

25 *"no disrespect"*: See Lempinen, "Connerly Widens Anti-Affirmative Action Campaign," *San Francisco Chronicle*, Jan. 16, 1997, p. A17; also see Chavez, "Connerly New Prop. 209 Push Draws Fire," *Sacramento Bee*, Jan. 12, 1997, p. A3.

25 *"the state shall not discriminate against"*: *Los Angeles Times*, Nov. 4, 1997, p. A1.

26 *"concrete universal"*: Hegel, *Hegel's Logic* and *Hegel's Science of Logic*. Also see Kolb, *The Critique of Pure Modernity*, esp. pp. 60–69.

26 *"stand in the doorways"*: *Los Angeles Times*, op. cit.

26 When civil rights leaders protested: *Sacramento Bee*, Oct. 25, 1996, p. A5.

27 *"The use of King"*: Ibid.

27 *"Every citizen should have an equal"*: *New York Times*, Jan 16, 1997, p. A16.

27 on *"the surface"*: King, *Why We Can't Wait*, p. 134.

27 *"it is obvious that if a man"*: Ibid.

27 *"the difficult problem of"*: Ibid.

27 *"become unpopular to exhibit"*: Ibid.

27 *"million of rupees"*: Ibid., pp. 134–135.

27 *" 'Well it may be' "*: Ibid., p. 135.

27 *"seek its own ways of atoning"*: Ibid.

28 *"people consider the fact"*: Ibid., p. 137.

28 *"No amount of gold"*: Ibid.

28 *"millions of [the] white poor"*: Ibid., p. 138. Stewart Burns, an opponent of such measures, argues that if the basis of compensation for blacks is racially rooted, it makes no moral sense to extend benefits to poor whites. He contends that King's "corollary argument seemed a bit specious, since a justification that might have been appropriate for a 'chosen people' liberated from slavery did not have the same moral charge when applied to a larger group that did not share this heritage" (Burns, "From the Mountaintop," p. 13). But Burns's argument is compelling only if one discounts King's universal moral vision that was complex and capable of entertaining two apparently contradictory claims: racial compensation and economic justice. For King, the one did not necessarily rule out the other. A moral imperative to help *all* poor did not deny the specific facts of the *black* poor, whose poverty was exacerbated by their race. Likewise, a moral imperative to seek justice for blacks did not deny the economic inequality confronted by poor whites. Most analysts commit a logical error when they contend that one cannot be at once an advocate of measures of racial compensation such as affirmative action while also promoting economic justice for all Americans. For some analysts, it is an either-or proposition. Such binaristic thinking depends on faulty reasoning; its advocates commit a category mistake by confusing race and class. Hence, they argue that it is unfair to practice racial compensation when poor whites are unfairly treated, especially in relation to those blacks who are benefited by such compensatory measures. But this is to confuse cause and effect: racial compensation did not cause the economic inequality experienced by poor whites. Further, racial compensation addresses a specific circumstance in American history: the racial inequality and systematic discrimination that denied all blacks social justice. To claim that racial compensation creates economic inequality among whites is to misdiagnose the origins of class division and income disparities in our society. As Adam Fairclough argues, King began to see "racism as an instrument of class privilege, a means of dividing the working class by giving whites marginal economic advantages and encouraging their psychological pretensions to superiority. Both black and white labor was thus more easily exploited and

cheapened" (Fairclough, "Was King a Marxist?" p. 120). King never believed that granting justice to blacks through compensatory measures was unfair to whites, even poor whites. (After all, even well-to-do blacks were denied basic rights that poor whites could take for granted.) Although racial and economic justice certainly overlapped, they were distinct if interrelated social issues that demanded specific remedies in redressing the injustice and oppression that flowed from their occurrence in our nation.

28 *"moral justification"*: King, *Why We Can't Wait*, p. 138.

29 *"chained by the weight"*: Ibid.

29 *"more evil for"*: Ibid.

29 *"raising the Negro from backwardness"*: Ibid.

29 the *"concept of supremacy"*: King, *"Playboy* Interview: MLK," in King, *A Testament,* p. 375.

Chapter 2: "Most Americans Are Unconscious Racists"

30 *"Most Americans Are Unconscious Racists"*: Halberstam, "When 'Civil Rights' and 'Peace' Join Forces" (originally published as "The Second Coming of Martin Luther King" in *Harper's Magazine,* Aug. 1967), in Lincoln, ed., *Martin Luther King, Jr.,* p. 202.

30 *jail in Selma*: C. King, *My Life,* pp. 256–258; Garrow, *Bearing the Cross,* pp. 392–393; Branch, *Pillar of Fire,* 578–579; Oates, *Let the Trumpet Sound,* pp. 340–341.

30 *they ran into each other*: Cone, *Martin and Malcolm,* pp. 2–3.

30 *"impressed by his"*: King, *My Life,* p. 256.

30 *"I want Dr. King to know"*: Ibid. According to David Garrow, when Coretta reported to her husband in his Selma jail that Malcolm made this statement, King "didn't react too much one way or the other" (Garrow, *Bearing the Cross,* p. 393). Later, however, King seems to have appreciated Malcolm's gesture. In 1967, King recalls that Malcolm "came down to Selma and said some pretty passionate things against me, and that surprised me because after all it was my own territory down there. But afterwards he took my wife aside, and said he thought he could help me more by attacking me than praising me. He thought it would make it easier for me in the long run." (Halberstam, "When 'Civil Rights' and 'Peace' Join Forces," p. 211).

30 *They sparred each other*: Cone, *Martin and Malcolm,* p. 2.

30 *encouraged blacks to be self-reliant*: Ibid., pp. 105–110. Also see Dyson, *Making Malcolm,* pp. 170–171.

30 *Malcolm had a dramatic change of heart*: Malcolm X, with Haley, *The Autobiography of Malcolm X,* pp. 348–397; Cone, *Malcolm and Martin,* pp. 198–212; Dyson, *Making Malcolm,* pp. 12–14, 63–72.

31 *an element of Malcolm's thinking*: Cone, *Martin and Malcolm,* pp. 244–259.

31 *King had been broadly trusting of whites*: Ibid., pp. 120–150.

31 *he doubted if whites could respond adequately*: Halberstam, "When 'Civil Rights' and 'Peace' Join Forces," p. 202; Garrow, *Protest at Selma,* pp. 220–236.

32 *The distinction is crucial*: I am not arguing that many whites did not bravely confront Southern apartheid. Some even gave their lives in the struggle for black liberation. But I am arguing that many white liberals did not encourage the massive civil disobedience of liberal white communities that might lead to the sort of violence, and sometimes death, routinely suffered by black activists. Furthermore, one may arguably see the link between this refusal to suggest large-scale white liberal suffering for black liberation in the antiaffirmative action postures of some contemporary liberals, neoliberals, or former liberals. Such figures are unwilling to view compensatory measures as the just fulfillment of the civil rights movement's push for true equality. For such figures, neither physical suffering in the sixties nor minimal economic sacrifice in the nineties appears to be a viable means to realizing the goal of racial justice.

32 *In the early days:* Lasch, *The True and Only Heaven,* pp. 406, 409.

32 *"great resources of goodwill":* King, cited in ibid., p. 396.

33 *King wanted to improve black life:* Thelen, "Conversation Between Cornish Rogers and David Thelen," esp. pp. 50–51, 59.

33 *widely heralded year-long bus boycott:* King, *Stride Toward Freedom;* Robinson, *The Montgomery Bus Boycott and the Women Who Started It;* Parks, with Haskins, *Rosa Parks,* pp. 108–160; Abernathy, *And the Walls,* pp. 131–188; C. King, *My Life,* pp. 108–148: Gray, *Bus Ride to Justice;* Raines, ed., *My Soul,* pp. 37–70; Graetz, *Montgomery;* Fields, *The Montgomery Story;* Wright, *Birth of the Montgomery Bus Boycott;* Garrow, ed., *The Walking City;* Burns, ed., *Daybreak of Freedom.*

33 *his theology, a simmering gumbo:* There has been an evolution of thinking about King's theology, in four stages. The first stage suggested that King's religious and social philosophy was shaped primarily by his white seminary training with its liberal outlook on biblical criticism and theology. See, for instance, Smith and Zepp, *Search for the Beloved Community.* The second stage dug deeper into the neo-orthodox views of theologian Reinhold Niebuhr, and the personalist philosophy of Edgar Brightman, and the social gospel of Walter Rauschenbush, in outlining King's theological vision of social justice. See, for instance, Ansbro, *Martin Luther King, Jr.* The third stage excavates and emphasizes King's black church heritage and his roots in black culture, arguing that King was much more powerfully influenced by African-American rituals, customs, rhetorical habits and moral perspectives than previously acknowledged in King studies. See, for instance, Cone, *Martin and Malcolm* and *Risks of Faith,* and Lewis Baldwin, *There Is a Balm,* and *To Make the Wounded Whole.* The just-emerging fourth stage accentuates the arguments of the previous stages, especially the emphasis on King's black church heritage, while also arguing for King's prominent, though marginal, position within black religious thought, as an advocate of the fusion of faith and progressive social and political philosophy. The fourth stage emphasizes as well King's challenge to cherished conventions in black church life and black religious thought. See, for instance, Carson, "Reconstructing the King Legacy," in Albert and Hoffman, eds., *We Shall Overcome,* pp. 239–248; Cone, *Risks of Faith,* and my emphasis on King's participation in the radical remnant of the black church, in Chapter 6.

33 *his belief that whites really wanted to change:* Cone, *Martin and Malcolm,* pp. 58–88.

33 *white soul slumped to repressed guilt:* King said that segregationists "know in their hearts" that segregation is "morally wrong and sinful. If it weren't, the white South would not be haunted as it is by a deep sense of guilt for what it has done to the Negro—guilt for patronizing him, degrading him, brutalizing him, depersonalizing him, thingifying him; guilt for lying to itself." (King, *Playboy* interview: Martin Luther King, Jr.," in King, *A Testament,* pp. 357–358).

34 *was proof enough to his black critics:* Elijah Muhammad and Malcolm X argued that black self-love was the predicate of true social and racial equality. Hence, any philosophy of racial reconstruction that began outside the arc of this fundamental insight was doomed to lead blacks to the worship of whites and the corollary self-harted of blacks. See Malcolm X, with Halley, *The Autobiography of Malcolm X,* esp. pp. 165–347; Cone, *Martin and Malcolm,* pp. 89–119; Clegg, *An Original Man;* Dyson, *Making Malcolm,* pp. 79–92.

34 *King believed that the Negro's mission:* From the beginning of his public ministry, King articulated the belief that black folk could, through heroic deeds, courageous practices, and sacrificial actions, redeem the soul of America, the subtitle of his SCLC. King appealed to white Christian historian Arnold Toynbee to ground his belief that the Negro might contain the seed of salvation for American society and Western culture. Moreover, King's assignment of onerous duties to blacks—that they could withstand beatings, whippings, stonings, lynchings and other forms of murder—drew from his belief in the use of black moral skill and ethical talent by divine providence to achieve the goals of black liberation as the fulfillment of God's will. Thus, King fused divine will and black struggle, which is

why he could claim that black folk had "cosmic companionship" in their fight for racial justice. Further, in his first major speech, on December 5, 1955, at the start of the bus boycott—his famous "Holt Street Address"—King exhorted his congregation by reminding them that "here in Montgomery when the history books are written in the future, somebody will have to say, 'There lived a race of people, of black people, fleecy locks and black complexion, of people who had the moral courage to stand up for their rights. And thereby they injected a new meaning into the veins of history and of civilization.' " "MIA Mass Meeting at Holt Street Baptist Church," in Carson, ed., *The Papers of Martin Luther King, Jr.*, Vol. 3: *Birth of a New Age*, p. 74. Also see Lischer, *The Preacher King*, p. 121.

34 *for blacks out of the racial chaos of Birmingham:* Lewis, *King*, pp. 171–209; Garrow, *Bearing the Cross*, pp. 231–264; Fairclough, *To Redeem*, pp. 111–139; Branch, *Parting the Waters*, pp. 708–802.

35 *that their struggle was not between white and black:* King, in "Remaining Awake Through a Great Revolution," preached that "we will not ever allow this struggle to become so polarized that it becomes a struggle between *black* and *white* men" (quoted in Lischer, *The Preacher King*, pp. 121–122). But this sermon, preached in Cincinnati early in his career, is not to be confused with the sermon of the same title that was the final Sunday sermon King delivered, on March 31, 1968, at the National Cathedral (Episcopal) in Washington, D.C. There King reminded the congregation of the "unhappy truth that racism is a way of life for the vast majority of white Americans, spoken and unspoken, acknowledged and denied, subtle and sometimes not so subtle—the disease of racism permeates and poisons a whole body politic. And I can see nothing more urgent than for America to work passionately and unrelentingly—to get rid of the disease of racism" (in King, *A Testament*, p. 270). Also see Carson and Holloran, eds., *A Knock at Midnight*, p. 208.

35 *"unearned suffering is redemptive":* King, "Suffering and Faith," in King, *A Testament*, p. 41.

36 *may be a lie, it's a vital lie:* Cited in Dyson, *Making Malcolm*, p. 154.

36 *therapeutic for many Southern whites:* Many of King's critics view this as a negative quality. His therapeutic presence is seen as being exercised at the expense of black self-determination. Also, it placated whites while relieving the burden of confronting their own severe shortcomings. After all, if a black leader argued that assaulted blacks should love whites despite the barbarity of white violence, then whites could indulge their most vicious inclinations toward blacks and fear neither legal nor moral reprisal. Further, by fastening onto King, whites were able to avoid the explosive rage contained in the breasts and brains of those blacks who operated largely outside King's circle of love. Malcolm X said that whites "use King to satisfy their own fears," and that by magnifying King's influence beyond its actual proportions, they ignore "the powder keg in their house." Instead of trying to "defuse the powder keg, they're putting a blanket over it, trying to make believe that this is no powder keg; that this is a couch that we can lay on and enjoy" (Malcolm X, quoted in Cone, *Martin and Malcolm*, p. 245).

36 *They were joined by the Bible and the ham hock:* For a discussion of the segregated world that white and black Southerners inhabited, the regional meanings they shared, and the social conflicts that grew from their common Southern heritage, see Woodward, *Origins* and *Strange Career;* Williamson, *The Crucible of Race;* King, *A Southern Renaissance;* Tindall, *The Emergence;* and Hale, *Making Whiteness*.

36 *convinced they were inferior:* In seeking to answer why, according to an *Ebony* poll, only one out of ten Negroes had been physically involved in social protest, King said that "there are millions of Negroes who have never known anything but oppression, who are so devoid of pride and self-respect that they have resigned themselves to segregation" (King, "*Playboy* Interview: Martin Luther King, Jr.," p. 370).

36 *King temporarily moved his family to a Chicago slum:* C. King, *My Life*, pp. 275–288.

36 *a run at Yankee apartheid:* Ralph, *Northern Protest*; Abernathy, *And the Walls,* pp. 362–399; Garrow, *Bearing the Cross,* 431–525; Young, *An Easy Burden,* pp. 372–421.

36 *than he had met in all his years in the South:* King told a television newsman that "I've never seen anything like it. I've been in many demonstrations all across the south, but I can say that I have never seen—even in Mississippi and Alabama—mobs as hostile and as hate-filled as I've seen in Chicago" (quoted in Oates, *Let the Trumpet Sound,* p. 413). In Chicago, the public choreography of hatred seemed to be a reflection of family values, in sharp contrast to the outlaw style of Southern bigotry. As Stephen Oates says of the policemen who protected the marchers in Chicago, they "were stunned. Many of them were second-generation Poles, Italians, and Germans themselves; these were *their* people stoning and calling them 'nigger lovers,' *their* people sporting Rebel flags and banners of the American Nazi party and battling them in the streets long after the marchers were gone, *their* people who were rioting now" (Oates, *Let the Trumpet Sound,* p. 413). Andrew Young said that "in the South we faced mobs, but it would be a couple of hundred or even fifty or seventy-five. The violence in the South always came from a rabble element. But these were women and children and husbands and wives coming out of their homes becoming a mob—and in some ways it was far more frightening" (in Hampton and Fayer, eds., *Voices of Freedom,* pp. 312– 313).

37 *King sought to expand the scope:* Garrow, *Bearing the Cross,* pp. 357–430, and Oates, *Let the Trumpet Sound,* pp. 387–419. King said that "I am appalled that some people feel that the civil rights struggle is over because we have a 1964 bill with ten titles and a voting rights bill" (quoted in Oates, *Let the Trumpet Sound,* p. 390). Also see Ralph, *Northern Protest.*

38 *"we had not evaluated the depth of resistance":* Quoted in Lasch, *The True,* p. 402.

38 *what doesn't appear to be broken:* King said the northern white, "having had little actual contact with the Negro, is devoted to an abstract principle of cordial interracial relations. The North has long considered, in a theoretical way, that it supported brotherhood and the equality of man, but the truth is that deep prejudices and discriminations exist in hidden and subtle and covert disguises. The South's prejudice and discrimination, on the other hand, has been applied against the Negro in obvious, open, overt and glaring forms—which make the problem easier to get at. The southern white man has the advantage of far more actual contact with Negroes than the northerner. A major problem is that this contact has been paternalistic and poisoned by the myth of racial superiority" ("*Playboy* Interview: Martin Luther King, Jr.," p. 358).

38 *"psychological and spiritual genocide":* Quoted in Garrow, *Bearing the Cross,* p. 598.

38 *"I'm tired of marching for something":* King, quoted in ibid., p. 515. Garrow quotes King as saying "mine at first," which sounds like what King said, and which I heard him saying as I listened to the speech over the years. But a close check of the *Eyes on the Prize* videotape reveals King saying "mine at *birth.*"

38 *"Chicago hasn't* seen *a demonstration":* King, quoted in Oates, *Let the Trumpet Sound,* p. 415.

38 *"tired of race":* King, "Who Is My Neighbor?" quoted in Lischer, *The Preacher King,* p. 161.

38 *"destructive cutting edge":* King, "Showdown for Nonviolence," in King, *A Testament,* p. 64.

38 *Our nation was born:* King, *Why We Can't Wait,* pp. 130–131.

38 *"nation that got started like that":* Quoted in Lischer, *The Preacher King,* p. 158.

38 *"You know why":* Ibid., p. 159.

39 *And you know what, a nation:* Ibid.

39 *"terrible ambivalence in the soul":* Ibid., pp. 158–159.

39 *"yes it is true . . . America":* Ibid., p. 159. Also see p. 202. Halberstam, "When 'Civil Rights' and 'Peace' Join Forces."

39 *And so we go this way:* Quoted in Lischer, *The Preacher King,* pp. 121–122.

39 *"For years I labored with the idea"*: Halberstam, "When 'Civil Rights' and 'Peace' Join Forces," pp. 201–202.

39 *"most Americans are unconscious racists"*: Quoted in Halberstam, "When 'Civil Rights' and 'Peace' Join Forces," p. 202.

39 *"fact is that there has never been any single"*: King, "America's Chief Moral Dilemma," quoted in Smith, "The Radicalization of Martin Luther King, Jr.," p. 272.

40 *"I am sorry to have to say"*: King, "Which Way Its Soul Shall Go," quoted in Smith, "The Radicalization of Martin Luther King, Jr.," p. 272.

40 *King was dissatisfied with the important:* King, "Frogmore Speech," quoted in Smith, "The Radicalization of Martin Luther King, Jr.," p. 274. In the speech, King said that "we must admit it: the changes that came about during this period were at best surface changes, they were not really substantive changes" ("Frogmore Speech," p. 6).

40 *America's schizophrenia vexed King:* King remarked on "schizophrenia that the South will suffer until it goes through its crisis of conscience" (*"Playboy* Interview: Martin Luther King, Jr.," p. 358). He also said that ever "since the Founding Fathers of our nation dreamed this noble dream, American has been something of a schizophrenic personality, tragically divided against herself. On the one hand we have proudly professed the principles of democracy, and on the other hand we have sadly practiced the very antithesis of those principles. Indeed slavery and segregation have been strange paradoxes in a nation founded on the principle that all men are created equal" (King, "The American Dream," in Washington, ed., *A Testament,* pp. 208–209).

41 *"the ways of white folk"*: Hughes, *The Ways of White Folks.*

41 *incidents such as the infamous Texaco case:* see Roberts, *Roberts vs. Texaco.*

41 *America has rarely willingly acknowledged:* King, "America's Chief Moral Dilemma," May 10, 1967, cited in Smith, "The Radicalization of Martin Luther King, Jr.," p. 273, n. 4.

41 *the spirit of Frederick Douglass:* Douglass famously said, "Power concedes nothing without a demand. It never did and it never will" (Douglass, "West Indian Emancipation," *Life and Writings of Frederick Douglass,* p. 437).

42 *including figures like:* Tomasky, *Left for Dead;* T. Jacoby, *Someone Else's House;* Lasch, *The True and Only Heaven;* Gitlin, *The Twilight of Common Dreams;* Sleeper, *The Closest of Strangers* and *Liberal Racism;* and Thernstrom and Thernstrom, *America in Black and White.*

43 *"King upheld nonviolence both as a tactic"*: Lasch, *The True,* p. 409.

44 *blacks rioted in the streets:* Ibid.

44 *"addressing their oppressors not only"*: Ibid., p. 396.

44 *"who supported busing and affirmative action"*: Ibid., p. 409.

45 *"America will make no sense"*: Sleeper, *Liberal Racism,* p. 175.

45 *"searing moral force"*: Ibid., p. 181.

45 *"ultimately there can be only transcendence"*: Ibid.

46 *"than anyone" was "responsible for the blossoming"*: Jacoby, *Someone Else's House,* p. 48.

46 *"color coding"*: Ibid., p. 541.

46 *"young black woman"*: Ibid., p. 1.

46 *The words jumped out at me:* Ibid.

46 *"kids who seemed to feel no sense"*: Ibid., p. 2.

46 *"privileged insider"*: Ibid.

47 *The Rage of a Privileged Class:* Cose, *The Rage of a Privileged Class.*

47 *"playing with fire"*: Jacoby, *Someone Else's House,* p. 541.

47 *"who understands what makes America great"*: Ibid.

47 *At home, on the weekend:* Ibid.

48 *made blacks exceptions to:* Dyson, *Race Rules,* p. 18.

49 *the dismantling of de jure segregation:* Dyson, "Integration and the New Black American Dilemma," pp. G6, G15.

49 *O. J. Simpson:* Dyson, *Race Rules,* pp. 1–46.

50 *the full stature of the title he loved best:* King said that in "the quiet recesses of my heart, I am fundamentally a clergyman, a Baptist preacher," in "The UnChristian Christian," *Ebony Magazine,* Aug. 1965, p. 77. In a 1967 sermon, "Thou Fool," King said that "I have no ambitions in life but to achieve excellence in the Christian ministry . . . I don't plan to do anything but remain a preacher" (Garrow, *Bearing the Cross,* p. 576). And Andrew Young said that King "was a preacher. And whenever we argued, he'd get to preaching. You never won an argument because he would take off on flights of oratory, and you'd forget your point trying to listen to him" (Oates, *Let the Trumpet,* p. 289).

Chapter 3: "As I Ponder the Madness of Vietnam"

51 *"As I Ponder the Madness of Vietnam":* King, "A Time to Break Silence," in King, *A Testament,* p. 234.

51 *a tape-recorded excerpt of one of his last sermons:* "The Drum Major Instinct," in ibid., pp. 259–267. All further quotations in this section are from the same source.

52 *he was a profound pacificist:* At one point, King believed that war "could serve as a negative good in the sense of preventing the spread and growth of an evil force. War, I felt, horrible as it is, might be preferable to surrender to a totalitarian system. But more and more I have come to the conclusion that the potential destructiveness of modern weapons of war totally rules out the possibility of war ever serving again as a negative good." See King, "Pilgrimage to Nonviolence," in King, *A Testament,* p. 39.

52 *"a great spiritual leader":* "Conversation with Martin Luther King" in King, *A Testament,* p. 658.

52 *Several myths cloud:* Fairclough, "Martin Luther King, Jr., and the War in Vietnam," pp. 21–22 (hereafter cited as "King and Vietnam").

53 *In contrast to such civil rights figures:* Ibid., p. 21; Anderson, *Bayard Rustin,* esp. pp. 57–149; Anderson, *A. Philip Randolph;* Pfeffer, *A. Philip Randolph,* pp. 21, 43, 63–65.

53 *"strict pacifist":* Fairclough, "King and Vietnam," p. 21.

53 *"just war theory":* Walzer, *Just and Unjust Wars.*

53 *application of nonviolence to international affairs:* King, "Pilgrimage to Nonviolence," p. 39.

53 *"the power of nonviolence in group conflicts":* Ibid.

53 *I felt that while war could never:* Ibid. Also see Friedly and Gallen, *Martin Luther King,* p. 448.

53 *"realistic pacifism":* King, *A Testament,* p. 39.

53 *"claim to be free":* Ibid.

53 *"cannot remain silent while mankind":* Ibid.

54 *"Rolling Thunder":* McNamara, Blight, and Brigham, et al., *Argument Without End,* pp. 173, 189, 208, 216, 336, 337, 342, 347, 379; Logevall, *Choosing War,* pp. 344, 363; Schulzinger, *A Time for War,* pp. 171–173; Van De Mark, *Into the Quagmire,* pp. 91, 97–98.

54 *prodded King to reexamine:* McKnight, *The Last Crusade,* p. 11; Noer, "Martin Luther King, Jr., and the Cold War," p. 118. Fairclough, "King and Vietnam," p. 22. Although King wrestled seriously with his views on pacifism, it would still take him two years to take a sustained public stand against the war. As Fairclough says, perhaps "the most surprising aspect of King's commitment to the peace movement was the fact that it took him so long to make it. The bombing of North Vietnam and the massive buildup of American forces commenced in February 1965; it was only in February 1967 that King devoted an entire speech to the war." Fairclough, "King and Vietnam," p. 22.

54 *"morally and politically wrong":* Fairclough, "King and Vietnam," p. 22.

54 *by two factors:* Ibid., p. 24. Also see Noer, "Martin Luther King, Jr., and the Cold War," pp. 118–120.

54 *"accomplishing nothing":* Cited in Garrow, *Bearing,* p. 394.

54 *"we must negotiate with the Vietcong":* Cited in Garrow, ibid., pp. 429–430.

54 *Without the prior approval of his board:* Noer, "Martin Luther King, Jr., and the Cold War," p. 118.

54 *North Vietnam would drop its demand:* Ibid.

54 *King pledged to write letters:* Ibid.; Fairclough, "King and Vietnam," p. 24; Garrow, *Bearing,* p. 438.

55 *the value of an SCLC resolution:* Garrow, *Bearing,* p. 437.

55 *He was rebuffed by SCLC's board:* Fairclough, "King and Vietnam," p. 24; Garrow, *Bearing,* p. 437; Lewis, *King,* pp. 295–96.

55 *to antagonize the man:* Fairclough, "King and Vietnam," p. 24.

55 *"too far in the international arena":* Cited in Garrow, *Bearing,* p. 438.

55 *"we have an obligation":* Ibid.

55 *"issued a statement disassociating the organization":* Noer, "Martin Luther King, Jr., and the Cold War," p. 118; Garrow, *Bearing,* p. 438; Fairclough, "King and Vietnam," p. 26.

55 *"civil rights groups [do not] have enough information":* Cited in Fairclough, "King and Vietnam," p. 25.

55 *"Johnson needs a consensus":* Cited in McKnight, "The Last Crusade," p. 12.

55 *His own aides:* Fairclough, "Martin Luther King, Jr.," p. 24; Noer, "Martin Luther King, Jr., and the Cold War," p. 118.

55 *Johnson was in private:* Noer, "Martin Luther King, Jr., and the Cold War," p. 119; Lentz, *Symbols,* p. 176.

55 *Johnson was noticeably frosty:* Lentz, *Symbols,* p. 176.

55 *Johnson encouraged King to meet:* Ibid.; Garrow, *Bearing,* p. 443; Noer, "Martin Luther King, Jr., and the Cold War," p. 119; Fairclough, "King and Vietnam," p. 26.

56 *Goldberg postponed:* Garrow, *Bearing,* p. 443.

56 *"very urgent to work":* Ibid.

56 *King disavowed:* Ibid.

56 *"war is obsolete":* Ibid.; Friedly and Gallen, *Martin Luther King, Jr.,* p. 449.

56 *Goldberg told King that secret negotiations:* Fairclough, "King and Vietnam," p. 26; Lentz, *Symbols,* p. 176.

56 *"public utterances":* Fairclough, "King and Vietnam," p. 26.

56 *Both Goldberg and King:* Garrow, *Bearing,* p. 445.

56 *"absolutely no competence":* Cited in Noer, "Martin Luther King, Jr., and the Cold War," p. 119; Fairclough, "King and Vietnam," p. 25.

56 *"alienated much of the support":* Fairclough, "King and Vietnam," p. 25; Noer, "Martin Luther King, Jr., and the Cold War," p. 119; Garrow, *Bearing,* p. 445.

56 *King believed that Johnson was behind:* Friedly and Gallen, *Martin Luther King, Jr.,* p. 434.

56 *the media assault in the wake of his criticism:* Garrow, *Bearing,* p. 445.

56 *a modest proposal:* Lentz, *Symbols,* p. 176.

56 *especially the news magazines:* Ibid.

57 *"just bombarded with criticism":* Cited in ibid., p. 176; Young, *An Easy Burden,* p. 430.

57 *"King should have . . . kept silent":* Lentz, *Symbols,* p. 176.

57 *"drawling bumpkin":* Ibid., p. 177.

57 *"Confusing the Cause":* *Time,* July 16, 1965, p. 20, cited in Fairclough, "Martin Luther King, Jr.," p. 25.

57 *"coalition of conscience":* Cited in Lentz, *Symbols,* p. 178.

57 *"opportunistic and meddling":* Ibid.

57 *"painted King as an opportunist":* Ibid., p. 180.

57 *a self-described temporary withdrawal:* Friedly and Gallen, *Martin Luther King, Jr.,* p. 435.

57 *He decided to drop his letter-writing campaign:* Ibid., pp. 434–435; Garrow, *Bearing,* p. 445; Noer, "Martin Luther King, Jr., and the Cold War," p. 120.

57 *I am convinced that the press:* Friedly and Gallen, *Martin Luther King, Jr.,* pp. 434–435.

57 *"to withdraw temporarily":* Ibid., p. 435.

57 *"They told me I wasn't an expert":* Cited in Fairclough, "King and Vietnam," p. 26.

57 *"put his pen":* Ibid.

57 *1966 saw two forces:* Ibid., p. 27; Noer, "Martin Luther King, Jr., and the Cold War," 121; McKnight, *The Last Crusade,* p. 12.

57 *Congress cut funds for community action programs:* Fairclough, "King and Vietnam," p. 27; McKnight, *The Last Crusade,* p. 14.

58 *"a distracted, uncaring President":* McKnight, *The Last Crusade,* p. 14. For an insightful sociological treatment of the cultural, social, and intellectual assault on the poor, see Gans, *The War Against the Poor.*

58 *"poverty . . . and social progress are ignored":* Fairclough, "King and Vietnam," pp. 27–28.

58 *His sermons and speeches reflected his disgust:* Ibid., p. 27; Garrow, *Bearing,* pp. 461, 469.

59 *many SCLC staff members:* Fairclough, "King and Vietnam," p. 28.

59 *got the SCLC board to take a public stand:* Garrow, *Bearing,* pp. 469–470, 502.

59 *Spock had approached King:* Ibid., p. 453; Oates, *Let the Trumpet Sound,* p. 381.

59 *his encounter with Spock:* Garrow, *Bearing,* p. 453.

59 *King's consent to run as a presidential candidate:* Ibid., p. 542.

59 *his first speech devoted exclusively to Vietnam:* King, "The Casualties of the War in Vietnam," cited in Fairclough, "King and Vietnam," p. 29. Also see Fairclough, *To Redeem,* p. 336.

59 *"supporting a new form of colonialism":* King, "Casualties of the War." Also see Fairclough, *To Redeem,* p. 336.

59 *a multicultural gaggle of activists:* Garrow, *Bearing the Cross,* pp. 556–557.

59 *King spoke extensively about Vietnam:* King, "Speech at Staff Retreat, Frogmore, S.C.," May 1967, cited in Fairclough, "King and Vietnam," p. 33.

60 *"weapon of spurious patriotism to galvanize":* King, "The Domestic Impact of the War," speech to National Labor Leadership Assembly for Peace, Chicago, Nov. 11, 1967, cited in Fairclough, "King and Vietnam," p. 33.

60 *"When a Hollywood performer, lacking distinction":* Ibid., p. 35.

60 *"opposing [the] government's policy":* King, "A Time to Break Silence," p. 231.

60 *"the apathy of conformist thought":* Ibid.

60 *"Vietnam War is an enemy of the poor":* Ibid., p. 233.

60 *"extraordinarily high proportion":* Ibid.

60 *Studies in the early 1970s show that:* MaClear, *The Ten Thousand Day War,* p. 232, cited in Darby and Rowley, "King on Vietnam," pp. 43–44.

60 *in 1965, the military lowered its:* Foner, *Blacks and the Military,* pp. 202–204, cited in Darby and Rowley, "King on Vietnam," p. 44.

61 *"guarantee liberties in Southeast Asia":* King, "A Time to Break Silence," in King, *A Testament,* p. 233.

61 *"a revolution of values":* Ibid., p. 242.

61 *"rededicate ourselves to the long":* Ibid., p. 243.

61 *"greatest purveyor of the violence in the world today":* Ibid., p. 233.

61 *"Martin Luther King, that goddamned":* Young, *An Easy Burden,* p. 434.

61 *as if he had discovered that King had raped:* Ibid., p. 472.

61 *The polls were against King as well:* Brink and Harris, *Black and White,* pp. 272–276; Fairclough, "King and Vietnam," p. 25.

61 *"attempt to merge the civil rights":* NAACP press release, Apr. 15, 1967, cited in Fairclough, *To Redeem,* p. 465, n. 14.

61 *Massachusetts senator Ed Brooke:* Darby and Rowley, "King on Vietnam and Beyond," p. 49. Also see Rowan, "The Consequences of Decision," in Lincoln, *Martin Luther King, Jr.,* p. 213.

62 *"grave injury":* "A Tragedy," *Washington Post,* Apr. 6, 1967, p. A20. Also see Rowan, "The Consequences of Decision," p. 213.

62 *"fusing of two public problems that are distinct":* "Dr. King's Error," *New York Times,* Apr. 7, 1967, sec. 1, p. 36.

62 *"Dr. King's Disservice to His Cause":* Life 62, Apr. 1967, p. 4.

62 *"demagoguery":* Lentz, *Symbols,* p. 239.

62 *"the entire cause of nonviolent Negro":* Ibid., pp. 239–240.

62 *"was ignorant of the best course to follow:* Ibid., p. 241.

63 *the promising achievements of Reconstruction:* Fairclough, "King and Vietnam," p. 22.

63 *"forget our special grievances and close ranks":* Cited in ibid., p. 22. Although Du Bois made these arguments in his famous "Close Ranks" editorial in the NAACP's magazine, *The Crisis,* he grew to regret his comments in light of the "Red Summer" of 1919, when seventy blacks were lynched, including ten uniformed soldiers. For an excellent discussion of the history of black arguments for and against involvement in the war in relation to the Vietnam War, especially as viewed through the lens of Muhammad Ali's career and antiwar activism, see Marqusee, *Redemption Song,* esp. pp. 162–252.

63 *A. Philip Randolph threatened a massive march on Washington:* Fairclough, "King and Vietnam," p. 23; Pfeffer, *A. Philip Randolph,* pp. 133–168.

64 *criticized Du Bois for capitulating:* Pfeffer, *A. Philip Randolph,* p. 9.

64 *they were briefly jailed in 1918:* Ibid., pp. 9–10.

64 *Coretta Scott King played a crucial role:* Young, *An Easy Burden,* p. 424; Fairclough, "King and Vietnam," p. 28; Oates, *Let the Trumpet Sound,* p. 381; King, *The Autobiography of Martin Luther King, Jr.,* p. 35.

64 *She was an earlier:* Oates, *Let the Trumpet Sound,* p. 381; Fairclough, "King and Vietnam," p. 28.

64 *She addressed a major antiwar rally in California:* Oates, *Let the Trumpet Sound,* p. 431.

64 *Coretta Scott King exhorted:* Ibid., p. 440.

65 *SCLC staffer James Lawson:* Fairclough, "King and Vietnam," p. 24.

65 *Lawson and four SCLC colleagues formed:* Ibid., p. 28.

65 *"a bunch of crazies":* Hampton and Fayer, eds., *Voices of Freedom,* p. 343.

65 *"band wagon that's playing a 'square' tune":* Cited in Fairclough, "King and Vietnam," p. 24.

65 *only a long-term strategy:* Ibid.

65 *Young became deeply committed:* Friedly and Gallen, eds., *Martin Luther King, Jr.,* p. 436.

65 *mystical theologian:* Halberstam, "When 'Civil Rights' and 'Peace' Join Forces," in Lincoln, *Martin Luther King, Jr.,* p. 204.

65 *he was offered the position:* Ibid.

65 *making King realize the importance:* Young, *An Easy Burden,* p. 425.

65 *"Lord can't hear our prayers":* Halberstam, "When 'Civil Rights' and 'Peace' Join Forces," p. 204. As Andrew Young recalls, at the time of Bevel's comments, "the U.S. military was contemplating a bombing action that would destroy the dikes that enabled rice production in the Mekong Delta, erasing the efforts of centuries of civilization. To prevent this, he [Bevel] reasoned, perhaps optimistically, that the U.S. military wouldn't drop bombs on American citizens. But it is a testament to Bevel's brilliance that his digestion anticipated a strategy that the peace activists would later use in Central America to protect the targets of death squads—accompaniment. During the war in El Salvador, courageous Americans would accompany leaders of the democracy movement who were

targeted by right-wing death squads on the theory that the presence of an American would protect them." Young, *An Easy Burden*, p. 425.

65 *"masterminded"*: Fairclough, "King and Vietnam," p. 28.

65 *"Andy, we have got to stop"*: Young, *An Easy Burden*, p. 425.

66 *It was Young who encouraged Bevel*: Ibid., pp. 425–426. The Bevel visit to King coincides with the often repeated story of King's being finally convinced to oppose the war because of reading an article, "The Children of Vietnam," by William Pepper in *Ramparts* magazine accompanied by photographs of Vietnamese children who had been burned by napalm dropped by American planes. Aide Bernard Lee recalls the moment King read the article in Jamaica in January 1967, on a rare four-week break from his tedious schedule: "When he came to *Ramparts* magazine he stopped. He froze as he looked at the pictures from Vietnam. He saw a picture of a Vietnamese mother holding her dead baby, a baby killed by our military. Then Martin just pushed the plate of food away from him. I looked up and said, 'Doesn't it taste any good?,' and he answered, 'Nothing will ever taste any good for me until I do everything I can to end that war.'" Cited in Garrow, *Bearing*, p. 543. Also see Lee's description of this incident in Hampton and Fayer, eds., *Voices of Freedom*, pp. 342–343. The author of the article that moved King, William Pepper, would have at least three more interesting connections to King. First, he was part of the National Conference for New Politics (NCNP), a largely white leftist organization whose antiwar passions led them to try to force King's hand in their bid to get him to run with pediatrician Benjamin Spock on a 1968 presidential ticket. Pepper told the *New York Times* in 1968 that his group "was negotiating with Dr. King" about a potential presidential bid, angering King and Andrew Young (Garrow, *Bearing*, p. 559). Second, Pepper authored a book about a conspiracy to murder King that included private and governmental forces. See Pepper, *Orders to Kill*, which, in its paperback edition published by Warner Books, includes a foreword by King's youngest son and King Center head, Dexter Scott King. For a book that rebuts Pepper's thesis of a widespread conspiracy that exonerates convicted King assassin James Earl Ray, see Posner, *Killing the Dream*. Third, after a 1978 interview with Ray, William Pepper, an attorney, subsequently became Ray's lawyer and participated in a 1993 mock trial, aired on HBO, arguing his client's innocence, a view that Dexter King, because of Pepper's influence, has adopted. As King writes in his foreword to Pepper's book, Pepper's "exhaustive research sheds new light on critical questions, including the extent of the involvement of government intelligence agencies, military units and organized crime in the assassination, the motives behind it, and the individuals who ordered and participated in it." King, Foreword to Pepper, *Orders to Kill*, p. xxiv.

66 *I was serving as chairperson of SNCC*: Hampton and Fayer, eds., *Voices of Freedom*, p. 340.

66 *Carmichael's relentless criticism of the war*: Lentz, *Symbols*, p. 242.

66 *"King, Carmichael & Co."*: Ibid., p. 241.

67 *"What are you doing?"*: Cited in Hampton and Fayer, eds., *Voices of Freedom*, pp. 346–347.

67 *"one of the most profound speeches"*: Ibid., p. 347.

67 *The key figure behind King's analytical genius*: Ibid., p. 344; Garrow, *Bearing*, p. 711, n. 30.

67 *Harding addressed a long letter*: Hampton and Fayer, eds., *Voices of Freedom*, p. 336.

67 *"to put themselves out in the open"*: Ibid.

67 *prepared a memo on Vietnam for King*: Ibid., p. 344; Abelove et al., eds., *Visions of History*, p. 229.

68 *"much of what I believed"*: Ibid., p. 337.

68 *what I was doing was really*: Hampton and Fayer, *Voices of Freedom*, p. 344.

68 *"had been unbalanced"*: Garrow, *Bearing*, p. 554.

68 *"spent a full afternoon thinking about"*: Cited in ibid.

68 *"white people sending black people"*: Cited in Marqusee, *Redemption Song*, p. 218.

68 *He is perhaps the best speaker*: Halberstam, "When 'Civil Rights' and 'Peace' Join Forces," p. 187.

69 *But as his biographer points out*: Anderson, *Bayard Rustin*, p. 300.

69 *"demonstrated to King the depth"*: Noer, "Martin Luther King, Jr. and the Cold War," p. 121.

69 *the strong reactions against the war in Northern ghettoes*: Ibid.

69 *younger and poorer black Americans*: Ibid.

69 *"he gets more cheers in Negro colleges"*: Friedly and Gallen, eds., *Martin Luther King, Jr.*, p. 533.

70 *antiwar sentiment was a predominantly white*: Marqusee, *Redemption Song*, pp. 166–167.

70 *Opinion polls*: Ibid., p. 166.

70 *25 percent of blacks supported withdrawal*: Ibid.

70 *"blacks, low-income families"*: Ibid.

70 *"There is more discontent"*: Friedly and Gallen, eds., *Martin Luther King, Jr.*, p. 533.

70 *Martin's decision to oppose the war*: Young, *An Easy Burden*, p. 427.

70 *Muhammad Ali*: Marqusee, *Redemption Song*, p. 223.

70 *"I ain't got no quarrel"*: Cited in ibid., p. 173.

70 *He was convicted of draft evasion*: Ibid., p. 227.

70 *denied at least $10 million*: Remnick, *King of the World*, pp. 285–291; Marqusee, *Redemption Song*, pp. 227–252.

70 *the U.S. Supreme Court overturned his conviction*: Marqusee, *Redemption Song*, p. 262.

71 *"a diffusion of interests"*: Graham and Singh, eds., *Conversations with Ralph Ellison*, p. 244.

71 *"let them off the hook"*: Ibid.

71 *"some of the defection of energies"*: Ibid., pp. 244–245.

72 *"injustice anywhere is a threat"*: "Letter from Birmingham Jail," in King, *A Testament*, p. 290.

72 *"strange liberators"*: King, "A Time to Break Silence," p. 235.

72 *"live out the true meaning"*: "I Have a Dream," in King, *A Testament*, p. 219.

72 *"I have worked too long now"*: King, *Trumpet of Conscience*, in King, *A Testament*, p. 636.

73 *"justice is indivisible"*: Ibid.

73 *"in a pulpit it's one thing"*: Graham and Singh, eds., *Conversations*, p. 245.

73 *"America's soul becomes totally poisoned"*: King, "A Time to Break Silence," p. 234.

73 *"can never be saved so long as it destroys"*: Ibid.

73 *"alarming imperialists in all countries"*: King, "Honoring Dr. Dubois," *Freedomways* 8, Spring 1968, reprinted in Foner, ed., *W.E.B. Du Bois Speaks*, Vol. I, *Speeches and Addresses, 1890–1919*.

73 *"would readily see the parallel"*: Ibid.

74 *greater support of the Gulf War among whites*: London *Financial Times*, Jan. 23, 1991, sec. 1, p. 4; *Daily Telegraph*, Jan. 26, 1991, p. 3.

74 *but only 43 percent of blacks*: Ibid. (both articles).

74 *King's January 15 birthday was chosen*: *Los Angeles Times*, Jan. 22, 1991, A29.

74 *"I'd like to see"*: Ibid.

74 *all criticized the Gulf War*: London *Financial Times*, Jan. 23, 1991, sec. 1, p. 4; *Los Angeles Times*, Feb. 16, 1991, A3; *Atlanta Journal-Constitution*, Jan. 22, 1991, C6.

74 *Jackson argued that tens of billions of dollars*: London *Financial Times*, Jan. 23, 1991, sec. 1, p. 4.

74 *"a moratorium on the crippling"*: *Los Angeles Times*, Feb. 16, 1991, A3.

74 *a cease-fire in the Persian Gulf: Atlanta Journal-Constitution*, Jan. 22, 1991, C6.

74 *"doesn't even have to be":* Ibid.

74 *many whites believed that blacks:* Ibid.

74 *"Let's set the record straight":* Ibid.

74 *"Black men and women": Daily Telegraph*, Jan. 26, 1991, p. 3.

75 *"retired black generals":* Ibid.

75 *"cannon-fodder":* Ibid.

75 *"outraged": St. Louis Dispatch*, Jan. 22, 1991, p. 1A.

75 *"the double whammy":* Ibid.

75 *"racism, classism":* Ibid.

75 *a group of black civil rights: Los Angeles Times*, Feb. 16, 1991, part A3.

75 *The Marines were composed of:* Ibid.

76 *"people who simply": Boston Globe*, Feb. 6, 1991, p. 15.

76 *Thus, many African-Americans, regardless of income:* Ibid.

77 *triplets of social misery:* Garrow, *Bearing the Cross*, p. 708, n. 13, and Young, *An Easy Burden*, p. 429.

Chapter 4: "America Must Move Toward a Democratic Socialism"

78 *"America Must Move":* King, "Frogmore Speech," in Smith, "The Radicalization of Martin Luther King, Jr.," p. 275.

78 *"It is criminal":* ABC-TV Special, "The Century: Memphis Dreams: Searching for the Promised Land," hosted by Peter Jennings, 1999. All the quotations from King in this section are from the same source.

79 *"He said to me":* Ibid. All the quotations from Lawson in this section are from the same source.

79 *"manipulation of the poor":* King, "A Time to Break Silence," p. 233.

79 *"Martin Luther King was a troublemaker":* ABC-TV Special, "The Century: Memphis Dreams: Searching for the Promised Land."

80 *"the most dangerous Negro":* Fairclough, *To Redeem*, p. 155; Friedly and Gallen, *Martin Luther King, Jr.,* p. 38. The statement was actually made by William Sullivan, the FBI's assistant director, who, after King's "I Have a Dream" speech (which he termed "demagogic"), said that he was "the most dangerous and effective Negro leader in the country" (Friedly and Gallen, *Martin Luther King, Jr.,* p. 38). Sullivan's words perfectly capture Hoover's sentiments. See Garrow, *The FBI and Martin Luther King, Jr.*; McKnight, *The Last Crusade*.

80 *"an action-oriented Marxist":* Garrow, "The Helms Attack on King," p. 14.

81 *There was no need to name:* Goodwin, *Black Migration*; Grossman, *Land of Hope*; Ralph, *Northern Protest*; Reed, *The Chicago NAACP*; Spear, *Black Chicago*; Travis, *Autobiography of Black Chicago*.

81 *"no earth-shaking victories":* King, "The President's Address to the Tenth Anniversary Convention of the Southern Christian Leadership Conference, Atlanta, Georgia, August 16, 1967," in Scott and Brockriede, eds., *The Rhetoric of Black Power*, p. 149.

81 *"will renovate deteriorating buildings":* Ibid., p. 150.

81 *"most dramatic success":* Ibid.

82 *"Negro-controlled financial institutions":* Ibid.

82 *"if you respect my dollar":* Ibid., p. 151.

82 *In Cleveland, Operation Breadbasket:* Ibid.

82 *"hold great possibilities":* Ibid.

83 *his moves to unionize ghetto citizens:* Ralph, *Northern Protest*.

83 *"basic social and economic problems":* Cited in Lasch, *The True and Only Heaven*, p. 401.

83 *"the old plantations in the South":* King, "The President's Address to the Tenth Anniversary Convention," p. 156.

83 *"strength required to bring about"*: Ibid.

83 *"dislocations in the market operations"*: Ibid., p. 157.

83 *"the Movement must address"*: Ibid., p. 161.

83 *"raising questions about the economic system"*: Ibid.

83 *"question[ing] the capitalistic economy"*: Ibid.

83 *alienated him from most of the few allies who remained*: King's radical social philosophy, his antiwar statements, and his change of perspective on racism caused a great deal of tension between King and other leaders. This was exacerbated by King's earlier fame as the most prominent civil rights leader in America, especially after the March on Washington. For a discussion of the jealousy toward King early on, see Anderson, *Bayard Rustin*, pp. 241, 246–247; and Rowan, *Breaking Barriers*, p. 261.

84 *"a restructuring of the very architecture"*: King, "Frogmore Speech," p. 273, n. 7.

84 *A nation that will keep people in slavery*: King, "The President's Address to the Tenth Anniversary Convention," p. 163.

84 *the Kerner Commission*: *Report of the National Advisory Commission on Civil Disorders*, 1968. The riot statistics that follow are from that report, as cited in Cook, *The Least of These*, p. 164.

85 *the uprisings as a "holocaust"*: King, "Next Stop: The North," in King, *Testament*, p. 192. For an astute appraisal of King's pilgrimage to Watts, see Horner, *Fire This Time*, pp. 183–184, 298–299.

85 *A study of the Watts uprising*: Cited in Wyatt, *Five Fires*, pp. 212–213..

85 *"a riot is [at bottom] the language of the unheard"*: King, *Where Do We Go?* p. 112.

85 *"the looting in Watts was a form of social protest"*: King, "Next Stop: The North," p. 192.

85 *"Negroes [who] created the theory"*: King, "Negroes Are Not Moving Too Fast" in King, *A Testament*, p. 179.

85 *"to perceive that nonviolence"*: Ibid.

85 *"Nothing in the theory"*: Ibid., p. 180.

85 *conversation with activist Marian Wright*: Hampton and Fayer, *Voices of Freedom*, pp. 453–454. (She was a King associate.)

85 *"the invisible poor"*: Harrington, *The Other America*.

85 *King's plan*: King, "Showdown for Nonviolence," in King, *A Testament*, pp. 64–72. Also see Colaiaco, *Apostle of Nonviolence*, pp. 188–191; Garrow, *Bearing the Cross*, pp. 575–624; and Fairclough, *To Redeem*, pp. 357–383.

86 *"if this campaign succeeds"*: King, "Showdown for Nonviolence," p. 65.

86 *"nonviolence will be discredited"*: Ibid.

86 *"massive nonviolence"*: Ibid. Also see King, *Trumpet of Conscience*, pp. 14–15; Smith, "The Radicalization of Martin Luther King, Jr.," pp. 280–285; and Lentz, *Martin Luther King*, pp. 263–280.

86 *"disruptive dimensions"*: King, "Showdown for Nonviolence," p. 68.

86 *"powerful enough, dramatic enough"*: Ibid., p. 66.

86 *Nonviolence must be adapted*: Cited in Smith, "The Radicalization of Martin Luther King, Jr.," p. 282.

87 *"go for broke"*: Garrow, *Bearing the Cross*, p. 582.

87 *"we've gone for broke before"*: Ibid.

87 *"In a sense, you could say"*: José Yglesias, "Dr. King's March on Washington, Part II," *New York Times Magazine*, Mar. 21, 1967, cited in Colaiaco, *Militant Apostle of Nonviolence*, p. 190.

87 *analyses like those of William Julius Wilson*: Wilson, *The Declining Significance of Race*; *The Truly Disadvantaged*; and *When Work Disappears*.

87 *"black underclass"*: King, "Why We Must Go to Washington," cited in Smith, "The Radicalization of Martin Luther King, Jr.," p. 274.

87 *"we have an underclass"*: Ibid.

87 *"legislative and judicial victories"*: Ibid. Also, "'Face to Face' Television News Interview," in King, *A Testament*, p. 404.

87 *"penetrate the lower depths"*: Smith, "The Radicalization of Martin Luther King, Jr.," p. 274; "'Face to Face' Television News Interview," in King, *A Testament*, p. 404.

87 *"the changes that came about"*: Smith, "The Radicalization," p. 274.

87 *"limited mainly to the Negro middle class"*: King, "Frogmore Speech," p. 274. Also see "'Face to Face' Television News Interview," p. 404.

87 *"the plight of the Negro poor"*: King, "Pre-Washington Campaign," cited in Smith, "The Radicalization of Martin Luther King, Jr.," p. 274.

87 *"the roots [of economic injustice]"*: King, "The State of the Movement," cited in Smith, "The Radicalization of Martin Luther King, Jr.," p. 275.

87 *"We are now making demands"*: King, "Frogmore Speech," p. 275.

88 *"turn off the tape recorder"*: Garrow, *Bearing the Cross*, pp. 591–592.

88 *"didn't believe that capitalism"*: Ibid., p. 592.

88 *"going to allow anybody"*: King, "Frogmore Speech," p. 275.

88 *"Dr. King had a genius"*: Hampton and Fayer, eds., *Voices of Freedom*, p. 450.

88 *"certainly wouldn't use"*: Ibid.

88 *"say such things from the pulpit"*: Garrow, *Bearing the Cross*, p. 717, n. 19.

88 *"wanted me to know"*: Ibid.

88 *"a man whose ideas"*: Ibid.

88 *"statement that [King] could no longer speak"*: Lasch, *The True*, p. 404.

89 For instance, James Bevel: Colaiaco, *Apostle of Nonviolence*, pp. 190–191; Garrow, *Bearing the Cross*, pp. 589–595.

90 *arrogance and amnesia that the liberal left:* Historian Robin D. G. Kelley writes: "The fact is, the American Left rarely claims King as a visionary for their movements—he's either dismissed as a reformer or treated as if he 'finally came around.' The fact is, he was ahead of the curve and understood, like many radicals in his day, the organic relationship between the military industrial complex and poverty; pacifism and socialism were two sides of the same coin." Kelley, private letter in author's possession.

90 *Was King, as Helms claimed:* Helms's remark is based on supposed records in the possession of the FBI. As David Garrow writes, the FBI's "still 'Top Secret' quotation of King saying 'I am a Marxist' probably would be discounted by most observers as something King could never have said." But Garrow contends that it might not be suprising after all for King to make such a remark in the light of King's "distaste of the American economic order" dating back to the 1950s. Garrow says that in private "he made it clear to close friends that economically speaking he considered himself what he termed a Marxist" (Garrow, *The FBI and Martin Luther King, Jr.*, pp. 213–214).

90 *"metaphysical materialism" and "ethical relativism"*: Carson, ed., *The Autobiography of Martin Luther King, Jr.*, pp. 20–21.

90 *"next to Abernathy"*: Fairclough, *To Redeem*, pp. 165–166.

90 *Wyatt Tee Walker:* "15 Greatest Black Preachers," *Ebony*, November, 1993, p. 156.

90 *"Uncle Tom"*: Garrow, *Bearing*, 465. Sometimes, however, the teasing turned violent. Martin Luther King would sometimes kid Young, greeting him once, "How ya doing, Tom." But on another occasion, Hosea Williams remembers that "Andy jumped on me physically one day and fought me and whopped me all up side the head. I [had] called him a white Uncle Tom" (Garrow, *Bearing*, p. 464).

91 *encouraged King to adopt even more radical tactics:* Fairclough, *To Redeem*, p. 358.

91 *"are ready and willing to pay the price"*: "The Racial Crisis: A Consensus," *Newsweek*, Aug. 21, 1967, pp. 15–18, cited in Fairclough, *To Redeem*, p. 358.

91 *"lying on highways"*: Garrow, *Bearing*, p. 582.

91 *"underclass that is locked out"*: Ibid., p. 583.

91 *isn't sufficiently crisis packed:* Ibid., p. 584.

92 *"I quantify revolution in dollar terms"*: Jacoby, *Someone Else's House*, p. 524.

92 *"down-to-earth" view*: Ibid.

92 *His new idea of how to get to the future*: Ibid.

93 *"support the development"*: Young, *An Easy Burden*, p. 420.

93 *"than build public housing projects"*: Ibid., pp. 420–21.

93 *social engineering*: Jacoby, *Someone Else's House*, p. 524. For excellent treatments of Jackson, see Reynolds, *Jesse Jackson*; and Frady, *Jesse*.

93 *"there is a problem with the staff"*: Garrow, *Bearing*, p. 590.

93 *"greatest doubters"*: Ibid., pp. 592, 593.

93 *hung up on what Martin called*: Young, *An Easy Burden*, p. 444.

94 *"dealt with neighborhood businesses"*: Ibid.

94 *"was convinced that a substantial increase"*: Ibid.

94 *"Memphis is the Washington campaign"*: Young, *An Easy Burden*, p. 458.

94 *"Everyone here wants to drag me"*: Ibid.

94 *"they were really feeling their oats"*: Ibid.

94 *"Look," King spoke sharply to Jackson*: Ibid., p. 458.

95 *"move toward a massive coalition"*: Gates, "Interview: Jesse Jackson," *Frontline: Online*, 1998, p. 5.

95 *working class black people*: Ibid.

95 *"most poor people are not"*: Ibid.

95 *"Most poor people work every day"*: Ibid.

95 *"the welfare debate has been stimulated"*: Ibid.

95 *So I remember distinctly in 1960*: Ibid., p. 6.

96 *social democrat William Julius Wilson*: *The Declining Significance of Race*; *The Truly Disadvantaged*.

96 *"like urban ghettoes and barrios"*: Jackson, "Leave No One Behind," *Liberal Opinion Weekly*, September 28, 1998; *The Post* (An Independent Daily Newspaper, Ohio University), September 8, 1998, p. 1.

97 *to work with businesses, labor, and government*: "Speech to Second Annual Wall Street Project Conference," January 14, 1999, p. 4 (speech in author's possession).

98 *Perhaps what he did that day*: Ibid., p. 2.

98 *"So here we are on Wall Street"*: Ibid.

98 *"thirty-one years later"*: Ibid.

99 *King refused to view any political ideology*: Lewis, *King*, p. 35.

99 *"to do God's will"*: King, "I See the Promised Land," in King, *A Testament of Hope*, p. 286.

100 *"pork-chop nationalists"*: Newton, *To Die for the People*, p. 92.

Chapter 5: "We Did Engage in a Black Power Move"

101 *"We Did Engage"*: King, "Conversation with Martin Luther King," in King, *A Testament of Hope*, p. 664.

101 *not 1966, when such rhetoric*: Williams, *The King God Didn't Save*, p. 176, where Williams quotes journalist Louis Lomax as he reported on the names hurled at King after he left an Albany jail earlier than planned: "'Sellout!' 'Uncle Tom Nigger!' 'Jive Cat!' 'Martin Loser!'"

101 *my book on Malcolm X*: Dyson, *Making Malcolm*.

102 *the question of racial inauthenticity*: The question of racial authenticity is one of the most hotly debated topics in black popular culture, especially around the issue of black masculinity, the politics of racial identity, and the intersection of class, gender, and sexuality in shaping black cultural identities. See Dent, *Black Popular Culture*; Dyson, *Reflecting Black*, pp. xiii-111; Rose, *Black Noise*; Boyd, *Am I Black Enough for You?* Neal, *What the Music Said*.

102 *early Motown:* George, *Where Did Our Love Go?* Early, *One Nation Under a Groove;* Gordy, *To Be Loved.*

102 *niggas like Clarence Thomas:* Morrison, ed., *Race(ing) Justice.*

103 *a figure we can't critically interrogate:* Even King's first scholarly biographer, David Levering Lewis, admits that he had a rough time in the black community because of his willingness to examine King's life and career through a lens that wasn't rosy or romantic. Lewis writes: "I shot myself in the foot badly with the King family and much of the African-American community by writing imprudently in the preface of my initial skepticism about Dr. King and by choosing for the biography's title—*King: A Critical Biography.* Bill Weatherby [a Penguin editor] and I both overlooked the negative connotation of 'critical' in American English. Mrs. King uttered a frosty appraisal. The Ministerial Alliance of Baltimore ordered parishioners not to read it—thereby making it a best-seller in Baltimore. Columbia's distinguished professor of government, Charles Hamilton, managed to write a politically correct review in the *Sunday Times Book Review* that said little about the biography and much about his own association with the Kings" (Lewis, "From Eurocentrism to Polycentrism," in Cimbala and Himmelberg, eds., *Historians and Race,* pp. 80–81).

103 *enormous guilt:* Garrow, *Bearing the Cross.*

103 *"class suicide":* Cabral, *Unity and Struggle.*

103 *"house Negroes":* Malcolm X, in Goodman, ed., *The End of White World Supremacy,* p. 137, and "The House Negro and the Field Negro," in Clark, ed., *Malcolm X: The Final Speeches,* pp. 26–28. The latter reference is the last portion (and the only part caught on tape) of the speech that Malcolm X gave in Selma at the invitation of SNCC as King and other colleagues were in jail, after which he expressed to Coretta King his desire to help King in his work.

103 *conservative cultural currents:* Moses, *The Golden Age of Black Nationalism,* and Vandeburg, ed., *Modern Black Nationalism.*

103 *recent debates about school integration:* Dyson, "Integration and the New Black American Dilemma," *Newsday,* Sunday, July 13, 1997, pp. G6, G15.

104 *"twentieth-century Uncle Tom":* Cited in Dyson, *Between God,* p. 97. Also see Clark, *King, Malcolm, Baldwin,* pp. 42–43, and Cone, *Martin and Malcolm,* pp. 99, 108, 263.

104 *a moderate who catered to "whitey":* Cited in "Conversation with Martin Luther King," in King, *A Testament,* p. 660.

104 *And some youth:* Dyson, *Between God and Gangsta Rap,* p. 98.

104 *Malcolm X eventually changed his mind:* Malcolm X and Halley, *The Autobiography of Malcolm X,* pp. 364–373.

104 *would disobey Muhammad on other matters:* Ibid., pp. 315–347.

105 *"psychic numbing":* Lifton, *History and Human Survival,* pp. 115, 339, 376.

105 *he took too readily to the language of pathology:* King, "An Address by Dr. Martin Luther King, Jr.," in Rainwater and Yancey, *The Moynihan Report,* pp. 402–409.

105 *blacks acted quite differently around whites:* The phenomenon of how powerless and oppressed folk behave in the presence and public of dominant society—how they exercise agency, exert their own kind of power, and preserve the dignity of masked response, and hence, their survival—has been explored in Scott, *Domination and the Arts of Resistance,* and Kelley, *Race Rebels.*

105 *Blacks gave their songs double meanings:* Levine, *Black Culture and Black Consciousness;* Scott, *Domination and the Arts of Resistance* and *Weapons of the Weak;* Kelley, *Race Rebels.* For an exploration of the intriguing way that blacks used patterns on quilts to signal the route to freedom on the Underground Railroad and the most auspicious time to flee see Tobin and Dobard, *Hidden in Plain View.*

106 *"signifyin'":* Gates, *The Signifying Monkey.*

106 *The spirituals are a perfect example:* Thurman, *Deep River;* Fisher, *Negro Slave Songs in the United States;* Cone, *The Spirituals and the Blues* and *Risks of Faith;* Newman, *Go Down Moses.*

106 *New Breed Negro:* Guralnick, *Sweet Soul Music,* pp. 220–245.

106 *displaced kinship and degrading social structures:* Drake and Cayton, *Black Metropolis;* Lemann, *The Promised Land.*

106 *The Great Migration:* Groh, *The Black Migration;* Grossman, *Land of Hope;* Lemann, *Promised Land;* Griffin, *Who Set You Flowin'?*

106 *myth of the authentic Negro:* Dyson, *Reflecting Black,* pp. xiii–xxv. Also see Dent, *Black Popular Culture;* Rose, *Black Noise;* Boyd, *Am I Black Enough for You?* Neal, *What the Music Said.*

106 *a culture full of bluster and boast:* Levine, *Black Culture and Black Consciousness;* Kelley, *Yo' Mama's Disfunktional,* pp. 15–42. Abrahams, *Deep Down in the Jungle;* and Baugh, *Black Street Speech.*

106 *bustling suburb of Mississippi:* Cayton and Drake, *Black Metropolis;* Grossman, *Land of Hope;* Lemann, *Promised Land.*

107 *Gospel music:* Heilbut, *The Gospel Sound;* Boyer, *How Sweet the Sound.*

107 *The blues:* Oliver, *Blues Fell This Morning,* and *Gospel Blues;* Spencer, *Blues and Evil.*

107 *"We are not asking for an end":* Cited in Lasch, *The True,* p. 405.

107 *never wanted to leave to chance:* This is why King and his colleagues insisted on extensive preparation and training in nonviolence, and the signing of an oath, a pledge card, to subscribe to the rules of the movement. See King, *Stride Toward Freedom.*

108 *slaves in the fields:* Blassingame, *Slave Community;* Berlin, Favreau, and Miller, eds., *Remembering Slavery;* Berlin, *Many Thousands Gone.*

108 *sharecroppers company on tenant farms:* Brown, *Coming Up Down Home;* Caldwell and Bourke-White, *You Have Seen Their Faces;* Conrad, *The Forgotten Farmers;* Kester, *Revolt Among the Sharecroppers;* Stimpson, *My Remembers.*

108 *indigenous black leaders:* Mills, *This Little Light of Mine;* Grant, *Ella Baker.*

108 *the unity of black selves:* Cone, *Martin and Malcolm,* pp. 120–150.

109 *their heritage was more numerous and ancient:* Moses, *The Golden Age of Black Nationalism;* Vandeburg, *Modern Black Nationalism;* Bracey et al., eds., *Black Nationalism.*

109 *For many black nationalists:* I am not suggesting that black nationalism is either monolithic or generic. Neither am I arguing that no variety of black nationalism accepted or attempted to exploit the hustler ethic at the heart of black secular urban life. I am simply arguing that the most prominent offices of black nationalism, including the Nation of Islam, fought tooth and nail against the sort of capitulation to the surrounding white culture that degraded black identity. See Malcolm X and Halley, *The Autobiography of Malcolm X,* esp. pp. 184–289; Cone, *Martin and Malcolm,* esp. pp. 151–180.

109 *carved from a masculine worldview:* Carson, *In Struggle,* pp. 147–148; Wallace, *Black Macho and the Myth of the Superwoman;* M. King, *Freedom Song;* James, *Transcending,* pp. 83–112; Giddings, *When and Where,* pp. 314–324; White, *Too Heavy a Load,* pp. 177–211.

109 *dynamic expressions of black popular culture:* Kelley, *Race Rebels,* pp. 161–181.

110 *"Rev. Dr. Chickenwing":* Cited in Cone, *Martin and Malcolm,* p. 99.

110 *"Martin Loser King":* Oates, *Let the Trumpet Sound,* p. 449.

110 *Malcolm viewed King as the antithesis:* Cone, *Martin and Malcolm,* p. 112. Malcolm said that "real men don't put their children on the firing line" (cited in ibid.).

110 *King's repression of rage:* Ibid., pp. 174–177.

111 *"nourished by the contemporary frustration":* King, "Letter from Birmingham Jail," in King, *A Testament,* pp. 296–297.

111 *"the more excellent way":* Ibid., p. 297.

111 *a will to self-creation:* Cone, *Martin and Malcolm,* pp. 107–119; Dyson, *Making Malcolm,* pp. 79–106.

111 *"Black Power":* Carmichael and Hamilton, *Black Power;* and Scott and Brockriede, eds., *The Rhetoric of Black Power.*

111 *"We feel that integration is irrelevant"*: Cited in "Black Power Bends Martin Luther King," in Scott and Brockriede, eds., *The Rhetoric of Black Power*, p. 169.

111 *"less vulnerable [to misunderstanding]"*: King, *Where Do We Go?* in King, *A Testament*, p. 574.

111 *words "'black' and 'power' together"*: Ibid.

111 *"the ready appeal"*: Ibid.

112 *"The shattering blows on the Negro family"*: King, "An Address by Dr. Martin Luther King, Jr.," in Rainwater and Yancey, eds., *The Moynihan Report*, p. 407.

112 *Moynihan report: The Negro Family: The Cause for National Action*, full text in Rainwater and Yancey, eds., *The Moynihan Report*, pp. 41–124.

112 *"dangers and opportunities"*: King, cited in Tomasky, *Left for Dead*, p. 104.

112 *"problems will be attributed to innate Negro"*: Ibid.

112 *"jammed up, neurotic, psychotic Negroes"*: The phrase is actually Andrew Young's, as he spoke in Chicago before a meeting of the Chicago Real Estate Board (Garrow, *Bearing the Cross*, p. 510).

112 *"I have never seen"*: Cited in Lasch, *The True*, p. 399.

112 *"Negroes of Chicago"*: Ibid.

112 *they "don't participate in"*: Ibid.

112 *"integration is out"*: *Newsweek*, July 11, 1966, p. 31, cited in Scott, "Black Power Bends Martin Luther King, Jr.," in Scott and Brockriede, eds., *The Rhetoric of Black Power*, p. 171.

113 *"Over the last ten years"*: King, "The President's Address to the Tenth Anniversary Convention," in Scott and Brockriede, eds., *The Rhetoric of Black Power*, p. 148.

113 *"stood up and confronted"*: Ibid., p. 147.

113 *"gained manhood in the nation"*: Ibid., p. 148.

113 *"the ghetto is a domestic colony"*: Ibid., p. 152. Also see Blauner, *Racial Oppression in America*.

113 *"psychological and spiritual genocide"*: Garrow, *Bearing the Cross*, p. 598.

113 *"tendency to ignore the Negro's contribution"*: King, "The President's Address to the Tenth Anniversary Convention," p. 155.

113 *"cultural homicide"*: Ibid.

113 *many Afrocentric scholars*: Vandeburg, ed., *Modern Black Nationalism*.

113 *"movement for the Negro's freedom"*: King, "The President's Address to the Tenth Anniversary Convention," p. 155.

113 *as "long as the mind is enslaved"*: King, "The President's Address to the Tenth Anniversary Convention," p. 155.

113 *"Psychological freedom"*: Ibid.

113 *The Negro will only be free*: Ibid., pp. 155–156.

114 *"psychological call to manhood"*: "Conversation with Martin Luther King." pp. 663–665.

114 *"All too many"*: Ibid., p. 664.

114 *"we did engage"*: Ibid.

114 *"can pool our resources"*: Ibid., p. 665.

114 *When we see integration*: Ibid., p. 666.

116 *prior to its 1997 convention*: Dyson, "Integration and the New Black American Dilemma," pp. G6, G15.

116 *James Baldwin*: Baldwin, *The Fire Next Time*.

117 *dropped dramatically in the South between 1964 and 1972*: Dyson, "Integration and the New Black American Dilemma," pp. G6, G15.

118 *Black and Latino children are consistently scapegoated*: Ibid.

119 *"against association with ourselves"*: cited in Dyson, "Integration and the New Black American Dilemma," pp. G6, G15. A recent study sponsored by the NAACP and

conducted by New York's Hamilton College and the polling firm Zogby International found that about "half of young adults believe that separation of the races is acceptable as long as there are equal opportunities for everyone." Nearly 50 percent of whites who were surveyed replied that separation is acceptable, while nearly 40 percent of blacks found it acceptable. "Race Separation Accepted in Poll," *Dallas Morning News*, Aug. 17, 1999.

119 *What we must remember:* Ibid.

120 *full of figures, admittedly on the margins:* Wilmore, *Black Religion and Black Radicalism.*

120 *"Before I'd be a slave":* "O, Freedom," in Newman, *Go Down Moses*, p. 103.

Chapter 6: "I Had to Know God for Myself"

123 *"I Had to Know God For Myself":* King, "Why Jesus Called a Man a Fool," in Carson and Holloran, eds., *A Knock at Midnight*, p. 162.

123 *The sight of Rev. Henry Lyons:* "Tearful Baptist Leader Is Given 5½ Year Term in Graft Case," *New York Times*, April 1, 1999, p. A19.

123 *Lyons stepped down:* Ibid.

123 *National Baptist Convention:* Washington, *Frustrated Fellowship*, and Higginbotham, *Righteous Discontent.*

123 *convicted of racketeering and theft: Jet*, March 15, 1999, p. 16; *New York Times*, April 1, 1999, p. A19; *Atlanta Journal-Constitution*, June 19, 1999, p. 1B.

123 *sentenced Lyons to five-and-a-half years: New York Times*, op cit.; *Atlanta Journal-Constitution*, op cit.

123 *harshly mistreated Martin Luther King, Jr.:* Branch, *Parting the Waters*, pp. 500–507.

123 *the brilliantly conservative leadership of Joseph H. Jackson:* Ibid., pp. 101–102, 335–339, 500–507. Branch observes the historical irony of Jackson's visits to the King household when Martin Luther King, Jr., was a child, and his father was one of Jackson's trusted lieutenants in the convention. Branch writes that young King "knew and revered Jackson from the time he was ten years old, unaware that the famous orator was destined to crush him within the church as a blood enemy" (Branch, *Parting*, p. 56).

123 *the Progressive Natoinal Baptist Convention:* Booth, *The Progressive Story*, and Garrow, *Bearing the Cross*, p. 166.

123 *sponsored by the Ford Foundation:* Garrow, *Bearing the Cross*, p. 598.

123 *"To Minister":* Cited in Smith, "The Radicalization of Martin Luther King., Jr.," p. 275. The following quotations from King in this section are from this speech.

124 *the tenor of so much contemporary black religion:* Franklin, *Another Day's Journey*, pp. 53–82. There are of course many black churches that are culturally conscious, socially involved, and politically aggressive. For several outstanding examples, see Billingsley, *Mighty Like a River.*

125 *radical remnant of the black church:* Wilmore, *Black Religion and Black Radicalism.*

125 *black folks' conversion to Christianity:* Frey and Cotton, *Come Shouting to Zion*, and Raboteau, *Slave Religion*. Also see Raboteau, *Fire in the Bones*, pp. 17–102.

125 *"many good, religious colored people":* Douglass, *Life and Times*, p. 85.

125 *their religion encouraged them to rebel:* Nat Turner, for instance, believed that the spirit of God motivated him to lead other blacks to rebel violently against slavery. In a remarkable passage, Turner describes in vivid biblical symbolism the holy thrust to assault the white dominions of the wicked. "The Spirit that spoke to the prophets in former days,—and I was greatly astonished, and for two years prayed continually, whenever my duty would permit; and then again I had the same revelation, which fully confirmed me in the impression that I was ordained for some great purpose in the hands of the Almighty. Several years rolled around, in which many events occurred to strengthen me in this my belief. . . . And about this time I had a vision—and I saw white spirits and black spirits engaged in battle, and the

sun was darkened—the thunder rolled in the heavens, and blood flowed in streams—and I heard a voice saying, 'Such is your luck, such you are called to see; and let it come rough or smooth, you must surely bear it' . . . And on the 12ᵗʰ of May, 1828, I heard a loud noise in the heavens, and the Spirit instantly appeared to me and said the Serpent was loosened, and Christ had laid down the yoke he had borne for the sins of men, and that I should take it on and fight against the Serpent, for the time was fast approaching when the first should be last and the last should be first." Turner, *The Confessions of Nat Turner.*

125 *one of the reasons:* Frey and Cotton, *Come Shouting to Zion.*

125 *Snobbish Anglicans viewed early Southern white:* Raboteau, "The Black Experience in American Evangelicalism," in Raboteau and Fulop, *African-American Religion,* pp. 89–106.

125 *Gospel of Freedom:* Raboteau, *Fire in My Bones,* and Hildebrand, *The Times.*

125 *Gabriel Prosser, Denmark Vesey, and Nat Turner:* Wilmore, *Black Religion and Black Radicalism,* pp. 77–98. See also Robertson, *Denmark Vesey.*

125 *Harriet Tubman:* Tubman—as were Catherine Harris, Thomas James, Frederick Douglass, Jermain Louguen, and Sojourner Truth—was "associated with Zionite activity against slavery" (Wilmore, *Black Religion,* p. 113). Also see Painter, *Sojourner Truth,* p. 201; Bradford, *Harriet Tubman;* and Conrad, *Harriet Tubman.*

125 *"case of Nat Turner":* Cited in Harding, "Religion and Resistance Among Antebellum Slaves," in *African-American Religion,* p. 118.

125 *"the greatest of all public nuisances":* Ibid. p. 119.

125 *other ways to resist:* Frey, *Water from the Rock;* Frey and Cotton, *Come Shouting to Zion;* Wilmore, *Black Religion.*

126 *"kept them submissive":* Mays, *The Negro's God as Reflected in His Literature,* p. 26, cited in Harding, "Religion and Resistance Among Antebellum Slaves," in Raboteau and Fulop, eds., *African-American Religion,* p. 110.

126 *"to a world after death":* Frazier, *The Negro Church,* p. 45.

126 *"so absorbed in a future good":* King, *Where Do We?* p. 124.

126 *Figures like Bishop Henry McNeal Turner:* Wilmore, *Black Religion and Black Radicalism,* pp. 149–157.

126 *black women formed the black church's revival culture:* Frey and Cotton, *Come Shouting to Zion,* p. xii.

126 *In Memphis, decades before King:* Honey, *Southern Labor.* The information in this paragraph draws from Honey's study.

127 *"an anthem for southern unionism":* Ibid., p. 138.

127 *Rev. Ernest Fields:* Ibid., p. 180.

127 *detailed histories:* Carson, *In Struggle;* Morris, *Origins;* Norrell, *Reaping the Whirlwind;* Chafe, *Civilities and Liberties;* Colburn, *Racial Change and Community Crisis;* Payne, *I've Got the Light of Freedom;* Fairclough, *Race and Democracy;* and Dittmer, *Local People.*

127 *not as famous as their male counterparts:* Mills, *This Little Light of Mine;* Grant, *Ella Baker;* Robinson, *The Montgomery Bus Boycott;* Clark, *Echo in My Soul;* Clark, *Ready from Within;* McFadden, "Septima Clark and the Struggle for Human Rights," in Crawford, Rouse, and Woods, eds., *Women in the Civil Rights Movement;* and Brown-Nagin, "The Transformation of a Social Movement into Law?" pp. 81–137.

127 *shed the fundamentalist garbs:* King, "Pilgrimage to Nonviolence," in King, *A Testament,* p. 35.

127 *King was profoundly influenced by the militant minority:* I am not suggesting that King was able consciously to embrace all of the radical elements within black Christianity, for example, those black religious figures like James Cone who were deeply influenced by Black Power and who soon after his death articulated Black Theology. Still, King's most radical moments both reflected such a groundswell of black religious dissent and was, in truth, one of its most powerful inspirations (see Cone, *Risks of Faith*). As Gayraud Wilmore notes, studies are needed "to show how black power

and the mid-twentieth-century expression of theology that was closely related to it illuminate the dialectical character of African American religion that was implied by King's leadership. He was never prepared to acknowledge those implications or admit that he had made a contribution to the radical rethinking of black Christianity. The new black theology, nonetheless, was grounded in the liberation tradition of one important segment of the mainstream church to which he belonged. It sought to learn from and assimilate the values of the black consciousness form of the survival tradition that King captured by his appeal to the urban masses" (Wilmore, *Black Religion*, pp. 274–275).

128 *"You meant evil against me":* Genesis 50:20.

128 *A crucial function of the black preacher:* W.E.B. Du Bois writes: "The Preacher is the most unique personality developed by the Negro on American soil. A leader, a politician, and orator, a 'boss,' an intriguer, an idealist—all these he is, and ever, too, the centre of a group of men, now twenty, now a thousand in number. The combination of a certain adroitness with deep-seated earnestness, of tact with consummate ability, gave him his preeminence, and helps him maintain it" (Du Bois, *Souls of Black Folk*, p. 141). Also see Hamilton, *The Black Preacher,* and Dyson, *Between God,* pp. 40–55.

128 *"God Almighty has spoken":* King, *Stride Toward Perfection,* p. 160. Also see Dyson, *Reflecting Black,* pp. 286–319.

128 *the state should be the black church's ally:* Dyson, *Reflecting Black,* pp. 303–309.

129 *faith should be quarantined from politics:* Franklin, *Another Day's Journey,* pp. 69–72.

129 *King used the language of civic piety:* Dyson, *Reflecting Black,* pp. 221–246, 303–309.

129 *He sought to transform society:* Ibid. Also see R. King, *Civil Rights and the Idea of Freedom.*

129 *seeking to enshrine his faith as law:* Reed, *Active Faith;* Robertson, *New World Order;* Falwell, *Strength for the Journey.*

129 *but he ingeniously interpreted that action:* Lischer, *The Preacher King,* and Miller, *Voice of Deliverance.*

129 *rhetorical resistance:* Dyson, *Making Malcolm,* pp. 15–17.

130 *King shrewdly appealed to the Constitution:* Dyson, *Reflecting Black,* pp. 231–232.

132 *Justice is what love sounds like:* King said that "justice is love in calculation," in his famous 1955 Holt Street Address. See Ayres, *The Wisdom of Martin Luther King, Jr.,* p. 126.

132 *According to a 1984 National Black Election Survey:* Cited in Smith, *We Have No Leaders,* pp. 314–315, n. 40.

132 *in a 1983 survey of eighteen hundred black ministers:* Lincoln and Mamiya, *The Black Church in America,* p. 198.

132 *nostalgic hunger for a golden era of "family values":* Coontz, *The Way We Never Were.*

133 *as white conservative evangelicals aggressively pursue:* Reed, *Active Faith;* Robertson, *New World Order;* Falwell, *Strength for the Journey.*

133 *"positive-thought materialism":* Franklin, *Another Day's Journey,* pp. 50–52.

133 *race specific without being race exclusive:* Dyson, *Race Rules.*

133 *left-leaning figures like Todd Gitlin:* Gitlin, *The Twilight of Common Dreams;* Tomasky, *Left for Dead;* Rorty, *Achieving Our Country.*

134 *a minister was pushed from an auditorium stage:* Branch, *Parting the Waters,* p. 502.

134 *Lyons first came under severe scrutiny:* Dyson, "When Preachers Prey," p. 120; *Jet,* March 15, 1999, p. 16; *New York Times,* April 1, 1999, p. A19; *Atlanta Journal-Constitution,* June 19, 1999, p. 1B.

135 *Sinclair Lewis's novel:* Lewis, *Elmer Gantry; The Apostle,* 1998.

135 *most preachers won't be convicted:* Dyson, "When Preachers Prey"; *Jet,* op cit.; *New York Times,* op cit.; *Atlanta Journal-Constitution,* op cit.; and Hundley, "Lyons Victims Seeking Shelter from Creditors." Lyons's downfall is even more tragically ironic in the light of his initial intent to set National Baptist Convention (NBC) business in order. Apparently the culture of

fiscal and erotic privilege was too seductively powerful and overmatched Lyons's resolve to correct NBC's shameful excesses. When Lyons assumed office in 1994, he revealed that the convention had run a $765,000 deficit and was unable to meet its financial obligations. Lyons further revealed that the convention had no written budget nor did it have a full-time executive director to handle the business of running the convention. Lyons claimed that in the past NBC leadership had greatly swollen its membership when it claimed that it had 8.2 million members with 33,000 affiliated churches. Lyons stated that the NBC had 3,000 churches with approximately 700,000 members. These facts were reported in the *Richmond Free Press*, Jan. 12–14, Feb. 16–18, 1995, and cited in Smith, *We Have No Leaders*, p. 315, n. 41.

135 *the culture of sexual privilege:* Dyson, "When Preachers Prey," pp. 120–122, 190, 192, 194, and Dyson, *Race Rules*, pp. 77–108.

135 *rail against the sexual deviance:* Dyson, *Between God and Gangsta Rap*, p. 185, and *Race Rules*, pp. 102–104.

135 *justice for women is the rule:* Dyson, "When Preachers Prey," p. 194. Higginbotham, *Righteous Discontent*.

135 *black women are largely excluded from leadership:* Dyson, *Between God and Gangsta Rap*, p. 185.

136 *King insisted that he was unworthy:* Garrow, *Bearing the Cross*, p. 588.

Chapter 7: "Somewhere I Read of the Freedom of Speech"

137 *"Somewhere I Read of the Freedom of Speech":* King, "I See the Promised Land," in King, *A Testament*, p. 282.

137 *known in my circles as "National Rent-a-Negro Month":* Dyson, "The Cruellest," p. 33.

139 *torn straight from the transcript:* Dyson, *Race Rules*, p. 81.

139 *an idea ripped off from theologian Karl Barth:* Barth, *Christ and Adam* and *The Word of God and the Word of Man*.

139 *the practices of black Baptist preachers:* Pipes, *Say Amen Brother!* Mitchell, *Black Preaching*; Davis, *I Got the Word in Me*; Pitts, *The Old Ship of Zion*; Boulware, *The Oratory of Negro Leaders*; Thomas, *They Always*; Rosenberg, *Can These Bones Live?* Raboteau, *Fire in the Bones*, pp. 141–151; Hamilton, *The Black Preacher*; Spencer, *Sacred Symphony*.

139 *the recent revelation that Martin Luther King, Jr., borrowed:* Wall Street Journal, Nov. 9, 1990, pp. A:1, 6; *New York Times*, Nov. 10, 1990, p. A10; *Atlanta Journal-Constitution*, Nov. 11, 1990, p. A8; *USA Today*, Nov. 13, 1990, p. A11; *Bloomington* [Indiana] *Herald-Times*, Nov. 16, 1990, p. A6; *Chicago Tribune*, Nov. 18, 1990, p. V2; *Washington Post*, Nov. 18, 1990, p. C5; *San Jose Mercury-News*, Nov. 19, 1990, p. A1; *Newsweek*, Nov. 19, 1990, p. 61; *Chronicle of Higher Education*, Nov. 21, 1990, p. A8; *New York Amsterdam News*, Dec. 1, 1990, p. 24; *Time*, Dec. 3, 1990, p. 126; *Los Angeles Times*, Dec. 11, 1990, p. E1; *New Republic*, Jan. 28, 1991, pp. 9–11; *Journal of American History*, June 1991, pp. 11–123.

140 *"converting King's blemish":* Higham, "Habits of the Cloth," p. 109.

140 *in his insightful:* Miller, *Voice of Deliverance*.

140 *He ingeniously seized on:* Ibid., esp. pp. 1–28, 41–141.

140 *the black oral art of "voice-merging":* Ibid., esp. pp. 142–158.

140 *His brilliantly argued:* Lischer, *The Preacher King*.

141 *King's real voice was edited out:* Ibid., esp. pp. 8, 93–118.

141 *"in his plagiarism King was simply adhering":* Ibid., p. 63.

141 *it "is one thing":* Ibid.

141 *overstates the extent:* Ibid., pp. 106–111.

141 *the reflection back to liberal white America:* Miller, *Voice of Deliverance*, pp. 67–85, 186–197.

141 *King's borrowing helped to subvert:* Lischer, *The Preacher King*, esp. pp. 142–162.

142 *King constructed a public persona:* Miller, *Voice of Deliverance,* pp. 169–197. Also see Miller, "Composing Martin Luther King, Jr.," pp. 70–82..

142 *Miller's notion of self-making:* Lischer, *The Preacher King,* pp. 112–113.

142 *to be "an American, a Negro":* The phrase is in Du Bois, *The Souls of Black Folk,* p. 45.

143 *Many critics are skeptical:* Lewis, "Failing to Know Martin Luther King, Jr.," p. 82; Genovese, *The Southern Front,* p. 174.

143 *to include Lincoln and Jefferson:* Coretta King claims that her husband, in his "I Have a Dream" speech, "intended to echo some of the Lincolnian language," speaking of Abraham Lincoln's Emancipation Proclamation to which King made early reference in his oration (C. King, *My Life,* p. 236). The same speech famously extends Jefferson's majestic words by giving them moral immediacy in the nation's racial drama. King implored America to "live out the true meaning of its creed—we hold these truths to be self-evident, that all men are created equal" (King, "I Have a Dream," in King, *A Testament,* p. 219). King claims to have been profoundly influenced by Gandhi in his beliefs about nonviolence ("Pilgrimage to Nonviolence," in Washington, ed., *A Testament,* pp. 38–39). Keith Miller, however, argues that "Gandhi exerted very little direct influence on King," since King had "learned nonviolence almost entirely from American sources" (Miller, *Voice of Deliverance,* p. 88). But however he got hold of Gandhi's ideas, there is little doubt that they profoundly influenced King's beliefs and behavior. Finally, King paid homage to Du Bois's greatness, and the influence on him of some of Du Bois's ideas, in King, "Honoring Dr. Du Bois," *Freedomways* 8, Spring 1968, reprinted in *W.E.B. Du Bois Speaks,* Vol. 1, *Speeches and Addresses, 1890–1919* (Foner, ed.).

143 *Prathia Hall and Archibald Carey:* Prathia Hall was the student whose prayer in Albany at a service King attended included the phrase "I have a dream" (Lischer, *The Preacher King,* p. 93). As Lischer notes, her inspired prayer was charged by a resonant notion in black communities of a dream or vision animating civil rights activists. King, moved by her prayer, seized its central metaphor and enlarged its yearning into a prophetic vision of hope for racial justice. Archibald Carey was the Chicago preacher, jurist, banker, and politician whose speech to the Republican National Convention gave King a galvanizing image for his "I Have a Dream" speech (Miller, *Voice of Deliverance,* p. 146). After quoting from "America the Beautiful," Carey rose to oratorical splendor: "That's exactly what we mean—from every mountain side, let freedom ring. Not only from the Green Mountains and White Mountains of Vermont and New Hampshire; not only from the Catskills of New York; but from the Ozarks in Arkansas, from the Stone Mountain in Georgia, from the Blue Ridge Mountains of Virginia—let it ring not only for the minorities of the United States, but for . . . the disinherited of all the earth—may the Republican Party, under God, from every mountainside, LET FREEDOM RING!" (cited in Miller, *Voice of Deliverance,* p. 146). King snatched this passage nearly word for word from Carey to cap his most famous oration.

144 *Miller's insistence that King was weighed down:* Miller, *Voice of Deliverance,* pp. 192–193.

144 *to produce a book of sermons:* King, *Strength to Love.*

144 *to consolidate King's white liberal audience:* Lischer, *The Preacher King,* pp. 4–5.

144 *unedited audiotapes of King's sermons and speeches:* Ibid.

144 *more Miles Davis than Milli Vanilli:* In truth, however, the case of Milli Vanilli, the multimillion record selling pop duo who won 1990's Grammy Award for best new artist, is not as simple as it seems. The duo, composed of black Europeans Rob and Fab, went down in infamy after it was revealed that they hadn't sung a note on their award-winning album, and they were subsequently forced to return their Grammy. Rob and Fab were talented and handsome performers. Desperate to land a record deal, they agreed to be the faces for a studio-produced album of songs engineered by a manipulative white European producer. Neither the duo nor their producer had any idea that the album

would do so well and that it would garner Milli Vanilli international fame and fortune. Disagreements between the duo and their "producer"—especially over Rob and Fab's desire to represent their own work on wax—led to a falling out that forced the duo to confess their mendacity publicly. Despite their extreme embarrassment and shame, Rob and Fab eventually were able to make an album featuring their own work, proving that they had genuine talent. By then, however, their downfall had eclipsed widespread interest in their work. Later, they split up, and in 1998, Rob committed suicide after several unsuccessful attempts. Their story is not simply one of the massive attempt to defraud the public while capitulating to the seductions of fame, fortune, and women. It is as well a bitter and tragic update of an old phenomenon: a white music executive exploiting vulnerable black artists for commercial gain. The tragedy is that Rob and Fab's authentic artistry was buried beneath the scandal of their misdeed. See "Behind the Music," VH1, March 28, 1999.

144 *even in his undergraduate days at Morehouse College:* Carson, et al., eds., *The Papers of Martin Luther King, Jr.,* Volume 1: *Called to Serve, January 1929–June 1951,* and Vol. 2: *Rediscovering Precious Values, July 1951–November 1955;* Genovese, *The Southern Front,* p. 162.

144 *trial sermon:* Branch, *Parting,* p. 66. Branch says that King borrowed his first sermon from Harry Emerson Fosdick's "Life Is What You Make It."

145 *often distinguished enough to earn him high marks:* Martin Luther King, Jr., Papers Project, "The Student Papers of Martin Luther King, Jr.," pp. 28–29; Lewis, *King,* pp. 37–38; Branch, *Parting the Waters,* pp. 72, 76; Garrow, "King's Plagiarism," p. 90.

145 *King's formal citation habits:* Martin Luther King, Jr., Papers Project; Genovese, *The Southern Front,* p. 162.

145 *King put his own stamp on personalist theology:* Genovese, *The Southern Front,* pp. 164–168, 173.

145 *it is now evident that King plagiarized large portions:* Martin Luther King, Jr., Papers Project, pp. 23–31.

145 *written just three years before King's thesis:* Ibid., p. 27.

145 *words for at least three reasons:* Genovese, *The Southern Front,* pp. 157–191, esp. p. 173; Martin Luther King, Jr., Papers Project, p. 24. Also see Carson, Holloran, Luker, and Russell, "Martin Luther King, Jr., as Scholar."

146 *"curious feature":* Genovese, *The Southern Front,* p. 173. It is also interesting to note that during his second fall in Boston as a graduate student, King received a D+ on a philosophy paper, which had scribbled over it caustic comments from his professor. King subsequently earned three straight A's on papers about Descartes, William James, and Mahayana Buddhism (Branch, *Parting the Waters,* p. 96). As with many other students, the awful embarrassment and ego deflation of a poor grade perhaps drove King to redouble his efforts, or perhaps it reinforced his habit of borrowing other's work to express his ideas.

146 *"exceptional intellectual ability":* Martin Luther King, Jr., Papers Project, p. 29; Garrow, *Bearing the Cross,* p. 41.

146 *Pappas's edited volume:* Pappas, ed., *Martin Luther King Plagiarism Story.*

146 *"repeated act of self-betrayal":* Lewis, "Failing to Know Martin Luther King, Jr.," p. 81.

146 *"angst of strivers":* Ibid., p. 83.

146 *"finding himself highly rewarded":* Ibid., p. 85.

146 *"wholly incredulous":* Ibid., p. 82.

147 *"alter our understanding":* Garrow, "King's Plagiarism," p. 86.

147 *"was far more deeply":* Ibid.

147 *"the black freedom movement was in no way":* Ibid.

147 *Like James Cone, Lewis Baldwin, and Taylor Branch:* Cone, "Martin Luther King, Jr., Black Theology—Black Church," pp. 409–420; Cone, "The Theology of Martin Luther

King, Jr.," pp. 21–39; Cone, *Martin and America* and *Risks of Faith*; Baldwin, "Understanding Martin Luther King, Jr., Within the Context of Southern Black Religious History," pp. 1–26; Baldwin, "Martin Luther King, Jr., the Black Church, and the Black Messianic Vision," *Journal of the Interdemoninational Theological Center* 12, Fall 1984–Spring 1985, pp. 93–108; Baldwin, *There Is a Balm* and *To Make the Wounded Whole;* Branch, *Parting the Waters,* esp. pp. 1–26; Miller, *Voice of Deliverance,* esp. pp. 13–40, 169–185; Lischer, *The Preacher King.*

147 *as Lewis and Genovese argue:* Lewis, "Failing to Know Martin Luther King, Jr.," pp. 84–85; Genovese, *The Southern Front,* p. 175. The second reader of King's dissertation, S. Paul Schilling, denied that there was "favoritism toward black students and therefore a lowering of standards for them," and in response to a question about whether King "was given a free ride because of reverse racism," responded "I would reject that completely" (Thelen, "Conversation Between S. Paul Schilling and David Thelen," pp. 65, 77). It may be true that King's thesis adviser, L. Harold DeWolf, was in King's case a "lax mentor who did not demand of King the analytical precision that might have prepared him for a career of scholarly writing" (Carson, Holloran, Luker, and Russel, "Martin Luther King, Jr.," p. 101). But that contradicts what other students knew about DeWolf. "Once he took them under his wing . . . he really worked with them," Cornish Rogers says. "He saw to it that all of them lived up to a certain quality that he demanded. And he kept after them until they did." Furthermore, Rogers rejects the reverse racism argument, saying of DeWolf and Schilling, "I knew how tough they were on me. I had taken courses from both of them." Therefore, it would be both unfair and inaccurate to overlook *the* plausible reason for DeWolf's strict inattention to King: DeWolf was overburdened as one of the few Boston University professors who was willing to work with black students. Rogers says that DeWolf "took on a lot of dissertations from, especially, black students or others whom other professors would not take on. If you were willing to be guided by him, he would take on students whose topics were not in his field. I got the impression that he helped a lot of folks who had difficulty getting someone to be their readers" (Thelen, "Conversation Between Cornish Rogers and David Thelen," pp. 53–55). Thus, the greater threat to black students was not racial paternalism, as bad as that might have been, but racist neglect, a far more harmful factor in the intellectual lives of black graduate students.

147 *distinguished scholars like:* Lischer, *The Preacher King,* p. 58.

147 *"first and foremost a young dandy":* Garrow, "King's Plagiarism: Imitation, Insecurity, and Transformation," p. 90.

147 *The most highly gifted black student:* "Moreover, although many black scholars had passed through Boston University's doctoral program in religion, one peculiar and tragic legacy of racism involved the pernicious self-doubts that could have plagued any developing black scholar. Qualities of self-worth, competence, talent, and skill are not developed in a vacuum, but are in part socially constructed and reproduced. In the mid-fifties it is certainly conceivable that a young talented black doctoral student who was uncertain of his real worth, despite the encouragement of his professors and colleagues . . . could be tempted to rely on work that had already been accepted and viewed as competent" (Dyson, *Reflecting Black,* p. 242). Also see Jerry Watt's brief but powerful discussion of the sometimes crippling self-doubt and insecurity that can smother even the most able budding scholar. Watts, *Heroism and the Black Intellectual,* p. xii.

148 *"a rather immature and insecure man":* Garrow, "King's Plagiarism," p. 90.

148 *world-historical figure:* Hegel, *The Philosophy of History* and *Phenomenology of Spirit.* Also see King, *Stride Toward Freedom,* pp. 95, 100–101.

148 *"King told me":* Thelen, "Conversation Between Cornish Rogers and David Thelen," p. 50.

148 *"changed his perspective":* Ibid.

148 *"alien in the sense":* Ibid., pp. 50–51.

149 *major cachet from his degree:* John Williams captures the significance of the degree for those times when he writes: "And if a young man could take graduate studies in the white universities of the North, his status was increased manyfold. Morehouse College has sent countless numbers of its graduates north where an overwhelming majority of them have made good in professional and academic circles. The A.B. soon enough became almost nothing in terms of status; the M.A. became the target, and finally, the Ph.D. How grand to roll around on the tongue the word 'doctor'! How marvelous to be addressed as 'doctor'!" (Williams, *The King God Didn't Save,* p. 152).

149 *whose plagiarism was far worse than King's:* Thelen, "Conversation Between S. Paul Schilling and David Thelen," pp. 76–77.

149 *sought to "straddle":* Reagon, "Nobody Knows the Trouble I See," pp. 113–117. Reagon says that in black culture, those who straddle "are born in one place, and we are sent to achieve in the larger culture, and in order to survive we work out a way to be who we are in both places or all places we move. . . . King was a straddler; he was who he was wherever he was—in the African-American church, on the march, in a rally, in jail, at the great and small universities, in Stockholm. We, his people, could look at him and feel him and know that he was one of us. *He succeeded in embracing the sound of our forefathers, and he never left that sound; no matter where he was, he was in the pulpit"* (ibid., pp. 114, 116).

150 *aversion, one shared by many black students:* Lischer, *The Preacher King,* p. 58. Lischer says that in "the fifteen years from 1942 to 1957 only five Boston students completed doctoral dissertations on race-related topics. King was not among them."

150 *"King passed over the chance to take courses":* Genovese, *The Southern Front,* p. 173. It should be noted that King is not now known for his facility with Plato, Hegel, formal logic, or modern philosophy—all of which proved to be in his hands little more than rhetorical fodder for Sunday sermons and inspired speeches. As David Lewis writes, King "was not an original philosopher, although, after Morehouse, it was perhaps the thing he most desired to be. There are legions of audiences that spent Sunday mornings, convocation periods, and evenings in auditoriums listening to him rhapsodically enumerate the principal ideas of Western philosophy from Thales to Miletus to Camus. . . . Such displays of encyclopedic knowledge sprang partly from a Baptist preacher's love of showmanship, and Mike [Martin] was a super actor. Partly, too, this was the venial intellectual arrogance of a young man who held a doctorate from one of the nation's better universities. But there was, undeniably, also an element of self-deception and self-mystification as to his philosophical acumen" (Lewis, *King,* pp. 44–45). King is known, however, for his brilliant abilities to translate the meanings of grand thinkers into the stuff of human action, thus enfleshing ideas with a genius that few others have possessed. It might have done King some good to have wrestled intellectually within the province of ideas that would motivate him to take to the streets out of disgust with merely thinking about the world. Some courses on Gandhi and race relations might have given him even deeper insight into the nature of the beast he was to confront when he left graduate school. As Marx famously said, many philosophers have thought about the world. The point was to change it. King took that imperative seriously and thus became a derivative philosopher but a world-class activist and a pioneer in social democracy.

150 *"not even mention racism":* Cone, *Martin and Malcolm,* p. 30.

150 *"six years at Crozer and Boston":* Ibid., p. 31.

150 *Dialectical Society:* Thelen, "Conversation Between Cornish Rogers and David Thelen," pp. 46–49. Also see Garrow, *Bearing,* p. 48; Branch, *Parting the Waters,* pp. 93–94. Apparently, however, these issues were not strongly enough debated for students like George Thomas, who was "one of a tiny minority of Negro students who lost interest in the Dialectical Society precisely because Jim Crow and other political matters were relegated to the joke period [held after the formal meeting]" (Branch, *Parting,* p. 93).

150 *"appeared to be glad merely":* Cone, *Martin and Malcolm* , p. 31.

150 *"the only reason many students stuck around"*: Thelen, "Conversation Between Cornish Rogers and David Thelen," p. 50.

151 *knew then that he would become*: Lewis, "Failing to Know Martin Luther King, Jr.," p. 85. More exactly, Lewis states of King and his professors that "neither he nor they knew who Martin Luther King was then." On that basis, it is easy enough to see that in not knowing who King was then, they had no knowledge of who he would become.

151 *Studies by Stanford University psychologist Claude Steele*: "Thin Ice: 'Stereotype Threat' and Black College Students," in *Atlantic Monthly*, Vol. 284, No. 2, Aug. 1999, pp. 44–54.

151 *"the national college-dropout rate"*: Ibid., p. 44.

151 *"the under-performance of black"*: Ibid.

151 *"uncomfortably finger-pointing"*: Ibid., p. 45.

152 *"stereotype threat"*: Ibid., p. 46.

152 *terribly tense, unable to escape the fact*: Oates, *Let the Trumpet Sound*, p. 24.

153 *But however just it may be*: New York Times, Nov. 13, 1990, p. A30.

154 *violate black women as a matter of course*: Lerner, ed., *Black Women in White America*, pp. 149–193; Jones, *Labor of Love, Labor of Sorrow*, p. 157; Hine, *Hine Sight*, pp. 37–47.

Chapter 8: "There Is a Civil War Going on Within All of Us"

155 *"There Is a Civil War Going on Within All of Us"*: Garrow, *Bearing the Cross*, p. 376.

155 *a moment comparable to Michael Jordan fending off*: Jet, June 29, 1998, p. 53.

155 *"King allegedly rendezvoused with two women"*: In 1993 Adjua Abi Naantaanbuu brought a defamation of character suit against the estate of Ralph David Abernathy, Harper & Row Publishers, and editor Daniel Bial. Naantaanbuu claimed that she was libeled by Abernathy's suggestion that she had an affair with Martin Luther King, Jr., the night before he was assassinated. Naantaanbuu was the woman at whose house King had dinner the night before his death. Abernathy's description of that night suggested that an unnamed woman and King had been intimate. The U.S. District Court for the Southern District of New York ruled that Naantaanbuu was "a private rather than a public figure with respect to the present lawsuit," but that "there was no showing" that the defendants had "acted in a 'grossly irresponsible manner' as required for liability under New York law." The court concluded that Naantaanbuu "has not produced sufficient information to demonstrate the possibility that Abernathy acted with some degree of culpable conduct, if in fact his version of events was false. She has come forward with information to make it a genuine issue of fact as to whether Abernathy was telling the truth about the events of the evening of April 3. That is, she produced her own affidavit and that of her sister, both of which contradict Abernathy's version of events." In short, the truth or falsity of Abernathy's claims was not resolved, but the court found that he had no malicious intent to harm Naantaanbuu and therefore found Abernathy inculpable of the charge of libel. *Naantaanbuu v. Abernathy*, 816 F. Supp. 218 (S.D.N.Y. 1993), 218, 229–230.

155 *a formidable one-two line-up*: Lewis, *King*; Oates, *Let the Trumpet Sound*; Garrow, *Bearing the Cross*; Fairclough, *To Redeem*; Branch, *Parting the Waters* and *Pillar of Fire*; Colaiaco, *Apostle of Militant Nonviolence*; Young, *An Easy Burden*.

156 *"best friend that I have in the world"*: "I See the Promised Land," in King, *A Testament*, p. 45.

156 *best-selling autobiography*: Abernathy, *And the Walls Came Tumbling Down*.

156 *Abernathy loved King even as he was jealous*: Garrow, *Bearing the Cross*, p. 366; Branch, *Parting the Waters*, pp. 898–899, and *Pillar of Fire*, pp. 540–543; Young, *An Easy Burden*, pp. 174, 281, 320, 461–462.

156 *"let Americans—particularly black Americans"*: Abernathy, "Introduction to the Paperback Edition, in *And the Walls Came Tumbling Down*, p. xiv.

156 *"wanted to show the private man"*: Ibid.
156 *"wanted to portray Martin"*: Ibid.
156 *"Washington, Lincoln, and a handful"*: Ibid., p. xv.
156 *"legends are important"*: Ibid.
157 *to his own philandering*: Branch, *Parting the Waters*, pp. 237–240. Abernathy neglects to mention this incident or even refute Branch's story in his own autobiography. As historian Jimmie Franklin concludes, one "has to assume reasonably that such a serious charge would have drawn a sure rebuttal in this book if it were false" (Franklin, "Autobiography, the Burden of Friendship, and Truth," p. 97). Franklin argues that since Abernathy "has judiciously refused to stand witness to much of his own past," his omission raises "difficult questions about the author's intent and about historical truth," suggesting that such "careful selectivity places the alert historian on guard" (ibid.). Franklin's point is compelling, especially since, as he pointed out earlier in his review of Abernathy's book, the latter's decision to tell about King's infidelity, as opposed to the goings-on at the Willard Hotel where *both* ministers were under FBI surveillance, is problematic. Legitimate questions about Abernathy's believability and motives for telling the "truth" about King's affairs can be usefully raised. However, to dismiss Abernathy out of hand as a liar (or traitor) because he has revealed uncomfortable aspects of his closest friend's sex life is equally troublesome. We should treat Abernathy's revelations as possibly, even plausibly, true, given his closeness to King and his intimate knowledge of King's personal life. Moreover, Abernathy's depiction of King is on balance a touching, moving, generous portrait of the man who in Abernathy's book comes off as a sacrificial, courageous, humane, and *human* leader. As Bernice Reagon writes: "It is time for society to reckon with the fallacy of turning our heroes and heroines into godlike inhuman figures. Martin Luther King, Jr., needs to become— through our work as historians—the human being he was. . . . I think all of us already know somewhere inside ourselves that those in human history who carry the mantle of being outstanding are also always flawed. However, popular and academic chroniclers have a way of reshaping reality so that the warts and pimples get smoothed off" (Reagon, "Nobody Knows the Trouble I See," p. 111).
157 *"will grow in the hearts of future Americans"*: Abernathy, *And the Walls Came Tumbling Down*, p. xv.
157 *"What business has the public"*: Cited in McWhorter, "Images of King," *St. Louis Post-Dispatch*, Jan. 21, 1991, p. 1D.
157 *reared in a preacherly culture where good sex*: Dyson, "When Preachers Prey," pp. 120–122, 190, 192, 194; Dyson, *Race Rules*, pp. 77–108.
157 *it surely gave King and others ample opportunity*: Abernathy, *And the Walls Came Tumbling Down*, p. 471; Dyson, *Race Rules*, p. 102.
158 *"pure in heart"*: Matthew 5:8.
158 *"make an idol of their commitments"*: Thurman, "The Dilemma of Commitment," a sermon preached at Riverside Church, New York City, Aug. 7, 1965.
158 *King often spoke against the sins he committed*: Friedly and Gallen, eds., *Martin Luther King, Jr.: The FBI File*, pp. 453–454; Garrow, *Bearing the Cross*, p. 577.
159 *double life as gay, cross-dressing "Mary"*: Summers, *Official and Confidential*.
159 *David Garrow has brilliantly documented*: Garrow, *The FBI and Martin Luther King, Jr.* Also see McKnight, *The Last Crusade*; Friedly and Gallen, *The FBI File*.
159 *"compulsive sexual athleticism"*: Garrow, *Bearing the Cross*, p. 375.
159 *"the campaign against Martin and the movement"*: Young, *An Easy Burden*, p. 471.
159 *Deeply buried but intense sexual fear*: Ibid.
160 *"chronic avocation among evangelical divines"*: Lewis, review of *Bearing the Cross*, p. 482.
160 *the sweet reward of spiritual servants*: Dyson, *Race Rules*, pp. 100–104.
160 *"exploit this power [over women]"*: Dyson, "When Preachers Prey," p. 120.

160 *King was a sexual magnet for women:* Garrow, *Bearing the Cross*, p. 375; Abernathy, *And the Walls Came Tumbling Down*, p. 471; Oates, *Let the Trumpet*, p. 283.

160 *private and public spaces acquired heightened importance:* Black Public Sphere Collective, ed., *The Black Public Sphere*.

161 *He spent nearly twenty-seven days:* Garrow, *Bearing the Cross*, p. 375; Oates, *Let the Trumpet*, p. 282. In a brief preface to a January 1965 *Playboy Magazine* interview he conducted with Martin Luther King, Alex Haley noted that King "works twenty hours a day, travels 325,000 miles and makes 450 speeches a year throughout the country" ("Playboy Interview: Martin Luther King, Jr.," in King, *A Testament*, p. 341).

161 *both tortured by his adultery:* Branch, *Pillar of Fire*, p. 557; Garrow, *Bearing the Cross*, p. 375.

161 *"loose sex relations and problems":* Friedly and Gallen, *The FBI File*, p. 453.

161 *"the past, too often":* Ibid.

161 *I think it is also necessary to bring:* Ibid., pp. 453–454.

162 *"go out this morning saying":* King, "Unfulfilled Dreams," in Carson and Holloran, eds., *A Knock at Midnight*, p. 198. Unlike David Garrow, Richard Lischer doesn't see such comments by King as veiled confessions of his sexual sins. "In the sexual realm," Garrow writes, "King viewed himself as a sinner, a theme he sometimes touched upon in his sermons" (Garrow, *Bearing the Cross*, p. 587). Lischer writes that if King "was laboring under a burden of shame because of his secret sins and the contradiction between his public and private life, the sermons do not indicate it. With the exception of a few oblique references to 'habits' that destroy personality and relationships, the sermons give little evidence that he was engaged in a moral struggle with his own infidelity or the casual sex practiced by many of the Movement's leaders, including the preachers" (Lischer, *The Preacher King*, p. 169). I fall between Garrow and Lischer. Although King made no explicit confession in his sermons, he certainly wrestled with his libido and his conscientious duty to God and his family. It is certainly reasonable to expect that such a struggle might seep into his homilies, in much the same way that adultery became for King a metaphor of racial apartheid. King was quoted in the *Time* magazine story that named him Man of the Year as saying that segregation "is the adultery of an illicit intercourse between injustice and immorality," and it "cannot be cured by the Vaseline of gradualism" (*Time*, Jan. 3, 1964).

162 *"each of us is two selves":* Garrow, *Bearing the Cross*, p. 376.

162 *"I'm fucking for God":* Branch, *Pillar of Fire*, p. 207. Branch explains that this quotation, as well as the quotation on the next page, are from FBI surveillance tapes of King. In interviews that Branch conducted with three FBI officials, he says that they reported having heard the bugging tapes. They claim to have heard King make the statements quoted here. Branch himself did not hear the tapes, which are sealed along with other FBI surveillance until 2027.

163 *"promised never to leave me":* King, "Unfulfilled Dreams," in Carson and Holloran, eds., *A Knock at Midnight*, p. 199.

163 *"if I make my bed in hell":* Psalm 139:8, King James Version.

163 *"fucking's a form of anxiety reduction":* Garrow, *Bearing the Cross*, p. 375.

163 *"I'm not a Negro tonight":* Branch, *Pillar of Fire*, p. 207.

163 *"He looked at me as if doubting":* Ibid.

164 *"an FBI director who is suspected of being a homosexual":* Ibid.

164 *"whenever black men gather":* Ibid.

164 *what we otherwise know about his sexual behavior:* Another indication of the possible insinuation of homoerotic behavior involving King occurs in a discussion in John Williams's book on King, *The King God Didn't Save*. At the same time, the passage seems to suggest that King did not engage in the same-sex activity implied by circumstantial evidence. In the second part of his book, Williams quotes several anonymous sources by labeling them as Person A, Person B, and so on. Williams quotes Person C as saying the fol-

lowing: "There were two pictures. One showed me sitting on the floor beside the bathtub in which Martin sat, naked. From the angle of the photo, it looks as though I was doing something. The other photo showed me sitting on the bed beside Martin, who's laying there, nude. Now in both cases, I was conferring with Martin in the only time available to me. Nothing, absolutely nothing took place" (p. 190). Later, Person C is quoted as being in Scandinavia with King (on his Nobel Peace Prize tour of Europe) and of being summoned to quash a potential controversy: "I was sleeping when they called me from downstairs and said that I had to come down to the desk at once. I pulled on my robe and went down. The police were there with a woman later said to be the biggest whore in town. And they had caught her coming out of the hotel with watches and wallets belonging to some of the people in our party. Well, she was there. There had been other women running through the hotel like chickens without their heads, looking for Martin. And all the guys were putting it to them that, if the girls gave them some pussy first, they'd see that she got to Martin. The whore? I thought it better to let her go with everything she had rather than embarrass ourselves and our hosts" (p. 198). From what we know about King's tour of Europe to collect his Nobel Peace Prize, Bayard Rustin coordinated the trip (Garrow, *Bearing the Cross*, p. 357; Oates, *Let the Trumpet*, p. 318; Branch, *Pillar of Fire*, pp. 524–525; Anderson, *Bayard Rustin*, p. 275). Further, we know that in Scandinavia, Bayard Rustin was summoned "as the group's coordinator," to "put a stop to some of the wilder activities" (Garrow, *Bearing the Cross*, p. 366). Apparently some of King's entourage had become involved with what Garrow termed "several scantily clad women," identified by Branch as "Norwegian prostitutes," who had attempted to rob the men after partaking in fleshly delight (Garrow, *Bearing the Cross*, p. 367; Branch, *Pillar of Fire*, p. 543). In fact, the women had "been promised Martin Luther King himself in exchange for favors to his unscrupulous associates" (Branch, *Pillar of Fire*). Rustin alerted hotel security, who quickly moved to take them into custody and return the stolen goods to their owners, including King's brother, A.D. Rustin demurred. He didn't "want these girls talking, let them have it. As far as I'm concerned, they've earned it. And get them out" (Garrow, *Bearing the Cross*, p. 367). In the light of Garrow and Branch's corroboration of the activities described by Williams, it seems likely that Rustin was Person C. Rustin was gay (Anderson, *Bayard Rustin;* Garrow, *Bearing the Cross*, p. 66; Branch, *Pillar of Fire*, pp. 172–173). His sexuality is of interest here because if, as I surmise, Rustin is Person C, then his disclaimers about King hold weight. Person C/Rustin claims that nothing took place between King and him on either occasion that photos (from surveillance cameras?) were taken. In each case, King was nude, and presumably Person C/Rustin was clothed. Still, as Person C/Rustin's comments suggest, the photos by themselves may be misleadingly interpreted—hence his assertion that "nothing, absolutely nothing took place." If that is true—and there is no reason to doubt Rustin's word—it seems to suggest that King's sexual transgressions, at least in this case (and in every case about which there is corroborating evidence), were heterosexual in nature.

164 *the context of the repressive sixties:* I am referring here to the repression of gay sexuality, even as the liberation of heterosexuality from its Victorian principles flourished in the sixties. See Duberman, *Cures*, and Delaney, *The Motion of Light in Water*.

165 *when they are unsealed:* The FBI surveillance tapes on King have been legally sealed until 2027. See my discussion, in Chapter 11, of Reagan's (and Jesse Helm's) mistaken belief that the tapes contain politically damaging—and not merely sexually explicit—materials.

165 *lie about their sexual powers:* Levine, *Black Culture and Black Consciousness;* Gates, *The Signifying Monkey;* Abrahams, *Deep Down in the Jungle*.

165 *"All this stuff about King's sexual appetite":* Rowan, *Breaking Barriers*, p. 306.

166 *live most of his life on the road:* Dyson, *Race Rules*, p. 102. In his sermon, "Standing by the Best in an Evil Time," King confessed that "I'm tired of all this traveling I have to do. I'm killing myself and killing my health, and always away from my children and my family" (Cited in Lischer, *The Preacher King*, p. 167).

166 *must be wrested away from* virtuecrats: I have in mind here figures like Bill Bennett who have extracted virtue from a discussion of the complicated forces that shape the moral life and energize our notions of the good, the just, and the beautiful. Bennett forgets that "the development of virtues, and the attendant skills that must be deployed in order to practice them effectively, is contingent upon several factors: where and when one is born, the conditions under which one must live, the social and communal forces that limit and define one's life, etc. These factors color the character of moral skills that will be acquired, shape the way in which these skills will be appropriated, and even determine the list of skills required to live the good life in different communities" (Dyson, *Reflecting Black*, p. 108, n. 13).

166 *Character can only be glimpsed in a sustained story:* MacIntyre, *After Virtue*; Sherman, *Making a Necessity of Virtue*; Thiemann, *Constructing a Public Theology*.

168 *our nation's first black president:* cited in Randall Kennedy, "Is He a Soul Man? On Black Support for Clinton," in *The American Prospect*, March–April, 1999, p. 26.

169 *"undue gratitude":* Ibid., p. 28.

169 *"special" concern "with racial justice for blacks":* Ibid.

169 *"progressive jurists to the Fourth Circuit Court of Appeals":* Ibid.

169 *"with a depth of feeling I had reserved":* Cited in O'Reilly, *Nixon's Piano*, p. 408.

170 *He knew it by heart:* Ibid.

170 *flagged by the FBI:* Ibid., p. 409.

171 *nine rounds of golf a day after the Illinois:* Ibid., p. 410.

171 *"photo-op execution":* Christopher Hitchens, cited in ibid., p. 411.

171 *When he and Al Gore published:* Ibid., p. 411.

171 *"I mean if black people kill black people every day":* Cited in ibid., p. 413.

171 *Trust me, you never get that lucky:* Cited in ibid., p. 415.

172 *Clinton knows all three verses:* Conversation with Tavis Smiley, July 4, 1999.

172 *welfare reform: Los Angeles Times*, Jan. 7, 1994, A23; "Ending the Democratic Party as We Know It," *In These Times*, Aug. 19, 1996–Sept. 1, 1996, p. 2; "Move 'Em Out," *In These Times*, Nov. 3, 1997–Dec. 14, 1997, p. 27; Derrick Z. Jackson, "Half the Story on Welfare Reform," *Boston Globe*, Aug. 11, 1999, p. A19. While Clinton was policing the lives of poor people, huge corporations were benefiting from billions of dollars of public largesse without a comparable attack by the Clinton administration. Expenditures on welfare pale in comparison to the layouts extended to American business. For a superb journalistic exposé of these legal but manipulative practices, see the four-part *Newsweek* series on welfare, Donald L. Barlett and James B. Steele: "States at War," Nov. 9, 1998, pp. 40–54; "Fantasy Islands: And Other Perfectly Legal Ways That Big Companies Manage to Avoid Billions in Federal Funds," Nov. 16, 1998, pp. 79–93; "Paying a Price for Polluters: Many of America's Largest Companies Foul the Environment but Clean Up on Billions of Dollars in Tax Benefits," Nov. 23, 1998, pp. 72–82; and "The Empire of the Pigs: A Little-Known Company Is a Master at Milking Governments for Welfare," Nov. 30, 1998, pp. 52–66.

172 *Clinton went before a conservative body:* Douglas Jehl, "Clinton Delivers Emotional Appeal on Stopping Crime," *New York Times*, Nov. 14, 1993, sec. 1, p. 1. To underscore my contention how Clinton uses racially coded themes in a subtle way to reinforce his standing with moderate and conservative white constituencies, I suggest a column by political commentator E. J. Dionne, Jr., about a Clinton speech delivered a year after his Memphis speech to black Pentecostals: "Why, you might reasonably ask, were two politicians— President Clinton and former vice president Dan Quayle—lecturing the nation last week on the horrors of out-of-wedlock births? Isn't it the job of preachers and priests and rabbis and parents to say, as Clinton did, that 'you shouldn't have a baby before you're ready and you shouldn't have a baby when you're not married'? . . . There are plenty of cynical explanations for why Clinton and Quayle did the 'family values' number last week. Clinton, it is said, is desperate for some new issues and wants to sound like a 'New Demo-

crat' again by focusing like a laser beam on those tried-and-true values of community, opportunity and responsibility. The best speech of his term so far was his address to a group of black ministers in Memphis last year in which he also preached on these themes. What better way to get out of a deep hole than by trying Memphis II?" (E. J. Dionne, Jr, "Bill & Dan & Murphy Brown," *Washington Post*, Sept. 13, 1994, p. A21). Two things are worth noting. First, Clinton's preaching against out-of-wedlock births was, by the time he delivered his speech, a well-established and widely accepted manner of attacking black families without explicitly having to say so. Clinton was able to send a signal to his neoliberal Democratic base that he had not forsaken their interests, including containing the scourge of pathology associated with uncontrolled black reproduction. Second, it is disturbing to observe that often when Clinton has been in crisis, he has launched attacks against black values—or their absence— in the American social structure and polity. This allows him to deliver a well-received reprimand to black communities for their destructive habits (Dionne praises him for giving the best speech of his term to the black Memphis religious gathering) while consolidating his moderate to conservative white suburban base. Even more disturbing, Clinton has attacked black family values through three public assaults on black women: Sister Souljah (for her hateful rage against whites); Lani Guinier (for her supposedly antidemocratic advocacy of weighted voting, a measure, ironically enough, that was later championed in a judicial opinion by conservative Supreme Court justice Clarence Thomas); and Jocelyn Elders (for her boundary-breaking suggestion of directly addressing the AIDS crisis in black communities by practicing safer sex, including masturbation). In an abstract sense, Clinton was of course on solid ground with his comments on Sister Souljah. But in the concrete political context of his comments, he cynically deployed Souljah to further his problematic racial politics. Clinton's treatment of Guinier is especially harmful because of his personal disloyalty to a friend, as well as his refusal to grant her a hearing in the public domain where she was attacked, something that George Bush did for Clarence Thomas when he was under much heavier attack. And Clinton's attack on Elders is strikingly hypocritical in the light of his subsequent sexual failures. Elders's sin seems to be that she was willing to be honest and open about sex in a way that the judgmental Clinton failed to appreciate. He cynically dismissed her without acknowledging, much less helpfully addressing, the crisis in black sexual practices among youth that fueled her comments.

172 *"a report card on the last 25 years"*: "President Clinton's Speech to Black Ministers in Memphis: Excerpts," *New York Times*, Nov. 14, 1993, p. 24.

172 *"I did not live and die to see"*: Ibid.

173 *A great man need not be virtuous:* Santayana, *Winds of Doctrine.*

173 *As King knew, character should never be judged:* In his last sermon to his Ebenezer congregation, "Unfulfilled Dreams," King reveals his perspective on the assessment of character. His words may easily apply to his own situation, an awareness that may have driven King to emphasize this point in his sermon: "Some weeks ago somebody was saying something to me about a person I have great, magnificent respect for. And they were trying to say something that didn't sound too good about his character, something he was doing. And I said, 'Number one, I don't believe it. But, number two, even if he is, he's a good man because his heart is right.' And in the final analysis, God isn't going to judge him by that little separate mistake that he's making, because the bent of his life is right" (Carson and Holloran, eds. *A Knock At Midnight*, pp. 197–198).

174 *While black youth easily embraced Malcolm X:* Dyson, *Making Malcolm*, pp. 79–96.

Chapter 9: "I Have Walked Among the Desperate, Rejected, and Angry"

175 *"I Have Walked Among the Desperate"*: King, "A Time to Break Silence," in King, *A Testament*, p. 233.

175 *"Professor Dyson, what's the answer?":* Meet the Press, Sunday, May 2, 1999.

175 *"That might lead to a resolution":* Ibid.

175 *"Molotov cocktails and rifles":* King, "A Time to Break Silence," p. 233.

176 *"I think that the reality is that all of us":* Meet the Press, May 2, 1999.

176 *"social pathology of racism":* Ibid.

176 *"And in black communities":* Ibid.

176 *"Littleton, Colorado, is not an exception":* Ibid.

177 *"If we were to be fair":* Ibid.

177 *I have too often been involved in panels:* Dyson, *Race Rules,* pp. 109–112; Dyson, "Statement of Michael Eric Dyson," in *Hearing before the Subcommittee on Juvenile Justice of Committee on the Judiciary, United States Senate to Examine the Effects of Violent and Demeaning Imagery in Popular Music on American Youth,* Feb. 23, 1994, Serial No. J-103043 (S. Hrg. 103–1005), pp. 21–34.

177 *white youth are taken to task:* Males, *The Scapegoat Generation* and *Framing Youth.*

177 *they are not reprimanded with nearly as much anger:* Rose, "Rap Music and the Demonizing of Young Black Men," in Golden, ed., *Black Male,* pp. 149–157.

177 *He would at least attempt to understand:* I base this assertion on the fact that King was willing to go into ghettoes and speak to alienated black youth, challenging them only after listening to tales of their pain and suffering. See King, "A Time to Break Silence," p. 233; Halberstam, "When 'Civil Rights' and 'Peace' Join Forces," in Lincoln, ed., *Martin Luther King, Jr.,* pp. 197–200. Halberstam describes a meeting King had with young black nationalists in Cleveland who had described him as a "Tom." Halberstam says King "talked with them, but more important he listened to them, and it went surprisingly well. While he spoke nonviolence to them he did tell them to be proud of their black color, that no emancipation proclamation, no act of Lyndon Johnson, could set them free unless they were sure in their own minds they liked being black. And of course he talked with them on Vietnam, and they liked that also. *The most important thing, however, was the simple act of paying attention to them*" (p. 198).

177 *They both smoked and drank:* Garrow, *Bearing the Cross,* p. 603 ("He liked to bend his elbow a little bit, and he could do that in very few places," Garrow says King friend Deenie Drew remembered). Oates, *Let the Trumpet Sound,* pp. 210ff. for the only publicly available picture that captures King smoking, as he awaits a plane at the Chicago airport with Andrew Young; Alexander and Cuda, *Got Your Back,* pp. 75–76, 77, 111–113. Tupac smoked marijuana and Newport cigarettes; his drinks of choice were Hennessy, Crystal, and Alize. Among King's favorite drinks was Cherry.

177 *waged a "war on sleep":* Young, *An Easy Burden,* p. 133; Alexander and Cuda, *Got Your Back,* p. 112.

177 *King and Shakur cursed, told lewd jokes:* Abernathy, *And the Walls,* p. 436; Garrow, *Bearing the Cross,* pp. 373, 550; Oates, *Let the Trumpet Sound,* p. 284. According to Abernathy, King scolded a female friend not to "say a goddamn thing about Ralph." Garrow reports on the FBI surveillance tape sent to King that included "dirty jokes and bawdy remarks King had made a year earlier at Washington's Willard Hotel" (Alexander and Cuda, *Got Your Back*).

177 *some of their friends as "nigger":* Young, *An Easy Burden,* p. 463; Alexander and Cuda, *Got Your Back; Vibe* Magazine, *Tupac Shakur.* Andrew Young says about two hours before he was assassinated, King jokingly reproved him for being gone all day without contacting him, by saying, "Lil' nigger, where you been?"

177 *had fierce rivals:* Garrow, *Bearing the Cross,* pp. 269–270; Lewis, *King,* p. 358. Roy Wilkins was famously jealous of King's leadership and resented that King got much of the ink and credit for achievements that Wilkins felt his own NAACP had brought about (see Farmer, *Lay Bare the Heart,* p. 218; Anderson, *Bayard Rustin,* pp. 245–246). And, as Garrow writes, King's elevation after his Birmingham campaign to preeminent black leader status

"meant that King's SCLC, rather than the long-established NAACP, would be the chief financial beneficiary of this new interest in civil rights." Lewis, as have others, records one of King's ugliest public disputes: an improvised fracas over Vietnam he had with Urban League head Whitney Young at a Long Island fund-raiser. Young told King that one of his speeches against Vietnam was unwise because it might alienate Lyndon Johnson. "'Whitney,' Martin shouted, 'what you're saying may get you a foundation grant [which it later did], but it won't get you into the kingdom of truth. . . .' Looking at King's expensive suit and burnished alligator shoes, he shot out, 'You're eating well!' Friends separated the eminent leaders before more damagingly quotable words could be exchanged" (also see Garrow, *Bearing the Cross,* p. 546). As a hip-hop artist, it was par for the course to have, indeed, nurture, enemies. Such hostility between two rappers drove record sales, promoted personal appearances, and generated more interest in their art and careers. But Tupac's battles were decidedly more violent than the norm, especially in the light of his being shot five times in an attempted robbery and due to his subsequent and still unsolved murder. Tupac most famously battled rival rap star Biggie Smalls and his producer/label president and artist, Sean "Puffy" Combs, or Puff Daddy. See Alexander and Cuda, *Got Your Back,* and *Vibe* Magazine, *Tupac Shakur,* esp. pp. 80, 101–103.

177 *grew up in public at the height of their fame:* Bennett, *What Manner of Man?* Lewis, *King;* Oates, *Let the Trumpet;* Garrow, *Bearing the Cross;* Fairclough, *To Redeem;* Branch, *Parting the Waters;* Alexander and Cuda, *Got Your Back;* Vibe Magazine, *Tupac Shakur;* White, *Rebel for the Hell of It.*

177 *shared women with their friends:* Branch, *Parting the Waters,* p. 239. Branch writes that King had confided to James Farmer that "he not only had known of Abernathy's extramarital liaisons in Montgomery but had joined in some of them himself." King's assertion, if true, means that Abernathy is even more dishonest in his dutiful revelation of King's affairs while neglecting to tell of his own erotic mishaps. Then, too, King's confession to Farmer confirms his marital indiscretions. Such a confirmation might lessen the assault on writers who choose to deal with King's erotic indiscretions as much because they happened and feature prominently in his life as because they have been so widely reported on and are now part of the public record on King. Too often, however, his sexual life is treated with little interpretive sophistication. I intend in this chapter to confront King's sexual blunders while attempting to understand their meaning for him and their function in his life, as well as to probe how his sexuality was tied up with prevailing racial beliefs. For Tupac, see Alexander and Cuda, *Got Your Back,* and *Vibe* Magazine, *Tupac Shakur,* esp. p. 21.

177 *were sexually reckless:* Garrow, *The FBI and Martin Luther King, Jr.,* pp. 101–172; Alexander and Cuda, *Got Your Back,* esp. pp. 80–122; *Vibe* Magazine, *Tupac Shakur,* esp. pp. 21, 33.

177 *wanted to be number one in their fields:* Williams, *The King God Didn't Save,* p. 189. Quoting a woman King was allegedly having an affair with, Williams writes about King's response to a *Newsweek* poll of 1963 that reflected his status as the preeminent black American leader. "'Martin got up and rushed to the newsstand. He had that copy of *Newsweek* already opened to the poll. He kept looking at it, and after a while, he must have sensed that I thought it was all disgusting, so he closed up the magazine. He pretended to be contrite. He said, "I know I shouldn't care what they think about me. I just ought to pay it no mind and do what I must. I shouldn't be so vain." But he was feeling good because he was first.'" For an analysis of *Newsweek*'s 1963 poll and a subsequent one in 1966, see Brink and Harris, *The Negro Revolution* and *Black and White.* For Tupac, see Alexander and Cuda, *Got Your Back,* and *Vibe* Editors, *Tupac Shakur.*

177 *occasionally hung out with women of ill repute:* Young, *An Easy Burden,* pp. 436–437. Young reports that when King was in Cleveland (to help elect Carl Stokes mayor), his car passed through a district where a prostitute peeped into his briefly stopped car and said, "There's that Uncle Tom, Martin Luther King. What's *he* doing here?" King demanded that his driver turn the car around so King could speak to her. King invited the woman

and her friends to his hotel to discuss why he was in Cleveland. Young reports that when "we returned to the hotel there was a delegation of ladies in waiting in the lobby! They had told the desk clerk they were waiting to meet with Martin Luther King! We arranged for a meeting room and ordered coffee, and Martin began a discussion on the necessity for them to register and vote if they ever hoped to get off the street" (Alexander and Cuda, *Got Your Back*).

177 *as youth like nice clothes and cars:* Lewis, *King*, pp. 15, 32; Branch, *Parting the Waters*, p. 59; Alexander and Cuda, *Got Your Back*.

177 *were obsessed with their own deaths:* Garrow, *Bearing the Cross*, p. 602; *Vibe* Editors, *Tupac Shakur;* White, *Rebel for the Hell of It.*

177 *allegedly got physical with at least one woman:* Abernathy, *And the Walls*, p. 436; *Vibe* Editors, *Tupac Shakur*, pp. 19, 21, 30–31, 33, 48–50, 63. Tupac was convicted of sexual abuse in 1994 and sentenced in early 1995 to up to four and a half years in prison at Rikers Island penitentiary, where he served seven months until he was released on a $1.4 million bond. Abernathy claims that on the morning of his death, King argued with a female friend, who had in turn blamed Abernathy in King's presence for failing to tell King the truth about his poor treatment of her. Abernathy writes: "'Don't you say a goddamn thing about Ralph,' he shouted and knocked her across the bed. It was more of a shove than a real blow, but for a short man, Martin had a prodigious strength that always surprised me. She leapt up to fight back, and for a moment they were engaged in a full-blown fight, with Martin clearly winning. Then it was all over."

177 *had their last work published posthumously:* King's book, *Trumpet of Conscience*, based on his 1967 Massey lectures on the Canadian Broadcasting Corporation, was published after his death in 1968. Shakur has had many posthumous releases, including his album *The Don Killuminati: The 7 Day Theory Makevelli*, released nearly two months after his November 5, 1997, death.

178 *His name was legally changed from Michael to Martin:* Branch, *Parting the Waters*, p. 44; Lewis, *King*, p. 6.

178 *King preferred the company of light-skinned black women:* Williams, *The King God Didn't Save*, p. 151; Garrow, *Bearing the Cross*, p. 375.

178 *accused of fathering a child out of wedlock:* Garrow, *Bearing the Cross*, p. 689, n. 18. Garrow writes that the "FBI also considered some harassment regarding 'a woman with whom King was involved and a child born to her in 1965, reportedly fathered by King.'"

178 *twice attempted to commit suicide:* Lewis, *King*, pp. 13–14; Branch, *Parting the Waters*, pp. 48–49, 57.

178 *deeply depressed:* Garrow, *Parting the Waters*, pp. 531–532, 602–604.

178 *"loved Tupac and Biggie":* Rock, *Rock This!* pp. 18–19.

178 *"Biggie Smalls was assassinated":* Ibid., p. 19.

179 *He drank from the roots:* Lischer, *The Preacher King*, pp. 1–70.

179 *"poet laureate of the American pulpit":* Dyson, *Between God and Gangsta Rap*, pp. 40–55.

179 *revivalist and civil rights activist C. L. Franklin:* Franklin, *Give Me This Mountain* (Titon, ed.), Lischer, *The Preacher King*, pp. 136, 254.

179 *Hip-hop's obsession with word-play:* Rose, *Black Noise;* Potter, *Spectacular Vernaculars;* Dyson, *Reflecting Black*, pp. 16–17, 277, and *Race Rules*, pp. 120–121.

179 *indebted to secular elements of black music:* Neal, *What the Music Said;* Rose, *Black Noise;* George, *Hip-Hop America;* Dyson, *Race Rules*, pp. 121–122.

179 *embrace of blues themes:* Dyson, *Reflecting Black*, pp. 8–10, and *Race Rules*, p. 121.

179 *celebration of irreverent folk and popular identities:* Kelley, *Race Rebels*, pp. 183–227; Boyd, *Am I Black Enough for You?*

179 *fuses the rhythmic and percussive elements:* Rose, *Black Noise*, 65–74; Dyson, *Race Rules*, pp. 120–121.

180 *C. L. Franklin's sermons are characterized:* Franklin recorded over sixty albums on Chess records, which display his mastery of the chanted sermon. See also Franklin, *Give Me This Mountain* (Titon, ed.). As with any other great preacher, Franklin must be heard in order to grasp his greatness and his supreme execution of his craft. For an excellent exploration of the cultural and rhetorical dimensions of the chanted sermon, see Raboteau, *Fire in the Bones*, pp. 141–151.

180 *Caesar Clark's preaching:* Some of Clark's sermons are available on vinyl; many more are available on tapes, which may be bought at his church, Good Street Baptist Church in Dallas, Texas, and at the annual meeting of the National Baptist Convention.

180 *gangsta rap genre:* Dyson, *Between God and Gangsta Rap*, pp. 172–186; Kelley, *Race Rebels*, pp. 183–227.

180 *severe criticism for its practice of "sampling":* Rose, *Black Noise*, pp. 90–93; Dyson, *Reflecting Black*, pp. 14–15.

180 *Because early hip-hop producers:* Dyson, *Race Rules*, pp. 120, 121, 122–123.

180 *early rap its rhythmic backbone:* Dyson, *Reflecting Black*, pp. 14–15.

181 *Harry Emerson Fosdick:* Miller, *Voice of Deliverance*, p. 76.

181 *the masculine emphasis:* Wallace, *Black Macho and the Myth of the Superwoman;* hooks, *Ain't I a Woman?* Giddings, *When and Where I Enter*, pp. 261–324; Collins, *Black Feminist Thought;* Hine, *Hine Sight*, pp. 16–26; White, *Too Heavy a Load*, pp. 176–211; Dyson, *Race Rules*, pp. 175–182, 197–212; James, *Transcending*, pp. 83–97; Rose, *Black Noise*, pp. 171–172; Dyson, *Making Malcolm*, pp. 92–98, 107–128, 166–173; Boyd, *Am I Black Enough for You?*

182 *"ultimate way to diminish our problems":* King, *Where Do We Go?* p. 125.

182 *Theodicy attempts to understand:* Jones, *Is God a White Racist?* Kushner, *When Bad Things Happen to Good People;* Pinn, *Why Lord?*

182 *examined at least four solutions:* DeWolf, *A Theology of the Living Church*, pp. 130–143, cited in Ansbro, *Martin Luther King*, pp. 53–54. My reading of DeWolf in this paragraph is heavily dependent on Ansbro's analysis.

183 *My personal trials have also taught me:* (the essay is 1960) King, "Suffering and Faith," in King, *A Testament*, p. 41.

183 *making a virtue of necessity:* Sherman, *Making a Necessity of Virtue.*

183 *"cosmic companionship":* cited in Oates, *Let the Trumpet*, p. 285.

183 *"if you use violence":* King, "The American Dream," in King, *A Testament*, p. 214.

183 *"stark, grim and colossally real":* King, *Strength to Love*, p. 58.

184 *Max Weber, conceived theodicy as the effort:* Sadri, *Max Weber's Sociology of Intellectuals*, pp. 44, 45, 65–66.

184 *Malcolm believed in mutual bloodshed:* Cone, *Martin and Malcolm and America*, p. 262; Dyson, *Reflecting Black*, p. 258.

184 *Colin Powell and Louis Farrakhan have urged blacks:* Dyson, *Race Rules*, pp. 150–195.

184 *They celebrate the outlaw:* Kelley, *Race Rebels*, pp. 183–227; Boyd, *Am I Black Enough?* Also, Eric Hobsbawn talks about the outlaw in Western society in Hobsbawm, *Bandits and Primitive Rebels.*

185 *"Where might I find a gracious God?"* Luther, cited in Thielicke, *The Waiting Father* and *Life Can Begin Again.*

185 *"justify the ways of God to men":* Milton, *Paradise Lost*, p. 6.

185 *rarely credited with such moral complexity:* Kelley, *Race Rebels*, pp. 183–227; Dyson, *Between God and Gangsta Rap*, pp. 172–186.

185 *Some religious thinkers have argued:* Jones, *Is God a White Racist?* Pinn, *Why Lord?* and *Varieties of Black Religious Experience*, pp. 154–185.

186 *Many hip-hop artists are obsessed with death:* White, *Rebel for the Hell of It;* Sartwell, *Act Like You Know*, pp. 173–178.

186 *The hip-hop jeremiad:* For insightful examination of the jeremiad, see Bercovitch, *American Jeremiad*, and Howard-Pitney, *Afro-American Jeremiad.*

187 *"lyrics do not glorify violence":* Sartwell, *Act Like You Know,* p. 174.

187 *"tell about violence, mourn it, object to it":* Ibid.

187 *Ice Cube's "Dead Homiez":* Dyson, *Between God and Gangsta Rap,* p. 173.

187 *In Scarface's "Never Seen a Man Cry":* For a powerful examination of this song, see Sartwell, *Act Like You Know.*

187 *Snoop Doggy Dogg's "Murder Was the Case":* See ibid. for an insightful exploration of this song.

188 *We will always be willing to talk:* King, "The Rising Tide of Racial Consciousness," in Washington, ed. *A Testament,* p. 149.

188 *If I were constantly worried about death:* King, "*Playboy* Interview: Martin Luther King, Jr.," in Washington, ed., *A Testament,* pp. 355–356.

188 *"no martyr complex":* Cited in Garrow, *Bearing the Cross,* p. 515.

189 *"I've told you all that I don't expect":* Ibid., p. 311.

189 *"somebody you can sit with":* Ibid., p. 604.

189 *"I have my moments of frustration":* Ibid., p. 717, n. 24.

189 *"profoundly weary and wounded spirit":* Ibid., p. 599.

189 *"was just a different person":* Ibid.

189 *"was depressed":* Ibid., p. 602.

189 *"last year or so":* Ibid.

189 *could relax only in a room:* Lischer, *The Preacher King,* p. 171.

190 *well publicized and widely denounced:* Hearing before the Subcommittee on Juvenile Justice of Committee on the Judiciary, United States Senate to Examine the Effects of Violent and Demeaning Imagery in Popular Music on American Youth, Feb. 23, 1994, Serial No. J-103043 (S. Hrg. 103–1005).

190 *Hip-hop has been rebuked:* Ibid. Also see Dyson, *Between God and Gangsta Rap,* pp. 172–186; Dyson, *Race Rules,* pp. 100–101, 112–113, 117–119, 125–149; Kelley, *Race Rebels,* pp. 183–227.

190 *an earlier epoch of moral discipline:* Dyson, *Race Rules,* pp. 109–149.

191 *"often plunges men's minds":* Cited in Garrow, *Bearing the Cross,* p. 104.

191 *criminal sexual acts against blacks:* Lerner, ed., *Black Women in White America,* pp. 149–193; Jones, *Labor of Love, Labor of Sorrow,* p. 157; Hine, *Hine Sight,* pp. 37–47.

191 *The best safeguards blacks could manage:* Dyson, *Race Rules,* pp. 84–86, 91–101.

192 *under constant surveillance:* Davis and Riddick, "Los Angeles," pp. 37–60; Davis, *City of Quartz.*

192 *resentment of the black bourgeoisie:* Dyson, *Race Rules,* pp. 110–111.

192 *"keepin' it real":* Powell, *Keepin' It Real.*

193 *King enjoyed sharp suits and light-skinned women:* Lewis, *King,* pp. 15, 32; Williams, *The King God Didn't Save,* p. 151; Garrow, *Bearing the Cross,* p. 375.

193 *Nicknamed "Tweedie":* Branch, *Parting the Waters,* p. 59.

193 *"M.L. could get involved with girls":* Garrow, *Bearing the Cross,* p. 36.

193 *"Robinson and Stevens":* Ibid.

193 *King confessed to Coretta:* Ibid., p. 47.

193 *King "loved beautiful women":* Ibid., p. 375.

193 *"as a man":* Williams, *The King God Didn't Save,* p. 185.

193 *"said that he was willing to fight and die":* Ibid., p. 151. Williams also says that "King's color consciousness seems to have been a direct throwback to the social values of black Atlanta." Later he writes that like "so many of us, King in his speeches took on the sketching of black power. He used the term 'Negro' and 'black people' interchangeably; black became beautiful, although his secret distaste for black women remained constant" (p. 206). King seems to have lessened his revulsion to blackness near the end of his life. In a painful but luminous scene in a Cleveland restaurant, eight local ministers had gathered to discuss King's crusade there in 1968. "Finally there is some mild joking and one of

the preachers, very dark in skin, points to another and says how much darker the other is. There is almost a reproach in King's remark: 'It's a new age,' he says, 'a new time. Black is beautiful'" (Halberstam, "When 'Civil Rights' and 'Peace' Join Force," p. 196). Still, color considerations loomed large after King's death. Ralph Abernathy, King's successor, describes the difficulties he faced in the light of King's shadow, both figuratively and in terms of skin tone, quite literally. "I was not, after all, Martin Luther King, Jr.; and as far as the white press was concerned, that made quite a difference. For one thing, I didn't have as many degrees as he did and I didn't have his polish. In addition, my skin was darker, a more important factor in dealing with the white press than anyone would dare admit. As Andrew Young put it, in advising me during those first days as president: 'Now the national press isn't going to be as kind to you as they were to Martin. You're not the fair-skinned boy. Your ancestors weren't 'house niggers,' so they'll treat you differently" (Abernathy, *And the Walls Came Tumbling Down*, p. 499).

194 *King's sexual pace did not slow:* Garrow, *The FBI and Martin Luther King, Jr.,* pp. 101–172.

194 *"had a chick in every town":* Williams, *The King God Didn't Save,* p. 129.

194 *"All the guys were putting it to them":* Ibid., p. 198.

194 *"Cease know":* Biggie Smalls, "I'm Fucking You Tonight," on *Life After Death.*

194 *"segregation is the adultery":* "Man of the Year," *Time,* Jan. 3, 1964, cited in Branch, *Pillar of Fire,* p. 212.

195 *"Do you nag?":* Cited in Garrow, *Bearing the Cross,* p. 104.

195 *"the primary obligation of the woman":* Ibid., p. 99.

195 *"would have had a lot to learn":* Raines, ed., *My Soul Is Rested,* p. 433.

195 *"somewhat uncomfortable around assertive women":* Giddings, *When and Where I Enter,* p. 312.

195 *"There would never be any":* Ella Baker, interview, Civil Rights Documentation Project, Moorland-Spingarn Collection, Howard University, Washington, D.C., pp. 34–35, cited in ibid., p. 312. Also see White, *Too Heavy a Load,* p. 233.

195 *"had a hard time with domineering women":* Ibid.

195 *She was never publicly saying:* Ibid., p. 313.

196 *the allegation that King may have engaged in a shoving match:* Abernathy, *And the Walls Came Tumbling Down,* p. 436.

Chapter 10: "The Primary Obligation of the Woman Is That of Motherhood"

197 *"The Primary Obligation of the Woman":* Cited in Garrow, *Bearing the Cross,* p. 99.

197 *"Did you get the flowers?":* King, *My Life,* p. 308.

197 *"I was touched by his gesture":* Ibid.

197 *"beautiful red carnations":* Ibid.

197 *"In all the years we had":* Ibid.

198 *ideas and practices that were common:* Giddings, *When and Where I Enter,* pp. 217–275; Hine, *Hine Sight,* pp. 59–145; Jones, *Labor of Love, Labor of Sorrow,* pp. 196–301; White, *Too Heavy a Load,* pp. 110–175.

198 *spark the rise of modern feminism:* M. King, *Freedom Song;* Carson, *In Struggle,* pp. 147–148.

198 *"our three Queens":* Quoted in Zook, "A Manifesto of Sorts for a Black Feminist Movement," *New York Times Magazine,* Nov. 12, 1995.

198 *Myrlie Evers-Williams:* Lyman, *Great African-American Women,* pp. 69–71.

198 *Dr. Betty Shabazz:* Ibid., pp. 200–202.

199 *sexist character of black culture:* Hull, Scott, and Smith, eds., *All the Women Are White;* Wallace, *Black Macho and the Myth of the Superwoman;* hooks, *Ain't I a Woman?*

Collins, *Black Feminist Thought;* Ransby and Matthews, "Black Popular Culture"; James, *Transcending,* pp. 115–129.

199 *before the seventies simply lumped together:* See all references in the previous note.

199 *the National Association of Colored Women:* Giddings, *When and Where I Enter,* pp. 93–94, 95, 116–117; Hine, *Hine Sight,* pp. 14, 44–45, 70, 120–121; White, *Too Heavy a Load,* pp. 21–141.

199 *the National Welfare Rights Organization:* Giddings, *When and Where I Enter,* pp. 312–313, 326; White, *Too Heavy a Load,* pp. 210–211, 228–229, 232–236, 237–240.

200 *From the beginning of black America:* Lerner, *Black Women in White America,* pp. 3–87, 288–292, 361–375, 435–440, 523–533, 561–572; Giddings, *When and Where I Enter,* pp. 33–83; Jones, *Labor of Love, Labor of Sorrow,* pp. 3–78.

200 *They have also been systematically excluded:* Lerner, *Black Women in White America,* pp. 345–352; Jones, *Labor of Love, Labor of Sorrow,* pp. 232–321; Carson, *In Struggle,* pp. 147–148; Morris, *Origins;* Crawford, Rouse, and Woods, eds., *Women in the Civil Rights Movement;* Payne, *I've Got the Light of Freedom;* James, *Transcending,* pp. 83–97, 115–129; Brown-Nagin, "The Transformation of a Social Movement into Law," pp. 81–137; Higginbotham, *Righteous Discontent.*

200 *Mary Church Terrell:* Terrell, *A Colored Woman in a White World;* Sterling, *Black Foremothers: Three Lives,* pp. 118–158; Giddings, *When and Where I Enter,* pp. 18–19, 97–98, 105–107, 109–110, 213, 218–219; Hine, *Hine Sight,* pp. 14–15, 44; White, *Too Heavy a Load,* pp. 21–27, 64–65, 77–78, 90–96, 106–107; Lyman, *Great African-American Women,* pp. 215–217. The information on Terrell in this section draws from these sources.

200 *"keep on insisting":* Sterling, *Black Foremothers: Three Lives,* p. 155.

201 *"required all eating-place proprietors":* Jones, "Mary Eliza Church Terrell," pp. 1158–1159, cited in Lyman, *Great African-American Women,* p. 217.

201 *The same is true of Mary McCloud Bethune:* Giddings, *When and Where I Enter,* pp. 197–230, 243–246; Hine, *Hine Sight,* pp. 16–17, 113; White, *Too Heavy a Load,* pp. 60, 106–107, 152–157; Lyman, *Great African-American Women,* pp. 22–24. The information on Bethune in this section draws from these sources.

202 *the social imagination of Rosa Parks:* Raines, *My Soul Is Rested,* pp. 43, 50; Giddings, *When and Where I Enter,* pp. 257, 261–265; Garrow, *Bearing the Cross,* pp. 15–16, 51, 98; Branch, *Parting the Waters,* pp. 124–125; Parks and Haskins, *Rosa Parks,* pp. 55–107.

203 *solidly anchored:* See all works cited in the previous note. Also see Payne, *I've Got the Light of Freedom,* pp. 71–72, 416–417; Grant, *Ella Baker,* pp. 101–102.

203 *organized in 1946 by Mary Fair Burks:* Giddings, *When and Where I Enter,* p. 264 (Giddings refers to her as Mary Burke); Garrow, *Bearing the Cross,* p. 14.

203 *under the presidency of Jo Ann Robinson:* Giddings, *When and Where I Enter,* pp. 264–265; Robinson, *The Montgomery Bus Boycott;* Garrow, *Bearing the Cross,* pp. 14–16, 18–19, 21; Branch, *Parting the Waters,* pp. 131–132, 147, 159. Robinson, along with other King loyalists, was forced to resign from her job in 1960 when Alabama governor Patterson sought retribution against King after he was acquitted in a perjury trial involving income taxes (Branch, *Parting the Waters,* p. 312).

203 *"not to just teach a lesson":* Giddings, *When and Where I Enter,* p. 264.

203 *King barely recognized WPC's achievements:* King, *Stride Toward Freedom.*

203 *E. D. Nixon:* Baldwin and Woodson, *Freedom Is Never Free;* Raines, *My Soul Is Rested,* pp. 37–39, 43–51; Garrow, *Bearing the Cross,* pp. 12–23.

203 *"little boys":* Raines, *My Soul Is Rested,* p. 48; Carson, ed., *The Autobiography of Malcolm X,* p. 57.

204 *"What the hell you talkin' about?":* Raines, *My Soul Is Rested,* p. 49.

204 *"You guys have went around":* Ibid.

204 *"with a choice of confronting":* Giddings, *When and Where I Enter,* p. 266.

204 *Ella Baker:* Grant, *Ella Baker;* Garrow, *Bearing the Cross,* pp. 84–86, 103–118, 120–121, 131–137, 141, 150, 163, 166–167; Giddings, *When and Where I Enter,* pp. 257, 267–269, 274–275, 284, 296; Hine, *Hine Sight,* pp. 22–23; Jones, *Labor of Love, Labor of Sorrow,* pp. 256, 267, 276, 282; Lerner, *Black Women in White America,* pp. 345–352; Anderson, *Bayard Rustin,* pp. 195, 197–201, 259; James, *Transcending the Talented Tenth,* pp. 83–84, 87–88, 97.

204 *Baker lent her expertise:* Grant, *Baker,* pp. 100–102.

204 *she often stayed with Rosa Parks:* Ibid., p. 102.

204 *ideologically committed to the empowerment:* Lerner, *Black Women,* pp. 345–352.

204 *When Baker, Rustin, and Levison:* Grant, *Baker,* pp. 102–103.

205 *"were willing to do something I had never seen":* Ibid., p. 103.

205 *"face up to the potential":* Ibid.

205 *"so all you need to do":* Ibid.

205 *"I think they would have been willing":* Ibid.

205 *King pressed Rustin to take the leadership:* Ibid., p. 104; Anderson, *Bayard Rustin,* pp. 198–199.

205 *she agreed to head the Crusade for Citizenship:* Grant, *Baker,* pp. 104–105; Anderson, *Bayard Rustin,* p. 199.

205 *"to set up at the local level":* Grant, *Baker,* p. 106.

205 *"reports from the cities I have reached":* Ibid., p. 107.

206 *Baker was encouraged by SCLC board members:* Ibid.

206 *Baker clashed with SCLC's cult of personality:* Ibid. Also see Lerner, *Black Women,* p. 351; Anderson, *Bayard Rustin,* pp. 199–200; Payne, *I've Got the Light of Freedom,* pp. 92–93; James, *Transcending,* p. 87.

206 *The group was driven:* Fairclough, *To Redeem the Soul of America.* Also see Branch, *Parting the Waters,* p. 301.

206 *"She wasn't church":* Grant, *Baker,* p. 122.

206 *Baker believed in group-centered leadership:* Lerner, *Black Women,* pp. 345–352; Grant, *Baker,* pp. 107–111; Payne, *I've Got the Light of Freedom* , pp. 92–93; James, *Transcending the Talented Tenth,* pp. 87–88; Lewis, *Walking with the Wind,* 114, 182, 189.

206 *She was extremely critical of King's leadership style:* Grant, *Baker,* pp. 105–124.

206 *faced in SNCC the same sexism:* Carson, *In Struggle,* pp. 147–148; Giddings, *When and Where I Enter,* pp. 277–297; White, *Too Heavy a Load,* p. 219.

206 *legendary grass-roots activist Fannie Lou Hamer:* Mills, *This Little Light of Mine;* Hamer, "It's in Your Hands," in Lerner, ed., *Black Women in White America,* pp. 609–614; Carson, *In Struggle,* pp. 73–74, 125–126; Giddings, *When and Where I Enter,* pp. 287–290, 293–294, 301; Jones, *Labor of Love, Labor of Sorrow,* pp. 275, 281, 283–284, 286–287, 311; Payne, *I've Got the Light of Freedom,* pp. 154, 227–228, 258–259, 425–426; James, *Transcending,* pp. 150–151.

207 *Hamer helped to form the Mississippi Freedom Democratic party:* Mills, *This Little Light of Mine,* p. 105; Lerner, ed., *Black Women in White America,* p. 609; Carson, *In Struggle,* p. 109.

207 *At a staff retreat in Waveland, Mississippi:* Carson, *In Struggle,* pp. 147–148; Lewis, *Walking with the Wind,* p. 298.

207 *"Assumptions of male superiority":* Cited in Carson, *In Struggle,* p. 147.

207 *"force the rest of the movement":* Ibid., p. 148.

207 *"Prone":* Ibid.; Giddings, *When and Where I Enter,* p. 302; Jones, *Labor of Love, Labor of Sorrow,* p. 283.

207 *"the paper on women effected no noticeable":* Carson, *In Struggle,* p. 148.

207 *"staged what they called a 'pussy strike' ":* Lewis, *Walking with the Wind,* p. 92.

208 *"other women brought many of the values":* Carson, *In Struggle,* p. 148.

208 *depended largely on the labor of poor:* Jones, *Labor of Love, Labor of Sorrow,* p. 279. The ideas in this paragraph are derived from Jones's excellent study.

208 *King met in 1967 with several welfare activists:* Giddings, *When and Where I Enter,* pp. 312–313; White, *Too Heavy a Load,* pp. 214–215.

208 *"had actually come up with the idea":* Giddings, *When and Where I Enter,* p. 312.

208 *were outraged that the Poor People's Campaign:* White, *Too Heavy a Load,* p. 214.

208 *their organization in 1968 exceeded ten thousand members:* Giddings, *When and Where I Enter,* pp. 312–313.

208 *"jumped on Martin like no one ever had before":* Cited in White, *Too Heavy a Load,* p. 214.

208 *she "means the Anti-Welfare Bill":* Cited in Giddings, *When and Where I Enter,* p. 313.

209 *"Where were you . . . when we were down":* Cited in ibid., p. 313.

209 *"You know, Dr. King":* Ibid., p. 313; White, *Too Heavy a Load,* p. 214.

209 *"You're right, Mrs. Tillmon":* White, *Too Heavy a Load,* p. 215.

209 *King's philosophy of material sacrifice:* Oates, *Let the Trumpet,* pp. 281–282; Garrow, *Bearing the Cross,* pp. 114–115, 164, 421–422; Branch, *Parting the Waters,* pp. 588–589.

209 *"when I first met him":* C. King, "Thoughts and Reflections," in Albert and Hoffman, eds., *We Shall Overcome,* p. 253.

209 *And he talked about working within the framework:* Ibid., p. 254.

209 *thought she was "bourgie":* Branch, *Parting the Waters,* p. 100.

209 *the daughter of poor Alabama farmers:* C. King, *My Life,* pp. 20–45; King, *Autobiography of Martin Luther King, Jr.,* pp. 35–37; Young, *An Easy Burden,* pp. 344–345.

209 *King, by his own admission, enjoyed:* Carson, ed., *The Autobiography of Martin Luther King, Jr.,* p. 5.

210 *King family lived in a rented home until 1965:* Garrow, *Bearing the Cross,* p. 421.

210 *King was ashamed of what he felt:* Ibid., p. 422.

210 *"nothing fashionable about his neighborhood":* Young, *An Easy Burden,* p. 163.

210 *barely keep the children in adequate shoes:* Ibid.

210 *his enormous guilt in being featured:* Garrow, *Bearing the Cross,* p. 588.

210 *he gave the movement most of his income:* King, "*Playboy* Interview: Martin Luther King, Jr.," in King, *A Testament of Hope,* p. 371.

210 *"the huge speaking fees of today":* Young, *An Easy Burden,* p. 282.

210 *King gave over three hundred speeches a year:* Alex Haley says that King gave over 450 speeches a year, in "*Playboy* Interview: Martin Luther King, Jr.," p. 341.

210 *to provide life insurance for his son:* Garrow, *Bearing the Cross,* p. 417.

210 *donate the entire purse to the civil rights movement:* Ibid., pp. 357, 368; Branch, *Pillar of Fire,* pp. 516, 520; Young, *An Easy Burden,* p. 326.

211 *King's decision greatly disappointed Coretta:* Garrow, *Bearing the Cross,* pp. 357, 374. Also see Branch, *Parting the Waters,* pp. 516, 520.

211 *a compromise of sorts:* Branch, *Pillar of Fire,* p. 520.

211 *the Abernathys insisted that they be treated:* Garrow, *Bearing the Cross,* p. 366; Branch, *Pillar of Fire,* pp. 541, 543. Also see Young, *An Easy Burden,* p. 320.

211 *"Martin . . . was absolutely a male chauvinist":* Garrow, *Bearing the Cross,* pp. 375–376.

211 *"very easily and smoothly":* C. King, *My Life,* p. 54.

211 *"You know every Napoleon":* Ibid. Also see Branch, *Parting the Waters,* p. 94; Schulke and McPhee, *King Remembered,* p. 23.

211 *"That's absurd":* Branch, *Parting the Waters.* Also see C. King, *My Life,* p. 54; Schulke and McPhee, *King Remembered,* p. 23.

211 *"grow in stature":* Ibid., pp. 54–55.

211 *"Do you know something":* Ibid., p. 55.

212 *"He was always popular with the girls":* Ibid., p. 56.

212 *"You know women are hero-worshipers":* Ibid.

212 *"an odd mixture of romance and pragmatism":* Branch, *Parting the Waters,* p. 96.

212 *"the first discussion we had":* Carson, ed., *The Autobiography of Martin Luther King, Jr.,* p. 35.

212 *"Martin had, all through his life"*: C. King, *My Life*, p. 60.

213 *"But when it came"*: Ibid.

213 *"how difficult it is to find a stable"*: Ibid., p. 70.

213 *"there was never a moment"*: Ibid.

213 *"amazing and wonderful and terrible things"*: Ibid.

213 *a recurring nightmare*: Oates, *Let the Trumpet Sound*, p. 128.

213 *"This is what is going to happen to me"*: C. King, *My Life*, p. 244; Oates, *Let the Trumpet Sound*, p. 270.

214 *she demanded that Martin Luther King, known affectionately as Daddy King*: Branch, *Parting the Waters*, p. 101. Coretta King, however, said that it was both King's and her decision to forgo the obedience vow. See C. King, *My Life*, pp. 73–74.

214 *"allowed me to be myself"*: King, "Thoughts and Reflections," in Albert and Hoffman, eds., *We Shall Overcome*, p. 255.

214 *"takes a toll on the family"*: Oates, *Let the Trumpet Sound*, p. 161.

214 *"frustrating aspects"*: Carson, ed., *The Autobiography of Martin Luther King, Jr.*, pp. 38–39.

214 *"with great difficulty that he kept her"*: Cited in Garrow, *Bearing the Cross*, p. 669, n. 7.

214 *Coretta became increasingly angry at King*: Ibid., pp. 165, 236, 308, 328, 339, 375, 617.

215 *"the side of a man who would change"*: C. King, "Thoughts and Reflections," p. 251.

215 *"I spoke to my husband about it"*: Garrow, *Bearing the Cross*, p. 165.

215 *"a household where my mother"*: Ibid., p. 236.

215 *"I've never been on the scene"*: Ibid., p. 308.

215 *King had promised to call home to check*: Ibid., p. 339.

215 *King even confessed in a 1965 sermon*: Cited in ibid., p. 698, n. 18.

215 *King and Coretta in full throttle*: Ibid., p. 328. Also see Branch, *Pillar of Fire*, p. 325.

215 *Klan death threats in his St. Augustine campaign*: Garrow, *Bearing the Cross*, p. 328; Branch, *Pillar of Fire*, p. 325.

216 *"Every now and then he gets peeved"*: Cited in Garrow, *Bearing the Cross*, p. 683, n. 39.

216 *During our whole marriage we never had*: Ibid., p. 374.

216 *her worried telephone calls with her husband's*: Ibid., p. 371.

216 *"one single discussion"*: Ibid., p. 374.

216 *the FBI sent King a cut-and-spliced tape recording*: Garrow, *The FBI and Martin Luther King, Jr.*, pp. 125–126; Garrow, *Bearing the Cross*, pp. 372–374; Branch, *Pillar of Fire*, pp. 556–557.

217 *"I couldn't make much out of it"*: Cited in Garrow, *Bearing the Cross*, p. 374. Also see Raines, *My Soul Is Rested*, pp. 427–430; Young, *An Easy Burden*, p. 329.

217 *"such accusations never seemed to touch her"*: Abernathy, *And the Walls*, pp. 472–473.

217 *King had established relationships of significant affection*: Garrow, *Bearing the Cross*, p. 375.

217 *"gulped"*: Ibid., p. 586.

217 *"That poor man was so harassed at home"*: Ibid., p. 617.

218 *"the marriage wouldn't have survived"*: Ibid.

218 *"Coretta King was most certainly"*: Ibid.

218 *former Kentucky state senator*: Davis, *I Shared the Dream*.

218 *"If Dr. King had been an ordinary man"*: Ibid., p. 3.

218 *"When Dr. King's life is researched"*: Ibid., p. 4.

218 *Before she wrote her book*: According to Davis, she got a call from the Associated Press when Abernathy's book came out inquiring about her relationship with King. This hardly qualifies as a media deluge. Further, she says that it had "always been my constant fear that one of King's close associates would talk about our relationship" and expresses surprise that it was Abernathy who did. "Then, when I finally read the account, I was further discouraged that he had not told the truth." While Davis's book is her version of the truth, it seems

that an article might have turned the trick. Of course, her very interesting and important life merits a book-length manuscript, but since its predicate of interest—even, it seems, in her own mind—is her covert sexual relationship with King, her other accomplishments are viewed as derivative or, worse, subordinate to her sexual intimacy with King.

218 *"a black woman"*: Abernathy, *And the Walls*, p. 436.

218 *"visited with Mrs. Davis"*: Cited in Rowan, *Breaking the Barriers*, p. 306.

219 *King on countless occasions had*: As Coretta King herself said a few days after her husband's death, as she asked America to eliminate poverty: "If this can be done, then I know that his death will be the redemptive force that he so often talked about in terms of one giving his life to a great cause and the things he believed in" (C. King, *My Life*, p. 346). And in his eulogy for King, mentor and former Morehouse president Benjamin Mays closed his oration with "what Martin Luther King, Jr., believed, that if *physical death was the price he had to pay to rid America of prejudice and injustice, nothing could be more redemptive* (italics in original, cited in C. King, *My Life*, p. 358; also see Mays, *Disturbed About Man*, p. 15).

220 *Although Coretta is mocked as "My husband"*: Boston Globe, Jan. 15, 1997, p. 1.

220 *lobbying the government to celebrate*: Lyman, *Great African-American Women*, p. 148.

220 *only four days after her husband's assassination*: C. King, *My Life*, 327–328.

220 *keynote speech at the Cardozo High School Auditorium*: See Abernathy, *And the Walls*, p. 511; Fairclough, *To Redeem the Soul*, pp. 385–386.

221 *In a poll of the attendees*: Walters and Smith, *African American Leadership*, pp. 205, 270, n. 4.

221 *Coretta gave speeches, wrote nationally syndicated news columns*: Lyman, *Great African-American Women*, p. 148.

221 *a prominent anti-apartheid activist*: Ibid.

222 *the powerful forces of historical amnesia*: Harding, *Martin Luther King*, pp. 58–68.

222 *he was no Safe Negro*: King said in 1967 that Northern mayors like Daley (Chicago) and Yorty (Los Angeles) used to tell him how great he was. And Cleveland mayor Locher was "damning me now and calling me an extremist, and three years ago he gave me the key to the city and said I was the greatest man of the century. That was as long as I was safe from him down in the South" (Halberstam, "When 'Civil Rights' and 'Peace' Join Forces," in Lincoln, ed., *Martin Luther King, Jr.*, p. 193). Also see Dyson, *Reflecting Black*, pp. 221.

Chapter 11: "Be True to What You Said on Paper"

225 *"Be True to What You Said on Paper"*: King, "I See the Promised Land," in King, *A Testament of Hope*, p. 282.

225 *In 1964, as a private citizen*: Marable, *Speaking Truth to Power*, pp. 88–91; Weisbrot, *Freedom Bound*, pp. 303–304; Branch, *Pillar of Fire*, p. 242.

225 *"Traces of bigotry still mar America"*: Reagan, "Remarks of the President at the Signing Ceremony for Martin Luther King, Jr. Holiday Legislation," *Ebony Magazine*, Jan. 1986, p. 37.

225 *little sympathy for blacks*: Marable, *Speaking Truth to Power*.

226 *"We'll know in about 35 years"*: Cited in Garrow, "The Helms Attack on King," p. 15.

226 *FBI surveillance of King that was sealed*: Ibid., p. 13; Branch, "Uneasy Holiday," *New Republic*, Feb. 3, 1986, p. 24.

226 *hoodwinked by Jesse Helms*: As Branch writes, the "sealed records from King's FBI file do not address the question of King's political allegiance. Those records, by the tens of thousands of pages, are available for public inspection in the FBI Reading Room. The sealed ones are about King's personal life, especially his extramarital sex life, as intercepted by FBI bugs and wiretaps" (Branch, "Uneasy Holiday," p. 24).

226 *Reagan called King's widow . . . to apologize*: Garrow, "The Helms Attack on King," p. 15.

226 *"the same reservations you have"*: Ibid.

226 *American's revolutionary birthright could be extended:* King said in his last speech that he was glad to have been around "in 1960, when students all over the South started sitting-in at lunch counters. And I knew that as they were sitting in, they were really standing up for the best in the American dream. And taking the whole nation back to those great wells of democracy which were dug deep by the Founding Fathers in the Declaration of Independence and the Constitution" (King, "I See the Promised Land," p. 286).

227 *Under the ruthless rule of J. Edgar Hoover:* Garrow, *The FBI and Martin Luther King, Jr.;* McKnight, *The Last Crusade;* Friendly and Gallen, *The FBI File;* McKnight, *The Last Crusade.* Also see J. Edgar Hoover, *Masters of Deceit* and *On Communism.*

227 *the red scare seized the political horizon:* Halberstam, *The Fifties,* pp. 49–59; Friendly and Gallen, *The FBI File,* pp. 88–99.

227 *Joseph McCarthy:* Rovere, *Senator Joe McCarthy.* For a bizarre attempt to rehabilitate McCarthy's image as a reasonable conservative, see William Buckley's novel, *Redhunter.*

227 *Hoover had a more damaging effect:* Garrow, *The FBI and Martin Luther King, Jr.;* O'Reilly, *Racial Matters;* McKnight, *The Last Crusade;* Friendly and Gallen, *The FBI File;* Marable, *Race, Reform, and Rebellion.* As Manning Marable argues, "The impact of the Cold War, the anticommunist purges, and near-totalitarian social environment, had a devastating effect upon the cause of blacks' civil rights and civil liberties" (p. 18).

227 *King became Hoover's most hated:* See all references in the previous note. As McKnight says, what the "public record reveals about the FBI's King file makes it hard to resist the appalling conclusion that this Nobelist and one of the most recognized, respected, and honored Americans of the twentieth century was at the time of his death probably *the most harassed, hounded, and investigated citizen in the history of the Republic*" (italics added, McKnight, *The Last Crusade,* p. 6).

227 *King did not attract much notice:* Garrow, *The FBI and Martin Luther King, Jr.,* pp. 21–26; Friendly and Gallen, *The FBI File,* pp. 20–22.

227 *Benjamin Davis's donation of blood to King:* Garrow, *The FBI and Martin Luther King, Jr.,* p. 24; Friendly and Gallen, *The FBI File,* p. 21.

228 *New York lawyer Stanley Levison:* Garrow, *The FBI and Martin Luther King, Jr.,* pp. 21–77; Friendly and Gallen, *The FBI File,* pp. 23–28, 33–36, 156–157; McKnight, *The Last Crusade,* pp. 16–17.

228 *The Kennedys feared that King's contact:* Garrow, *The FBI and Martin Luther King, Jr.,* pp. 44, 59–63, 87, 94; Friendly and Gallen, *The FBI File,* pp. 34–41.

228 *"no matter what a man was":* Cited in ibid, p. 28.

228 *"crippling totalitarianism":* Cited in ibid., p. 30.

228 *there was never any proof:* Ibid., p. 27. David Garrow, however, concludes that although it is "doubtful any positive answer ever will be possible" in Levison's case, "a more critical examination of Levison's own story shows that he probably did at one time have the involvement in CP financial dealings that the Bureau believed he had" (Garrow, *The FBI and Martin Luther King, Jr.,* p. 97).

228 *"denounced the State Dept. ban on travel":* Cited in Friendly and Gallen, *The FBI File,* p. 29.

229 *its major ideologues:* Bell, ed., *The Radical Right;* Redekop, *The American Far Right;* Theyer, *The Farther Shores of Politics;* Epstein and Forester, *The Radical Right;* Wander, "The John Birch Society and Martin Luther King Symbols in the Radical Right," pp. 4–14.

229 *It's Very Simple:* Stang, *It's Very Simple,* p. 118, cited in Wander, "The John Birch Society," p. 8.

229 *Dan Smoot praised Alabama governor:* Ibid., p. 9.

229 *"King's 'non-violent' agitation triggered violence":* Smoot, "Voting Rights Bill," *The Dan Smoot Report,* May 10, 1965, p. 147, cited in Wander, "The John Birch Society," p. 9.

229 *"was obviously about revolution"*: Stanley, "Revolution: The Assault on Selma," *American Opinion* 8, no. 5, 1965, pp. 1–10, cited in Wander, "The John Birch Society."

229 *"we must continue telling the truth about Martin Luther King"*: Stang, *It's Very Simple,* p. 6, cited in Wander, "The John Birch Society," p. 10.

229 *that spawn figures like Timothy McVeigh:* For background on the radical right, Timothy McVeigh, and the militia and antipatriot movements, see: Steve Lipsher, "The Radical Right," *Denver Post,* Jan. 22, 1995, A1; Phil Reeves, "Embittered 'Patriots' at Heart of America," *Independent (London),* Apr. 28, 1995, p. 13; Mark Sauer and Jim Okerblom, "Patriotism or Paranoia? Videos, Radio, Internet All Used to Spread Fears of the Far Right That Government Poses Danger," *San Diego Union-Tribune,* May 4, 1995, p. E1; Michael Booth and Jeffrey A. Roberts, "Militias More Bark Than Bite in Colorado, Factions Brandish Constitution," *Denver Post,* May 7, 1995, p. A1; Malcolm Gladwell, "At Root of Modern Militias: An American Legacy of Rebellion," *Washington Post,* May 9, 1995, A1; Christopher Cox, "Are Modern-Day Militia Members . . . ; Neo-Patriots or Anti-American Warriors?" *Boston Herald,* Apr. 17, 1996, p. 34; Scott Canon, "McVeigh Called a Patriot, Model Soldier Who Was Troubled by the Siege at Waco," *Kansas City Star,* June 17, 1997, p. A1; Rasheeda Crayton, "Lead Prosecutor in McVeigh Trial Talks on Terrorism," *Kansas City Star,* Apr. 10, 1998, A11. Also see Dees and Corcoran, *Gathering Storm,* and Neiwert, *In God's Country.*

230 *"part of the world Communist conspiracy"*: Cited in Garrow, "The Helms Attack on King," p. 12.

230 *"there is some Communist conspiracy"*: Cited in ibid.

230 *"out of respect for the important"*: Ibid.

230 *"kept around him as his principal advisers"*: Ibid., p. 13.

230 *"King may have had an explicit"*: Ibid.

230 *"King has no real interest"*: Stang, "The King and His Communists," in Welch, ed., *Two Revolutions at Once,* p. 50, cited in Wander, *The John Birch Society,* p. 10.

230 *But two different Ford administration:* Garrow, "The Helms Attack on King," p. 13. Also see Branch, "Uneasy Holiday," p. 24.

230 *Apart from Paul Robeson, Benjamin Davis:* Duberman, *Paul Robeson;* Horne, *Black Liberation/Red Scare;* Lewis, *W.E.B. Du Bois;* Naison, *Communists in Harlem During the Depression;* Record, *The Negro and the Communist Party;* Painter, *The Narrative of Hosea Hudson;* Kelley, *Hammer and Hoe* and *Race Rebels.*

231 *"are as many Communists in this freedom movement"*: "*Playboy* Interview: Martin Luther King," in King, *A Testament of Hope,* p. 362.

231 *"I think with all of the weakness and tragedies"*: King, "Love, Law, and Civil Disobedience," in King, *A Testament of Hope,* p. 45.

231 *"would break with communism"*: Ibid.

231 *"that capitalism has often left a gulf"*: King, *Where Do We Go?* in King, *A Testament,* pp. 629–630.

231 *"is found neither in traditional"*: Ibid., p. 630.

231 *Moreover King believed that unjust laws must be broken:* King, "Letter from Birmingham Jail," in King, *A Testament,* p. 293.

232 *Civil disobedience was not a wanton disregard:* King, *Trumpet of Conscience;* quoted in King, *A Testament,* pp. 647–648.

232 *civil disobedience was a hopeful social practice:* King, "Love, Law, and Civil Disobedience," in King, *A Testament,* p. 52.

233 *just law is a law that squares:* Ibid., p. 49. Also see King, "Letter from Birmingham Jail," in King, *A Testament,* pp. 293–294.

233 *somebody says that that does not mean anything to me:* King, "Love, Law, and Civil Disobedience," p. 49.

234 *individuals who stand up on the basis:* Ibid.

234 *Reed criticized liberals:* San Diego Union-Tribune, Oct. 6, 1995, pp. 1, 6, 7, 8.
235 *as abolitionism in the 1830s:* Ibid.
235 *"centerpiece" of the Christian Coalition's legislative agenda:* Los Angeles Times, Jan. 31, 1997, p. 22.
235 *"The Samaritan Project is a bold":* Ibid.; Mar. 1, 1997, B4.
235 *ease racial tension:* Ibid. (both articles in the previous note).
235 *"If we went out and talked about abortion":* Ibid., Mar. 21, 1997, B4.
236 *"window dressing":* Ibid., Jan. 31, 1997, p. 22.
236 *Jesse Jackson accused Reed:* Ibid., Mar. 1, 1997, B4.
236 *"The moment was so pregnant":* Ibid., Mar. 21, 1997, B4.
236 *"We in the black community":* Ibid., Jan. 31, 1997, p. 22.
236 *I draw much of my own inspiration:* Reed, Active Faith, pp. 280–281.
237 *the coalition's goal of securing government-supported:* Los Angeles Times, Jan. 31, 1997, p. 22.
237 *The coalition advocated a $500 tax credit:* Ibid., B4.
238 *founded upon the same:* Reed, Active Faith, p. 28.
238 *"always acknowledged that hearts and souls":* Ibid., pp. 270–271.
239 *"the vision and leadership":* Ibid., p. 57.
239 *just as he spoke as a black man:* Ibid., p. 64.
240 *were immeasurably greater than those taken:* To his credit, Reed concedes this point. He writes that "there is nothing like a crisp moral equivalence between the civil rights movement of the 1960s and the pro-life, pro-family movement of today. We can never know the suffering and outrages endured by those who struggled against racism. Some, like Mississippi NAACP leader Medgar Evers, lost their lives. Others were beaten, jailed, or fired from jobs, had their homes blown up or their children mowed down with fire hoses" (Reed, Active Faith, p. 64). It is unfortunate that such beliefs are not more widely shared or more broadly acted on in the crafting of conservative religious practice or political activism.
240 *I endorse it:* King, "Playboy Interview: Martin Luther King, Jr.," in King, A Testament, p. 373.
241 *often cite Martin Luther King and the civil rights movement:* Boston Globe, Oct. 28, 1988, p. 25; Los Angeles Times, Sept. 7, 1989, pt. 2, p. 1; San Diego Union-Tribune, Sept. 17, 1989, p. B10; Atlanta Journal-Constitution, Aug. 26, 1991, A13.
241 *to dramatize the plight of the unborn:* Terry, "Operation Rescue: The Civil-Rights Movement of the Nineties," Policy Review, 47, Winter 1989, pp. 82–83. I thank Ann Pellegrini for pointing out the use of King by the radical antiabortion movement.
241 *staging a series of blockades:* Boston Globe, Oct. 28, 1988, p. 25.
241 *confronted forces of oppression:* Los Angeles Times, Sept. 7, 1989, pt. 2, p. 1.
241 *"And what did these people have in common?":* Ibid.
241 *At a 1989 California antiabortion rally:* San Diego Union-Tribune, Sept. 17, 1989, p. B10.
242 *"acts of civil disobedience, which we call rescues":* Terry, "Operation Rescue," p. 82.
242 *"such as the Underground Railroad":* Ibid.
242 *by enlisting the black church leadership:* Ibid.
243 *"This is not a game":* San Diego Union-Tribune, Sept. 17, 1989, p. B10.
244 *the connection between European colonialism:* Noer, "Martin Luther King Jr. and the Cold War," p. 113.
244 *that has accounted for the new sense:* King, "The Rising Tide of Racial Consciousness," in King, A Testament, p. 146.
245 *"I am absolutely convinced":* Cited in Garrow, Bearing the Cross, p. 118.
245 *"The nations of Asia and Africa":* Noer, "Martin Luther King Jr. and the Cold War," p. 114. Also see King, "Letter from Birmingham City Jail," p. 293.
246 *"thrive on sneer and smear":* "Playboy Interview: Martin Luther King, Jr.," p. 362.

246 *"from the prodigious hilltops of New Hampshire"*: It is intriguing to consider the possibility that King was making a sly reference to Woody Guthrie's folk anthem, "This Land Is Your Land." Guthrie was writing for the Communist party's *Daily Worker* in the forties when he wrote the song. Its verses make references to "from California to the New York Island; from the Redwood Forest to the Gulf Stream Waters." King had already been deeply influenced by Pete Seeger's rendition of "We Shall Overcome," which he heard for the first time when the singer performed the song at the twenty-fifth anniversary celebration of the Highlander Folk School, which offers training sessions for activists (Garrow, *Bearing the Cross*, p. 98). At Highlander, Seeger, Zilphia Horton, Guy Carawan, and others "collected and adapted slave songs, gospel songs, folk songs, labor songs, and new songs, and taught them to the young activists" (Kasher, *The Civil Rights Movement*, p. 72). Given that Guthrie's song had filtered into progressive communities—labor, civil rights, and the like—it is reasonable to believe that King was familiar with it. Further, King had a keen ear for melodic phrases that evoke American patriotism. (We know, for instance, that King had pinched Archibald Carey's 1952 Republican Convention speech for his "I Have a Dream" peroration, which I am now suggesting was also influenced by Guthrie.) This is especially true when patriotism was claimed, challenged, and expanded by figures on the margins of American political life who, because of their leftist politics, were deemed by the right to be un-American. Given the similar sounds of Guthrie's verse and King's peroration, it is at least possible that King may have taken up the singer-songwriter's defiance of those reactionary forces that seek to define loyalty to America narrowly. This land is our land, too, Guthrie was saying, and was surely not the exclusive preserve of conservative forces. That is an idea with which King was profoundly sympathetic. For an explanation of Guthrie's song, see Seeger, *Where Have All the Flowers Gone?* I thank Robin D. G. Kelley for suggesting this line of interpretation.

246 *in a commencement address in 1961*: King, "The American Dream," p. 208.

246 *"American dream reminds us"*: Ibid.

246 *"sat down at lunch counters"*: King, "I See the Promised Land," p. 286.

247 *"be true to what"*: Ibid.

247 *"I'm not going anywhere"*: King, "Why Jesus Called a Man a Fool," in Carson and Holloran, eds., *A Knock at Midnight*, p. 154.

247 *"America is essentially a dream"*: King, "The American Dream," p. 208.

247 *"the true saviors of democracy"*: Ibid., p. 209.

247 *except, perhaps, Lincoln's*: Donald, *Lincoln*.

Chapter 12: "I Won't Have Any Money to Leave Behind"

249 *"I Won't Have Any Money to Leave Behind"*: "Drum Major Instinct," in King, *A Testament of Hope*, p. 267.

249 *one of the few places that accommodated black lodgers*: New York Times, Jul. 1, 1991, sec. A, p. 1.

249 *motel had languished for years*: Ibid.

249 *White businesses and foundations*: Ibid.

250 *"To not have this museum in Memphis"*: Jackson sermon, cited in ibid.

250 *"These people are playing with history"*: Ibid.

250 *"I think my grandfather and Martin Luther King"*: Ibid. The irony is that one scholar reported that he was "pitched out" of the King Center archives after Coretta Scott King attended a movie premiere for the film *Gandhi* and listened to the Mahatma's heirs "express shock that she was not selling access to the material." See *Boston Globe*, Jan. 15, 1995, p. 1.

250 *risen to royal status in black America*: I base this in part on the King family's frequent appearances as the first family of civil rights—and symbolically of black America as King's

heirs—in *Ebony Magazine*, the nation's leading black magazine. For a small sample, see *Ebony Magazine*, Jan. 1986 (*The Living King*: "The Real Meaning of the King Holiday," by Lerone Bennett, Jr., p. 31; "The Crusade for a King Holiday," p. 36; "Remarks of the President and Mrs. Coretta Scott King at the Signing Ceremony for Martin Luther King Jr. Holiday Legislation," p. 37; "In Memory of Martin Luther King Jr.," pp. 64–68, 70–72; "The World Honors MLK Through Stamps," p. 82–84; "Martin's Legacy," by Coretta Scott King, pp. 105–106, 108). Also see *Ebony Magazine*, Jan. 1995 (*New Generation of Kings Take Over*: "Dexter King Is Named CEO of the King Center," pp. 25–26, 28; "The Rev. Bernice A. King Continues the Family's Preaching Legacy," pp. 30, 32, 34), and *Ebony Magazine*, Jan. 1997 ("Dexter's Dream," pp. 27–28, 30). The *Boston Globe* says that the King family was "treated as sacrosanct for a generation" (*Boston Globe*, Jan. 15, 1995, p. 1), while *U.S. News & World Report* says that around "the world she [Coretta Scott King] is greeted like royalty (*U.S. News & World Report*, Jan. 16, 1995, pp. 54, 57). Former Black Panther and author Elaine Brown argues that the King family are the "heirs of the only black icon America acknowledges" (*Atlanta Journal-Constitution*, Jan. 26, 1997, p. 6B). Finally, Dexter King admitted that his family had been a "sacred" subject in Atlanta circles (*New York Times*, Aug. 19, 1997, p. 1). It may be argued that what was once true of Atlanta was also true for most of the country, especially in black communities. As *Ebony Magazine* proclaimed, "The Kings, after all, are Black America's royal family" ("Dexter's Dream," pp. 27–28).

251 *Coretta King sued Boston University*: *Boston Globe*, Apr. 21, 1993, p. 29, Apr. 22, 1993, p. 29; *Chicago Tribune*, Apr. 22, 1993, p. 4; *New York Times*, Apr. 30, 1993, p. A12.

251 *more than 100,000 King papers*: *Washington Post*, Mar. 12, 1988, p. C1; *Atlanta Journal-Constitution*, Apr. 28, 1993, p. A10.

251 *After six years of legal maneuvers*: *Washington Post*, Apr. 8, 1988, p. D1; *Boston Globe*, Apr. 21, 1993, p. 29, Apr. 21, 1993, p. 4, May 7, 1993, p. 1; *New York Times*, Apr. 30, 1993, p. A12.

251 *a countersuit by Boston University*: *Washington Post*, Apr. 8, 1988, p. D1; *San Diego Union-Tribune*, Apr. 7, 1988, p. A12.

251 *At the two-week trial, Coretta testified*: *Boston Globe*, Apr. 22, 1993, p. 4, Apr. 24, 1993, p. 27, Apr. 28, 1993, p. 26; *New York Times*, Apr. 30, 1993, p. A12.

251 *With their home being bombed*: *Boston Globe*, Apr. 21, 1993, p. 29, Apr. 22, 1993, p. 29; *Atlanta Journal-Constitution*, Apr. 28, 1993, p. A10; *Washington Post*, May 6, 1993, p. A3.

251 *Coretta argued that her husband had no intention*: *Boston Globe*, Apr. 28, 1993, p. A10, Apr. 29, 1993, p. 28, May 3, 1993, p. 13; *Atlanta Journal-Constitution*, Apr. 29, 1993, p. A10.

252 *preferring instead a Southern black institution*: In her lawsuit, Coretta King said that before his death, Martin Luther King expressed the desire that his papers be kept in an "institution dedicated to the education of black students, the preservation of black history and promotion of the civil rights movement" in the South, where the struggle for black equality had been largely fought. See *Boston Globe*, Apr. 21, 1993, p. 29. During cross-examination of Coretta King by a Boston University lawyer, she asserted that her husband had a "nagging conflict of whether he had done the right thing" in temporarily giving his papers to Boston University. In response, the lawyer, Earle Cooley, responded: "And that nagging conflict is whether he had done the right thing in placing them with his alma mater, a white university, as opposed to his undergraduate alma mater, a black university," a statement with which Coretta King agreed (*Boston Globe*, Apr. 28, 1993, p. 26). That assertion was not only a key to Coretta King's claim that her husband's papers should be returned to her in the South, but, as we shall later see in this chapter, it was one of the strongest arguments against the King family's subsequent move to sell the papers to a white institution outside the South. Also see *New York Times*, Apr. 30, 1993, p. A12.

252 *brusque demeanor, intemperate rhetoric, and demagogic style*: Giroux, *Fugitive Cultures*, pp. 7–8. Also see Wilkie, "Silber Style," *Boston Globe*, Oct. 14, 1990, p. 41.

252 *Silber testified that his concern:* Boston Globe, Apr. 28, 1993, p. 23.

252 *Coretta King's assertion that one of the reasons:* Ibid., May 1, 1993, p. 24, May 4, 1993, p. 21.

252 *"I pitched her a hardball":* Ibid., May 4, 1993, p. 21.

252 *"could work together":* Ibid., Apr. 28, 1993, p. 23.

252 *"cordial relationship":* Ibid.

252 *"no trace of anger or disappointment":* Ibid., May 4, 1993, p. 21.

252 *never reconcile their schedules in four years:* Ibid.

252 *"very, very hostile":* Ibid., Apr. 28, 1993, p. 23; Atlanta Journal-Constitution, Apr. 28, 1993, p. A2.

252 *Silber summarily dismissed:* Boston Globe, Apr. 28, 1993, p. 23.

252 *"that claim seriously in the absence":* Ibid., May 4, 1993, p. 21.

252 *"some strange reason":* Ibid.

253 *Coretta said Martin Luther King felt awkward:* Ibid., May 4, 1993, p. 21.

253 *a committee at SCLC to obtain the papers:* Ibid., Apr. 21, 1993, p. 29, Apr. 22, 1993, p. 29; Atlanta Journal-Constitution, Apr. 28, 1993, p. A2; New York Times, Apr. 30, 1993, p. A12; Washington Post, May 6, 1993, p. A3.

253 *But a lawyer for Boston University argued:* Atlanta Journal-Constitution, Apr. 28, 1993, p. A2.

253 *never mailed a letter:* Ibid.

253 *"Before I could finish":* Boston Globe, Apr. 28, 1993, p. 23.

253 *"very distressed":* Ibid., May 4, 1993, p. 21.

253 *"as if she didn't know I had it":* Ibid.

253 *When she claimed at trial:* Atlanta Journal-Constitution, Apr. 28, 1993, p. A2.

253 *"I still don't recall having seen":* Ibid.

253 *implied that Coretta King was lying:* As reported in Minneapolis's Star Tribune, an "attorney for Boston University stopped short of accusing Coretta Scott King . . . of lying but disputed her contestation that her husband wanted back 83,000 documents that he deposited at the school." *Minneapolis Star Tribune,* May 6, 1993, p. 7A. And Boston University lawyer Earle Cooley "asserted that it was Coretta King who changed her mind and asked to have the papers back." *Washington Post,* May 6, 1993, p. A3. (Of course, Silber had testified that he didn't believe King when she told him in 1985 that her husband wanted to have his papers returned to the South.) Although he contended that "this case is not about anybody lying," Cooley accused her of wish projection as he stated that the "case is about something both beautiful and perverse, the human condition . . . how easy it is to believe with your heart and soul that something is the truth because it is your desire." But as King attorney Rudolph Pierce rightly concluded in his closing argument to the jury, "To discount the evidence meant the jury would have to believe that not only Mrs. King, but also some of Rev. King's advisers, were lying." Boston Globe, May 6, 1993, p. 26.

253 *which included two blacks and a Latino:* Boston Globe, May 7, 1993, p. 1.

253 *voted ten to two in favor of Boston University:* Ibid.; Courier-Journal (Louisville, Kentucky), May 7, 1993, p. 2A; Boston Globe, May 8, 1993, p. 20.

253 *the copyright to her husband's papers:* Boston Globe, May 7, 1993, p. 1.

253 *She appealed to the state supreme judicial court:* Ibid., Apr. 13, 1995, p. 1; Fort Lauderdale Sun-Sentinel, Apr. 13, 1995, p. 3A. Before she could appeal to the supreme judicial court, Coretta Scott King had to file a motion for a "judgment notwithstanding the jury verdict," a request for the judge to set aside the jury verdict. Boston Globe, May 8, 1993, p. 20.

253 *"decision is tragic":* Boston Globe, Apr. 13, 1995, p. 1.

253 *"moral justice":* Ibid., May 7, 1993, p. 1.

254 *"in the real world it's a legal one":* Ibid., May 6, 1993, p. 26.

254 *"seems tragic that one would have to legally"*: Ibid., Apr. 22, 1993, p. 29.

254 *"It's really about ownership"*: Ibid., May 6, 1993, p. 1.

254 *"It's like saying the Pyramids"*: Ibid.

254 *"When you think about the civil rights struggle"*: Ibid.

254 *"is dedicated to keeping alive the work"*: Chronicle of Higher Education, July 20, 1988, p. A6.

254 *"center is a gold mine"*: Ibid.

254 *it holds the papers of the Congress*: Ibid.; New York Times, July 16, 1997, p. A10. The King Center also houses organizational records for the Coordinating Council of Community Organizations, 1964–1968; the Delta Ministry, 1963–1971; the Episcopal Society for Cultural and Racial Unity (ESCRU), 1959–1970; the Mississippi Freedom Democratic Party (MFDP), 1964–1965; the National Lawyers Guild (NLG), 1936–1968; and the United States National Students Association—Southern Project, 1957–1969.

255 *files collected by the FBI surveillance of King*: Chronicle of Higher Education, July 20, 1988, p. A6. The King Center also has an audiovisual and oral history collection that includes the Civil Rights Film Collection; the Civil Rights Oral History Collection; Conversations from Widespread Collection; the James Forman Collection; the Martin Luther King, Jr., Center Tape Collection; the Martin Luther King, Jr., Center Speaks Collection; the Anne Romaine Oral History Collection; the Donald H. Smith Oral History Collection; the Maggie Wanza Collection; the Wesleyan Tapes; and the Hosea Williams Collection.

255 *personal papers of civil rights veterans*: Ibid.; New York Times, July 16, 1997, p. A10. The King Center also holds the papers of J. T. Alexander, 1891–1960s; Randolph Battle, 1962–1968; Ben Brown, 1952–1970; Johnnie Carr, 1956–1979; Hazel Gregory, 1956–1965; and Howard Moore, 1964–1968.

255 *"King Papers Belong in the South"*: Atlanta Journal-Constitution, Apr. 28, 1993, p. A10.

255 *"it was never [King's] intent"*: Ibid.

255 *King was flattered by the offer*: Branch, Pillar of Fire, p. 305. Also see Boston Globe, Apr. 22, 1993, p. 29.

255 *Mays had refused to place King*: Ibid.

255 *So Mays claimed that he avoided*: Ibid.

255 *King was disappointed and insulted*: Ibid.

256 *"It's not a question of whether these papers"*: Ibid., May 6, 1993, p. 1.

256 *Only scholars with longstanding requests*: New York Times, Jul. 16, 1997, p. A10, Aug. 19, 1997, p. 1; Atlanta Journal, July 18, 1997, p. 3C.

256 *a request from former King Center archivist Louise Cook*: Boston Globe, May 1, 1993, p. 24.

256 *"substantial damage"*: Ibid.

256 *"a professional scandal"*: Ibid.

256 *"I didn't think, in good conscience"*: Ibid.

256 *"perfectly usable"*: Ibid.

257 *"This is about control"*: Ibid. Branch said that he was "hardly alone in wanting to sound a warning about the abuse of the control that the King family already has. If they gained control of all the papers, there's every reason to believe the monopoly would only get worse." Chronicle of Higher Education, May 19, 1993, p. A14. Later, Branch would complain that the writing of history "would grind to a halt" if the Kings exercised unreasonably strict control over their intellectual property, including King's written work and filmed speeches. New York Times, Jan. 15, 1997, p. A10.

257 *"no commercial or proprietary"*: Boston Globe, Jan. 15, 1997, p. 1.

257 *"I thought their demands for payment"*: New York Times, Aug. 19, 1997, p. 1.

257 *"It's a question of ethics"*: Boston Globe, May 3, 1993, p. 13.

257 *crown jewel*: Ibid.; Washington Post, May 6, 1993, p. A3.

257 *worth a mere eighteen thousand dollars: Boston Globe,* Apr. 21, 1993, p. 29. Boston University's reluctance to turn over the papers was certainly a measure of its investment over the years. Typically universities "spend hundreds of thousands of dollars on special collections—on building space to house the papers, acid-free folders and storage boxes, catalogues, and reference aides to assist scholars. The longer the papers are in one place, the greater the investment." *Boston Globe,* May 6, 1993, p. 13.

257 *"Coretta King failed to live up to pledges":* Although Coretta Scott King may have failed to keep her pledge to move papers from her home to the King Center in the 1970s and 1980s, many "of the documents have apparently been moved in recent years." *New York Times,* Aug. 19, 1997, p. 1.

258 *"Mrs. King always said to me": New York Times,* Aug. 19, 1997, p. 1.

258 *the King estate has recently decided to sell off: Houston Chronicle,* Jan. 20, 1997, p. 1; *New York Times,* July 16, 1997, p. A10; *Richmond Times Dispatch,* Aug. 17, 1997, p. A1.

258 *"someplace where proper care":* Ibid.

258 *Emory University, in making the same argument:* Rudolph P. Byrd, director of African-American Studies at Emory University, argued that "it would be unimaginable for them [the King papers] to be in any other location than the South. I think it would create a rupture in our collective memory that would have unknown and far-reaching consequences." *New York Times,* July 16, 1997, op cit.

258 *"Dexter King and I": Atlanta Journal-Constitution,* July 18, 1997, p. C3.

259 *"It's not a Southern situation for us": New York Times,* July 16, 1997, op cit.

259 *a leaky roof threatens:* Ibid., Aug. 19, 1997, p. 1.

259 *"these black kids killing each other": Atlanta Journal-Constitution,* op cit.

259 *Jones said that the papers:* Ibid.

259 *"My own personal opinion":* Ibid.

260 *"So this fear about the papers":* Ibid.

260 *"in principle":* Ibid.

260 *"I do not determine what is right and wrong":* King, "Remaining Awake Through a Great Revolution," in King, *A Testament,* p. 276.

260 *King family successfully litigated the violation: Washington Post,* Jan. 8, 1981, p. A18.

260 *legally established the King family's inheritance: Boston Globe,* Jan. 15, 1995, p. 1; *New York Times,* Jan. 15, 1997, p. A10.

260 *filed suit in Los Angeles Superior Court: Los Angeles Times,* Nov. 7, 1992, p. B8.

260 *They have waged legal war on companies: New York Times,* Jan. 15, 1997, p. A10.

261 *The King estate sued CBS:* Ibid., and Aug. 19, 1997, p. 1.

261 *five-part documentary:* Ibid., Jan. 15, 1997, p. A10.

261 *"Just as it is important to cover":* Ibid.

261 *copyright law makes an exception:* Ibid.

261 *the federal court decided in 1998: Jet,* May 31, 1999, p. 39.

261 *appealed the decision:* Ibid.

261 *sued USA Today: New York Times,* Jan. 15, 1997, p. A10; *Boston Globe,* Jan. 15, 1997, p. 1; *New York Times,* Aug. 19, 1997, p. 1.

261 *the King estate sent a letter threatening: Boston Globe,* Jan. 15, 1997, p. 1.

261 *A German television charged:* Ibid.

261 *"wanted to have $4,000":* Ibid.

261 *"viciously attack[ing]":* Ibid.

262 *King himself copyrighted his speech: New York Times,* Jan. 15, 1997, p. A10.

262 *"Dr. King had a literary agent":* Ibid.

262 *On October 3, 1963:* FBI files: Friedly and Gallen, *The FBI File,* pp. 172–173.

262 *"I get a fairly sizable but fluctuating":* "*Playboy* Interview: Martin Luther King," in King, *A Testament of Hope,* p. 371. Andrew Young had to defend King to critics who spread the rumor that King had cash stored away in a Swiss bank account. One such

critic was the FBI, and Young recalls what he said in defense of King. "It's just impossible that Martin Luther King is confiscating any money. . . . Virtually all the money we have in the organization is raised from his speeches and books anyway. This is how our salaries are paid. He doesn't even *take* a salary from SCLC, his only salary is from Ebenezer. Martin gave away the Nobel Prize money to SCLC and other civil rights organizations. He never has any money, he has to borrow money from his Daddy to pay his taxes every year. SCLC covers his expenses, and I can tell you just what they are, if you're interested. If he stays in a suite when he travels, it's usually the group he spoke for that paid for the suite. The idea of a secret bank account in Switzerland is totally ridiculous" (Young, *An Easy Burden*, p. 330).

262 *as the one it took against Blackside, Inc.:* Boston Globe, Jan. 15, 1995, p. 1.

263 *widely used in American classrooms:* Ibid.

263 *refrained from showing the series:* Ibid.

263 *Hampton offered the family $100,000:* Ibid.

263 *"an aggressive attempt to get":* Ibid.

263 *"had a chilling effect on Blackside's":* Ibid.

263 *an attack on his family:* Ibid.

263 *"our documentary was usurped":* Ibid.

263 *"were being sold at Blockbuster Video":* Ibid.

264 *an out-of-court settlement for what both figures:* Ibid.

264 *"regenerated Dr. King's role":* Ibid.

264 *the King family banned the National Park Service:* U.S. News & World Report, Jan. 5, 1995, p. 16, Jan. 16, 1995, pp. 54, 57; Boston Globe, Jan. 15, 1995, p. 1; Jet, Jan. 16, 1995, p. 12; Time, Jan. 16, 1995, p. 37; Richmond Times Dispatch, Aug. 17, 1997, p. A1; New York Times, Jan. 15, 1997, p. A10; New York Times, Aug. 19, 1997, p. 1.

264 *the third most popular historic attraction:* Time, Jan. 16, 1995, p. 37.

264 *alleviate the severe shortage of parking:* Ibid.

264 *the King family claims it was excluded:* Ibid.; Boston Globe, Jan. 15, 1995, p. 1.

265 *the visitor center would cut into the King family:* Jet, Jan. 16, 1995, p. 12; Time, Jan. 16, 1995, p. 37; New York Times, Aug. 19, 1997, p. 1.

265 *Dexter King consulted with Oppenheimer Capital:* Time, Jan. 16, 1995, p. 37.

265 *demanded the Park Service triple its annual:* Boston Globe, Jan. 15, 1995, p. 1; Richmond Times Dispatch, Aug. 17, 1997, p. A1.

265 *spread false stories:* Boston Globe, Jan. 15, 1995, p. 1.

265 *"trying to sell off the Historic District":* Ibid.

265 *"The same evil forces that destroyed":* Jet, Jan. 16, 1995, p. 12; Time, Jan. 16, 1995, p. 37; U.S. News & World Report, Jan. 16, 1995, pp. 54, 57.

265 *"I don't think there is this continued level":* Richmond Times Dispatch, Aug. 17, 1997, p. A1.

265 *visitor center would slash the crucial revenues:* U.S. News & World Report, Jan. 16, 1995, pp. 54, 57.

265 *even Interior Secretary Bruce Babbitt:* Ibid. and Jan. 9, 1995, p. 16.

266 *"None of us who marched with Dr. King":* Ibid.

266 *"up for sale like soap":* New York Times, Jan. 9, 1997, p. A14.

266 *"If the Park Service gets its way":* Time, Jan. 16, 1995, p. 37.

266 *"to annex this area to control":* Jet, Jan. 16, 1995, p. 12.

266 *it had earlier spied on him:* Atlanta Journal-Constitution, Mar. 22, p. A3, which alleges "that the U.S. Army spied on the late Dr. Martin Luther King Jr. and three generations of his family with everything from U-2 spy planes to Green Beret commando teams." Also see Garrow, *The FBI and Martin Luther King, Jr.;* Friedly and Gallen, *The FBI File;* McKnight, *The Last Crusade.*

266 *The Kings, by their own admission, were instrumental:* U.S. News & World Report, Jan. 16, 1995, pp. 54, 57. Also see Time, Jan. 16, 1995, p. 37.

267 *"If they are the repository"*: New York Times, Aug. 19, 1997, p. 1.

267 *"The center is not addressing"*: Ibid.

267 *"it is incumbent upon"*: Ibid.

267 *"high-handed, dictatorial and undemocratic"*: Boston Globe, Jan. 15, 1995, p. 1.

267 *"History is all right"*: Richmond Times Dispatch, Aug. 17, 1997, p. A1.

267 *"years of shortsighted leadership"*: Atlanta Journal-Constitution, Jan. 19, 1997, p. R5. (Also see New York Times, Aug. 19, 1997, p. 1; Boston Globe, Jan. 15, 1995, p. 1; Richmond Times Dispatch, Aug. 17, 1997, p. A1.) In a letter to the editor of the Atlanta Journal, former Black Panther and author Elaine Brown took strong issue with Tucker. She accused Tucker's "crusade against the family of Rev. Martin Luther King Jr." as "but fodder for racists. Disingenuously asking whether the words of King should belong to his family or history, she postured as the voice of history." Brown claimed that history's interests lie precisely in the King family's publishing all of King's words and that the "only genuine question here is the legal ownership of his intellectual property. The only response is King and his heirs." Brown also criticized Tucker's "ethnic shading" of the "spurious claims on King's words made just last week by the Atlanta Journal-Constitution on behalf of itself and other media, particularly CBS." Brown said this was little more than "fawning support of the established media's scheme to deny the King family its legitimate legacy so as to themselves exploit and profit from King's words." Brown concludes by comparing the Kings to the vaunted legacy of another legendary clan, the Kennedys. "Tucker assailed the King family, heirs of the only black icon America acknowledges, while she was silent on whether the 'legacy' of John F. Kennedy, for example, belongs to his family or history—a resounding silence, in light of the recent Sotheby's sale of Jacqueline Kennedy Onassis's property. Neither did Tucker call the Richard Nixon family to task—a glaring omission given that the so-called Nixon papers, documents from his presidency when he was on the public payroll, are still claimed by the Nixon estate" (Atlanta Journal-Constitution, Jan. 26, 1997, p. 6B). Brown raises some powerful issues, most of which I attempt to address in relation to King below. But a crucial distinction between King, and Kennedy and Nixon, is that King was a private citizen, while Kennedy and Nixon were elected officials. In this light, it might be argued that the King family has even more of a proprietary claim to King's intellectual property, since Kennedy and Nixon were politicians whose words belong to the public. By contrast, King's words belong in a private domain of private ownership. But there are at least two problems. First, as a private citizen, King was also a public figure whose words were shaped and shared in intimate contact with a variety of groups, organizations, and publics. This does not negate all, or even primary, claims to ownership of King's intellectual property by his heirs. But it does mitigate against assigning as the primary meaning of King's words a commercial interest that neglects their social context and public purposes. Of all private citizens with a public profile, King more than any other figure—including, perhaps, Kennedy and Nixon—"belongs" to the nation in precisely the way he sought to serve the public: as an instrument of liberation and enlightenment. In short, a consideration of the publicly useful functions of King's words should be a central feature in discussing "ownership" of King's intellectual property. His memory should not be divorced from his moral vision in deference to money. Second, King was most interested in preserving the precious principles of justice, freedom, and equality through the spoken word. His public performances and speech acts were aimed at bringing democracy more vividly into existence. Hence, the utility of his speech should be a significant means by which we characterize the ownership of King's words. By giving primacy to private ownership over public use, King's heirs threaten the very legacy they claim to protect.

267 *"are trying to polish and protect"*: Boston Globe, Jan. 15, 1995, p. 1.

268 *"We hardly see any of these people"*: Time, Jan. 16, 1995, p. 37.

268 *"we have seen no plans"*: Ibid.

268 *"that this [Park Service dispute] came up"*: Boston Globe, Jan. 15, 1995, p. 1.

268 *"The trouble with Mrs. King"*: U.S. News & World Report, Jan. 16, 1995, pp. 54, 57.

268 *Nelson Mandela, with whom she danced:* Ibid.

268 *as did President Clinton:* Ibid.

268 *"I believe the dream is still alive"*: Ibid.

268 *"This line about my family"*: Ibid.

268 *She accuses the park service:* Ibid.

269 *When checks poured into the SCLC:* Young, An Easy Burden, p. 478.

269 *largely insensitive to her need for help:* Ibid.

269 *There were a lot of contestants:* Ibid., pp. 478–479.

269 *"painful to see people that Martin nurtured"*: Ibid., p. 479.

270 *eventually grew to seventy employees:* New York Times, Oct. 23, 1994, p. 30, Nov. 26, 1994, p. A8, Aug. 19, 1995, p. 1; Time, Jan. 17, 1995, p. 37.

270 *nearly a million dollars in aid:* New York Times, Aug. 19, 1995, p. 1.

270 *the King Center ran a deep deficit:* Time, Jan. 17, 1995, p. 37; New York Times, Aug. 19, 1997, p. 1.

270 *"I was ready before"*: Ebony Magazine, Jan. 1995, p. 25.

270 *appointing them to a majority of the board's seats:* New York Times, Aug. 19, 1997, p. 1.

270 *engineered the early closing:* Ibid.

270 *streamline the King Center operations:* Ibid.

270 *he shifted the focus of the Center:* Ibid.

270 *created a separate unit:* New York Times, Aug. 19, 1997, p. 1.

270 *"We were not being very effective"*: Ibid.

271 *"cash-only business"*: Ibid.

271 *"I used to get knots in my stomach"*: Ibid.

271 *"Everybody for the most part"*: Ibid.

271 *"determined that the King Center"*: Atlanta Journal-Constitution, July 18, 1997, p. 3C.

271 *"would prefer the center become institutionalized"*: Ibid.

271 *"programming is very localized"*: Ibid.

271 *"new paradigm"*: Ibid.

271 *"I have never seen myself"*: New York Times, Aug. 19, 1997, p. 1.

272 *the King family has refused to lend it:* Ibid.

272 *out to protect Martin Luther King, Incorporated:* This notion on the surface is offensive to Dexter King, who, in defending his move to commercialize King's image, ironically calls on his father's own behavior to justify the King family ventures: "We have a responsibility to follow the conduct my father did. In his death, his work became so much more valuable, and the administration of that process is costly. But I don't believe we're blatantly commercializing the legacy. We're not starting a business called Martin Luther King Inc." Boston Globe, Jan. 15, 1995, p. 1.

272 *The family agreed to license merchandising:* Atlanta Journal-Constitution, Feb. 4, 1996, p. 6G.

272 *movie possibly directed by Oliver Stone:* Richmond Times Dispatch, Aug. 17, 1997, p. A1; New York Times, Aug. 19, 1997, p. 1.

272 *to pay the King estate 6 percent to 10 percent royalty:* Atlanta Journal-Constitution, Feb. 4, 1996, p. 6G.

272 *"high-quality and tasteful"*: Ibid.

272 *more than a thousand requests:* Ibid.

272 *"I want it clear that all of this"*: Ibid.

272 *(The younger King did, however, visit Graceland):* Richmond Times Dispatch, Aug. 17, 1997, p. A1.

272 *"We're going to start"*: Atlanta Journal-Constitution, Feb. 4, 1996, p. 6G.

273 *"You run the risk"*: Ibid.

273 *a 1997 blockbuster deal with Time Warner:* Reuters North American Wire, Jan. 8, 1997; *Augusta* (Georgia) *Chronicle,* Jan. 9, 1997, p. B6; *Los Angeles Times,* Jan. 9, 1997, p. E3; *New York Times,* Jan. 9, 1997, p. A14, Jan. 15, 1997, p. A10, Aug. 19, 1997, p. 1; *Richmond Times Dispatch,* Aug. 17, 1997, p. A1; *Publishers Weekly,* Jan. 13, 1997, p. 14.

273 *new books of King's writings:* See all works cited in previous note. See also Carson, ed., *The Autobiography of Martin Luther King, Jr.;* and Carson and Holloa, eds., *A Knock at Midnight.*

273 *"a national treasure":* Publishers Weekly, Jan. 13, 1997, p. 14.

273 *"a distinctive relationship":* Los Angeles Times, Jan. 9, 1997, p. E3; *Publishers Weekly,* Jan. 13, 1997, p. 14.

273 *"I don't think you've had":* New York Times, Jan. 9, 1997, p. A14.

273 *"Today is a great day for the legacy":* Ibid.; *Los Angeles Times,* Jan. 9, 1997, p. E3.

274 *"I think the family has some right":* New York Times, Jan. 15, 1997, p. A10.

274 *"What you see is more and more":* Richmond Times Dispatch, Aug. 17, 1997, p. A1.

274 *"He was far more universal in scope":* Ibid.

274 *Ford, British Petroleum, and Coca-Cola withdrew:* Ibid.

274 *"If people are going to exploit it":* Atlanta Journal-Constitution, Feb. 4, 1996, p. 6G.

274 *"People look with a jaundiced eye":* New York Times, Aug. 19, 1997, p. 1.

275 *"Martin had to spend most of his life":* Ibid., Jan. 15, 1997, p. A10; *Atlanta Journal-Constitution,* Feb. 4, 1996, p. 6G.

275 *he was accustomed to and avidly indulged:* Branch, "Uneasy Holiday," New Republic, Feb. 3, 1986, p. 26.

275 *His father, Martin Luther King, Sr.:* King and Riley, *Daddy King;* C. King, *My Life,* pp. 75–83; Lewis, *King,* pp. 6–11; Oates, *Let the Trumpet Sound,* pp. 3–9; Garrow, *Bearing the Cross,* pp. 32–35; Branch, *Parting the Waters,* pp. 34–59.

275 *Alfred Daniel Williams:* King and Riley, *Daddy King,* pp. 69, 70–71, 72, 75, 81–86, 89, 91, 100–101; C. King, *My Life,* p. 78; Lewis, *King,* pp. 4–5; Garrow, *Bearing the Cross,* pp. 32–33; Branch, *Parting the Waters,* pp. 30–40.

276 *"met a fine chick in Phila":* Carson, Luker, and Russell, eds., *The Papers of Martin Luther King, Jr.,* Vol. 1: *Called to Serve, January 1929–June 1951,* p. 161.

276 *"Yes, if you want to say":* "Drum Major Instinct," in Washington, ed., *A Testament of Hope,* p. 267. King's profound material sacrifice, in conjunction with the palpable danger he constantly confronted, drove Harry Belafonte to get life insurance for King's family. As Andrew Young says, Belafonte "was so concerned about the danger Martin was facing that after the Birmingham campaign he personally took out one-hundred-thousand-dollar life insurance policies on Martin for each of Martin's children. Stan Levison set up the policies and Harry paid the premiums. Harry knew that Martin had no money to leave the children if he were to be killed" (Young, *An Easy Burden,* p. 331).

276 *I believe as sincerely as I believe anything:* "Playboy Interview: Martin Luther King, Jr.," in Washington, ed., *A Testament of Hope,* p. 371.

278 *how disastrously things worked for Ralph Abernathy:* Fairclough, *To Redeem the Soul of America,* pp. 385–405; Abernathy, *And the Walls,* pp. 494–539, 579–586.

279 *Michael Jordan is the least likely of champions:* Naughton, *Taking to the Air;* Greene, *Hang Time;* Jordan, *For the Love of the Game;* Halberstam, *Michael Jordan.*

280 *"Because they are King's blood":* Richmond Times Dispatch, Aug. 17, 1997, p. A1.

280 *Prathia Hall:* Lischer, *The Preacher King,* p. 93. Hall has been hailed as one of the fifteen greatest black women preachers (in fact, she tied Carolyn Knight and Vashti McKenzie). See Kinnon, "Fifteen Greatest Black Women Preachers," p. 102.

281 *Archibald Carey:* Miller, *Voice of Deliverance,* pp. 146–148.

Chapter 13: "If I Have to Go Through This to Give the People a Symbol"

282 *"If I Have to Go Through This"*: Garrow, *Bearing the Cross*, p. 428.

282 *James Forbes*: Dyson, *Reflecting Black*, pp. 274–275; Kinnon, "Fifteen Greatest Black Preachers," p. 156.

282 *Charles Adams*: Kinnon, "Fifteen Greatest Black Preachers," p. 156.

282 *Frederick Sampson*: Ibid. Also see Dyson, *Between God and Gangsta Rap*, pp. 52, 131–132.

283 *"I was somewhat taken aback"*: Adams, "Faith Critiques Faith," sermon at Riverside Church, July 19, 1998.

283 *"They mandated"*: Ibid.

283 *"Now why did Ronald Reagan"*: Ibid.

284 *Denmark Vesey, Gabriel Prosser, Nat Turner*: Wilmore, *Black Religion and Black Radicalism*, pp. 79–98. Also see Turner, *The Confessions of Nat Turner*.

284 *Sojourner Truth, and Harriet Tubman*: Gilbert and Titus, *Narrative of Sojourner Truth*; Painter, *Sojourner Truth*; Bradford, *Harriet Tubman*; Conrad, *Harriet Tubman*.

284 *Frederick Douglass and Booker T. Washington*: Douglass, *Narrative of the Life of Frederick Douglass; My Bondage and Freedom,* and *The Life and Times of Frederick Douglass;* Washington, *Up from Slavery.*

284 *Henry Highland Garnett*: Wilmore, *Black Religion and Black Radicalism*, pp. 52, 62, 120, 199, 268.

284 *Henry McNeal Turner*: Ibid., pp. 149–157, 163–167, 198–199.

284 *Collective memory was a crucial means*: For work on collective memory, see Schwartz, "Social Change and Collective Memory," pp. 221–236; and Halbwachs, *The Collective Memory.*

284 *"the end of the Civil War"*: Foner, *Reconstruction*, pp. 78–79.

284 *"kept African-Americans outside the mainstream"*: Kamen, *Mystic Chords of Memory*, p. 13.

284 *"the mid-1880s onward"*: Ibid.

285 *It is not well to forget*: Douglass, cited in ibid., pp. 121–122.

286 *"a historical reenactment of the drama"*: Wiggins, *O Freedom*, p. 134.

286 *"second time in a little more than a century"*: Ibid.

286 *"their demands to have this date declared"*: Ibid.

286 *"blacks and whites, men and women"*: Ibid., pp. 134–135.

287 *"his presence is felt in pictures"*: Ibid., p. 135.

288 *"a thoroughly bad piece of legislation"*: Senate Committee on the Judiciary, and House Committee on Post Office and Civil Service, p. 34, cited in ibid., pp. 141–142.

288 *"not the caliber of person"*: Ibid., p. 142.

288 *"would be very costly"*: Ibid.

289 *The cost? What are the costs*: Ibid.

289 *"hundreds of years of economic"*: Ibid., p. 143.

289 *"there have been many black historical figures"*: Ibid., p. 147.

289 *"closely connected with the"*: Ibid.

289 *"collaborated intimately with the Communists"*: Ibid.

293 *"obviously prefer less threatening . . . depictions"*: Merelman, *Representing Black Culture*, p. 89.

293 *"thus help to project"*: Ibid.

293 *"little black resistance"*: Ibid.

293 *"leader of black resistance"*: Ibid., p. 88.

293 *To be sure, blacks as victims*: Ibid., p. 89.

294 *mass picketing, public protests*: Ibid., p. 91.

294 *racial progress was an inevitable feature*: Dyson, *Reflecting Black*, pp. 152–153.

294 *the point is to acknowledge the depth*: Dyson, *Race Rules*, esp. pp. 1–46, 185–195, 213–224.

295 *in the cultural consensus that was needed*: Weisbrot, "Celebrating Dr. King's Holiday," *New Republic*, Jan. 30, 1984, pp. 10–12, 15–16; Branch, "Uneasy Holiday," *New Republic*, Feb. 3, 1986, pp. 22, 24–27.

296 *"eventful" and "event-making"*: Hook, *The Hero in History*, p. 153.

296 *"the individual to whom we can justifiably"*: Ibid.

296 *"eventful man in history"*: Ibid., p. 154.

296 *"event-making man is an eventful man"*: Ibid.

296 *"a hero is great not merely in virtue"*: Ibid.

296 *"create an event the time"*: Bennett, *What Manner of Man*, p. 131.

296 *In Birmingham, King approached*: Ibid.

297 *with the exception of writers who are unearthing*: Dittmer, *Local People*; Chafe, *Civilities and Civil Liberties*; Carson, *In Struggle*; Morris, *Origins*; Payne, *I've Got the Light of Freedom*; Fairclough, *Race and Democracy*.

297 *SNCC organizers had been working in Albany*: Carson, *In Struggle*, pp. 56–65; Lewis, *Walking with the Wind*, pp. 182, 186–187, 191, 195, 210, 217.

297 *widely regarded as one of his greatest defeats*: Lewis, *King*, pp. 140–170; Oates, *Let the Trumpet Sound*, pp. 180–200; Fairclough, *To Redeem*, pp. 85–109; Garrow, *Bearing the Cross*, pp. 173–230; Branch, *Parting the Waters*, pp. 608, 631–632.

297 *"I don't think that anybody appreciates"*: Lewis, *Walking with the Wind*, p. 196.

298 *"I have always thought what is"*: Baker, "Developing Community Leadership," in Lerner, *Black Women*, p. 352.

298 *"strong people don't need strong leaders"*: Cantarow, *Moving the Mountain*, p. 351.

298 *I have always felt it was a handicap*: Baker, "Developing Community Leadership," p. 351.

298 *"cult of personality"*: Grant, *Baker*, p. 107.

298 *"our great leader"*: Ibid., 108.

298 *"Well, I can't help"*: Ibid.

299 *"I know that you would"*: Ibid., pp. 108–109.

299 *"did not envision the SCLC"*: Ibid., p. 117.

299 *"very noble concept"*: Lewis, *Walking with the Wind*, p. 189.

299 *"Anarchy and chaos"*: Ibid., p. 291.

299 *"democratic charisma"*: Wills, *Cincinnatus*, esp. pp. 1–84.

299 *SNCC was able to do more*: Carson, *In Struggle*; Fairclough, *To Redeem the Soul of America*.

299 *far less than local, largely anonymous*: Payne, *I've Got the Light of Freedom*, esp. pp. 265–283; Dittmer, *Local People*; Fairclough, *Race and Democracy*.

300 *there was a key difference between*: Moses, "Commentary," in Albert and Hoffman, eds., *We Shall Overcome*, pp. 73–74.

300 *Finding Dr. King to take the leadership*: Payne, *I've Got the Light of Freedom*, pp. 417–418.

301 *"the most perceptive King-centered studies"*: Carson, "Reconstructing the King Legacy: Scholars and National Myths," in Albert and Hoffman, eds., *We Shall Overcome*, p. 245.

301 *"the tendency of many Americans"*: Ibid.

301 *"I never thought of the movement"*: Moses, "Commentary," p. 76.

301 *"through that history of the movement"*: Ibid., p. 73.

301 *"trying to understand King"*: Ibid.

301 *"frustration with young people"*: Ibid.

301 *"interchangeable parts"*: Huggins, "Commentary," in Albert and Hoffman, eds., *We Shall Overcome*, p. 87.

301 *"just as the charismatic individual"*: Ibid., p. 92.

301 *"If it's misguided to wait"*: Ibid.

302 *"Fight on Amos"*: Burns, "From the Mountaintop," p. 16, n. 4.

302 *"You are becoming a prophet"*: Ibid.

302 *"I have longed for a Baptist"*: Ibid.

302 *"He who was nailed to the cross"*: Ibid.

303 *"You're a leader"*: Ibid.

303 *"if I had to die tomorrow"*: Cited in Garrow, "Martin Luther King, Jr., and the Spirit of Leadership," in Albert and Hoffman, eds., *We Shall Overcome*, p. 22.

303 *"I just want to do God's will"*: "I See the Promised Land," in King, *A Testament of Hope*, p. 286.

304 *"the movement made Martin"*: Garrow, *Bearing the Cross*, p. 625.

304 *But the Civil Rights Movement*: Lischer, *The Preacher King*, pp. 197–198.

305 *"injustice anywhere is a threat"*: "Letter from a Birmingham Jail," in King, *A Testament of Hope*, p. 290.

305 *"an inconvenient hero"*: Harding, *An Inconvenient Hero*.

306 *claim his brand of heroism*: for an incisive look at what King's heroism means in an era of expanded cultural definitions and expectations of heroism, see Julian Bond, "Remember the man and the hero, not just half the dream," in *Seattle Times*, April 4, 1993.

Epilogue: "Lil' Nigger, Just Where You Been?"

307 *"Lil' Nigger, Just Where You Been?"*: Young, *An Easy Burden*, p. 463.

307 *took his first bow on the national stage*: Hale, *Making Whiteness*, pp. 279, 283. Also see Oates, *Let the Trumpet Sound*, p. 11, and Branch, *Parting the Waters*, pp. 54–55.

307 *the film's black actors were barred*: Hale, *Making Whiteness*, p. 278.

307 *singing, if not the songs of Zion*: The singers, composed of the Ebenezer Baptist Church choir, sang four spirituals, with Mrs. King (Martin's mother) directing. The choir was dressed in aprons and "Aunt Jemima bandannas." Following their Monday performance, Martin Luther King, Sr., was reprimanded by the local Baptist minister's association, the Atlanta Baptist Minister's Union. King and his choir were taken to task for both their participation in a degrading segregated event and for partaking in a sinful occasion where drink and dance were featured, strong taboos in Baptist circles. See Branch, *Parting the Waters*, p. 55.

307 *"happy darky"*: Hale, *Making Whiteness*, p. 283.

308 *sue the hip-hop group Outkast*: *Jet*, Apr. 26, 1999, p. 24.

308 *"You have her name associated"*: Ibid.

308 *"inspired our music"*: Ibid.

308 *DiMaggio was quite peeved*: "Paul Simon, the Silent Superstar," *New York Times*, March 9, 1999, p. A23.

309 *"I understand that I am a symbol"*: Parks and Haskins, *Rosa Parks*, p. 185.

309 *"a victim of both the forces"*: King, *Stride Toward Freedom*, in Washington, ed., *A Testament*, p. 424.

309 *"spent much of her adult life"*: Payne, *I've Got the Light of Freedom*, p. 416.

310 *"but so many young people"*: Parks and Haskins, *Rosa Parks*, p. 170.

310 *They didn't know who I was*: Ibid.

Books

Abelove, Henry, et al. *Visions of History*. Manchester: Manchester University Press, 1983.

Abernathy, Ralph. *And the Walls Came Tumbling Down: An Autobiography*. New York: Harper & Row, 1989.

Abrahams, Roger D. *Deep Down in the Jungle: Negro Narrative Folklore from the Streets of Philadelphia*. Chicago: Aldine, 1970.

Albert, Robert J., and Hoffman, Ronald, eds. *We Shall Overcome: Martin Luther King Jr. and the Black Freedom Struggle*. New York: Pantheon Books, 1990.

Alexander, Frank, with Cuda, Heidi S. *Got Your Back: The Life of a Bodyguard in the Hardcore World of Gangster Rap*. New York: St. Martin's Press, 1998.

Anderson, Jervis. *Bayard Rustin: Troubles I've Seen*. New York: HarperCollins, 1996.

Ansbro, John J. *Martin Luther King, Jr.: The Making of a Mind*. Maryknoll, N.Y.: Orbis Books, 1982.

Ayres, Alex. *The Wisdom of Martin Luther King, Jr.: An A–Z Guide to the Ideas and Ideals of the Great Civil Rights Leader*. New York: Meridian, 1993.

Baldwin, James. *The Fire Next Time*. New York: Dial Press, 1963.

Baldwin, Lewis. *There Is a Balm in Gilead: The Cultural Roots of Martin Luther King, Jr*. Minneapolis: Fortress Press, 1991.

————. *To Make the Wounded Whole: The Cultural Legacy of Martin Luther King, Jr*. Minneapolis: Fortress Press, 1992.

Baldwin, Lewis, and Woodson, Aprille. *Freedom Is Never Free: A Biographical Portrait of E. D. Nixon, Sr*. Atlanta: Williams Printing Company, 1992.

Barrett, Michele. *The Politics of Truth: From Marx to Foucault*. Cambridge: Polity Press, 1991.

Barth, Karl. *Christ and Adam*. New York: Collier, 1992.

————. *The Word of God and the Word of Man*. Gloucester, Mass.: P. Smith, 1978.

Baugh, John. *Black Street Speech: Its History, Structure, and Survival*. Austin: University of Texas Press, 1983.

Beifuss, Joan Turner. *At the River I Stand: Memphis, the 1968 Strike, and Martin Luther King, Jr*. Brooklyn, N.Y.: Carlson Pub., 1989.

Bell, Daniel. *The Religious Right*. Garden City, N.Y.: Doubleday, 1964.

Bennett, Lerone. *What Manner of Man: A Biography of Martin Luther King, Jr*. Chicago: Johnson Pub. Co., 1968.

Bercovitch, Sacvan. *American Jeremiad*. Madison: University of Wisconsin Press, 1978.

Berlin, Ira. *Many Thousands Gone: The First Two Centuries of Slavery in North America*. Cambridge, Mass: Harvard University Press, 1998.

Berlin, Ira, et al. *Remembering Slavery: African Americans Talk About Their Personal Experiences of Slavery and Freedom*. New York: New Press, 1998.

Bernstein, Richard. *Dictatorship of Virtue: Multiculturalism and the Battle for America's Future*. New York: Knopf, 1994.

Billingsley, Andrew. *Might Like a River: The Black Church and Social Reform*. New York: Oxford University Press, 1999.

Black Public Sphere Collective, ed. *The Black Public Sphere: A Public Culture Book*. Chicago: University of Chicago Press, 1995.

Blassingame, John W. *Slave Community: Plantation Life in the Antebellum South.* New York: Oxford University Press, 1982.

Blauner, Bob. *Racial Oppression in America.* New York: Harper & Row, 1972.

Booth, William D. *The Progressive Story: New Baptist Roots.* St. Paul, Minn.: Braun Press, 1981.

Boulware, Marcus Hanna. *The Oratory of Negro Leaders, 1900–1968.* Westport, Conn.: Negro Universities Press, 1969.

Bowen, William G., and Bok, Derek. *The Shape of the River: Long-Term Consequences of Considering Race in College and University Admissions.* Princeton, N.J.: Princeton University Press, 1998.

Boyd, Todd. *Am I Black Enough for You? Popular Culture from the 'Hood and Beyond.* Bloomington: Indiana University Press, 1997.

Boyer, Horace. *How Sweet the Sound: The Golden Age of Gospel.* Montgomery: Black Belt Communications Group, 1995.

Bracey, John, et al. *Black Nationalism in America.* Indianapolis: Bobbs-Merrill, 1970.

Bradford, Sarah H. *Harriet Tubman: The Moses of Her People.* New Jersey: Citadel Press, 1974.

Branch, Taylor. *Parting the Waters: America in the King Years, 1954–63.* New York: Simon & Schuster, 1988.

———. *Pillar of Fire: America in the King Years, 1963–65.* New York: Simon & Schuster, 1998.

Brink, William, and Harris, Louis. *Black and White: A Study of U.S. Racial Attitudes Today.* New York: Simon & Schuster, 1967.

———. *The Negro Revolution in America: What Negroes Want, Why and How They Are Fighting, Whom They Support, What Whites Think of Them and Their Demands.* New York: Simon & Schuster, 1964.

Brown, Cecil. *Coming Up Down Home: A Memoir of Southern Childhood.* Hopewell, N.J.: Ecco Press, 1993.

Buckley, William F. *Redhunter: A Novel Based on the Life of Joe McCarthy.* Boston: Little, Brown, 1999.

Burns, Stewart, ed. *Daybreak of Freedom: The Montgomery Bus Boycott.* Chapel Hill: University of North Carolina Press, 1997.

Cabral, Amilcar. *Unity and Struggle: Speeches and Struggle.* New York: Monthly Review Press, 1979.

Cahn, Steven M., ed. *The Affirmative Action Debate.* New York: Routledge, 1995.

Caldwell, Erskine, and Bourke-White, Margaret. *You Have Seen Their Faces.* Athens, Ga.: University Press of Georgia, 1995.

Cantarow, Ellen. *Moving the Mountain: Women Working for Social Change.* New York: Feminist Press, 1981.

Carson, Clayborne, and Holloran, Peter, eds. *A Knock at Midnight: Inspiration from the Great Sermons of Martin Luther King, Jr.* New York: Intellectual Properties Management in Association with Warner Books, 1998.

Carson, Clayborne, ed. *The Papers of Martin Luther King, Jr. Vol. 1: Called to Serve, January 1929–June, 1951.* Berkeley: University of California Press, 1992–.

———, ed. *The Papers of Martin Luther King, Jr. Vol. 2: Rediscovering Precious Values, July 1951–November 1955.* Berkeley: University of California Press, 1992–.

———, ed. *The Papers of Martin Luther King, Jr. Vol. 3: Birth of a New Age, December, 1955–December, 1956.* Berkeley: University of California Press, 1992–.

———. *In Struggle: SNCC and the Black Awakening of the 1960s.* Cambridge, Mass.: Harvard University Press, 1981.

Chafe, William. *Civilities and Civil Rights: Greensboro, North Carolina, and the Black Struggle for Freedom.* New York: Oxford University Press, 1980.

Churchill, Ward, and Vander Wall, Jim. *Agents of Repression: The FBI's Secret Wars Against the Black Panther Party and the American Indian Movement.* Boston: South End Press, 1988.

Cimbala, Paul A., and Himmelberg, Robert F., eds. *Historians and Race: Autobiography and the Writing of History.* Bloomington: Indiana University Press, 1996.

Clark, Kenneth. *King, Malcolm, Baldwin: Three Interviews.* Middletown, Conn.: Wesleyan University Press, 1985.

Clark, Septima Poinsette. *Ready from Within: Septima Clark and the Civil Rights Movement.* Edited, with an introduction, by Cynthia Stokes Brown. Navarro, Calif.: Wild Trees Press, 1986.

Clegg, Claude Andrew. *An Original Man: The Life and Times of Elijah Muhammad.* New York: St. Martin's Press, 1997.

Colaiaco, James A. *Martin Luther King, Jr.: Apostle of Militant Nonviolence.* New York: St. Martin's Press, 1988.

Colburn, David R. *Racial Change and Community Crisis: St. Augustine, Florida, 1877–1980.* New York: Columbia University Press, 1985.

Collins, Patricia Hill. *Black Feminist Thought: Knowledge, Consciousness, and the Politics of Empowerment.* Boston: Unwin Hyman, 1990.

Cone, James H. *Martin and Malcolm and America: A Dream or a Nightmare.* Maryknoll, N.Y.: Orbis, 1991.

———. *Risks of Faith: The Emergence of Black Theology of Liberation 1968–1998.* Boston: Beacon Press, 1999.

———. *The Spirituals and the Blues: An Interpretation.* New York: Seabury Press, 1972.

Cone, James H., and Wilmore, Gayroud S., eds. *Black Theology: A Documentary History.* Maryknoll, N.Y.: Orbis Books, 1993.

Conrad, David Eugene. *The Forgotten Farmers: The Story of Sharecroppers in the New Deal.* Urbana: University of Illinois Press, 1965.

Conrad, Earl. *Harriet Tubman.* Washington, D.C.: Associate Publishers, 1943.

Cook, Anthony E. *The Least of These: Race, Law, and Religion in American Culture.* New York: Routledge, 1997.

Coontz, Stephen. *The Way We Never Were: American Families and the Nostalgia Trap.* New York: Basic Books, 1992.

Cose, Ellis. *The Rage of a Privileged Class.* New York: Basic, 1993.

Crawford, Vicki L., et al.. *Women in the Civil Rights Movement: Trailblazers and Torchbearers, 1941–1965.* Brooklyn, N.Y.: Carlson Pub. Co., 1990.

Curry, George, ed. *The Affirmative Action Debate.* Reading, Mass.: Addison-Wesley, 1996.

Datcher, Michael, and Alexander, Kwame. *Tough Love: The Life and Death of Tupac Shakur, Cultural Criticism and Familial Observations.* Alexandria, Va.: Alexander Pub. Group, 1997.

Davis, Angela. *Angela Y. Davis Reader.* Edited by Joy James. Malden, MA: Blackwell, 1998.

Davis, Gerald. *I Got the Word in Me and I Can Sing It, You Know: A Study of the Performed African-American Sermon.* Philadelphia: University of Pennsylvania Press, 1985.

Davis, Mike. *City of Quartz: Excavating the Future in Los Angeles.* London: Verso, 1990.

Dees, Morris, and Corcoran, James. *Gathering Storm: America's Militia Threat.* New York: Harper-Collins, 1996.

Delany, Samuel. *The Motion of Light in Water: Sex and Science Fiction Writing in the East Village, 1957–1965.* New York: Arbor House/William Morrow, 1988.

Dent, Gina, ed. *Black Popular Culture.* Seattle, Wash.: Bay Press, 1992.

Dittmer, John. *Local People: The Struggle for Civil Rights in Mississippi*. Urbana: University of Illinois Press, 1994.

Donald, David Herbert. *Lincoln*. New York: Simon & Schuster, 1995.

Dorrien, Gary. *The Democratic Socialist Vision*. Totowa, N.J.: Rowman & Littlefield, 1986.

Douglass, Frederick. *The Life and Writings of Frederick Douglass*, vol. II, *Pre–Civil War Decade, 1850–1860*. Edited by Philip Foner. New York: Industrial Publishers, 1950.

Drake, St. Clair, and Cayton, Horace. *Black Metropolis: A Study of Negro Life in a Northern City*. New York: Harcourt, Brace, 1945.

Duberman, Martin. *Cures: A Gay Man's Odyssey*. New York: Dutton, 1991.

———. *Paul Robeson*. New York: Knopf, 1988.

Du Bois, W.E.B. *W.E.B. Du Bois, A Reader: 1868–1963*. Edited by David Levering Lewis. New York: H. Holt, 1995.

———. *The Souls of Black Folk*. New York: Modern Library, 1996.

———. *W.E.B. Du Bois Speaks: Speeches and Addresses*, vol. 1 (1970), *1890–1919*, vol. 2 (1977), *1920–1963*. Edited by Philip S. Foner. New York: Pathfinder Press.

Dyson, Michael Eric. *Reflecting Black: African-American Cultural Criticism*. Minneapolis: University of Minnesota Press, 1993.

———. *Making Malcolm: The Myth and Meaning of Malcolm X*. New York: Oxford University Press, 1995.

———. *Between God and Gangsta Rap: Bearing Witness to Black Culture*. New York: Oxford University Press, 1996.

———. *Race Rules: Navigating the Color Line*. Reading, Mass.: Addison-Wesley, 1996.

Early, Gerald. *One Nation Under a Groove: Motown and American Culture*. Hopewell, N.J.: Ecco Press, 1995.

Ellison, Ralph. *The Collected Essays of Ralph Ellison*. Edited, with an introduction, by John F. Callahan. New York: Modern Library, 1995.

Epstein, Benjamin R., and Forster, Arnold. *The Radical Right: Report on the John Birch Society and Its Allies*. New York: Vintage Books, 1967.

Eze, Emmanuel Chukwudi. *Race and the Enlightenment*. Cambridge, Mass.: Blackwell, 1997.

Ezorsky, Gertrude. *Racism and Justice: The Case for Affirmative Action*. Ithaca: Cornell University Press, 1991.

Fairclough, Adam. *To Redeem the Soul of America: The Southern Christian Leadership Conference and Martin Luther King, Jr.* Athens: University of Georgia Press, 1987.

———. *Race and Democracy: The Civil Rights Struggle in Louisiana, 1915–1972*. Athens: University of Georgia Press, 1995.

Falwell, Jerry. *Strength for the Journey*. New York: Simon & Schuster, 1987.

Fields, Uriah J. *The Montgomery Story: The Unhappy Effects of the Montgomery Bus Boycott*. New York: Exposition Press, 1959.

Fisher, Miles Mark. *Negro Slave Songs in the United States*. New York: Citadel Press, 1963.

Franklin, C. L. *Give Me This Mountain: Life History and Selected Sermons*. Edited by Jeff T. Titon. Champaign, Ill.: University of Illinois Press, 1989.

Franklin, Robert M. *Another Day's Journey: Black Churches Confronting the American Crisis*. Minneapolis: Ausburg Fortress Publishers, 1997.

Frazier, Edward Franklin. *The Negro Church in America*. New York: Schocken Books, 1964.

Frey, Sylvia R. *Water from the Rock: Black Resistance in a Revolutionary Age*. Princeton, N.J.: Princeton University Press, 1991.

Frey, Sylvia, and Wood, Betty. *Come Shouting to Zion: African-American Protestantism in the American South and British Caribbean to 1830*. Chapel Hill: University of North Carolina Press, 1998.

Friedly, Michael and Gallen, David. *Martin Luther King, Jr.: The FBI File*. New York: Carroll & Graf, 1993.

Fulop, Timothy E., and Raboteau, Albert J., eds. *African-American Religion: Interpretive Essays in History and Culture*. New York; London: Routledge, 1997.

Gans, Herbert. *The War Against the Poor: The Underclass and Antipoverty Policy*. New York: Basic Books, 1996.

Garrow, David J. *Protest at Selma: Martin Luther King, Jr., and the Voting Rights Act of 1965*. New Haven, Conn.: Yale University Press, 1978.

———. *The FBI and Martin Luther King, Jr.: From "Solo" to Memphis*. New York: Norton, 1981.

———. *Bearing the Cross: Martin Luther King, Jr. and the Southern Christian Leadership Conference*. New York: Random House, 1986.

———, ed. *The Walking City: The Montgomery Bus Boycott, 1955–56*. Brooklyn, N.Y.: Carlson Pub., 1986.

Gates, Henry Louis. *The Signifying Monkey: A Theory of African-American Literary Criticism*. New York: Oxford University Press, 1988.

Genovese, Eugene. *The Southern Front: History and Politics in the Cultural War*. Columbia: University of Missouri Press, 1995.

George, Nelson. *Where Did Our Love Go? The Rise and Fall of Motown Sound*. New York: St. Martin's Press, 1985.

———. *Hip-Hop America*. New York: Viking, 1998.

Giddings, Paula. *When and Where I Enter: The Impact of Black Women on Race and Sex in America*. New York: Morrow, 1984.

Gilbert, Olive, and Titus, Frances W. *Narrative of Sojourner Truth*. New York: Arno Press, 1968.

Giroux, Henry. *Fugitive Cultures: Race, Violence and Youth*. New York: Routledge, 1996.

Gitlin, Todd. *The Twilight of Common Dreams: Why America Is Wracked by Culture Wars*. New York: H. Holt, 1995.

Golden, Thelma, ed. *Black Male: Representations of Masculinity in Contemporary American Art*. New York: Whitney Museum of American Art, 1994.

Goodwin, Marvin E. *Black Migration in America from 1915 to 1960: An Uneasy Exodus*. Lewiston, Me.: E. Mellen Press, 1990.

Gordy, Berry. *To Be Loved: The Music, the Magic, the Memories of Motown: An Autobiography*. New York: Warner Books, 1994.

Graetz, Robert S. *Montgomery: A White Preacher's Memoir*. Minneapolis: Augsburg Fortress Publishers, 1991.

Graham, Maryemma, and Singh, Amritjit., eds. *Conversations with Ralph Ellison*. University Press of Mississippi, 1995.

Grant, Joanne. *Ella Baker: Freedom Bound*. New York: Wiley, 1998.

Gray, Fred D. *Bus Ride to Justice: Changing the System by the System, the Life and Work of Fred D. Gray*. Montgomery, Ala.: Black Belt Communications Group, 1995.

Griffin, Farah Jasmine. *Who Set You Flowin'? The African-American Migration Narrative*. New York: Oxford University Press, 1995.

Groh, George W. *The Black Migration: The Journey to Urban America*. New York: Weybright and Talley, 1972.

Grossman, Richard. *Land of Hope: Chicago, Black Southerners, and the Age of Migration*. Chicago: University of Chicago Press, 1989.

Guinier, Lani. *The Tyranny of the Majority: Fundamental Fairness in Representative Democracy*. New York: Free Press, 1994.

Guralnick, Peter. *Sweet Soul Music: Rhythm and Blues and the Southern Dream of Freedom.* New York: Harper & Row, 1986.

Halberstam, David. *The Children.* New York: Random House, 1998.

———. *The Fifties.* New York: Villard Books, 1993.

Halbwachs, Maurice. *On Collective Memory.* Translated from French by J. Ditter, Jr. and Vida Yazdi Ditter. New York: Harper Colophon, 1980.

Hale, Grace Elizabeth. *Making Whiteness: The Culture of Segregation in the South, 1890–1940.* New York: Pantheon Books, 1998.

Hamilton, Charles V. *The Black Preacher in America.* New York: Morrow, 1972.

Hampton, Henry, and Fayer, Steve, eds. *Voices of Freedom: An Oral History of the Civil Rights Movement from the 1950s through the 1980s.* New York: Bantam Books, 1990.

Harding, Vincent. *Martin Luther King, the Inconvenient Hero.* Maryknoll, N.Y.: Orbis Books, 1996.

Harrington, Michael. *The Other America: Poverty in the United States.* New York: Macmillan, 1962.

Hegel, George Wilhelm Friedrich. *Hegel's Logic.* Translated by William Wallace and John Findlay. Oxford: Oxford University Press, 1975.

———. *Hegel's Science of Logic.* Translated by Arnold Miller. London: Allen & Unwin, 1969.

———. *The Philosophy of History.* Translated by J. Sibree, 1899. New York: Dover, 1956.

———. *Hegel's Phenomenology of Spirit.* Translated by Arnold Miller. Oxford: Oxford University Press, 1977.

Heilbut, Anthony. *The Gospel Sound: Good News and Bad Times.* New York: Limelight Editions, 1985.

Herrnstein, Richard J., and Murray, Charles. *The Bell Curve: Intelligence and Class Structure in American Life.* New York: Free Press, 1994.

Hicks, John D. *Evil and the God of Love.* San Francisco: Harper, 1978.

Higginbotham, Evelyn Brooks. *Righteous Discontent: The Women's Movement in the Black Baptist Church, 1880–1920.* Cambridge, Mass.: Harvard University Press, 1993.

Hildebrand, Reginald Francis. *The Times Were Strange and Stirring: Methodist Preachers and the Crisis of Emancipation.* Durham, N.C.: Duke University Press, 1995.

Hine, Darlene Clark. *Hine Sight: Black Women and the Re-Construction of American History.* Brooklyn, N.Y.: Carlson Pub., 1994.

Hobsbawm, Eric. *Primitive Rebels: Studies in Archaic Forms of Social Movements in the 19th and 20th Centuries.* New York: Praeger, 1953.

———. *Bandits.* New York: Delacorte Press, 1963.

Honey, Michael. *Southern Labor and Black Civil Rights: Organizing Memphis Workers, 1929–1955.* Champaign: University of Illinois Press, 1993.

Hook, Sidney. *The Hero in History: A Study in Limitations and Possibility.* New York: The John Day Co., 1943.

hooks, bell. *Ain't I a Woman? Black Women and Feminism.* Boston: South End Press, 1981.

Hoover, J. Edgar. *Masters of Deceit.* Cutchogue: Bucanner Books, 1994.

Horne, Gerald. *Black Liberation/Red Scare: Ben Davis and the Communist Party.* Newark, Del.: University of Delaware Press, 1994.

———. *Fire This Time: The Watts Uprising in the 1960s.* Charlottesville: University Press of Virginia, 1995.

Howard-Pitney, David. *Afro-American Jeremiad: Appeals for Justice in America.* Philadelphia: Temple University Press, 1990.

Hughes, Langston. *The Ways of White Folks.* New York: Knopf, 1947.

Jacoby, Russell, and Glauberman, Naomi, eds. *The Bell Curve Debate: History, Documents, Opinions.* New York: New York Times Books, 1995.

Jacoby, Tamar. *Someone Else's House: America's Unfinished Struggle for Integration.* New York: Free Press, 1998.

James, Joy. *Transcending the Talented Tenth: Black Leaders and American Intellectuals.* New York: Routledge, 1997.

Jennings, Peter, and Brewster, Todd. *The Century.* New York: Doubleday, 1998.

Jensen, Arthur R. *Genetics and Education.* London: Methuen, 1972.

———. *Bias in Mental Testing.* New York: Free Press, 1980.

———. *Straight Talk About Mental Tests.* New York: Free Press, 1981.

Johnson, Lyndon B. *Vantage Point: Perspectives of the Presidency, 1963–1969.* New York: Holt, Rinehart, and Winston, 1971.

Jones, Jacqueline. *Labor of Love, Labor of Sorrow: Black Women, Work, and the Family from Slavery to the Present.* New York: Basic Books, 1985.

Jones, William R. *Is God a White Racist? A Preamble to Black Theology.* Boston: Beacon Press, 1998.

Kammen, Michael. *Mystic Chords of Memory: The Transformation of Tradition in American Culture.* New York: Knopf, 1991.

Kasher, Stephen. *The Civil Rights Movement: A Photographic History, 1954–1968.* New York: Abbeville Press, 1996.

Kelley, Robin D. G. *Hammer and Hoe: Alabama Communists During the Great Depression.* Chapel Hill: University of North Carolina Press, 1990.

———. *Race Rebels: Culture, Politics, and the Black Working Class.* New York: Free Press, 1994.

———. *Yo' Mama's Disfunktional! Fighting the Culture Wars in Urban America.* Boston: Beacon Press, 1997.

Kester, Howard. *Revolt Among the Sharecroppers.* New York: Covici, Friede, 1936.

King, Coretta Scott. *My Life with Martin Luther King, Jr.* New York: Holt, Rinehart, and Winston, 1969.

King, Martin Luther, Jr. *Stride Toward Freedom: The Montgomery Story.* New York: Harper, 1958.

———. *Strength to Love.* New York: Harper & Row, 1963.

———. *Why We Can't Wait.* New York: New American Library, 1964.

———. *Where Do We Go from Here: Chaos or Community?* New York: Harper & Row, 1967.

———. *Trumpet of Conscience.* New York: Harper & Row, 1968.

———. *The Words of Martin Luther King, Jr.* Selected by Coretta Scott King. New York: Newmarket Press, 1983.

———. *A Testament of Hope: The Essential Writings of Martin Luther King, Jr.* Edited by James Melvin Washington. New York: Harper & Row, 1986.

———. *Autobiography of Martin Luther King, Jr.* Edited by Clayborne Carson. New York: Warner Books, 1998.

King, Martin Luther, Sr., with Clayton Riley. *Daddy King: An Autobiography.* New York: William Morrow, 1980.

King, Mary. *Freedom Song: A Personal Story of the 1960s Civil Rights Movement.* New York: Morrow, 1987.

King, Richard H. *A Southern Renaissance: The Cultural Awakening of the American South, 1930–1955.* New York: Oxford University Press, 1982.

———. *Civil Rights and the Idea of Freedom.* New York: Oxford University Press, 1992.

Kolb, David. *The Critique of Pure Modernity: Hegel, Heidegger, and After.* Chicago: University of Chicago Press, 1986.

Kushner, Harold S. *When Bad Things Happen to Good People*. New York: Simon & Schuster, 1983.

Lasch, Christopher. *The True and Only Heaven: Progress and Its Critics*. New York: Norton, 1991.

Lawrence, Charles R., and Matsuda, Mari J. *We Won't Go Back: Making the Case for Affirmative Action*. Boston: Houghton Mifflin, 1997.

Lemann, Nicholas. *The Promised Land: The Great Black Migration and How It Changed America*. New York: Knopf, 1991.

Lentz, Richard. *Symbols, the News Magazines, and Martin Luther King*. Baton Rouge: Louisiana State University Press, 1990.

Lerner, Gerda. *Black Women in White America: A Documentary History*. New York: Pantheon Books, 1972.

Levi, Peter. *Tennyson*. London: Macmillan, 1993.

Levine, Lawrence. *Black Culture and Black Consciousness: Afro-American Folk Thought from Slavery to Freedom*. New York: Oxford University Press, 1977.

Lewis, David Levering. *King: A Critical Biography*. New York: Praeger, 1970.

———. *W. E. B. Du Bois: Biography of a Race, 1868–1919*. New York: H. Holt, 1993.

Lewis, John, with Michael D' Orso. *Walking with the Wind: A Memoir of the Movement*. New York: Simon & Schuster, 1998.

Lewis, Sinclair. *Elmer Gantry*. New York: Harcourt, Brace, 1927.

Lifton, Robert Jay. *History and Human Survival: Essays on the Young and Old, Survivors and the Dead, Peace and War, and on Contemporary Psychohistory*. New York: Random House, 1961.

Lincoln, C. Eric, ed. *Martin Luther King, Jr.: A Profile*. New York: Hill & Wang, 1970.

Lincoln, C. Eric, and Mamiya, Lawrence. *The Black Church in the African-American Experience*. Durham, N.C.: Duke University Press, 1990.

Lind, Michael. *The Next American Nation: The New Nationalism and the Fourth American Revolution*. New York: Free Press, 1995.

Lischer, Richard. *The Preacher King: Martin Luther King, Jr. and the Word That Moved America*. New York: Oxford University Press, 1995.

Logevall, Fredrik. *Choosing War: The Lost Chance for Peace and Escalation of War in Vietnam*. Berkeley, Calif.: University of California Press, 1999.

Lyman, Darryl. *Great African-American Women*. Middle Village: Jonathon David Pub., 1973.

MacIntyre, Alasdair. *After Virtue: A Study in Moral Theory*. Notre Dame, Ind.: University of Notre Dame Press, 1984.

MaClear, Michael. *The Ten Thousand Day War: Vietnam, 1945–1975*. New York: Avon, 1981.

Malcolm X, with Haley, Alex. *The Autobiography of Malcolm X*. New York: Ballantine Books, 1965.

———. *The End of White World Supremacy: Four Speeches*. Edited by Benjamin Goodman. New York, Merlin House, 1971.

———. *February 1965: The Last Speeches*. Edited by Steve Clark. New York: Pathfinder Press, 1992.

Males, Mike. *Framing Youth: Ten Myths About the Next Generation*. Monroe, Me.: Common Courage Press, 1998.

———. *The Scapegoat Generation: America's War on Adolescents*. Monroe, Me.: Common Courage Press, 1996.

Marable, Manning. *Black Leadership*. New York: Columbia University Press, 1998.

———. *Race, Reform, and Rebellion*. Jackson, Miss.: University Press of Mississippi, 1991.

———. *Speaking Truth to Power: Essays on Race, Resistance, and Radicalism*. Boulder, Colo.: Westview Press, 1999.

Marqusee, Mike. *Redemption Song: Muhammad Ali and the Spirit of the Sixties*. London: Verso Press, 1999.

Marx, Karl, and Engels, Friedrich. *The Communist Manifesto*. Edited with an introduction by David McLellan. Oxford; New York: Oxford University Press, 1998.

———. *On Religion*. New York: Schocken Books, 1964.

Maultsby, Eileen. *The Black Christian Worship Experience*. Atlanta: Journal of the Interdenominational Theological Center, 1992.

Mays, Benjamin E. *Born to Rebel: An Autobiography*. Athens: University of Georgia Press, 1987.

———. *Disturbed About Man*. Richmond, Va.: John Knox Press, 1969.

———. *The Negro's God, as Reflected in His Literature*. New York: Russell and Russell, 1968.

McCormick, John. *George Santayana: A Biography*. New York: Knopf, 1987.

McKnight, Gerald. *The Last Crusade: Martin Luther King, Jr., the FBI, and the Poor People's Campaign*. Boulder, Colo.: Westview Press, 1998.

McNamara, Robert S., Blight, James, and Brigham, Robert, with Thomas Biersteker and Col. Herbert Schandler. *Argument Without End: In Search of Answers to the Vietnam Tragedy*. New York: Public Affairs, 1999.

Merelman, Richard M. *Representing Black Culture: Racial Conflict and Cultural Politics in the United States*. New York: Routledge, 1995.

Miller, Keith D. *Voice of Deliverance: The Language of Martin Luther King, Jr., and Its Sources*. New York: Free Press, 1992.

Mills, Kay. *This Little Light of Mine: The Life of Fannie Lou Hamer*. New York: Dutton, 1993.

Milton, John. *Paradise Lost*. Edited by James Robert Boyd. New York: A. S. Barnes & Co., 1856.

Mitchell, Henry. *Black Preaching*. Philadelphia: Lippincott, 1970.

Morris, Aldon. *Origins of the Civil Rights Movement: Black Communities Organizing for Change*. New York: Free Press, 1984.

Morrison, Toni, ed. *Race(ing) Justice, (En)Gendering Power: Essays on Anita Hill, Clarence Thomas, and the Construction of Social Reality*. New York: Pantheon Books, 1992.

Moses, William Jeremiah. *The Golden Age of Black Nationalism, 1850–1925*. Hamden, Conn.: Anchor Books, 1978.

Naison, Mark. *Communists in Harlem During the Depression*. Urbana: University of Illinois Press, 1983.

Neal, Mark Anthony. *What the Music Said: Black Popular Music and Black Popular Culture*. New York: Routledge, 1999.

Neiwert, David A. *In God's Country: The Patriot Movement and the Pacific Northwest*. Pullman, Wash.: Washington State University Press, 1999.

Newman, Richard. *Go Down Moses: A Celebration of the African-American Spiritual*. New York: Clarkson Potter, 1998.

Newton, Huey P. *To Die for the People: The Writings of Huey P. Newton*. New York: Random House, 1972.

Norrell, Robert J. *Reaping the Whirlwind: The Civil Rights Movement in Tuskegee*. New York: Random House, 1972.

Oates, Stephen B. *Let the Trumpet Sound: The Life of Martin Luther King, Jr*. New York: Harper & Row, 1982.

Oliver, Paul. *Blues Fell This Morning: Meaning and the Blues*. New York: Cambridge University Press, 1990.

———. *Gospel Blues*. New York: Norton, 1997.

O'Reilly, Kenneth. *Racial Matters: The FBI's Secret File on Black America, 1960–1972*. New York: Free Press, 1989.

————. *Black Americans: The FBI Files.* New York: Carroll and Graf, 1994.

————. *Nixon's Piano: Presidents and Racial Politics from Washington to Clinton.* New York: Free Press, 1995.

Painter, Hosea Irvin. *The Narrative of Hosea Hudson: The Life and Times of a Black Radical.* Edited by Nell Irvin Painter. New York: Norton, 1993.

Painter, Nell Irvin. *Sojourner Truth: A Life, a Symbol.* New York: Norton, 1996.

Pappas, Theodore. *Plagiarism and the Culture War: The Writings of Martin Luther King Jr. and Other Prominent Americans.* New York: Hallberg Publishing Corp., 1998.

Parks, Rosa, with Jim Haskins. *Rosa Parks, My Story.* New York: Dial Books, 1992.

Payne, Charles M. *I've Got the Light of Freedom: The Organizing Tradition and the Mississippi Freedom Struggle.* Berkeley: University of California Press, 1995.

Pepper, William. *Orders to Kill: The Truth Behind the Murder of Martin Luther King.* New York: Carroll and Graf, 1995.

Perkins, William Eric, ed. *Droppin' Science: Critical Essays on Rap Music and Hip Hop Culture.* Philadelphia: Temple University Press, 1996.

Pfeffer, Paula F. *A Philip Randolph: Pioneer of the Civil Rights Movement.* Baton Rouge: Louisiana State University Press, 1990.

Pinn, Anthony B. *Varieties of African-American Religious Experience.* Minneapolis: Fortress Press, 1998.

————. *Why Lord? Suffering and Evil in Black Theology.* New York: Continuum, 1995.

Pipes, William H. *Say Amen Brother: Old Time American Negro Preaching, a Study in American Frustration.* Detroit: Wayne State University Press, 1992.

Pitts, Walter. *Old Ship of Zion: The Afro-Baptist Ritual in the African Diaspora.* New York: Oxford University Press, 1993.

Porter, Jean. *Moral Action and Christian Ethics.* New York: Cambridge University Press, 1995.

Posner, Gerald. *Killing the Dream: James Earl Ray and the Assassination of Martin Luther King, Jr.* New York: Random House, 1998.

Potter, Russell A. *Spectacular Vernaculars: Hip-Hop and the Politics of Postmodernism.* Albany: State University of New York Press, 1995.

Power, Georgia Davis. *I Shared the Dream: The Pride, Passion, and Politics of the First Woman Senator from Kentucky.* Far Hills, N.J.: New Horizon Press, 1995.

Powell, Kevin. *Keepin' It Real: Post MTV Reflections on Race, Sex, and Politics.* New York: Ballantine Books, 1997.

Raboteau, Albert J. *Fire in the Bones: Reflections on African-American Religious History.* Boston: Beacon Press, 1995.

————. *Slave Religion: The "Invisible Institution" in the Antebellum South.* New York: Oxford University Press, 1998.

Raines, Howell, ed. *My Soul Is Rested: Movement Days in the Deep South Remembered.* New York: Putnam, 1977.

Rainwater, Lee, and Yancey, William L. *The Moynihan Report and the Politics of Controversy.* Cambridge, Mass.: MIT Press, 1967.

Ralph, James. *Northern Protest: Martin Luther King, Jr., Chicago, and the Civil Rights Movement.* Cambridge, Mass.: Harvard University Press, 1993.

Rauschenbush, Walter. *A Theology for the Social Gospel.* Louisville: Westminster John Knox Press, 1997.

Record, Wilson. *The Negro and the Communist Party.* New York: Simon & Schuster, 1971.

Redekop, John Harold. *The American Far Right: A Case Study of Billy James Hargis and the Christian Crusade.* Grand Rapids, Mich.: W. B. Eerdman's Publishing Co., 1968.

Reed, Christopher. *The Chicago N.A.A.C.P. and the Rise of Black Professional Leadership, 1910–1966.* Bloomington, Ind.: Indiana University Press, 1997.

Reed, Ralph. *Active Faith: How Christians Are Changing the Soul of American Politics.* New York: Free Press, 1996.

Roberts, Ellen B. *Roberts vs. Texaco: A True Story of Race in Corporate America.* New York: Avon Books, 1998.

Robertson, David. *Denmark Vesey.* New York: Knopf, 1999.

Robertson, Pat. *New World Order.* Dallas: World Press, 1991.

Robinson, Jo Ann Gibson. *The Montgomery Bus Boycott and the Women Who Started It: The Memoir of Jo Ann Gibson Robinson.* Edited by David Garrow. Knoxville: University of Tennessee Press, 1987.

Rock, Chris. *Rock This!* New York: Hyperion, 1998.

Rorty, Richard. *Achieving Our Country: Leftist Thought in Twentieth Century America.* Cambridge, Mass.: Harvard University Press, 1998.

Rose, Tricia. *Black Noise: Rap Music and Black Culture in Contemporary America.* Hanover, N.H.: Wesleyan University Press, 1994.

Rosenberg, Bruce A. *Can These Bones Live?* Urbana: University of Illinois Press, 1988.

Rovere, Richard. *Senator Joe McCarthy.* New York: Harcourt, Brace, 1959.

Rowan, Carl T. *Breaking Barriers: A Memoir.* Boston: Little, Brown, 1991.

Rubinstein, Michael. *Music to My Ear: Reflections on Music and Digressions on Metaphysics.* Salem House Pub, n.d.

Sadri, Ahmed. *Max Weber's Sociology of Intellectuals.* Oxford University Press, 1994.

Sartwell, Crispin. *Act Like You Know: African-American Autobiography and White Identity.* Chicago: University of Chicago Press, 1998.

Schulke, Flip, and McPhee, Penelope. *King Remembered.* New York: W. W. Norton, 1986.

Schulzinger, Robert D. *A Time for War: The United States and Vietnam, 1941–1975.* New York: Oxford Press, 1997.

Scott, James C. *Domination and the Arts of Resistance: Hidden Transcripts.* New Haven, Conn.: Yale University Press, 1990.

———. *Weapons of the Weak: Everyday Forms of Peasant Resistance.* New Haven, Conn.: Yale University Press, 1985.

Scott, Robert L., and Brockriede, Wayne, eds. *The Rhetoric of Black Power.* New York: Harper & Row, 1969.

Seeger, Pete. *Where Have All the Flowers Gone? A Singer's Stories, Songs, Seeds, Robberies.* Bethlehem, Penn.: Sing Out, 1993.

Sharpton, Al, and Walton, Anthony. *Go and Tell Pharaoh: The Autobiography of Reverend Al Sharpton.* New York: Doubleday, 1996.

Sherman, Nancy. *Making a Necessity of Virtue: Aristotle and Kant on Virtue.* New York: Cambridge University Press, 1997.

Shockley, William B. *Shockley on Eugenics and Race: The Application of Science to the Solution of Human Problems.* Washington, D.C.: Scott-Townsend Publishers, 1992.

Smith, Kenneth L., and Zepp, Ira G. *Search for the Beloved Community: The Thinking of Martin Luther King, Jr.* Valley Forge, Penn.: Judson Press, 1974.

Smith, Robert. *We Have No Leaders: African-Americans in the Post–Civil Rights Era.* Albany: State University of New York Press, 1996.

Spencer, John Michael. *Sacred Symphony: The Chanted Sermon of the Black Preacher.* Westport, Conn.: Greenwood Press, 1987.

———. *Blues and Evil.* Knoxville: University of Tennessee Press, 1993.

Spear, Allan H. *Black Chicago: The Making of a Negro Ghetto, 1890–1920.* Chicago: University of Chicago Press, 1967.

Steele, Shelby. *Content of Our Character: A New Vision of Race in America*. New York: St. Martin's Press, 1990.

Sterling, Dorothy. *Black Foremothers: Three Lives*. Old Westbury, N.Y.: Feminist Press, 1979.

Stimpson, Eddie. *My Remembers: A Black Sharecropper's Recollection of the Depression*. Denton, Tex.: University of North Texas Press, 1995.

Summers, Anthony. *Official and Confidential: The Secret Life of J. Edgar Hoover*. New York: G.P. Putnam's Sons, 1993.

Terrell, Mary Church. *A Colored Woman in a White World*. Salem, N.H.: Ayer Co., 1998, c. 1940.

Terry, Wallace, ed. *Bloods: An Oral History of the Vietnam War*, by Black Veterans. New York: Random House, 1984.

Thayer, George. *The Farther Shores of Politics: The American Political Fringe Today*. New York: Simon & Schuster, 1967.

Thielicke, Helmut. *The Waiting Father: Sermons on the Parables of Jesus*. New York: Harper, 1959.

———. *Life Can Begin Again: Sermons on the Sermon on the Mount*. Philadelphia: Fortress Press, 1963.

Thiemann, Ronald. *Constructing a Public Theology: The Church in a Pluralistic Culture*. Westminster: John Knox Press, 1991.

Thomas, Frank. *They Never Like to Quit Praisin' God: The Role of Celebration in Preaching*. Cleveland: United Church Press, 1997.

Thurman, Howard. *Deep River*. Richmond, Va.: Friends United Press, 1975.

Tindall, George B. *The Emergence of the New South, 1913–1945*. Baton Rouge: Louisiana State University Press, 1967.

Tobin, Jacqueline L., and Dobard, Raymond G. *Hidden in Plain View: The Secret Story of Quilts and the Underground Railroad*. New York: Doubleday, 1999.

Tomasky, Michael. *Left for Dead: The Life, Death, and Possible Resurrection of Progressive Politics in America*. New York: Free Press, 1996.

Travis, Dempsy. *Autobiography of Black Chicago*. Chicago: Urban Research Institute, 1981.

Tucker, David M. *Black Pastors and Leaders: Memphis, 1819–1972*. Memphis: Memphis State University Press, 1975.

Turner, Nat. *The Confessions of Nat Turner and Related Documents*. Edited by Kenneth S. Greenberg. Boston: Bedford Books of St. Martin's Press, 1996.

Vandeburg, William L. *Modern Black Nationalism: From Marcus Garvey to Louis Farrakhan*. New York: New York University Press, 1997.

———. *New Day in Babylon: The Black Power Movement and American Culture, 1965–1975*. Chicago: University of Chicago Press, 1992.

Van De Mark, Brian. *Into the Quagmire: Lyndon Johnson and the Escalation of the Vietnam War*. New York: Oxford University Press, 1995.

Vibe Magazine, eds. *Tupac Amaru Shakur, 1971–1996*. New York: Crown, 1997.

Wallace, Michele. *Black Macho and the Myth of the Superwoman*. New York: Dial Press, 1979.

Walters, Ronald W., and Smith, Robert C. *African American Leadership*. Albany: State University of New York Press, 1999.

Walzer, Michael. *Just and Unjust Wars: A Moral Argument with Historical Illustrations*. New York: Basic Books, 1977.

Washington, Booker T. *Up from Slavery: An Autobiography*. Garden City, N.Y.: Doubleday, 1953.

Washington, James Melvin. *Frustrated Fellowship: The Black Baptist Quest for Social Power*. Macon, Ga.: Mercer, 1986.

Watts, Jerry G. *Heroism and the Black Intellectual: Ralph Ellison, Politics, and Afro-American Intellectual Life*. Chapel Hill, NC: University of North Carolina Press, 1994.

Weisbrot, Robert. *Freedom Bound: A History of America's Civil Rights Movement*. New York: Norton, 1990.

White, Armond. *Rebel for the Hell of It: The Life of Tupac Shakur*. New York: Thunder's Mouth Press, 1997.

White, Deborah G. *Too Heavy a Load: Black Women in Defense of Themselves, 1894–1994*. New York: Norton, 1999.

Wiggins, William H. *O Freedom! African-American Emancipation Celebrations*. Knoxville: University of Tennessee Press, 1987.

Wilkins, Roger. *A Man's Life*. New York: Simon & Schuster, 1982.

Williams, Delores S. *Sisters in the Wilderness: The Challenge of Womanist God-Talk*. Maryknoll, N.Y.: Orbis Books, 1993.

Williams, John A. *The King God Didn't Save: Reflections on the Life and Death of Martin Luther King, Jr*. New York: Coward-McCann, 1970.

Williamson, Joel. *The Crucible of Race: Black/White Relations in the American South Since Emancipation*. New York: Oxford University Press, 1986.

Wills, Gary. *Cincinnatus: George Washington and the Enlightenment*. Garden City, N.Y.: Doubleday, 1984.

Wilmore, Gayraud. *Black Religion and Black Radicalism*. Garden City, N.Y.: Doubleday, 1972.

Wilson, William Julius. *The Declining Significance of Race: Blacks and Changing American Institutions*. Chicago: University of Chicago Press, 1980.

———. *The Truly Disadvantaged: The Inner City, the Underclass and Public Policy*. Chicago: University of Chicago Press, 1987.

———. *When Work Disappears: The World of the New Urban Poor*. New York: Knopf, 1996.

Wofford, Harris. *Of Kennedys and Kings: Making Sense of the Sixties*. New York: Farrar, Strauss, and Giroux, 1980.

Woodward, C. Vann. *Origins of the New South, 1877–1913*. Baton Rouge: Louisiana State University Press, 1953.

———. *Strange Career of Jim Crow*. New York: Oxford University Press, 1955.

Wright, Roberta H. *Birth of the Montgomery Bus Boycott*. Southfield, Mich.: Charro Book Company, 1991.

Wyatt, David. *Five Fires: Race, Catastrophe, and the Shaping of California*. Reading, Mass.: Addison-Wesley, 1997.

Young, Andrew. *An Easy Burden: The Civil Rights Movement and the Transformation of America*. New York: HarperCollins, 1996.

Journal Articles

Alzoie, Nicholas O. "Political Tolerance Hypotheses and White Opposition to a Martin Luther King Holiday in Arizona." *Social Science Journal*, 32, January 1995, pp. 1–16.

Baldwin, Lewis. "Martin Luther King, Jr., the Black Church, and the Black Messianic Vision." *Journal of the Interdenominational Theological Center*, 12, Fall 1984–Spring 1985, pp. 93–108.

———. "Understanding Martin Luther King, Jr., Within the Context of Southern Black Religious History." *Journal of Religious Studies*, 13, 1987, pp. 1–26.

Brown-Nagin, Tomiko. "The Transformation of a Social Movement into Law," *Women's History Review*, 8, 1999, pp. 81–137.

Burns, Stewart. "From the Mountaintop: The Changing Political Vision of Martin Luther King, Jr." *History Teacher*, 27, November 1993, pp. 7–18.

Carson, Clayborne. "Martin Luther King, Jr.: Charismatic Leadership in a Mass Struggle." *Journal of American History*, 74, September 1987, pp. 448–454.

Carson, Clayborne, with Holloran, Peter, Luker, Ralph E., and Russell, Penny. "Martin Luther King, Jr., as Scholar: A Reexamination of His Theological Writings." *Journal of American History*, 78, June 1991, pp. 98–111.

Colaiaco, James A. "The American Dream Unfulfilled: Martin Luther King, Jr., and the 'Letter from Birmingham Jail.'" *Phylon*, 45, March 1984, pp. 1–18.

Cone, James. "Martin Luther King, Jr., Black Theology—Black Church." *Theology Today*, 40, January 1984, pp. 409–420.

———. "The Theology of Martin Luther King, Jr." *Union Seminary Quarterly Review*, 40, January 1986, pp. 21–39.

Darby, Henry E., and Rowley, Margaret N. "King on Vietnam and Beyond." *Phylon*, 47, March 1986, pp. 43–50.

Davis, Mike, and Riddick, Sue. "Los Angeles: Civil Liberties Between the Hammer and the Rock." *New Left Review*, July–August 1988, pp. 37–60.

Fairclough, Adam. "Was Martin Luther King a Marxist." *History Workshop Journal*, no. 15, Spring 1983, pp. 117–125.

———. "Martin Luther King, Jr. and the War in Vietnam." *Phylon*, 45, January 1984, pp. 19–39.

Franklin, Jimmie Lewis. "Autobiography, the Burden of Friendship, and Truth." *Georgia Historical Quarterly*, 74, pp. 84–98.

Garrow, David. "King's Plagiarism: Imitation, Insecurity, and Transformation." *Journal of American History*, 78, June 1991, pp. 92–97.

Higham, John. "Habits of the Cloth and Standards of the Academy." *Journal of American History*, 78, June 1991, pp. 106–110.

Jensen, Arthur R.. "How Much Can We Boost I.Q. and Scholastic Achievement?" *Harvard Educational Review*, 39, pp. 1–124.

Kennedy, Randall. "Is He a Soul Man? On Black Support for Clinton." *The American Prospect*, March–April 1999, pp. 26–30.

Lewis, David Levering. "Bearing the Cross." *Journal of American History*, 74, September 1987, pp. 482–484.

———. "Failing to Know Martin Luther King, Jr." *Journal of American History*, 78, June 1991, pp. 81–91.

Martin Luther King, Jr., Papers Project. "The Student Papers of Martin Luther King, Jr.: A Summary Statement on Research." *Journal of American History*, 78, June 1991, pp. 23–31.

Miller, Keith D. "Composing Martin Luther King, Jr." *PMLA*, 10, January 1990, pp. 70–82.

———. "Martin Luther King, Jr., and the Black Folk Pulpit." *Journal of American History*, 78, June 1991, pp. 106–110.

Noer, Thomas. "Martin Luther King, Jr. and the Cold War." *Peace & Change*, 22, April 1997. pp. 111–131.

O'Brien, Michael. "Old Myths/New Insights: History and Dr. King." *History Teacher*, 22, November 1988, pp. 49–65.

Ransby, Barbara, and Mathews, Trayce. "Black Popular Culture and the Transcendence of Patriarchal Illusions." *Race and Class*, 35, 1993.

Reagon, Bernice Johnson. "'Nobody Knows the Trouble I See:' or 'By and By I'm Gonna Lay Down My Heavy Load.'" *Journal of American History*, 78, June 1991, pp. 113–117.

Rogers, Cornish. "Conversation Between Cornish Rogers and David Thelen." *Journal of American History*, 78, June 1991, pp. 41–62.

Schilling, Paul S. "Conversation Between S. Paul Schilling and David Thelen." *Journal of American History,* 78, June 1991, pp. 63–86.

Schwartz, Barry. "Social Change and Collective Memory: The Democratization of George Washington." *American Sociological Review,* 56, Apr. 1991, pp. 221–236.

Smith, Kenneth L. "The Radicalization of Martin Luther King, Jr.: The Last Three Years." *Journal of Ecumenical Studies,* 26, September 1989, pp. 270–288.

Starosta, William J. "A National Holiday for Dr. King? Qualitative Analysis of Arguments Carried in the *Washington Post* and *New York Times.*" *Journal of Black Studies,* 18, March 1988, pp. 358–378.

Stump, Roger W. "Toponymic Commemoration of National Figures: The Cases of Kennedy and King." *Names,* 36, September–December 1988, pp. 203–217.

Thelen, David. "Conversation Between Cornish Rogers and David Thelen." *Journal of American History,* 78, June 1991.

Wander, Philip C. "The John Birch and Martin Luther King Symbols in the Radical Right." *Western Speech,* 35, Winter 1971, pp. 4–14.

Magazine Articles

"15 Greatest Black Preachers." *Ebony,* Nov. 1993, p. 156.

"Dexter King Is Named CEO of the King Center." *Ebony,* Jan. 1995, pp. 25–28.

"Dexter's Dream." *Ebony,* Jan. 1997, pp. 27–30.

"Dr. King." *National Review,* Feb. 13, 1987, pp. 20–21.

"Henry Lyons Found Guilty of Racketeering, Grand Theft." *Jet,* Mar. 15, 1999, p. 16.

"King Holiday Observed as Dexter King Takes Over as King Chairman." *Jet,* Jan. 16, 1995, p. 6.

"Martin Luther King, Jr.: Never Again Where He Was." *Time,* Jan. 3, 1964.

"Rev. Bernice A. King Continues Family's Preaching Legacy." *Ebony,* Jan. 1995, pp. 30, 32, 34.

"The Unchristian Christian." *Ebony,* Aug. 1965.

"The World Honors Martin Luther King Through Stamps." *Ebony,* Jan. 1986.

Babington, Charles. "Embargoed; Martin Luther King, Jr., Plagiarism Story Cover-Up." *New Republic,* Jan. 28, 1991, p. 9.

Bennett, Lerone, Jr. "The Real Meaning of the King Holiday." *Ebony,* Jan. 1986, p. 31.

Branch, Taylor. "Uneasy Holiday." *New Republic,* Feb. 3, 1986, pp. 22–27.

Breindel, Eric. "King's Communist Associates." *New Republic,* Jan. 30, 1984, p. 14.

Carey, John. "Behind the Bell Curve." *Business Week,* Nov. 7, 1994, p. 36.

Coughlin, Ellen K. "Researchers Debate Jury's Decision to Award King Papers to Boston U." *Chronicle of Higher Education,* May 19, 1993, p. A14.

Dyson, Marcia L. "When Preachers Prey." *Essence,* May 1988, pp. 120–122, 190–194.

Dyson, Michael Eric. "The Cruellest." *New Yorker,* Feb. 17, 1997, p. 33.

———. "Integration and the New Black American Dilemma." *Newsday,* July 13, 1997, pp. G6, G15.

Eddings, Jerelyn. "Coretta King's Lonely Days." *U.S. News & World Report,* Jan. 16, 1995, pp. 54, 57.

Galloway, Joseph, et al. "Dr. Shockely and Mr. Hyde." *U.S. News & World Report,* Aug. 28–Sept. 4, 1989, p. 16.

Garrow, David J. "The Helms Attack on King." *Southern Exposure,* 12, Mar.–Apr. 1984, pp. 12–15.

Goodman, Ellen. "Whatever His Failings, King Remains a Hero." *Newsday*, Nov. 16, 1990, p. 88.

Heller, Scott. "Essays That Live On." *Chronicle of Higher Education*, Apr. 2, 1999, p. A20.

Jet. June 29, 1998, p. 53.

King, Coretta Scott. "Martin's Legacy." *Ebony*, Jan. 1986, pp. 105–108.

King, Martin Luther. "John F. Kennedy." *Transition*, 15, July–Aug. 1964, pp. 27–28.

Kinnon, Joy. "15 Greatest Black Women Preachers." *Ebony*, Nov. 1997, p. 102.

McMillian, John C. "King's Radical Legacy." *In These Times*, Feb. 21, 1987.

Mills, Nicolaus. "Heard and Unheard Speeches," *Dissent*, Summer 1988.

Paul, Angus. "Scholars Tend to Favor Martin Luther King, Jr. Center over Boston U. as the Home for All of King's Papers." *Chronicle of Higher Education*, July 20, 1988, p. A1.

Reagan, Ronald. "Remarks of the President at the Signing Ceremony for Martin Luther King, Jr. Holiday Legislation," *Ebony Magazine*, Jan. 1986.

Reid, Calvin. "King Family in Multi-Million Dollar Deal with Warner." *Publishers Weekly*, Jan. 13, 1997, p. 14.

Schneiderman, Howard G. "The Martin Luther King, Jr., Plagiarism Story." *Society*, Feb. 14, 1996, pp. 80–85.

Starr, Mark. "Archie Bunker with a Ph.D." *Newsweek*, Jan. 18, 1990, p. 19.

Terry, Randall A. "Operation Rescue: The Civil Rights Movement of the Nineties." *Policy Review*, 47, Winter 1989, pp. 82–83.

Watanabe, Paul. "The Politics of Independence: Where Independents Have Made a Difference: The Case of Massachusetts." *Public Perspective*, 2, Nov. 1990, pp. 27–29.

Weisbrot, Robert. "Celebrating Dr. King's Birthday." *New Republic*, Jan. 30, 1984, pp. 10–16.

White, Jack. "Texaco's High-Octane Racism Problems." *Time*, Nov. 25, 1996, pp. 33–34.

Newspaper Articles

"Dr. King's Error," *New York Times*, Apr. 7, 1967, sec. 1, p. 36.

"Dr. King's Widow Finally Has Her Day in Court," *New York Times*, Apr. 30, 1993, EDT, p. A12.

"King Papers Belong in the South," *Atlanta Journal-Constitution*, Apr. 28, 1993, EDT, p. A10.

"King Trial Excerpts," *Boston Globe*, Apr. 28, 1993, EDT, p. 26.

"Martin Luther King's Moral Authority," *New York Times*, Jan. 21, 1991, EDT, p. A16.

"Suit on King Busts," *Washington Post*, Jan. 8, 1981, EDT, p. A18.

"Tearful Baptist Leader Is Given 5 1/2-Year Term in Graft Case," *New York Times*, Apr. 1, 1999, p. A19.

"Yummy's Legacy." *Chicago Sun-Times*, EDT, Apr. 25, 1997, p. 39.

Associated Press. "Boston U. Seeks King Documents in Counterclaim," *San Diego Union Tribune*, Apr. 7, 1988, p. A12.

Baker, William O. "The Legacy of Martin Luther King, Jr." *Atlanta Journal-Constitution*, Jan. 26, 1997, p. 6B.

Belluck, Pam. "With a New Image, Jackson Campaigns Outside 200 Race." *New York Times*, July 28, 1999, p. A12.

Black, Chris, and McGrory, Brian. "Some Faculty Members Fear for BU's Reputation." *Boston Globe*, Mar. 16, 1993, p. 16.

Bond, Julian. "Remember the Man and the Hero, Not Just Half the Dream." *Seattle Times*, Apr. 4, 1993.

Booth, Michael, and Roberts, Jeffery A. "Militias More Bark Than Bite in Colorado, Factions Brandish Constitution." *Denver Post,* May 7, 1995, p. A1.

Brodie, Ian. "Clinton's Foe Is Linked to Racist Group." (Oversea News), *The Times* (London), Jan. 15, 1999.

Bryant, Tim. "Holiday Turns to War Talk . . . Slain Leader Would be Saddened by World Events, Speakers Say." *St. Louis Post-Dispatch,* Jan. 22, 1991, p. A1.

Canon, Scott. "McVeigh Called a Patriot, Model Soldier Who Was Troubled by the Siege at Waco." *Kansas City Star,* June 7, 1997, p. A1.

Carson, Clayborne. "King's Ties to Atlanta Shaped His Career." *Atlanta Journal-Constitution,* Jan. 19, 1992, p. D1.

Chavez, Ken. "Connerly's New Prop. 209 Push Draws Fire." *Sacramento Bee,* Jan. 12, 1997, p. A3.

Confino, Jonathon. "The Gulf War: Race Split Feared as US Blacks Oppose War." *Daily Telegraph,* Jan. 26, 1991.

Cotlair, Sharon. "Second Teen Accused in Boy's Slaying Gets 60-Year Term." *Chicago Sun-Times,* Apr. 23, 1997, p. 25.

Cox, Christopher. "Are Modern-Day Militia Members New Patriots or Anti-American Warriors?" *Boston Herald,* Apr. 17, 1996, p. 34.

Crayton, Rasheeda. "Lead Prosecutor in McVeigh Trial Talks on Terrorism." *Kansas City Star,* Apr. 10, 1998, p. A11.

Cummings, Judith. "Is There Nothing Left to Lose to Urban Despair?" *Los Angeles Times,* Sept. 30, 1994, p. B7.

Daly, Christopher B. "King Kept Titles to Papers, Jury in BU Case Is Told." *Washington Post,* May 6, 1993, p. A3.

Dean, Paul. "The Paper Chase; Scholarship: The Martin Luther King Research Team Warns Against Distorting Its Findings of Plagiarism; The Dream and the Dreamer Will Survive, They Say." *Los Angeles Times,* Dec. 11, 1990, p. 1–4.

Depalma, Anthony. "Plagiarism Seen by Scholars in King Dissertation." *New York Times,* Jan. 15, 1997, A10.

Dunne, Nancy. "The Gulf War: Television Presents War with a White Face to US Blacks." *London Financial Times,* Jan. 23, 1991, Sec. 1, p. 4.

Durcanin, Cynthia. "King's Pulpit for World Peace Becomes a Platform to End War in Persian Gulf." *Atlanta Journal-Constitution,* Jan. 22, 1991.

Farley, Christopher John. "King, Malcolm X Leave Legacy of Tactics." *USA Today,* Feb. 21, 1991, p. 4D.

Flint, Anthony. "Not Just King's Papers, but Also Legacy at Stake." *Boston Globe,* May 6, 1993, p. 1.

————. "Prestige Is at Stake in King Papers Trial; Writings of the Famous Prized in Academia." *Boston Globe,* May 3, 1993, p. 13.

————. "State High Court's Ruling Lets BU Keep King Papers." *Boston Globe,* Apr. 13, 1995, p. 1.

Fulwood, Sam III. "Black Activists Urge Bush to Declare Cease-Fire." *Los Angeles Times,* Feb. 16, 1991, p. 3.

Fulwood, Sam III, and Lin, Judy. "Two in GOP Join in Fight Against Racist Group." *Los Angeles Times,* Mar. 19, 1999, p. A22.

Garrow, David. "How King Borrowed; Reading the Truth Between Sermons and Footnotes." *Washington Post,* Nov. 18, 1990, p. C1.

Gladwell, Malcolm. "At Root of Modern Militias: An American Legacy of Rebellion." *Washington Post,* May 9, 1995, p. A1.

Glalagher, Kirsten. "Professor: Rhetoric Can Hide Messages of King, Malcolm X." *Orlando Sentinel Tribune,* Jan. 30, 1992, p. B3.

Hundley, Kris. "Lyons Victims Seeking Shelter from Creditors." *St. Petersburg Times,* June 2, 1991, p. A1.

Jackson, Derrick Z. "A Lopsided Volunteer Military." *Boston Globe,* Feb. 6, 1991, p. 15.

Johnson, Mark. "King's Legacy Is Losing Its Luster in Atlanta; Heirs Chastised for Harping on Finances Instead of Issues." *Richmond Times-Dispatch,* Aug. 17, 1997, p. A1.

Lang, Perry. "Black Students Rally Against the Gulf War." *San Francisco Chronicle,* Feb. 23, 1991, p. A5.

Leisner, Pat. "Fraud Earns Minister Jail Time, Fine." *Atlanta Journal-Constitution,* June 19, 1999, p. 1B.

Lempinen, Edward W. "Connerly Widens Anti-Affirmative Action Campaign; He Announces New Effort on King Birthday." *San Francisco Chronicle,* Jan. 16, 1997, p. A17.

Lesher, Dave. "Governments Step Unsurely Toward 'Colorblind' Goal." *Los Angeles Times,* Nov. 4, 1997, p. A1.

Lipsher, Steve. "The Radical Right." *Denver Post,* Jan. 22, 1995, p. A1.

May, Lee. "King Day Celebrations Include Calls for Cease-Fire in Persian Gulf War." *Los Angeles Times,* Jan. 22, 1991.

McMillian, John. "The Radical Rev. King." *Boston Globe,* Jan. 18, 1999, p. A13.

McWhorter, Darrell. "Images of King." *St. Louis Post-Dispatch,* Jan. 21, 1991, p. 1D.

Merina, Victor. "Outline of King Speech to be Sold Despite Heirs' Suit." *Los Angeles Times,* Nov. 7, 1992, p. B8.

Milloy, Courtland. "Let King Rest in Peace." *Washington Post,* Nov. 22, 1990, p. J1.

Pogrebin, Robin. "Time Warner to Publish Martin Luther King's Works." *New York Times,* Jan. 9, 1997, p. A14.

Pomerantz, Gary. "King Papers' New Chapter." *Atlanta Journal-Constitution,* July 18, 1997, p. C3.

Rankin, Bill. "Angry Words over King Papers; Slain Leader's Change of Mind Key to Atlanta-Boston Struggle." *Atlanta Journal-Constitution,* Apr. 28, 1993, p. A2.

————. "Mrs. King Papers Poorly Kept at Home; Documents Once Stored in Basement." *Atlanta Journal-Constitution,* Apr. 29, 1993, p. A10.

Reeves, Phil. "Embittered 'Patriots' at Heart of America." *London Independent,* Apr. 28, 1995, p. 13.

Rezendes, Michael. "The Battle over King's Papers; Widow, Boston U. at Odds and in Court." *Washington Post,* Mar. 12, 1988, p. C1.

————. "Boston U. Sues to Obtain King's Papers; Action Seeks Widow's Holdings." *Washington Post,* Apr. 7, 1988, p. D1.

Rimer, Sara. "An Effort to Honor Dr. King Moves a Mostly White Town." *New York Times,* Jan. 20, 1997, p. A1.

Sack, Kevin. "Battles Flare over King's Lucrative Legacy." *New York Times,* Jan. 14, 1997, p. A10.

————. "King Estate Battle over Licensing." *Houston Chronicle,* Jan. 20, 1997, p. 1.

————. "Sheen of the King Legacy Dims on New, More Profitable Path." *New York Times,* Aug. 19, 1997, pp. A1, A16.

————. "Two Universities Vie for King Center's Papers." *New York Times,* July 16, 1997.

Sauer, Mark, and Okerblom, Jim. "Patriotism or Paranoia? Videos, Radio, Internet All Used to Spread Fears of the Far Right That Government Poses Danger." *San Diego Union-Tribune,* May 4, 1995, p. E1.

Simon, Paul. "The Silent Superstar." *New York Times,* Mar. 9, 1999, p. A23.

Smothers, Ronald. "Living and Shaping Legacy of Civil Rights Leader." *New York Times,* Nov. 26, 1994, sec. 1, p. 8.

———. "Son of Slain Civil Rights Leader Succeeds Mother as Head of Group." *New York Times,* Oct. 23, 1994, p. A30.

Starr, John R. "King's Accomplishments Stand." *Arkansas Democrat-Gazette,* Aug. 23, 1994, p. B7.

Sweeny, Ann. "Rosa Parks' Attacker Pleads Guilty; Prosecution Seeks 15-Year Term." *Detroit News,* June 15, 1995, p. D3.

Tabor, Mary B. W. "King's Dream Lives Again at Site of His Death." *New York Times,* July 1, 1991, p. A1.

Towns, Hollis R. "'Tasteful' Marketing of MLK Heirs Agree to License the Words, Images, of Martin Luther King, Jr." *Atlanta Journal-Constitution,* Feb. 4, 1996, p. G6.

Wilkie, Curtis. "Family Faces Turmoil over King Legacy." *Boston Globe,* Jan. 15, 1995, p. 1.

———. "Silber Style: Few Apologies for Tough Talk." *Boston Globe,* Oct. 14, 1990, p. 41.

Wong, Doris Sue. "Author Testifies to King Papers' Condition at BU." *Boston Globe,* May 1, 1993, p. 24.

———. "BU, Family Argue in Court over King Papers." *Boston Globe,* Apr. 22, 1993, p. 29.

———. "BU Wasn't Told to Return Papers, King Concedes." *Boston Globe,* Apr. 29, 1993, p. 28.

———. "Coretta King's Lawyer Will Ask Judge to Set Aside BU Verdict." *Boston Globe,* May 8, 1993, p. 20.

———. "Court Hears 1964 Tape in BU-King Case." *Boston Globe,* Apr. 24, 1993, p. 27.

———. "Jury Rules BU Rightful Owner of King Papers." *Boston Globe,* May 7, 1993, p. 1.

———. "Jury Selection Begins Today in Dispute over King Papers." *Boston Globe,* Apr. 21, 1993, p. 29.

———. "King Calls Silber 'Hostile'; Testifies BU Head Angry over Papers." *Boston Globe,* Apr. 28, 1993, p. 23.

———. "Silber Disputes King Widow's Account; Denies Being Hostile, Says Papers Belong to BU." *Boston Globe,* May 4, 1993.

I wish to begin the way people in my community of faith often begin their testimonies in public: Giving honor to God, who is the head of my life. That is truly the key to my existence and the foundation of my faith and the work I do. I want to thank two colleagues who read an earlier version of this manuscript and offered critical comments that have substantially improved it: Robin D. G. Kelley, my dear friend and a towering historian, and D. Soyini Madison, my closest friend, a brilliant cultural critic and a peerless wisewoman whose counsel has saved me from foolish errors, personal and professional. I also thank the talented John McMillian for his invaluable research assistance. Susan Taylor and Kephra Burns have blessed my family with their love, their genius, their courage, and their commitment to bringing the best of black life to this nation. Thank you—and Clarence Smith and Ed Lewis—for including us in your plans. Bill Hunter, a brilliant thinker, an imaginative leader, and a man of huge talent and courage, and his lovely wife, Janice, a bright and wonderful woman whose penetrating questions forced me to make my points plain, have blessed me in untold ways. Richard Plepler, an astonishing visionary, gifted conversationalist, and man of boundless integrity, has been a source of inspiration and has provided a crucial outlet for my thinking. And my dear friend Zan Holmes, a great pastor, brilliant preacher, and wonderful teacher, and his late wife, Dorothy, a wise and gifted woman who made her transition near the end of this work, provided me a space in their hearts and congregation to renew my spirit.

I am grateful to the University of North Carolina at Chapel Hill, which gave a young scholar the opportunity to spread his wings. I especially thank Dick McCormick, then a Provost, who made it possible for me to go there, and my dear friend Bill Balthrop (and my colleagues in Communication Studies), the kindest, smartest, most humane department chair I have known, for his support of my vision and work. I am also grateful to Leith Mullings and Manning Marable (and Daria and Diane, too, who took good care of me!) for their ingenious scholarship, intellectual zeal, social activism, and cherished friendship. Because of Manning, I was able to spend two years in New York at Columbia, a crucial period in writing my book. And to President Father Jack Minogue (who gave the green light), Vice President Dick Meister (who made it possible), and Dean Mike Mezey (who makes it work), I am grateful for the love and support, and for a great new home at DePaul University, where I can truly be myself.

Finally, I want to thank my editors and my family. Liz Maguire is so much more than a daring and gifted editor. She is one of my dearest friends and an intellectual soul mate whose vision, energy, and rigor have sustained me for years. Without her, this book would not exist. I also thank Chad Conway for his superb attention to details, Beverly Miller for her fine copyediting, and Edith Lewis for her careful shepherding of this manuscript into its final form. My family has been invaluable to me. My mother Addie Mae Dyson is our sustaining soul; and to my brothers and nieces and nephews, I am grateful for your love and support. My children are my heart: Michael (my main Jigga!), Maisha (girl, you fly!), Mwata (soon-to-be-doc!), and Virgil (CEO-in-the-making). I reserve my greatest thanks for Marcia Dyson, to whom this book is dedicated. She has been my most diligent research assistant, tracking down articles, books, and footnotes into the wee hours of the morning. She has offered invaluable criticism and support, and has lived this book with me from beginning to end. It is truly her book as much as it is mine. I owe her a debt of gratitude for her intellectual imagination, her spiritual genius, and for the way she makes our family thrive and work. Without her, this book could never have been written.

One day the King archives will be widely available for scholarly use. Because my book is a critical reinterpretation of King's legacy and his reception in the larger culture, a wide array of articles, books, magazines, and films provided the grist of my interpretative mill. Only those with longstanding requests are granted access to the King archives, which renders them virtually inaccessible to people writing books like mine; in the future, their ready availability will greatly enhance all King studies.

Abernathy, Ralph David, 59, 65, 89, 90, 155–156, 164, 189, 203, 211, 217, 218, 250, 269, 278, 304

Abortion, 241–244

Active Faith (Reed), 236–237

Adams, Charles, 282–283

Adams, John Hearst, 75

"Advice for Living" columns (King), 191, 195

Affirmative action, 3, 14, 22–27, 44, 169

Ali, Muhammad, 70–71

"American Dream, The" (King), 19–20

"America's Chief Moral Dilemma" (King), 39

And the Walls Came Tumbling Down (Abernathy), 156

Anthony, Susan B., 241

A&P grocery store chain, 82

Apostle, The (film), 135

Appalachia, 96–97

Atlanta Journal-Constitution, 255, 261

Autobiography of Malcolm X, The, 103

Autobiography of Martin Luther King, Jr., The (ed. Carson), 273

Babbitt, Bruce, 266

Baker, Ella, 73, 108, 127, 195, 204–206, 298–299, 304

Baker, Jim, 135

Baldwin, James, 116, 306

Baldwin, Lewis, 147, 254

Barnett, Ross, 230

Barry, Rick, 278

Barth, Karl, 139, 145

Bayh, Birch, 288–289

Becker, Ernest, 36

Belafonte, Harry, 59, 220

Bennett, Lerone, 296

Bernstein, Richard, 23–24

Bethune, Mary McCloud, 201–202

Bethune-Cookman College, 201

Bevel, James, 59, 65–66, 89, 90, 93, 304

Big Boi, 308

Bill of Rights, 25

Bill of Rights for the Disadvantaged (proposed), 28–29

Black church, 120, 123–136, 147, 200, 297

Black History Month, 137, 263

Black nationalism, 100, 103–105, 109–116, 120

Black Panthers, 170

Black Power, 66, 72, 111–114

Blacks, in military, 60–61, 63, 74–76

Blackside, Inc., 262–265

Blyden, Edward Wilmot, 109

Bond, Julian, 58, 254, 256, 258, 267, 293, 299, 304

Boozer, Jack, 145

Borders, William Holmes, 179

Boston University, 145, 147, 148, 150, 251–260

Braden, Ann, 229

Braden, Carl, 227, 229

Branch, Taylor, 147, 212, 256–257

Breaking Barriers (Rowan), 163

Brightman, Edgar, 145

Brooke, Ed, 61–62

Brown, James, 180, 289

Brownback, Sam, 175

Brown v. Topeka Board of Education (1954), 117, 201

Bunche, Ralph, 62

Burks, Mary Fair, 203

Bush, George, 74, 171, 279

Busing, 44, 117, 118

Butts, Calvin, 75, 134

Carey, Archibald, 143, 281

Carmichael, Stokely, 5, 59, 66–68, 111–113, 207

Carson, Clayborne, 207–208, 258, 259, 271, 273, 301

Carter, Jimmy, 279, 287

Case, Steve, 175

"Casualties of the War in Vietnam" (King), 59

CBS (Columbia Broadcasting System), 261

Chaney, James, 304

Chavis, Benjamin, 75

Chicago, Illinois, 37, 38, 80–82, 93, 110, 112

Christian Century, 182

Christian Coalition, 234–241

"Christmas Sermon on Peace, A" (King),
    21
Church burnings, 235
Civil Rights Act of 1964, 25, 37, 87, 113
Civil rights movement, 11–13, 23, 30,
    32–34, 36–40, 50, 53–56, 71–73
  black church and, 127, 129, 130
  Chicago movement, 37, 38, 80–82, 93,
    110, 112
  Crusade for Citizenship, 205–206
  King's nonviolent philosophy and, 30,
    32–35, 37, 43–44, 52, 53, 73, 84–87,
    105, 107–112, 130, 229, 232–234,
    242–243
  King's symbolic leadership of, 295–302
  Memphis sanitation workers' strike,
    78–79, 93, 94
  Montgomery bus boycott, 33, 53, 56,
    201, 203, 204, 249, 302
  Operation Breadbasket, 81–82, 93
  Poor People's Campaign, 11, 77, 79, 85,
    89–94, 208, 220
  Selma to Montgomery march, 20, 310
  women's role in, 195, 198, 200, 202–208
Civil War, 63, 304
Clark, Caesar, 180
Clark, Jim, 274
Clark, Septima, 127, 255, 293, 304
Cleveland, Ohio, 38, 81, 82, 114
Clinton, Bill, 167–173, 268, 279
Clinton, George, 171
Clinton, Hillary Rodham, 168
Coffin, William Sloane, 59
Collins, Addie Mae, 304
Color-blindness, 13–15, 22, 24, 35
Color-coding, 46, 47
Colored Woman in a White World, A (Ter-
    rell), 201
Colored Women's League, 200
Communism, King and, 89, 90, 159, 160,
    226, 228–231, 289
Communist party USA (CPUSA), 228
"Comparison of the Conceptions of God
    in the Thinking of Paul Tillich and
    Henry Nelson Wieman, A" (King)
Cone, James, 147, 150, 254
Congress of Racial Equality (CORE), 254,
    300
Congress of Women's International
    League for Peace and Freedom
    (1919), 200
Connerly, Ward, 25–27
Connor, Bull, 34, 104
Conservatives, 6, 7, 12–14, 22–28
Constitution of the United States, 18, 25,
    38, 130, 231, 246
Content of Our Character (Steele), 24

Conyers, John, 286
Cook, Louise, 256–258
Coppola, Francis Ford, 185
Cotton, Betty, 126
Cotton, Dorothy, 189, 195, 196, 304
Council for United Civil Rights Leader-
    ship, 210
Cox, Harvey, 283
Cox, Oliver, 73
Crawford, Evans, 147, 150
Crawford, Kenneth, 62
Criminal justice system, 49
Crozer Theological Seminary, Chester,
    145, 150, 276
Crummell, Alexander, 109
Crusade for Citizenship, 205–206
Curry, Izola Ware, 227

Daley, Richard J., 37
Davis, Angela, 304
Davis, Benjamin, 73, 227, 230
Davis, Georgia, 218–219
"Dead Homiez" (Ice Cube), 187
Declaration of Independence, 18, 38–39,
    72, 130, 231, 246
De facto segregation, 25, 117, 118
De jure segregation, 25
Delaney, Martin, 109
Democratic National Convention (1968),
    207
DeWolf, L. Harold, 145, 182, 251, 253, 255
Dexter Avenue Baptist Church, Mont-
    gomery, 33, 148
Dialectical Society, Boston University, 150
Diallo, Amadou, 176
Diem, Ngo Dinh, 72
DiMaggio, Joe, 308
Dodd, Thomas, 56
Doggystyle (Snoop Doggy Dogg), 185
"Domestic Impact of the War in Vietnam,
    The" (King), 60
Douglass, Frederick, 41, 109, 125, 200,
    284, 285
Downs, Hugh, 161
Dre, 308
Drew, Deenie, 189
"Drum Major Instinct, The" (King), 20,
    51–52, 276
Du Bois, W.E.B., 63, 64, 73, 109, 119, 142,
    143, 227, 230
Dukakis, Michael, 171
Dyson, Marcia L., 160

Ebenezer Baptist Church, Atlanta, 20, 51,
    162, 251, 264
Ebony Magazine, 191, 195
Edwards, Bernice, 134

Elders, Jocelyn, 172
Ellison, Ralph, 71, 73
Elmer Gantry (Lewis), 135
Emancipation Proclamation, 18, 113, 286
Emory University, 258, 259
Engels, Friedrich, 131
Eskridge, Chauncey, 217
Evers, Medgar, 198, 304
Evers, Myrlie, 198
Eyes on the Prize (documentary), 263–264

Falwell, Jerry, 241
Farrakhan, Louis, 115, 117, 158, 184
Fauntroy, Walter, 238
FBI (Federal Bureau of Investigation), 69, 80, 89, 159, 163–165, 194, 215–217, 226–230
Fellowship of Reconciliation, 65, 76
Fields, Ernest, 127
Fisher, John, 79–80, 86
Foner, Eric, 284
Forbes, James, 282
Ford Foundation, 123
Fosdick, Harry Emerson, 181
Franklin, C.L., 179, 180, 282
Franklin, Robert, 133
Frazier, E. Franklin, 126
Frey, Sylvia, 126
Fruit of Islam, 104

Gandhi, Mohandas, 27, 76, 130, 143, 239, 250
Gandhi Society for Human Rights, 228
Garnett, Henry Highland, 238, 284
Garrow, David, 43, 146–148, 159, 256, 274
Garvey, Marcus, 109
Genovese, Eugene, 146, 147, 150
"Ghetto Won't Change, The" (Master P), 184, 185
Gibson, John, 189
Giddings, Paula, 204, 208
Gitlin, Todd, 42, 133
"Give Us the Ballot—We Will Transform the South" (King), 19
Godfather, The (film), 185
Goldberg, Arthur, 56, 58
Gone With the Wind (film), 307
Goodman, Andy, 304
Gordy, Berry, 102
Gore, Al, 171
Gray, Fred, 255
Gray, Victoria, 304
Gray, William, 238
Great Migration, 106
Great Society, 58, 60
Gregory, Dick, 254
Griffey, Ken, 279

Grossman, David, 175
Guinier, Lani, 172

Halberstam, David, 39, 68–69
Haley, Alex, 262, 276
Hall, Prathia, 143, 280
Hamer, Fannie Lou, 73, 108, 127, 206–207, 293, 304
Hampton, Henry, 263–265
Handcox, John, 127
Harding, Vincent, 67–68, 305
Harrington, Michael, 85, 88, 89
Harrison, Benjamin, 200
Hayden, Casey, 207
Haygood, Lawrence F., 236
Hegel, Friedrich, 26, 145, 148
Helms, Jesse, 80, 90, 155, 159, 169, 226, 230
Henning, C. Garnett, 75
Heschel, Abraham Joshua, 52
Heyward, Andrew, 261
Hip-hop culture, 177–188, 190–192, 194–196
Ho Chi Minh, 54, 56
Holmes, Bob, 265
Holmes, Hamilton, 255
Honey, Michael, 127
Hook, Sidney, 296
Hooks, Benjamin, 56
Hoover, J. Edgar, 80, 155, 159, 163–165, 194, 217, 227, 229, 288
Horn, Etta, 208
House, Eugene, 170
House Un-American Activities Committee (HUAC), 227
Hubbard, H.H., 203
Huggins, Nathan, 301–302
Hughes, Langston, 41

Ice Cube, 180, 187
"If the Negro Wins, Labor Wins" (King), 19
"I Have a Dream" (King), 5, 14–19, 21–22, 24, 26, 27, 29, 170, 246, 261, 262, 280–281
International Woodworkers of America, 127
"I See the Promised Land" (King), 1–2, 14, 21, 249–250, 303
I Shared a Dream (Davis), 218

Jackson, Derrick, 76
Jackson, Earl, 236
Jackson, Jesse, 74, 75, 81, 89, 90, 93–99, 132, 171, 236, 238, 250, 279, 304
Jackson, Joseph H., 123
Jackson, Maynard, 74

Jacoby, Tamar, 42, 46–47
James, Chappy, 289
James, C.L.R., 88
Japanese Americans, 39
Jefferson, Thomas, 7, 15, 143
John Birch Society, 229, 246
Johnson, Lyndon Baines, 6, 49, 54–56, 58, 61, 71, 89, 113, 173, 209
Johnson, Matthew, 134
Jones, Charles, 273
Jones, Clarence, 55, 228, 262
Jones, Major, 147, 150
Jones, Philip, 258–260, 262, 265, 271, 272
Jordan, Michael, 155, 278, 279
Just war theory, 53

Kammen, Michael, 284
Kant, Immanuel, 145
Kennedy, John F., 55, 95, 153, 213, 228, 279
Kennedy, Randall, 169
Kennedy, Robert F., 96, 228, 279
Kerner Commission (National Advisory Commission on Civil Disorders), 38, 84
King, Alberta, 275
King, Alfred Daniel, 218, 219, 275
King, Bernice, 261, 262
King, Christine, 275
King, Coretta Scott, 30, 74, 189
  background of, 209
  birthday legislation and, 287–289
  FBI tapes and, 216–217
  King's legacy and, 198, 219–221, 247–248, 250–281
  pacifism of, 53, 64
  relationship with King, 161, 193, 195–199, 209–221
King, Dexter, 221, 258, 261, 263, 265–267, 270–274, 277
King, Martin Luther, Jr.
  Abernathy and, 155–156
  "Advice for Living" columns, 191, 195
  affirmative action and, 3, 14, 22, 24–27
  "The American Dream" speech, 19–20
  "America's Chief Moral Dilemma" speech, 39
  assassination of, 1–3, 155, 229, 247, 249
  birthday holiday legislation and celebration, 60, 225, 230, 270, 281–284, 286–295, 303, 304
  black church and, 120, 123, 127–133, 147, 297
  "Casualties of the War in Vietnam" speech, 59
  Chicago movement and, 37, 38, 80–82, 93, 110, 112
  "A Christmas Sermon on Peace," 21

on colonialism, 244–245
communism and, 89, 90, 159, 160, 226, 228–231, 289
courtship of Coretta, 211–212
death, view of, 188–190, 303, 304
democracy and, 4, 7, 40, 72
democratic socialist principles of, 77, 80, 88, 90, 91, 99, 209
"The Domestic Impact of the War in Vietnam" speech, 60
"The Drum Major Instinct" sermon, 20, 51–52, 276
education of, 144–152
enlightened nationalism of, 104–105, 110, 113, 114, 120
FBI and, 69, 80, 89, 159, 163–165, 194, 215–217, 226–230
finances of, 210–211, 262, 276
funeral of, 51, 52
gender, view of, 198, 199, 208, 211–213, 221–222
"Give Us the Ballot—We Will Transform the South" speech, 19
as greatest American, 7, 305–306
hip-hop culture and, 177–179, 181, 194–196
homosexuality issue, 164–165
"If the Negro Wins, Labor Wins" speech, 19
"I Have a Dream" speech, 5, 14–19, 21–22, 24, 26, 27, 29, 170, 246, 261, 262, 280–281
international social vision of, 244–245
"I See the Promised Land" speech, 1–2, 14, 21, 249–250, 303
"Letter from Birmingham Jail," 246
Malcolm X and, 30, 101, 104, 110–111
March on Washington (1968) and, 85–87, 89
Marx and, 130
Memphis sanitation workers' strike and, 78–79, 93, 94
Montgomery bus boycott and, 33, 53, 56, 203, 204, 302
nickname of, 193, 275–276
Nobel Peace Prize awarded, 51, 57, 61, 210–211, 303
nonviolent philosophy of, 30, 32–35, 37, 43–44, 52, 53, 73, 84–87, 105, 107–112, 130, 229, 232–234, 242–243
"Our God Is Marching On!" speech, 20
as patriot, 4, 72, 226–227, 231, 234, 246–247
plagiarism by, 136, 139–154, 157, 158, 166, 168, 178, 280–281
on poverty, 11–12, 21
press and, 6, 56–57, 62

problem of evil and, 182–183
proposed Bill of Rights for the Disadvantaged and, 28–29
on race riots, 84–85
on racism, 4, 29, 31–46, 48, 49
radicalism of, 80, 82–85, 87–90, 92, 99, 124, 303
relationship with Coretta, 161, 193, 195–199, 209–221
religious beliefs of, 4, 22, 126–129, 189, 192, 222, 231–234
religious right's appropriation of, 234–241
"Remaining Awake Through a Great Revolution" sermon, 20–21
"The Roots of Racism Are Very Deep in America" speech, 260
on school prayer, 240
Southern roots of, 35
suicide attempts of, 178
"The Three Dimensions of a Complete Life" sermon, 144
"A Time to Break Silence" speech, 20, 60–62, 67
"To Minister to the Valley" sermon, 123–124
upbringing of, 275–276
Vietnam War, opposition to, 6, 20, 49–62, 64–74, 76–77, 173, 175, 245
"Where Do We Go from Here?" speech, 20, 66, 231
"Which Way Its Soul Shall Go" speech, 40
"Why We Must Go to Washington" speech, 87
womanizing by, 136, 154–163, 165, 166, 168, 178, 189, 193–196, 216–219
Young, Andrew and, 90–91
King, Martin Luther, Sr., 20, 195, 214, 255, 275
King, Martin Luther, III, 254
King, Mary, 207
King, Yolanda "Yoki," 215
King Center for Nonviolent Social Change, 221, 251, 254–260, 263–267, 269–274, 278, 287
King Historic District, Atlanta, 251, 264, 265
Kirschbaum, Larry, 273
Knock at Midnight, A (ed. Carson), 273
Kool Moe Dee, 190
Ku Klux Klan, 201, 215

Labor movement, 126, 127
Labor Youth League, 228
Lasch, Christopher, 32, 42–45, 88, 89
Last Man Standing (film), 185

Lawson, James, 53, 65, 79
Lee, Bernard, 211
Lentz, Richard, 57, 62
"Letter from Birmingham Jail" (King), 246
Levin, Gerald, 273
Levison, Stanley, 55, 59, 68, 69, 91, 204–205, 228
Lewinsky, Monica, 168
Lewis, David Levering, 146, 147, 151, 160
Lewis, John, 207, 238, 266, 293, 299, 304
Lewis, Sinclair, 135
Liberals, 6–7, 13, 19, 31, 32, 40–45
Life After Death (Notorious B.I.G.), 187
"Life Goes On" (Shakur), 187
Life Magazine, 62, 214
Lifton, Robert Jay, 105
Lincoln, Abraham, 7, 55, 113, 143, 247, 286, 304
Lincoln, C. Eric, 147, 150
Lind, Michael, 24
Lischer, Richard, 140–144, 148, 257, 304
Littleton school shooting, 175, 177
Liuzzo, Viola, 304
Lorraine Motel, Memphis, 1, 249, 250
Loury, Glenn, 24
Lowenstein, Allard, 59
Lowery, Joseph, 74, 75, 217
Luther, Martin, 184–185
Lyons, Henry, 123, 134–136

Malcolm X, 5, 30–31, 73, 101, 103, 104, 110–111, 113, 174, 184, 198, 199, 227, 304
Mandela, Nelson, 221, 268, 283
March on Washington (1941), 202
March on Washington (1963), 11, 15, 18, 26, 77, 229, 288
March on Washington (1968), 85–87, 89
Marsalis, Wynton, 8
Marshall, Thurgood, 117
Martin Luther King Plagiarism Story (Pappas), 146
Marx, Karl, 80, 90, 130–131, 133, 145, 239
Master P., 184, 185
Matalin, Mary, 171
Mays, Benjamin E., 126, 255
Mboya, Tom, 244, 245
McCarthy, Joseph, 227
McDonald, Larry P., 288
McKissick, Floyd, 59, 66
McNair, Denise, 304
McVeigh, Timothy, 229
McWilliams, Carey, 59
Meet the Press, 175–177
Memphis sanitation workers' strike, 78–79, 93, 94
Merelman, Richard, 292–294

Miller, Keith D., 140–144, 148
Milliken v. *Bradley* (1973), 118
Mitchell, Margaret, 307
Montgomery bus boycott, 33, 53, 56, 201, 203, 204, 249, 302
Montgomery Improvement Association (MIA), 204
Montgomery to Memphis (documentary), 263–264
Moore, Harry, 304
Morehouse College, 144, 193, 255–256, 262, 275
Morrison, Toni, 168
Moses, Bob, 293, 299–301, 304
Moss, Thomas, 200
Motown, 102
Movement to End Slums, 93
Moynihan report (1965), 112
Muhammad, Elijah, 104, 109, 110
Multiculturalism, 23–24
"Murder Was the Case" (Snoop Doggy Dogg), 187
Murphy, Laura W., 236
Muste, A.J., 59, 65
Myrdal, Gunnar, 116

Nash, Diane, 65, 299, 304
Nation, The, 59, 227
National Association for the Advancement of Colored People (NAACP), 61, 115–117, 198, 202, 204
National Association of Colored Women (NACW), 199–202
National Baptist Convention, 115, 123, 131, 134–135
National Black Election Survey (1984), 132
National Campaign Against Affirmative Action, 25
National Civil Rights Museum, Memphis, 249
National Committee for a Sane Nuclear Policy (SANE), 64
National Council of Negro Women (NCNW), 202
National Emergency African-American Leadership Summit on the Persian Gulf War, 75
National Institute for Community Empowerment, 270
National Park Service, 264–268, 272
National Welfare Rights Organization (NWRO), 200, 208
National Youth Administration (NYA), 202
Nation of Islam, 104, 110, 111, 117
Nehru, Jawaharlal, 27

Neoseparatism, 117–118
Neusner, Jacob, 146
"Never Seen a Man Cry" (Scarface), 187, 188
Newsweek, 6, 8, 57, 62, 91, 112
Newton, Huey, 100, 304
New York Times, The, 62, 153
Niebuhr, Reinhold, 145, 302
Nietzsche, Friedrich, 145
Nixon, E.D., 203–204
Nobel Peace Prize, 51, 57, 61, 210–211, 303
Noer, Thomas, 245
Notorious B.I.G., 178, 180, 183, 186, 187, 194

O'Dell, Hunter Pitts "Jack," 228, 229, 230
Office of Economic Opportunity, 58
"On Being Fit" (Fosdick), 181
O'Neill, Tip, 288
"Only God Can Judge Me" (Shakur), 186, 188, 190
Operation Breadbasket, 81–82, 93
Operation Rescue, 241–243
Oppenheimer Capital, 265
"Our God Is Marching On!" (King), 20
Outkast, 308–311
Owen, Chandler, 64

Pappas, Theodore, 146
Parks, Rosa, 201–204, 241, 249, 307–311
Patriarchy, 109, 110, 135, 195
Payne, Charles, 300
Payne, David, 109
Pendergrass, Coakley, 74
Persian Gulf War, 74–76
Personalist theology, 145
Pippen, Scottie, 155
"Place of Reason in Paul Tillich's Conception of God, The" (Boozer), 145
Playboy Magazine, 231, 276
Plessy v. *Ferguson* (1896), 117
"Point Tha Finga" (Shakur), 184
Pomerantz, Gary, 280
Poor People's Campaign, 11, 77, 79, 85, 89–94, 208, 220
Positive-thought materialism, 133
Powell, Adam Clayton, 104, 110, 238
Powell, Colin, 76, 184
Preacher King, The (Lischer), 140–141
Presley, Elvis, 272
Proctor, Samuel, 147, 150
Progressive National Baptist Convention, 123
"Progress of Colored Women, The" (Terrell), 200
Proposition 14, 225

Proposition 209, 25
Prosser, Gabriel, 125, 284
Psychic doppleganger, 105–109
Public Broadcasting Company (PBS), 263
Puff Daddy, 180
Putting People First (Clinton and Gore), 171

Race riots, 3, 21, 84–85
Racial evasionists, 42–45
Rainbow/PUSH Coalition, 95
Randolph, A. Philip, 53, 63, 64, 76, 202
Ransom, Reverdy C., 126
Rap music, 177–188, 190–192, 194–196,
    308–310
Ray, James Earl, 249
Ray, Sandy, 179
Reader's Digest, 62
Reagan, Ronald, 60, 155, 170, 221,
    225–226, 230, 283, 286–289
Reagon, Bernice Johnson, 149
Reagon, Cordell, 297
Recalcitrant amnesia, 291–292, 295
Reconstruction, 63, 284
Rector, Rickey Ray, 171
Reddick, Lawrence, 27
Redlining, 81
Reeb, James, 304
Reed, Gregory, 308
Reed, Ralph, 234–241
Reisman, David, 257
"Remaining Awake Through a Great Rev-
    olution" (King), 20–21
Repentant amnesia, 291, 293, 295
Republican party (California), 26–27
Resistant amnesia, 292, 295
Resurrection City, 85, 220
Revelation Corporation, 115
Reverential amnesia, 290, 293, 295
Revisionist amnesia, 290–291, 293–295,
    297
Reynolds, William Bradford, 22
Rittenhouse, E. Stanley, 288
Roberts, Joseph, 267, 274
Robertson, Carole, 304
Robertson, Pat, 234, 241
Robeson, Paul, 73, 227, 230
Robinson, Jackie, 62
Robinson, Jo Ann, 127, 203
Rock, Chris, 168, 178
Rockefeller, Nelson, 239
Rogers, Cornish, 147, 148, 150
Rooney, John, 163, 164
Roosevelt, Franklin Delano, 63, 202
"Roots of Racism Are Very Deep in
    America, The" (King), 260
Rorty, Richard, 133
"Rosa Parks" (Big Boi and Dre), 308–310

Rosenbergs, the, 227
Rowan, Carl, 62, 72, 163–165, 218
Russert, Tim, 175, 176
Rustin, Bayard, 53, 55, 69, 76, 89, 194,
    204–206, 229, 304
Rutherford, Bill, 217

Safe Negro Leadership, 6
Samaritan Project, 235
Sampson, Frederick, 282
Sanders, Beulah, 208
Sandifer, Yummy, 176
Santayana, George, 173
Sartwell, Crispin, 187
Satcher, David, 175
Scarface, 187, 188
Schilling, S. Paul, 145, 149
School desegregation, 103–104, 115–119
Schwerner, Mickey, 304
Scott, Edythe, 213
Seale, Bobby, 170
Sealtest, 82
Self-segregation, 118–119
Selma to Montgomery march (1965), 20,
    310
Shabazz, Betty, 198–199
Shakur, Tupac, 177, 178, 183–188, 190
Sherrod, Charles, 304
Shuttlesworth, Fred, 255
Silber, John, 251–253
Simon, Paul, 308
Simpson trial, 49
Sleeper, Jim, 42, 45, 46
Smalls, Biggie, 178
Smith, Jacqueline, 250
Smoot, Dan, 229
Snoop Doggy Dogg, 180, 183, 185,
    187–188, 193
Sobell, Morton, 227
Souljah, Sister, 171
South Africa, 220, 221, 245
Southern Christian Leadership Confer-
    ence (SCLC), 20, 30, 54–56, 59, 60,
    65, 81–84, 87, 90–91, 94, 205, 206,
    210, 228, 254–255, 269
Spiller, Howard, 268
Spock, Benjamin, 59
Spring Mobilization to End the War in
    Vietnam (1967), 59, 64, 65, 68
Stanford University, 258, 259
Stang, Alan, 229, 230, 289
Stanley, Scott, Jr., 229
Starnes, Debi, 268
Steele, Claude, 151, 152
Steele, Shelby, 24
Steering, 81
Steinberg, Arnold, 27

Stokes, Carl, 114
Stone, Oliver, 272
Stop the Violence Movement, 190
Strategic deracialization, 96
Strength to Love (King), 144
Stride Toward Freedom (King), 203
Student Nonviolent Coordinating Committee (SNCC), 30, 58, 66, 206, 207, 255, 297, 299, 300
Supreme Court rulings, 117, 118, 128, 201, 240
Swaggart, Jimmy, 135
Swift, Jonathan, 15

Taylor, Gardner, 179
Terrell, Mary Church, 200–201
Terrell, Robert Heberton, 200
Terry, Randall, 241–242
Thernstrom, Abigail, 42
Thernstrom, Stephan, 42
Thieu-Ky regime, 73
"Things Done Changed" (Notorious B.I.G.), 186
Thomas, Clarence, 102, 103, 173
Thomas, Norman, 59
Thomson, Meldrim, 226
"Three Dimensions of a Complete Life, The" (King), 144
Thugs N Harmony, 183
Thurman, Howard, 158
Thurmond, Strom, 230, 288
Till, Emmett, 304
Tillich, Paul, 145
Tillmon, Johnnie, 208–209, 304
Time, 6, 57, 62, 66
"Time to Break Silence, A" (King), 20, 60–62, 67
Time Warner, 273–275
Today Show, The (NBC), 161
Tomasky, Michael, 42, 43, 133
"To Minister to the Valley" (King), 123–124
True Lies (film), 185
Truth, Sojourner, 284
Tubman, Harriet, 125, 284
Tucker, C. Delores, 198
Tucker, Cynthia, 267
Turner, Henry McNeal, 109, 126, 284
Turner, Nat, 125, 284
20th Century with Mike Wallace, The (CBS), 261
"2Pacalypse Now" (Shakur), 185

Untouchables, in India, 27
Urban League, 202
U.S. News & World Report, 57, 62, 268–269
USA Today, 261, 262

Vanity Fair, 168
Vesey, Denmark, 125, 284
Vietnam War, 6, 20, 49–62, 64–74, 76–77, 173, 175, 245
Vivian, C.T., 206, 274–275
Voice of Deliverance (Miller), 140
Voting Rights Act of 1965, 37, 55, 87

Wachtel, Harry, 55, 57–58, 68, 253
Walker, David, 109
Walker, William "Sonny," 271
Walker, Wyatt Tee, 90
Wallace, George, 229, 240
Wall Street Project, 97–98
Walters, Alexander, 126
Ward, Mrs., 218
War on Poverty, 58, 60
Washington, Booker T., 109, 284, 289
Washington, Harold, 287
Washington Post, The, 62
Weber, Max, 184
Welch, Robert, 229
Wells-Barnett, Ida B., 73
Wesley, Cynthia, 304
"Where Do We Go from Here?" (King), 20, 66, 231
"Which Way Its Soul Shall Go" (King), 40
White, E.B., 15
Whitman, Walt, 306
Why Can't We Wait (King), 28
"Why We Must Go to Washington" (King), 87
Wieman, Henry Nelson, 145
Wiggins, William, 286
Wilkins, Roger, 189
Wilkins, Roy, 55, 61, 304
Williams, Alfred Daniel, 275
Williams, Hosea, 59, 65, 89, 91, 304
Williams, Jasper, 134
Williams, Larry, 193
Wills, Gary, 146
Wilson, William Julius, 87, 96
Women's International League for Peace and Freedom, 64
Women's Political Council (WPC), Montgomery, 203
Wonder, Stevie, 286–288
Wright, Marian, 85

Yglesias, José, 87
Young, Andrew, 55, 65–66, 70, 74, 89–94, 159–160, 195–196, 208, 210, 214, 217, 238, 255, 268, 269, 274, 304
Young, Whitney, 55, 61, 72, 304
Youngblood, Mtamanika, 267–268
"You're Nobody Til Somebody Kills You" (Notorious B.I.G.), 187